THE SOCIOLOGY AND
PROFESSIONALIZATION OF
ECONOMICS

BRITISH AND AMERICAN ECONOMIC ESSAYS
A. W. Bob Coats

ON THE HISTORY OF
ECONOMIC THOUGHT
VOLUME I

THE SOCIOLOGY AND PROFESSIONALIZATION
OF ECONOMICS
VOLUME II

THE HISTORIOGRAPHY AND METHODOLOGY
OF ECONOMICS
VOLUME III

THE SOCIOLOGY AND PROFESSIONALIZATION OF ECONOMICS

British and
American economic essays
Volume II

A. W. Bob Coats

London and New York

First published 1993
by Routledge
11 New Fetter Lane, London EC4P 4EE

Simultaneously published in the USA and Canada
by Routledge
29 West 35th Street, New York, NY 10001

© 1993 A. W. Bob Coats

Typeset in Baskerville by Intype, London

Printed and bound in Great Britain by
Mackays of Chatham PLC, Chatham, Kent

British Library Cataloguing-in-Publication Data

A catalogue record for this book is available from the British Library.

ISBN 0-415-06716-2

Library of Congress Cataloging in Publication Data

Coats, A. W. (Alfred William), 1924–
  The sociology and professionalization of economics / A.W. Bob
Coats.
      p.   cm. — (British and American economic essays ; v. 2)
  Simultaneously published in the USA and Canada.
  Includes bibliographical references and index.
  ISBN 0-415-06716-2
  1. Economics—History.   2. Economics—Social aspects.
3. Government economists.   I. Title.   II. Series: Coats, A. W.
(Alfred William), 1924–   British and American economic essays; v.
2.
HB87.C63   1993
330'.09—dc20
                                                                          93-16563
                                                                             CIP

CONTENTS

CONTENTS

Part II Institutions, their history and activities

Part III The economics profession and the role of economists in government

CONTENTS

NOTES ON CHAPTERS

All but one of the chapters comprising this volume have been published before, appearing between 1960 and 1991. Chapter 3 has been published only in Swedish. Chapters 24 and 27 were published jointly with Alan Booth and Chapter 18 with my wife, Sonia E. Coats. Both have kindly agreed to this republication. Given below is a listing of sources.

thought – *American Economic Review*, vol. LI, no. 4 (September 1961), pp. 624–37.

13 The American Economic Association, 1904–29 – *American Economic Review*, vol. LIV, no. 4, pt 1 (June 1964), pp. 261–85.

14 The American Economic Association's publications: an historical perspective – *Journal of Economic Literature*, vol. VII, no. 1 (March 1969), pp. 57–68.

15 The origins of the 'Chicago School(s)'? – *Journal of Political Economy*, vol. LXXI, no. 5 (October 1963), pp. 487–93.

16 John Elliotson Symes, Henry George and academic freedom in Nottingham during the 1880s – *Renaissance and Modern Studies*, vol. VII (October 1963), pp. 110–38.

17 The origins and early development of the Royal Economic Society – *Economic Journal*, vol. LXXVIII (June 1968), pp. 349–71.

18 The changing social composition of the Royal Economic Society 1890–1960 and the professionalization of British economics – *British Journal of Sociology*, vol. 24, no. 2 (June 1973), pp. 165–87.

19 Alfred Marshall and the early development of the London School of Economics: some unpublished letters – *Economica*, vol. 34, no. 136 (November 1967), pp. 408–17.

20 The distinctive LSE ethos in the inter-war years – *Atlantic Economic Journal*, vol. X, no. 1 (March 1982), pp. 18–30.

21 Economics as a profession – *Companion to Contemporary Economic Thought*, D. Greenaway, M. Bleaney and I. Stewart (eds) (London, Routledge: 1991), pp. 119–42.

22 The development of the agricultural economics profession in England – *Journal of Agricultural Economics*, vol. XXVII, no. 3 (September 1976), pp. 381–92.

23 The American Economic Association and the economics profession – *Journal of Economic Literature*, vol. XXIII, no. 4 (December 1985), pp. 1697–727.

24 The market for economists in Britain, 1945–75: a preliminary survey – *Economic Journal*, vol. 88, no. 3 (September 1978), pp. 436–54.

25 Introduction to *Economists in government: an international comparative study*, A. W. Coats (ed.) (Durham, N.C.: Duke University Press, 1981), pp. 3–26. Also in *History of Political Economy*, vol. 13, no. 3 (Fall 1981), pp. 341–64.

26 Britain: the rise of the specialists – *Economists in government: an international comparative study*, A. W. Coats (ed.) (Durham, N.C.: Duke University Press, 1981), pp. 24–66. Also in *History of Political Economy*, vol. 13, no. 3 (Fall 1981), pp. 365–404.

27 Some wartime observations on the role of the economist in government – *Oxford Economic Papers*, vol. 32, no. 2 (July 1980), pp. 177–99.

28 The changing role of economists in Scottish government since 1960 – *Public Administration*, vol. 57 (Spring 1979), pp. 399–424.
29 Economists in government: an historical and comparative perspective – *Canberra Bulletin of Public Administration*, vol. 53 (December 1987), pp. 45–55.

ACKNOWLEDGEMENTS

For permission to reproduce the materials in this volume, acknowledgement is due to the following sources: JAI Press Inc. for 'The sociology of knowledge and the history of economics' © 1984 by JAI Press Inc.; *Kyklos* for 'Is there a "structure of scientific revolutions" in economics?'; Duke University Press and *History of Political Economy* for the following four articles: 'The economic and social context of the marginal revolution of the 1870s', 'The culture and the economists: some reflections on Anglo-American differences' © 1980 by Duke University Press, the Introduction to *Economists in government: an international comparative study* edited by A. W. Coats, and 'Britain: the rise of the specialists'; *Journal of Law and Economics* for 'The role of authority in the development of British economics'; *Journal of Political Economy* for the following two articles: 'Sociological aspects of British economic thought (*ca.* 1880–1930)' © 1967 by the University of Chicago, and 'The origins of the "Chicago School(s)"?' © 1963 by the University of Chicago; *Journal of Economic Literature* for the following three articles: 'The role of scholarly journals in the history of economics: an essay', 'The American Economic Association's publications: an historical perspective' and 'The American Economic Association and the economics profession'; *Economic Notes by Monte dei Paschi di Siena* for 'The learned journals in the development of economics and the economics profession: the British case'; *American Economic Review* for the following three articles: 'The first two decades of the American Economic Association', 'The Political Economy Club: a neglected episode in American economic thought' and 'The American Economic Association, 1904–29'; *Renaissance and Modern Studies* for 'John Elliotson Symes, Henry George and academic freedom in Nottingham during the 1880s'; *Economic Journal* for 'The origins and early development of the Royal Economic Society'; *British Journal of Sociology* for 'The changing social composition of the Royal Economic Society 1890–1960 and the professionalization of British economics'; *Economica* for 'Alfred Marshall and the early development of the London School of Economics: some unpublished letters'; *Atlantic Economic Journal* for 'The distinctive LSE ethos in the inter-war years'; Omega Scientific for 'Economics as a profession' in *Companion to*

ACKNOWLEDGEMENTS

Contemporary Economic Thought edited by D. Greenaway, M. Bleaney and I. Stewart; *Journal of Agricultural Economics* for 'The development of the agricultural economics profession in England'; *Economic Journal* for 'The market for economists in Britain, 1945–75: a preliminary survey'; *Oxford Economic Papers* for 'Some wartime observations on the role of the economist in government'; *Public Administration* for 'The changing role of economists in Scottish government since 1960'; *Canberra Bulletin of Public Administration* for 'Economists in government: an historical and comparative perspective'.

1

INTRODUCTION

The chapters in this volume represent an economic and social historian's approach to the history of economics.[1] This involves a shift away from the customary preoccupation with the history of economic theory towards broader, less precise and more elusive matters, such as the interrelationships between economic ideas and their historical context, the influence of economic ideas on policy, and the public reputation, organization and professionalization of economics as an academic discipline and/or science.

It is easy to explain why most historians of economics have unduly neglected, or at least inadequately explored, such matters. Even in these days of intense academic specialization there are few full-time scholars in the field, largely because most practising professional economists attach little value to work of this kind, and consequently graduate students regard it as an unsound basis for a career. Most of the leading contributors to the history of economics have been trained as economists, rather than historians; and generally speaking this is desirable, for broad expanses of late-twentieth-century economics are inaccessible to those without any, or with outdated qualifications in the discipline, as I can personally attest! As economists, historians of the subject are naturally fascinated by the development of economic theory, since this is usually regarded as the foundation of economics' claim to be the most 'scientific' of the social sciences; and the fact that some of the discipline's greatest masters have displayed a serious interest in the history of theory (e.g. Marx, Marshall, Schumpeter, Mitchell, Viner, Keynes, Samuelson, Hicks) has given it a certain cachet.[2] But, unfortunately, the history of economics has too often been treated as a subordinate or spare-time activity, so that it has infrequently been pursued with sufficient dedication and persistence.

For economists who treat the history of their discipline as a part-time activity or avocation, more comprehensive studies of the sources, development and impact of economic ideas are simply too demanding of time and energy. Joseph Schumpeter's massive *History of Economic Analysis* (1954), to cite an outstanding example, gives some indication of the magnitude of the task, for he never succeeded in integrating the 'analysis' – ostensibly his main focus – with the historical background and what he called the 'intellectual scenery', to which he devoted so much space. Moreover, he expressly denied any interest in the history of economic policy. Another notable example of the sheer amount of work involved in writing what might loosely be termed an historian's history of economics (though the author was a distinguished economist) is Wesley Mitchell's classic lectures on *Types of Economic Theory* (1967, 1969). In his case the attempt to combine the history of economics with more general history effectively broke down when he reached the later nineteenth- and twentieth-century literature. Like Keynes, Schumpeter and Mitchell were, of course, much more than mere economists; whereas in recent times those with up-to-date training in economics tend to be much narrower in their scholarship, a state of affairs discouraging them from undertaking ambitious historical studies.

An economic and social historian's approach to the history of economics entails no denial of either the intellectual attractions or the importance of economic theory. Nor does it imply that those who study what Schumpeter termed 'the filiation of scientific ideas' (i.e. economic analysis) are necessarily less adequate as historians – except in so far as they examine economic ideas in isolation from their historical setting. There is room for a division of labour here, as elsewhere. It is simply that there is much more to the history of economics than the evolution of theory, even when the subject is treated solely as an academic discipline or professional activity. And this assertion is even more true if we broaden the definition to include the history of economic thought or opinion, for then it is difficult to draw the line between the development of economic ideas and general intellectual history, not to mention other branches of historical study.

While continuing to plead the case for a broader, more comprehensively historical and explicitly sociological approach to the history of economics, I have never claimed that this is the only route to be followed, or that my own approach and choice of subjects should be regarded as exemplary. My intellectual interests have in fact evolved in an almost haphazard fashion.[3] There has been no consistent or coherent plan. Most of the essays in this volume resulted simply from a desire to learn something about aspects of the history of economics neglected by others. My publications on the American Economic Association, for example, originated in my aim of converting my Ph.D. dissertation into a book, which was modified under the benign influence of Harold Williamson, the organization's Secretary and a leading economic historian, who was reluctant to embark on the official history he was so admirably equipped to undertake. Likewise, my initial vague interest in the role of economists in British government was stimulated and encouraged by Sir Alec Cairncross, who did not however entirely approve of my decision to include agricultural economists and statisticians, as well as economic generalists. This work was a logical development of my research on economic methodology and the philosophy of economics, for the epistemological questions, 'In what sense, if any, is economics a science?' and 'What do economists know?', led naturally to the occupational question, 'Why should anyone employ an economist, rather than some other expert or professional?' Even when the question is couched in the simplest terms, there remains the problem of specifying what economists actually 'do' in non-academic settings – i.e. how they utilize their training and special skills. And the investigation of these activities takes the history of economics right out of academia (except in so far as 'inning' and 'outing' are regular practices) into the 'real' world, as it is so quaintly termed.

If this volume required an additional subtitle, the triad 'ideas, individuals, institutions' would be apt. Generally speaking, historians have paid ample attention to the first two – with some reservations when 'individuals' is extended to include groups, schools of thought, and research traditions. But the character and significance of the institutional contexts in which economists have acquired their qualifications and performed their functions, whether academic or non-academic, have on the whole been sorely neglected. With respect to qualifications, universities have been the overwhelmingly preponderant qualifying institutions during the past century or so; and it is clear from the multi-country project on the institutionalization of political economy undertaken a few years ago, that they have been in the business of teaching economics, in one form or another, at least since the mid-eighteenth century.[4] Nevertheless, few historians of economics have taken a serious interest in the history of higher education, either in general or in particular, although there have been revolutionary changes in this sector since the later nineteenth century.[5] The scope for comparative studies of academic systems and styles of teaching and research in economics is considerable.

With respect to functions, academic economists of course perform as teachers, researchers and administrators; but outside academia economists are to be found in a bewildering variety of workplaces. Their activities in government have indeed attracted some scholarly attention, and there is a rich literature produced by ex-government economists (mainly in the UK and the USA), some of whom have written about their experiences extensively and perceptively. The last five chapters in this volume address various general and particular aspects of this type of activity; but as yet we have only scratched the surface, and for most countries the available archival evidence has been deplorably underutilized.[6] In my view, the literature on the role of economists in government should be used as an integral component in the vocational preparation of graduate economists. It is not only often entertaining, and intrinsically interesting from an historical standpoint; it also provides valuable insights into an important part of the economics profession's collective learning experience, especially since World War II.

When we turn to the private sector the research possibilities are even more open. As the chapters on the American Economic Association in this volume reveal, businessmen made a significant impact on that organization at least up to the late 1920s, while as late as 1960 businessmen constituted the largest single category among the Royal Economic Society's members.[7] Yet we still know remarkably little about businessmen's interest in economics or economists' activities in private enterprises – in manufacturing, commerce and finance. Here again there is tremendous scope for revealing research if we seek to understand the economists' contribution to society.

As noted elsewhere,[8] my focus on the sociology and professionalization of economics, which is unusual among historians of economics, was a long-term by-product of my fascination with Anglo-American differences in the development of economic ideas, and in the structure and functioning of the discipline. At an early stage in my career I was privileged to review Schumpeter's *History of Economic Analysis*,[9] part I of which proved a lasting stimulus, while a decade or so later Michael Polanyi's *Personal Knowledge* (1958) and T. S. Kuhn's *Structure of Scientific Revolutions* (1962) sensitized me to the interdependence of the history, philosophy and sociology of science. I realized that the philosophical debate in the 1960s about the relative importance of 'internal' and 'external' influences on the growth of knowledge obviously applied to the development of economics, both in general and in specific terms, and this influenced my papers on Kuhn's *magnum opus*; on the economic and social context of the marginal revolution – where I devoted some attention to the problem of historical explanation; and on the role of 'authority' in British economics[10] – an article which subsequently led to research on the tariff reform movement, Pigou's appointment as Marshall's successor, and broad reflections on the cultural context of British and American economics.[11]

There is an obvious link between these writings and the second and third chapters in this volume which were designed to introduce historians of economics to the growing sociology of science (knowledge) literature. I have never felt the urge to develop a comprehensive framework or systematic theory of the sociology of economics, desirable though this might be. The existing theories seemed for the most part to be either too one-sided or unduly influenced by ideological prejudices. However it is worth noting that a philosopher–economist, Uskali Maki, has recently been attempting to rectify this situation in two stimulating essays, having complained with some justification that 'the literature on the sociology of economics is very scarce, and often conceptually hazy'.[12] I wish him every success in this endeavour; and wholeheartedly endorse his cautious 'minimum suggestion . . . that the methodologists of economics would do wisely to recognize and analyze and tentatively apply the varieties of social theories of science suggesting a number of ways in which science may be socially conditioned'. While seeking a *via media* between 'asocial or weakly social theories of science' and 'antirealist relativisms', Maki believes economists may pursue both social and epistemic goals.[13] This topic, together with the interrelationships between methodology and professionalism, will be considered at some length in Volume III of this series.

In principle, the sociology of economics is virtually unlimited in scope since it embraces every facet of the two-way interactions between the discipline and society at large. In practice, however, the recent scholarly preoccupation with the internal sociology of economics has diverted attention away from broader, more amorphous, and consequently less manageable questions about the impact of economics on society. This is one reason for welcoming the economists' increasing awareness of the nature and significance of the professionalization process, especially since the so-called crisis of the late 1960s and early 1970s, for this subset of the sociology of economics has both internal and external dimensions.[14] The former predominate in the now very large literature on the scholarly economics journal output which yields many insights into the intra-disciplinary communications network and the structure of the discipline, as well as being a sensitive indicator of the current state of knowledge at any time as well as past and future research trends.[15] The characteristic academic predilection for navel-gazing is clearly apparent when one compares this voluminous literature with the dearth of scholarly studies of economics in the newspapers, popular magazines, radio, television, and other media of communication between economists and the general public.[16] The past history of these media is another vast territory hitherto almost entirely ignored by historians of economics.

As a final point, one major link between the internal and external dimensions of the profession is the education of economics graduates, which has recently been the subject of close scrutiny and active debate.[17] This issue raises crucial questions about the profession's responsibilities to society, as well as to the present and future development of economic knowledge.

NOTES

1 For the evolution of my approach see the 'Introduction: "First kick up a dust . . ."' to my *On the History of Economic Thought*, British and American Economic Essays vol. I (London and New York: Routledge, 1992), pp. 1–26.

2 Faced with this list of luminaries, which could easily be extended, it is amusing to recall Alfred North Whitehead's dictum that 'a science which hesitates to forget its founders is lost'.

3 Cf. note 1, *supra*.

4 The following publications have already emanated from this project: Levan Lemesle (ed.), *Les problèmes de l'institutionnalisation de l'Économie Politique en France aux XIXe siècle*, Oeconomia (Paris: Presses Universitaire de Grenoble, 1988); M. Augello, M. Bianchini, G. Gioli and P. Roggi (eds), *The Academic Institutionalisation of Political Economy in Italy, 1750–1900* (Milan: Franco Angeli, 1988) (in Italian); Chuhei Sugiyama and Hiroshi Mizuta (eds), *Enlightenment and Beyond,*

Political Economy Comes to Japan (Tokyo: Tokyo University Press, 1988); N. Waszek (ed.), *Die Institutionalisierung der Nationalökonomie an Deutschen Universitäten, Zur Erinnering an Klaus Heinrich Hennings (1837–1896)* (St Katherinen: Scripta Mercaturae Verlag, 1988); William J. Barber (ed.), *Breaking the Mould: Economists and Academic Higher Learning in the Nineteenth Century* (Middletown, Conn.: Wesleyan University Press, 1991); Thomas A. Boylan and Timothy P. Foley, *Political Economy and Colonial Ireland. The Propagation and Ideological Functions of Economic Discourse in the Nineteenth Century* (London and New York: Routledge, 1992). Also forthcoming: Istvan Hont and Keith Tribe (eds), *Trade, Politics and Letters: The Rise of Economics in British University Culture, 1755–1905* (London and New York: Routledge). A closely related study, not a direct outcome of the project, is Keith Tribe, *Governing Economy. The Reformation of German Economic Discourse, 1750–1840* (Cambridge: Cambridge University Press, 1988).

5 See, for example, my essay on 'The Educational Revolution and the Professionalization of American Economics', in Barber, op. cit., pp. 340–75. Two-thirds of the essays published in the present volume consider the institutional context of economic thought either directly or indirectly.

6 The collection of essays on *Economists in Government: An International Comparative Study* (Durham, N.C.: Duke University Press, 1981), also published as a complete issue of *History of Political Economy* vol. 13 (Fall 1981), from which Chapters 25 and 26 in this volume are taken, gives some indication of the possibilities in the ten countries represented. See also the collection I edited on *Economists in International Agencies: An Exploratory Study* (New York: Praeger International, 1986). The subtitle is appropriate. There are also many private research institutes and non-profit organizations employing economists.

7 Cf. especially Chapter 18 in this volume; and Chapters 11–14. Needless to say, not all of the AEA or RES members were economists in any strict sense of the term.

8 See note 1, *supra*.

9 *Economica* N. S. vol. 22 (May 1955), pp. 171–4.

10 Chapters 4, 5 and 6 in this volume. See also my 'Explanations in Economics and History', *Social Research*, Summer 1989 (reprinted in vol. III in this series).

11 See 'Political Economy and the Tariff Reform Campaign of 1903', pp. 284–337 in vol. I in this series, and the references to subsequent literature on p. 334. 'The Culture and the Economists: Some Reflections on Anglo-American Differences' is Chapter 8 in this volume.

12 See his 'Social Conditioning of Economics', pp. 65–104, and my 'Commentary', pp. 105–10, in Neil de Marchi (ed.), *Post Popperian Methodology of Economics: Recovering Practice* (Boston, Dordrecht and London: Kluwer, 1992); and 'Social Theories of Science and the Fate of Institutionalism in Economics', in U. Maki, B. Gustaffson and C. Knudsen (eds), *Rationality, Institutions and Economic Methodology* (London: Routledge, 1993), pp. 76–109. The quotation in the text is from p. 77 of this essay.

It amuses me to recall that when I submitted my 'Sociological Aspects' paper (Chapter 7 in this volume) to the *Journal of Political Economy* it was accepted, subject to cuts, despite the comments of a referee (almost certainly George Stigler) that it was not 'systematic sociology' and 'only amusing gossip'. I accept the first stricture, but would claim that the second was but a partial truth. That paper has had some constructive influence on the work of Alon Kadish, Gerard Koot, John Maloney and John Wood who, collectively, have greatly enriched our knowledge of the period.

13 Maki, 'Social Theories of Science', in Maki *et al.*, op. cit., pp. 104–5, 106; cf. p. 77.
14 Aspects of the economics profession are considered in Chapters 21–4 in this volume. The 'crisis' in economics is discussed in Chapter 22 in vol. I in this series.
15 See Chapters 9, 10 and 14 in this volume. Also the 'Bibliography of Scholarly Articles on Economics Journals', in *Economic Notes by Monte dei Paschi di Siena* vol. 20 (1991), pp. 181–8.
16 David C. Colander and A. W. Coats (eds), *The Spread of Economic Ideas* (Cambridge: Cambridge University Press, 1989, 1993). This volume contains essays on 'From Economists to the Lay Public' and 'From Economist to Policymaker', but they constitute only a small step in the right direction.
17 See, for example, Arjo Klamer and David Colander, *The Making of an Economist* (Boulder, Colo.: Westview Press, 1990); *Report of the Commission on Graduate Education in Economics, Journal of Economic Literature* vol. 29 (September 1991), pp. 1035–53; H. Kasper *et al.*, 'The Education of Economists. From Undergraduate to Graduate Study', *Journal of Economic Literature*, vol. 29 (September 1991), pp. 1088–109; David Colander and Reuven Brenner, *Educating Economists* (Ann Arbor: Michigan University Press, 1992); A. W. Coats, 'Changing Perceptions of American Graduate Education in Economics, 1953–1991', *Journal of Economic Education* vol. 23 (Fall 1992), pp. 341–52 and accompanying comments on pp. 353–61.

ROUTLEDGE

11 New Fetter Lane
London EC4P 4EE
Telephone: 071-583 9855
Fax: 071-583 4519

We have much pleasure in sending you the accompanying book for review

Title: **Sociology & Profess.
of Economics**

Author: **Coats**

ISBN: Hb   **0 415 06716 2**

Pb

Publication Date:

28.10.93

Published Price: £   **45.00**   Hb

£   Pb

A copy of the review would be greatly appreciated.
Reviews should not appear in the press prior to the
date of publication.
For further information please contact:

Andrew Beavon

Part I

THE SOCIOLOGY OF ECONOMICS

2

THE SOCIOLOGY OF KNOWLEDGE AND THE HISTORY OF ECONOMICS

I INTRODUCTION

The sociology of knowledge has never been applied systematically to the history of economics. This chapter is designed to reveal some of the abundant research possibilities inherent in such an undertaking.

There are two principal reasons for embarking upon this enterprise. The first is simply that the twentieth-century expansion of economics as a discipline has been so rapid and complex that conventional, old-fashioned modes of historical explanation in terms of 'great men' (persons?) and 'great ideas' are no longer adequate – if, indeed, they ever were. New methods of handling and interpreting the proliferating literature are required if the historian is not only to keep abreast of the subject but also to present it succinctly and persuasively to current and future generations of students, professional practitioners, and laymen. Given the widespread recognition that economics is currently in a state of confusion, if not crisis, the performance of this task is of special interest and importance. The second, or 'external', reason reinforces this contention, for recent research in the sociology of knowledge (or science) constitutes an invaluable source of insights and hypotheses that can be serviceable to historians of economics in their present predicament.

No brief survey can do justice to the richness and variety of the sociology of science literature. The following account necessarily reflects my personal interests and the limitations of my knowledge. The emphasis is on what the sociologists of science have been doing, rather than on the implications of their research for the history and philosophy of science – although these fields are closely interrelated – for an examination of these wider issues would require a lengthy research monograph. Comparatively little space will be devoted to the applicability of the sociology of science to the history of economics as such, for many of the potential applications cited at the end of this essay will be obvious to specialists in the field. Indeed, one may well ask: Why have they been so reluctant to seize the available opportunities?

This question is the more surprising given the pioneering example of Joseph A. Schumpeter's classic *History of Economic Analysis* [60], which contained many perceptive comments on the sociology of economics and intellectual activity in general. His opening sections on economic sociology and the sociology of economics (chap. 4) constitute a rare example of serious scholarly interest in such topics by an economist. However, although the book contained a considerable volume of material on economic, political, and social history, Schumpeter's basic viewpoint was 'absolutist' rather than 'relativist' – that is, he focused on the cumulative progress of economic theory rather than the changing relationships between economic ideas and the historical context in which they developed. When Schumpeter was writing, many historians of ideas were unfavourably disposed to the sociology of knowledge, which had usually been presented in a simplistic and deterministic fashion emphasizing, for example, the social class determinants of ideas at any given time or place.[1] Moreover, the approach was predominantly macrosociological and insufficiently sensitive to the available historical evidence.

The situation is very different now, both in the sociology of knowledge and in the history and philosophy of science literature. Simplistic and deterministic explanations are out; and despite the profound influence of such 'Weltanshauungen analyses' as T. S. Kuhn's *The Structure of Scientific Revolutions* [41], which combined philosophy, history, and sociology of science in a fascinating, albeit controversial manner, the emphasis in all three fields is shifting toward more precise, small-scale studies of scientific ideas and practices. Even the philosophers now consider that

> the key to developing an adequate philosophical understanding of science as an epistemic enterprise is the detailed examination of actual scientific practice from which one generalizes and evaluates the reasoning patterns encountered.[2]

Whether such investigations acknowledge the relevance of psychological or sociological factors in scientific work is a fundamental disputed issue. Nevertheless a microphilosophical study which exposes the role of reason in scientific work is likely to be more appealing to historians of economics than one couched in the broad abstract terms to be found in earlier philosophical writings.

The relationship between the epistemological and sociological dimensions of science will be referred to later, especially in connection with the so-called 'strong' programme in the sociology of knowledge (sections II and III). At this point, however, it is appropriate to note the general argument for a more sociological approach to the history of economics, which is indispensable in dealing with recent periods. As economics has grown and proliferated, the role of individual achievement and creativity may indeed be as great as in earlier periods, but it is certainly more difficult to isolate and evaluate. Rather than the new paradigms, imaginative leaps, crucial experiments, or other intellectual breakthroughs which figure so prominently in conventional histories, the growth of a modern academic discipline must be seen as a collective phenomenon, a relatively continuous or evolutionary process shaped by many hands. In depicting this process we must perforce resort to more sociological methods, as, for example, with the aid of the statistical techniques pioneered in our field by that well-known sociologist, George Stigler [64, pp. 31–50; see also 8, 14, 22, 23]. There have already been studies of the communications network, career patterns, reward system, and social stratification in economics, especially through the analysis of the content and status of scholarly journals. As most of these exercises have been concerned with recent developments they have, naturally enough, been ignored or at least underutilized by historians of economics; and it must be conceded that the quantitative data for much earlier periods is either more sparse or lacking, and probably less reliable. Nevertheless, this does not excuse the neglect of the available information on the late nineteenth and early twentieth century. This statistical material is only the tip of an iceberg which merits much deeper investigation. Such topics as the origins, nature, and significance of doctrinal schools, movements, and other groupings; the rise (and fall?) of specialist fields or subdisciplines; the influences on and changing character of the recruitment, training, and socialization of new entrants; mechanisms of institutional rivalry and leadership, both national and international; the significance of demographic changes for career and promotion prospects and intergenerational differences and conflicts; national styles of academic organization and their effects on teaching and research; and the interrelationships between the various economics 'professions' (i.e., academic, business, and government economics) and society (see section IV).

The list of relevant research topics is potentially endless, and the bibliography of existing writings on the sociology of economics – most of which are occasional in character and limited in scope – is already substantial. It is now time to attempt to draw together and build upon the existing scattered and uneven stock of material and to make more consistent and systematic use of the concepts, research methods, and findings already available in the sociology of science literature. The scope and significance of this undertaking can only be outlined in this chapter, and it is first of all necessary to provide some kind of preliminary intellectual framework. As the so-called strong programme in the sociology of knowledge is the most provocative and assertive part of the sociology of science literature it will provide a suitable starting point.

II THE 'STRONG' PROGRAMME IN THE SOCIOLOGY OF KNOWLEDGE

The 'strong' programme (hereinafter SP) emanates from a group of scholars at the University of Edinburgh, which includes Barry Barnes, David Bloor, and Steven Shapin. Their objective is to generalize on the basis of numerous empirically oriented studies in the history of science, and their work helps to fill the substantial gap between the philosophers' account of science and the descriptive investigations of how scientists actually go about their work. This parallels the notorious discrepancy between economists' practices and their methodological preachings, teachings, and prescriptions, which Mark Blaug, for example, has demonstrated so devastatingly in his recent study [10]. Advocates of the SP proceed in a direction opposite to that usually adopted, i.e., they go from actual practice to methodological principle, and key terms in their vocabulary include *local*, *contingent*, and *context dependent*, referring to what scientists actually believe and do in specific situations, as contrasted with the supposedly universal and immutable correct principles which have hitherto figured so prominently in methodological and philosophy of science literature. They admit, and even rejoice in, their relativism, decrying the abstract philosophical absolutism underlying the conventionally agreed conception of the scientific mode. Thus the SP reverses the usual relationship, making logic and methodology the subordinate partner and sociology the dominant one.

A few quotations will convey the flavour of this approach. For example, Barnes attacks what he calls 'the Manichean myth of knowledge' which draws a sharp distinction between science and its social context, denies the role of social contingencies, and depicts scientific judgement as proceeding 'entirely by reference to timeless, universal "rules of reason"'. . . . Great effort is expended upon protecting science from the threats of pollution which empirical studies of its development invariably present' [3, pp. 117–18]. Barnes maintains that the familiar distinction between the internalist (superior) and externalist (inferior) interpretations of the growth of knowledge is derived from the same epistemological preconceptions. Whereas the former emphasizes 'the forces of light within the esoteric scientific context – observation, experiment, rational inference', the latter purportedly invokes 'such dark outside agencies as interests and social biases for the same explanatory task. The two approaches are regarded as incompatible, the former being the ideal, and the latter the *bête noir* of much historiographical rhetoric' [ibid.]. According to Bloor, the classification internal = rational vs. external = sociological presupposes a false dichotomy:

> As well as an *external* sociology of knowledge there is also an *internal* sociology of knowledge . . . where broad social factors are not involved, narrow ones take over. . . . [That is,] the social factors

concerned may be ones which derive from the narrowly conceived interests or traditions or routines of the professional community. . . . Much that goes on in science can be plausibly seen as a result of the desire to maintain or increase the importance, status and scope of the methods and techniques which are the special property of a group. . . . To claim that scientists are educated and socialized into a certain community and address their communications to their peers, is most certainly *not* . . . to invoke a trivial mode of social involvement. The claim only appears trivial if it is attended by a shallow or uncertain grasp of the social processes in question. Properly understood, training, socialization and communication are deep and complex and revealing phenomena.[3]

It is in the analysis of the 'internal' sociology of knowledge (to use their terminology) that exponents of the SP come into their own. Instead of limiting themselves to the institutional framework of science and the social forces affecting its growth or direction, they contend that the sociology of knowledge should investigate and can explain the very content and nature of scientific knowledge.[4] 'The internal values and pressures of the discipline' [*64*, p. 22] – the methodological rules, heuristic principles, basic norms and conventions adopted by any scientific group – have no unique, absolute, or universal validity and significance. They are merely means to an end (or ends); and both means and ends are largely, if not entirely, local, contingent, and context dependent. Evidently nothing is sacred, not even logic itself, for there is no unique logical system:

> As a body of conventions and esoteric traditions the compelling character of logic, such as it is, derives from certain narrowly defined purposes and from custom and institutionalised usage. Its authority is moral and social, and as such it is admirable material for sociological investigation and explanation. In particular, the credibility of logical conventions, just like everyday practices which deviate from them, will be of an entirely local character. . . . The rationalist goal of producing pieces of knowledge that are both universal in their credibility *and* justified in context-independent terms is unattainable.[5]

The same considerations apply to the language employed by scientists, their systems of classification, and their inferences and judgements, all of which have to be learnt within the scientific community or, more precisely, within the relevant segment of that community.[6] Instead of defining a theory in the conventional manner as 'a system of statements perhaps, or a formal mathematical structure, from which particular solutions are deduced or logically derived . . . the tables are turned, and a theory . . . is defined by its applications: it is simply the cluster of what are called its "applications" ' or problem solutions [*3*, p. 121].

The SP is a logical extension of tendencies already apparent in methodological literature which have not yet come fully within the economist's ken. The end result is a form of extreme relativism which is easily reached by venturing beyond Kuhn's concept of the incommensurability of paradigms, through the problems of theory testing and intertheoretic criticism and comparison, to an awareness of the conventional character of language, and finally to the ethnomethodologists' conclusion that there are no objective and unambiguous procedures for applying social rules since the meanings of particular actions are indexical, or context dependent, rather than dependent on any invariant general principles.[7] According to Barnes and Bloor, the concept of a 'rational bridgehead' or

> common core of belief shared by all cultures, turns out to be a purely imaginary construct with no empirical basis. . . . The distinction between the parts of the culture that belong to the core, and the parts that are specific and variable is just another version of the idea that observational predicates are qualitatively different from theoretical predicates . . . it is a plea for a single pure observation language. Of all the dualisms of epistemology, this must be the most discredited. Surely we all recognise that although we may well share the same unverbalised environment, there are any number of reasonable ways of speaking about it.
>
> [5, pp. 39–40; in reply to 29, pp. 67–86]

The SP embodies a radically relativistic sociological interpretation of the scientific community and its knowledge-producing practices which can be summarized, albeit with some unavoidable oversimplification, in the following main concepts: naturalism, radical conventionalism, tradition, finitism, validation, and instrumentalism.

According to this approach there is a general correspondence between knowlege and 'reality' (naturalism), but reality can be perceived, described, and interpreted in a variety of ways.[8] There is no single criterion of truth acceptable in all cultures, and scientific concepts, theories, paradigms, tests, judgements, etc. are simply conventions approved by the scientific community (radical conventionalism).[9] However, this does not mean that these conventions are either arbitrary or lax: on the contrary, they derive from stringent rules and procedures which cannot easily be mastered or changed. Science is based on order, continuity, authority, and control, and although it is neither rigid nor inflexible the scope for novelty and innovation is strictly limited by the recognized conventions (tradition) and by the specific circumstances of the scientist's field [cf. 26, 39]. Tradition governs the accepted theories, methods, and techniques in any discipline, and also the selection, training, qualification, and socialization of entrants into the relevant segment of the scientific community.

Viewed from this standpoint, Kuhn's dramatic account of scientific

16

'revolutions' is less revealing than his conception of 'normal' science, which is 'of *fundamental* theoretical importance since it describes many characteristics of cognition and culture which it is difficult to imagine could be otherwise' [*3*, p. 57; italics in original]. Radical criticism is possible 'only where there are more than one set of standards and conventions and more than one conceivable definition of reality' [*11*, p. 38]. This does not mean that normal science is static. In practice acceptable scientific usage is 'developed step by step in a succession of on-the-spot judgments. Every instance of use, or proper use, of a concept must in the last analysis be accounted for separately, by reference to specific, local, contingent circumstances' [*3*, pp. 30–1]. The corollary of this view (finitism) is the denial 'that inherent properties or meanings attach to concepts and determine their future applications', and that

> truth and falsity are inherent properties of statements. 'True' and 'false' are terms which are interesting only as they are used by a community itself, as it develops and maintains its own accepted patterns of concept application.

> [Ibid.]

Associated with this is the SP's most controversial contention that in science 'there is no basis for validation superior to the collective contingent judgment of the paradigm-sharing community itself' (validation) [*42*, p. 51]. All species of knowledge are transmitted, sustained, and undermined by the same social processes, and they are differentiated according to 'the particular social interests they are related to and the manner in which they are actively employed' (instrumentalism) [*2*, p. 83]. Thus the SP seeks to obliterate the sharp distinction customarily drawn between science and other kinds of knowledge. Science is bounded by social credibility and practical utility, and influenced by an overt interest in prediction and control and a covert interest in rationalization and persuasion. Ideologically determined knowledge, on the other hand, is not irrational, but rather a naturally rational response to the need for legitimation, and the dichotomy is further undermined by acknowledging the extent to which science itself embodies a disciplinary or professional ideology.

Spokesmen for the SP strenuously deny that their model is deterministic; that it equates social factors with irrational 'external' macrosociological influences; or that it rejects 'the contention that scientific knowledge is empirically grounded in sensory output from natural reality' [*61*, p. 197; cf. *46*, p. 205]. It simply seeks to make due allowance for the variety of contingent interests and conditions affecting scientific work and the variety of verbal formulations utilized in historical and sociological explanations. Of course, this variety is not unlimited or haphazard. By studying exemplars or paradigmatic concrete problem solutions the student or apprentice is initiated into understanding of the 'disciplinary matrix' comprising sym-

17

bolic generalizations, shared commitments to particular models, and shared values, which, taken together, help to account for the relatively unproblematic character of professional communication and relative unanimity of judgement in a 'normal' scientific community [*42*, p. 307; cited in *3*, pp. 35–6]. To advocates of the SP, this scientific subculture 'is far more than the setting for scientific research; it is the research itself' [*42*, p. 10].

III CRITIQUE OF THE STRONG PROGRAMME, AND AN ALTERNATIVE SOCIOLOGICAL APPROACH

In its more extreme form the SP asserts the primacy of sociological over all other interpretations of scientific knowledge and procedures, and it is hardly surprising that some historians and philosophers resist and resent it as an attempted imperialist takeover by presumptuous predatory sociologists. Curiously enough, both the proponents of SP and contemporary philosophers of science focus their attention on scientific 'fields' or 'domains' rather than science in general, but the central tendency in contemporary philosophy of science, according to Suppe, is the strong commitment to a metaphysical and epistemological realism which virtually precludes sociological views of knowledge of the kind embodied in the Weltanschauungen analyses referred to earlier.[10] This commitment is postpositivist in the sense that it stresses the role of rationality in the growth of scientific knowledge, whereas the SP involves a regression to radical empiricism in its naturalistic refusal to take account of the epistemological basis and implications of the scientist's activity. To Dudley Shapere, for instance,

> the systematic examination of the 'reasoning patterns' actually employed in science is a primary source of information about the nature of scientific knowledge and the theories, models, and conceptual devices science employs [and this formulation] requires no reference to psychological or sociological factors, and their operation in concrete cases is, or can be, independent of such factors.[11]

The qualifying phrase 'or can be' suggests that some reconciliation of the two approaches may be possible, though at present the battle lines are still sharply drawn. From another standpoint the distinction is one between 'Rationality and Relativism', or between the variability of scientific concepts, modes, theories, procedures, and interpretations highlighted in the SP literature and the philosopher's question

> whether concepts, propositions, reasoning patterns, and methods that prove to be stable in the history of science and govern the ways changes of ideas take place are stable because they are independent of the *content* of science at any stage.

[*67*, p. 684; cf. *30*, *passim*]

This passage serves as a bridge between the SP and other, less radical interpretations of the sociology of science which do not rely on the 'symmetry' thesis [*29*, p. 68, based on *11*], i.e., the contention that the explanation of beliefs is independent of their status, whether true or false, scientific or nonscientific. Ernest Nagel once characterized science as 'an institutionalized mechanism for sifting warranted beliefs' [*48*, p. 490], and any adequate account of this activity must incorporate both an epistemological theory or criterion by which to differentiate between valid and invalid hypotheses and/or conclusions and a sociological strategy which explains how scientific communities or groups arrive at their collective judgements. According to Richard Whitley[12] the SP is deficient on both counts: it obscures the crucial epistemological distinction between science and other kinds of knowledge, consequently failing to provide a sociological explanation of the emergence of modern science as a peculiar and important species of understanding; and its descriptions of scientific work are too particularistic. Admittedly scientists are not seeking 'truth' in the abstract philosophical sense of that term; they are seeking particular kinds of truth which emerge in the course of pursuing particular research procedures and practices. Nevertheless, despite some sociologists' tendency to treat the social process of knowledge production as chaotic, which makes the eventual emergency of agreement on results appear either mysterious or inexplicable, it is necessary to provide a generalized comprehensible account of scientific work and its significance both for the growth of knowledge and for society. Contrary to Shapere and other philosophers, Whitley denies that the concepts, propositions, reasoning patterns, and methods employed by any group of scientists are independent of the content of science at any stage, and this forms the starting point of his suggestive typology of scientific fields or disciplines (to be considered in the following paragraphs). The SP, Whitley argues, depicts scientists' judgements and scientific change merely as epiphenomena of material causes and interests, a radical empiricist interpretation which provides no theoretical foundation for the evaluation of scientific beliefs. Rather than beliefs being simply dependent on 'interests' – which consequently appear as 'external' to the processes of science – scientists' interests and beliefs are reciprocally interrelated and

> the sociology of knowledge should concern itself with the configuration of relations linking beliefs, rationalities, social structures, and the organization of knowledge production. Sociological accounts of the genesis, elaboration and acceptance of scientific beliefs ... need to reconstruct the procedures and practices through which it made sense to particular groups to believe one theory or set of statements rather than another.
>
> [*75*, p. 694; cf. ibid., pp. 687–94]

Such reconstructions are to be found in many of the works cited by advocates of SP, and the methods employed in these studies are fully compatible with the procedures conventionally utilized by historians of economics.

One of the central features of modern science, Whitley maintains, is the use of knowledge to create new knowledge, and the ability of some intellectual producers to exert a measure of control over this process. The workers in any scientific field are institutionally committed to constructing intellectual innovations – only 'new' knowledge is considered publishable – and the extent of such innovations is restricted by making reputations, and hence rewards, dependent upon the use made of them for others' research. The scientists acquire positive intellectual reputations and coordinate their work through a public communication system which forms a 'reputational system' of work organization and control in any given field. The emergence of distinct work control and organizational patterns in different scientific fields is determined, to a significant degree, by the content of each field. Consequently we need studies of

> the organisation of research in different situations and historical circumstances, of how intellectual fields become distinguished and separated, and how such fields as socio-intellectual structures become established, exert control over research, reproduce themselves, and change.

> [Ibid., p. 708]

It is neither possible nor appropriate to provide a detailed account of Whitley's impressive effort to construct a typology of scientific fields in terms of their organizational structures and internal relationships. For the present purpose it is sufficient to concentrate on two cases only: economics, for obvious reasons, and physics, which possesses very distinct features and has long been regarded as the 'icon of scientificity' [25, p. ix] by many economists and natural scientists. Before doing so, however, it may be helpful to specify the four key variables in Whitley's model [76, pp. 14–28]:

a. *The degree of mutual dependence among scientists*, which subdivides into two components: (i) *functional dependence* – the extent to which workers in any field need to coordinate task outcomes and demonstrate adherence to common competence standards; and (ii) *strategic dependence* – the extent of the need to coordinate research strategies and convince colleagues of the centrality of particular concerns to collective goals.
b. *The degree of task uncertainty*, which also subdivides into two components (i) *technical task uncertainty* – the extent to which work techniques are well understood and produce reliable results; and (ii) *strategic task uncertainty* – the extent to which problems are organized into a stable hierarchy of importance according to common standards of significance.

According to Whitley, physics is unique among contemporary sciences owing to its combination of technical control, problem uniformity and stability, and high mutual dependence among its practitioners. The quest for formal coherence and mathematical unity (which also inspires some economists) is associated with a high degree of theoretical and strategic certainty and a relatively low degree of task uncertainty, so that the growth of specialization and differentiation within the discipline has occurred without fragmentation. Subdisciplines and specialisms are easily distinguishable, yet interdependent, and disputes centre not on the general framework but on the way it is used to integrate and order reputations among subfields. In physics theoretical work has emerged as a distinct occupational identity which has no counterpart in other sciences. Nevertheless theoretical work is not divorced from applied or experimental activity because coordination and integration

> can be carried out by scientists who are separate from the actual production and assessment of experimental results just as the coordination and control of production in mass production industries is a separate activity from the direct supervision of the production process.
>
> [*74*, p. 52]

Disputes centre not on the basic framework but on the way it is used to integrate and order reputations among subfields, and as there are restricted opportunities to participate in the most prestigious activities competition centres on access to facilities and resources and the relative merits of competing expansions and extensions of the 'theory core'. Specialization enables physicists to produce original work within the dominant framework, but each area has to demonstrate its importance for 'real' physics if it is to provide prestigious reputations. Consequently the relationship between the core and peripheral or 'deviant' areas is a critical concern, and the physicists'

> policing of intellectual boundaries and fears of 'pollution' from 'applied' issues and goals are as marked as those of economists, especially in European countries, and are a strong contrast to the more relaxed attitudes of chemists.
>
> [Ibid., p. 53]

In Whitley's scheme physics exemplifies the category of 'conceptually integrated bureaucracies' whereas economics, which he examines at some length, falls within the class of 'partitioned bureaucracies'.[13] In economics, as in physics, the theoretical core dominates textbooks, training programmes, the communication system, and academic reputations, posts, and honours. Moreover:

> Within analytical economics there is a high degree of mutual dependence among practitioners, a high degree of formalisation and stan-

dardisation of work procedures, assessment standards and problem formulations and a high degree of task differentiation.[14]

[Ibid., p. 33]

However economics is distinct from other scientific fields in its combination of a high level of technical task uncertainty with a low level of strategic task uncertainty. Despite the dominance of the established body of economic analysis there is, unlike the situation in physics, a marked division between theoretical and empirical work.[15] This is partly owing to the lack of technical control over empirical work, which limits the applied economist's dependence on the theorist (again unlike what happens in physics), and also because of the existence of other relevant audiences outside the theoretical establishment and, indeed, outside the scientific and/or professional community. The low level of strategic task uncertainty means that competition within the central core, though intense, is restricted to technical refinements and extensions of the analytical scheme to novel problems which can be tackled with existing techniques.[16] High reputations for significant work are based on theoretical sophistication and demonstrations of the consistency and generality of the dominant framework.

The partitioning of theoretical from empirical economics has not, however, ensured the empiricists' autonomy, for the degree of segmentation of applied fields is limited by the dominance of the established theoretical goals.[17] This dominance does not work equally well in all the subdisciplines, for

the degree of impersonality and formalisation of coordination and control procedures varies between sub-units as the relatively intractable and unpredictable nature of empirical phenomena restricts the extent to which systematic comparison and validation of task outcomes can be accomplished through the formal communications system.

[74, p. 30]

The heterogeneity of applied fields, though high, is constrained by 'rigid delimitation' of the sorts of problems deemed legitimate and important; yet deviations on the periphery can be largely ignored by the intellectual élite who control the dominant communication media and training programmes.

Like many other commentators, Whitley observes that owing to the gap between theoretical and empirical work in economics the student learns to solve artificial analytical problems rather than those posed by everyday economic events. Moreover, there are persistent disputes about the relationship of formal economics to the real world, partly owing to the lack of means whereby empirical studies feed back into the theoretical corpus (unlike the situation in physics). The results of applied work make little impact either on academic reputations or on the received doctrine, which

22

is preserved without substantial modification even when contradictions and errors are admitted. Because there is less monolithic control over work goals in the applied areas there is some scope for theoretical deviance, as in industrial and labour economics, and the discipline as a whole can absorb additional personnel partly by extending the range of applications to new subject-matter, e.g., the economics of the arts, crime, the family, etc.:

> No other field in the social sciences and humanities comes close to economics in its combination of theoretical uniformity and technical uncertainty. Attempts at formalizing and standardizing fields have usually failed because of the difficulties of establishing a high restricted understanding of their subject matter and/or the plurality of possible audiences and resource providers which has limited the degree of dependence of scientists upon each other for reputations and material rewards. Generally, the closeness of most areas to common sense concerns and concepts has severely hampered movements to 'professionalize' them and render lay judgements totally irrelevant to reputations.
>
> [74, p. 34]

Despite its powerful and relatively autonomous theoretical core, and its battery of sophisticated measurement procedures, economics has not yet emancipated itself from the influence of 'lay images'.[18] This is obviously due in part to the economists' collective inability to resist the many opportunities to participate in and shape public discussion and the extent to which they have become an advisory profession[19] – much more so, it should be noted, than other social scientists.

IV THE APPLICABILITY OF WHITLEY'S MODEL TO THE HISTORY OF ECONOMICS

Many historians of economics will probably have reservations about Whitley's ambitious attempt to locate economics within his generalized sociology of science framework. Some may object to the very idea of a typology of disciplines, while others may consider parts of his account either trite, obvious, or incorrect. Nevertheless, it is usually illuminating 'to see ourselves as others see us', and Whitley's framework points the way to future research by revealing the progress already made toward an understanding of the differing characteristics within and the changing relations among scientific fields and academic disciplines.

There are both sociological and epistemological reasons why economists (and historians of economics) are inclined to resist the adoption of a sociological interpretation of their discipline. In one sense the relevance of sociological factors is too obvious and disconcerting. Few economists cherish the illusion that they are immune from exogenous societal influences, yet they cling to the ideal of scientific autonomy while at the same time seizing the available opportunities to participate in public policy discussion and decision making. On the other hand, their neglect (at least until recently; *vide infra*) of social influences within the disciplinary matrix is probably due to the fact that the subject had its modern origins in liberal-rationalist moral philosophy and its concomitant epistemological optimism, according to which there was

> no need for any man to appeal to authority in matters of truth because each man carried the sources of knowledge in himself: either in his power of sense perception which he may use for the careful obser-vation of nature, or in his power of intellectual intuition which he may use to distinguish truth from falsehood by refusing to accept any idea which is not clearly and distinctly perceived by the intellect.
>
> [53, p. 5]

Against this excessively individualistic view sociologists of science propose to shift attention from the traditional preoccupation with unchanging regularities and laws to the study of diachronic sequences of developing concepts and forms of thought. As Norbert Elias has suggested, in scientific concept formation the human 'subject' is not

> an isolated individual abstracting on its own common properties from a number of 'concrete' objects by comparing them, but an intergener-ational process formed by many individuals – an unplanned process whose direction is functionally related to that of societies providing continuity for this knowledge process . . . the terminological separ-ation to which we are used, between the structure of knowledge, the genesis of knowledge, and the structure and development of the human groups which store, administer, and produce knowledge is unreal and misleading . . . [for] it is particularly clear how *inextricably interwoven and interdependent are the social values and thus the status and power ratio of groups of scientists and the cognitive value of the scientific knowledge produced by them.*[20]

A purely descriptive SP-style sociology of economics may be unattainable in principle. Nevertheless, sociological analysis can provide a bridge linking economic methodology with the history of economics, two fields customarily dismissed – with some justification – as unduly abstract and remote from professional practice. However, when methodology is viewed as the study and evaluation of the procedural rules, heuristic principles, and scientific conventions utilized by economists, and doctrinal history is focused on the origins, development, and significance of changing styles of professional activity (rather than the study of disembodied ideas or outstanding indi-vidual figures), their convergence and relevance to the current and future

24

state of the discipline immediately become apparent. As noted earlier, an academic discipline or science is an ongoing collective enterprise, and the rise, scientific characteristics, survival capacity, and influence of particular intellectual groups, movements, and schools, and their interrelationships should be a primary focus of inquiry. In the case of economics, for example, even such hackneyed subjects as the Ricardians, Marxians, Austrians, and Keynesians, have not yet been examined from a systematic sociological standpoint, partly because historians of economics have usually been unwilling to go beyond the conventional history of ideas. Consequently, even in such a heavily worked-over topic as J. M. Keynes and Cambridge, on which there is a vast literature of theoretical analysis, interpretation, and textual exegesis, casual empiricism, *obiter dicta*, and personal reminiscence have tended to predominate in accounts of the origins, evolution, reception, influence, and scientific importance of the *General Theory*, although it is widely acknowledged that a fascinating combination of personality, beliefs, behaviour, social background, academic location, career experience, sociopolitical attitudes, colleagues in Cambridge, and contemporary events, all played a significant part. If, as seems clear, there has been no comprehensive and systematic investigation of the historical and sociological, as well as the intellectual context of the most important single economics book published in this century, the case for the sociology of economic science requires no further support.[21]

With the recent resurgence of rival economic doctrines and schools since the end of the Keynesian hegemony, there is a pressing need for careful historical and sociological studies of the contending professional groups and interests that will take into account their ideological preconceptions, institutional affiliations, professional networks and goals, as well as their assumptions, scientific criteria, methods, techniques, doctrines, and policy recommendations. There is, of course, a considerable volume of published work on recent economic thought and policy which contains many useful hints, hypotheses, and source materials for prospective researchers, ranging in scope from Harry G. Johnson's [32] stimulating but highly impressionistic discussion of national 'styles' in economic research (a lamentably neglected topic),[22] through Benjamin Ward's intriguing and potentially subversive exploration of *The Ideal Worlds of Economics* [70] (which argues that there are three concurrent, self-contained incommensurable paradigms or Weltanschauungen in contemporary economics), to the narrower focus of Melvin Reder's penetrating analysis of the Chicago school [54]. None of these is entirely satisfactory from a sociological standpoint – nor, it should be added, is it intended so to be. For example, although Reder's valuable article brings the reader close to the heart of the Chicago version of economic science and contains illuminating glimpses of the leading personalities and their institutional context, it is not intended to be either comprehensive or exhaustive. A systematic investigation of the recruitment, careers, research activities, and publications of Chicago-oriented economists and their students and disciples over the past four or five decades, supplemented by a collective biography based on systematic interviews, the use of survey research methods, and historical study of the University of Chicago Economics Department's records, would shed considerable new light on the evolution, nature, and impact of this very influential component in the contemporary economics profession. Hopefully, such a study would be accompanied by comparable research on the other leading past and present centres of economic teaching and research.[23]

Work of this kind would not go far beyond the range and methods employed by previous researchers in the history of economics. More innovative, however, and more problematic, is Whitley's agenda for study of the 'dimensions of contexts' of a scientific field, which includes such items as the following:

1. Reputational autonomy over the setting of performance standards, significance standards, problem formation, and descriptive concepts
2. Concentration of control over access to critical resources, including the degree of
   a. horizontal control over access to funds, journal space, and jobs by a reputational élite, through its ability to set standards and assess performance; and
   b. vertical control by leaders of employment units over appointments, promotions, submissions to journals, funding agencies, research strategies
3. Audience structures – including the variety of audiences and their goals; and the extent to which different audiences are equivalent or form a stable hierarchy [76, pp. 45–9].

How far studies of these 'dimensions of contexts' can be fruitfully pursued in the case of economics is the most challenging question posed by Whitley's model, for it is central to the discipline's distinctive division between theoretical and empirical work (see section III, above). In my view Whitley overstates the coherence of and control exercised by the dominant theoretical core in economics and seriously underestimates the significance and influence of the perennial dissenting tradition within and on the fringes of the professional establishment. These are matters of degree and judgement which cannot be fully explored here; but their role and importance can be appreciated by reference to the concepts of 'closure' and 'restrictions' cited by Whitley and others [9, 46, 49, 56, 71, 73].

Generally speaking, the less 'restricted' a science and the more complex its objects of study, the more open and varied is the research process, and this, in turn, is directly linked to the central issues of organization and control through the key variables of functional and strategic dependence, technical and strategic task uncertainty. Or, to translate the same issue into terms familiar to historians of economics, it raises the central problem of the relationship between the main orthodox (classical and neoclassical) stream of thought and its heterodox rivals (especially historical and institutional economics).

As is well known, during the past half century the so-called mathematical-quantitative revolution in economics has brought the theoretical core of the subject much closer to the ideal of a 'restricted' discipline, an ideal which has dominated the natural sciences for more than a century. At least since the marginal revolution of the 1870s, mainstream economists have sought to enhance their intellectual authority and autonomy by excluding certain questions which were either sensitive (such as the distribution of income and wealth, and the role of economic power in society) or incapable of being handled by their preferred methods and techniques, or both. These are precisely the questions which are emphasized by their professional and lay critics and, more recently, by many economists who cannot be dismissed by their professional colleagues as either ignorant or incompetent.[24] One such economist cited by Whitley is Nicholas Georgescu-Roegen [27], whose distinction between arithmomorphic and dialectical (nonarithmomorphic) disciplines exposes the connections between basic ontological and epistemological commitments, on the one hand, and systems of scientific production, on the other. 'The arithmomorphic ideal of working with objects constituted by simple elements that can be aggregated and disaggregated as one wishes' is associated with

> the scientific goal of universalism (requiring standardization) . . . and the social and cultural goal of Western civilization to increase its control over nature and man. Within science, successful control is institutionalized through the reproduction of procedures and experimental set-ups; the first requires much skill and tacit knowledge, but after a time in a more standardized way and supported by regular training.
>
> [56, p. 229]

The relevance of this description to post-1945 developments in graduate training in mathematical and quantitative economics need not be elaborated here, but it is worth juxtaposing the contrasting judgements of its effects on the scientific quality of the discipline expressed by two leading practitioners, Paul Samuelson and Harry Johnson. According to Samuelson, the Ph.D. is crucial to the existence, let alone the maintenance, of high standards in economics:

> This is not at all because our average doctoral dissertation is a substantial contribution to scholarship, a work of art, or even a literate document. To look at a thesis is to miss the point; it is only the exposed peak of a submerged iceberg. If the Ph.D. programme had

27

never existed we should now have to invent it – for the simple reason that it *gives us the excuse to carry on advanced instruction in economics*.

[*59*, p. 1741; italics in original (this passage dates from 1966)]

But to Johnson there was a much more serious likelihood that the narrowing of the economics training in Ph.D. programmes, which was an almost inevitable concomitant of academic specialization, would impair the scientific progress of the discipline:

One of the intellectually safe and relatively riskless ways of producing a successful Ph.D. thesis, or a post-Ph.D. thesis, or a post-Ph.D. article, is to do more elegantly and with greater generality a piece of work previously done by someone else in the same institution – because if B does better than A something A got a Ph.D. for, it is very difficult for the staff who approved A's thesis to turn down B's. This is one reason why so many promising young Ph.D.-stage economists are never heard of again. Without someone else's shoulders to stand on, they get lost in the crowd of intellectual midgets.

[*36*, p. 502]

Many of the intellectual advances of the early postwar years, he maintained,

represented the working out, by sustained application of many intelligences, of ideas explicit or obviously implicit in the thinking of the past great economists, thinking transmitted to the post-World War II generation of economists as a consequence of the scholarly knowledge of the literature of the pre-World War I period and 1920's and early 1930's. With the prolonged studied neglect of the history of the subject that has come to characterize the Ph.D. preparation stage and the immediately ensuing publication stage of a professional career, the subject is very likely to deteriorate sharply intellectually, unless revivified by fresh and deep draughts of literary scholarship on the works of the great economists of the past. This, however, is likely to occur more or less automatically, as the sterility of purely technologically-based work becomes increasingly obvious.

[Ibid., p. 507]

Whether Johnson's long-run optimism was more or less securely grounded than his short-run pessimism is a suitable topic for research, though his explanation is, at least in part, obviously congenial to historians of economics. According to one pessimistic commentator, in the academic community:

the power to appoint and, if not dismiss, then *dis*appoint potential and actual members is vested with the leading elite (the 'invisible college') of each disciplinary profession. It does not follow that these academic authorities are necessarily 'stooges' of the state. They certainly do feel some degree of responsibility in keeping the academic order in line with the broadest aims and objectives of the society; but outside this broader framework they enjoy a substantial degree of autonomy in exercising their power. This autonomous power enables the leading elite of each discipline to draw purely academic lines between proper and improper conduct. In practice, proper academic conduct is to operate within the established framework (or, as the popular expression has it, 'toe the line') and improper conduct is to search for new ones. Hence the slowness of the pace of intellectual progress. This, too, is a function of size. The growth in the number and size of the institutions of the academic profession has made an important contribution to this process by increasing the anonymity and irrelevance of the individual academic. . . . The contemporary professional academic is less free and more secure than he has ever been in the entire history of the modern academic progression.

[*38*, pp. 126–7]

It is unnecessary to accept this account in detail, but it represents a logical – or, more properly, a coherent sociological – interpretation of the effects on economics of recent developments in the knowledge-producing process. As with more familiar accounts of the effects of specialization and the division of labour on the wage earner in a modern industrialized economy, the possibility of alienation among professionals cannot be lightly dismissed. Indeed, the potential threat to the mental worker may be even greater than that to the manual worker:

In the case of material production the conveyor belt mediates between the activities of numerous specialists in giving rise to the final, integrated product: the motor car is certain to leave the factory in one piece for all the world to see. But there is no such mediating agent for the highly specialized efforts of intellectual workers. Each one digs further and further into a small corner of the problem apart from the others, without there being an automatic or impersonal or even institutional agency which would bring all the pieces together and integrate the solution in one piece. . . . The professional academic who himself is a tiny link in this gigantic socio-technological structure can hardly be expected to apprehend its full dimensions – to cope with it, let alone to criticize, direct and reconstruct it. . . . Only when there is a total breakdown is he asked to diagnose and prescribe; to search for a real solution to a real problem – he is not even allowed to anticipate the problem and suggest ways of preventing it. In any case he is generally ill-equipped to do so, morally, intellectually and professionally.

[Ibid., pp. 129–30]

29

This is neither the time nor the place to embark upon an analysis of the perennial tensions between the arithmomorphic (quantitative, mechanistic) and the dialectical (qualitative, historical, institutionalist, evolutionary) conceptions of and components in economics,[25] although no student of the history and sociology of the natural sciences will be surprised to learn that when the former standpoint is (perhaps temporarily) under widespread attack, the latter will be undergoing a revival, as at present. The important point to stress here is that these changes affect not only the cognitive but also the regulative level of the discipline. Disputes centre not merely on issues of methodology, theory, techniques, and policy (a dimension that is particularly sensitive and of growing importance in economics); they also have to be seen in the broader terms encompassed in contemporary sociology of science.

It would be possible to conclude this essay with a checklist of research topics in the sociology of economics, but this seems unnecessary (see section I). Instead it may be fitting to end with a forceful declaration from George Stigler, a distinguished, tough-minded economist noted both for his scholarship in the history of the discipline and for his confidence in the orthodox tradition:

> The sociology of science is a field of high challenge and vast promise: it is intrinsically at least as interesting for a scholar to understand scholarship as to understand other parts of the world. This young field will not begin to gather results and influence, however, until it accepts standards of rigor and evidence which are routine in scientific research.
>
> [66, pp. 336–7]

It is time the torch passed from those who, like Schumpeter, regarded the sociology of economics as fit only for a 'tired or spent economist', and from contemporary professionals whose impressionistic outbursts and reflections stemmed from impatience or frustration, to the historians of the discipline, who are equipped to respond to Stigler's challenge.

NOTES

1 There are traces of determinism in Schumpeter's linkage of economic ideas to the thinkers' 'social location' [cf. 60, p. 36].

Arthur Smithies shed some light on Schumpeter's attitude by recalling that, despite Schumpeter's brilliant performance in his *Capitalism, Socialism, and Democracy* 'and his insistence on its importance, he persisted in regarding sociology as the proper occupation for a tired or spent economist' [63, p. 630]. This attitude was probably representative of 'positive' economists and is similar to that encountered among philosophers and historians of science, as will be indicated below. For further discussion of Schumpeter's views see, for example, the helpful unpublished paper by Hans Jensen [3].

30

2 [67, p. 683 (Suppe)] For an earlier expression of this view see also Stephen Toulmin [68, p. 109], who emphasized the need to bring philosophical and historical investigations to bear 'on the practical business in which working scientists are engaged'. This is a key motif in the 'strong' programme considered here in Sections II and III. Suppe applies the term Weltanschauung analysis to the works of Toulmin, T. S. Kuhn, Sir Karl Popper, D. Böhm, and Paul K. Feyerabend in a very disparaging analysis [67, pp. 125–221].

3 [12, pp. 203–4; italics in original.] Imre Lakatos was a great champion of internalist history of science [42a]. Historians of economics have often been made to feel mildly guilty when they are unable to explain the development of ideas (i.e., theory or analysis rather than 'thought') solely by reference to rational processes. However, advocates of the SP show that sociological factors are powerfully at work amid what George Stigler has termed 'the internal values and pressures of the discipline' [64, p. 22].

4 This is Bloor's initial claim [11, p. 1], one that is strenuously denied by many philosophers of science, who are naturally determined to defend their disciplinary domain.

5 [5, pp. 44, 45, 46.] Elsewhere Barnes argues against 'the myth that knowledge has direct inherent logical implications', so that detailed empirical study is required to explain how a given scientific theory has been developed or applied [4, pp. 107, 103].

6 Note the suggestive discussion by Polanyi [50] and his concept of the 'tacit dimension' [51]. The point is especially important in accounting for the gap between formal and informal accounts of scientific work [see, e.g., 28].

7 For an indication of the relationship of some of these issues to contemporary economic methodology, see my [19, pp. 29–33]. The case for relativism, or rather Feyerabendian anarchism, has now been made with a vengeance by Donald McCloskey [44]; also the reply by Caldwell and Coats [15].

8 [2, p. 25] On the relationship between 'science' and 'reality', Steven Shapin remarks: 'If scientific representations were simply determined by the nature of reality, then no sociological accounts of the production and evaluation of scientific knowledge could be offered. Perhaps one might attempt to understand why certain features of reality were selectively attended to at different periods and in different social settings, but of the resulting knowledge nothing of sociological interest could be said' [61, p. 159].

9 For example, Popper's concept of a 'demarcation criterion' [52, pp. 37–8]. Of course, to recognize the role of conventions does not logically entail the adoption of a radical conventionalist philosophy.

10 See section I and Suppe [67, pp. 652, 649]. The most seductive of the Weltanschauungen interpretations is Toulmin's 'intellectual ecology' which presents internal and external history, sociology of science, the psychology of scientific research, and philosophy of science in an evolutionary framework. Unfortunately his first volume [69] of a projected trilogy still stands alone and has been exposed to severe criticism [cf. 67, p. 127 et seq.]. For a somewhat parallel, if less ambitious approach, see [57, pp. 440–55].

11 Suppe [67, p. 683], paraphrasing and quoting Shapere [67, p. 564]. Shapere's entire essay [pp. 518–70] is relevant to the present issue.

12 The remainder of this section is largely a paraphrase and summary of Whitley's work. Citations have been kept to a minimum. The most accessible brief statement of his model is in [76].

13 The other types of scientific fields are the following: fragmented adhocracies, polycentric oligarchies, professional adhocracies, polycentric professions, and

technologically integrated bureaucracies. The key variables involved are the degree of functional and strategic dependence and the degree of technical and strategic uncertainty. Some critical comments on Whitley's interpretation of economics are provided here in section IV.

14 The role of textbooks in this situation is strategic. Whitley cites Kuhn's perceptive remarks on this topic in [42, pp. 179–92, 228–39]; see also [74, pp. 38–9]. The subject of the evolution of economics textbooks, including the competition between rival texts, has been much neglected by historians of economics.

15 Whitley [74, p. 2] quotes Phyllis Deane's Presidential Address to the Royal Economic Society [21, p. 6]: 'the leading theorists left little doubt that progress in economic science (as opposed to political economy) could take place only at the theoretical core. . . . Questions of empirical validity . . . simply did not arise at the theoretical level. They could be relevant only within the more flexible periphery of applied economics.'

16 This has been conspicuous in the case of the Chicago school [cf. 54].

17 For an original attempt to analyse the relationship between the core and the periphery in economics see [55, pp. 76–91].

18 For a suggestive discussion of this aspect see [43].

19 An especially important aspect of this situation is examined in [18a, passim; also 16].

20 [24, pp. 20, 61, 62; italics in original.] Elias argues that the 'linchpin' of the intellectual revolution required is 'the re-thinking of our theory of knowledge in terms of evolving figurations of people, of developing groups of interdependent individuals as the subject of knowledge rather than that of an isolated individual of the homo clausus type' [ibid., p. 62].

21 It is to be hoped that the publication of Robert Skidelsky's biography, John Maynard Keynes, vol. 1: Hopes Betrayed, 1883–1920 (London: Macmillan, 1983), will initiate a new phase in the literature on the man and his ideas.

22 Toward the end of his life Johnson published a number of significant studies of the organization, social structure, and quality of the economics profession. Some examples are cited in [32–7].

23 It is unnecessary to enumerate such obvious candidates as Berlin, Vienna, and Cambridge in the nineteenth century, and Oslo, Rotterdam, London, Oxford, Cambridge, Harvard, Wisconsin, Berkeley, and Austin, Texas, more recently. More challenging still would be an examination of the similarities and differences between academic economics and that practised in research institutes, government departments, and international agencies [cf. 18a].

24 According to Joan Robinson, 'The cranks and critics flourish because the orthodox economists have neglected the great problems that everybody else feels to be urgent and menacing.' The failure to deal with such issues as distribution and inflation reveals 'the bankruptcy of economic theory' [58, pp. 8–10]. Similar views could be cited from economists of a variety of doctrinal and ideological positions.

25 For a stimulating analysis of the failure of recent orthodox (neoclassical) efforts to take over institutional economics, see [47]. The fundamental issue of the historicity of economics is too large a subject to be examined here, but the need to synthesize the orthodox and heterodox approaches is widely acknowledged.

REFERENCES

1 Barnes, B., *Scientific Knowledge and Social Theory*. London and Boston: Routledge & Kegan Paul, 1974.

2 ——, *Interests and the Growth of Knowledge*. London and Boston: Routledge & Kegan Paul, 1977

3 ——, *T. S. Kuhn and Social Science*. New York: Columbia University Press, 1982.

4 ——, 'On the Implications of a Body of Knowledge', *Knowledge: Creation, Diffusion, Utilization*, September 1982, *4*, 95–110.

5 ——, and D. Bloor, 'Relativism, Rationalism, and the Sociology of Knowledge', in Hollis and Lukes, cited *infra* [*30*, pp. 21–47].

6 ——, and Steven Shapin, eds., *Natural Order: Historical Studies of Scientific Culture*. Beverly Hills, Calif.: Sage Pub., 1979.

7 Bell, D., and I. Kristol, *The Crisis in Economic Theory*. New York, Basic Books, 1981.

8 Berg, S. B., 'Increasing the Efficiency of the Economics Journal Market', *Journal of Economic Literature*, September 1971, *9*, 798–813.

9 Bhaksar, R., *A Realist Theory of Science*. Leeds: Leeds Books, 1975.

10 Blaug, M., *The Methodology of Economics: How Economists Explain*. London and New York: Cambridge University Press, 1980.

11 Bloor, D. *Knowledge and Social Imagery*. London and Boston: Routledge & Kegan Paul, 1976.

12 ——, 'The Strengths of the Strong Program', *Philosophy of the Social Sciences*, 1981, *2*, 119–213.

13 Blume, S. S., *Perspectives in the Sociology of Science*. New York: Wiley, 1977.

14 Bordo, M. D., and D. Landau, 'The Pattern of Citations in Economic Theory, 1945–68: An Explanation Towards a Quantitative History of Thought', *History of Political Economy*, Summer 1979, *2*, 240–53.

15 Caldwell, B., and A. W. Coats, 'Comment on McCloskey', *Journal of Economic Literature*, June 1984, *22*, 575–8.

16 Coats, A. W., 'The Economists' Role: An International Perspective', in Skoie, cited *infra* [*62*].

17 ——, 'The Current "Crisis" in Economics in Historical Perspective', *Nebraska Journal of Economics and Business*, Summer 1977, *16*, 3–16. Reprinted in vol. I in this series.

18 ——, 'Methodology and Professionalism in Economics: A Subordinate Theme in Machlup's Writings', in *Breadth and Depth in Economics: Fritz Machlup – The Man and His Ideas*, edited by Jacob S. Dreyer, Lexington, Mass.: Heath (Lexington Books), 1978, pp. 23–35.

18a ——, ed., *Economists in Government: An International Comparative Study*. Durham, N.C.: Duke University Press, 1981.

19 ——, 'Half a Century of Methodological Controversy in Economics, as Reflected in the Writings of T. W. Hutchison', in *Methodological Controversy in Economics: Historical Essays in Honor of T. W. Hutchison*, edited by A. W. Coats. Greenwich, Conn.: JAI Press, 1983, pp. 1–33. Reprinted in vol. III in this series.

20 Colvin, P., 'Ontological and Epistemological Commitments and Social Relations in the Sciences: The Case of the Arithmomorphic System of Scientific Production' in Mendelsohn *et al.*, cited *infra* [*46*], pp. 103–28.

21 Deane, P. 'The Scope and Method of Economic Science', *Economic Journal*, March 1983, *93*, 1–12.

22 Eagly, R. V., 'Contemporary Profile of Conventional Economists', *History of Political Economy*, Spring 1974, *6*, 76–91.

23 ——, 'Economics Journals as a Communication Network', *Journal of Economic Literature*, September 1975, *12*, 878–88.

24 Elias, N., H. Martins, and R. Whitley, *Scientific Establishments and Hierarchies*. Dordrecht, Netherlands: Reidel, 1982.

25 ——, and R. D. Whitley, 'Introduction', in Elias *et al.*, cited *supra* [*24*].

26 Gallie, W. B., 'What Makes a Subject Scientific?' *British Journal for the Philosophy of Science*, August 1957, *8*, 118–39.

27 Georgescu-Roegen, N., *The Entropy Law and the Economic Process*. Cambridge, Mass.: Harvard University Press, 1971.

28 Gilbert, N., and M. Mulkay, 'Contexts of Scientific Discourse: Social Accounting in Experimental Papers', in Knorr *et al.*, cited *infra* [*40*, pp. 269–94].

29 Hollis, M., and S. Lukes, 'The Social Destruction of Reality', in Hollis and Lukes, cited *infra* [*30*, pp. 67–86].

30 ————, eds., *Rationality and Relativism*: Oxford: Blackwell, 1982.

31 Jensen, H., 'New Lights on J. A. Schumpeter's Theory of the History of Economics', in *Research in the History of Economic Thought and Methodology*, vol. 5, Ed. W. Samuels. Greenwich, Conn.: JAI Press, 1987, pp. 117–48.

32 Johnson, H. G., 'National Styles in Economic Research: The United States, The United Kingdom, Canada, and various European Countries', *Daedalus*, Spring 1973, *102*, 65–74.

33 ——, 'The State of Theory', *American Economic Review*, May 1974, *64*, 323–4.

34 ——, 'The Current and Prospective State of Economics', *Australian Economic Papers*, June 1974, *13*, 1–27.

35 ——, 'The American Tradition in Economics', *Nebraska Journal of Economics and Business*, Summer 1977, *16*, 17–26.

36 ——, 'Methodologies of Economics', in *The Organization and Retrieval of Economic Knowledge*, edited by M. Perlman. Boulder, Colo.: Westview Press, 1977, pp. 496–509.

37 ——, *The Shadow of Keynes: Understanding Keynes, Cambridge and Keynesian Economics*. Chicago: University of Chicago Press, 1978.

38 Katouzian, H., *Ideology and Method in Economics*. London: Macmillan, 1980.

39 King, M. D., 'Reason, Tradition and the Progressiveness of Science', *History and Theory*, 1971, *10*, 3–32.

40 Knorr, K. D., R. Krohn, and R. D. Whitley, *The Social Process of Scientific Investigation*. Dordrecht, Netherlands: Reidel, 1981.

41 Kuhn, T. S., *The Structure of Scientific Revolutions*. Chicago: University of Chicago Press, 1962 (2nd ed., 1970).

42 ——, *The Essential Tension: Selected Studies in Scientific Tradition and Change*. Chicago: University of Chicago Press, 1977.

42a Lakatos, I., 'History of Science and its Rational Reconstruction', in *PSA 1970: In Memory of Rudolf Carnap. Boston Studies in the Philosophy of Science*, edited by R. C. Buck and R. S. Cohen, vol. VIII. Dordrecht, Netherlands: Reidel, 1971, pp. 91–136.

43 Lammers, C., 'Mono- and Poly-paradigmatic Developments in Natural and Social Sciences', in *Social Processes of Scientific Development*, edited by R. Whitley. London and Boston: Routledge & Kegan Paul, 1974, pp. 123–47.

44 McCloskey, D. N., 'The Rhetoric of Economics', *Journal of Economic Literature*, June 1983, *21*, 481–516.

45 McKenzie, D. and B. Barnes, 'Scientific Judgment: the Biometry–Mendelism Controversy', in Barnes and Shapin, cited *supra* [*6*, pp. 119–201].

46 Mendelsohn, E., P. Weingart, and R. D. Whitley, *The Social Production of Scientific Knowledge*. Dordrecht, Netherlands: Reidel, 1977.

47 Mirowski, P., 'Is There a Mathematical Neo-institutional Economics?' *Journal of Economic Issues*, September 1981, *15*, 593–613.

48 Nagel, E., *The Structure of Science: Problems in the Logic of Scientific Explanation*. New York: Harcourt Brace Jovanovich, 1961.

49 Pantin, C. F. A., *The Relations Between the Sciences*. London and New York: Cambridge University Press, 1968.

50 Polyani, M., *Personal Knowledge: Towards a Post-critical Philosophy*. Chicago: University of Chicago Press, 1958.

51 ——, *The Tacit Dimension*. London and Boston: Routledge & Kegan Paul, 1967.

52 Popper, K. R., *The Logic of Scientific Discovery*. London: Hutchinson, 1959.

53 ——, *Conjectures and Refutations*. New York: Basic Books, 1963.

54 Reder, M., 'Chicago Economics: Permanence and Change', *Journal of Economic Literature*, March 1982, *20*, 1–38.

55 Remenyi, J., 'Core Demi-core Interaction: Toward a General Theory of Disciplinary and Sub-disciplinary growth', *History of Political Economy*, Spring 1974, *6*, 76–91.

56 Rip, A., 'The Development of Restrictedness in the Sciences', in Elias *et al.*, cited *supra* [*24*, pp. 219–38].

57 Robinson, J., 'The Second Crisis of Economic Theory', *American Economic Review*, May 1972, *62*, 1–10.

58 Rosenberg, C., 'Toward an Ecology of Knowledge: on Discipline, Context, and History', in *The Organization of Knowledge in Modern America*, edited by A. Oleson and J. Voss. Baltimore: Johns Hopkins University Press, 1979, pp. 440–55.

59 Samuelson, P., 'Economic Thought and New Industrialism', in *The Collected Scientific Papers of Paul Samuelson*, edited by J. Stiglitz, vol. 2. Cambridge, Mass.: MIT Press, 1966.

60 Schumpeter, J. A., *History of Economic Analysis*. London and New York: Oxford University Press, 1954.

61 Shapin, S., 'History of Science and Its Sociological Reconstructions', *History of Science*, 1982, *20*, 157–211.

62 Skoie, H., ed., *Scientific Expertise and the Public*. Oslo: Institute for Studies in Research and Higher Education, 1975.

63 Smithies, A., 'Joseph Alois Schumpeter, 1883–1950', *American Economic Review*, September 1950, *40*, 628–48.

64 Stigler, G. J., *Essays in the History of Economics*. Chicago: University of Chicago Press, 1965.

65 ——, *The Economist as Preacher and other Essays*. Chicago: University of Chicago Press, 1982.

66 ——, Review of R. V. Eagly, *Events, Ideology, and Economic Theory: The Determinants of Progress in the Development of Economic Analysis* (Detroit: Wayne State University Press, 1968), in *Journal of Economic History*, June 1969, *29*, 336–7.

67 Suppe, F., ed., *The Structure of Scientific Theories*. Urbana: Illinois University Press, 1977.

68 Toulmin, S., *Foresight and Understanding: An Inquiry into the Aims of Science*. Bloomington: Indiana University Press, 1961.

69 ——, *Human Understanding*. Princeton, N.J.: Princeton University Press, 1972.

70 Ward, B., *The Ideal Worlds of Economics: Liberal, Radical and Conservative World Views*. New York: Basic Books, 1979.

71 Whitley, R. D., 'Changes in the Social and Intellectual Organization of the Sciences: Professionalization and the Arithmetic Ideal', in Mendelsohn *et al.*, cited *supra* [*46*, pp. 143–69].

72 ——, 'The Sociology of Scientific Work and the History of Scientific Developments', in Blume, cited *supra* [*13*, pp. 21–50].

73 ——, 'The Establishment and Structure of the Sciences as Reputational Organizations', in Elias *et al.*, cited *supra* [*24*, pp. 313–57].

74 ——, 'The Organizational Structure of Scientific Fields', unpublished ms.; now chap. 5 of book cited *infra* [*77*].

75 ——, 'From the Sociology of Scientific Communities to the Study of Scientists' Negotiations and Beyond', *Social Science Information*, 1983, *22*, 681–720.

76 ——, 'The Development of Management Studies as a Fragmented Adhocracy', Manchester Business School and Centre for Business Research, Working Paper Series no. 84, 1983.

77 ——, *The Intellectual and Social Organization of the Sciences*. London and New York: Oxford University Press, 1984.

3

THE SOCIOLOGY OF SCIENCE
Its application to economics*

This paper starts from two premises: that economcs is a 'science', in the broader sense of that weasel word; and that the sociology of science offers many fruitful hypotheses and research topics for historians of economics, especially for those interested in twentieth-century developments.

I

During the past two decades or so there has been a great surge of scholarly work on the history, philosophy and sociology of science, and on the interrelationships between these three dimensions of the growth of knowledge. So far, however, aside from various efforts to identify Kuhnian paradigms or revolutions or Lakatosian research programmes, specialist historians of economics have displayed little interest in these matters. This is both regrettable and surprising – the latter because the recent sustained cries of anguish about the state and prospects of the subject have been accompanied by many stimulating, shrewd, albeit usually casual and impressionistic, reflections on the organization, structure and functioning of economics as a discipline and a profession. Historians of economics have made no effort to draw systematically on these scattered hints and suggestions or on the many small-scale studies of economics bearing on the larger theme, presumably because they are focused on current or recent past conditions and developments, and therefore fall outside the historian's conventional time frame. This paper is designed to reveal some of the missed opportunities, and to encourage readers to draw upon the rich vein of historical insights in the sociology of science literature.

The following account takes many things for granted or passes over others in a summary fashion.[1] It focuses attention on one very recent comprehensive approach to the sociology of science, and then presents a number of practical applications to economics.

Historians sceptical of new fashions may be reassured by the reminder that the application of the sociology of knowledge science to economics is not new. It permeates Schumpeter's great *History*, so much so that a

37

stimulating hour or so could be spent simply citing from his work.[2] However there are traces of determinism in Schumpeter's approach which reflect his intellectual background and milieu, whereas recent sociology of science literature is more self-consciously relativist, and contextualist, and genuinely historical in its goals and methods than earlier versions.

David Bloor and his Edinburgh colleagues advocate what they call the 'strong' programme, which gives priority to the sociology, as against the history and philosophy, of science. But while their work has been both provocative and constructive it is possible to favour a sociology of science approach without embracing their position *toto coelo*. The Edinburgh approach is especially useful is exploring the much neglected links between methodology and professionalism in economics[3] – i.e. where criteria of theory choice, methods of testing, and the interpretation and application of research findings involve divergent conceptions of professional standards, norms, values and ethics. Indeed, the persistence of methodological debate in economics, an activity generally held in low esteem, is itself a suitable topic for sociological (or collective psycho-sociological) investigation.

II

There is a well-known cautionary tale about a sociologist who spent several months studying the work patterns, career conditions and personal relationships of a group of laboratory scientists, but who, when his report was completed, was unable to say what they had actually been working on! One of the most constructive features of contemporary sociology of science literature is its sensitivity to the links between the structure, institutional organization and *content* of science,[4] while at the same time emphasizing that the particular ways in which research topics are conceived and connected are historically contingent and variable.

This is the historian's entry point. The more restricted,[5] standardized, uniformitarian and cumulative a science the narrower the scope for historical investigation of blind alleys, red herrings, watersheds, breakthroughs and turning-points; and the greater the importance of 'internal' as against 'external' determinants of its development. As in Kuhn's so-called 'normal' phases, scientific advances in such cases will be relatively predictable, multiple discoveries or roughly simultaneous solutions to puzzles will be more likely to occur,[6] and control will be more effectively maintained by the scientific élite (or other employers) who command access to qualifications, career opportunities, communication networks and resources. Such a science, according to Richard Whitley, will probably demonstrate:

1 low technical and strategic task uncertainty;
2 high functional and strategic dependence among its practitioners;

3 high reputational autonomy over performance and significance standards, problem formulations and descriptive terms; and

4 low audience variety and high audience equivalence.

These unfamiliar terms refer to the main variables whose nature and interdependencies are skilfully and persuasively elaborated in Whitley's *The Intellectual and Social Organization of the Sciences* (1984), an ambitious attempt to provide a systematic approach to the sociology of science which combines 'internal' and 'external' factors, with a wealth of illustrations. While it is obviously impossible to reproduce his analytical framework in detail here, its relevance is enhanced by his substantial discussion of economics as a distinctive, if not unique, specimen among the 'human sciences'.

The conception of science as a factor of production is familiar to economists, both in connection with human capital and, more broadly, in Fritz Machlup's ambitious *The Production and Distribution of Knowledge* (1962). To Whitley, science involves the use of knowledge to create new knowledge. Scientists are institutionally committed to producing intellectual innovations, a process limited by the fact that reputations and rewards are dependent on the use made of such innovations in other scientists' research. Reputations are acquired through a public communications network which forms a 'reputational system' of work organization and control in any field, the nature of which is determined largely by the content of the field. Thus a major objective of the sociology of science is to reveal

the organisation of research in different situations and historical circumstances . . . how intellectual fields become distinguished and separated, and how such fields as socio-intellectual structures become established, exert control over research, reproduce themselves, and change.[7]

By combining the degrees of functional and strategic dependence with the degrees of technical and strategic task uncertainty, Whitley's typology contains sixteen possible types of scientific fields, of which 'only seven seem to be stable and distinct reputational systems of knowledge production and control'.[8] Among these, 'Anglo-Saxon' economics is cited as a unique example of a 'partitioned bureaucracy', in which

the level of mutual dependence is rather high because of the uniformity of undergraduate training, the hierarchical communication system, and the high value attached to analytical and theoretical elaboration at the expense of empirical 'applications' of the dominant approach. Low strategic task uncertainty is maintained here, by strict controls over skills and the partitioning of empirical work from the theoretical orthodoxy.

Whitley cites Phyllis Deane's Presidential Address to the Royal Economic

Society, in which she stresses the leading theorists' contentions that progress in economics 'could take place only at the theoretical core' and that 'questions of empirical validity . . . simply did not arise at the theoretical level. They could be relevant only within the more flexible periphery of applied economics.'[9] Of course this is a point frequently made by critics of economic orthodoxy. Whitley's study makes it clear how unusual is this state of affairs among the recognized sciences.

Whitley focuses on four main components of knowledge production in science: training, employment, reputational assessment and funding; and it may be helpful to review briefly certain broad features of the history of modern economics in these terms.

The late nineteenth century witnessed the emergence of Anglo-American 'economics' from 'political economy' as a leading component in the academicization of the social sciences, which were then in the process of splitting into more or less distinct academic disciplines – incidentally, at a time when the mutual dependence between fields in the natural sciences was probably growing in most countries.[10] Academicization meant that the university became the principal intellectual and social context for the advancement of scientific economics; academic values and reputations became dominant; and notwithstanding the growing international links among economists in the major countries involved there were significant differences in the number, organization, structure and control of and within academic institutions which directly affected the discipline's evolution in different locations – e.g. as between the UK, continental Europe and the USA.[11] By comparison with the natural sciences, which had been expanding rapidly and gaining in intellectual prestige and organizational complexity during the nineteenth century, especially in Germany, it was a comparatively short time before economics came under the influence of two basic changes which had already occurred in the natural sciences:

1 a rapid growth in the number and variety of non-academic employment opportunities (in economics especially in business and government from the 1930s); and
2 the emergence of major research organizations and non-academic funding agencies. (In economics the National Bureau of Economic Research and Brookings were outstanding among many social science research bodies in the USA before World War II. During that period the private research foundations were very influential, whereas the federal government became heavily involved during and after the war. Comparable developments in other countries were usually much slower and less dramatic.)

The longer run implications of these developments may become clearer if we note the effects of the growth of 'big science' in the natural sciences. According to Whitley:

As the system of knowledge production has expanded and transcended the university structure the inculcation and certification of skills [e.g. via research training and postgraduate degrees] have become differentiated from the employment and direction of researchers, so that scientific fields are no longer coterminous with academic disciplines and intellectual goals are less determined by purely academic considerations.[12]

Under these circumstances, while knowledge production and validation remain under the control of employees (i.e. the scientists) a 'dual system of work control' has emerged between academic and non-academic science, and 'control over how research is conducted and assessed is shared between employers and intellectual élites'. The relationships between these two controlling groups will depend on:

1 the degree to which employers' goals are oriented towards public reputational ones (i.e. those of the scientific community, especially the élite in any given field);
2 the degree to which employers' personnel policies follow the verdicts and standards of reputational groups; and
3 the degree to which employers' reward systems are dependent upon the standards and values of a single reputational élite in the field.

At present we are seriously ignorant about the criteria of selection, activities, performance standards and evaluation of economists and their employers in business, government and international agencies. Historians of economics have grossly neglected the study of these organizations and their effects on work processes, types of research and the prevailing conceptions of the strategic importance of the various tasks and problems on which economists are engaged – not to mention the feedback effects on the academic community. The general relevance of Whitley's analysis to these spheres requires no emphasis. The lack of technical control over empirical work, which severely limits the theorists' influence on applied economics, enhances the non-academic employer's capacity to exert an influence over the goals, performance standards and even the criteria of validation of his economist employees' work – though this will probably vary according to the degree of technical and esoteric knowledge required. With respect to reward systems, and performance and significance standards, it is well known that not only academic employers but also academic and non-academic economist employees often question the value and relevance of much of the economic theory and techniques which constitute the basis of the economist's claim to be treated as a professional, with substantial autonomy and authority in the work place. Thus, in so far as academic and non-academic employers and employees attach markedly different values to specific components in the economist's knowledge and skills, the scope for dominance by a reputational élite is correspondingly undermined. (This helps to account for the anxieties recently displayed in the innumerable commentaries on the 'crisis' in economics and on the education of economists.)

The partitioning of economic theory from applied economics, which stands out in Whitley's synoptic survey, and which has been so incessantly emphasized by critics of economic orthodoxy, has protected the basic analytical apparatus from the feedback effects of results that are unstable and difficult to interpret, and from the implications of task outcomes that are difficult to coordinate and subject to controversial and conflicting interpretations. Likewise, the narrowing of the scope of economics during the academicization phase referred to earlier, served to sharpen the lines between economics and its neighbour disciplines, thereby strengthening the economists' claims to exclusive rights over their restricted domain, and excluding certain problems they were unwilling or unable to tackle – e.g. the distribution of wealth, the role of economic power in society, etc. This partitioning also helps to explain one of the most puzzling features of the history of economics – the remarkable survival capacity of the central corpus of theory despite almost two centuries of shrewd and seemingly persuasive attacks on its unrealism, abstractness and irrelevance to contemporary problems. This is perhaps a modest price to pay for the preservation of the established reputational system, with its high degree of mutual dependence among its practitioners. In most of the other human and social sciences there is a significantly greater degree of technical and strategic task uncertainty than in economics; the importance of problems is unclear, and different groups assess them in opposing ways, together with appropriate theoretical strategies; intellectual structures are highly fluid and unstable; individual practitioners have a considerable degree of autonomy from any single dominant group in formulating a research strategy; and audiences are diverse, are rapidly changing, and adopt various evaluation criteria.[13] Despite the persistence of conflict among economists over priorities and methods, the stability of the whole field is preserved by the control exercised by the reputational élite through its power over the training system, the communications network, and access to research resources and employment opportunities.

It is now time to provide more specific examples of the applicability of this approach to economics.

III

According to Harry G. Johnson, after World War II American economics,

which had been something of a condescendingly patronized country-bumpkin cousin of European city slicker economic sophistication,

42

rapidly became the leader of the world profession of economics. In the process, the distinguishing characteristics of American economists became, naturally enough, the distinguishing characteristics of good professional economics.[14]

This sweeping and provocative statement is obviously debatable; but it is a good place from which to start, for like Schumpeter, Johnson was a remarkably pungent, prolific and penetrating commentator on the social and intellectual structure and functioning of economics in a number of countries. Both men were economists of international stature with direct knowledge of the workings of several markedly different academic communities. Though neither could be termed a marginal man (typically a fruitful source of sociological insights into any group), both were in a sense outsiders as well as insiders. Johnson's background as a Canadian, from the periphery of the Anglo-Saxon economic world, was reinforced by his international interests and peregrinations, and the extraordinary energy that enabled him both to write prolifically within his fields of professional expertise and to play the role of the committed participant-observer. The connections he perceived, and so frankly exposed, between the internal and the external conditions, beliefs and forces affecting the content as well as the structure of the economics discipline and profession are especially pertinent here. Unfortunately only brief glimpses of his ideas can be provided on this occasion.

Johnson's bitter and incisive criticisms of post-1945 Cambridge (UK) and British economics in *The Shadow of Keynes*[15] are probably well known. Yet his highly personal and impressionistic papers on national styles of research in economics,[16] despite their obvious limitations, are even more suggestive, since they brought together psychological, occupational, demographic and institutional variables into a sweeping explanation of certain broad features of the postwar period. For example, in referring to the differences between the Anglo-American and continental European academic traditions, Johnson noted the emergence in economics of 'a new type of personality, broader in social origins and experience, and pragmatic and professional rather than scholastic in its approach, one result being greatly to reduce the gulf created by the traditional university between the academic scholar and the man of affairs'.[17] The growth of non-academic employment opportunities for economists, Johnson argued, had had mixed results. While providing obvious scope for increased specialization and division of labour within the academic community, and an increased number of students from which to recruit future academic talent, government employment also afforded a safe alternative to those failing to make the academic grade, thereby encouraging the conservatism manifested among economists during the late 1960s student unrest. The American government's practice of treating economists as hired professional experts had had substantially beneficial effects by providing immediate research incentives, specific topics and deadlines for delivery, and sustained supervision by and contact with other researchers. In the UK, however, the practice of in-house government research and civil service secrecy had distracted 'good economists from regular academic research without yielding substantial benefits to the advancement of the subject in the form of published research results'. In Canada, government work had tended 'to divert professional attention away from theoretical and/or "curiosity-oriented" research, thus making the Canadian profession less independent and less interesting to economists in other countries than it could be'. By contrast, in Australia, where the British amateur tradition had survived more strongly, there had been more original basic theoretical work in economics during the first two postwar decades than in Canada, a state of affairs that might change as a result of the increasing percentage of Australians undertaking graduate work in the USA.[18]

Few if any of Johnson's contemporaries have offered such confident generalizations about national differences in economics, a subject deserving of careful comparative investigation.[19] On other matters – for example, his concern about the low and declining returns resulting from excessive mathematization and empirical quantification; the trivialization of research resulting from the Ph.D. process; and the narrowing of scope in advanced training – we are on much more familiar ground. Especially congenial to historians of economics is Johnson's conviction that as the rapid intellectual advances of the early postwar years were built on the foundations laid in the pre-1914 period, the 1920s and early 1930s,

> with the prolonged studied neglect of the history of the subject that has come to characterize the Ph.D. preparation stage and the immediately ensuing publication stage of a professional career, the subject is very likely to deteriorate sharply intellectually, unless revivified by fresh and deep draughts of literary scholarship on the works of the great economists of the past.[20]

Here, indeed, is yet another challenge for the historian of economics.

Many of the recent sociologically-oriented commentaries on the state of economics have emanated from those concerned about or hostile to the prevailing pressures to conformity[21] within the discipline and the control exercised by the dominant neoclassical orthodoxy. According to Whitley, a detached observer, a relatively small élite group at a relatively small number of élite departments controls access to prestigious journal space, a situation reinforced by the concentration of training and certification establishments. Those trained in the leading schools are more likely to obtain academic jobs in high ranking universities, which tend to recruit their own products, publish articles, and make highly valued contributions to the most prestigious sub-fields.[22]

For a variety of reasons, most of the protests about and the evidence for this state of affairs have emanated from and have been focused on the USA. Apart from its current leading world position, American scholars have long been more self-conscious about professional matters than their European counterparts.[23] The scale and structure of academic disciplines have changed more rapidly in the USA than elsewhere; and in the case of economics there has been a long-standing dissenting tradition in opposition to the disciplinary establishment – i.e. institutionalism. How far similar features and trends can be found in other countries, and in other social science disciplines is not yet clear.

For those historians who are sceptical about sweeping attacks on a monolithic professional 'establishment' there is ample scope for research on a less exalted plane, e.g. in relation to particular schools or movements in economic thought[24] or, more fruitfully still, on the nature, timing, structure and development of particular sub-disciplines, specialities, fields or domains within economics. These have been proliferating during the past half century and they form convenient units of study which provide revealing insights into the inner workings of the scientific community. Here, too, research in the history and sociology of science offers valuable guideposts for historians of economics.

Needless to say, not all sub-disciplines or fields are equally prestigious. Benjamin Ward has suggested that there is a clear hierarchy in economics,[25] in descending order:

1 micro- and macrotheory, and econometrics;
2 international trade, public finance, money and banking;
3 labour, industrial organization and economic history; and
4 history of economic thought, economic development and comparative economic systems.

Any such classification is necessarily somewhat arbitrary, and the respective rankings will change over time, and differ from place to place. As might be expected from Whitley's account, generally speaking prestige in economics is positively correlated with the level of abstraction, the degree of theoretical and technical difficulty (in which mathematization and sophisticated quantification play crucial roles), and inversely correlated with breadth of subject-matter and degree of interdisciplinarity. Within any given level policy relevance may be an asset, but it cannot go far in explaining the different levels.

Recent research on the internal structure of the economics discipline has concentrated intensively on the nature and significance of publications, especially journal literature rather than books, and it has been highly quantitative. One of the pioneers in this work was George J. Stigler, with his essay 'Statistical Studies in the History of Economic Thought' (1964).[26] But there were earlier articles on the institutional affiliations of participants in the American Economic Association's programmes and contributors to professional journals,[27] and during the past decade or so there has been a veritable explosion of bibliometrics in economics.[28] Most of the studies have been piecemeal, limited in scope and time, and no systematic effort has been made to draw general conclusions or trace broad development patterns. Space limitations, not to mention the audience's attention span, precludes even a list of the subjects covered in these exercises. But for those seeking manageable research topics for postgraduate students the possibilities are endless, for most of the work undertaken so far has been on American materials; the scope for comparative and longitudinal studies is immense; and there is much to be learnt from earlier examples in the natural sciences where abstracting services and citation indexes have been available much longer than in the social sciences.[29]

The choice of an appropriate unit of study has been one of many points of disagreement among contemporary sociologists of science, and given the current vogue for empiricism there have been numerous efforts to identify and generalize about the 'natural history' of particular fields, specialities, domains, sub-disciplines, research schools, communications networks, invisible colleges, etc. (there is considerable terminological individualism in the literature). There has also been parallel work on specific research teams, laboratories and research institutes. Some of the profoundly contentious epistemological and methodological issues entailed in this work will be noted later.[30] But historians of economics have much to learn from the depth and subtlety of analysis and the detailed documentation displayed in these studies. The concurrent interest in reflexivity, not to mention the perennial narcissism among intellectuals, makes it tempting to take our own speciality of the history of economics as an example.[31] However, let me instead cite a modest exercise, apparently innocent of recent sociology of science research, focused on the history, development, and prospects of research on the soviet economy, which identifies four distinct generations of specialists; notes changes in the content and division of their labour – the availability of data being one key factor; traces personal and institutional linkages, job opportunities, and sources of funding; and even refers to the geo-political factors affecting the volume and type of scholarly activity.[32] Closer to my own interest, and somewhat more ambitious in its scope and implications, is the rise (and fall?) of the 'new' economic history,[33] a peculiarly American phenomenon in its origins and character, though its influence has been felt in many other lands. This resulted from a complex interaction of intellectual fashion, new ideas and techniques, academic hardware, institutional structures and functioning, generational changes, and the climate of public opinion, which directly affected the availability of funding and the prevailing research interests and opportunities. Many other examples could be quoted, some clearly more promising and appealing than others. Nor is there any reason why more abstract themes should be excluded,[34] and for those seeking a more formal and explicit intellectual framework there is Joseph Remenyi's core/demi-core/periphery structure, closely allied to the Kuhn–Lakatos sequence which has already proved seductive to some historians of economics.[35] Some will of course view such frameworks as too abstract or constricting, but the recent sociology and history of science literature can be raided for specific hypotheses or checklists of 'factors' suggestive to any scholar wishing to draw implications from his or her research.[36] More generally, enough has been said to indicate that we have much to learn about how and why the component parts of economics have emerged, flourished, and/or withered and declined in various intellectual and institutional contexts. Even more obvious is the scope for systematic research on particular 'schools' of thought.

Research areas have been approached from a novel standpoint by a group of scholars who focus their attention on how scientists construct accounts of what is going on during the research process. In conformity with the current tendency to treat this process as problematic, they argue that 'reality' cannot be separated from the scientists' account of it, and that by analysing scientific discourse they can not only illuminate such familiar topics as the nature of discovery, theory choice, scientific consensus, and the role of norms in scientific work, but also provide insights into such neglected topics as accounts of error, the structure of formal texts, the use of pictorial representations, the practical applications of scientific knowledge, and even the role of scientific jokes.[37] Like some other contemporary work, this 'social accounting' approach emphasizes the substantial gap between what scientists actually do and how they present their work as public knowledge. We are all familiar with the expression 'writing up' research, and this phrase has acquired added depth and significance through studies emphasizing that scientific knowledge does not emerge spontaneously in a pristine, objective form, but is consciously *constructed* in accordance with the researchers' aims, interests and conception of conventionally accepted procedures and results.[38]

Some of this is already familiar to economists. One may cite, for example, George Stigler's wry observations on 'The Nature and Role of Originality in Scientific Progress'.[39] The wide gulf between scientific practice and methodological preaching is a hardy perennial; and Edward Leamer has very recently opened up a rich vein with his iconoclastic 'Let's Take the Con out of Econometrics'.[40] Yet here as with so many other topics, we have much to learn from the sociologists of science. With respect to discourse *proprement dites* we can go beyond Donald McCloskey's casual and inadequately developed distinction between the 'official' and the 'workaday' rhetoric of economics[41] to the more systematic analysis offered by Arjo Klamer, which suggests many new possibilities.[42] Using the full range of sources available to historians we can gain new insights into the processes of presentation, persuasion and legitimation which have an especially

47

important place in the so-called policy sciences. The relations between style and audience have been grossly neglected, and as the social character of research is now a central focus the social character of language in economics needs no special emphasis here. Indeed this is now a more active subject of discussion among economists than ever before.[43]

The proponents of discourse analysis view it as an indispensable means of circumventing the interpretative difficulties arising from the remarkable variety in scientists' accounts of their actions and beliefs, but this is an illusion. As one critic has observed, there are no grounds for claiming privileged status for any given species of data, and the problem of interpretation is inescapable.[44] An even more radically empiricist and relativist approach to scientific work is Karin Knorr-Cetina's 'constructivist' programme, which involves microscopic internalist studies of scientists' behaviour on the grounds that research is essentially idiosyncratic, contingent and context-dependent. Such a programme, it should be added, is viewed not as an end in itself but as a means to a deeper (and ultimately more general?) understanding of the nature and processes of scientific knowledge production.[45] The methodological and epistemological implications of this and some other contemporary sociology of science work will be considered briefly in the concluding section of this paper.

IV

That there is currently a ferment of debate among sociologists of science with respect to the nature, methods and objectives of their discipline and its relationships to more conventional history and philosophy of science will be obvious from the foregoing account, which makes no pretensions to completeness. The general attractions of this literature for social scientists should also be obvious, since it contributes to the demystification of the natural sciences (with some occasional debunking thrown in for good measure), and it reminds us that the two categories of intellectual disciplines are neither as homogeneous nor as wide apart in their character, aims and procedures as is often suggested in methodological treatises and economics textbooks. Like economists, natural scientists are human and fallible, and while they may seem to present a united front to outsiders, among themselves they often disagree strongly with respect to the appropriateness of assumptions and research procedures, the reliability of experiments, the replicability of research and the significance of new 'results'. Moreover, as with economists, there are leading scientists who appear as partisan advocates in major public controversies over such matters as nuclear policy, pollution, energy resources, weapons systems, experiments on human subjects and sociobiology. Hence, it is no surprise to find complaints of the 'deprofessionalization' of science, or claims that: 'In becoming involved in the definition and solution of societal and political problems science as an institution loses its boundaries and thus its identity.'[46]

A central message of recent sociology and history of science publications is that scientific research, when closely scrutinized, appears much more contingent and *ad hoc* than hitherto supposed. Blinded by the scientists' achievements, outsiders have generally underestimated the degree of task uncertainty in scientific knowledge production and exaggerated the extent to which it is highly methodical and systematic in its technical procedures, and stable and explicable in its results. To that extent the constructivist approach has been illuminating.

To stop at this point, however, would be to gloss over the fundamental epistemological and methodological problems currently under active discussion -- especially the question of relativism, and the crucial relationship between the social influences on (and in) science and the content and validity of scientific work. As Johan Galtung has noted in a brilliant and ambitious comparative analysis:

> there has to be some kind of correspondence between general social structures and the structure of the scientific community, and there also has to be some kind of correspondence between the structure of the scientific community and the structure of the scientific product, that is the mixture of paradigm analysis/proposition production/ theory formation/commentary ultimately produced.[47]

The general nature of these correspondences has, for the time being, been relegated to a subordinate place by sociologists of science, for they have turned away from the broader issues posed by Robert Merton and his disciples. In a challenging attack on the relativist/constructivist programme, which provoked a long series of replies and rejoinders, the Mertonian Thomas F. Gieryn argued that

> the *constitutive* historical question of the sociology of science is: what explains the origins of modern science in the seventeenth century (or so), and its ascendence in four centuries to a position of cognitive monopoly over certain spheres of decisions? To answer this historical question requires inquiry into the constitutive analytical question: what makes science unique among culture-producing institutions?[48]

The sociologists of science considered in the paper have, for the most part, either rejected or brushed aside the Mertonian question: 'How does the institution of science establish and maintain its cognitive authority?'[49] They consciously avoid basic epistemological issues, and in some cases deliberately blur or ignore the conventional question of the demarcation between science and other forms of knowledge.[50] Yet they disagree strongly with respect to the proper objectives of research and the appropriate methods to be employed. To H. M. Collins, for example, relativism is a methodological prescription, a heuristic or regulative rule for the sociologist of science. In advocating his 'special relativism' he recognizes that

> in one set of circumstances 'correct scientific method' applied to a problem would precipitate result p whereas in another set of social circumstances 'correct scientific method' applied to the same problem would precipitate result q where, perhaps, q implies not-p.[51]

But he is not prepared to take a firm stand on matters of epistemological and methodological principle.

Collins denies that his relativism is incompatible with empiricism, arguing that technically competent field studies designed to reveal how pieces of knowledge gain acceptance within science 'may have a bearing on how scientific knowledge as a whole has gained canonical status'.[52] There is, indeed, a curious parallel between Collins's contention that 'the approach we favour is to push the relativistic heuristic as far as possible: where it can go no further "nature" intrudes',[53] and Lakatos's counter contention that externalist explanations of science should begin only after the possibilities of internal rational reconstruction have been exhausted. Undoubtedly relativism entails the risk that in seeking to discover precisely how far knowledge production is determined by social factors, rather than 'nature' (or reality), the general may be lost in the pursuit of the particular. This is especially so in the case of constructivism, which adopts an anthropological approach that threatens to degenerate into crude descriptivism. As one of its sharper critics has observed, in disregarding 'the systematic, trans-local and intersubjective aspects of knowledge' it entails a return to 'the most primitive and naive positivistic positions'.[54] It is essential to recognize the broader disciplinary and environmental constraints on knowledge production, as well as the local and contingent variables at work.

The sociology of science literature considered here has been described as a second post-Kuhnian wave, and it is evidently in a highly unstable and transitional state. To some of the participants the current diversity of opinion represents chaos; unresolvable issues abound;[55] and critics recognize the dangers of sociological reductionism amid the strenuous efforts to study science 'as it happens'. However, none of this need unduly trouble historians of economics, who can draw upon this lively and impressive research programme without becoming involved in the deeper epistemological and methodological issues.[56] Despite the extraordinary survival capacity of orthodox classical and neoclassical economics, few of its exponents have been disposed to regard it as canonical or entitled to unique institutional or epistemological status. The sociology of science is complementary, not a rival, to other approaches to the history of our discipline, and should be welcomed as a means of adding depth and rigour to our subject.

NOTES

* Originally delivered at the History of Economic Thought Conference, University of Surrey, Guildford, September 1984, and at Uppsala University, Sweden.

1 'The Sociology of Knowledge and the History of Economics', in vol. 2 of *Research in the History of Economic Thought and Methodology* ed. Warren Samuels (Greenwich, Conn.: JAI Press, 1985) pp. 211–34 (reprinted in this volume, pp. 11–36).

2 See, for example, the sections on Economic Sociology and Sociology of Economics, in *History of Economic Analysis* (New York: Oxford University Press, 1954), ch. 4.

3 Cf. my 'Methodology and Professionalism in Economics: A Subordinate Theme in Fritz Machlup's Writings', in Jacob Dreyer, *Breadth and Depth in Economics* (Boston: D. C. Heath, 1978).

4 In Karl Mannheim's *Wissenssociologie* 'logico-mathematical and natural scientific knowledge' was excluded from the 'sociology of knowledge' on the assumption that scientific thought is governed purely by reason and logic, not by social factors, and this view permeated Robert Merton's functionalist approach and much of the work of Joseph Ben David and others prior to Thomas S. Kuhn's influential *The Structure of Scientific Revolutions* (Chicago: University of Chicago Press, 1962; 2nd ed. 1970). For penetrating discussions of the implications of the change brought about since the early 1960s see, for example, M. D. King, 'Reason, Tradition and the Progressiveness of Science', *History and Theory* vol. 10 (1971), pp. 3–32; and Herminio Martins, 'The Kuhnian "Revolution" and Its Implications for Sociology' in A. H. Hanson, T. Nossiter, and Stein Rokaan (eds), *Imagination and Precision in Political Analysis: Essays in Honor of Peter Nettl* (London: Faber & Faber, 1972), pp. 13–58.

5 On this characteristic see, for example, A. Rip, 'The Development of Restrictedness in the Sciences', in Norbert Elias, Herminio Martins, and Richard Whitley (eds), *Scientific Establishments and Hierarchies* (Dordrecht, Netherlands: Reidel, 1982), pp. 219–38. (This is vol. 6 of the Sociology of the Sciences yearbook, a series which contains many fascinating sociology of science essays.) Economics has become increasingly restricted with the post-1945 so-called mathematical-quantitative revolution. Cf. *infra*, p. 44.

6 As applied to economics see, for example, George J. Stigler, 'Merton on Multiples, Denied and Affirmed', in *The Economist as Preacher and Other Essays* (Chicago: University of Chicago Press, 1982), pp. 98–103.

The conventional positivist distinction between 'the context of discovery' and 'the context of justification' breaks down when we focus on the recognition of discovery rather than its origin. Mere subjective originality or temporal priority is not enough. As Augustine Brannigan has noted, 'multiple discoveries present a very complex mix of attributions made by the researchers themselves, their colleagues and their contemporaries as well as their successors' and the organizational arrangements in the field 'constitute an important set of intervening variables between the production of innovation and its attribution of discovery status'. Cf. his *The Social Basis of Scientific Discoveries* (Cambridge: Cambridge University Press, 1981), pp. 173, 176. Also Stigler, op. cit., pp. 102–3. The scope for innovation in science is strictly limited by current knowledge and accepted standards of scientific practice (i.e. tradition). According to Kuhn, scientists and artists have radically different conceptions of the value of innovation for innovation's sake. 'Science has its élite, and may have its rearguard, its producers of kitsch. But there is no scientific avant garde, and the existence of one would threaten science', which preserves its identity by pursuing unsuspected possibilities suggested by existing knowledge. T. S. Kuhn, 'Comment', in *Com-*

parative Studies in Society and History vol. 11 (October 1969), p. 411; also Michael Polanyi, 'The Growth of Science in Society', *Minerva* vol. 5 (1956–7), p. 539, and his *The Tacit Dimension* (New York: Doubleday, 1966), pp. 75–6.

7 Richard Whitley, 'From the Sociology of Scientific Communities to the Study of Scientists' Negotiations and Beyond', *Social Science Information* vol. 22 (1983), p. 708.

8 *The Intellectual and Social Organization of the Sciences* (London and New York: Oxford University Press, 1984), pp. 206–7. The list comprises: fragmented adhocracies (e.g. management studies); polycentric oligarchies (e.g. British social anthropology); partitioned bureaucracies (e.g. Anglo-Saxon economics); professional adhocracies (e.g. bio-medical science); polycentric professions (e.g. experimental physiology); technologically integrated bureaucracies (e.g. twentieth-century chemistry); and conceptually integrated bureaucracies (e.g. post-1945 physics).

9 Ibid., pp. 154–5. Cf. Phyllis Deane, 'The Scope and Method of Economic Science', *Economic Journal* vol. 93 (March 1983), p. 6.

10 Whitley, op. cit., p. 276.

11 For some general observations on this aspect see, for example, my 'The Culture and the Economists: Some Reflections on Anglo-American Differences', *History of Political Economy* vol. 12 (Spring 1980), pp. 588–609 (reprinted in this volume, pp. 134–54); also the articles by Harry G. Johnson referred to *infra*, notes 15–20.

12 Whitley, op. cit., p. 302.

13 Ibid., pp. 240–2, 277–9.

14 'The American Tradition in Economics', *Nebraska Journal of Economics and Business* vol. 16 (Summer 1977), p. 23.

15 Elizabeth S. Johnson and Harry G. Johnson, *The Shadow of Keynes, Understanding Keynes, Cambridge, and Keynesian Economics* (Chicago: University of Chicago Press, 1978). The bitterness of some of these essays, especially those directed towards some of his erstwhile Cambridge colleagues and the British Keynesian establishment, should not be allowed to detract from their value as a contribution to the internal sociology of modern economics. I accept Elizabeth Johnson's suggestion that the attack on Cambridge probably owed less to her husband's disappointment at his failure to obtain a Cambridge chair than to the inevitable disillusionment stemming from the unrealistically high expectations he brought to the university in the early postwar years.

16 'National Styles in Economic Research: The United States, the United Kingdom, Canada, and various European Countries', *Daedalus* vol. 102 (Spring 1973), pp. 65–74; 'The State of Theory', *American Economic Review* vol. 64 (May 1974), pp. 323–4; 'The Current and Prospective State of Economics', *Australian Economic Papers* vol. 13 (June 1974), pp. 1–27; 'The American Tradition in Economics', op. cit.

Johnson's explanation of national differences was couched in very broad terms, including such factors as national character, general cultural traditions, social structure, demography, educational institutions, career and employment opportunities, political and even geo-political conditions.

17 'The Current and Prospective State of Economics', *Australian Economic Papers* vol. 13 (June 1974), p. 15.

18 Ibid., pp. 13–15.

19 Routledge is publishing a series on the history of economic thought in various countries. Volumes include: Tessa Morris-Suzuki, *A History of Japanese Economic Thought* (1989); Bo Sandelin (ed.), *A History of Swedish Economic Thought* (1990);

Peter Groenewegen and Bruce McFarlane, *A History of Australian Economic Thought* (1991); and Robin Neill, *A History of Canadian Economic Thought* (1991).

20 'Methodologies of Economics', in Mark Perlman (ed.), *The Organization and Retrieval of Economic Knowledge* (Boulder, Colo.: Westview Press, 1977), p. 507.

21 For example, J. K. Galbraith, in his Presidential Address to the American Economic Association, complained that instead of the earlier censorship of economic ideas there is nowadays 'a new despotism. That consists in defining scientific excellence as whatever is closest in belief and method to the scholarly tendency of the people that are already there. This is a pervasive and oppressive thing not the less dangerous for being, in the frequent case, both righteous and unconscious.' 'Power and the Useful Economist', *American Economic Review* vol. 63 (March 1973), p. 2. Another President, and Nobel prizewinner, complained from a very different standpoint that the existing institutional arrangements in the profession discouraged interdisciplinary collaboration. Tjalling C. Koopmans, 'Economics Among the Sciences', *American Economic Review* vol. 69 (March 1979), p. 13. Other leading figures, such as Kenneth Boulding, Wassily Leontief, and Joan Robinson, have complained of the waste and misallocation of intellectual resources in economics.

Of course many critics of economic orthodoxy have advanced similar arguments. For a useful recent sampler from a post-Keynesian perspective see the essays in Alfred S. Eichner (ed.), *Why Is Economics Not Yet A Science?* (Armonk, NY: M. E. Sharpe, 1983). Also the penetrating, if somewhat overstated, critique in Homa Katouzian, *Ideology and Methodology in Economics* (London: Macmillan, 1980), especially pp. 126–31.

22 Whitley, op. cit., p. 248: 'In the 1950's, for example, six university departments in the United States: Berkeley, Chicago, Columbia, Harvard, MIT, and Wisconsin, produced nearly one-half of the Ph.D.'s in economics and two-thirds of these obtained academic jobs and published articles. Many of these papers were in the central sub-fields and most of the present reputational leadership of present U.S. economics came from those schools.' Moreover, my own research suggests that there was a similar concentration in earlier periods, see 'Economics in the United States, 1920–70', in volume 1 in this series, pp. 413–14. Whitley cites George J. Stigler and Claire Friedlander's fascinating article, 'The Citation Practices of Doctorates in Economics', reprinted in Stigler, *The Economist as Preacher and other Essays* (Chicago: University of Chicago Press, 1982), pp. 192–222. For a comparable analysis, from which the authors draw much less dispassionate conclusions, see E. Ray Canterbery and Robert J. Burkhardt, 'What Do We Mean By Asking Whether Economics Is A Science?', in Eichner, op. cit., especially pp. 26–31. See also *infra*, pp. 45–46.

23 See, for example, the sources cited in Coats, op. cit.

24 As the role of 'schools' in economics is familiar to historians it will not be considered here. For a notable recent example, which still leaves many questions unanswered, see Melvin Reder, 'Chicago Economics: Permanence and Change', *Journal of Economic Literature* vol. 20 (March 1982), pp. 1–38. The same applies to other schools and groups. Cf. *infra*, pp. 46–47.

25 *What's Wrong with Economics* (New York: Basic Books, 1972), ch. 1.

26 See his *Essays in the History of Economics* (Chicago: University of Chicago Press, 1965), pp. 31–50; also the three quantitative studies reprinted in his *The Economist as Preacher*, op. cit., pp. 173–243.

27 For example, D. R. Fusfeld, 'Program of the American Economic Association Meetings', *American Economic Review* vol. 46 (September 1956), pp. 642–4, F. R. Cleary and D. J. Edwards, 'The Origins of the Contributors to the AER during

the Fifties', *American Economic Review* vol. 50 (December 1960), pp. 1011–14; Pan A. Yotopoulos, 'Institutional Affiliation of the Contributors to Three Professional Journals', American Economic Review vol. 51 (September 1961), pp. 665–70.

28 For a comprehensive, yet doubtless incomplete, listing see A. W. Coats, 'Bibliography of Scholarly Articles on Economic Journals', *Economic Notes by Monte dei Paschi di Siena* vol. 20 (1991), pp. 181–8. For some of the broader issues see, for example, the work of Machlup, op. cit., and Perlman, op. cit.; and Richard and Nancy Ruggles, 'Communication in Economics: The Media and Technology', *Annals of Economic and Social Measurement* vol. 1/2 (1972), pp. 217–31. The issue of *Economic Notes* cited earlier is devoted to the learned journals in the development of economics and the economics profession. It includes contributions from the editor, Axel Leijonhufund, and R. Whitley, H. Hagemann, M. Perlman, A. Graziani, and D. N. McCloskey. My own contribution is reprinted in this volume.

29 For a useful introduction from a sociology of science standpoint see Marc de Mey, *The Cognitive Paradigm. Cognitive Science, a Newly Explored Approach to the Study of Cognition Applied in an Analysis of Science and Scientific Knowledge* (Dordrecht, Netherlands: Reidel, 1982), especially part II dealing with 'Bibliometrics and the Structure of Science', 'Informal Groups and the Origins of Networks', and 'The Life Cycle of Scientific Specialities'. His references (on p. 112) to the 'econometrics' of products of intellect, and 'social epistemology' as 'the analysis of the production, distribution and utilization of intellectual products' should appeal to economists.

It should, of course, be unnecessary to point out the dangers of an overenthusiastic reliance on quantification in this as in other subjects. Cf., for example, David Edge, 'Quantitative Measures of Communication in Science: A Critical Review', *History of Science* vol. 17 (1979), pp. 102–34.

30 *Infra*, pp. 49–50.

31 Cf. my 'The First Decade of HOPE (1968–79)', *History of Political Economy* vol. 15 (Fall 1983), pp. 303–19 (reprinted in vol. III in this series). This paper now strikes me as unimaginative and excessively descriptive. In so saying I completely exempt the accompanying paper by Neil de Marchi and John Lodewijks on 'HOPE and the Journal Literature in the History of Economic Thought' from guilt by association.

32 James R. Millar, 'Where are the Young Specialists on the Soviet Economy and What are they Doing?' *Journal of Comparative Economics* vol. 4 (September 1980), pp. 317–29; also Abram Bergson's 'Comment', *Journal of Comparative Economics* vol. 5 (March 1981), p. 119. Millar was evidently worried by the idea that 'fields die from the top'.

Although Schumpeter recognized intergenerational differences of attitudes in economics he did not consider training in the discipline rigorous enough to condition these attitudes. Cf. *History of Economic Analysis*, pp. 46, 1181n. *Plus cq change . . . ?*

33 Cf. my 'The Historical Context of the "New" Economic History', *Journal of European Economic History* vol. 9 (Spring 1980), pp. 185–207 (reprinted in vol. III in this series); also the unpublished Ph.D. thesis by Steven Wentworth, 'Marginalized History: A Contribution to the Critique of New Economic History', Uppsala, 1984, which contains an excellent bibliography.

34 For example, Heinz Arndt, *The Rise and Fall of Economic Growth, A Study in Contemporary Thought* (Melbourne: Longman Cheshire, 1978), which has little systematic reference to sociological and institutional influences. The same criticism applies to Paul McNulty's useful study of *The Origins and Development of*

Labor Economics, a Chapter in the History of Social Thought (Cambridge, Mass.: MIT Press, 1980).

35 See Remenyi's 'Core Demi-Core Interaction: Toward a General Theory of Disciplinary and Sub-Disciplinary Growth', *History of Political Economy* vol. 11 (Spring 1979), pp. 30–63. The specific example he selected was development economics.

For two contrasting case studies from outside economics see Arnold Thackray, 'The Pre-History of an Academic Discipline: The Study of the History of Science in the United States, 1891–1941', *Minerva* vol. 18 (1980), pp. 448–73; and Nicholas C. Mullins, 'The Development of Specialities in Social Science: The Case of Ethnomethodology', *Science Studies* vol. 3 (1973), pp. 245–73. Mullins specifies four stages in the emergence of new disciplines: normal, network, cluster, and speciality or discipline; and contends that theory development is always preceded by social development. More generally see C. Lemaine, R. Macleod, M. Mulkay and P. Weingart, *Perspectives on the Emergence of Scientific Specialities* (The Hague: Mouton, 1976).

36 Thus two studies suggest fourteen or fifteen factors accounting for the success or failure of particular research schools. Some are obviously irrelevant to economics (e.g. simple and readily exploitable experimental techniques) whereas other relevant factors have been either largely or wholly neglected by historians of economics (e.g. access to graduate students; cognitive overlaps between innovators and established practitioners; conflict with established or parent discipline; clear identity, single 'audience'; funding). Cf. Gerald L. Gieson, 'Scientific Change, Emerging Specialities, and Research Schools', *History of Science* vol. 19 (1981), pp. 24–5. He emphasizes the distinction between conceptual growth and scientific change, arguing that new specialities are more often associated with the latter than the former. New specialities may emerge because of resistance to scientific innovation on the part of established groups.

37 Michael Mulkay and G. Nigel Gilbert, 'What is the Ultimate Question? Some Remarks in Defence of the Analysis of Scientific Discourse', *Social Studies of Science* vol. 12 (1982), pp. 309–19; also their earlier 'Contexts of Scientific Discourse: Social Accounting in Experimental Papers', in Karin D. Knorr, Roger Krohn, and Richard Whitley, *The Social Process of Scientific Investigation*, Sociology of the Sciences Yearbook vol. IV (1980) (Dordrecht, Netherlands: Reidel, 1981), pp. 269–94; and *idem*, 'Joking Apart: Some Recommendations Concerning the Analysis of Scientific Culture', *Social Studies of Science* vol. 12 (1982), pp. 585–613.

38 This will be considered in the section on historiography in vol. III in this series.

39 Stigler, *Essays in the History of Economics*, especially pp. 4–6: 'The Technique of Persuasion'.

40 *American Economic Review* vol. 73 (March 1983), pp. 31–43. If a joke is permissible here, according to the grapevine Leamer is preparing a follow-up paper, 'Let's Take the Tricks out of Econometrics'.

41 'The Rhetoric of Economics', *Journal of Economic Literature* vol. 21 (June 1983), pp. 481–587. In support of the disparaging comment in the text see Bruce Caldwell and A. W. Coats, 'The Rhetoric of Economics: A Comment on McCloskey', *Journal of Economic Literature* vol. 22 (June 1984), pp. 575–8. As the sociology of science literature demonstrates, rhetoric is much more than a matter of figures of speech and methodological prejudice.

42 'Levels of Discourse in New Classical Economics', *History of Political Economy* vol. 16 (Summer 1984), pp. 283–90; see also his *Conversations with Economists: New Classical Economists and Their Opponents Speak Out on the Current Controversy in Macroeconomics* (Totowa, N. J.: Rowman & Allanheld, 1983). For a very different

approach to economic discourse see Keith Tribe, *Land Labour and Economic Discourse* (London: Routledge & Kegan Paul, 1978).

43 On this see vol. III in this series.

44 Cf. *infra*, p. 49ff, for further discussion.

45 'The Constructivist Programme in the Sociology of Science: Retreats or Advances?' *Social Studies of Science* vol. 12 (1982), p. 323. See also her 'Relativism – What Now?', *Social Studies of Science* vol. 12 (1982), pp. 133–6; and her *The Manufacture of Knowledge: An Essay on the Contructivist and the Contextual Nature of Science* (Oxford: Pergamon Press, 1981).

46 Peter Weingart, 'The Scientific Power Elite', in Norbert Elias, Herminio Martins, and Richard Whitley (eds), *Scientific Establishments and Hierarchies*, p. 85.

47 'Structure, Culture, and Intellectual Style: An Essay Comparing Saxonic, Teutonic, Gallic, and Nipponic Approaches', *Social Science Information* vol. 6 (1981), p. 834.

48 'Relativist/Constructive Programmes in the Sociology of Science: Redundance and Retreat', *Social Studies of Science* vol. 12 (1982), p. 281. Emphasis in original.

49 Thomas F. Gieryn, 'Not-Last Words: Worn-Out Dichotomies in the Sociology of Science' (Reply), *Social Studies of Science* vol. 12 (1982), p. 332.

50 This is one of the main charges against the 'strong' programme, whose proponents deny that 'truth and falsity are inherent properties of statements . . . terms which are interesting only as they are used by a [scientific] community itself, as it develops and maintains its own patterns of concept application . . . there is no basis for validation superior to the collective contingent judgment of the paradigm-sharing community'. Barry Barnes, *T. S. Kuhn and Social Science* (New York: Columbia University Press, 1982), pp. 30–1. See also supra p. 14ff.

51 'The Place of the "Core-Set" in Modern Science: Social Contingency with Methodological Propriety in Science', *History of Science* vol. 19 (1981), pp. 6–7. Critics maintain that a strictly relativist programme cannot explain results which are both surprising and compelling. One commentator argues in favour of distinguishing between 'results which intrude themselves on a surprised researcher, those observations available only to observers with an alerting framework, those available only with extra scrutiny, and those available only to those thoroughly trained in the relevant technique'. Roger Krohn, 'On Gieryn on the Relativist/Constructivist Programme in the Sociology of Science: *Naïveté* and Reaction', *Social Studies of Science* vol. 12 (1982), p. 327. Another critic is uncertain how far Collins's programme implies the relativity of truth and rationality. Cf. Thomas Nickles's review essay, 'A Revolution that Failed: Collins and Pinch on the Paranormal', *Social Studies of Science* vol. 14 (1984), p. 307.

52 Gieryn, 'Not-Last Words', p. 330, citing Collins. In his reply to Gieryn, Collins posed intriguing questions about the interrelationship between the supposed epistemological uniqueness of science and its powerful normative structure. Cf. H. M. Collins, 'Knowledge, Norms and Rules in the Sociology of Science', *Social Studies of Science* vol. 12 (1982), p. 301.

53 H. M. Collins and G. Cox, 'Recovering Relativity: Did Prophecy Fail?' *Social Studies of Science* vol. 6 (1976), p. 439. For a response to this see Nickles, op. cit., p. 308 n. 4.

54 Gad. Freudenthal, 'The Role of Shared Knowledge in Science: The Failure of the Constructivist Program in the Sociology of Science', *Social Studies of Science* vol. 14 (1984), p. 293. Also ibid., p. 286: 'the internal logic of constructivism inevitably leads to an extreme, obviously absurd, form of positivism and solipsism.'

55 Mulkay and Gilbert argue that discourse analysis has the merit of focusing on

modest and answerable questions. Knorr-Cetina would probably make the same point for constructivism.

56 This evasive observation reflects the epistemological scepticism commonly found among historians and sociologists.

4

IS THERE A 'STRUCTURE OF SCIENTIFIC REVOLUTIONS' IN ECONOMICS?

According to well-informed observers, we are now in the midst of a 'revolution' in the historiography of science. The conventional 'uniformitarian' conception of scientific progress as a continuous process of stockpiling facts and techniques is being challenged by a 'catastrophist' view that the process has been subject to periodic breakdowns and changes of direction, discontinuities obscured by historians who have unconsciously interpreted the past in the light of their own epistemological preconceptions. The leading advocate of the catastrophist veiwpoint is Thomas S. Kuhn, whose brilliant book *The Structure of Scientific Revolutions* (1962), has provoked considerable controversy among historians of science;[1] and this paper is designed to draw the attention of economists to his stimulating central thesis.

It is appropriate to compare the history of economics with the history of the natural sciences, not only because economists have persistently striven to emulate the natural scientists' methods but also because any signs of an antipositivist movement among historians of science are obviously of interest to those engaged in the interminable debate about 'positive' economics, as well as to historians.[2] Moreover, both groups may derive intellectual stimulus from Kuhn's effort to synthesize epistemology, the sociology of knowledge and the study of science as a profession.

From a sociological viewpoint, science may be regarded as 'an institutional mechanism for sifting warranted beliefs', a process controlled by a group of persons known as 'scientists'; and there are obvious reasons why the 'self-corrective mechanisms of science as a social enterprise "have functioned less effectively in economics than, say, in physics" '.[3] It is a field in which the authority of tradition has been strong, well-defined standards of scientific or technical competence have been lacking, and those seeking conclusive empirical tests of hypotheses have encountered serious technical and methodological difficulties.[4] The history of economics has been punctuated by recurrent bitter methodological disputes, disputes influenced by policy issues as well as by purely scientific considerations. Nevertheless it is widely recognized that the differences between economics and the natural sciences are differences of degree rather than kind, and as Kuhn demon-

58

strates, methodological disputes in any branch of science are often marred by the conspicuous irrationality of the disputants for, as Karl Popper has observed, the 'criterion of demarcation' by which scientific propositions are distinguished from non-scientific propositions is fundamentally based on 'a proposal for agreement or convention – a decision going beyond rational argument'.[5]

Although Kuhn's approach to the history of science was influenced by his awareness of the differences between the social and the natural sciences, any economist who reads his book will be struck by certain marked similarities. Kuhn maintains that 'normal' science is dominated by 'paradigms' which he defines as 'universally recognized scientific achievements that for a time provide model problems and solutions to a community of practitioners' (p. x), and the paradigm's function is regulative (i.e. normative) as well as cognitive since it provides the scientist not only with 'a map, but also with some of the directions essential for map-making' (p. 108). A paradigm is not simply a theory; it incorporates 'accepted examples of scientific practice' which include 'law, theory, application and instrumentation together' (p. 10); and it enables the scientists in that field to take the foundation of their knowledge for granted and concentrate their attention on the solution of more concrete problems, or 'puzzles'. Obviously no paradigm is complete; if it were, 'normal' scientific activity would cease, for there would be no unsolved puzzles; and as 'normal' research proceeds unexpected or anomalous results appear. For a time these will be ignored, or dismissed as irrelevant or accidental, because 'the scientist who pauses to examine every anomaly he notes will seldom get any significant work done' (p. 82). But as the anomalies grow in number and importance, they eventually become 'critical'; a sense of crisis develops as the inadequacy of the ruling paradigm becomes increasingly apparent, and research is diverted from puzzle-solving to paradigm-testing (pp. 91, 82–4). However, any serious challenge to an established paradigm will provoke a reaction, which is both natural and healthy since the challengers are threatening the established scientific tradition, with its concomitant network of commitments to specific concepts, theories, instruments, and standards of scientific performance (p. 42). In the ensuing debate all the scientific passions are aroused; and if the ruling paradigm is overthrown its defeat will be due to a 'conversion experience', a 'transfer of allegiance', rather than to 'the logical structure of scientific knowledge', for the change is dependent on the possibilities inherent in the new paradigm rather than any demonstrable proof of its superiority (pp. 94, 150, 156–7).

This bald summary does scant justice to Kuhn's cogent and subtle argument, which is buttressed by a wealth of historical illustrations; but it should be enough to suggest its relevance to economics. Have there been phases of crisis and paradigm-change in economics, and if so have they resulted from the failure of crucial experiments or from extra-scientific sources? Kuhn himself doubts whether there have been any paradigms in the social sciences (p. 15), but this remark suggests the ambiguity of the paradigm concept, for it may be interpreted as a specific book or style of exposition, a 'basic theory', a *Weltanschauung*, or the entire range of scientific activity.[6] Fortunately this definitional difficulty creates no fundamental problems for the social scientist for he is much less concerned with instruments, apparatus, and applications of theory than the natural scientist, and in the social science context a paradigm may be defined as a 'basic theory'. From this standpoint economics may be regarded as more 'uniformitarian' than the natural sciences, for despite persistent and often penetrating criticism by a stream of heterodox writers (e.g. socialists, evolutionists, institutionalists) it has been dominated throughout its history by a single paradigm – the theory of economic equilibrium via the market mechanism.[7] According to Kuhn's criteria economists may be said to have enjoyed considerable success in two phases of the 'normal' scientific activity of actualizing the promises inherent in their paradigm, i.e. extending the knowledge of 'relevant' facts, and improving the 'articulation' of the paradigm itself (p. 24). However, their efforts to improve the match between the facts and the paradigm's predictions have met with only limited success, although this is understandable in view of the virtual absence of 'instrumental expectations'.[8] Does this not mean that by comparison with the natural sciences economics has not yet passed beyond the 'developmental' or pre-paradigm stage?

The application of Kuhn's approach to economics does not merely involve the translation of a few methodological commonplaces into a new language; it provides a new interpretive framework – a basis from which to re-examine the precise scientific importance of successive theoretical advances. By emphasizing the regulative as well as the cognitive functions of paradigms Kuhn suggests new relationships among the ingredients in familiar debates. The process of pardigm change in the natural sciences may be regarded as an ideal type which may be used to clarify the inter-relationships between the terminological, conceptual, personal, ideological and professional (i.e. careerist) elements in the development of scientific knowledge. This approach provides a framework, not a straitjacket. Kuhn explicitly denies that science is monolithic; and although competing paradigms can co-exist in any given scientific field only during crisis periods, not all theories achieve paradigm status, and there are many specialized overlapping and interpenetrating paradigms (pp. 61, 77, 94, 49–51).

Needless to say, the structure of scientific revolutions is much less readily discernible in economics than in the natural sciences. Economic theories (whether paradigms or sub-paradigms) are usually less rigid and compelling than their natural science equivalents, hence they rarely represent an obvious challenge to the established scientific tradition. Instead of outright hostility they more often encounter neglect, scepticism, or even anti-intellectual scorn. However, the most striking example of paradigm-change in economics, the Keynesian revolution of the 1930s, possessed many of the characteristics associated with Kuhn's 'scientific revolutions'. There were unrecognized precursors of Keynes, a growing concern about the inadequacy of existing theory, and a change of psychological outlook on the part of many economists virtually amounting to a 'conversion experience'. The revolution was led by a band of youngsters (apart from the Peter Pan-like figure of Keynes himself) who encountered fierce resistance from their elders; but within a remarkably short time the new paradigm had won an almost complete victory.[9] As with paradigm changes in the natural sciences, the initiative had come from *within* the scientific community – indeed, at its very heart, and its leader knew exactly what he was doing. There was certainly 'no standard higher than the assent of the relevant community' (p. 93), but it is now clear that the Keynesian paradigm was not 'incompatible' with its predecessor, and during the subsequent 'mopping-up operations' (p. 24) it proved necessary to devote considerable effort to the task of clarifying and systematizing Keynes's ideas. Yet he had undoubtedly provided his professional colleagues not only with a new 'map, but also with some of the directions essential for map-making' (p. 108); and the whole process would repay systematic study in terms of the cognitive and regulative functions attributed to Kuhn's paradigms.

The Keynesian revolution was unique in the history of economics, especially in regard to its regulative impact on the economics profession.[10] However, earlier revolutions have occurred, each of which has exhibited points of similarity with Kuhn's revolutions – much as the victory of classical economics via the Political Economy Club; the *Methodenstreit* between German and Austrian economists; and the more purely cognitive marginal utility revolution. Obviously Kuhn's model will not fit all these cases. But it adds precision to Schumpeter's conception of the 'classical situation', and serves as a healthy corrective to more deterministic sociological models.[11] If there is any discernible pattern in the development of economic science, it is one that combines ideas and events in a flexible manner; and the significance of Kuhn's approach stems from its demonstration of the mediating role played by the scientific community.

NOTES

1 Subsequent references to Kuhn will appear as page numbers in the text. For background discussion see Gerd Buchdahl, 'A Revolution in Historiography of Science', *History of Science*, vol. 4, 1965, pp. 56–69. Also C. C. Gillespie, 'Review of Joseph Agassi', in: *Isis*, vol. 55, 1964, pp. 97–9; and Walter F. Cannon, 'The Uniformitarian–Catastrophist Debate', *Isis*, vol. 51, 1960, pp. 38, 55.

2 See, for example, T. W. Hutchison, '*Positive Economics' and Policy Objectives*, 1964, and A. W. Coats, 'Value Judgements in Economics', *Yorkshire Bulletin of Economic*

and Social Research, vol. 16, 1964, pp. 53–67. (To be reprinted in vol. III in this series.)

3 The quotations are from Ernest Nagel, *The Structure of Science, Problems in the Logic of Scientific Explanation* (1961), p. 490.

4 For some illustrations, see A. W. Coats, 'The Role of Authority in the Development of British Economics', *Journal of Law and Economics*, vol. 7, 1964, pp. 88–95 (reprinted in this volume, pp. 82–104).

5 *The Logic of Scientific Discovery* (1961), pp. 37–8.

6 Cf. Buchdal's critical comments, op. cit., pp. 58–9. Also the reviews of Kuhn by Dudley Shapere in the *Philosophical Review*, vol. 73, 1964, pp. 383–94, and H. V. Stopes-Roe in *The British Journal for the Philosophy of Science*, vol. XV, 1964, p. 159.

7 Donald Gordon concludes his comments on Kuhn somewhat complacently by claiming that the persistence of this economic paradigm is 'a tribute to the supremacy of purely positivistic forces'. Cf. 'The Role of the History of Economic Thought in the Understanding of Modern Economic Theory', *American Economic Review*, vol. 55, 1965, p. 124. To my knowledge, this was the first published attempt to relate Kuhn's views to economics. Cf. my unpublished monograph, *The Role of Value Judgements in Economics* (University of Virginia, Thomas Jefferson Center for Studies in Political Economy), Mimeo, May 1964, pp. 56–61.

8 Cf. Kuhn, p. 67, and the comments on econometrics in Henry W. Briefs, *Three Views on Economic Method* (1960), pp. 29–30.

9 For some characteristically penetrating observations on this episode see Joseph A. Schumpeter, *History of Economic Analysis* (1954), pp. 1180–1. The older generation's opposition, Schumpeter noted, did not merely stem from arteriosclerosis, for they were the beneficiaries as well as the victims of their training. They had acquired, among other things, 'analytic experience. And in a field like economics, where training is often defective and where the young scholar very often simply does not know enough, this element in the case counts much more heavily than it does in physics where teaching, even though possibly uninspiring, is always competent.' See also, R. F. Harrod, *The Life of John Maynard Keynes* (1952), pp. 451–67, for valuable personal and methodological insights into the Keynesian revolution.

10 According to one bitter critic, 'most of the younger sceptics who expressed misgivings about the "new" economics began to be eliminated from academic life. There was no inquisition, no discernible or intentional suppression of academic freedom; but young non-conformists could seldom expect promotion. They appeared rather like young physicists who were arrogant enough to challenge the basic validity of revolutionary developments which they did not properly understand. To suggest that Keynes was all wrong was like questioning the soundness of Einstein or Bohr. The older economists could declare their doubts without serious loss of prestige, but any dissatisfaction on the part of the younger men seemed to be evidence of intellectual limitations.' W. H. Hutt, 'Critics of the "Classical Tradition" ', *South African Journal of Economics*, vol. 32, 1964, p. 81. For interesting earlier comments see his *The Economists and the Public* (1936), p. 245.

11 Cf. Schumpeter, op. cit., pp. 51, 87, 143, 380; also W. A. Stark, 'The "Classical Situation" in Political Economy', *Kyklos*, vol. 12, 1959, pp. 57–63.

5

THE ECONOMIC AND SOCIAL CONTEXT OF THE MARGINAL REVOLUTION OF THE 1870s

I

This essay is focused on a particular aspect of a general philosophical problem, i.e., the problem of explanation in history.* The fundamental question at issue is this: From what standpoint, in what terms, and to what extent, can the historian of economics 'explain' the marginal revolution? As the title indicates, I do not believe it can be adequately explained solely in terms of the immanent development of the logic of economic theory. But, on the other hand, none of the familiar environmentalist theories has proved convincing, for as George Stigler has justly complained, exponents of this approach have usually failed 'to offer hypotheses on the portions of the social environment which do or do not influence economic theorizing. Of course the environment has some influence, but until we can specify when and where we only have a *deus ex machina*.'[1]

The problem of explanation in science and history has been the subject of considerable scholarly controversy in recent decades.[2] Without entering into the details of the debate it may be said that the prerequisite of any explanation is a clear definition of the explanandum. A survey of the historiography of economic thought reveals innumerable competing, overlapping, and conflicting interpretations of the nature and significance of the marginal revolution of the 1870s. It may therefore clear the ground for subsequent discussion if I express my support for the conventional view that despite the existence of numerous earlier versions of the marginal concept, the combined achievements of Jevons, Menger, and Walras in the early 1870s did constitute a significant intellectual breakthrough in the development of economic analysis and may be regarded as revolutionary in their implications, if not in their novelty or in the speed of diffusion.[3] The changes included not only a major shift in the focus of economic theory – towards an emphasis on subjective factors, on demand and consumption rather than supply, production, and distribution; they also laid the basis for a comprehensive systematization of the subject matter of economics, including the elaboration and eventual completion of competitive price theory, the integration of value, production, and distribution theories, the refinement of economic logic, and the extension of mathematical modes of analysis. As Mark Blaug has observed, 'The theory of utility supplied most of the excitement of discovery in the seventies and eighties, but it was the introduction of marginal analysis as such that marked the true dividing line between classical theory and modern economics. The significance of marginal utility theory was that it provided the archetype of the general problem of allocating given means with maximum effect.'[4]

In considering how to account for this breakthrough in economic analysis the first problem is the choice of perspective. This is largely a subjective matter, but to my mind a satisfactory explanation must encompass the common characteristics of the ideas and experiences of the three cofounders of modern marginalism and must also place their work in its wider intellectual and socioeconomic setting. According to Blaug, previous explanations have fallen into four broad categories, regarding the marginal revolution respectively as (i) an autonomous intellectual development within the discipline of economics, (ii) the product of philosophical currents, (iii) the result of definite institutional changes in the economy, and (iv) a counterblast to socialism, particularly to Marxism.[5] These four categories are not mutually exclusive, and recent research in the history, philosophy, and sociopsychology of science points the way to a further type of explanation which incorporates logic, methodology, personality, and environmental factors in fruitful new combinations. To say this is not, of course, to suggest that a 'complete' explanation is available, or is ever likely to be; nor does it mean that the new approach is entirely novel. Nevertheless, as it is a source of fruitful hypotheses, it merits some consideration in a volume devoted to the history of marginalism in economics.

II

The sociology of science (or the science of science) is a subdivision of the sociology of knowledge, which is a field of research rather than a specific theory. The sociology of knowledge may be defined as 'the branch of sociology which studies the relations between thought and society ... [it] attempts to relate the ideas it studies to the socio-historical settings in which they are produced and received';[6] and as this approach has sometimes been associated with rigid deterministic theories of the influence of events upon ideas, it should immediately be noted that there are in fact numerous competing theories of the relationship between thought and society, some loose, idealistic, and sweeping (macrosociological), others more precise and empirically grounded (microsociological). The current orthodoxy among students of the history and sociology of science supports the contention that endogenous (or internal) influences largely explain the growth of scientific knowledge. Indeed one authority, after commenting on the 'virtual disappearance' since World War II 'of attempts to explain the content and theories of science on the basis of social conditions', adds:

> Historical studies of the development of scientific thought, and socio-logical investigation of the way scientists work, have unquestionably shown that the problems investigated by scientists are overwhelmingly determined by conditions internal to the scientific community, such as the 'state of the art' and the resources for and organization of scientific work. This is not to say that general philosophical ideas and social concerns may not influence science at all, but that the growth of scientific knowledge cannot be *systematically* explained as resulting from such external conditions.[7]

However, before directly applying this generalization to the marginal revolution in economics, two significant qualifications must be noted. Most work in the sociology of science is concerned with the natural sciences rather than the social sciences, which are, on the whole, much less self-contained bodies of knowledge; and even with the natural sciences there has been considerable disagreement as to where the boundary line should be drawn between 'internal' and 'external' conditions. Secondly, statements derived from twentieth-century conditions are not necessarily applicable to earlier periods, when the 'scientific community', if it existed at all, was much smaller and less tightly organized.

One further preliminary observation is in order. While it is true that current research in the history and philosophy of science favours expla-nations of scientific change in terms of 'conditions internal to the scientific community', there has nevertheless been a significant shift in the prevailing interpretation of those conditions. While turning away from such broad exogenous influences as the state of the economy, the social structure, ideology, and class bias, scholars have tended to emphasize the variety and complexity of factors at work within the scientific community. It is no longer fashionable to accept the logical empiricists' clear-cut distinction between the sociology of scientific knowledge and the philosophy of science, a distinction sometimes expressed as a dichotomy between the 'context of discovery' and the 'context of justification'. Instead, attention is increasingly focused on actual scientific practice rather than correct scientific method, the latter representing an ideal seldom attained in practice. Likewise, it is increasingly recognized that 'theoretical and philosophical factors are presupposed in every aspect of scientific inquiry . . . in the meanings of observational and theoretical terms, in the characterization of the problems tackled by a science, and in what is to count as solutions to those prob-lems'.[8] It remains to be seen how far this new species of microsociological analysis can contribute to a reappraisal of the marginal revolution of the 1870s.

65

III

Sociological analysis of the marginal revolution can begin at any one of a number of points, for example, the concept of multiple discoveries in science.[9] As the subjective originality of the three cofounders is not in question, the approximate similarity and contemporaneity of their achievements link the creativity of the individual innovator to the mainstream of scientific knowledge, thereby strengthening the impression that the growth of knowledge has an organic life of its own. This aspect illustrates the problem of perspective mentioned earlier: when we view the process of scientific development as it were from a distance, the common characteristics seem relatively more important; whereas on closer inspection, the idiosyncratic features of the individual innovators assume greater significance; and there can be no single uniquely correct perspective. Of course the extent to which an apparent multiple is in fact a genuine one is a matter for detailed historical investigation; but the very existence of multiples in the history of economics[10] helps to distinguish the field as a scientific discipline from less systematic areas of intellectual endeavour, the assumption being that in economics, as contrasted with the creative arts, if one scientist does not 'discover' something there is a reasonable expectation that somebody else will.[11] In this sense the extent and speed of recognition of a multiple tell us something about the level of intellectual coherence and organization of the research area in which it occurs. As any given science becomes more institutionalized, and as increasing numbers of specialists are at work on the same or closely related problems, any given discovery is increasingly likely to be made independently more than once. Swift recognition of a multiple is, of course, a function of the efficiency of communication among specialists in the field;[12] and in the case under consideration the contacts between Jevons and Walras reveal the existence of an embryonic international network of scientific economists in the 1870s.[13]

The occurrence of a multiple naturally invites the historian of ideas to investigate the intellectual context from which it emerged.[14] He should, for example, consider whether the discovery was unexpected by contemporaries or sprang from an acknowledged intellectual 'crisis' – and in the latter case he should examine the nature of that crisis and the extent to which the discovery represented a genuine solution of the intellectual difficulties recognized at the time. Unlike natural scientists, economists are rarely confronted with crises resulting from an accumulation of experimental results which conflict with existing theories;[15] indeed, their theories have rarely been subjected to rigorous empirical testing, and it is consequently more difficult for the historian to determine the precise reasons why one economic theory displaced another. Two or more rival theories often coexist,[16] and it rarely happens that one is superior to its competitors in all respects – e.g., generality, manageability, and congruence with reality.[17] A shift of allegiance from one theory to another may result from a change of intellectual fashions, the emergence of a new and ambitious school of writers, or a shift in the range of problems thought to be important.[18] There seems to be no reason to believe that the marginal revolution of the 1870s was the product of an acute sense of intellectual crisis; on the contrary, as Schumpeter observed, many of the cofounders' 'fellow scientists felt no attachment to the old doctrines'.[19]

This state of affairs can be explained in a variety of ways. On a purely intellectual level emphasis may be laid on the manifest theoretical and empirical shortcomings of the received doctrines – though this calls for an explanation of the revival of interest after a phase of intellectual stagnation.[20] On the other hand, the absence of a sense of crisis may also be due to the loose social structure of the scientific community of economists, especially the small number of scientific practitioners and the low level of 'social acoustics' in the field.

While we recognize the interdependence of logical, psychological, and sociological elements in the marginal revolution, it is nevertheless essential to attempt a precise estimate of the scientific nature and importance of the changes involved. How far, for instance, did the subjective-value theorists accept the classical economists' 'scientific vision'?[21] Which theoretical and empirical propositions of classical economics were (i) accepted *in toto*, (ii) modified and if so, how drastically, (iii) rejected, by the marginalists? To put the matter differently: while agreeing that the marginal revolution represented a breakthrough in theory and technique, rather than the applications of theory, we may still enquire whether it constituted a breakthrough in methodology, in the content and focus of theory, in the conceptual language employed (e.g., the use of mathematics), and in the extent to which theory became congruent with reality, amenable to verification, or relevant to policy. An attempt to answer these (somewhat rigidly taxonomic) questions would enable us to judge how far the classicists and marginalists were employing 'incommensurable' conceptual frameworks, and how far the revolution involved genuine scientific disagreement rather than the rhetorical exaggeration so often associated with assertions of scientific novelty.[22] Of course, no final answers to these questions can be given, not merely because there is no uniquely correct historical perspective but also because the historian's judgement is itself influenced by his philosophical and methodological preconceptions.[23]

As already noted, the occurrence of multiple discoveries highlights the relationship between the general growth of scientific knowledge and the contributions of individual scientific innovators, and it is appropriate to consider each of these aspects in turn. The innovator's role is commonly regarded as analogous to that of a biological mutation in the evolutionary process of nature,[24] and from this standpoint science appears as a special type of adaptive social system – what Ernest Nagel has termed 'a social mechanism for sifting warranted beliefs'.[25] This mechanism connects the subjective activity of the individual scientific researcher to the collective quest for objective knowledge, and this relationship has become familiar to historians of economics largely through T. S. Kuhn's analysis of the behaviour of scientific groups in so-called 'normal' and 'revolutionary' periods of scientific advance. It has been well said that Kuhn's scientist is 'a man engaged in the interpretation, elaboration, modification, and even on occasions overthrow of a professional tradition of practice, rather than an automaton whose activities are finally monitored by a fixed inexorable logic';[26] and although Kuhn has been criticized for overemphasizing psychological and sociological aspects, and minimizing the importance of rational elements in scientific practice (a contention he has strenuously denied),[27] his approach is compatible with a kind of 'epistemological agnosticism' according to which some of the more vexing, theoretical difficulties in the philosophy of science can be allowed to recede into the background.

The sociology of science is a fruitful source of hypotheses about the immediate social context of the marginal revolution. For example,

> Who were the people taking part in scientific activity? What were their numbers, education, social position, means of livelihood, personal motives and opportunities, means of communication, institutions? What critical audience was there to be convinced by, use, transmit, develop, revise or reject their conclusions? What social pressures were there within the scientific community itself to affect the consensus of opinion in favour of the old or the new?[28]

Obviously if a 'scientific community'[29] of economists can be said to have existed in the early 1870s, it was much smaller, less tightly organized, and less immune to external influences than the twentieth-century body of natural scientists, with which so much recent work in the sociology of science has been concerned. Nevertheless, the degree of social organization required need not be elaborate; indeed, the mere recognition of a 'problem area' within a scientific discipline may be a sufficient condition, since this problem area can be regarded as the prototype of a more formal and stable organization designed to produce and foster innovation. The essential need is for a 'social circle' or scientific group – a 'critical mass' comprising 'an audience of sufficient size and competence to provide an adequate feedback' in the form of professional recognition.[30] Once this exists, the establishment of common scientific values, standards, and goals, with the concomitant attributes of 'conviviality' and 'commitment' so vividly portrayed by Michael Polanyi,[31] cannot be far behind.

These remarks may help to point the way towards a more systematic comparative study of the sociointellectual context of the marginal revolution, an undertaking which can only be hinted at here. Such a study would seek to identify the principal differences between the personal histories, scientific backgrounds, and intellectual beliefs and objectives of the three cofounders. On a broad level it would show that when they published their major works they were all comparatively young[32] members of the moderately well-to-do social class which had access to higher education in nineteenth-century Europe, and they were all brought up in the mainstream of European ideas which laid the foundations for the growth of modern science.[33] However, there were, at the same time, significant differences in their backgrounds and knowledge, for example, in the extent to which a professional tradition of economic thought existed in their respective countries during the 1860s and the extent to which each cofounder could be regarded (or could regard himself) as a deviant from his inherited intellectual beliefs. While the academic community was doubtless more open and flexible in Jevons' England than on the European continent, Jevons faced a more powerful and firmly entrenched corpus of economic ideas than either Menger or Walras, both of whom suffered from lack of congenial and stimulating scientific colleagues until after they had produced their major works. From this point it would be appropriate to examine how far their academic backgrounds and connections shaped their approach to economics, for it has often been noted that from the 1870s most of the significant advances in economics were made by academics. If this is in fact the case, we should surely examine the changing university environment in which this occurred and endeavour to assess its precise influence on the development of economic ideas.

A comparative study of the type indicated would need to consider the psychological dimensions of the marginal revolution, in addition to the social situation within the scientific community, for these two levels of discourse necessarily interact. To recall the evolutionary analogy mentioned above, if the scientific innovator resembles a biological mutant, then in psychological terms 'learning, perception and other increases in knowledge at the individual level, and increases in the accuracy and scope of scientific knowledge, are part processes of the more general case of increases in the adaptive fit of organism to environment'.[34] How far any given scientist will strive to advance knowledge in his special field will, of course, depend on a subtle combination of circumstances, some intrinsic to the individual, others reflecting the pressures and opportunities presented by his particular sociocultural environment.

In the past the process of scientific discovery has too often been regarded as a mystery, the product of some inherently unanalysable characterological traits summed up in the expression 'creative genius'. More recently, however, efforts have been made to study this phenomenon as a social process, and although it is impossible to explain the specific content of mental phenomena in terms of physical facts,[35] it is nevertheless possible to shed light on the more general influences bearing on multiple discoveries. Thus numerous efforts have been made to specify the characterological traits to be found in the representative innovator – such qualities as insight and motivation, personal attributes such as erudition, xenophilia (love of the unexpected), visualization (e.g., insight into logical, spatial, or mechanical relationships), alertness, and consistency of purpose.[36] Research in this area is still in its infancy; for instance, there is much to be learnt about the elements in motivation, such as the role of curiosity, aggressiveness, self-esteem, vanity, power;[37] and there is obviously no unique scientific 'type', for there are many different functions to be performed by members of the scientific community.[38]

Historians of economics differ markedly in the importance they attach to the role of biographical factors in the development of their subject. For example, while George Stigler is inclined to think that 'biography distorts rather than illuminates the understanding of scientific work',[39] William Jaffé has argued that

> a great original discovery or a great innovation, be it in economics or in any realm of scientific or artistic endeavour, is not a composite product, but the product of the imagination of some one individual whose identity marks the achievement indelibly in a thousand and one subtle ways, giving it, to be sure, a bias. . . . We miss some essential trait of an argument, or of a theory, or even of a piece of description in economics, if we ignore the distinctive individuality of its author. One does not need to be an out-and-out Marxist to concede that the particular social status of the economist must exert influence directly or indirectly on his ideas and interests; nor need one be an out-and-out Freudian to acknowledge the impact of childhood experience and education on his fundamental attitudes.[40]

This is surely a claim that needs to be tested by historians of economics – for example, as part of our proposed comparative study of the marginal revolution.[41] All three cofounders exhibited in striking fashion the psychological attributes commonly found among scientific innovators, while Jevons and Walras in particular were highly self-conscious about their scientific contributions.[42]

The interdependence between the subjective approach of the individual scientist and the collective judgement of the scientific community has been most perceptively depicted by Michael Polanyi. 'Discoveries are made,' he observes,

> by pursuing unsuspected possibilities suggested by existing knowledge. And this is how science retains its identity through a sequence of successive revolutions. . . . Only plausible ideas are taken up, discussed and tested by scientists. Such a decision may later be proved right, but at the time that it is made, the assignment of plausibility

is based on a broad exercise of intuition guided by many subtle indications, and *thus it is altogether undemonstrable. It is tacit.*

But while different scientists proceed on the basis of different methods, questions, and objectives,

> it is not rare for two or more scientists to make the same discovery independently – because different scientists can actualize only the same available potentialities; and they can indeed be relied on to exploit such chances.[43]

IV

These remarks take us back to our starting point – the relationship between individual scientific discovery and the corpus of knowledge from which it emerged. Can it be said that Jevons, Menger, and Walras actualized 'the same available potentialities' in economic theory? And if so, does this reveal significant parallels between scientific progress in nineteenth-century economics and the paradigm of natural science? Or, by suggesting that the marginal revolution was a break comparable to a biological mutation, have we implied that the new departure was by no means an inevitable product of the organic growth of scientific knowledge? How far can the marginal revolution be regarded as a typical example of the 'learning process' in scientific work, and how far do explanations of this type depend on the assumption that economics, like natural science, is a comparatively closed intellectual system?

It is at least conceivable that a study of the marginal revolution in economics will shed light on the general process of intellectual innovation in economics and, indeed, in other branches of the social sciences. It may also even shed new light on the age-old question of the similarities and differences between the natural and social sciences, especially with respect to their developmental patterns.[44]

APPENDIX

Any attempt to explain the marginal revolution (or, indeed, any other historical occurrence) as a product of environmental influences must be specific if it is not to be merely tautological, for in its broadest sense the term 'environment' embraces all the possible antecedent causes of the phenomenon to be explained. Many hypotheses about the interrelationships between events and ideas have been advanced, but most have been partial and selective and seldom has any serious effort been made to explicate the underlying logical structure.

The difficulties involved in the environmentalist's approach are exemplified by Werner Stark's interpretation of the marginal revolution as an instance of what Schumpeter termed a 'classical situation'. To Stark, this state of affairs was no mere intellectual phenomenon but a 'life situation', for the 1870s was a time when 'capitalism was so to speak most fully and clearly itself, in which social and economic reality approached, comparatively speaking, most closely to a state of integration in a determinate equilibrium'. There was, he admitted, no *social* equilibrium in the early 1870s; indeed, the existence of a sociopolitical gulf between capitalist and proletarian helps to explain the theoretical economist's 'retreat' to an abstract concept of economic equilibrium: 'In Walras' day competition was as perfect as it is possible in the nature of things, . . . the economies of the leading countries came as near then to the realization of a free, automatically functioning market as never before and never since. Chapter and verse for this assertion can be found in any textbook of economic history', and this bold claim was backed by references to free trade, the general existence of free competition, and the absence of obstacles to international payments or controls over the labour market and the wage contract.[45]

The foregoing example may be too extreme to be taken seriously; yet its very excesses serve to highlight the difficulties inherent in the environmentalist approach. Stark's account is couched in such vague and general terms that it is virtually impossible to decide what empirical evidence, if any, could be cited to confirm or refute his claims. Notwithstanding his confident assertion about economic history textbooks, there is ample evidence incompatible with his contention that society approximated a state of 'perfect competition' when 'the utility theory of values arose'.[46] Indeed, if 'perfect competition' is a purely mental construct, should we seek an empirical counterpart? And if the answer is in the affirmative, where should we look, and when? Are we to infer from Stark's account that competition was more nearly perfect in Jevons' England, Menger's Austria, and Walras's Switzerland (or France) than elsewhere? And if not, why were marginal utility theories absent from other countries? Would any serious economic historian suggest that economic and social conditions were essentially similar in England, Austria, and Switzerland (or France) when it is well known that the first of these three was by far the most advanced industrially?[47] How should we account for the fact that earlier versions of marginal utility theory were enunciated in several widely differing historical settings? If we accept Stark's contention that ideas appear in historical perspective not merely as 'conditioned by reality' but also 'determined by it – provided that we do not forget that the formation of ideas has never been subject to absolute necessity in its time',[48] we must presumably seek causal connections, not merely correlations, between events and ideas. But what particular connections should we expect to find between an individual thinker and his socioeconomic environment? Is there any reason to expect the same parallels in the cases of all the codiscoverers of an important theoretical concept or system? Should we seek clues in the individual's life history, in that of his family or social group, or in the broader background of his national culture? Again, what time lags should we expect to discover between the (slowly or rapidly) changing socioeconomic environment and the intellectual products to which it gives rise?

A more subtle example of the environmentalist approach is Nikolai Bukharin's contention that the Austrian School's version of marginal utility economics reflected the individualistic outlook that represented a fundamental trait of the bourgeoisie, while the emphasis on the psychology of the consumer was characteristic of the *rentier* class. Bukharin's Marxist standpoint embraced methodological, historical, sociological, and logical elements, for he was anxious to disassociate himself from the antitheoretical biases of the German historical school. As a Marxist he advocated recognition of 'the priority of society over the individual', the essentially 'temporary nature of any social structure', and the 'dominant part played by production' in economic life, whereas the Austrian School was characterized by 'extreme individualism in methodology, by an unhistorical point of view, and by its taking consumption as a point of departure'. While acknowledging the need for abstraction in economic science, Bukharin nevertheless argued that psychology was the basis of logic, and the psychology of the *rentier* was present-minded, whereas the proletarian viewpoint was dynamic and forward-looking – presumably up to the classless utopia. The consuming *rentier* stood apart from the processes of production and trade; he was concerned only with luxury consumption such as 'riding mounts, with expensive rugs, fragrant cigars, the wine of Tokay'. Thus the historical conditions favourable to the growth of subjective value theories included 'the rapid evolution of capitalism, the shifting of social groupings and the increase in the number of the class of rentiers, all these produced in the last decades of the nineteenth century all the necessary sociopsychological presuppositions for bringing these delicate plants to efflorescence'.[49]

Like Stark's account, Bukharin's explanation was couched in general terms; but he was at least aware of the crucial distinction between the genesis, the formulation, and the diffusion of marginal utility theory. After noting the works of some earlier and later forerunners he commented that 'only at the beginning of the decade 1870–80 did the theory of marginal utility find a sufficient prop in the "social public opinion" of the ruling scientific circles and rapidly become *communis doctorum opinio*.' It is not entirely clear whether the triumvirate – Jevons, Menger, and Walras – were thought to be fully aware of their historical mission, though it is clear that subsequent authors used their theories 'in order to justify the modern order of society'. However, Bukharin avoided some of the more specific environmentalist difficulties by emphasizing that the Austrian School was not distinctively *Austrian* at all, adding that it had 'actually become the scientific implement of the international bourgeoisie of *rentiers* regardless of their domicile'.[50]

Reverting to the basic issue stated in the second sentence of this essay, we must again ask what kind of 'explanation' is required. Is it necessary to embrace all the dimensions of Bukharin's approach – methodological, historical, sociological, and logical – or would any two or three dimensions suffice? According to Mark Blaug, 'it is not far-fetched to see a connection between changes in the economic structure of society around the middle of the century and the theoretical innovations of the subjective value trio';[51] but precisely what kind of connection must be sought? The most constructive discussion of this problem is George Stigler's article on 'The Influence of Events and Policies on Economic Theory',[52] in which he endeavoured to specify the points at which the environment impinged on economic theory. While recognizing the multiplicity of possible connections, he contended that the majority of events, whether of major or minor importance, have been routine with respect to economic theory in the period since economics became 'a discipline pursued by professional scholars' (p. 19). Indeed, he regarded this comparative immunity from external influences as a mark of the maturity of the discipline. Prior to 1870, however (and the date is obviously significant with respect to the marginal revolution), economists were oriented toward contemporary problems and institutions, and economics was 'dominated by controversies over policy' (ibid.). For a problem to affect the main corpus of economic theory it must be pervasive, persistent, and of 'vast importance' in relation to the conditions of all economies at all times. Otherwise theory (though not other parts of economics) would be unaffected, since 'the dominant influence upon the working range of economic theorists is the set of internal values and pressures of the discipline' (p. 22). Facts do, of course, influence the economic theorist's work; indeed the 'pedestrian, even vulgar' fact 'of diminishing marginal utility of objects' influenced Jevons, Menger, and Walras (pp. 22–3); but facts are increasingly being provided through the professional expertise of the empirical research economist. Public policy, on the other hand, is a separable part of the environment and is not closely geared to events. Once again, only 'general and persistent policy questions are likely to call forth permanent advances in theory' (p. 25), and the classical problems of tariffs, monetary standards, monopoly, control of business fluctuations, the role of government and unions in labour markets, the incidence of taxes, and the treatment of the indigent fall into this category. 'The development of related disciplines' is also part of the environment within which economic theory evolves, and this is felt mainly through the progress of such technical subjects as mathematics and statistics and through the development of other substantive fields (e.g., Darwinian theory and positivism) on the economist's 'scientific vision'.

Hence, on the whole, Stigler emphasized 'the immense degree of autonomy that any successful science must apparently possess' (p. 29). However, if this argument is accepted, the question remains: How far was economics intellectually autonomous in the period immediately prior to the marginal revolution?

NOTES

* This article is based on a paper designed to provide a background for the conference discussions. It therefore poses questions rather than offering solutions and is reproduced substantially as originally presented. The conference proceedings were published as *The Marginal Revolution in Economics. Interpretation and Evaluation*, eds. R. D. Collison Black, A. W. Coats, and Crawford D. W. Goodwin (Durham, N. C., 1973) and in *History of Political Economy* 4 (Fall 1972): 603–24.

1 Review of Robert V. Eagly, *Events, Ideology and Economic Theory* (Detroit, 1968) in the *Journal of Economic History* 29 (June 1969): 337. In an earlier paper, 'The Influence of Events and Policies on Economic Theory', reprinted in his *Essays on the History of Economics* (Chicago, 1965), pp. 16–30, Stigler attempted to identify those parts of the environment which exerted an influence both on economic theory and on other branches of economics. For a brief résumé of his argument and comments on two environmentalist theories see the Appendix at the end of the present article.

2 See, for example, Patrick Gardiner, ed., *Theories of History* (Glencoe, Ill., 1959); Robert Brown, *Explanation in Social Science* (London, 1963); William H. Dray, ed., *Philosophical Analysis and History* (New York, 1966); and Leonard I. Krimerman, ed., *The Nature and Scope of Social Science* (New York, 1969), for selections from a large and growing literature. Against this background one may well question the meaning of George Stigler's protest at 'the peculiar belief that intellectual history is exempt from the requirements of respectability of proof, which are imposed on all scientific work'. Review of Eagly, pp. 336–7. The concept of 'respectability of proof' is sociological or psychological, rather than logical, and is dependent on the currently recognized methodological rules or decisions. For further discussion of this matter see n. 27 below.

3 For a recent contrary opinion see George J. Stigler, 'Does Economics Have a Useful Past?' *History of Political Economy* 1 (Fall 1969): 225: 'the marginal utility revolution of the 1870's replaced the individual economic agent as a sociological or historical datum by the utility-maximizing individual. The essential elements of the classical theory were affected in no respect.'

4 Mark Blaug, *Economic Theory in Retrospect*, 2d ed. (Homewood, Ill., 1968), p. 299. Sentence order reversed.

5 Ibid., pp. 304–8. As the significance of the marginal revolution was recognized only after an appreciable time lag, an attempt to account for this breakthrough should, strictly speaking, include the first two decades or so of the diffusion process. However, as that phase has been admirably treated in Richard S. Howey, *The Rise of the Marginal Utility School* (Lawrence, Kans., 1960), I shall concentrate on the conditions of production rather than the reception of the new ideas.

6 Lewis Coser, 'The Sociology of Knowledge', in *International Encyclopedia of the Social Sciences* (New York, 1968), 8: 428; also Robert Merton, *Social Theory and Social Structure*, 2d ed. (New York, 1957), chap. 12; W. Stark, *The Sociology of Knowledge* (London, 1958). As Merton has noted, 'each type of imputed relation between knowledge and society presupposes an entire theory of sociological method and social causation' (p. 476).

7 Joseph Ben-David, 'Introduction' to the Sociology of Science issue of the *International Social Science Journal* 22 (1970): 19–20. Italics supplied.

8 R. G. A. Dolby, 'Sociology of Knowledge in Natural Science', *Science Studies* 1 (Jan. 1971): 9. This article contains a useful survey of recent research. Robert K. Merton accepted the logical empiricists' distinction as embodied in the works of R. Carnap, H. Reichenbach, C. G. Hempel, E. Nagel, and K. R. Popper, whereas the newer approach can be found in the writings of N. Hanson, P. K. Feyerabend, S. Toulmin, and T. S. Kuhn, among others. There is a penetrating critique of the contrasting views of Merton and Kuhn in M. D. King, 'Reason, Tradition and the Progressiveness of Science', *History and Theory* 10 (1971): 3–32. I have drawn heavily on this article, and on my discussions with the author.

9 The concept of multiple discoveries is, of course, especially associated with the work of Robert Merton. Cf. his 'Singletons and Multiples in Scientific Discovery: A Chapter in the Sociology of Science', *Proceedings of the American Philosophical Society* 105 (Oct. 1961): 470–86; and 'Resistance to the Systematic Study of Multiple Discoveries in Science', *Archives Européenes de Sociologie* 4 (1963): 237–82. For some comments on the relevance of this notion to economics see Stigler, 'Does Economics Have a Useful Past?' pp. 225–7. While acknowledging the importance of multiples, Stigler emphasizes the difficulties in assessing the significance of discoveries widely spaced in time.

10 Alfred Marshall's views on multiples are especially interesting considering his emphasis on the continuity of economic ideas and the fact that he may have been an independent, but inadequately recognized, codiscoverer of the marginal utility idea. 'The substance of economic thought cannot well be to any great extent the work of one man. It is the product of the age. Perhaps an exception should be made for Ricardo: but everything of importance that was said in the five generations 1740–65, 1765–90, 1815–40, 1840–65, 1865–90, seems to me to have been thought out concurrently more or less by many people.' To L. L. Price, 19 Aug. 1892, in *Memorials of Alfred Marshall*, ed. A. C. Pigou (London, 1925), pp. 378–9.

11 'There is only one world to discover, and as each morsel of perception is achieved the discoverer must be honored or forgotten. The ivory tower of the artist can be a one-man cell; that of the scientist must contain many apartments so that he may be housed among his peers.' Derek J. de Solla Price, *Little Science, Big Science* (New York, 1963), p. 69. More recently, however, it has been suggested that science and art are less different than formerly supposed. Cf. the contributions by J. S. Ackerman, E. M. Hafner, G. Kubler, and T. S. Kuhn, to *Comparative Studies in Society and History* 2 (1969): 371–412. In a well-known survey, 'Marginal Utility Economics', in the *Encyclopedia of the Social Sciences* (New York, 1931), 5: 357–63, Frank H. Knight argued that owing to the 'wreck' of the classical system by the late 1860s, 'a new start became inevitable'. However, he did not maintain that marginal utility was the only possible foundation of a new system, merely a very likely one: 'The utility theory should be seen as the culmination, historically and logically, of the rationalistic and individualistic intellectual movement of which the competitive economic system itself is one aspect and modern science and technology are others. To its admirers it comes near to being the fulfilment of the eighteenth-century craving for a principle which would do for human conduct and society what Newton's mechanics had done for the solar system.'

12 With perfect communication there would be no separate independent discoveries; the original innovator's achievement would be instantly recognized everywhere and subsequent rediscoveries would be forestalled. As Merton has put it,

'There, but for the grace of swift diffusion, goes a multiple.' 'Singletons and Multiples', p. 478. For a preliminary discussion of the diffusion process see, for example, Joseph J. Spengler, 'Notes on the International Transmission of Economic Ideas', *History of Political Economy* 2 (Spring 1970): 133–51. Spengler distinguishes between the source, the media of transmission, the content transmitted, and the receiver. For a relevant case study see T. W. Hutchison, 'Insularity and Cosmopolitanism in Economic Ideas, 1870–1914', *American Economic Association Papers and Proceedings*, May 1955, pp. 1–16. The rate of acceptance of a new idea may be a function of the rate at which new, and presumably young and receptive, persons enter the field.

13 See, for example, the correspondence in William Jaffé's magnificent edition, *Correspondence of Léon Walras and Related Papers* (Amsterdam, 1965), vol. 1, 1857–83. An investigation of the growth and scientific importance of this international network of economists in the nineteenth century would be a fruitful topic of research. Such a project might, indeed, begin with a detailed examination of the sources cited in the early works and correspondence of Jevons, Menger, and Walras.

14 Neil de Marchi's examination of the British background to Jevons' *Theory of Political Economy* [see his 'Mill and Cairnes and the Emergence of Marginalism in England', *History of Political Economy* 4 (Fall 1972): 344–63] provides an admirable illustration of this point. I have profited greatly from reading and discussing his work.

15 For a penetrating discussion of intellectual crises of this kind see Thomas S. Kuhn, *The Structure of Scientific Revolutions*, rev. ed. (Chicago, 1970), chaps. 7–9. Kuhn's critics have not merely objected to his notion of paradigm change on the grounds that the paradigm concept is vague and misleading; they have also questioned the validity of his fundamental distinction between 'normal' and 'revolutionary' phases in the history of science. For example, while Karl Popper considers that Kuhn has exaggerated the distinction, he nevertheless regards it as of 'great importance'. Stephen Toulmin, on the other hand, believes that the notion of revolution is useful as a descriptive label, but useless as an explanatory concept. Imre Lakatos, a disciple of Popper, adopts an intermediate position which assimilates many of Kuhn's ideas. See the discussion of these problems in Imre Lakatos and Alan Musgrave, eds., *Criticism and the Growth of Knowledge* (Cambridge, 1970), esp. pp. 41, 52, 93ff.

16 One of Kuhn's more vigorous and effective critics, Imre Lakatos, maintains that competition between rival theories is endemic and healthy in the natural sciences, especially in periods of rapid advance. 'Instant rationality', he argues, is impossible in practice: one theory does not supplant another overnight, nor is the full significance of a new theory quickly appreciated. Even in the natural sciences anomalies do not (as Kuhn claims) accumulate until they become intolerable, and so-called 'crucial experiments' do not immediately establish the superiority of one theory over its rivals, for there is usually a substantial time lag before the significance of such experiments is recognized. Like other philosophers of science (e.g., Karl Popper, M. Polanyi, and Morris Cohen), Lakatos recognizes the 'principle of tenacity' – the legitimate desire to retain a theory of proven value despite the accumulation of anomalies and counterexamples. Cf. Lakatos' long essay, 'Falsification and the Methodology of Scientific Research Programmes', in Lakatos and Musgrave, pp. 91–195. A penetrating review of this essay by David Bloor appears in *Science Studies* 1 (Jan 1971): 101–15.

17 These characteristics of successful theories are discussed by George J. Stigler in his classic article, 'The Development of Utility Theory', reprinted in his *Essays,*

pp. 148–55. Other characteristics could be suggested, for example, simplicity, elegance, fruitfulness, 'heuristic power'. Cf. Lakatos and Musgrave, pp. 132ff.

18 This list of possible causes is by no means exhaustive. For a valuable account of the wide range of factors involved see Joseph J. Spengler, 'Exogenous and Endogenous Influences in the Formation of Post-1870 Economic Thought: A Sociology of Knowledge Approach', in *Events, Ideology and Economic Theory, the Determinants of Progress in the Development of Economic Analysis*, ed. Robert V. Eagly (Detroit, 1968), pp. 159–87. On fashions cf. R. D. Collison Black, *Economic Fashions* (Belfast, 1963). For an interpretation of the history of science in terms of shifts in what does not need to be explained, see Stephen Toulmin, *Foresight and Understanding: An Inquiry Into the Aims of Science* (London, 1961), chaps. 3 and 4.

19 Cf. his essay on Eugen Böhm-Bawerk in *The Development of Economic Thought: Great Economists in Perspective*, ed. Henry W. Spiegel (New York, 1952), p. 570. This assertion needs careful documentation.

20 Joseph J. Spengler has advanced the notion of a 'conceptual freeze' which may be broken by the emergence of 'intractable policy problems, flaws in consensual explanations, new empirical findings, and technological and methodological developments (for example, computers, input–output) which consensual explanations cannot effectively incorporate'. See his 'Economics: Its History, Themes, Approaches', *Journal of Economic Issues* 2 (March 1968): 21.

21 In the nineteenth century an economist's attitude to the value problem was often regarded as providing a clue to his entire outlook. For example F. von Wieser, *Natural Value*, ed. W. Smart (1893), p. xxx: 'As a man's judgment about value, so, in the last resort, must be his judgment about economics.... Every great system of political economy up till now has formulated its own peculiar view on value as the ultimate foundation in theory of its applications to practical life, and no new effort at reform can have laid an adequate foundation for these applications if it cannot support them on a new and more perfect theory of value'; J. S. Mill, *Principles of Political Economy* (Toronto, 1965), 2: 456: 'Almost every speculation respecting the economical interests of a society ... implies some theory of Value: the smallest error on that subject infects with corresponding error all our other conclusions; and anything vague or misty in our conception of it, creates confusion and uncertainty in everything else.' These statements serve as a reminder that value theory occupied a central place in late nineteenth-century economics.

22 The 'technique of persuasion' is discussed in George J. Stigler, 'The Nature and Role of Originality in Scientific Progress'; cf. his *Essays*, pp. 4ff.

23 For a provocative treatment of this problem see Imre Lakatos, 'History of Science and Its Rational Reconstructions', in PSA 1970, in memory of Rudolf Carnap, *Boston Studies in the Philosophy of Science*, vol. 8, ed. Roger C. Buck and Robert S. Cohen, pp. 91–136; also the accompanying 'Notes on Lakatos' by Thomas S. Kuhn, ibid., pp. 137–46.

24 Cf. Kuhn, *Structure of Scientific Revolutions*, pp. 170–3; Karl Popper, *The Logic of Scientific Discovery* (London, 1959), p. 108; also his *Conjectures and Refutations* (London, 1963), p. 52.

25 Ernest Nagel, *The Structure of Science: Problems in the Logic of Scientific Explanation* (New York, 1961), p. 489.

26 King, 'Reason, Tradition', p. 25.

27 Lakatos, for example, attacks Kuhn's emphasis on the importance of the collective judgement of the scientific community as 'mob psychology', but stresses the crucial role of methodological decisions, such as the decisions which deter-

mine whether a particular proposition should be viewed as a fact or a theory in the context of a given 'research programme'; what part of a scientific programme is to be regarded as the 'irrefutable' hard core; and what constitute acceptable criteria of falsification of a scientific theory. He concedes that his approach tends to blur the dividing line between science and metaphysics, a line that was carefully drawn by positivist philosophers, and rejects what he calls naive or dogmatic falsificationism. While insisting that 'experience' is the impartial arbiter of scientific controversy, he readily admits the difficulty of knowing what experience proves or disproves. Lakatos, 'Falsification', and the comments by Popper, Feyerabend, and Kuhn, in Lakatos and Musgrave. See also Bloor's review article referred to in n. 16 above; and the Lakatos–Kuhn exchange cited in n. 23 above.

28 Cf. A. C. Crombie, ed., *Scientific Change* (London, 1963), p. 10. These remarks draw attention to the processes of professionalization and academicization which were repeatedly referred to in the conference discussions. Cf. 'Retrospect and Prospect', sec. III, *History of Political Economy* 4 (Fall 1972): 603–24.

29 The term 'scientific community' was introduced by Michael Polanyi to describe the way scientists enforced strict discipline amidst a great deal of individual freedom through training, refereeing of publications, and purely informal sanctions of approval and disapproval. He also showed how this informal system was related to the intrinsic characteristics of research. Cf. Joseph Ben-David, 'Introduction', p. 12.

30 Cf. Norman Storer, 'The Internationality of Science and the Nationality of Scientists', *International Social Science Journal* 22 (Feb. 1970): 92; also his book *The Social System of Science* (New York, 1966); and Warren O. Hagstrom, *The Scientific Community* (New York, 1965). The development of a 'social circle' of marginalists after 1871 has been traced by Richard S. Howey, *Rise of the Marginal Utility School*. In the present context, however, it is more pertinent to ask, To what audience did Jevons, Menger, and Walras address themselves?

31 See especially his *Personal Knowledge* (Chicago, 1958), chaps. 7, 10.

32 The major creative achievements of Jevons, Menger, and Walras compare favourably with other performances in economics and political science analysed in Harvey C. Lehman, *Age and Achievement* (Princeton, 1953), esp. pp. 137–8, 296–7, 302–3. Such achievements tended to occur later in the nineteenth century than nowadays because innovators usually derived less aid from their teachers and were more dependent on the development of their own intellectual tools. Moreover, the pecuniary rewards and prestige value of innovativeness are probably higher now.

33 Cf. the comment by F. H. Knight cited in n. 11 above.

34 Donald T. Campbell, 'Objectivity and the Social Locus of Scientific Knowledge', Unpublished paper. Despite considerable efforts, including checking two comprehensive bibliographies of Campbell's writings, I cannot find this as a publication. It is not in the Boston volumes. My quotation is taken from a mimeod script (which Campbell sent me) and which is in my Nottingham home. There is no reference in Psychological Abstracts to the Presidential Address. A Duke colleague has been unable to solve this mystery. For an extended discussion of the links between psychology and the philosophy of science with special reference to the problem of scientific discovery, see also Campbell's 'Evolutionary Epistemology', in *The Philosophy of Karl R. Popper*, ed. P. A. Schilpp, Library of Living Philosophers vol. 14 (La Salle, Ill., 1974), pp. 413–63. Campbell emphasizes the 'blind-variation-and-selective-retention process' in scientific enquiry: 'What is characteristic of science is that the selective system which weeds out among the

variety of conjectures involves deliberate contact with the environment through experiment and quantified prediction, designed so that outcomes quite independent of the preferences of the investigator are possible.'

35 This is forcefully argued in F. A. von Hayek, *The Sensory Order* (London, 1952), pp. 192–3.

36 Cf. 'Great Men and Scientific Progress', in *History, Psychology and Science: Selected Papers by Edwin G. Boring*, eds. Robert I. Watson and Donald T. Campbell (New York, 1963), pp. 29–49. See also Bernice T. Eiduson, *Scientists: Their Psychological World* (New York, 1962).

37 Watson and Campbell, Editor's Foreword, p. vii.

38 As George Stigler noted in a pioneering essay, much valuable scientific work – the testing of hypotheses, the accumulation of knowledge, the refinement or elaboration of economic theory – requires little or no originality; and there may even be an excess of originality which impedes the essential process of 'scientific fermentation'; cf. 'Originality in Scientific Progress', pp. 12–14. The less original phases of scientific activity are reminiscent of Kuhn's conception of 'normal' scientific puzzle-solving. As is well known, Jevons was an 'ideas' man, a man of immense intellectual fertility in a variety of fields, who was eager to flick his ideas at the world rather than to work them out fully and painstakingly. In the conference discussions it became clear that Walras often chose to concentrate his attention on relatively limited problems which could be fully solved, whereas Menger's *Grundsätze* was far more open-minded and consequently provided many hints and incompletely worked-out ideas which his disciples could refine and elaborate.

39 Cf. his review of *The Evolution of Modern Economic Theory* by Lord Robbins, in *Economica* 37 (Nov. 1970): 426.

40 William Jaffé, 'Biography and Economic Analysis', *Western Economic Journal* 3 (Summer 1965): 227. See also Spengler, 'Economics: Its History', pp. 26–8.

41 This point was vigorously debated at the conference. Cf. 'Retrospect and Prospect', sec. IV, *History of Political Economy* 4 (Fall 1972): 603–24.

42 Thus Jevons discussed the 'Character of the Experimentalist' in his book *The Principles of Science: A Treatise on Logic and Scientific Method* (London, 1874), chap. 26.

43 'The Growth of Science in Society', *Minerva* 5 (1966–7): 539, 536, 542, reprinted as chap. 5 in his volume of essays, *Knowing and Being* (London, 1969). Italics are in the original.

44 In the first (1962) edition of *The Structure of Scientific Revolutions*, Kuhn began by emphasizing the differences between the natural and the social sciences, and he has since described the latter as 'proto-sciences – in which practice does generate testable conclusions but which nevertheless resemble philosophy and the arts rather than the established sciences in their developmental patterns'. Cf. Lakatos and Musgrave, p. 244; also the 'Postscript – 1969' to the 2d edition (1970) of Kuhn's *Structure*, esp. pp. 207–10, and his 'Comment' in *Comparative Studies in Society and History* 11 (1969): 403–12.

45 W. Stark, 'The Classical Situation in Political Economy', *Kyklos* 12 (1959): 59, 62–3. Cf. Joseph A. Schumpeter, *History of Economic Analysis* (Oxford, 1954), pp. 51, 87, 143, 380.

46 Cf. W. Stark, *The History of Economics in Its Relation to Social Development* (London, 1944), p. 56. There is, of course, room for dispute as to when 'the utility theory of values *arose*'. Although Stark considered it a remarkable coincidence that the first edition of Walras's *Eléments* appeared in the years which show 'a maximum approach to a free economy in practice' ('The Classical Situation', p. 62) it is

noteworthy that another, more subtle environmentalist has emphasized that Walras's theory was entirely in conflict with contemporary economic conditions. Cf. Leo Rogin, *The Meaning and Validity of Economic Theory* (New York, 1956), p. 438.

47 The operative term here, of course, is 'essentially'; i.e., in what crucial respect was there similarity of 'conditions'?

48 Stark, *History of Economics*, p. 7.

49 *The Economic Theory of the Leisure Class* (London, 1927), pp. 36, 26, 34. The book was substantially written in 1914, and a Russian edition appeared in 1919 or 1920.

50 Ibid., p. 34. For further discussion of the role of environmental influences see 'Retrospect and Prospect', sec. IV, *History of Political Economy* 4 (Fall 1972): 603–24.

51 Blaug, p. 306. For comments on this subject see also S. G. Checkland, 'Economic Opinion in England as Jevons Found It', *Manchester School* 19 (May 1951): 151–2; and his *The Rise of Industrial Society in England* (London, 1964), pp. 428–9. For an explanation in ideological terms see Daniel R. Fusfeld, 'Neo-Classical Economics and the Ideology of Capitalism', *Papers of the Michigan Academy of Science, Arts and Letters* 43 (1958): 191–202.

52 Reprinted in his *Essays in the History of Economics*, pp. 16–30. Subsequent page references are included in the text in parentheses.

6

THE ROLE OF AUTHORITY IN THE DEVELOPMENT OF BRITISH ECONOMICS

I

During the past few decades, the impact of science on society has increased enormously, and as an inevitable by-product there has been a marked growth of scholarly interest in the history and sociology of science. As yet, this intellectual fashion has exerted little or no influence upon historians of economics, which is somewhat surprising in view of the fact that the question of the scientific character and status of economics has long been the subject of debate. The present article aims not to revive dead issues in the methodology of economics, but to throw new light on the development of the subject as a scientific and professional discipline by considering the changing role of authority in the history of British economic thought. The geographical restriction is necessary in order to pin down a somewhat elusive theme, and this case is especially suitable because there has been a striking degree of continuity in the intellectual leadership of the British community of economists. There can be no doubt, however, that international comparisons would yield some highly interesting conclusions.

The question of the role of authority in economics has been unduly neglected in the past, but it has not been entirely ignored, as the following pages will reveal. In particular, it was systematically examined in one chapter of W. H. Hutt's *The Economists and the Public*.[1] But Hutt, as his title suggests, was chiefly concerned with the relationships between the economists and the community at large, rather than with the function of authority within the community of scholars, and his account was, in any case, so preoccupied with the defence of 'orthodox' economics and the political and ethical premises and implications of that doctrine, that it can scarcely be regarded as a satisfactory presentation of the main issues.

At first sight, many economists are likely to reject the notion that authority can play any legitimate part in the development of their discipline, for modern economic analysis had its origins in the liberal-rationalist moral philosophy of the eighteenth century, and this tradition is still influential enough to lead economists to believe that reason and authority are antithetical forces. Nor is this view wholly superficial, for economic thought has long been grounded upon what Karl Popper has termed 'epistemological optimism', the view that there was

> no need for any man to appeal to authority in matters of truth because each man carried the sources of knowledge in himself; either in his power of sense-perception which he may use for the careful observation of nature, or in his power of intellectual intuition which he may use to distinguish truth from falsehood by refusing to accept any idea which is not clearly and distinctly perceived by the intellect.[2]

The validity of this epistemological doctrine need not be examined here; we are more concerned with the sociological than with the philosophical aspects of the matter. Nevertheless the philosophical issue cannot be wholly ignored, for in any scholarly and scientific activity the ultimate intellectual authority is truth, and the accepted view of the nature and criteria of valid knowledge can therefore never be a matter of indifference. This, of course, largely explains why methodological disagreements have been so common in economics, for it is a discipline in which the criteria of valid knowledge have been difficult to define and to apply, and in which ideological and other non-logical influences have been highly influential.

Although liberal epistemological optimists generally assume that there is a necessary antithesis between authority and reason, authority necessarily plays an indispensable role in any intellectual discipline. As A. J. Balfour (a philosopher, statesman, and one-time Vice-President of the Royal Economic Society) observed: 'It is from Authority that Reason itself draws its most important premises', and 'it is Authority which supplies us with essential elements in the premises of science'.[3] In the development of any branch of scientific activity, it soon becomes impossible for any individual to master more than a tiny fraction of the knowledge relevant to his own field of interest or research, and he is therefore obliged to rely upon his fellow scientists for most of his assumptions, for his methods of reasoning, and for the starting point of his inquiry – which is usually determined by the existing lacunae or problems within his particular province. As modern science has grown in size and scope, its organization has necessarily become more complex, and at the same time the role of authority has increased and has become the object of systematic study. Only qualified scientists can serve as reliable guides to the state of scientific knowledge in any field, or can be allowed to determine whether or not new discoveries are to be rejected or incorporated into the recognized corpus of established findings. And, as Michael Polanyi has observed:

> This group of persons – the scientists – administer jointly the advancement and dissemination of science. They do so through the control of university premises, academic appointments, research grants, scien-

tific journals and the awarding of academic degrees which qualify their recipients as teachers, technical or medical practitioners, and opens to them the possibility of academic appointment. Moreover, by controlling the advancement and dissemination of science, this same group of persons, the scientists, actually establish the current meaning of the term 'science', determine what should be accepted as science, and establish also the current meaning of the term 'scientist', and decide what they themselves and those designated by themselves as their successors should recognize as such. The cultivation of science by society relies on the public acceptance of these decisions as to what science is and who are the scientists.[4]

This passage is both pertinent and vivid; but it depicts a state of affairs strikingly different from that obtaining in economic science during the greater part of its history. Even now it is not fully applicable even in the USA, where the organization of economic knowledge is more complex than elsewhere, although within the past two decades or so there has been an international trend towards the provision of a more standardized professional training for apprentice economists.

The history of the economics 'profession' has yet to be written, and anyone brave enough to undertake the task will soon find himself grappling with a number of intractable problems of definition and scope. The following survey of the changing role of 'authority' in the history of British economics will, however, give some indication of the main outlines of the story, both as regards the public prestige of the discipline and the role of authority within the circle of 'qualified practitioners' or scientists. In this discussion the term 'authority' will be used mainly in the sense of 'power to influence action, opinion, belief', rather than as 'power to enforce obedience',[5] for in intellectual affairs (at least one may hope) the influence of respect usually outweighs that of coercion.

II

The first group of British economists to regard themselves and to be regarded by important sections of the public as qualified scientific experts were the Ricardians, and it was during the second and third decades of the nineteenth century that the problem of authority in political economy first became a matter of serious interest to its practitioners. Before that date, economic writing was normally either subordinate to some other literary or scholarly pursuit (such as moral philosophy), or the work of political pamphleteers or journalistic hacks. Seventeenth- and eighteenth-century authors usually listed the names and works of any predecessors whose support might be thought to add weight to their contentions, but they doubtless realized that these citations soon became tiresome and were far less effective a means of establishing their claims to authority than an appeal to established scientific laws, principles, or conclusions. In an age when the authority of revealed religion was in disrepute and the embryonic science of political economy was virtually unknown there was, however, no satisfactory alternative, and Professor Letwin has recently provided an illuminating discussion of the devices employed by seventeenth-century economic writers in their vain endeavours to convince their readers of the disinterestedness of their motives and the validity of their conclusions.[6]

In the decade or so after Waterloo, economic questions were in the forefront of public discussion, and it was both the timeliness and the complexity of the issues examined in their writings that enabled the economists to enhance the prestige of their discipline, for they were obviously dealing with important problems beyond the layman's comprehension. Ricardo himself was the very epitome of the scientific intellectual, and he soon became recognized both by the *cognoscenti* and by the laity as the leading economic authority of the day, largely because of the skill, lucidity, and detachment with which he analysed technical problems of currency, banking, and trade, both in his published writings and in his House of Commons speeches. There was, of course, no clear demarcation between those who were qualified to write on economic subjects and those who were not; and despite Carlyle's famous gibe about 'the gloomy professors of the dismal science', most of the leading economists spent only a small proportion of their lives in academic chairs, and academic training in political economy was woefully inadequate.[7] Even among those with serious claims to be regarded as qualified economists there were sharp disagreements on matters of theory and policy, and it was clearly recognized that these disagreements tended to rouse doubts as to the scientific status of political economy, especially where matters of principle were involved. There were repeated references to the need to avoid unnecessary controversy,[8] but at a time when principles, policies, and politics were intimately connected this was no easy task, and recent historians of economic thought have conducted a lively debate as to whether the reputation of Ricardian economics was waxing or waning after the mid-1820s.[9]

The issues at stake in this debate have, unfortunately, been blurred by a failure to distinguish between theory and policy, for while the theoretical foundations of Ricardian economics had been seriously undermined, if not completely destroyed, by the early 1830s, the influence of Ricardian policy recommendations remained powerful until the mid-century. This was largely the result of successful propaganda conducted by James Mill and J. R. McCulloch, Ricardo's two most ardent disciples, who disseminated Ricardo's ideas in such influential publications as the *Encyclopedia Britannica*, the *Edinburgh Quarterly*, and the *Westminster Review*, thereby creating a façade of unity among the leading economic writers. Likewise, the founding of the Political Economy Club of London in 1821, which was an integral part of this campaign, was an important landmark in the early history of the economics profession in England, even if it is an overstatement to describe it as a 'political act'.[10]

It is clearly impossible, in a broad survey of this kind, to provide many detailed examples of early nineteenth-century references to the problem of authority in political economy. Ricardo, for instance, was comparatively open-minded, for although his works contain numerous comments on the soundness and the qualifications of other economic writers, and occasional references to the 'heretical principles' advanced by Malthus or Torrens, he was usually much more respectful towards the public than either Mill or McCulloch, remarking on one occasion that both he and Malthus should submit their views to the public, 'that we might have some able heads engaged in considering it'.[11] Ricardo's disciples, however, conducted a lively campaign in print against the literati, such as Coleridge and the romantics, who had the temerity to reject doctrines they were unable to grasp, and they were equally scathing in their condemnation of the 'Tory' political economy of the *Quarterly Review* and the views of 'practical men' who, according to Mill, 'are always the most obstinate and presumptuous of all theorists'.[12] Of much greater interest, however, are the views of Robert Torrens, who was delicately poised on the periphery of the Ricardian circle and was therefore in a position to view the problem of authority in political economy with insight and detachment.

An able, if somewhat contentious character, Torrens was too independent-minded to swallow the straight Ricardian line handed down by Mill and McCulloch; but although he complained of the 'premature generalizations and pure abstractions of the Ricardian school' in an uncompromising way that would have been unthinkable in one who counted himself a full member of the group, he was anxious to protect the public reputation of political economy, and he deplored Ricardo's revised views on the influence of machinery on the demand for labour, describing them as 'fundamental and dangerous errors' that were calculated to retard the 'progress of the science'.[13] Torrens attacked those who questioned the validity of the doctrines of political economy on the grounds of the persistent disputes among the 'celebrated masters' of the subject. Current controversy, he declared, was but a transitional stage characteristic of any branch of science, one that preceded the period of unanimity about fundamental principles which, he predicted, would obtain in political economy 'twenty years hence'.[14]

From his position as a founder member and regular contributor to the Political Economy Club, and yet a dissenter whose views commanded the respect of his fellow economists, Torrens was better equipped than most of his contemporaries to appreciate the role of authority in intellectual affairs.

As the mechanical divisions of employment compel us to receive the greater part of our physical enjoyments from the hands of others, so the intellectual divisions of employment constrain us to receive the greater portion of our opinions from the minds of others. . . . On intricate questions, requiring long and patient investigation, the opinions even of the most enlightened class will have their origin, in a majority of cases, not in knowledge but in faith. Hence, principles are received upon trust, doctrines become creeds, authority is implicitly followed, and blind leaders are enabled to assume the guidance of the blind.[15]

Yet Torrens sometimes betrayed concern about his own 'professional' reputation. On one occasion, in a letter to the press, he cited his previous writings and his membership of the Political Economy Club as evidence of his claims to respectful attention; and in the postscript to one of his works he confessed:

I am fully aware that questions of this nature must be decided, not by authority, but upon their own intrinsic evidence, and I have made this reference to the highest authorities only for the purpose of removing the preliminary reluctance to the consideration of my views, which would naturally arise were it supposed that I was advancing novel theories at variance with the established principles of economical science.[16]

Even though the term 'professional' still lacks a precise meaning,[17] it would be inappropriate to describe the Ricardians as a 'professional group'. Nowadays, the would-be economist must undergo a fairly extended, if not unduly rigorous academic training, and as Schumpeter once remarked, this process may well influence his views on matters outside his professional competence.[18] In the early nineteenth century there was no such training; but it could be said that most of the leading economists shared common value presuppositions about the ends of economic activity, and although the boundaries of the profession were extremely blurred, there was at least a clearly demarcated line between the economists and their most articulate intellectual opponents, the literary critics.[19] It is, therefore, of some interest that the only man who crossed the gulf that separated the two groups, Thomas de Quincey, appears to have been fully aware of the problem we are considering. From 1809 onwards, de Quincey studied political economy and formed an opinion of French and English writing on the subject that was in complete accord with the lakeland setting of his literary endeavours.

I saw, that these were generally the very dregs and rinsings of the human intellect, and that any man of sound head, and practised in wielding logic with a scholastic adroitness, might take up the whole academy of modern economists and throttle them between heaven and earth with his finger and thumb, or bray their fungus heads to powder with a lady's fan.[20]

Later, however, he became an ardent admirer of Ricardo, and though not an uncritical disciple, an expositor of elementary political economy on unmistakably Ricardian lines. By this time he had not only altered his assessment of the quality of Ricardo's performance (he compared Ricardo to Kepler, 'who, because he introduced new laws of motion and new forces into the mechanism of the heavens, was not in debt to any disciple of Tycho or of Ptolemy for a perfect scheme of the heavenly appearances'[21]), but he had also acquired a keen awareness of the nature and terminology of our problem. He spoke of Ricardo's 'professional' mode of explanation, and declared that

> it was the *clerus*, not the *populus*, whom Ricardo addressed: he did not call attention from the laity, who seek to learn, but from the professional body who seek to teach. To others, to uninitiated students, he needs a commentary.[22]

It was such a commentary that de Quincey sought to supply, first in his *Dialogues of Three Templars on Political Economy*, published in *Blackwoods Magazine*, and subsequently in *The Logic of Political Economy*.

De Quincey maintained that his own reasoning was superior to Ricardo's because he was himself trained in 'scholastic logic',[23] and the point is important because there was little agreement among the Ricardians as to the criteria of valid knowledge in political economy – a state of affairs that undoubtedly weakened its scientific authority. Torrens occasionally asserted that his own arguments constituted 'proof amounting to strictly mathematical demonstration', suggesting a purely logical discipline, whereas McCulloch, who defined political economy as a science of 'fact and experiment', appreciated that its doctrines could not be expected to attain apodictic certainty.[24] In a methodological article on the 'usefulness of political economy', James Mill revealed his awareness of this issue, for he spoke confidently of the need to apply 'the criteria and tests of a science' before deciding whether political economy should be accorded scientific recognition; but unfortunately he did not specify what those tests were, and it did not help to say that

> the science of political economy, if propriety of speech is observed, means, a combination of true propositions respecting the supply, distribution and consumption of the articles or things composing the wealth of nations.[25]

In fact, it was not until the early 1840s after his son, John Stuart, had published his *Logic*[26] and his essay 'On the Definition of Political Economy; and On the Method of Philosophical Investigation in that Science',[27] that there was a sound basis for agreement about the epistemological foundations of political economy and the tests of valid knowledge applicable to it; and in view of the importance of this matter, it is interesting to note that Mill himself hoped that

> the essay, even if for that end it should remain unpublished for twenty years, should become classical and of authority . . . as I am persuaded that the *foundation* of the truth is here.[28]

One further aspect of the role of authority in political economy during the Ricardian era remains to be considered, namely its function in connection with matters of definition. Malthus was especially interested in this question, possibly as a result of his protracted debates with Ricardo, in which terminological differences figured prominently; and in his *Definitions in Political Economy*[29] he made a serious effort to prescribe rules designed to eliminate purely verbal disagreements among economists. 'In the case of a proposition the nature of which admits of a logical proof,' he declared, 'authority is of no consequence; but in a question which relates to the meaning to be attached to any particular term, it is quite incredible that any person should thus have ventured to disregard it.'[30] In definitional matters, he claimed, five rules should be followed:

(a) the best and most desirable authority was the 'common conversation of educated persons';
(b) the usage adopted by 'the most celebrated writers' in any discipline should be followed, especially if one such writer was regarded as its founder;
(c) the authority of the past could not, however, be treated as binding, and in 'the less strict sciences' changes were sometimes unavoidable, and usually easy to defend;
(d) any change of definition should be 'demonstrably beneficial in the whole';
(e) any new definition should be consistent with previously established definitions which were to be left unchanged.[31]

These rules, Malthus added, were obvious enough; but they were often neglected in practice, with the effect of creating unnecessary dissension; and although his treatise left no lasting mark on the subject, subsequent efforts to achieve the same end[32] suggest that he was addressing himself to a genuine problem.

III

For a quarter century or more after the publication of John Stuart Mill's *Principles* in 1848, the authority of the main stream of English classical economics became firmly established in the public mind, and perhaps the most significant indication of its prestige is the fact that Mill himself felt obliged to publish a formal recantation when he changed his mind about the 'wages fund' doctrine, which was widely regarded as one of the central pillars of doctrinal orthodoxy.[33] By 1871, when W. S. Jevons published the first edition of his pathbreaking *Theory of Political Economy*, the dead hand of the past in English political economy was so heavy that he felt impelled to conclude his treatise with a brief section on 'The Noxious Influence of Authority', in which he declared:

> I think there is some fear of the too great influence of authoritative writers in Political Economy. I protest against deference for any man, whether John Stuart Mill, or Adam Smith, or Aristotle, being allowed to check inquiry. Our science has become far too much a stagnant one, in which opinions rather than experience and reason are appealed to.[34]

The reasons for this sorry state of affairs are well known: a combination of a restrictive academic power structure; the leadership of a few individuals who 'had gained authority before they had developed competence';[35] and a period of economic prosperity which was often falsely regarded as affording proof of the beneficial effects and hence the validity of the reigning creed. But soon after Jevons' protest the situation changed dramatically. Major theoretical advances occurred with the so-called 'marginal revolution'; there was a serious methodological assault on doctrinal orthodoxy by supporters of the German Historical School; the untimely decease of several of the leading exponents of the old orthodoxy brought new leadership to the profession; and a severe depression shook the complacency of the majority of British economic and social thinkers.

It is not our purpose to re-examine this story here. The background is necessary, however, if we are to grasp the significance of the view of authority (especially with regard to doctrinal orthodoxy) that prevailed among members of the next generation of British economists. Its leaders were extremely anxious to correct the widely-held belief that political economy was a rigid doctrinaire science in which new ideas were unwelcome. Admittedly Alfred Marshall, who exerted a greater influence in his day than any other single economist, was unduly deferential to the great figures of the past, extremely slow to publish his own ideas, and very careful not to exaggerate the novel features of his own writings or those of his contemporaries. There was, in his outlook, much of what he once termed the 'Chinese element',[36] and by constantly impressing on his pupils the conviction that the development of economic ideas was a slow evolutionary process he may have unintentionally inhibited the progress of theoretical speculation. But when it came to a choice between respect for the past and scientific advance Marshall's sympathies were in the right place, and a revealing illustration of his open-mindedness is afforded by his attitude towards the British Economic Association (later the Royal Economic Society) which was founded in 1890.[37]

At that time there was still only a handful of academic posts in economics in the British Isles, and an association that confined its membership to college and university teachers would necessarily have been tiny and lacking in public influence. But once it was decided to adopt a wider membership policy the question arose whether the organization should be open to all comers on payment of a nominal subscription, like the American Economic Association, or whether some restriction of membership should be imposed. The discussion of this apparently trivial matter was complicated by the fact that three distinct but interrelated issues were involved, namely, what should be the nature and functions of the Association; what, if any, should be the minimum technical (that is, professional) qualifications for membership; and how could the establishment of a new doctrinal orthodoxy be avoided?

The object was, as Henry Sidgwick put it, to make the Association 'as unexclusive as it could be consistently with its scientific aims',[38] but some of the founder-members feared that, if anyone could join, the organization would lack intellectual and scientific authority, there would be little chance of harmonious cooperation, and it would be undesirable to hold frequent meetings and discussions, lest they should become occasions for methodological controversy or political propaganda, either of which would be damaging to the reputation of the Association. Even Marshall, who worked strenuously towards an open society and appealed for an 'absolutely catholic basis', expressed the hope that they would 'include every school of economists which was doing *genuine* work',[39] a statement that was interpreted by a non-academic member, the Liberal Member of Parliament, Leonard Courtney, as meaning that 'there must be authority somewhere, and that some opinions must be excluded'.[40] Edgeworth warned that if any test of economic orthodoxy were to be adopted, 'if some were to be excluded because they appeared unsound to others . . . the list of members would be very small',[41] but the Chancellor of the Exchequer, James Goschen, who was Chairman of the inaugural meeting, agreed with Courtney, for he 'saw in certain quarters men who called themselves political economists, but who had not the slightest idea what economics were . . . groups of men who seemed to disbelieve in the possibility of any economic science whatever'.[42] Marshall had expressed the hope that the Association would exert a 'wholesome influence' by simply welcoming 'the criticisms of all people who knew what they were talking about',[43] but Goschen drew cheers from the assembled company when he stressed the importance of 'the common diffusion of economic knowledge in the interest of the country at large, and quite apart from the more scientific desires and aspirations of economists themselves' and despite Marshall's warning against emphasizing 'wholesome influence' and sound ideas, he affirmed his belief that economic study 'would lead to the diffusion of truths which appeared to him to be extremely necessary to the happiness and prosperity of the nation'.[44]

These opinions reveal the different and partly incompatible motives of the academics and the politicians, and yet the status of economics at the time was such that a collaboration of both groups was necessary to the success of the new society. As Foxwell remarked, in Ricardo's day 'the economists were perhaps too immersed in current business and politics' but now 'the theorist was apt to become academic in the bad sense of that word, perhaps even pedantic; the man of affairs was apt to be shortsighted in his action, and deficient in imagination and breadth of view', and he hoped that the organization would facilitate the meeting of theorists and practical men, promote scientific advance, and exert an influence in social progress and reform.[45] On this compromise platform various interests were reconciled, and the membership difficulty was solved by following the example of the Royal Statistical Society, by requiring prospective members to obtain the written support of two existing members (which proved to be a purely nominal process) and to pay a small subscription. Henry Sidgwick probably expressed the general feeling when he said that 'it was quite desirable that a reserve power should be placed in the hands of the council to reject any obviously objectionable applicant'[46] – a power that has apparently never been used.

IV

The relations between the academic and the non-academic economists at the turn of the century would repay systematic study; but while the question of professional standards in British economics appears to have receded into the background in subsequent years, the problem of authority flared up again in 1903, when it was the subject both of scholarly analysis and of public controversy. These two aspects were, moreover, interrelated, for although the tone of James Shield Nicholson's paper *The Use and Abuse of Authority in Economics* was detached and impartial, and its content general and retrospective, it nonetheless represented a response to a heated public controversy about the validity of the free trade doctrine which had flared up some five months earlier in *The Times* and elsewhere.[47] Nicholson's paper was neither radical nor anti-Marshallian: indeed in some ways it even seems conservative, for he especially complained of the recent tendency in economic literature to strain after novelty and to underrate previous work. 'The legitimate appeal to authority is simply the recognition that every science must advance by slow gradations or, in other words, by little increments. . . . And that means that we must first of all consult the recognized authorities.'[48] It is legitimate to emphasize 'the use of scientific methods'; but

it is an abuse of authority to quote opinions of economists, even the most eminent in the past or the most fashionable in the present, as if such opinions were as binding as the decisions of the House of Lords as a final court of appeal. . . . A writer who has made a reputation either as an expounder of general principles or by some particular enquiry, may himself enter the arena of social or political reform, not simply as an individual with a certain training but as a representative, so to speak, of the authority of the science in general or of his particular field. This assumption of authority, it may be noted, is more often made by the disciple than by the master, by the follower than by the leader of thought.[49]

It was precisely this kind of abuse of authority that Nicholson and thirteen other prominent economists had been accused of when they expressed their views on 'certain matters of a more or less technical character' in the correspondence columns of *The Times*, on August 15th, 1903. Declaring their ardent sympathies towards the objectives sought by advocates of imperial preference, they nevertheless questioned the wisdom of Joseph Chamberlain's fiscal proposals on the grounds that the means selected would not achieve the desired ends. They were not only concerned at 'the prevalence of certain erroneous opinions' in support of protection, which they rejected 'partly for reasons of the same kind as those which, as now universally admitted, justified the adoption of free trade'; they also warned that the evil consequences of such a policy would not merely be economic, for it 'brings in its train the loss of purity in politics, the unfair advantage given to those who wield the powers of jobbery and corruption, unjust distribution of wealth, and the growth of "sinister interests" '. In support of their contentions they appended seven observations, of which only the first, and most confident, need be quoted here:

> It is not true that an increase of imports involves the diminished employment of workmen in the importing country. The statement is universally rejected by those who have thought about the subject and is completely refuted by experience.[50]

During the next month or so *The Times* printed about thirty letters and several editorial comments on the economists' 'manifesto' most of which (in line with that newspaper's support for Chamberlain) criticized their arguments or raised questions about the issue of principle involved in their action. The so-called 'fourteen professors' were accused of trying to stifle free discussion by peremptorily deciding the tariff debate before Chamberlain's proposals were fully known, and their views were denounced as pure theory, and as evidence of their ignorance and their neglect of practical experience. This correspondence revealed to *The Times*' readers the division of opinion among the economists, for Foxwell, W. A. S. Hewins, and L. L. Price were among those who explicitly rejected the manifesto, while other correspondents cited the names of contemporary British, European, and American protectionist economists. The professors' critics also mustered some apt quotations from the works of such economists as Adam Smith, Ricardo, the Mills, Sidgwick, and Nicholson, one of the most effective of which was the previously quoted extract from Jevons' 'On the Noxious Influence of Authority'.[51]

On the question of authority, some critics declared that the fourteen economists had damaged their professional and scientific reputations and brought their subject into disrepute by thus exceeding their legitimate academic function, while the editor of *The Times* poked fun at

> The spectacle of these fourteen dervishes emerging from their caves and chanting in solemn procession their venerable incantations against the rising tide of inquiry . . . it is quite certain that the day has gone by when the professors of political economy can impose opinions upon the country by the weight of authority, if, indeed, that day ever dawned. . . . A more scientific conception of their own science, which pretends to be, but never is, an experimental science, would save professors from the painful discovery that they convince nobody who stands in need of conviction.[52]

This unfavourable impression was probably strengthened by Foxwell's letter, for he objected to the manifesto because 'the vital issues involved are more political than scientific, [and] I do not think that economists have any right to attempt to prejudge these issues by a pronouncement which assumes scientific authority, though nearly every sentence is obviously and necessarily political'. He wished to correct any misconception that his department at University College, London, might be in some way committed to an approval of this document simply because one former and two current members had signed it, and added, somewhat ponderously, that

> we shall never object to inquiry into any economic tradition however popular or venerable, and we shall never pronounce or appear to pronounce upon any economic proposal coming from responsible persons until the details of that proposal are before us.[53]

Only two of the signatories replied to the attacks upon their letter. Pigou denied that he had in any way committed, or intended to commit the department of economics at University College, London, to any views on fiscal policy,[54] while Bowley gave his blessing to any inquiry into the tariff problem, provided that it was undertaken by a qualified and impartial commission.[55] The most important statement for the defence, however, came from Sydney Chapman, Professor of Political Economy at Manchester, who declared that he would have signed but for his absence abroad. He conceded that economics professors should not lend their scientific authority to dogmatic pronouncements on highly political and controversial matters, but denied that the manifesto fell into this category. Economists, he continued

> ought not surely to feel themselves debarred from expressing their opinions on such matters, especially when the economic considerations involved are of almost predominant importance. In advancing their opinions, however, they should separate, as far as it is possible to do so, their conclusions upon the question as a whole, where the political elements play a large part, from their views, which can be expressed with a greater degree of certitude, upon the more specifically economic components of the problem. This appears to me to have been done in the manifesto, and in signing it I wish to be taken as drawing such a distinction ... it seems to me that much of the popularity of the proposed new policy is due to a failure to recognize, or appreciate fully, the 'unseen' effects which would be brought about by its adoption. Upon the general question I should express myself in this way; but upon the truth or falsity of certain economic sequences which have been implied in the course of discussion in the last few weeks economists can speak, and should speak, with more certainty and authority – for instance, as to the relation between imports and exports, the effect of imports upon employment at home (etc.)....
> These latter are matters of economic cause and effect, and while no man can prophesy in detail in such a mutable world as this, economic science does lay claim to the power of indicating the possible results of a given course of action and roughly estimating their degrees of probability.[56]

This passage has been cited at length because it focuses attention on the economist's dual responsibility – as a scholar and as a citizen, a duality that presents acute problems in times of intense public controversy, especially in situations where academic freedom is insecure. As a citizen he can hardly be expected to remain silent on matters within the sphere of his professional competence; but controversial economic questions usually possess important non-economic aspects and implications, and it is the scholar's duty not only to be cautious, detached, and impartial, but also to avoid lending the weight of his professional or scientific authority to opinions about matters on which he has no special expertise. It is beyond the scope of this paper to consider the merits of the argument involved in the tariff reform controversy; the economists' letter was a nine-days wonder and appears to have left no permanent scars on the development of the subject, although the incident probably discouraged the leading economists from making other concerted efforts to influence public opinion.

V

During the first three decades of this century the development of economics as an organized academic discipline proceeded apace in Britain, as elsewhere: there was a striking growth in the number of students, degrees granted, university and college teaching posts, and professional publications. Consequently, by the time Keynes' *General Theory* was published in 1936, the organization of academic economics resembled Polanyi's above-quoted description of the physical sciences somewhat more closely than it had done at the turn of the century,[57] and it is, therefore, easy to understand why Keynes addressed himself to his academic colleagues, rather than to the general public. Indeed, one of the most significant (and to professional conservatives, one of the most regrettable) features of the so-called Keynesian revolution was the fact that its leader was himself one of the outstanding products of the academic tradition that he so outspokenly attacked.

This is not the place to provide even a thumbnail sketch of the history of British economics from Marshall to Keynes; but apart from its intrinsic importance, the appearance of Keynes' *General Theory* happened to coincide with the publication of W. H. Hutt's extended apologia for the 'orthodox' tradition, in the course of which he devoted more space to the question of the role of authority in economics than any previous writer had done.[58] Unfortunately, Hutt's book is, in many respects, unsuitable to our purpose, for in his defence of the nineteenth-century liberal economic and social philosophy he did not examine the essential logical distinction between political conservatism and what might be called professional conservatism. Hutt believed that the low public reputation of economics in the 1930s was largely due to the fact that the previous generation of academic economists had compromised their scholarly integrity by bending before the wind of popular socialism; and while it may be true that political and professional conservatism (or radicalism) in economics have often been associated in practice,[59] the problem of intellectual authority, which relates solely to the latter, is one that merits examination in its own right.

Up to a point, professional conservatism is characteristic of all scholarly activity, for apprentice scholars are taught to respect the views and achievements of the established leaders in their field and to avoid overstating the originality of their own work. This outlook is reinforced by the accepted conventions of scholarly behaviour, which enjoin detachment, impartiality, and a readiness to suspend judgement until the evidence has been sifted and a determined effort has been made to test alternative hypotheses and to trace cause and effect relationships. Needless to say, these conventions are not always heeded; and independent-mindedness is a psychological trait common among scholars. Despite what Polanyi has termed the research student's 'act of affiliation' to his teacher and the mature scholar's responsiveness to the 'conviviality' of the scientific consensus,[60] respect for authority is never binding, for each individual reserves the right to make his own judgement as to the validity of those results which most directly affect his scientific vision of reality. Nevertheless, the weight of the past can be overwhelming. As Schumpeter is said to have remarked, there may be 'too many scholars and not enough fools' who are prepared to rush in and challenge the accepted views.[61] As Hutt said:

> Any social scientist must know from introspection that we are all dominated by ideas which we have inherited uncritically and unquestioningly from some part of current tradition. Once we are past the undergraduate stage it may require a mental shock of a rare kind to cause us even to exercise the mildest scepticism concerning what are the accepted commonplaces of the people with whom we associate or of the orthodox exposition of our science. And it may be that the largest sources of error are to be found in notions that we are never prompted to doubt.[62]

It was Keynes' awareness of this kind of intellectual inertia that induced him to attack the classical tradition so vigorously, for, unlike Hutt, he did not believe that 'the great body of economic *theory* may possibly be *relatively* free from this charge' of uncritical acceptance of the past, doubtless because he did not share Hutt's view that 'what have been called "economic laws" are simply deductions from axioms, and these axioms are "obvious" in the sense that it is impossible for the student to imagine a world in which they are not operative'.[63]

However, as a study in the role of authority in economics Hutt's book is distinctive not because of his political beliefs or his metaphysical predilections, but because he endeavoured to define the criteria by which the authority of a scientific economist should be gauged, and prescribed a series of recommendations for restoring the economists' reputation with the public. The scientific economist, he maintained, must:

(i) 'have devoted much study and thought to the subject-matter of economics';

(ii) have 'an adequate acquaintance with equilibrium economics';

(iii) be able to master the specific technical difficulties of any given problem about which his advice is sought, though he need not possess any special aptitudes or mental powers, or much 'experience of the practical world', since 'the practical man's relevant experience can always be communicated to the "theorist" who can alone grasp the full significance of the facts in complex questions';

(iv) hold an academic appointment in a university; and, above all,

(v) be 'exempt from personal interest' in the effects of his pronouncements, and must not be either an advocate of a creed or a member of a doctrinal school whose leader is actively engaged in politics or business.[64]

In order to restore public confidence in their science, Hutt proposed that economists should be neither active politicians nor members of political parties, and even added that the terms of academic appointments should include a renunciation of the right to stand for Parliament. Economists should be permitted to give advice to businessmen, financiers, or to the press, but should accept no payment for their services, and any academic economist who possessed substantial private means should ensure that his assets were widely distributed so as to avoid the accusation that he was swayed by any specified vested interest. Provided that these conditions were fulfilled, Hutt maintained, the individual's birth, background, and beliefs would be unlikely to impair his scientific judgement; and the reputation of the profession would be greatly strengthened if a number of such economists were to form a society and publish 'an authoritative journal' which reflected the expertise and disinterestedness of its members, rather than 'all shades of economic opinion' and the views of 'all schools of thought' – which was the avowed object of the *Economic Journal*.[65]

These proposals sound somewhat naive and utopian; and they might even be regarded as having a sinister aspect when one reads that it is those economists usually termed 'orthodox' who constitute 'the body of expert opinion which the community might be expected to accept as authoritative'.[66] Nevertheless, despite the element of special pleading, Hutt's ideas have been too long neglected, especially by historians of economics, for they raise complex and important questions about the organization of the economics profession – for example, questions of professional ethics, academic freedom, and the changing relationship between the academic economists and the public.[67] Hutt's pioneer work enables us to perceive some of the issues in the sociology of economics which lie behind those now unfashionable, but still by no means completely forgotten, controversies between 'orthodox' and 'heterodox' viewpoints, and about the relationships between theory and applied economics. A systematic study of the nature, criteria, and functions of intellectual authority in economics would, it is submitted, help to reveal the connection between the perennial problem of scientific method in economics and the kind of world in which the practising economist actually functions.

NOTES

1 Hutt, *The Economists and the Public* (1936), especially ch. X, Sanctions for the Economists' Authority.
2 Popper, Conjectures and Refutations 5 (1963). This is from a paper entitled *On the Sources of Knowledge and Ignorance*.
3 Balfour, *The Foundations of Belief* 237, 238 (8th ed. 1902).

4 Polanyi, *Personal Knowledge, Towards a Post-Critical Philosophy* 216–17 (1958). No single quotation can hope to convey the depth and subtlety of Polanyi's analysis. See, e.g, ch. 7, Conviviality. For a brief discussion of the implications of Polanyi's views in this and earlier works see Jouvenal, The Republic of Science, in *The Logic of Personal Knowledge* 131–41 (1961), an unedited Festschrift.

5 These are Oxford Dictionary definitions. Hutt drew heavily upon George Cornewall Lewis's forgotten but valuable *Essay on the Influence of Authority in Matters of Opinion* (1849). According to Lewis, the principle of authority is 'the principle of adopting the belief of others, on a matter of opinion, without reference to the particular grounds on which that belief may rest'. Matters of opinion were said to include disputed questions of fact and 'general propositions or theorems relating to laws of nature or mind, principles and rules of human conduct, future probabilities, deductions from hypotheses, and the like, about which a doubt may reasonably exist'. Resort to authority can never 'produce any increase or improvement of knowledge, or bring about the discovery of new truths', and 'when a person derives an opinion from authority, the utmost he can hope is to adopt the belief of those who, at any time, are the least likely to be in error' – hence the importance of the qualified expert, the professional. Id. at 7, 3, 8.

6 Letwin, *The Origins of Scientific Economics; English Economic Thought, 1660–1776*, ch. 3 (1963). It should be noted that Professor Letwin uses the term 'authority' in several different ways (Cf. 80–3, 86, 209–11) and that he evidently regards authority and reason as mutually exclusive (Cf. 87).

7 See Checkland, The Advent of Academic Economics in England, 19 *The Manchester School* 43 (1951).

8 Most of the references were casual; but James Mill elaborated the point in his last published article, Whether Political Economy is Useful? 30 *Westminster Rev.* 553 (1836), claiming that half a dozen writers publicized their objections to political economy while a far greater number who accepted its doctrines remained silent. 'Among those who have so much knowledge on the subject as to entitle their opinion to any weight, there is wonderful agreement.' On the 'great points' there is 'general concord'; on 'all the great doctrines' there is 'perfect concurrence'; and there was only 'any dispute' on 'some of the minor questions involved', etc., etc. (id. at 569–71). Yet a few years earlier, in a caustic review of the doctrines published in the *Quarterly Review*, he had scathingly remarked that 'in political economy there is no opinion, however absurd, whether on a question of fact or of principle, which may not easily be proved from competent authority'. On the Essay on Political Economy, 3 *Westminster Rev.* 213, 230 (1825). As we shall see, the key questions were, of course: who are the 'competent authorities'; and what are the criteria of valid knowledge?

9 For example, see Blaug, Ricardian Economics (1958), especially ch. 3; Checkland, The Propagation of Ricardian Economics in England, 16 Economica N.S. 40 (1949); Grampp, *The Manchester School* (1960); Meek, The Decline of Ricardian Economics in England, 17 *Economica* N.S. 43 (1950).

10 Checkland, op. cit. *supra* note 9, at 51.

11 Ricardo, 7 Works and Correspondence 71 (Sraffa ed. 1952). Cf. id. at 35–6; 8 id. at 142.

12 Mill, War Expenditure, 2 *Westminster Rev.* 45 (1824). 'A reasoner must be hard pressed, when he is driven to quote practical men in aid of his conclusions. There cannot be a worse authority, in any branch of political science, than that of merely practical men.' Ibid. This is a characteristic device used by those seeking to set themselves apart from and, of course, above the laity. In this case

Mill aimed to exalt 'those principles which are deduced from a general and enlarged experience'.

13 Torrens, *An Essay on the External Corn Trade xiii* (1829 ed.); *An Essay on the Production of Wealth xi–xii* (1821). At other times he severely criticized Malthus, Senior, and J. S. Mill – usually with justification. For a general assessment of his work see Robbins, *Robert Torrens and the Evolution of Classical Economics* (1958).

14 Torrens, *An Essay on the Production of Wealth xiii* (1821). Five years later he claimed there were already 'unequivocal signs of the approaching fulfilment of this prediction'. Torrens, *An Essay on the External Corn Trade xi* (1829 ed.). (This was first published in 1826.)

15 Torrens, *The Principles and Practical Operations of Sir Robert Peel's Act Explained and Defended iii–iv* (1858). Torrens was discussing J. S. Mill's views on currency, and concluded that as Mill was a co-candidate for Parliament with Thomas Tooke, the 'authority' of the two men must be regarded as equal. Tooke's views were 'but mirage-formations which a ray of analysis dissolves'.

16 Torrens, *The Budget on Commercial and Colonial Policy 332* (1844). For his letter to the Editor of the Examiner, see id. at 78. On another occasion he defined the problem of expertise even more clearly, for in a letter to Wilmot Horton, dated November 7, 1826, he argued that an economist should be appointed to the Board of Trade because 'it partakes of the nature of a professional appointment, requiring a peculiar course of study, and knowledge of an almost technical nature. . . . Though the time may not have actually arrived, yet it is rapidly approaching, when it will be deemed as necessary to select the members of the Board of Trade from the Economists, as it is to take the Bishops from the Church, or the Law Officers from the Bar.' O'Brien, The Transition in Torrens' Monetary Thought, 32 *Economica*, 272 (1965).

17 In their pioneer study, *The Professions 284–5* (1933), Carr-Saunders and Wilson regarded the dividing line between professional and non-professional vocations as too arbitrary to be definable. The term 'profession', they remark, stands for a 'complex of characteristics'.

18 Schumpeter, *History of Economic Analysis 47* (1954).

19 It is, perhaps, significant that the emergence of a literary 'profession' is clearly discernible at this time. See, e.g., Williams, *Culture and Society 49* (1958).

20 See the Editor's Preface, 9 *The Collected Writings of Thomas de Quincey 1* (Masson ed. 1890). The quoted passage was probably written about 1811.

21 De Quincey, Ricardo and Adam Smith, op. cit. *supra* note 20, at 113, 116. On his general position see Gherity, Thomas de Quincey and Ricardian Orthodoxy, 29 Economica, N.S., 269 (1962).

22 De Quincey, op. cit. *supra* note 21, at 117. Cf. de Quincey, The Logic of Political Economy 228 (184).

23 De Quincey, op. cit. *supra* note 20, at 41.

24 McCulloch, *A Discourse on the Rise, Progress, Peculiar Objects and Importance of Political Economy 9* (1824). Torrens, On Wages and Combinations 73 (1834).

25 Mill, Whether Political Economy is Useful? op. cit. *supra* note 8, at 554.

26 Mill, *Logic* (1843).

27 Mill, On the Definition of Political Economy, and on the Method of Philosophical Investigation in that Science, 26 *Westminster Rev.* 1 (1836).

28 The essay was probably written between 1829 and 1831 and first published in the *Westminster Review* in October 1836, but it became generally known to economists only after it was reprinted in Mill, *Essays on Some Unsettled Questions of Political Economy 120* (1844). The title was slightly altered to read On the Definition of Political Economy; and On the Method of Investigation Proper to

It, and there were minor revisions of the text. Mill's comments appear in a letter to John Pringle Nichol dated January 17, 1834, published in 12 *The Earlier Letters of John Stuart Mill 1812–1848*, at 209–12 (Mineka ed. 1963) (italics in original).

29 The full title of his monograph was *Definitions in Political Economy, Preceded by an Inquiry into the Rules which ought to guide Political Economists in their Definition and Use of their Terms. With Remarks on the Deviation from these Rules in their Writings* (1827).

30 Id. at 138. Earlier (id. at 124) he had remarked:

Till some steadiness is given to the science by a greater degree of care among its professors, not to alter without improving, – it cannot be expected that it should attain that general influence in society which (its principles being just) would be of the highest practical utility.

31 Id. at 4–5.

32 In the early 1890s the American Economic Association established a series of committees whose task was to reach some agreement on the use of terms. These committees were uniformly unsuccessful. A proposal for standardizing the use of symbols in economic models was made only recently. Cf. Mars, A Note on a Problem of Notation, 73 *Economic J.* 226 (1963).

33 The symbolic aspect of Mill's recantation is heightened by the fact that in retrospect it soon appeared as a work of supererogation. Cf., for example, Schumpeter, op. cit. *supra* note 18, at 671: 'the first English economist of the age had disavowed the hateful scarecrow.'

34 Jevons, *Theory of Political Economy* 275–6 (4th ed. 1911). 'In matters of philosophy and science authority has ever been the great opponent of truth. A despotic calm is usually the triumph of error. In the republic of the sciences sedition and even anarchy are beneficial in the long run to the greatest happiness of the greatest number. In the physical sciences authority has greatly lost its noxious influence. . . . In science and philosophy nothing must be held sacred. Truth indeed is sacred; but, as Pilate said, "What is Truth?".'

These remarks suggest that Jevons's conception of the role of authority was unduly narrow, and that his view of the benefits of sedition and anarchy was incompatible with the orderly growth of scientific knowledge. But his remarks are the characteristic outpourings of a frustrated intellectual innovator. From Jevons's economic writings and from his published correspondence, it is clear that he was conscious of being intellectually, emotionally, and geographically (especially in his Manchester days) out of touch with the main stream of contemporary economic ideas. In some ways, of course, this position was a source of intellectual strength.

35 Checkland, Economic Opinion in England as Jevons Found it, 19 *The Manchester School* 143, 168 (1951). Cf. id. at 153, 162. This article contains a thorough survey of the condition of the subject in the 1870s. See also Hutchinson, *A Review of Economic Doctrines 1870–1929*, ch. 1 (1953).

36 See Coats, Alfred Marshall and Richard T. Ely: Some Unpublished Correspondence, 28 *Economica* N.S. 193 (1961). Reprinted in vol. I in this series, pp. 253–6.

37 The following paragraphs are based on the account in 1 *Economic J.* 2–14 (1891). Extracts were reprinted, together with editorial comments in The Society's Jubilee 1890–1940, 50 *Economic J.* 401–9 (1940). See also Collet & Keynes, Obituary: Henry Higgs, and Miss Collet's important supplementary note, id. at 546–61.

38 1 *Economic J.* 10 (1891).

39 1 *Economic J.* 5 (italics supplied). Marshall did not explain the difference between fake and genuine work; but his motives are revealed in the following letter from Marshall to James Bonar dated July 25, 1890, reprinted in The Society's Jubilee 1890–1940, 50 *Economic J.* 401, 406 (1940):

My dear Bonar,
I am sorry you won't be present at the meeting; firstly because I think you might be converted to an open Society. No one, to whom I have spoken, except Foxwell, Edgeworth and yourself thinks a close society would be safe and the general opinion of those with whom I have conferred is that a close society would be inundated with Quacks, who could not be kept out, unless the society was so small as to be little more than a private club: but that Quacks would not care to come into a society which was open to all: and would not do much harm there, if they did come in.

Yours very truly,
Alfred Marshall.

It is worth noting that, on the whole, the non-academic founder-members, like Bonar, Higgs, Courtney, and Goschen, seem to have been initially more reluctant to lower the barriers to entry, possibly because they were less sensitive to the risks of establishing a new orthodoxy.

40 1 *Economic J.* 9 (1891). As an example of minimum standards of technical competence Courtney suggested that while they might legitimately consider whether gold alone or silver alone, or an amalgam of both should be the basis of the currency, they could not tolerate the view that 'an unlimited supply of paper would cover all the difficulties of the world'. The distinction between academic and non-academic men should not be pressed too strongly; Courtney was a former Professor of Political Economy at University College, London. See note 50 (*infra*).

41 Id. at 10.

42 Id. at 7.

43 Id. at 5.

44 Id. at 6.

45 Id. at 12.

46 Id. at 10.

47 Nicholson, The Use and Abuse of Authority in Economics, 13 *Economic J.* 554 (1903). An introductory footnote stated that the paper had been read to the Edinburgh University Economic Association, but no date was given. For a valuable recent study of the political aspects of the tariff reform controversy of 1903, see Gollin, *Balfour's Burden: Arthur Balfour and Imperial Preference* (1965), especially 89–90, where the author notes that the Prime Minister sought the advice of certain economists before adopting the middle-of-the-road position set forth in his *Economic Notes on Insular Free Trade*. For the King's suggestion that he should consult the experts (presumably including the professors), id. at 83.

48 Id. at 565.

49 Id. at 563.

50 The signatories of the letter, with their institutional affiliations, were given as follows (my abbreviations): C. F. Bastable (Prof. of Pol. Econ., University of Dublin); A. L. Bowley (Teacher of Statistics, London School of Economics); Edwin Cannan (Teacher of Econ. Theory, LSE); Leonard Courtney (formerly Prof. of Pol. Econ., University College, London); F. Y. Edgeworth (Prof. of Pol. Econ., Oxford); E. C. K. Gonner (Prof. of Econ. Sci., University of Liverpool); Alfred Marshall (Prof. of Pol. Econ., Cambridge); J. S. Nicholson (Prof. of Pol.

Econ., University of Edinburgh); L. R. Phelps (Editor of Econ. Review); A. Pigou (Lecturer, U. Coll., London); C. P. Sanger (Lecturer, U. Coll., London); W. R. Scott (Lecturer, University of St. Andrews); W. Smart (Prof. of Pol. Econ., University of Glasgow); Armitage Smith (Lecturer, Birkbeck Coll., and LSE).

According to Foxwell, it was James Bonar 'who introduced Marshall, against M's better judgment, and after M had twice refused, to sign the Professor's Manifesto. It was just because he felt his signature was a blunder, that he was so angry with me for attacking it.' Letter from Foxwell to W. R. Scott, 18 February, 1930, in Kress Collection, Harvard University.

51 Quoted by (Sir) Vincent Caillard in The Times, Aug. 18, 1903, p. 6.

52 The Times, Aug. 18, 1903, p. 7. Also on that day, Tariff Reformer ridiculed the 'remarkable phenomenon of so much learning and ability and so little output – two professors to one platitude'. Tariff Reformer was L. S. Amery. See his autobiography, My Political Life, Vol. 1, 243–6 (1953), in which he claims that despite the 'shattering effect of such an overwhelming barrage of the heaviest artillery on the morale of Chamberlain's supporters and, still more, on the great majority who were still undecided', his reply succeeded in making 'the pundits look ridiculous'.

53 The Times, Aug. 20, 1903, p. 10. Foxwell noted that 'with scarcely an exception, the historical group of English economists declined to sign the manifesto', but if this remark represented an effort to re-open old wounds it evidently failed. A somewhat similar letter appeared on the same day from W. A. S. Hewins, while on the following day another of Foxwell's colleagues at University College, the statistician G. Udny Yule, dissociated himself from the manifesto, describing it as 'both deplorable for the dogmatism of its tone and lacking in a sense of the character, the complexity, and the importance of the issues involved'. The Times, Aug. 20, 1903, p. 10; Aug. 21, 1903, p. 5.

The economic historian, William Cunningham, also expressed his strong disapproval of the manifesto. Cunningham, Richard Cobden and Adam Smith 33–4 (1904); The Wisdom of the Wise; Three Lectures on Free Trade and Imperialism 6–7 (1906); and The Case Against Free Trade 105 (1911).

In a letter to Bonar dated 22 November, 1903, Foxwell said:

I thought I was entitled to make a protest for fair play against what seemed to me an attempt to represent the proposals as condemned a priori by elementary economic principles: principles really almost wholly irrelevant to the issues ... but I do not see any means to do more than this unless officially requested – & this last is extremely unlikely, as the Manifesto has had the effect which so many of us foresaw at the time of putting economists out of court altogether. We are now hopelessly discredited: in fact political economy seems to me to have fallen back in public opinion to the position it held about the 70's. I hoped that the more realistic and liberal tone of the work of the last generation would have gained for English economists something of the respect which German economists enjoy in the world of affairs. However the mischief is done & silence is now the most fitting attitude for a 'professor'. . . .

Letter in Kress Library, Harvard University.

54 The Times, Aug. 24, 1903, p. 6. For further discussion of the tariff reform controversy see vol. I in this series, pp. 268–337.

55 The Times, Aug. 29, 1903, p. 5.

56 The Times, Sept. 17, 1903, p. 5.

57 See text accompanying note 4 *supra*.

58 *Supra* note 1.

59 For a recent discussion of this point see Stigler, The Politics of Political Econo-mists, 73 Q.J. Econ. 522 (1959), and Comments, 74 Q.J. Econ. 659, 666, 670 (1960).

60 Polanyi, op. cit. *supra* note 4, at 208. Much of chapter 7 is devoted to this theme.

61 Quoted by Richard Ruggles, Methodological Developments, in 2 A Survey of Contemporary Economics 425 (Haley ed. 1952).

62 Hutt, op. cit. *supra* note 1, at 48.

63 Ibid. (Italics in original.) Hutt distinguished between 'custom-thought' and 'power-thought' and argued that whereas economic theory was relatively free from the taint of the former both were influential in the discussion of economic policy.

64 Id. at 221–7.

65 Id. at 227–39. In an appendix to this chapter, written after the appearance of Keynes' General Theory, Hutt commented that it 'may easily prove to be the source of the most serious single blow that the authority of orthodox economics has ever suffered.' Id. at 245. For evidence that Hutt has not changed his mind see his Keynesianism – Retrospect and Prospect, A Critical Restatement of Basic Economic Principles 4–5 (1963).

66 Hutt, The Economists and the Public 236 (1936).

67 For studies of certain aspects of these questions as they have affected American economics see Dorfman, 4 The Economic Mind in American Civilization 208–10 (1958); Metzger, Academic Freedom in the Age of the University, chs. 3–5 (1961); Coats, The American Economic Association 1904–1929, 54 Am. Econ. Rev. 261 (1964) (reprinted in this volume, pp. 239–63).

7

SOCIOLOGICAL ASPECTS OF BRITISH ECONOMIC THOUGHT (*ca.* 1880–1930)

I

Textbook writers on the history of economics usually maintain that British economic thought was dominated by the Cambridge 'school' from the first appearance of Alfred Marshall's *Principles of Economics* in 1890 until shortly before J. M. Keynes's *General Theory* was published in 1936,[1] but in attempting to account for this state of affairs they concentrate on the development of analytical (especially Marshallian, or neo-classical) economics and pay insufficient attention to the role of personality, tradition, and the academic and social context. Such an approach not only underestimates important aspects of the intellectual scene; it also neglects the fact that a doctrinal 'school' is not merely the product of intellectual influences: it is a sociological phenomenon and, as such, can only be adequately understood by reference to the social situation from which it emerged. This was acknowledged by J. A. Schumpeter, who remarked, in his massive *History of Economic Analysis* (1954), that

> The professionals that devote themselves to scientific work in a particular field . . . tend to become a sociological group. This means that they have other things in common besides the interest in scientific work or in a particular science per se. . . . The group accepts or refuses to accept co-workers also for reasons other than their professional competence or incompetence. In economics this group took long to mature but when it did mature it acquired much greater importance than it did in physics. . . . [In late nineteenth-century England] the association of scientific work with teaching produced an economic profession in a fuller sense of the word and this economic profession developed attitudes to social and political questions that were *similar also for reasons other than similar scientific views*. This similarity of conditions of life and social location produced similar philosophies of life and similar value judgments about social phenomena.[2]

This article seeks to amplify and interpret Schumpeter's remarks, but in

105

a provisional (and, it is hoped, suggestive) rather than a comprehensive and definitive way, for there are serious gaps in our knowledge. In place of the usual discussion of Marshall's economic ideas and his conception of the nature and purpose of economics, we shall consider the influence of the Cambridge 'school' in terms of his personality, position, and qualities of leadership; the general academic environment; the range of potential rival ideas, individuals, and groups; and the size, composition, and social attitudes of the British economics 'profession'. This method necessarily implies that Marshall's importance cannot simply be attributed to his individual genius; but it is not our intention to derogate his achievement – indeed, in some respects, it seems all the more remarkable, given the academic milieu.

II

In 1885, when Marshall became professor of political economy at Cambridge, the condition of his subject was profoundly discouraging, and its immediate prospects seemed little better. Its public reputation had fallen, owing to the combined effects of a sharp public reaction against classical economics, an increased concern about current economic and social problems, and the disruptive methodological wrangles among the leading economic writers (Hutchison, 1953, chap. i; Coats 1954a), while in the universities there were few opportunities (or incentives) for specialist study or research. Political economy still formed only a minor element in a traditional curriculum dominated by classics and theology; where taught at all, it was usually taught by dons whose principal intellectual interests (if, indeed, they had any) lay elsewhere; and it was virtually ignored in the examination system of what has rightly been called an 'exam ridden' country. Moreover, unlike foreign universities, the ancient English universities provided an infertile soil for those hoping to sow intellectual seeds or plant a doctrinal 'school', for, as noted by the biographer of Marshall's distinguished Cambridge contemporary, F. W. Maitland, 'We are an economical race, and since advanced work does not pay in the Tripos, or in the careers to which the Tripos serves as a portal, it is left to the casual patronage of amateurs. Maitland thoroughly understood the limitations under which an English professor must work' (Fisher, 1910, pp. 170–1); and, as we shall see, so too did Marshall.

Yet although the situation was discouraging, it was by no means hopeless. The tide of economic opinion was turning away from methodological disputation, and the desire for a realignment and consolidation of forces was growing – a process that was ultimately aided by the recent decease of some of the leading protagonists. Whatever its deficiencies, Cambridge represented a good base for relief operations, since it was one of the two dominant institutions in a hierarchical and status-conscious educational pyramid. It adopted a more sympathetic attitude to university reform – including the expansion of science, mathematics, and 'modern' subjects – than Oxford; and there was a powerful tradition of rational, empirical philosophy that encouraged the quest for a more scientific approach to economic and social questions.[3] The existence of the moral sciences tripos, and the presence of men like Henry Sidgwick and H. S. Foxwell, undoubtedly facilitated Marshall's task, as did also his growing reputation as a thinker and lecturer. In 1887 Foxwell claimed that 'half the economic chairs in the United Kingdom are occupied by his [Marshall's] pupils, and the share taken by them in general economic instruction in England is even larger than this'; and a year later he performed a major service for Cambridge economics by discouraging John Neville Keynes from taking political economy at Oxford, arguing that 'it is much better that a study should be concentrated in a particular place. There arise many of the same advantages as in the localisation of an industry' (Foxwell, 1887, p. 92; Harrod, 1951, p. 9).

In due course, a belief in the superiority of Cambridge economics and economists seems to have emerged – though this is obviously difficult to document – and John Maynard Keynes, Neville's illustrious son, has been quoted as saying 'there isn't anyone else' (that is, outside Cambridge), a view that his biographer underlined by commenting, with characteristic British understatement, that Keynes doubtlessly 'made enemies among men who had established some reputation as practical economists even before he was ever heard of, by assuming that they were not worth consideration. . . . It was not so much the practice, however, as its elevation into a doctrine that may have done harm.'[4] Maynard Keynes was, of course, an exceptional man whose outlook cannot be regarded as typical; and even in Cambridge the Marshallian approach was questioned in Foxwell's lectures and vigorously attacked in print by the economic historian, William Cunningham (Cunningham, 1892; Marshall, 1892; Keynes, 1936, pp. 590–3). Nevertheless, the range and volume of dissent was far more limited than in Oxford, and the all-embracing Marshallian blend of induction and deduction, mathematical and non-mathematical analysis, theoretical and applied economics, disarmed the critics, and by 1910, when Dennis Robertson was a Cambridge undergraduate, there was apparently a consensus of opinion on fundamentals, including the important question of what problems were worth studying.[5] Despite the furore of contemporary methodological controversy among American economists, largely owing to the disturbing genius of Thorstein Veblen (Dorfman, 1949, chap. xix; Coats, 1954b), Robertson recalled an atmosphere of calm that now seems somewhat forced and unnatural as well as characteristically British in its insularity and complacency. Marshall had deliberately (and apparently successfully) endeavoured to protect his pupils from the profound methodological disagreements that had plagued his own generation, and the sense of continuity and local loyalty became so strong that as late as 1927 Maynard Keynes was still assiduously defending Cambridge economics against fundamental criticism from within;[6] and it was the legacy of the past that compelled him to exaggerate the extent of his subsequent breach with the Cambridge tradition and to dramatize his revolt by attacking Pigou, the embodiment of Marshallian influence. Pigou, in turn, reacted so strongly in defence of his 'Master' that he was unable to do justice to Keynes's contributions until after Keynes's death (Pigou, 1950, pp. 64–6). Indeed, the whole history of Cambridge economics in this century is a collectors' item for connoisseurs of the sociology of the social sciences.

By temperament, as well as by intellectual interest, Marshall was almost ideally suited to the role assigned him by providence and the Cambridge electors. Dignified, reserved, lofty, self-restrained, moderate in expression, learned but modest, he was equipped to exploit whatever advantages of prestige and authority attached to a chair at an ancient British university. His catholicity of outlook and his combination of analytical originality and insight with respect for historical evidence exerted a wide appeal; and the Marshallian synthesis was so generous and so broadly based that it afforded a platform on which moderate exponents of widely differing methodological persuasions could form a coalition against any outsiders who questioned the value of their contributions. Advanced students were attracted by his theoretical originality, for his writings and lectures contained enough novelty to suggest that economics possessed considerable potentialities for development. On the other hand, his awareness of the limitations of pure theory and his insistence on the importance of using non-technical language whenever possible were calculated to appeal to laymen, especially businessmen, for whom he had a high regard; while his emphasis on the merits of the economics of yesteryear endeared him to conservatives. Moreover, as Talcott Parsons brilliantly demonstrated,[7] Marshall shared the value assumptions commonly held by educated middle- and upper-class Victorians whose sons formed the bulk of his Cambridge audiences; and although his sociological assumptions, like his ethical preconceptions (which proved so irritating to Schumpeter and other continental readers), may be irrelevant to his technical economics and could usually be taken or left according to the reader's individual taste, they directly enhanced his effectiveness as the leader of a sociological group. Order and synthesis were badly needed, and Marshall's skill in applying new technical tools to the analysis of traditional problems in a traditional setting may well have appealed to certain deep-rooted traits in the British (or Anglo-Saxon, as he would have termed it) character. No serious student could ignore his repeated injunctions enjoining respect for the authority of the past, and as T. W. Hutchison has shrewdly observed, he became 'the great father figure of English economics, firmly upholding the virtue of respect for one's elders and betters in the family of economists. After the middle eighties there were in England patently no betters than Marshall himself, and, of course, as time passed, fewer and fewer comparable elders' (Hutchison, 1953, pp. 63–4).

As a leader, Marshall lacked the charismatic qualities of his Oxford contemporaries, Arnold Toynbee and T. H. Green, who won the hearts as well as the minds of a generation of undergraduates. He was more like Benjamin Jowett, the master of Balliol during Marshall's brief Fellowship, who influenced his career, and possibly his outlook, more than has usually been recognized. Jowett was tremendously influential, but Leslie Stephen despised him 'for being all things to all men and for commending "a good sort of roguery" which consists in never saying a word against anybody however they much deserve it' (Annan, 1951, pp. 138, 136–8). As an economist, Marshall certainly tried to be 'all things to all men', sometimes finding merit in most unlikely places; and he publicly appealed to his fellow economists to interpret each other's writings in the best possible sense – a suggestion that tended to inhibit certain types of criticism. Perhaps this was etiquette (or group solidarity) rather than 'roguery', for he himself made outspoken comments on his contemporaries in private (Seligman, 1930, p. 343); but, like Jowett, he may also have been something of an intellectual coward and a snob, for he intensely disliked controversy and was extremely sensitive to criticism, while ready to defer to 'the prejudices of those whom he wished to persuade', especially if they were, like Jowett, 'representatives of cultivated opinion'. As he admitted to the American economist, Richard T. Ely, 'our etiquette does not allow anyone to praise his own work, or even to claim originality, on penalty of being judged an offender against our rather artificial canons of reticence'; and this explains why he disapproved of Jevons' claims, why there are no 'labels of salesmanship' in the *Principles*, and why his 'references to the question of priority are extremely reserved' (Coats, 1961, pp. 193–4; Pigou, 1925, pp. 66–7).

By stressing deference to authority and respect for tradition, Marshall was, in effect if not in intention, reinforcing his own position, since he personified these qualities. 'Continuity of tradition [he once wrote] is important everywhere; it is nowhere more important than in our use of terms; while in our use of terms it is even more important as regards the *tone* or *flavour* which they connote, than as regards the boundaries marked out by their formal definition' (Marshall, 1898, p. 43); and the sociological significance of this distinction has not been fully appreciated. The Cambridge 'oral' tradition, which has been considered 'quite unique in the history of economics' (Seligman, 1963, p. 457), arose partly because Marshall's ideas were familiar in Cambridge long before they were published; and this inside knowledge contributed to his associates' sense of privilege and superiority. But, in addition, indoctrination into the subtle connotations of economic terms played an integral role in the training of Cambridge novitiates, and this could hardly be acquired except by personal contact with the fount of knowledge. Marshallian terminology was full of pitfalls for the uninitiated, for it was designed to combine the linguistic precision required by the expert with the comprehensibility demanded by the layman; and in evolving 'the Cambridge didactic style' (Fouraker, 1958), Marshallian economics invited exegesis by pupils and admirers who could explain what the master really meant. As Michael Polanyi has convincingly argued (Polanyi, 1958, chaps. iv. and v), scientific training calls for the acquisition of semi-intuitive skills of 'tacit knowledge' and 'connoisseurship' as well as more conventionally explicit kinds of understanding; and in Cambridge economics this applied, not merely to the connotation of terms, but also to the use of partial equilibrium analysis, the successful application of which depends on the analyst's skill in distinguishing relevant from irrelevant variables and in knowing how far to pursue the implications of a given problem (Briefs, 1960, pp. 13–17). Yet another feature of the Cambridge school was a distinctive mode of reasoning which Wassily Leontief once called 'implicit theorizing', a practice that led him to conclude that when Cambridge economists were accused of errors they were liable to defend themselves by adopting subtle shifts of meaning or by employing illegitimate modes of argument (Leontief, 1937).

Limitations of space preclude undertaking a detailed examination of these contentions; the present discussion merely seeks to amplify Marshall's claim that 'Cambridge has an idea of its own which asserts itself in spite of the partially non-Cambridge idiosyncrasies of one or two members of the staff. . . . The guiding principle of those Cambridge men who are . . . in my view the most truly Cambridge men . . . [is] the search for the One in the Many and the Many in the One' (Marshall to W. A. S. Hewins, October 12, 1899 [Hewins Papers]).

This is surely vague enough, even semi-mystical; nor is it significantly elucidated by quoting Marshall's dictum that 'the Mecca of the economist lies in economic biology rather than economic dynamics' (Marshall, 1920, p. xiv). However, 'biology' is a more organic concept than 'dynamics', one that calls for more intuitive understanding than the mechanistic logic of mathematical economics (for example, Walrasian general equilibrium analysis); and in this respect as in others, Marshallian economics possessed important semi-intuitive, extra-logical attributes that tended to limit its accessibility to others.

This is not to imply that Marshall deliberately set out to create a doctrinal 'school', for, curiously enough, he lacked some of the usual qualities of leadership, such as initiative, energy, assertiveness, ruthlessness, and organizing ability. He was loath to claim originality for his ideas, accustomed to employing the language of understatement, inordinately slow in publishing his findings, unwilling to assume offices of dignity – even when they were thrust upon him, excessively sensitive to the opinions of others, diffident when appearing before public bodies, reluctant to participate in public controversy, unwilling to edit or assume any responsibility for the

Economic Journal, and perennially anxious to be left alone to complete his 'magnum opus'.

It could indeed be said that he led British economics from the rear; but he nevertheless employed a number of subtle and indirect methods of exerting his influence, and occasionally, though perhaps rarely, used a more direct approach.[8] As Maynard Keynes recorded in his brilliant obituary essay (Keynes, 1963), Marshall exaggerated his own frailty and ill health; and his well-known sensitivity to criticism and distaste for controversy must surely have discouraged adverse comment and moderated disagreements on the part of his friends, pupils, and colleagues. Marshall consistently advocated intellectual freedom and toleration of heresy and dissent, but his desire for harmony among the economists represented a kind of protective device that helped to reduce opposition to his own ideas. He warned off hasty critics by letting it be known that he never published anything before giving it prolonged and profound consideration, and the innumerable modifications he made to successive editions of the *Principles* reveal his anxiety to meet every legitimate criticism, however minor. Marshall evidently inculcated a strong sense of loyalty in his pupils and associates, and in one remarkable instance he virtually accused F. Y. Edgeworth of treachery because the latter had published a criticism without consulting the author.[9] On one of the rare occasions when he replied to an attack, it was because he feared that a false impression of his own and Cambridge economics might be created by his antagonist, the economic historian William Cunningham, who, as a Cambridge man and a former pupil, appeared to speak with the authority of an insider.[10]

Yet, although Marshall enjoyed certain advantages at Cambridge, it is easy to underestimate the academic obstacles confronting him. Soon after his appointment to the chair he declared that political economy was 'the only subject of which the unsystematic study in the University exceeds the systematic, the only one which finds a great portion of the ablest and most diligent students among those who are preparing for, or have graduated in, Triposes in which it is not represented. I want to supply an Examination which, by offering public recognition of thorough work, will help to steady and systematize this unsystematic study' (Marshall, 1885–6).

As it transpired, it took him eighteen years to achieve his objective, with the inauguration of the economics tripos in 1903, and progress was so painfully slow because economic study did not and could not lead the way to a career as long as the existing conservative educational tradition persisted. 'Given the number of our students,' Marshall wrote to Neville Keynes in 1894, 'I think we make the most of them; because we encourage specialized inductive study only after and not before the B.A. degree' (Marshall to Keynes, June 10, 1894 [Marshall Papers]); but this was obviously inferior to a situation in which there was an undergraduate degree designed for economic specialists. In a later letter, written during the negotiations for the economics tripos, Marshall complained that although the moral sciences tripos had attracted postgraduate students from other universities there had been none of those 'fresh strong beautiful youthful minds that used to come'. The students taking history without economics were far superior to those taking moral science fresh from school, and he concluded that 'the oppression and suppression of economics by the incubus of Moral Sciences seems to me at once so cruel and so great a national evil that I should be a traitor to my trust if I allowed my personal regard for Keynes and others to prevent me from appealing to the judgment of the impartial University for redress' (Marshall to Foxwell, February 14, 1902 [Marshall Papers]).

Until the economics tripos was launched, Marshall recruited economists chiefly by attracting men from other disciplines, and in this way he secured such valuable catches as A. C. Pigou – his chief disciple and successor in the chair – from moral philosophy, and J. H. Clapham from history.[11] Nevertheless, the process was sometimes profoundly discouraging, as he feared that the 'empirical treatment' of economics would displace the 'scientific and analytical' treatment and believed that he and Neville Keynes were the only middle-aged English economists who were 'perfectly loyal' to the latter approach. (He discounted Edgeworth, who was 'so extreme'.)

> Put yourself in my position, I am an old man. For many reasons I wish I were out of harness now. I have no time to wait. Economics is drifting under the control of people like Sidney Webb and Arthur Chamberlain. And all the while, through causes for which no one is in the main responsible, *the curriculum to which I am officially attached has not provided me with **one single** high class man devoting himself* to economics during the sixteen years of my Professorship.
>
> I do not want to say so in public because I do not want to reflect on Edgeworth, but it is a fact that the crop of economists whom I got out of Oxford in a single year – Price, Harrison, and Gonner – is better than those whom I have got out of the Moral Sciences Curriculum proper in the last sixteen years. In fact McTaggart is the only first class man whom I have caught; and him I have only half caught.[12]

This outburst was unusually pessimistic; but the task of putting Cambridge economics on a sound footing must have been exhausting and time consuming; and had he been working in an academic environment more conducive to specialized teaching and research, Marshall might well have completed the additional volumes of the *Principles* which his contemporaries so eagerly awaited. His references to Webb and Chamberlain reveal his fears of competition from the London School of Economics (recently incorporated into the University of London) and the new School of Commerce at the University of Birmingham, headed by W. J. Ashley; and in general it seems that an effective Cambridge 'school' of economics did not emerge until the tripos was launched. This helps to explain why Marshall apparently canvassed so energetically for Pigou's election as his successor in 1908, for if the appointment had gone to either of Pigou's two principal rivals – Foxwell (aged 58, in contrast to Pigou's 30) and Ashley (aged 48) – the emphasis of Cambridge economics would have shifted more decisively in favour of those dynamic, statistical, and empirical studies which Marshall himself once described as the principal task of future generations (Pigou, 1925, p. 301; Hutchison, 1953, p. 22, n. 1). Yet analytical economics would doubtlessly have suffered for the sake of applied economics and economic history, and it seems ironic that the Cambridge 'school' eventually became identified with a species of theoretical reasoning that Marshall himself considered to be of secondary importance. Pigou undoubtedly did much to insure that Marshallian concepts, techniques of analysis, and problems dominated Cambridge economics until the appearance of Keynes's *General Theory*; and he was largely responsible for its somewhat introverted quality, especially the preoccupation with the elaboration and refinement of a given corpus of theoretical knowledge and the critical exegesis of Marshall's *Principles*. Foxwell or Ashley, on the other hand, would have received powerful support from Clapham, whose dissatisfaction with the narrowness and unrealism of Cambridge economics (Clapham, 1922) was in some respects more faithful to Marshall's spirit than the theoretical economics of Pigou and the later Cambridge 'school'.

III

The backward condition of British academic economics outside Cambridge constitutes one of the principal reasons why Marshallian economics appears, in retrospect, to have been so dominant at the turn of the century. Given the hierarchical character of British higher education, Oxford was the only conceivable base for an effective alternative to the Cambridge 'school' – at least until the London School of Economics was founded in 1895 (see below). Broadly speaking, the obstacles to serious economic study at Oxford were similar to those at Cambridge; but the climate of Oxford opinion favoured genteel culture and character formation rather than intellectual discipline, and the bias in favour of teaching and against specialization and research was greater, and the progress of science and other modern subjects was even slower, than at Cambridge. Marshall seems to have made a deep impression on those who attended his lectures at Oxford during his Balliol Fellowship, but during the 1880s many Oxford undergraduates came under the spell of Arnold Toynbee and T. H. Green, who emphasized citizenship and the moral aspects of social reform rather than the need for intellectual discipline. Though Green was 'not altogether free . . . of orthodox political economy', Toynbee roundly denounced the

113

Ricardian tradition and seemed to give general support to the vehement mid-Victorian criticisms of classical economics derived from Carlyle and Ruskin (cf. Toynbee, 1884, p. 1; Price, 1887; Richter, 1964, p. 77). Oxford economics lacked an effective intellectual leader, for the professor of political economy from 1868 to 1888 was Bonamy Price, a genial nonentity who denied that economics was a science and asserted that it was merely a practical, common-sense subject employing rule-of-thumb methods and enunciating familiar truisms (Price, 1878, pp. 15–16). Price's views tended to reinforce the complacent maxims emphasized by such inexpert tutors as Benjamin Jowett (cf. Symonds, 1925, p. 90; Theobald, 1935, p. 40; Faber, 1957), and the situation was little improved by Price's successor, the economic historian J. E. Thorold Rogers, who was a contentious individual, an active free-trade propagandist and politician as well as a scholar, and a caustic critic of classical economics and Oxford education in general. At the Political Economy Club's Wealth of Nations centennial dinner, Rogers denounced the scandalous 'monopoly' of teaching at Oxford (Political Economy Club, 1876, p. 35), and he undoubtedly stimulated Oxford critics of 'orthodox' political economy, some of whom, like W. J. Ashley, W. A. S. Hewins, and J. A. Hobson, subsequently became influential. But Rogers offered no viable alternative, for his own theories were derived from Ricardo and Mill, and his opinions were too vituperative and too idiosyncratic an amalgam of sense and nonsense to equip him for leadership of any doctrinal school.

Thus in the 1880s and early 1890s economic opinion at Oxford was decidedly hostile to theory and was dominated by idealistic philosophy and ethical social reform sentiment; and the character of one of its principal groups can be seen in the pages of the *Economic Review*, a journal sponsored by the Oxford branch of the Christian Social Union. Its first issue appeared only a few weeks before the *Economic Journal* was launched by the British Economic Association, and the two were necessarily rivals, since their subject matter, and hence their potential readership, overlapped to a substantial extent.[13] Some contemporaries doubtlessly regarded them as organs of two hostile factions or movements of economic thought; but this interpretation will not stand close analysis, if only because the *Journal* was not simply a Cambridge publication, and its editors made strenuous efforts (at least initially) to 'represent all schools of economic opinion'. Nevertheless, the *Economic Review* is significant, for its contents reveal how miscellaneous were the opinions arrayed against the methods, theories, and policies associated with classical and neo-classical economics. It reflects both the state of economic opinion at Oxford and the absence of any coherent, theoretically systematic alternative to the Marshallian approach.

With the appointment of F. Y. Edgeworth as Rogers' successor in 1891 things might conceivably have changed, for he was a brilliant economist who provided a necessary corrective to the predominantly anti-theoretical, ethical, and empirical climate of Oxford opinion. But Edgeworth was too far ahead of his contemporaries to exert much immediate influence, despite his originality. He was an outstanding exponent of the more refined species of mathematical economics and statistics, but the predominantly non-mathematical audiences at his lectures found them esoteric and difficult to follow. He wrote numerous abstruse papers which were of interest mainly to specialists, but no magisterial text; and despite his potentially strategic position as editor of the *Economic Journal* – a task which he performed with due impartiality – he gave comparatively little space to continental and American theories, thereby reinforcing the prevailing insularity of neoclassical economics. Methodologically orthodox, apart from his advocacy of mathematical analysis – which won few disciples – he was a protégé and fervent admirer of Marshall, and like his mentor he possessed a 'reverence for authority'.[14] Moreover, he was temperamentally unfitted to exercise active leadership, for he was personally somewhat eccentric and unworldly, indifferent to administration – if not positively inefficient – and unsympathetic toward contemporary radical and heterodox ideas; and Oxford economics is said to have languished during his tenure of the chair (Price, 1946, chap. iii, pp. 33–7).

Of course, any such judgement is necessarily subjective; but it demands serious consideration, since it was confirmed by one of Edgeworth's principal colleagues, L. L. Price, a middle-of-the-road man whose outlook illustrates the dangers of generalizing about Oxford economics. A favourite pupil of Marshall, who invited him, together with Neville Keynes, to read the first edition of the *Principles* in manuscript, Price was no uncritical admirer, though he wrote a highly favourable review in the *Economic Journal*. He sympathized with the anti-Marshallian elements in the writings of his fellow economic historians Cunningham and Ashley, and, like them and Foxwell, he was a prominent supporter of Chamberlain against Marshall and the orthodox free-trade view during the heated tariff reform debate of 1903.[15] Price's many reviews of works on economic theory reveal the practical and empirical cast of his mind; but though a moderate dissenter, he made no effort to form an alternative or rival doctrinal school. On the contrary, he formed a bridge between orthodoxy and heterodoxy, criticizing Ashley's new commerce curriculum at Birmingham because it overemphasized facts and underemphasized economic theory; and, significantly, it was he rather than Edgeworth who took the lead in agitating for an independent degree course at Oxford similar to the Cambridge economics tripos (Price, 1946, chap. iii, pp. 34, 47; Price, 1902; Price, 1908). But though some success was achieved, Oxford economics lacked a central core, a focus of interest, and a sense of unity and direction; and its impact on the development of British economics in this period is of interest mainly because Oxford men made disproportionate contributions to the success of Cambridge's chief rival, the London School of Economics (LSE).

115

IV

When Sidney Webb launched the LSE in 1895, with funds which had been donated for the propagation of Fabian socialism, he set out to encourage a type of economic instruction distinct from that provided elsewhere, though something other than a diet of socialist economics. F. A. Hayek admirably summarized the aims of the new institution in reporting:

> If Webb and Hewins [the first director] were guided by any one conviction it was mainly that the theoretical and individualist economics of Ricardo and Mill had kept their dominant position far too long and that it was time to give other schools a chance. They therefore drew largely on all the different opposition movements, however much these might differ among themselves. Politics entered no more than through Webb's conviction that a careful study of the facts ought to lead most sensible people to socialism; but he took great care to select the staff from all shades of political opinion, more anxious to bring promising men under the influence of the new institution than to have it dominated by any one kind of outlook. Although there may have been some justification for Alfred Marshall's reputed comment that the lecture list was determined more by the sort of people who were available than by educational considerations, it was hardly more so than was inevitable in an experimental new institution; and the best answer to Marshall's criticism is, perhaps, that the school was from the beginning designed to provide, not a general course for young beginners, but an introduction to independent research work for maturer people with some knowledge of the world [Hayek, 1946, p. 5; Hewins, 1929, vol. I, chap. v; Drake and Cole, 1948, pp. 84–95; Beveridge, 1960; Caine, 1963].

The choice of Hewins as head of the LSE is significant, for he was a non-socialist Oxford graduate and an outspoken critic of economic orthodoxy who had read some economics books before he went to the university and had 'disliked their theoretical outlook, their materialism leavened with sentiment and their remoteness from real events'. These views, so typical of the popular attitude toward political economy in the 1880s, were reinforced by his undergraduate studies, and he determined to 'substitute for, or at any rate to supplement, the theoretical system based upon an analysis of motives and the philosophy underlying orthodox economics. . . . Thorold Rogers discouraged me and told his experience at Oxford. He said it was impossible for me to make any headway against the economic views which were clearly established, and that if I tried to do so I should simply ruin my career' (Hewins, 1929, I, 15, 19, 20). At that time Rogers was in the wilderness, having not yet been re-elected to the Oxford political economy professorship which he had held prior to 1868, when he failed to secure re-election because of opposition to his liberal radical views (Rogers, 1888, p. ix; cf. Ashley, 1889). Hewins was not deterred by this advice and proposed to reorganize the teaching of economics by working through the University Extension movement, many of whose lecturers shared his distaste for classical economics; but despite his energy and optimism, and the sympathetic response of a number of young deviants and heretics who attended his Social Science Club at Oxford, including the founders of the *Economic Review*, Hewins failed to win much support; and his experience suggests that Oxford, the home of lost causes, was unlikely to become the home of a new doctrinal 'school' of economics.

Hoping for better things in London, Hewins applied for the Tooke Chair of Economics and Statistics at King's College in 1891, when Edgeworth moved to Oxford; but although his application was unsuccessful – he was only twenty-six – his elaborate scheme, designed to make the college the metropolitan centre of economic training, formed the basis of his later plans for the LSE (Hewins, 1929, I, 23–6). There were, however, certain peculiar problems apart from the usual financial constraints, for if the school was too one-sided, its scholarly reputation and effectiveness would be impaired; whereas if it was too impartial, ardent Fabians might complain that the initial endowment was being misapplied. Even before the school opened, G. B. Shaw complained to Beatrice Webb of the temporary suspension of Sidney's wits, insisting,

> First Hewins must be told flatly that he must, in talking to the Guild of St. Matthew and the other Oxford Socialists, speak as a Collectivist, and make it clear that the School of Economics will have a collective bias. Any pretence about having no bias at all, about 'pure' or 'abstract' research, or the like evasions and unrealities must be kept for the enemy. . . . Third, the collectivist flag must be waved, and the Marseillaise played if necessary in order to attract fresh bequests. If the enemy complains it must be told that the School has important endowments the conditions of which are specifically Socialist [Caine, 1963, p. 44; Cole, 1961, p. 71].

Nevertheless, Sidney was unmoved, for he wished to secure funds from a variety of sources and realized the need to avoid arousing any suspicion that academic freedom was being impaired. On the other hand, he and Hewins can hardly have been indifferent to the views of those they appointed; and it seems likely that if two men of roughly equal ability and qualifications were available, one of whom was an orthodox Cambridge economist, the other would have been appointed. The early list of economics lectures contains the names of disproportionately few Cambridge men; and the only prominent ones were Foxwell and Cunningham, both of whom were by this time decidedly critical of Marshallian economics.[16] On the other hand, the principal positions were occupied by Oxford men, especially

Edwin Cannan, who was responsible for the economic theory teaching during the school's first three decades.

Cannan may well have been selected because he was thought to be heterodox, for one of his early writings appeared under Fabian auspices (Robbins, 1931–40, p. 142). Nevertheless, his case illustrates Webb's and Hewins's difficulties, and sheds further light on the absence of serious doctrinal competition with Cambridge, for he turned out to be a good deal less unorthodox than appeared at first sight. An Oxford contemporary of Hewins and an able economic theorist, he was a penetrating and caustic critic of Marshallian economics, but he was a deviant rather than a radical opponent of economic orthodoxy. His relations with Cambridge economics were delightfully depicted by the economic historian, C. R. Fay, one of Marshall's later favourites, who took graduate work in London. Cannan kept Fay supplied with a regular stream of postcards referring to errors in Marshall's *Principles*, and on one occasion wrote, 'You Cambridge people will never be intelligible until you stop gibbering about consumer's surplus. I was horrified to hear you do it the other day. What is it? M[arshall] never says what it is but just starts talking about it.'[17] Cannan's persistent irreverence toward Cambridge is suggested by Fay's recollection that after he had proposed to his colleagues on the Cambridge History Board that a paper on social economics should be substituted for an existing paper on 'potted Marshall and sugared sticks of Hartley Withers', Cannan warned him to 'walk henceforth in a suit of chain plate and hire a private foodtaster'; and Fay confessed that under Cannan's influence his attitude toward Cambridge economics had 'swayed between veneration and minor revolt' during his first six years of teaching.[18]

Cannan was an incisive nonconformist rather than an outright rebel, and though he was an important source of informed theoretical criticism of Marshall at a time when such criticism was in short supply, it is misleading to claim him as an outrider of the 'institutionalist' movement, though his ideas bear some resemblances to that peculiarly American heterodoxy (Ayres, 1960, p. 55; cf. Cannan, 1934; and Boulding, 1957, p. 3). Although (as Lionel Robbins recalls) 'he sometimes made jokes at Marshall's expense when he was lecturing . . . his respect for Marshall was tremendous and woe betide the student who had not read the *Principles* and completely assimilated the main points'.[19] While fearlessly expressing severe independent appraisals of the work of his fellow economists, he was nevertheless 'determined to keep the field against the uninitiated', as is apparent from his complaints about the 'marginal men' who contributed to the *Economic Review*.

My dear Fay,
    Can't somebody be put up to slaughter J. S. Smith for writing such bosh in the *Economic Review*. I can't do it because I slaughtered A. J.

Carlyle, too, a short time ago – the knife still reeks. Carlyle has said very little ever since. It is quite true that the part of Marshall that Smith attacks is very bad, but that's no reason for not making an example of another of these outsiders. . . .

John Carter has written again to Pigou asking him to take the thing in hand, but as I say in my forthcoming work, you can't expect the Astronomer Royal to answer every crank who says the earth is flat. He might, however, put somebody on – an undergraduate by preference.[20]

V

Cannan's curt dismissal of Smith and Carlyle as 'outsiders' reminds us that although economics was gaining recognition as a distinct academic specialism in the early years of this century many, possibly most, college and university teachers of the subject were amateurs or part-timers, and whatever the disagreements among the leading experts and spokesmen for various 'schools' of economic thought, they demonstrated a growing sense of professional consciousness and solidarity as they strove to emancipate themselves from their dependence on moral philosophy and history, the two subjects with which political economy had hitherto been most closely associated. In 1894 an authoritative subcommittee of Section F of the British Association for the Advancement of Science reported on the urgent need to develop adequate training facilities in economics (British Association, 1894), and this undoubtedly stimulated efforts to establish independent degree courses in the leading academic centres. But degrees meant examinations, and examinations can function as devices for enforcing intellectual conformity as well as assessing academic ability; and as the establishment of independent degree courses roughly coincided with the rise of the Cambridge 'school' of economics, it is worth considering the influence of these new developments.

It would, of course, be easy to exaggerate the effects of the examination system, either by echoing the cries of 'monopoly' uttered by extremists like Thorold Rogers and Henry Dunning MacLeod, or by citing the unfortunate experiences of exceptional men like Jevons and Maynard Keynes, both of whom (probably rightly) thought that they knew more than their examiners (Political Economy Club, 1876; MacLeod, 1892; Harrod, 1951, p. 121; Keynes, 1963, pp. 292–3). On the other hand, the system clearly worked in favour of established or traditional views and against the interests of innovators like Hewins and Webb, and in this respect their opinions were supported by Cannan, who wrote in 1912: 'There were in 1902 no teachers who were not hampered by traditional standards and there are none now. This is partly due to the ordinary examination system, which checks progress by making teachers afraid to teach anything new because the examiners will not examine in it, and makes the examiners afraid to ask anything new because the teachers will not have taught it.' At the LSE, he continued, the teachers were at first entirely free from examinations, whereas later they became members of a university which adopted for its 'internal' side the principle that examiners should examine on what has been taught, in place of the old principle or practice that teachers should teach what is likely to be 'asked' (Cannan, 1912, p. 23).

On the whole, the examination system in economics was a centripetal force tending to counteract the effects of the disintegration of classical dogma, a process which might otherwise have proved destructive at a time when provincial centres of academic economics were growing. In Britain the ancient universities' influence (in this case, mainly Cambridge) was extended by dispatching eager young missionaries into the provincial back-woods, and sustained by the practice of appointing 'external' examiners, for, as a qualified American observer noted:

> it is essentially an 'internal' examination, in the sense that its scope, spirit, and technique are perfectly understood from college to college and from one university to another. . . . The universities of Oxford and Cambridge have for generations fixed the standards of English scholarship. Their teachers continue the tradition that they estab-lished as students and apply the same standards as those by which they rose to their own positions. The intellectual life both there and in other institutions largely modelled upon them is homogeneous and highly schooled in similar conceptions and measures of excellence. Its representatives tend, therefore, to agree in fundamental matters much as they do in their characteristic manner of speech, and a student is ultimately judged not by the individuals with whom he is in actual contact, but by a cloud of witnesses speaking through them [Learned, 1925, pp. 93–4].

As Sir Ernest Barker once remarked, the British examination system served as a partial substitute for the scholarly society, a species of organization that performed a much more important role in the USA, where the com-munity of scholars was much larger, more widely dispersed, more hetero-geneous in its ideals and standards, and more susceptible to anti-intellectual attacks from the general public (Barker, 1953, p. 103; Metzger, 1955, esp. chap. iv; Hofstadter, 1964). Even in Britain, however, there is at least one instance in which the authority of a Cambridge examiner in economics was appealed to by a professor whose career was in jeopardy because of his radical economic and social ideas (Coats, 1963, p. 129).

Apart from the examination system, a doctrinal 'school' can extend its sway by influencing academic appointments, and during our period a large miscellaneous body of 'outsiders' believed, whether rightly or wrongly, that academic economics was dominated by a self-perpetuating clique of 'orthodox' professors. This belief was more strongly held in the 1870s and 1880s than later, and it forms part of what W. S. Jevons termed the 'noxious influence of authority' (Jevons, 1871 [ed. 1911], pp. 275–6) exercised on behalf of 'the Mill–Ricardo tradition', a tradition that Marshall stoutly defended. In a discipline whose leading practitioners were engaged in a severe and painful process of critical self-examination, one in which, moreover, there were no generally accepted criteria of competence, such opposition was potentially disruptive. Up to the mid-1890s the most remarkable and consistently unsuccessful outsider was Henry Dunning MacLeod, an arrogant, opinionated man whom Schumpeter described as 'an economist of many merits who somehow failed to achieve recognition, or even to be taken seriously, owing to his inability to put his many good ideas into a professionally acceptable form' (Schumpeter, 1954, p. 1115). A Cambridge University statute enabled MacLeod to claim the right to be registered as a lecturer in political economy, but his academic career progressed no further, though certainly not for want of trying, since he made at least nine unsuccessful applications for chairs. The civil service commissioners rejected his repeated demand that his works on money and credit be included in their lists of recommended reading, and eventually desperation drove him to question the competence and impugn the motives of the professors of economics who had so long denied him his rights; and he eventually challenged the civil service commissioners to consult a higher court 'because Economics being essentially a Juridicial Science, I will submit to no arbitrament but that of the judges of England'.[21]

Another outsider whose credentials were rejected by university economists was J. A. Hobson, a far less eccentric and belligerent individual than MacLeod. Hobson was refused permission to teach economics as a London University Extension lecturer apparently because Edgeworth considered that *The Physiology of Industry* afforded proof of his incompetence in economic theory.[22] He was allowed to teach subjects other than economics, but he never obtained a full university post – nor, apparently, did he ever seek one. Nevertheless, the incident is curious, not only because Maynard Keynes in the *General Theory* subsequently elevated Hobson to the exalted company of his neglected predecessors (a not uncommon occurrence in the history of science), but also because Edgeworth had expressed doubts about the value of tests of economic orthodoxy when the qualifications for membership in the British Economic Association were under discussion (British Economic Association, 1891, p. 10).

Turning from the unsuccessful outsiders to those who obtained professorial appointments in economics, it is unfortunately impossible to assess the shifting combination of academic and lay influences at work, for virtually nothing is known of the proceedings of appointments committees. Marshall undoubtedly had a voice in most appointments in England (and possibly in Britain and the Commonwealth too) during his quarter-century as professor at Cambridge, but he appears to have made little effort to exploit his potentially commanding position. As previously noted, he was reluctant to speak ill of his fellow economists and was neither opinionated nor irresponsible. Had he wished, he could no doubt have ruined the chances of any candidate he strongly opposed, and certainly Ashley at Oxford in 1888 and William Smart at Glasgow in 1896 feared that Marshall would 'run' one of his own candidates.[23] In the event, the elections went to Thorold Rogers and Smart, respectively, neither of whom could be regarded as a Marshallian; and when the Birmingham chair of commerce was filled in 1900, Ashley, the successful contender, was delighted by Marshall's testimonial, despite the fact that his chief rival was Foxwell, Marshall's (admittedly somewhat contentious) Cambridge colleague (Ashley, 1932, p. 94 n.; Foxwell to Seligman, January 6, 1902, in Seligman Papers).

In the most important case of all, the election of his successor at Cambridge, Marshall apparently campaigned energetically on behalf of his protégé, Pigou, and the outcome undoubtedly served to confirm the suspicions of those who held that (apart from Birmingham) support for free trade was an essential qualification for a professorial appointment.[24]

Although some of Marshall's pupils seem to have been unduly deferential to his ideas[25] and perhaps to his wishes, British academic economics was far from monolithic, whatever the more naive 'outsiders' believed. The range of opinion was certainly narrow as compared with the USA, but it was significantly broader than in France; and despite the close network of personal relations among the leading economists, there is no evidence of any deliberate pressure toward intellectual conformity.[26]

VI

Up to this point attention has been focused on the obstacles and discouragements encountered by the late nineteenth-century academic economists, but it is nevertheless true that the leadership in economic thought was gradually passing into their hands during the early decades of the twentieth century.[27] Despite his comparatively low estimate of the intellectual and practical value of economic theory, W. J. Ashley rightly advised his Harvard students, in 1892, to acquire 'a considerable familiarity' with that body of knowledge 'because theoretical political economy is still so strong in the support of most teachers in England and America that it would be hardly fair to set a man against the current especially if his professional prospects as a teacher were at all involved' (Ashley, 1893, p. 4).

Fifteen years later, as dean of commerce at the new University of Birmingham, Ashley was still confidently pronouncing the obsequies of the old orthodoxy over a corpse that stubbornly refused to lie down; yet he acknowledged that economics was 'beginning to furnish a career' as a result of the creation of new university chairs, graduate schools, and scholarly journals. He was more than usually sensitive to 'the dangers of academic life', for he had a vested interest in strengthening the links between the university and the business community; but most academic economists would have endorsed his warm appreciation of the services of writers who, like 'Mr. Seebohm, Mr. [Charles] Booth, Mr. Rowntree, Mr. Palgrave, Mr. Webb, Mr. Hobson, Mr. [Chiozza] Money, Mr. Welsford . . . [were] unhampered by the duties of the professional teacher' (Ashley, 1907, p. 243).

But while the future lay with the academic economists, there was no sharp dividing line between the experts and the laymen, and it was still possible in the 1900s for an outstanding monetary theorist like Ralph Hawtrey to make his first serious contact with political economy at a 'crammers', while preparing for the civil service examinations after his Cambridge mathematics degree (Eshag, 1963; Guillebaud, 1964, p. 475). Moreover, members of the older 'pre-professional' generations still occupied prominent and powerful positions and were accorded a respectful hearing by the general public, whereas the academics were, more often than not, either ignored, dismissed as irrelevant, or attacked as presumptuous upstarts – as, for example, when the so-called fourteen professors had their knuckles sharply rapped for writing to the *Times* in 1903 expressing their disapproval, both on theoretical and on practical grounds, of Joseph Chamberlain's tariff reform proposals (see n. 15 above). The Prime Minister himself, A. J. Balfour, in his capacity as vice-president of the Royal Economic Society, warned the assembled economists at the society's annual dinner in 1904 that unless they were more careful in the future they would forfeit their 'scientific' reputations and be regarded as mere propagandists (Balfour, 1904, p. 350).

The trouble was that, as economics became recognized as a distinct intellectual expertise, its practitioners stressed the analytical and technical aspects of the subject; but its growing abstractness and complexity made it seem both less relevant to current affairs and less intelligible to the layman. As one historian has acutely observed, 'the "science" did not gain enough prestige to make the public willing to accept the recommendations of economists *without* understanding the analyses behind them' (Taylor, 1960, p. 327).

During the 1890s and early 1900s, the problem of the economists' relations with the public attracted far more attention at the annual meetings of the British Economic Association (later the Royal Economic Society) than discussions of the proper training and qualifications of economists, largely because full-time academics constituted but a small minority of the organization's six or seven hundred members, and one of its aims was to restore some of the prestige the subject had lost since the mid-nineteenth century. But while it was generally agreed that the bona fide economist enjoyed less respect and exerted less influence than was his due, there was no consensus of opinion as to the best method of rectifying this situation. Nor, as might have been expected, was there any clear-cut division of opinion between the academic and non-academic spokesmen (British Economic Association, 1891; cf. n. 13 above), a point which suggests that the gap between the two groups had not yet become very marked, though it was undeniably growing. On the whole, the British economists' organization was more casual, more informal, and less effectively organized for either scholarly or propaganda purposes than its American counterpart, for the American economists, generally speaking, were both intellectually and professionally less secure than their British colleagues. In the USA, genuine academic freedom had never been the rule, and economists were the principal victims of public attack in the 1890s and early 1900s, and, in self-defence, they developed a more active professional *esprit de corps* than would otherwise have arisen in a country of such vast extent with so heterogeneous an educational system. By contrast, a British academic economist enjoyed virtually complete freedom of expression and security of tenure once he had obtained a permanent college or university post, and the typical reaction to incidents, such as the public investigation of Richard T. Ely's opinions at the University of Wisconsin in 1894, was one of astonishment and outrage, coupled with the complacent thought that 'it couldn't happen here'.[28]

VII

Yet although the British economists were enjoying some improvement in their 'professional situation' early in this century, and displaying some sense of professional self-consciousness, they could hardly claim more than semi- or quasi-professional status. There were still no acknowledged standards of technical competence in economics, no uniform provisions for the training of apprentices, no standardized examinations or qualifications supervised by a recognized qualifying body, no codes of professional ethics, and no identifiable professional functions. Hence there was no unambiguous method of distinguishing fully qualified practitioners from those whose claims rested solely on practical experience or native wit (cf. Millerson, 1964, chap. i).

When the question of membership qualifications arose in the early days of the British Economic Association it was quietly shelved, partly because no acceptable criteria could be devised, but also because the founder-members feared that any attempt to be selective would invite accusations that they were being exclusive or sectarian, thereby weakening both their scientific and their public influence. In this situation, any attempt to identify the 'economists' as a social or professional group becomes exceedingly difficult, if not unrealistic; but it is nevertheless worth trying to classify the main 'groups' of contributors to British economic thought during our period, if only to provide some corrective to the usual practice of concentrating on a comparatively limited number of academics.

Since the vast majority of economic writers came from middle-class origins, and accepted middle-class social and intellectual values, and held middle-of-the-road political views, neither social nor ideological criteria of classification offer much help.[29] Even the primary distinction between academics and non-academics is somewhat difficult to apply in practice – for instance, with government officials like James Bonar and Henry Higgs, whose writings and leisure activities were distinctly academic; and ardent politicians (or statesmen) like Leonard Courtney, who had been professor of political economy at University College, London. Among the academics, even important members of the Cambridge 'school' like Sidgwick and Neville Keynes were not merely economists; and while it would be appropriate to include such Cambridge men as A. C. Pigou, D. H. Robertson, F. Lavington, and Maynard Keynes within the 'school', that category should be extended to embrace E. C. K. Gonner (Marshall's Oxford protégé); S. J. Chapman; the statistician, A. L. Bowley; the economic historian, J. H. Clapham; and possibly the mathematician-economists, A. Berry and H. Cunynghame. Naturally, it is difficult to draw the boundaries of a 'school', a phenomenon which includes 'zones of influence' and 'fringe ends' as well as a central core of disciples. Hence J. S. Nicholson of Edinburgh, though unquestionably 'orthodox', a Cambridge graduate, and an admirer of Marshall, was by no means a disciple; like C. F. Bastable of Dublin, he might more accurately be termed a Millian than a Marshallian; while Foxwell, Marshall's closest and oldest colleague, can best be regarded as a fringe member.

There was no 'school' of London economists, partly because the metropolitan teaching of economics was for long weak and decentralized, and partly because Edgeworth, Foxwell, and Cannan each lacked either the desire or the necessary qualities of leadership. The anti-doctrinaire features of the LSE reinforced this tendency, and the nearest thing to an academic 'group' was the London (originally the Junior) Economic Club, founded by Foxwell's students at University College, London (Collet, 1936, 1940), and consisting largely of empirically minded civil servants like H. Higgs, C. Collet, David Schloss (trained at Oxford), and G. Armitage Smith (later principal of Birkbeck College).

Outside the academic walls, the notion of an 'economist' becomes even more difficult to define, for some economic writers merely displayed their ignorance, while others who published little or nothing both understood the subject and exerted a direct and important influence on economic affairs. The range of competence involved can be indicated by mentioning, at one extreme, the Spencerian philosopher, J. B. Crozier, who wrote extensively and displayed all the psychological traits of an 'outsider' (Crozier, 1906, 1908); and at the other, the brilliant theorist, cleric, and Dante scholar, P. H. Wicksteed; while the lawyer and would-be professor, H. D. MacLeod, came somewhere in the middle. Another discernible, though not easily definable, group were the Fabians, G. B. Shaw, S. Webb, S. Olivier, and H. W. Macrosty, several of whom had close personal relations with the academics (McBriar, 1962, chap. ii). And finally we must take account of the non-academic members of the Political Economy Club and the British Association, some of whom have serious claims to attention, such as the Chancellors of the Exchequer Viscount Goschen and Sir Michael Hicks-Beach; public servants like Sir Robert Giffen, Sir Francis Mowat, and Lord Farrer; bankers like Sir R. H. Inglis Palgrave and J. B. Martin; and merchants like Sir Leo Chiozza Money.

Needless to say, such a list falls far short of a systematic social survey of the 'economics' profession (but cf. Stigler, 1965, pp. 31–50). Nevertheless it reveals the limitations of more conventional histories of economics which tend to concentrate on the stars rather than the supporting players; and it suggests that if we are to assess the influence of men like Marshall, we cannot afford to ignore the cranks, quacks, outsiders, and marginal men, who sometimes exert an important influence on the development of economic theory, and who, like the journalists and popularizers, play a vital role in the propagation of economic ideas. Beyond a certain point, analysis of the social composition and structure of the economics 'profession' must yield diminishing returns; but it may confidently be asserted that that point is still some way off.

NOTES

1 Cf. Hutchison (1953), pp. 62, 74, 70: 'for some time *theoretical* economics in England consisted very largely of discussion and interpretation, often textual, of Marshall's *Principles* . . . and the search for Marshall's hidden assumptions occupied a whole generation.' Also Schumpeter (1954), p. 829ff.

2 Schumpeter (1954), p. 47. Elsewhere he spoke of the Ricardians as a 'genuine school in our sense: there was one master, one doctrine, personal coherence; there was a core; there were zones of influence; there were fringe ends' (ibid., p. 470). Cf. Hutchison (1953), pp. 11–12.

3 For some idea of the differences between Cambridge rationalism and Oxford idealism, compare Annan (1951) and Richter (1964). I am indebted to T. W. Hutchison for suggesting that this point be emphasized.

4 Harrod (1951), pp. 322–3. The basis of this sense of superiority may have been laid in Marshall's Inaugural (see Pigou, 1925, pp. 171, 173).

5 Speaking of the 'topic of what sort of a study economics is, and what it is all about', Robertson recalled: 'To us, I think, it seemed a topic more suitable for discussion by Germans than by Englishmen. There was on our reading-list what I have since come to regard as a good, if dry, book about it, J. N. Keynes's *Scope and Method of Political Economy*, but to be quite honest I doubt if many of us read it. We thought we knew pretty well what sort of things we wanted to know about, and were glad enough to take the counsel given by Marshall himself near the beginning of the *Principles*, "the less we concern ourselves with

scholastic enquiries as to whether a certain consideration comes within the scope of economics the better" ' (Robertson, 1951, pp. 111–12). For curious parallels between British economics and historical studies, see Walsh (1962), p. 51.

6 In his inaugural lecture, delivered in the safe retreat of Cape Town, H. M. Robertson recalled how Keynes 'sailed into me' after a paper delivered at the Cambridge Political Economy Club in 1927, 'accusing me, indeed, of foolhardiness, if not of something almost akin to poor taste, because in Marshall's own University I had disparaged some of Marshall's leading ideas and commended the heretic Hobson in the same breath. . . . All the same, when I consider the almost revolutionary influence of Keynes after 1936 . . . I confess I find a certain piquancy in his later *volte face* upon Marshall and Hobson' (Robertson, 1950, pp. 6, 8).

7 Parsons emphasized Marshall's reliance upon a mid-Victorian ideal of character that led him to suppose that 'the whole process of social evolution leads to the production of the English businessman and artisan', adding that whatever the propriety and validity of this idea the question was 'whether such subjective ethical convictions should be allowed to colour the whole perspective of the past and present tendencies of social development. . . . The complete disregard of most other things which it entails is hardly compatible with the ideal of scientific objectivity' (Parsons, 1932, p. 335; also see Parsons, 1931; 1964, chap iv; Weisskopf, 1955; Annan, 1959, p. 13).

8 For example, when D. H. Macgregor, one of Marshall's pupils, confided to Edwin Cannan on December 22, 1908: 'Now about [consumer's] surplus. I have always been a bit discontented. In the first draft of my article I suggested we should drop both surplus and margin as confusing. . . . But (this is in confidence) Marshall was furious, and I got a good talking to. So I kept marginal, and thinned it down, as my paper shows. I have yet the whole question of surplus *sub judice* just now. Students cannot be got to understand it, though they pretend they do. My hesitation is due to the fact that I know how careful M. is before he puts anything in print.' Macgregor, then professor of economics at the University of Leeds, had published his article in the *Economic Journal* (1908).

9 'What I want to say is that I do not think you at all appreciate the deadly and enduring injury that A does to B if he reads rapidly a piece of hard argument on which B has spent an immense deal of work; and then believing that argument to be wrong, writes an article full of the most polite phrases, in which a caricature of that argument is held up to the most refined but deadly scorn. I fancy you think that the polite phrases diminish the mischief. Really it is that they cause the most harm. Their effect, though *certainly* not their intention, is that of a white flag under which the ship approaches close to another and rams or torpedoes it' (Marshall to Edgeworth, April 4, 1891 [Marshall Papers]). On Edgeworth, see part III below.

10 Marshall (1892), p. 518. Personal feelings were also involved, for on his return to Cambridge in 1885, Marshall had objected to Cunningham teaching economics. According to Cunningham's daughter, Edgeworth refused to print Cunningham's rejoinder in the *Economic Journal*, so he published letters in the *Academy* and the *Pall Mall Gazette* instead (Cunningham, 1950, pp. 64–6).

11 Marshall declined Lord Acton's invitation to contribute to the *Cambridge Modern History*, proposing Clapham instead, saying 'he has more analytic faculty than any other thorough historian that I have ever taught; his future work is still uncertain; a little force would I think turn him this way or that. If you could

turn him towards XVIII and XIX century economic history, economists would ever be grateful to you; and I am sure you would have no cause for regret' (Marshall to Acton, November 13, 1897 [Marshall Papers]). Despite Marshall's prescience, Acton had a much lower opinion of Clapham's potentialities and preferred W. A. S. Hewins.

12 Marshall to J. N. Keynes, January 30, 1902 (copy in Marshall Papers). For Sidney Webb (and the London School of Economics) and the views of L. L. Price, see parts III and IV below. (Sir) E. C. K. Gonner became lecturer (1888–91) and then professor of economic science at the University of Liverpool. F. C. Harrison (Balliol, 1882–4) joined the Indian Civil Service and wrote numerous articles in the *Economic Journal*. J. E. McTaggart turned to philosophy.

13 For an account of these matters, see Coats (1968*b*). Reprinted *infra* pp. 313–17.

14 See J. M. Keynes's *Economic Journal* obituary essay on Edgeworth, reprinted in Keynes (1963), especially pp. 236, 224. It may be significant that Edgeworth's interest in economics was first aroused by Jowett.

15 See Price (1946), chap. iii, p. 14. On this episode, see Coats (1968*a*). Reprinted in vol. I in this series.

16 Despite Shaw's above quoted letter to Beatrice Webb, it now appears that she was more anti-propagandist than her husband (Cole, 1961, p. 71). Sidney Webb subsequently explained that W. Acworth, the railway expert, and Cunningham had been deliberately chosen 'to counteract Marshall' (Hayek, 1946, p. 5). Other Cambridge 'economists' among the early lecturers were C. P. Sanger, who appeared only in a minor role, and A. L. Bowley, the statistician, who was far more important. Hewins's hopes are indicated in a letter to Webb of September 22, 1898 (Beveridge, 1960, p. 38): 'You may be gratified to know, if you don't know it already, that in Germany you and Mrs. Webb are held in the highest estimation of all English writers on economics. Marshall is nowhere. His book is not considered intrinsically important, and even amongst those who might be expected to agree with him his ideas are not considered original. Schmoller is very keen about the School, and we seem to be getting firm hold on the younger men. I think that the transference of the "centre of force" in economics from Germany to London is by no means impossible.' For Beatrice Webb's collectivist hopes, see Drake and Cole (1948), p. 145.

17 Cannan to Fay, December 17, 1908 (Cannan Papers). As late as 1931 Cannan described an exchange between J. M. Keynes and D. H. Robertson on saving as 'more like two Roman augurs disputing about the significance of the entrails of a goose' (Fay, 1937, p. 10). A longer manuscript version of this memoir is in the Cannan Papers.

18 Fay (1937), pp. 3–4. By contrast, F. Lavington showed true piety in response to Cannan's corrections: ' "Surely you don't contend that there's a mistake in Marshall's *Principles*", Lavington would say. For the thought to him was blasphemy unbelievable' (ibid., p. 4). Cf. the description of Lavington as 'unconditionally Marshallian' in Schumpeter, 1954, p. 1084.

19 Quoted (by permission) from a private letter from Lord Robbins, dated March 9, 1964. Fay's reminiscences confirm this point: ' "I'll show up Marshall before I've done" said the man who lectured on him more faithfully and fully than any other; and how we at Cambridge chuckled when to him succeeded two such exemplary Marshallians as Allyn Young and Lionel Robbins' (Fay, 1937, p. 9).

20 Cannan to Fay, October 28, 1913 (Fay, 1937, p. 11, with reference to Smith, 1913). Like Cannan, who continued to live in Oxford while holding his professorship in London, Carlyle (University College), Smith (Balliol), and Carter

(Exeter) were members of the Oxford Political Economy Club. Carlyle and Carter were clergymen and members of the group that published the *Economic Review* (see above). Curiously, the young 'executioner' chosen to dispatch Smith was P. Sargant Florence, who subsequently came under the influence of the American 'institutionalist', Wesley C. Mitchell (Florence, 1914; cf. Boulding, 1957).

21 MacLeod (1892), p. 12. He recommended the appointment of a Royal Commission to investigate the situation whereby 'Professors of Economics are appointed by the Board of Electors not one of whom ever gave the slightest proof of their capacity to judge on the subject. These Electors openly and avowedly pay not the slightest attention to the merits or the capacity of the Candidates, nor of the Testimonials they produce in their favour. When persons are thrust into Professorships of Economics in the Universities, not by an examination of their capacity, nobody is responsible for what they teach, and no human being pays the smallest heed to what they say.' See also MacLeod (1884), p. 11.

22 Hobson (1938), p. 30; Hutchison (1953), pp. 118–19. Hobson was also refused permission to give extension lectures on economics for Oxford and Birmingham (Harvey, 1942, p. 96).

23 Ashley to Richard T. Ely, February 2, 1888 (Ely Papers). Smart wrote for letters of support from several leading American economists, some of whom knew little of him or his work, in an effort to strengthen his claims. He not only feared Marshallian influence but also knew that his support for bimetallism and his sympathy toward trade unions made him suspect among Glasgow businessmen. In the event, although L. L. Price was a rival candidate, he was delighted by Marshall's testimonial. See Smart to Cannan, May 14, June 4, and June 26, 1896 (Cannan Papers).

24 See the sources referred to in n. 15 above. There is some evidence to justify the view that the professoriat was virtually unanimous in support of free trade, though Leo Amery exaggerated in saying 'It has been as easy in my lifetime for a professed protectionist to be appointed to an economics chair in this country as for an earnest Protestant to be elevated to the Cardinalate' (Amery, 1953, p. 52).

25 For example, Smart to Ely, December 28, 1895, in Ely Papers: 'I wish it were in my power to teach with a free hand as you do. But I am somewhat suspect in this great commercial centre. I must follow Marshall. And, indeed, I find that there is a great deal more in Marshall than meets the eye – perhaps more than he himself knows – and the time is not wasted in getting thoroughly into his mind. I wish, however, he were not so abominably cautious.'

T. S. Ashton recalls that as a student at Manchester under S. J. Chapman in 1908–10 'the word "orthodox" played a large part in our discussions. I am almost tempted to say we students were less concerned with whether an opinion was right or wrong than with whether or not it had the seal of Authority. Authority, to us, was Alfred Marshall.'

After citing one of several appeals to Marshall for guidance, he adds, 'We were concerned, above all, to be orthodox – at a time when there were few young economists about and very many ill informed critics. In my own case it led, I think, to undue respect for Authority and undue concern when my masters themselves seemed to go astray. Under Chapman we had been brought up as strong Free Traders, and had even been encouraged to lecture for the Free Trade Union. It was a shock when in 1932 Chapman became the chief architect of the new British tariff system' (quoted, by permission, from a private letter of September 10, 1966).

26 On the French situation, see Jaffé (1965). Any generalizations on the British situation must necessarily be tentative, but there seems to be a prima facie case for G. D. H. Cole's view that 'the main penalisation is not so much of those who have the jobs, as penalisation of those who are looking for them. Our older academicians and professional people and those who appoint to positions, are apt to choose candidates who do not look dangerous. . . . A good deal of the battle for academic freedom is actually lost before the appointments are made . . . to a substantial degree, the appearance of tranquility on the sea of English academic life is due to a very careful selection at the start' (see Cole, 1935, p. 14).

27 One indication is that the proportion of full-time academics among the officers and council members of the British Economic Association rose from 35 per cent in 1891 to 45 per cent in 1903 and 50 per cent in 1920.

28 The histories of the English civic universities contain many references to 'friction' between the teaching staff and non-academic members of the governing body, or the local community; but the evidence is usually unsatisfactory (however, cf. Coats, 1963). For the American situation, see Dorfman (1949), Coats (1960), and Metzger (1955).

29 I am indebted to Dr Royden Harrison for the warning that a more thorough analysis might lead to a modification of this statement. See Coats (1973) for an analysis of the RES membership.

REFERENCES

Amery, L. *My Political Life*. Vol. I. London: Hutchinson & Co., 1953.

Annan, N. *Leslie Stephen, His Thought and Character in Relation to His Time*. London: MacGibbon & Kee, 1951.

———. *The Curious Strength of Positivism in England*. London, 1959.

Ashley, A. *William James Ashley, a Life*. London: P. S. King & Son, 1932.

Ashley, W. J. 'James E. Thorold Rogers', *Polit. Sci. Q.*, IV (1889), 381–407.

———. 'On the Study of Economic History', *Q.J.E.*, VII (January, 1893), 115–36.

———. 'The Present Position of Political Economy in England', British Assoc. for the Advancement of Sci. (1907). Reprinted as 'A Survey of the Past History and Present Position of Political Economy', in R. L. Smyth (ed.). *Essays in Economic Method, Selected Papers Read to Section F of the B.A.A.S., 1860–1913*. London: Gerald Duckworth & Co., 1962, pp. 223–46.

Ayres, C. 'Institutionalism and Economic Development', *Southwest Soc. Sci. Q.*, XLI (June, 1960), 45–62.

Balfour, A. J. 'Speech at Annual Dinner', *Econ. J.*, XIV (September, 1904), 351–4.

Barker, E. *Age and Youth*. London: Oxford Univ. Press, 1953.

Beveridge, J. *An Epic of Clare Market, Birth and Early Days of the London School of Economics*. London: G. Bell & Sons, 1960.

Boulding, K. 'A New Look at Institutionalism', *A.E.R.*, XLVII (May, 1957), 1–12.

Briefs, H. W. *Three Views of Method in Economics*. Washington, D. C.: Georgetown Univ. Press, 1960.

British Association for the Advancement of Science. 'The Methods of Economic Training Adopted in This and Other Countries' (1894), pp. 365–91.

British Economic Association. 'Report of the Proceedings at the Inaugural Meeting', *Econ. J.*, I (March, 1891), 2–14.

Caine, Sir S. *The History of the Foundation of the London School of Economics and Political Science.* London: G. Bell & Sons, 1963.

Cannan, E. *The Economic Outlook.* London: T. Fisher Unwin, 1912.

——. 'Capital and the Heritage of Improvement', *Economica*, N. S., I (November, 1934), 381–92.

——. 'Papers', in British Library of Polit. and Econ. Sci., London School of Econ.

Clapham, J. H. 'Of Empty Economic Boxes', *Econ. J.*, XXXII (September, 1922), 305–14.

Coats, A. W. 'The Historist Reaction in English Political Economy, 1870–90', *Economica*, N. S., XXI (May, 1954), 143–53. Reprinted in vol. I in this series.

——. 'The Influence of Veblen's Methodology', *J. P. E.*, LXII (December, 1954), 529–37. Reprinted in vol. III in this series.

——. 'The First Two Decades of the American Economic Association', *A. E. R.*, L (September, 1960), 555–74. Reprinted in this volume, pp. 205–24.

——. 'Alfred Marshall and Richard T. Ely: Some Unpublished Letters', *Economica*, N. S., XXVIII (May, 1961), 191–4. Reprinted in vol. I in this series.

——. 'John Elliotson Symes, Henry George, and Academic Freedom in Nottingham during the 1880s', *Renaissance and Modern Studies*, VII (1963), 110–38. Reprinted in vol. I in this series.

——. 'Political Economy and the Tariff Reform Campaign of 1903', *J. Law and Econ.* (April, 1968), 181–229. (*a*). Reprinted in vol. I in this series.

——. 'The Origins and Early Development of the Royal Economic Society', *Econ. J.* LXXVIII (June, 1968), 349–71. (*b*). Reprinted in this volume, pp. 313–37.

——. 'The Changing Social Composition of the Royal Economic Society 1890–1960 and the Professionalization of British Economics', *Br. J. Soc.*, 24 (June, 1973), 165–87. Reprinted in this volume, pp. 338–60.

Cole, G. D. H. Report, in *Conference on Academic Freedom.* Oxford: W. Heffer & Sons, 1935.

Cole, M. *The Story of Fabian Socialism*, London: Heinemann, 1961.

Collet, C. 'Professor Foxwell and University College', *Econ. J.*, XLVI (December, 1936), 614–19.

——. 'Henry Higgs' (obituary), *Econ. J.*, L (December, 1940), 558–61.

Crozier, J. *The Wheel of Wealth, Being a Reconstruction of the Science and Art of Political Economy on the Lines of Modern Evolution.* London: Longmans, Green & Co., 1906.

——. *My Inner Life: Being a Chapter in Personal Evolution and Autobiography*, 2 vols. London: Longmans, Green & Co., 1908.

Cunningham, A. *William Cunningham.* London: SPCK, 1950.

Cunningham, W. 'The Perversion of Economic History', *Econ. J.*, XII (1892), 491–506.

Dorfmann, Joseph. *The Economic Mind in American Civilization*, vol. III: *1865–1918.* New York: Viking Press, 1949.

Drake, B. and Cole, M. I. (eds.). *Our Partnership, by Beatrice Webb.* London: Longmans, Green & Co., 1948.

Ely, R. T. 'Papers', in Wis. State Hist. Soc., Madison.

Eshag, E. *From Marshall to Keynes, an Essay in the Monetary Theory of the Cambridge School.* Oxford: Blackwell, 1963.

Faber, Sir G. *Jowett, a Portrait with Background.* London: Faber & Faber, 1957.

Fay, C. R. 'Edwin Cannan, the Tribute of a Friend', *Econ. Rev.*, XIII (June, 1937), 1–21.

Fisher, H. A. L. *Frederick William Maitland, a Biographical Sketch.* Cambridge: Cambridge Univ. Press, 1910.

Florence, P. S. 'Professor Smith and Dr Marshall', *Econ. Rev.*, XXIV (April, 1914), 170–85.

Fouraker, L. A. 'The Cambridge Didactic Style', *J. P. E.*, LXVI (February, 1958), 65–73.

Foxwell, H. S. 'The Economic Movement in England', *Q. J. E.*, II (October, 1887), 84–103.

Guillebaud, C. W. Review of Eshag, 'From Marshall to Keynes', *Econ. J.*, LXXIV (December, 1964), 475.

Harrod, R. F. *The Life of John Maynard Keynes.* London: Macmillan & Co., 1951.

Harvey, J. W. (ed.). *John Henry Muirhead. Reflections by a Journeyman in Philosophy on the Movements of Thought and Practice in His Time.* London: George Allen & Unwin, 1942.

Hayek, F. A. 'The London School of Economics, 1895–1945', *Economica*, N. S., XIII (February, 1946), 1–31.

Hewins, W. A. S. *The Apologia of an Imperialist.* 2 vols. London: Constable & Co., 1929.

——. 'Papers', in University of Sheffield, Library.

Hobson, J. A. *Confessions of an Economic Heretic.* London: George Allen & Unwin, 1938.

Hofstadter, R. *Anti-Intellectualism in American Life.* London: Jonathan Cape Ltd., 1964.

Hutchison, T. W. *A Review of Economic Doctrines, 1870–1929.* Oxford: Clarendon Press, 1953.

Jaffé, W. *Correspondence of Léon Walras and Related Papers.* 3 vols. Amsterdam: North-Holland Publishing Co., 1965.

Jevons, W. S. *The Theory of Political Economy.* London: Macmillan & Co., 1871 (ed. 1911).

Keynes, J. M. 'Herbert Somerton Foxwell' (obituary), *Econ. J.*, XLVI (December, 1936), 589–614.

——. *Essays in Biography.* New York: W. W. Norton & Co., 1963.

Learned, W. S. *The Quality of the Educational Process in the United States and in Europe.* New York: Carnegie Found., 1925.

Leontief, W. 'Implicit Theorizing: A Methodological Criticism of the Neo-Cambridge School', *Q. J. E.*, LI (February, 1937), 337–51.

McBriar, A. M. *Fabian Socialism and English Politics, 1884–1918.* Cambridge: Cambridge Univ. Press, 1962.

Macgregor, D. H. 'Earnings and Surpluses', *Econ. J.*, XVIII (December, 1908), 532–40.

MacLeod, H. D. *An Address to the Board of Electors to the Professorship of Political Economy in the University of Cambridge.* London: 1884.

——. *An Address to the Civil Service Commissioners on the Teaching of Economics in the Public Service.* London: 1892.

Marshall, A. 'Letter to the Vice Chancellor', *Cambridge Univ. Reporter* (1885–6), p. 579.

——. 'A Reply', *Econ. J.*, II (September, 1892), 507–19.

——. 'Distribution and Exchange', *Econ. J.*, VIII (March, 1898), 37–59.

——. *Principles of Economics.* 8th ed. London: Macmillan & Co., 1920.

——. 'Papers', in Marshall Library, Cambridge Univ.

Metzger, W. P. *Academic Freedom in the Age of the University.* New York: Columbia Univ. Press, 1955.

Millerson, G. *The Qualifying Associations, a Study in Professionalization.* London: Routledge & Kegan Paul, 1964.

Parsons, T. 'Wants and Activities in Marshall', *Q. J. E.*, XLVI (November, 1931), 101–40.

——. 'Economics and Sociology: Marshall in Relation to the Thought of His Time', *Q. J. E.*, XLVI (February, 1932), pp. 316–47.

——. *The Structure of Social Action.* 2d ed. New York: Free Press, 1964.

Pigou, A. C. (ed.). *Memories of Alfred Marshall.* London: Macmillan & Co., 1925.

——. *Keynes's 'General Theory', a Retrospective View.* London: Macmillan & Co., 1950.

Polanyi, M. *Personal Knowledge: Towards a Post-critical Philosophy.* Chicago: Univ. of Chicago Press, 1958.

Political Economy Club. *Revised Report of the Proceedings at the Dinner of 31st May 1876.* London: Longmans, 1876.

Price, B. *Chapters on Practical Political Economy.* London: Kegan Paul, 1878.

Price, L. L. *Industrial Peace, Its Advantages, Methods and Difficulties.* London: Macmillan Co., 1887.

——. *The Present Position of Economic Study in Oxford: A Letter to the Vice Chancellor of the University.* Oxford: Published privately, 1902.

——. *Position and Prospects of the Study of Economic History.* Oxford: Clarendon Press, 1908.

——. 'Memoirs and Notes on British Economists, 1881–1946'. Manuscript, Brotherton Library, Univ. of Leeds, 1946.

Richter, M. *The Politics of Conscience, T. H. Green and His Age.* London: Weidenfeld & Nicolson, 1964.

Robbins, L. 'Edwin Cannan', *Dictionary of National Biography, 1931–40.* New York: Oxford Univ. Press, pp. 141–3.

Robertson, D. H. 'Utility and All That', *Manchester School*, XIX (May, 1951), 111–42.

Robertson, H. M. *The Adam Smith Tradition.* (Inaugural lecture delivered before Univ. of Cape Town on October 13, 1950.) Cape Town: Oxford Univ. Press, 1950.

Rogers, J. E. T. *The Economic Interpretation of History.* London: T. F. Unwin, 1888.

Schumpeter, J. A. *History of Economic Analysis.* New York: Oxford Univ. Press, 1954.

Seligman, B. B. *Main Currents in Economics, Economic Thought since 1870.* New York: Free Press, 1963.

Seligman, E. R. A. 'Pareto and Pantaleoni: Personal Reminiscences of Two Italian Economists', *Polit. Sci. Q.*, XLV (September, 1930), 341–6.

——. 'Papers', in Columbia Univ. Library, New York.

Smith, J. A. 'On Some Fundamental Notions of Economics', *Econ. Rev.*, XXIII (October, 1913), 366–81.

Stigler, G. J. 'Statistical Studies in the History of Economic Thought', *Essays in the History of Economics.* Chicago: Chicago Univ. Press, 1965.

Symonds, M. *Out of the Past.* London: John Murray Ltd., 1925.

Taylor, O. H. *A History of Economic Thought.* New York: McGraw-Hill Book Co., 1960.

Theobald, Sir H. S. *Remembrance of Things Past.* Oxford: Blackwell, 1935.

Toynbee, A. *Lectures on the Industrial Revolution.* London: Longmans, Green & Co., 1884.

Walsh, W. H. 'History and Theory', *Encounter*, CV (June, 1962), 50–4.

Weisskopf, W. A. *The Psychology of Economics.* Chicago: Univ. of Chicago Press, 1955.

8

THE CULTURE AND THE ECONOMISTS

Some reflections on Anglo-American differences*

INTRODUCTION

Specialization is an inescapable concomitant of modern scholarship. Yet as Jacob Viner once wisely observed: 'Men are not narrow in their intellectual interests by nature; it takes special and rigorous training to accomplish that end';[1] and equally strenuous efforts may occasionally be required if we are to break out from the constraints of our accustomed mental perspective. The following account may, of course, merely demonstrate the limitations of such exercises, since it is designed to present some familiar features of the development of economics in Britain (especially in England) and the USA against the background of the general intellectual culture in each country, of which the economist's professional subculture forms a part. The purpose is not, I must insist, to advocate any form of cultural determinism, and I shall resist the temptation to employ an anthropological apparatus of the kind utilized in Axel Leijonhufvud's brilliant spoof article, 'Life among the Econ',[2] which focuses on the present state of mature (or perhaps decadent) professionalism. Instead, I propose to consider the evolution in economics of what Burton Bledstein has termed 'the culture of professionalism',[3] that is, the 'set of learned values and habitual responses' which includes both 'the set of internal values and pressures of the discipline', to cite George Stigler's well-known remark,[4] and the exogenous influences at work upon the academic community.

It is a textbook commonplace that from about the time of the 'marginal revolution' the leadership in economic science (i.e. theory or analysis) gradually passed from laymen to academics, and were the term not so barbarous it would be more accurate to speak of the 'academicization' of economics rather than its professionalization. Yet the discipline has rarely for long been an autonomous, self-contained intellectual activity, and academic communities are seldom entirely insulated from societal influences. Indeed, as is said to be the case with governments, nations usually get the universities they deserve, and on both sides of the Atlantic the development of higher education has both reflected and reacted upon the general cultural and socio-economic environment. The resources, structures, and objectives of higher education have helped to shape – though not exclusively to determine – the rate of expansion, the focus, and in varying degrees the content of academic disciplines, especially in the social sciences. Of course, the precise manner and degree to which academic economists have responded to extramural pressures and inducements has varied over time, and is itself a valid subject for historical investigation. Even in the post-1945 phase of vigorous academic growth and increasing professional autonomy and self-consciousness, exogenous influences have continued to be important.[5] The 'problematic' (to use a currently fashionable term) has been decisively shaped by an awareness of such broad issues as the obstacles to economic development in low-income countries, the social and economic impact of technological change, and the need for appropriate policies to achieve economic growth and stability in an increasingly interdependent world. Of course, these considerations have had less impact on the central corpus of economic theory than on what economists actually 'do' (to recall Viner's familiar definition of 'economics'). Nevertheless, the remarkable expansion of professional economists' employment opportunities in business and government, which often involves a movement of personnel back and forth between academic and non-academic life, makes it increasingly inappropriate to confine the professional or scientific part of economics to that practised in the academic community. Some revision of our conventional perspective is therefore unavoidable.

Since World War II there has been a marked trend towards the internationalization of economic knowledge through the dissemination of textbooks, research publications, and official reports; through the increased mobility of graduate students and the proliferation of global jet-set contacts; and through the activities of economists employed by businesses, governments, and international agencies.[6] The Americans and Russians have played the leading part in this process which, politics apart, reflects the diffusion of modern 'technology' in the enlarged, if somewhat amorphous, sense employed by Clarence Ayres.[7] And it remains unclear whether in the emerging post-industrial global society significant differences in national styles and cultures will gradually diminish and even eventually disappear.[8]

Whatever the future may hold, there is ample evidence of differences of national styles in economics during the past century or so – in pure theory and techniques as well as in their practical applications;[9] and there is considerable scope for research into these matters. In attempting to explore certain congruences between national cultures and development patterns in economics one must perforce proceed on a high level of generalization; and within the confines of a single article it is impossible to provide more than a general structure of argument, which in this case is applied more thoroughly to the formative period than to more recent decades, supported

135

by a few, hopefully well-chosen, illustrations. Yet even where these illustrations are familiar they may acquire fresh significance when viewed in a broader, less familiar perspective.

THE HISTORY OF ECONOMICS AND THE SOCIOLOGY OF KNOWLEDGE

During the past decade or so economists have displayed a discernible, if still limited, growth of interest in the sociology of their discipline – especially in such relatively parochial matters as the reward system, and the role and significance of current doctrinal schools, invisible colleges, and other communications networks.[10] There has, however, been much less investigation of the historical antecedents of these phenomena, or the wider question of the economist's position as a professional intellectual in society, in terms of the social role of the man of knowledge, his relations with the laity, and the extramural market for economic expertise. As a result a number of valuable studies by non-economists have been unduly neglected, even by historians of economics.

Here, as on so many other matters, it is convenient to begin with Schumpeter's classic *History of Economic Analysis*, in which he wrote a quarter of a century ago:

> The professionals that devote themselves to scientific work in a particular field . . . tend to become a sociological group. This means that they have other things in common besides the interest in scientific work or in a particular science per se. . . . The group accepts or refuses to accept co-workers for reasons other than their professional competence or incompetence. In economics this group took long to mature but when it did mature it acquired much greater importance than it did in physics. . . . [In late-nineteenth-century England] the association of scientific work with teaching produced an economic profession in a fuller sense of the word and this profession developed attitudes to social and political questions that were similar also for reasons other than similar scientific views. This similarity of conditions of life and social location produced similar philosophies of life and similar value judgements about social phenomena.[11]

Schumpeter did not elaborate this theme or utilize it as a basis for international comparisons, although there are various allusions to these matters in his writings. Nevertheless his remarks provide a foundation from which to view the history of economics as the development of the interests and activities of a distinctive, though not closed, sociological group within the culture of modern (as contrasted with traditional) professionalism. But before exploring this possibility it is appropriate to make some preliminary comments on the important, but generally neglected relationship between methodology and professionalism in economics.[12]

This relationship helps to explain why so much time and effort has been devoted to methodological controversy in economics, despite the low esteem in which this activity is usually held. The underlying motives have, of course, been mixed – including the desire to defend or assert the superiority of a particular method, approach, doctrine, school, policy, or ideology. But there has also invariably been present, whether overtly or covertly, the desire to establish, maintain, or justify certain approved procedures or standards of professional practice, a matter of no small significance in a discipline whose practitioners have often been both divided among themselves and in the forefront of public discussion.

Methodological writings in economics have two distinct but interrelated dimensions – the cognitive and the regulative. The former has generally received more attention from historians of ideas, including such questions as: What is valid knowledge in economics? How is it attained? How can its validity be tested or established? What are its limitations, especially when it is applied to problem solving or policy making? From a regulative standpoint, however, somewhat different issues become central, such as these: How can correct standards of scientific or professional practice be established, taught, and maintained? How are knowledge-seeking processes most effectively organized and controlled? How is knowledge most efficiently accumulated, preserved, disseminated, and applied?

Wherever methodological controversy occurs, professional values and standards are involved, either explicitly or implicitly. Scientific and scholarly activity is never absolutely value-free. Its supreme end – the pursuit of truth – also entails the adoption of subordinate procedural ideals or rules, some of which are purely instrumental (such as freedom of inquiry and the quest for certainty, exactness, universality, and system), while others are primarily aesthetic. However, 'all formal rules of scientific procedure must prove ambiguous, for they will be interpreted quite differently according to the particular conceptions about the nature of things by which the scientist is guided'.[13] And as the scientist or scholar is never quite entirely immune from societal influences the choices he makes will necessarily involve value judgements, some of which will reflect his personal experience and predilections, while others will be derived from broader community norms and standards, including those of the scientific community in which he was trained, on which he depends for material and psychological support, and to which he resorts for approval of his performance.

Viewed against this background the sharp contrast between the persistence and intensity of methodological controversy in American economics (especially from the 1870s to the early 1930s, but also more recently) and its comparative absence from Britain since the early 1890s (apart from a brief flare-up in the 1930s), is clearly a matter of more than merely passing interest. It cannot be explained solely in terms of the endogenous development of science (for example in terms of 'stages of development'), nor simply by reference to the differences between American cosmopolitanism and British insularity.[14] This latter point takes us part of the way; but it is also necessary to go deeper in order to expose the underlying differences in national history, intellectual styles, and the culture of professionalism in the two countries.

THE CITADEL:[15] AUTHORITY AND INSULARITY IN ENGLISH ECONOMICS

Most historians of economics would agree that the intellectual foundations of the discipline were laid by the British classical economists, but it was not until the last two decades of the nineteenth century that the professionalization process manifested itself clearly on both sides of the Atlantic. There is much truth in the dictum that 'an industrializing society is a professionalizing society',[16] and it is appropriate to ask why the professionalization of economics came so late in Britain, given the fact that industrialization began so much earlier there than in the USA.

To provide an adequate answer to this question would take us too far afield, hence it is necessary to focus attention on a few essential factors. First and foremost is the geographical fact that Britain is a small island physically separate from the European mainland with a comparatively continuous and homogeneous political, social, and cultural life. Just as the British political power structure successfully absorbed the nineteenth- and early twentieth-century pressures for modernization and the extension of the suffrage in the first industrial nation without the need for radical change or revolution, so too did the system of higher education adapt itself slowly, and in retrospect remarkably painlessly, to the need for new categories of trained personnel. The rise of professionalism, both within the academic community and in society at large, represented an effort by new specialist groups to gain social status and market power, and there was a marked contrast between the assertive competitiveness manifested in the USA (to be discussed later) and the 'controlled selection' that occurred in Britain.[17]

Professionalization in the USA, both for the traditional professions (e.g. law, medicine, and the church) and for their modern counterparts (including the social sciences), was an important avenue to élite status and increased influence in an undeferential society lacking a clear-cut social stratification. In Britain, by contrast, where social differentiation was clear and well understood, the slowly expanding corps of academic professionals experienced a combination of co-option and segregation into an intellectual aristocracy, especially in the ancient universities of Oxford and Cambridge, which were gradually adapting themselves in a sometimes reluctant effort to reconcile the traditional values and vested interests of the established social and intellectual élite with the emergent class structure of industrial capitalism. Training for the newer professions, such as accounting, engineering, surveying, etc., was initially provided outside the university system, and the academic authorities were reluctant to acknowledge the need for formal training and qualifications even in such obvious academic disciplines as History, English, and the Natural Sciences. In many instances the lead was taken by dissenting institutions (like University College, London, with its powerful Benthamite utilitarian associations) or by the civic universities, which were emerging in the later Victorian period.[18] Leading figures in the newly developing social sciences at Oxford and Cambridge were fully aware of these trends and were anxious to carve out a place for their disciplines within the slowly expanding curriculum, but they faced many institutional obstacles, not the least of which was the entrenched opposition of their academic colleagues, the 'dons', who enjoyed an oligarchical control over university affairs.[19] Challenges to the status quo there inevitably were, and some successes for the new subjects can be recorded. But given the slow pace of change and the limited numbers involved prior to World War II, there was never a sufficient number of brash, thrustful new recruits to mount a successful campaign against the existing academic hegemony. Admittedly in economics, a subject which made painfully slow academic progress in the first three quarters of the nineteenth century despite its prominence in the public mind, there is evidence of substantial dissent from the ruling classical orthodoxy. This was true even at Oxford, but more especially in London – initially at University College and much later at the London School of Economics;[20] and eventually the organizational bases for systematic opposition emerged, with recruits both from élite institutions and from those with a more plebeian background and a more overtly vocational conception of professionalism.[21] Yet given these circumstances, it seems all the more significant that when the received economic doctrines were at last successfully challenged, in the 1930s, the initiative came not from the expected sources but from J. M. Keynes, an outstanding member of the dominant school, trained in the established doctrines, who was already 52 years old when he made his decisive public break with the past.

As is well known, Keynes rebelled against the intellectual constraints imposed by the Ricardian, or 'classical' orthodoxy, and wilfully distorted the past as a method of emphasizing the novelty of his own contributions.[22] But it is impossible to fully grasp the psychological and sociological impact of his 'revolution' – or 'war of independence', as Harry Johnson so aptly termed it[23] – without reference to the strength of the received tradition and the accepted standards of debate in British economics. At this point some drastic simplification is unavoidable, and it is appropriate to begin with Dennis Robertson's revealing reminiscence about 'methodology' – or, significantly, what he preferred to describe as the question of 'what sort of a subject economics is, and what it is about'. As he recalled:

> This is a topic, which, when I started to read economics at Cambridge in 1910, it was not, I think, fashionable among us to think much about. . . . To us, I think, it seemed a topic more suitable for discussion by Germans than by Englishmen. We thought we knew pretty well what sort of things we wanted to know about, and we were glad enough to take the counsel given by Marshall near the beginning of the *Principles*, 'the less we concern ourselves with scholastic enquiries as to whether a certain consideration comes within the scope of economics the better'.[24]

This passage seems characteristically British – even characteristically Edwardian – in its complacent self-assurance, insularity, and deference to authority; and it can be taken as a fairly typical reaction to the methodological controversies of the 1870s and 1880s, which led most British economists to accept the eclectic compromise embodied in Marshall's *Principles* and the provisions of the armistice laid down in John Neville Keynes' *Scope and Method of Political Economy*.[25] The fact that these two volumes appeared just about the time that the first open scholarly society for British economists was formed, and the first two scholarly periodicals appeared, helps to account for the subsequent professional consensus dominated by the Cambridge school.[26] Nevertheless, that dominance was too persistent and too effective to be regarded merely as a coincidence.

According to H. S. Foxwell, a mildly dissenting Cambridge colleague of Marshall's (who was addressing an American audience in 1887), 'after the appearance of Mill's *Principles* English economists, for a whole generation, were men of one book';[27] and it is tempting to extrapolate this statement by observing ' 'twas ever thus'. There has certainly been a discernible proclivity among English economists – distinctly less apparent among the Scots and Irish – to regard a single great economics work as paradigmatic, from Smith through Ricardo to Mill, Marshall, and J. M. Keynes. Up to the 1860s there were innumerable extraordinarily confident assertions about the perfection and authoritativeness of the classical doctrines, even from J. S. Mill, who was on many matters so open-minded.[28] There were, of course, dissenters, some of them very distinguished, like Jevons, who protested against 'the noxious influence of authority' in economics.[29] Nor was this an isolated outburst. Yet even Marshall, who was in many respects so cautious, seems to have believed, after the publication of his *magnum opus*,

> that the fundamental principles of the subject were now fixed beyond dispute, and that the next generation of economists would be free to concern themselves mainly with the application of these principles in

all the bewildering variety of institutions and practices of the real world.[30]

Doubtless Pigou, Marshall's successor and favourite pupil, exaggerated in referring to 'the Marshallian dictatorship',[31] and chance circumstances help to explain how, as Terence Hutchison once put it, Marshall became

> the great father figure of English economics, firmly upholding the virtue of respect for one's elders and betters in the family of economists. After the middle eighties there were in England patently no betters than Marshall himself, and, of course, as time passed, fewer and fewer comparable elders.[32]

It was the strength of the Marshallian tradition that induced Maynard Keynes, another 'favourite son', to exaggerate his own break with the past, an exaggeration strongly deprecated by some of his collaborators and disciples, and one that seriously distorted the subsequent development of the subject for several decades thereafter. But as Keynes himself put it, the *General Theory* represented 'a struggle to escape from habitual modes of thought and expression'[33] which had sociological and professional implications as well as psychological and intellectual significance.

Of course there is much more to the history of British economics than the classical and neoclassical tradition through and beyond Keynes and the Keynesians. But the continuity and influence of this mainstream seems especially significant when it is contrasted with the American situation.

Keynes' career, like that of Marshall and other leading figures, reveals that there was scope for innovation *within* the British tradition; and it is worth recalling the well-known 'principle of tenacity', according to which scientific progress would be impossible if its practitioners too readily abandoned their paradigm or theoretical base immediately it came under serious attack. This would be a recipe for chaos. Like a political community, a scientific community must avoid the extremes of anarchy and rigid authoritarianism. There must be an appropriate combination of pressures for conformity and opportunities for change. Most scientists are thoroughgoing constitutionalists, reformers not revolutionaries; consequently, while scientific 'revolutions' may be intellectually momentous affairs, from a social standpoint they generally prove to be pretty innocuous, since 'scientists have no stomach for disorder'.[34] But just as there are differences among national political cultures, so too there are differences among national scientific or professional cultures.

Keynes' career exemplifies, albeit in heightened form, certain enduring features of British academic life as epitomized in Cambridge economics, which has recently been penetratingly, even ruthlessly, exposed by the late Harry Johnson.[35] In the cosy, complacent, deferential, and highly personalized British academic environment, prestige readily filtered down from an acknowledged great man to his disciples. What Marshall called the 'Chinese element' discouraged unduly novel speculation and excessive claims to originality.[36] It was implicitly assumed that informal networks of communication would suffice because everyone in a given field already knew everyone else worth knowing. This personalization is evident (not only in economics) in the management of journals and scholarly societies[37] and in the crucial process of making academic appointments.

Aside from the immediate aftermath of each of the world wars, and a brief period in the 1960s when several new universities opened, academic mobility has been low or non-existent; rank and emoluments have depended more on fixed salary scales and promotion by seniority than inter-institutional competition; and with the emphasis on undergraduate teaching, structural rigidities built into the serial and relatively specialized curriculum, and hierarchical control of policy in comparatively small departments, the scope for significant innovation has been much more limited than in the USA. There have, admittedly, been signs of change since 1945 – the entry of a new generation of academics with more varied social and cultural backgrounds; occasional gusts of fresh air from visiting overseas scholars and British graduates trained abroad; the expansion and growing strength of the provincial universities; the development of formal post-graduate training; and in economics, the rise of the Association of University Teachers of Economics to challenge the conservative policies and leadership of the Royal Economic Society, and the proliferation of periodical rivals to the *Economic Journal*, which is no longer managed from Cambridge as it was throughout the interwar years. Nevertheless, the process of change has been less than revolutionary, and if one accepts the judgement of one informed, cynical, and internationally minded observer, the legacy of the past still casts a dark shadow over the current professional situation and prospects.[38]

THE CARAVAN: THE STRUGGLE TO PROFESSIONALIZE AMERICAN ECONOMICS

As in Britain, the growth of professional self-consciousness among late-nineteenth-century American social scientists was but one manifestation of the increasing specialization and division of labour among the educated classes. But there were important differences, both because the cultural context was different and because the sheer pace of change in the USA accentuated and dramatized a process that had been taking place over a much longer period and less disruptively in Europe, where generations of academic tradition and established institutional constraints had to be circumvented or broken down.

In the post Civil War 'revolution' in American higher education the new state universities and land-grant colleges were, naturally enough, much more subject to community pressures and susceptible to the public service ideal than the old-established liberal arts colleges and new private foundations; but these last two categories were by no means immune.

As society became secularized the older colleges gradually shed their denominational characteristics and a number of major new private universities were launched and soon appeared to be permeated by business standards and values, a state of affairs alarming to Veblen and other progressives.[39] During the late nineteenth and early twentieth centuries the spirit of academic entrepreneurship flourished as never before among presidents, administrators, and professors, and the ideals of productivity and efficiency emerged as the source of the now familiar requirement to publish or perish. Within the academic community there was a marked, though protracted, shift of emphasis from teaching to research – the former being primarily inward-looking and client-centred, whereas the latter was increasingly outward looking and discipline-oriented, addressing itself to a national or even an international community of scholars. The well-known dictum 'those who can, do; those who can't, teach' was re-translated to read 'those who can, do research (or perhaps consulting); those who can't, teach'; and a degree of stratification emerged among academics between 'pedagogues' and 'producers', or 'locals' and 'cosmopolitans' – to cite a more familiar recent dichotomy. The intensifying competition for status, recognition, and emoluments rapidly acquired intra- and inter-institutional, inter-regional, and sometimes even international dimensions.

These tendencies were not, of course, manifested simultaneously and evenly throughout academia. The liberal arts college was, generally speaking, more resistant to change than the professional, vocational, or graduate school. But even in the older foundations the extension of the elective system rapidly undermined the traditional curriculum which had centred on the classics, theology, and moral philosophy. Under the new dispensation the social sciences, especially economics, seemed both attractive and relevant. They soon gained a foothold in the new curriculum and were, in general, more subject to extramural inducements and threats than the humanities, natural sciences, and technology. It is therefore no coincidence that during the transitional late-nineteenth- and early-twentieth-century period the focus of academic freedom cases shifted from theological heresy to economic heresy.[40]

As the economists appreciated, when they concentrated on abstract deductive theories, the public and university trustees were uninterested, and correspondingly disinclined to intervene. But when they made public pronouncements about such controversial issues as the currency, tariffs, public utilities, the trusts, or labour unions, they were liable to offend some individual or vested interest. Unlike the members of Oxford and Cambridge colleges, which were closed, self-perpetuating corporations, they tended to be regarded as hired hands who could be dismissed if they undermined or did not 'advertise' their institution.

Under these circumstances the central dilemma facing the late-nineteenth-century American social scientist, one which was of much less concern to his European counterpart, was how to demonstrate the relevance of his knowledge to contemporary life without, at the same time, endangering his reputation for scientific detachment and objectivity and possibly risking dismissal from his academic post. Somewhat similar pressures were evident, in a muted form, in some of the newer British provincial universities in the Victorian era, but they rarely led to dismissals.[41] Although Richard Hofstadter has very properly cautioned that academic freedom cases constitute the pathology of academic life, a study of these incidents undoubtedly sheds light on the healthy body, as well as on disease.[42]

There is neither the time nor the need to examine these well-documented affairs in detail. But it is appropriate to mention, if only in passing, Mary Furner's splendid study entitled *Advocacy and Objectivity: A Crisis in the Professionalization of American Social Science, 1865–1905*, in which economics plays a central role. As she has observed, the new generation of social scientists was in an anomalous position:

> As professors, they depended for livelihood on sources of financial support which they did not control. As scholars, they conducted investigations and developed critical theories which could adversely affect the very interests that supported them. Thus they were caught in a situation that inevitably produced conflict. As professionals, they wanted to defend colleagues against community pressure. Yet they needed to place reasonable restraints on restless performers who persisted in undermining community support.[43]

It was on this basis that Richard T. Ely and other besieged academics argued the right, on the grounds of their professional competence and expertise, to advocate reforms as well as merely to investigate contemporary economic and social problems.

Gradually, after much debate, indecision, and no little anguish, there emerged the rudiments of a consensus about the limits of permissible advocacy. As a result, moderation tended to become equated with objectivity and scholarly merit, and this involved a trend away from radicalism to conservatism. It was, however, a movement towards *professional* rather than *political* conservatism. By the early years of this century a recognizable consensus about professional behaviour and standards is apparent, especially as expressed by a dominant

> small highly professionalized elite which determined a model for younger, less self-conscious academics to follow . . . out of all the cases there emerged a rudimentary discipline which identified the degree and type of advocacy that was entitled to collective security. Within the limits where agreement could be reached on goals and tactics,

the economists had exchanged the capricious discipline provided by powerful external opponents, for the more steady influence of national professional control. . . . The academic freedom cases cut two ways. They established more autonomy than professional social scientists had enjoyed before. They also demonstrated the negative results of partisanship. For better or worse, these troubles taught many academics to conserve their image, and preserve their institutions, to prepare to defend themselves, but avoid the necessity, to exert influence quietly as experts rather than noisily as partisans.[44]

From a sociological standpoint, the growth of collective self-consciousness among late-nineteenth-century American academic social scientists was simply one manifestation of the 'culture of professionalism' resulting from the increasing specialization and division of labour among the educated classes in a society undergoing rapid modernization. In organizational terms this process was most strikingly revealed – much more so, for example, than in the British case – in the rise and fall of the American Social Science Association (ASSA), a familiar story which has recently been incisively reinterpreted in Thomas Haskell's ambitious book, *The Emergence of Professional Social Science: The American Social Science Association and the Nineteenth-Century Crisis of Authority*.[45] This umbrella association, founded in the 1860s by a group of New England gentlemen, educators, and men of affairs, who sought solutions to the social problems generated by rapid industrialization, immigration, and urbanization, lasted much longer than its English counterpart, the National Association for the Promotion of Social Science. But this earlier, élite, amateur generation was bound to give way before the rising tide of university professionals, and the shift from generalists to specialists is symbolized in the disintegration of the ASSA after it had given birth to separate national organizations of historians, economists, sociologists, and political scientists. According to Haskell, the epistemological foundations of this drive for cultural consolidation, which John Higham has likened to the trust movement in American business, was the need 'to establish or re-establish [intellectual] authority in face of profoundly disruptive changes in habits of causal attribution, in the criteria of plausibility, in the relation of the man of knowledge to his clientele – [and] finally, changes in the very notion of truth itself'.[46] This is, of course, an ambitious explanation, and it is doubtful whether his key concept of 'interdependence', which he defines as an 'intellectualization' of the '*direction* in which objective conditions were changing'[47] provides a sufficiently clear basis on which to distinguish between the declining amateur theorists and the rising professionals. But his study is suggestive in seeking a link between epistemology (i.e. methodology) and professionalization. And it is fascinating to contemplate an incident which he highlights, the moment when Daniel Coit Gilman, President of the Johns Hopkins

145

University, who stood 'on the very edge of the transition from amateur to professional social science',[48] had to decide whether to accept the proposed merger of the ASSA into his new institution, which for many observers symbolized and pioneered the introduction of Germanic scholarly ideals into American higher education. As it transpired, Gilman's rejection helped to seal the ASSA's eventual fate.

One further dimension of the story which differentiates the American from the British situation needs to be mentioned, a dimension that is much more familiar to historians of economics.

About the time of the marginal revolution of the 1870s there was a discernible growth in the international network of scholarly personnel and ideas. This is abundantly revealed in William Jaffé's superb edition of Léon Walras's *Correspondence and Related Papers*,[49] and in W. S. Jevons' preface to the second edition of his *Theory of Political Economy*, in which, as Terence Hutchison has noted, he 'threw open the windows on a vast new landscape of economic ideas, including the writings of one or two of those now recognised as among the most fundamental seminal pioneers in the history of the subject'.[50] At first this network was more a European than a trans-atlantic phenomenon, partly for reasons of distance but also because of the comparatively retarded condition of American intellectual life. But the situation changed rapidly owing to the remarkable exodus of thousands of American students to Europe, especially to Germany, for advanced study. From the 1880s, in economics, as in many other disciplines, the number of students rose rapidly, new academic posts were created, new scholarly publications and associations were launched, and the foundations of modern graduate training were laid.[51] In the next half-century or so Americans borrowed and adapted ideas from English, German, and Austrian sources, and there was a proliferation of new theories and competing textbooks, but no marked tendency to form doctrinal schools. It was in this period – during the early years of the American Economic Association in the 1880s and early 1890s when German historical ideas were becoming fashionable; and from the turn of the century when Veblen inspired a more distinctively American brand of heterodoxy which has survived in various guises ever since – that the proclivity to methodological controversy became a charac-teristic part of the national style in economics.[52] In the 1920s and 1930s any tendency towards economic and political isolationism was more than offset, in the intellectual sphere, by the influx of a distinguished group of European expatriates, many of whom were fleeing from fascist persecution.[53] There is, of course, some danger of presenting an idealized picture of the American academic scene. While Kenneth Boulding's career, for example, epitomizes the contrast between the constraints of Edinburgh, where he was a lowly assistant, and the freedom of Chicago, where, as a graduate student, his arguments with Frank Knight had led to publications on the 'period of production' which marked an important stage in his career, one must not gloss over the antisemitism of the prewar Ivy League colleges and the anti-intellectual Babbitry of some midwestern institutions.[54] And, of course, after World War II there were widespread threats to academic freedom experienced in the McCarthy period.[55] Nevertheless, with scholarly cooperation between immigrants and indigenous personnel, backed by vast American financial resources and academic facilities, it seems with hindsight that the post-1945 United States international leadership in economics, as in many other disciplines, was virtually inevitable.

CONCLUDING REFLECTIONS

Against this background it may be appropriate to ask why, given the resources of the country and the early development of professional self-consciousness in the social sciences, the supremacy of American economics was so long delayed. In attempting an answer, it must be admitted that even more sweeping generalizations are involved than in the earlier sections of this article.

One factor is that the professionalization process at the turn of the century was premature: it was forced upon the social scientists by a combination of personal insecurity and external threats to academic freedom, and despite the intrinsic interest of this episode, it is probably misleading as a general guide to contemporary academic standards of the time. The events depicted by Mary Furner, Walter Metzger, and others provide invaluable insights into the growth of professional ideals and self-consciousness – which is quite a different thing from standards of performance, which must not only be perceived but also implemented. In economics, for example, although the American Economic Association was always more active professionally than its British counterpart, its effectiveness was limited – except as a forum for discussion – until World War II.[56]

Secondly, although the size, competitiveness, and decentralization of academic life in the USA were a guarantee against monolithic domination of the economics discipline by any single doctrine or group and were, in the long run, a stimulus to scientific advance, in the short and medium term they were probably an impediment. From the early years of this century there was a need for consolidation in American economics, rather than continuing novelty. In contrast to Britain there was *insufficient* regard for intellectual leadership or authority; a tendency to what E. G. Nourse (the first Chairman of the Council of Economic Advisers) in the 1950s called 'super-individualism', echoing a view expressed, in somewhat different terms, by J. M. Clark in the late 1920s and J. L. Laughlin in the early 1900s.[57] Not only was there an excess of heterodoxy – associated mainly with the various species of institutionalism – but among the orthodox there was a restless tendency to pursue intellectual novelty for its own sake and, on the part of textbook writers, to indulge in excessive product differentiation in an effort to improve their sales. The development of high and relatively homogeneous standards of graduate training was impeded by the rapid growth of employment opportunities up to the depression of the 1930s, by the immense variety of institution and socio-economic conditions, by the heterogeneity of scholarly backgrounds, and by the difficulties of interregional communication. And it was not until the 1940s, with the spread of Keynesian economics, that there existed a solid doctrinal foundation for a professional consensus.

A third factor, which cannot be weighed precisely, is the contention that the intellectual quality of personnel entering American academic life was inferior to that in Europe. Controls on entry were lax, and some observers have argued that in a country given to anti-intellectualism a disproportionate number of outstanding individuals were attracted away from a life of scholarship and teaching by the higher rewards and prestige accorded to such occupations as business, law, medicine, and engineering.[58] Unfortunately, as we have no reliable measures of such phenomena, this view must remain conjectural, though if true, it helps to explain why the comparatively small number of outstanding immigrants from Europe made such an impact. But it is important to note that from the standpoint of the economics profession as a whole it is average rather than peak performance that concerns us, whereas the opposite is true when one is primarily concerned with scientific achievement. It is the depth and average quality of the economics profession in the USA during the past two or three decades that have so impressed more recent observers, and, as Paul Samuelson once remarked, if one wishes to maximize the average performance in any category the correct procedure is to eliminate all but the best performer[59] – in which case he is probably referring to himself!

Finally, two more familiar considerations may be added. One is that the conventional national predilection for useful knowledge and the social scientist's desire to be seen as an expert rather than as a pure theorist – what Morton White referred to as the revolt against formalism[60] – may have discouraged fundamental developments in economic theory. Here again the influence of social pressures seems important, for as George Stigler once noted, a successful science requires a substantial measure of autonomy if its practitioners are not to be constantly diverted from the pursuit of long-term goals by current problems and events.[61] Outstanding economic theorists and scientists like J. B. Clark, Irving Fisher, Henry Ludwell Moore, had few disciples, whereas a number of outstanding dissenters and iconoclasts flourished, like Veblen, Herbert Davenport, John R. Commons, and Frank H. Knight.

One significant exception to this short list of outstanding American economists, a man who was no great theorist, only a mild dissenter, but undeniably the founder of a professional tradition, was Wesley C. Mitchell. Mitchell's career not only exemplifies the oft-quoted American intellectual predilection for empiricism; it also illustrates the truth that the effort to construct a science from empirical foundations may ultimately be the most productive process but it is also the most roundabout. In Mitchell's work, and that of his followers, the theoretical substructure was deficient. Yet in the longer-run perspective, the solid data base of American economics has proved to be a great source of strength, whereas Keynes' distaste for this kind of work, as Don Patinkin has shown,[62] and reluctance to give it sufficient support (notwithstanding Richard Stone's defence)[63] undoubtedly proved to be a disadvantage in post-1945 British economics. Whether or not this reflects differences in the professional culture of the two societies, as seems likely, is too involved a subject to be considered at this late stage. It seems broadly true to state that up to World War II American economics was generally weaker in theory formulation than its British counterpart but much stronger in its data base. Since 1945 the Americans have undoubtedly surged ahead on both fronts.

NOTES

* This article represents a revised version of an invited address prepared for the History of Economics Conference at Urbana, Illinois, in May 1979. I have benefited from critical comments both on that occasion and when it was delivered at Auburn University and Emory University.

1 Jacob Viner, 'A Modest Proposal for Some Stress on Scholarship in Graduate Training', in *The Long View and the Short: Studies in Economic Theory and Policy* (Glencoe, Ill., 1958), p. 380.

2 Axel Leijonhufvud, 'Life among the Econ', *Western Economic Journal* 11 (Sept. 1973): 327–37. In addition to delightful satire, this article contains penetrating insights into the state of economics, including the observation that owing to the neglect of their history, 'Having lost their past, the Econ are without confidence in the present and without purpose and direction for the future' (p. 336).

3 Burton J. Bledstein, *The Culture of Professionalism: The Middle Class and the Development of Higher Education in America* (New York, 1976).

4 George J. Stigler, 'The Influence of Events and Policies on Economic Theory', *Essays in the History of Economics* (Chicago, 1965), p. 22. For a general survey see also Joseph J. Spengler, 'Exogenous and Endogenous Influences in the Formation of Post-1870 Economic Thought: A Sociology of Knowledge Approach', in Robert V. Eagly, *Events, Ideology, and Economic Theory: The Determinants of Progress in the Development of Economic Analysis* (Detroit, 1968), pp. 159–205, including comments by Eagly.

5 Cf. C. J. Lammers, 'Mono- and poly-paradigmatic developments in natural and social sciences', in R. Whitley, ed., *Social Processes of Scientific Development* (London, 1974), pp. 123–47, especially his discussion of 'lay images'.

6 The internationalization of economics is discussed by Harry G. Johnson in 'The American Tradition in Economics', *Nebraska Journal of Economics and Business* 16 (Summer 1977): 17–26, where he remarks that American economics, 'which had been something of a condescendingly patronized country-bumpkin cousin of European city-slicker economic sophistication, rapidly became the leader in the world profession of economics. In the process, the distinguishing character-

istics of American economics became, naturally enough, the distinguishing characteristics of good professional economics' (p. 23).

7 See for example Clarence Ayres, *The Theory of Economic Progress* (Chapel Hill, 1944). See also the essays on Ayres by William Breit and A. W. Coats in *Science and Ceremony: The Institutional Economics of C. E. Ayres*, ed. William Breit and William Patton Culbertson, Jr (Austin, Tex., 1976); the essay by Coats is entitled 'Clarence Ayres' Place in the History of American Economics: An Interim Assessment' and is reprinted in vol. I of this series.

8 For a discussion of this point see Kenneth E. Boulding, *The Meaning of the Twentieth Century* (New York, 1964).

9 For a discussion of the recent situation see Harry G. Johnson, 'National Styles in Economic Research: The United States, the United Kingdom, Canada, and various European Countries', *Daedalus* 102 (Spring 1973): 65–74. He distinguishes between three levels in the American economics community – according to the status of the graduate school, the extent of orientation to research and publication, and the quality of training. The élite engage in international conferences, pre-publication, and invisible colleges and adopt an international style which is primarily American in origin and outlook. They often face hostility or resentment from their colleagues and show a strong desire to found research institute with financial support from outside the university (p. 67).

10 There have, for example, been many articles on the functions and quality of economic journals, the composition and significance of contributions to scholarly meetings, the prestige ratings of individual departments, and the relationships between publication performance and career success in economics, to mention only a few related topics. See the essays in this volume, pp. 155–75 and 176–201.

11 Joseph A. Schumpeter, *History of Economic Analysis* (New York, 1954), p. 47.

12 For a more detailed discussion see my 'Methodology and Professionalism in Economics: A Subordinate Theme in Machlup's Writings', in Jacob S. Dreyer, *Breadth and Depth in Economics: Fritz Machlup – the Man and His Ideas* (Lexington, Mass., 1978), pp. 23–35. In his *Methodology of Economics and Other Social Sciences* (New York, 1978), Fritz Machlup draws a careful distinction between methodology, methods, logic, epistemology, and philosophy, by defining methodology as 'the study of the principles that guide students in any field of knowledge, and especially of any branch of higher learning (science) in deciding whether to accept or reject certain propositions as part of the body of ordered knowledge in general or of their own discipline' (p. 54). It is hardly necessary to emphasize the sociological aspects of this decision.

13 Michael Polanyi, *Personal Knowledge* (Chicago, 1958), p. 167.

14 T. W. Hutchison, 'Insularity and Cosmopolitanism in Economic Ideas, 1870–1914', *American Economic Review* 455 (May 1955): 1–16.

15 I have borrowed this term from Frank Thistlethwaite's suggestive paper, 'The Citadel and the Caravan: Anglo-American Relations in the Twentieth Century', reprinted in Hennig Cohen, *The American Experience: Approaches to the Study of the United States* (New York, 1968). It originally appeared in *American Quarterly* 9 (Spring 1957): 22–33. Thistlethwaite remarks: 'The Caravan is a society of traders committed to the journey; variously recruited; bound together by compelling but temporary loyalties; conscious that there will be other caravans, other companions; discounting yesterday's crises, anticipating tomorrow's opportunities, and navigating by the stars. The Citadel is a society of guardians protecting a crossroads of traffic; close in kin; governed by custom in an unquestioned hierarchy of authority; adapting inherited offices and chambers to changing uses, but conscious that the Citadel and its duties are fixed and permanent.'

16 William J. Goode, 'Encroachment, Charlatanism, and the Emerging Professions: Psychology, Sociology, Medicine', *American Sociological Review* 25 (1960): 902. According to Talcott Parsons, 'the professional complex . . . [is] the most important component in the structure of modern societies'. Cf. 'Professions', *International Encyclopedia of the Social Sciences*, 12 (1968): 545.

17 On the comparative development of late-nineteenth-century professionalism in Britain and the USA see Magali Sarfatti Larson, *The Rise of Professionalism: A Sociological Analysis* (Berkeley, 1978), pp. 79, 102. See also Bledstein, op. cit.; W. J. Reader, *Professional Men: The Rise of the Professional Classes in Nineteenth-Century England* (London, 1966); and Harold Perkin, *Key Profession: The History of the Association of University Teachers* (London, 1969). The aspiring late-nineteenth-century British professional economists were not dissimilar in important respects to Noel Annan's 'intellectual aristocracy' – an intelligentsia who conformed to and worked through existing institutions. They were tolerant of the older generation of dons, and although they relished the association with the real nobility and ruling class, they never confused themselves with that class: cf. Noel Annan, 'The Intellectual Aristocracy', in J. H. Plumb, ed., *Essays in Social History* (London, 1955), pp. 243–87.

18 W. H. G. Armytage, *Civic Universities* (London, 1955).

19 There are valuable insights into the changing intellectual climate in Oxford and Cambridge in Melvin Richter, *The Politics of Conscience: T. H. Green and His Age* (London, 1964), and Sheldon Rothblatt, *The Revolution of the Dons: Cambridge and Society in Victorian England* (London, 1968).

20 Some general comments on developments at Oxford and London are provided in my 'Sociological Aspects of British Economic Thought (*ca.* 1880–1930)', *Journal of Political Economy* 75 (Oct. 1967): 706–29 (reprinted in this volume, pp. 105–33), which needs to be supplemented and modified in the light of subsequent research, especially Alon Kadish, *The Oxford Economists in the Late Nineteenth Century* (Oxford, 1982), and John Maloney, *Marshall, Orthodoxy and the Professionalization of Economics* (Cambridge, 1985). The potential anti-Keynes movement at the London School of Economics in the 1930s, led by Lionel Robbins and F. A. von Hayek, needs to be considered. See for example Donald Winch, *Economics and Policy: An Historical Study* (London, 1969), especially ch. 9; and Don Patinkin and J. Clark Leith, eds., *Keynes, Cambridge, and the General Theory: The Process of Criticism and Discussion Connected with the Development of* The General Theory (Macmillan, 1977). See also Coats, 'The Distinctive LSE Ethos in the Inter-War Years', *Atlantic Economic Journal* 10 (March 1982): 18–30 (reprinted in this volume, pp. 372–92).

21 See, for example, the Fabian conception of professional expertise in Peter Clarke, *Liberals and Social Democrats* (Cambridge, 1978), especially pp. 34, 44, 119, 123, 262. The distinction between lower and upper middle-class conceptions of professionalism in England would repay systematic study. There are valuable insights in Roy and Kay MacLeod, 'Contradictions of Professionalism: Scientists, Trade Unionism and the First World War', in *Social Studies of Science* 9 (1979): 1–32, and in F. M. L. Thompson, *Chartered Surveyors: The Growth of a Profession* (London, 1968). The distinction between the upper-class conception of the leisured amateur or 'intelligent layman' was institutionalized in the British civil service, where the so-called Professional and Works Classes were accorded inferior status to the élitist Administrative Class. Before 1939 the two groups had separate organizations, known then, respectively, as the Second Division and First Division Associations. These designations and the respective class

structures among public servants have been changed so as to make them less invidious.

22 This is clear from the fascinating correspondence in vol. 13 of *The Collected Writings of J. M. Keynes* (London, 1973).

23 Harry G. Johnson, 'Keynes' *General Theory*: Revolution or War of Independence?', in Elizabeth S. Johnson and Harry G. Johnson, *The Shadow of Keynes, Understanding Keynes, Cambridge and Keynesian Economics* (Chicago, 1978), pp. 235–6.

24 Quoted in Hutchison, p. 12, from *Utility and All That* (1951), pp. 111–12.

25 On this subject see Coats, 'The Historist Reaction in English Political Economy, 1870–90', *Economica*, n.s. 21 (May 1954): 143–53 (reprinted in vol. I in this series). It is worth noting that Robertson's reminiscence refers to a period twenty years after the first edition of the *Principles* and two years after Marshall's retirement from the Cambridge chair.

26 For a general view of the character and importance of the Marshallian school see my 'Sociological Aspects of British Economic Thought (*ca.* 1880–1930)', *Journal of Political Economy* 75 (Oct. 1967): 706–29 (reprinted in this volume, pp. 105–33); also my 'The Origins and Early Development of the Royal Economic Society', *Economic Journal* 78 (June 1968): 349–71 (reprinted in this volume, pp. 313–37); also Maloney, *Marshall, Orthodoxy and the Professionalization of Economics*.

27 Herbert S. Foxwell, introduction to Anton Menger, *The Right to the Whole Produce of Labour* (London, 1899), p. xxviii.

28 Cf. the stimulating essay, 'Economists and the History of Economics: Revolutionary and Traditional Versions', by T. W. Hutchison, in his *On Revolutions and Progress in Economic Knowledge* (Cambridge, 1978), especially p. 221; also Schumpeter, p. 530, and Thomas Sowell, *Say's Law: An Historical Analysis* (Princeton, 1972), pp. 163–4.

29 W. S. Jevons, *Theory of Political Economy* (1871; 4th ed. 1911), pp. 275–6.

30 R. F. Harrod, *The Life of John Maynard Keynes* (London, 1951), p. 143.

31 Hutchison, 'Insularity and Cosmopolitanism', op. cit., p. 13. The expression is quoted from A. C. Pigou, *Essays in Economics* (London, 1952), p. 8. It is clear from the context (cf. p. 7) that he was referring to a 'moral dictatorship' rather than a purely intellectual one; Pigou considered that the situation had changed markedly by 1939 when, in place of Marshall as 'a centre of unity, of acquiescence, of quiescence', there were 'centres of disturbance' and a 'turmoil . . . a period of confusion'.

32 T. W. Hutchison, *A Review of Economic Doctrines, 1870–1939* (Oxford, 1953), pp. 63–4.

33 J. M. Keynes, *The General Theory of Employment, Interest and Money* (London, 1936), Preface, p. viii.

34 Here I have drawn freely on the penetrating analysis by M. D. King in his 'Reason, Tradition and the Progressiveness of Science', *History and Theory* 10 (1971): 3–32.

35 Cf. 'Cambridge in the 1950's', 'The Shadow of Keynes', and 'Keynes and British Economics', in Elizabeth S. Johnson and Harry G. Johnson, *The Shadow of Keynes, Understanding Keynes, Cambridge, and Keynesian Economics* (Chicago, 1978).

36 See A. W. Coats, 'Alfred Marshall and Richard T. Ely: Some Unpublished Letters', *Economica* n. s. 28 (May 1960): 193–4 (reprinted in vol. I in this series).

37 Cf Richard D. Whitley, 'The Formal Communication System of Science: A Study of the Organization of British Social Science Journals', *Sociological Review Monograph*, no. 16 (University of Keele, 1970); also, 'The Operation of Social

Science Journals: Two Case Studies in British Social Science', *Sociological Review* 18 (July 1970): 241–58.

38 Harry Johnson, *The Shadow of Keynes*, pp. 219–20.

39 Thorstein Veblen, *The Higher Learning in America: A Memorandum on the Conduct of Universities by Businessmen* (New York, 1918). For general background studies see Laurence R. Veysey, *The Emergence of the American University* (Chicago, 1965); Frederick Rudolph, *The American College and University* (New York, 1962); and the recent survey article by Edward Shils, 'The Order of Learning in the United States from 1865 to 1920: The Ascendancy of the Universities', *Minerva* 16 (Summer 1978): 159–95. Shils places more emphasis on the emergence of a hierarchy of American universities than seems appropriate to the present, broadly comparative, account. His essay has been reprinted in a valuable new collection edited by Alexandra Oleson and John Voss, *The Organization of Knowledge in Modern America 1860–1920* (Baltimore, 1979). See also A. W. Coats, 'The Educational Revolution and the Professionalization of American Economics', in William J. Barber, ed., *Breaking the American Mould. Economists and American Higher Learning in the Nineteenth Century* (Middletown, Conn.: Wesleyan University Press, 1988), pp. 340–75.

40 Richard Hofstadter and Walter P. Metzger, *The Development of Academic Freedom in the United States* (New York, 1955).

41 See A. W. Coats, 'John Elliotson Symes, Henry George, and Academic Freedom in Nottingham during the 1880s', *Renaissance and Modern Studies* 7 (1963): 110–38, (reprinted in this volume, pp. 289–312).

42 Hofstadter, p. ix.

43 Mary O. Furner, *Advocacy and Objectivity: A Crisis in the Professionalization of American Social Science 1865–1905* (Lexington, Ky., 1975), p. 145.

44 Ibid., pp. 257–8.

45 Thomas L. Haskell, *The Emergence of Professional Social Science: The American Social Science Association and the Nineteenth-Century Crisis of Authority* (Urbana, 1977).

46 Ibid., p. 65.

47 Ibid., p. 15.

48 Ibid., p. 160.

49 Léon Walras, *Correspondence and Related Papers*, ed. William Jaffé, 3 vols. (Amsterdam, 1965).

50 Hutchison, 'Insularity and Cosmopolitanism', p. 7.

51 Cf. the sources referred to above in n. 39.

52 See, for example, my unpublished Ph.D. thesis, 'Methodological Controversy as an Approach to the History of American Economics, 1885–1930' (Johns Hopkins, 1953); Joseph Dorfman, *The Economic Mind in American Civilization*, 3 (New York, 1949), ch. 9; *idem*, 'The Role of the German Historical School in American Economic Thought', *American Economic Review* 45 (May 1955): 17–28; A. W. Coats, 'The First Two Decades of the American Economic Association', *American Economic Review* 50 (Sept. 1960): 555–74 (reprinted in this volume, pp. 205–24).

53 Donald Fleming and Bernard Bailyn, eds., *The Intellectual Migration: Europe and America, 1930–1950* (Cambridge, Mass., 1969); Laura Fermi, *Illustrious Immigrants: The Intellectual Migration from Europe 1930–41* (Chicago, 1968).

54 Cf. the fascinating account in Cynthia Earl Kerman, *Creative Tension: The Life and Thought of Kenneth Boulding* (Ann Arbor, 1973), especially pp. 26–9, 243–7. Boulding's articles were published in the *Quarterly Journal of Economics* and *Economica*. On antisemitism see Paul A. Samuelson, 'Economics in a Golden Age: A Personal Memoir', in *The Twentieth Century Sciences: Studies in the Biography of*

Ideas, ed. Gerald Holton (New York, 1972), p. 170. On the general subject see Richard Hofstadter, *Anti-Intellectualism in American Life* (New York, 1962).

55 Cf. P. Lazarsfeld and W. Thielens, *The Academic Mind: Social Scientists in a Time of Crisis* (Glencoe, Ill., 1958); Robert MacIver, *Academic Freedom in Our Times* (New York, 1955).

56 This is an impressionistic judgement based on a reading of the AEA and Royal Economic Society records. Of course there are those who would contend that the AEA's effectiveness is still too limited. See A. W. Coats, 'The American Economic Association and the Economics Profession', *American Economic Association* 23 (Dec. 1985): 1697–727 (reprinted in this volume, pp. 433–73).

57 Cf. Hugh S. Norton, *The Role of the Economist in Government: A Study in Economic Advice Since 1920* (Berkeley, 1969), p. 58; J. M. Clark, 'Recent Developments in Economics', in E. C. Hayes, ed., *Recent Developments in the Social Sciences* (Philadelphia, 1927), p. 304; J. Laurence Laughlin, *Industrial America* (1906; New York, 1972), p. 228.

58 Among economists this view was expressed by J. L. Laughlin and J. A. Schumpeter. For a more general argument on these lines see Hofstadter, *Anti-Intellectualism*. However, falling average standards may simply have been an impression derived from the increase in numbers. It was an impression shared by Pigou; cf. his *Essays*, quoted above in n. 31.

59 Cf. Joseph E. Stiglitz, ed., *The Collected Scientific Papers of Paul A. Samuelson* (Cambridge, Mass., 1966), 2: 1653.

60 Morton A. White, *Social Thought in America: The Revolt Against Formalism* (Boston, 1957).

61 Stigler, 'Influence of Events', p. 29.

62 Don Patinkin, 'Keynes and Econometrics: On the Interaction Between the Macroeconomic Revolutions of the Interwar Period', *Econometrica* 44 (Nov. 1976): 1091–123.

63 Richard Stone, 'Keynes, Political Arithmetic and Econometrics', Seventh Keynes Lecture, delivered at the British Academy, 3 May 1978.

9

THE ROLE OF SCHOLARLY
JOURNALS IN THE HISTORY
OF ECONOMICS

An essay*

Several recent studies in the history, philosophy, and sociology of science have demonstrated the central, if subtle and complex, role of the publication process in the communication, scrutiny, and acceptance of new ideas [Polanyi, 1958; Kuhn, 1962; Hagstrom, 1965], yet comparatively little attention has hitherto been paid to this aspect of the development of economics. This is somewhat surprising, for economists, like other members of the academic community, are well aware of the sinister implications of the warning 'publish or perish' and their discipline, like others, has been profoundly affected by the explosion of scientific knowledge.[1]

I

Historians of economics have at their disposal that magnificent, but still largely unexploited source, *The A.E.A. Index of Economic Journals*, and this is not only an indispensable bibliographical aid but also a valuable mine for those inclined to employ statistical methods. George Stigler and Martin Bronfenbrenner have already made initial forays into this still uncharted territory [Stigler, 1965 and Bronfenbrenner, 1966], but the present article is the first to be based on a detailed analysis of a select group of economic journals.

To avoid misunderstandings, the purpose of this exercise must be explained at the outset. Initially conceived as an attempt to test the hypothesis that some editors have in the past exerted a discernible influence on the contents of particular economic journals,[2] it subsequently broadened into an empirical analysis of the changing characteristics of five leading English-language periodicals. Among these characteristics, attention has been focused on: long-run trends and short-term fluctuations in the distribution of contents both of individual journals and of the whole group; endogenous and exogenous influences on this distribution; and certain measures of the comparative innovativeness and quality of individual journals. Needless to say, the treatment is suggestive rather than exhaustive,

155

for the research possibilities in this field are almost endless; but some of the wider implications will be indicated at appropriate points. The statistical methods employed are elementary – if not downright crude – mainly because the raw data in the *Index* volumes (which were compiled for an entirely different purpose) do not readily lend themselves to more sophisticated techniques.[3]

II GENERAL FEATURES OF THE SELECTED JOURNALS

Despite certain obvious differences, the five journals in our sample possess several basic features in common.[4] They are all venerable and prestigious, though some inevitably more so than others; none has ever been deliberately restrictive with respect to subject matter; and at least four have experienced long spells of editorial continuity, especially at the beginning of their careers.[5] The fact that three are American and two British has necessarily had some effect on the choice of material, especially with regard to practical problems and policy issues, but the general similarities suggest that much the same influences were at work on both sides of the Atlantic. More important at first sight is the fact that while two of the journals are sponsored by organizations, the remainder are published by important university departments of economics; there is some evidence that the editors of departmental periodicals are more inclined to accept articles written by their faculty colleagues or by past students.[6] However, this is likely to exert a significant influence on the distribution of contents only in the case of a monolithic or narrow department, and no such differences have been found (or, admittedly, sought) in the present case. Unfortunately, our general knowledge of the influences affecting editors of economic journals is very deficient, owing to the dearth of editorial correspondence.[7] It seems likely that organization journal editors are subject to a different, and probably wider variety of psychological and professional pressures than their departmental counterparts – especially the desire to satisfy the diffuse and sometimes conflicting demands of their membership; but in the present state of our knowledge this can only be a matter for conjecture. There is no evidence of regular co-operation between the editors of the journals in our sample, and there was no systematic effort to 'divide the field'. Consequently it can be suggested, as an initial working hypothesis, that the selection of material in each case reflects broadly the same combination of endogenous and exogenous influences.

III LONG-RUN TRENDS

For the purposes of long-run analysis, the periodic system adopted in the *A.E.A. Index* has been taken as given, with one exception.[8] As the period 1886–1924 is so long, and the number of economic journals then being published so limited, period I has been divided at 1910 (into Ia: 1886–1910; Ib: 1911–24), to mark the advent of the AER in 1911.[9] As *Economica* appeared for only three years before the end of period I, it is approximately correct to say that period Ia covers three journals; period Ib, four; and periods II–V, five. For certain purposes other publications will also be considered, especially the *A.E.R. Supplement*, which contains the *Papers and Proceedings* of the annual meetings.

Table 1 Percentage distribution of articles in five 'general' economics journals

Category	Period Ia	Period Ib	Period II	Period III	Period IV	Period V
2	11	10	27	26	34	36
4	4	2	4	8	7.5	7
9	13	11	10.5	6.5	4	6
11	8	8	10.5	10	14	10
13	1	8	0.5	7	2	0.3
15	20	20	13	8	9	9
19	12	11	7	6	4	4.5
All other	31	30	38	28.5	25.5	25.5

Table 1 presents a summary of the long-term changes in the distribution of contents of the selected journals over the entire period 1886–1959. Only seven of the twenty-three main categories in the *Index* are shown separately as they comprised between 70 and 75 per cent of the total number of articles in most periods, a proportion that tended to increase with the passage of time, probably owing to the growth in the number of specialized journals.

It will be seen that the principal long-run trends included a striking increase in category 2 (Economic theory, including Monetary theory); a modest rise in categories 11 (International Economics) and 4 (History of Economic Thought); and a fall in categories 9 (Money, Credit and Banking), 15 (Industrial Organization and Public Policy) and 19 (Labour Economics). These changes were more or less continuous, whereas the marked fluctuations in category 13 (War and Defence Economics) reflected the predictable impact of two world wars.

Analysis of these long-run trends within each of our five selected journals reveals the broad similarities between them. Despite significant differences in the initial range and distribution of their contents, not to mention differences in sponsorship, location, and longevity, they all tended to concentrate their attention on the same few principal categories. Moreover, with the passage of time their content distribution tended to become more alike.[10] For example, the distinctive features of the *A.E.R.* and *Eca.*, which were quite marked when they were first published, subsequently disappeared. Moreover, the largest changes in the distribution of contents within any single journal between successive periods have been those which brought abnormally large or small categories closer to the general average; in the few instances when a particular journal diverged from the general trend in any period, such a movement proved to be only temporary.[11]

Comparing these results with Professor Bronfenbrenner's rough-and-ready measures [1966, p. 545] of the trends in articles published in all the journals included in the *Index*[12] we find several significant differences, most of which are directly attributable to differences in the scope and method of the two studies. In both cases there are broadly comparable trends in the five main categories – that is, a rise in 2 and 11, and a fall in 9, 15, and 19. However, the extent and direction of the movements of individual categories is not identical in both studies; for instance, the growth of category 2 was far more rapid in our sample than in the periodical literature as a whole. Also, as a result of the introduction of new journals, certain specialist and technical categories – e.g., Economic History (5), Mathematical and Statistical Tools (7), Social Accounting and Statistical Data (8), Business Organization and Managerial Economics (14) – have either diminished or remained insignificant in the general journals while occupying an increasing share of the total periodical literature. Conversely, the History of Economic Thought (4) increased its hold on the general journals while losing ground elsewhere.

As the five journals in our sample tended in the long run to conform to a common pattern, it is tempting to suggest that their editors were subject to forces beyond their control; that far from being dynamic academic entrepreneurs of the Schumpeterian type, they were merely passive recipients of a changing flow of manuscripts over which they exercised little or no editorial influence. There is, indeed, some evidence to support this interpretation. In the best documented example – the *A.E.R.* 1911–40 – despite Davis R. Dewey's original intention of leaving 'Theory' to the *Q.J.E.*[13] the percentage of articles in category 2 increased rapidly as in other general journals. In the case of the *J.P.E.*, on the other hand, although J. L. Laughlin claimed to be concentrating on 'practical questions' while the *Q.J.E.* specialized in 'theory',[14] there was in fact no clear-cut division of material between the two periodicals. Obviously either Laughlin was unable to implement his avowed policy, or else he was simply mistaken.

However, it would be wrong to deduce definite conclusions about editorial policy from the inadequate evidence available, for broad comparisons of content distribution constitute an insensitive index of editorial behaviour. Two examples will suffice to support the interpretation suggested above. First, an analysis of the *A.E.A. Papers and Proceedings* reveals trends somewhat similar to those in the general journals – including significant increases in categories 2 and 4, and decreases in categories 9 and 19. The parallels are not exact, for the *A.E.R./S.* published consistently less in category 2, and relatively more in categories 15 and 13 (especially in wartime) than the general journals.[15] Yet the differences are much smaller than might have been expected given the fact that the contents of the *A.E.R./S.* represent the outcome of the decisions of successive AEA presidents who were responsible for the selection of papers at the annual meetings.[16] The second, and more telling example, is the transfer of the *A.E.R.*'s editorship from Dewey to Paul Homan in the early 1940s, a change which undoubtedly rejuvenated the *Review* even though it left comparatively little trace on the distribution of its contents.[17] Homan was a far more energetic and positive person than his predecessor, and, unlike many editors of scholarly periodicals, he deliberately exercised his editorial initiative by soliciting contributions from the many economists then employed in wartime Washington. While he aimed to print articles on subjects of current and prospective significance, he was more concerned with quality than subject-matter – and in this respect his editorial attitude was probably typical. Except when launching a new periodical, or in a crisis, most academic editors would deem it inappropriate, if not positively undignified, to solicit material. Such efforts, however discreetly conducted, may prove self-defeating, being interpreted as a sign of weakness; hence, given these constraints, editors of scholarly periodicals have little choice but to adopt a somewhat passive role. If the flow of material is ample, much can be achieved by judicious selection from the items submitted for publication. But even if the results of their selections are detectable, they are unlikely to affect the long-term general trends presented in this section.

On the whole, the twenty-three *Index* categories are too blunt to be utilized for detailed analysis. They can, however, be used to display some of the broad differences between individual journals – for example, in the period following the inauguration of the *A.E.R.*, in 1911. This event was preceded by long and anxious discussions among editors of existing American economics journals and the officers of the American Economic Association [Coats, 1969, p. 58]; in the ensuing period the relations between the three main periodicals were more than usually self-conscious. Of course, not all the changes in content distribution of the *Q.J.E.* and *J.P.E.* in period Ib (1911–24) can be ascribed to the advent of a new competitor, for World War I largely explains the striking increase in category 13 (War and Defence Economics) in all three journals. It also accounts for the absence of growth in category 2 (which actually fell in the *Q.J.E.*) and the rise in category 15 in the *Q.J.E.* and *J.P.E.* – a trend reflecting the growth of wartime and post-war interest in public policy questions.[18] Nevertheless, the total number of American economics periodicals was small enough for the *A.E.R.* to make a perceptible difference.[19] It is therefore noteworthy that a comparison of the pre- and post-1911 periods reveals significantly greater changes in the *Q.J.E.* than in the *J.P.E.*, which suggests that F. W. Taussig, editor of the former, may have been deliberately helping Dewey to differentiate his new product. The two editors were certainly on friendly terms, and they lived in close proximity to one another. Furthermore,

Dewey consulted Taussig both before the beginning and during the early months of his editorship, and there is evidence of occasional collaboration between them.[20] By contrast, relations between Dewey and Laughlin (of the *J.P.E.*) were both physically and psychologically more distant; and in saying that he aimed to avoid duplicating the work of other journals, Dewey may have had the *Q.J.E.* in mind rather than the *J.P.E.* Given these circumstances, it is not surprising to find that in period Ib (1911–24) the content distribution of the *A.E.R.* was closer to that of the *J.P.E.* (and, incidentally, the *E.J.*) than that of the *Q.J.E.* This was also true in period II (1925–39), a fact which may reflect the continuity of editorial policies, for Taussig retired only shortly before, and Dewey shortly after the close of the 1930s.[21] During the period 1886–1959 there were several significant long-term changes in the content distribution within the individual journals in our sample, not all of which can be readily explained. However, no further examples will be discussed here, for we must now turn to a more fruitful topic – the analysis of short-term movements in economic literature.

IV SHORT-TERM ANALYSIS BY SUB-CATEGORY

The twenty-three categories which comprise the *Index* are broad in coverage and heterogeneous in content, and, as Professor Stigler has rightly observed [1965, p. 48], they 'reflect the categories of subjects which were fashionable in the 1960's'.[22] How far this renders them unsuitable as a basis for examining earlier periods is a matter for discussion, but it does not follow, as Stigler maintains [1965, p. 48],[23] that the *Index* is unsuitable for the analysis of fashions in economics. On the contrary, the fluctuating fortunes of particular topics can readily be discerned in the movement of the seven hundred or so sub-categories; and the compilation of a detailed inventory of articles by subject, date, and journal, widens the scope for analysis so greatly that only a few illustrative examples can be given. Thus, although category 2 expanded in successive periods in the five journals, there was a discernible decline of interest in such matters as economic motivation (2.01), and certain aspects of value and distribution theory (e.g., 2.10; 2.112; 2.20; 2.210; 2.2110; 2.220; 2.23), whereas the striking recent increase of activity in growth and development theory represents an important component part of the overall expansion of the category.[24] Clearly marked waves of interest can be detected in such cases as demand analysis and elasticity (2.113 and 2.114 in period II); oligopoly and bilateral monopoly (2.1333 in period III); investment by individual firm (2.213 in period III); quantity theory and price level (2.324 in period III); and investment theories of the cycle (2.332 in period II). In many instances the reasons for these small-scale movements are obvious enough. Yet they constitute the very stuff of which scientific progress is made; and in theoretical fields such as those covered in category 2 we are largely dealing with movements endogenous to the discipline, rather than those attributable to exogenous influences.[25]

Many of these short-term statistical patterns are familiar, and any tolerably well-read economist can immediately think of certain seminal articles which have provoked a flurry of academic controversy or generated a flow of research contributions. Likewise, there are short-term peaks and troughs in the literature resulting from such exogenous sources as wars, depressions, monetary crises, tariff measures, banking and monopoly legislation, and major strikes, any of which may leave an imprint on the journal literature. For example, in period I several phases of controversy on both sides of the Atlantic were reflected in sub-category 11.230 (Trade Policy, General). In the USA these peaks roughly coincided with new tariff legislation and the establishment of the US Tariff Commission in 1912, while in Britain, the hectic tariff reform controversy in the 1900s left clear traces in the *E.J.* (which printed 25 articles in this sub-category between 1900 and 1906). Throughout period I the *E.J.* published far more articles on trade policy than the American general journals, but in subsequent periods interest in this topic dwindled rapidly throughout our sample. A somewhat parallel movement is evident in sub-category 15.8 (Transportation), where the dramatic fall after period I was mainly due to a decline of interest in railroads. As this subject figured much more prominently in public controversy in the USA than in the UK, the *E.J.* published far fewer transportation articles than either the *Q.J.E.* or the *J.P.E.*[26] However, there was one exception to the general decline in later periods for the curious reason that from 1947 to 1953 a group of transportation economists managed to pre-empt a regular place on the AEA's annual programme, thereby helping to swell the number of transportation articles in the *A.E.R./S.* when it was generally declining in the other general periodicals.[27] And, incidentally, this case casts some doubt on the validity of the distinction between exogenously and endogenously influenced topics, both because several of the *A.E.R./S.* transportation articles were highly academic in content, and also because it shows that even in a policy-orientated field the number of articles may be influenced as much by academic politics as by public interest.

On the whole, waves of interest in questions of public importance are easier to account for than those in more academic subjects. However, sub-category 1.3 (Teaching of Economics) clearly reveals the effects of changes in editorial policy on the contents of individual journals. Until the early 1920s the *J.P.E.* led easily, largely owing to Laughlin who, in 1909, so successfully solicited contributions to a symposium on the teaching of economics that this journal printed 22 articles in this sub-category within the next five years. In 1917 his successor followed suit and published a seven-article symposium on graduate teaching, but thereafter the *J.P.E.* lost interest, and the lead passed to the AEA's periodicals. Four articles appeared in the *A.E.R./S.* in 1920–3, and seven more in the *A.E.R.* in 1922–3 (but one of many examples of interchange of ideas between these two publications), and after a long interval during which little was published on the subject there was a marked revival of interest in the 1940s, both in the *A.E.R./S.* and in the *A.E.R.*[28] Apparently by this time the Association had assumed the responsibility for a topic of general interest to the profession at large. However, it is worth noting that the other organization journal in our sample, the *E.J.*, did not do likewise, probably because the Royal Economic Society, unlike its American counterpart, has only very recently provided an open forum for professional discussion among British economists.

Of course, many other waves of interest in theoretical topics can be discerned in the *Index*, some of which are very familiar to historians of economics. For example, at the turn of the century the theory of distribution was prominent in all three general journals then being published, and the *Q.J.E.* led the field, not only because it was widely thought to be specializing in theory, but also because it had already acquired a 'corner' in distribution theory even before the *E.J.* and *J.P.E.* first appeared. Once established, such a lead tends to be self-perpetuating as long as the editor wishes, for some articles invite comments and replies, and authors tend to assume that the editor will welcome further contributions to a field in which his journal already has a reputation. However, such a 'corner' was never exclusive in our sample; nor was it usually maintained indefinitely. In distribution theory, for instance, the lead passed to the *A.E.R.* from period II – that is, at a time when the subject had lost some of its former excitement.[29] Transfers of interest of this kind from one journal to another are quite common and cannot easily be explained. In the case of growth models (sub-category 2.3401), for example, two seminal articles by Harrod (*E.J.* 1939) and Domar (*A.E.R.* 1947) were followed (after a time lag of 10 years in the *E.J.* and 5 years in the *A.E.R.*) by a swelling flood of imitators in the 1950s in several different journals.[30] It would obviously be foolish to study sequences of this kind simply by scrutinizing the titles of articles in a few selected periodicals. The filiation of ideas can only be traced in the texts themselves and, more especially, in the footnotes – a point to which we shall refer later. Nevertheless, the *Index* can serve as a valuable starting point for such inquiries – a source of working hypotheses rather than answers to questions.[31]

Only two further species of short-run analysis will be quoted, the first of which concerns the introduction of new journals. Despite the risks of *post hoc ergo propter hoc* reasoning, it may be assumed that the issue of a new journal will be followed by a decline in the number of articles published in its field by the general journals.[32] However, in practice this sequence is not as readily discernible as might be supposed, partly because of the long-term growth in the total number of articles; partly because author loyalties, like some consumer loyalties, are not readily transferable, especially as a newcomer takes some time to earn a favourable reputation. Moreover, a new journal is not simply a response to existing demand for publishing space: quite apart from the more sordid empire-building motives occasionally involved, it is also to some extent an active agent, encouraging the growth of research and publication in its field. This largely explains the growth of economic articles on particular areas which followed the introducton of such periodicals as *The Indian Economic Journal* (1916), *The Economic Record* (1925), *The South African Journal of Economics* (1933), and *The Canadian Journal of Economics and Political Science* (1935).[33]

In addition to the effects of new journals, short-run analysis can also reveal international differences between periodicals, thereby casting valuable new light on the origins and development of the international scientific community of economists. It can provide clues to the genesis, evolution, and diffusion of new theoretical concepts and technical tools; it can also serve as a basis for international comparisons of the application of economic ideas to the solution of practical problems.[34] Here, as elsewhere, the examination of *Index* entries will be only a prelude to serious research. But it will be a highly time-saving prelude. Unfortunately our sample is too small and too uneven (in a chronological sense) to reveal much of interest, though certain international differences have already been mentioned elsewhere in this article.

V SOME QUALITATIVE CONSIDERATIONS

In the two preceding sections we have seen that quantitative analysis of the *Index* can shed some light on changes in editorial policy. It now remains to show that it can also provide some basis for judgements of the respective merits of various journals. This is, of course, a sensitive area in which we must proceed with caution.

In the process of acquiring his professional qualifications, every fledgling economist is initiated into the prevailing occupational folklore, part of which consists of opinions about the aims, characteristics, and comparative prestige ratings of the various periodical publications in the field. Some of these opinions are vague, ephemeral, and highly subjective; as such, they hardly constitute adequate grist for the historian's mill. Nevertheless, their importance should not be underestimated, for they constitute an essential part of the shared 'tacit knowledge' which is indispensable to the smooth functioning of the scientific communications network.[35] These opinions necessarily influence the flow of manuscripts to academic journals; unfortunately we know far too little about this process. Even though some would-be contributors may be indifferent as between two alternative outlets for their work, it may be assumed *ceteris paribus* that the majority prefer to publish in the periodical with the greatest prestige and the largest circulation among specialists in their field (and, perhaps, also among academic administrators). There may also be a preference for publication in their own country and language.

These hypotheses, like many others concerning the role of scholarly journals, are not amenable to scientific testing owing to the dearth of evidence. Hence we may never know, for example, whether editors of economics journals have been 'gatekeepers' of the science in any but a passive sense of that expression. Nor can we readily discover what, if any, have been the effects of changes in the composition and functions of editorial boards.[36] Nevertheless, with the aid of the *Index* it is possible to form a rough impression of the extent to which the journals in our sample performed their primary function of advancing knowledge within their field.

In principle, the degree of 'innovativeness' can be demonstrated statistically by counting the number of times a given journal was the first to publish an article in any given *Index* sub-category. Clearly the importance of such innovations varies greatly from one case to another. A 'first' article may be vastly inferior to its successors, which may be quite independent of it. (Here citations will be a better clue to interdependence than mere similarity of classification by sub-category.) An article may be 'first' – especially if it is on a topic of 'current' interest – merely because of chance factors, such as variations in the dates and frequency of publication, printing delays, etc. (For instance, a 'good' journal may have a longer backlog of articles awaiting publication than an inferior one.) Some of these considerations will be offset by the size of our sample (i.e., the seven hundred or so distinct sub-categories in which firsts may occur), and the fact that there have been no great variations in the quality, timing, and publication policy of our five selected journals. On the other hand, while innovativeness is a desirable characteristic in a scientific publication, it is by no means the only one; and, as already noted, the editor's main function may simply be to accept articles for publication without either taking the initiative or even having much freedom of choice.

Before assessing the relative innovativeness of our selected journals, it will be useful to provide an illustration of the problem of tracing priorities. As an example we may consider sub-category 2.313 (Relation of Saving to Investment), a topic extensively discussed in the years before and after the publication of Keynes' *General Theory* (1936). Naturally enough, the *E.J.* figured prominently in this field as it was co-edited by Keynes himself, and the discussion effectively began in December 1931 with H. Somerville's 'Interest and Usury in a New Light', a note followed by a lengthy symposium in the March and June 1932 issues. After this date, however, the *E.J.* printed nothing more in this sub-category until 1937, although the subject was taken up vigorously by other journals. Moreover, Somerville's note – essentially a comment on Keynes' *Treatise on Money* (1930) – was not a genuine 'first' in our sense, for it was preceded by C. O. Hardy's substantial *J.P.E.* article on 'Savings, Investment, and the Control of Business Cycles', and this in turn was preceded by Hardy's important review of the *Treatise* in the March 1931 *A.E.R.* – an item not even listed in the *Index* under 2.313. Evidently there are risks involved in making casual attributions of priority based on the *Index*; this case confirms our earlier impression that while it is undoubtedly a useful starting point for research,[37] it is no substitute for a careful scrutiny of the literature.

However, despite these limitations, a statistical analysis of successive *Index* volumes can provide a rough indication of innovativeness, a characteristic which can be measured both within our selected group of journals and in the periodical literature as a whole.

Table 2 shows how the scope for innovativeness diminished with the passage of time in relation to the fixed number of *Index* categories. Period Ia has been excluded because the publication of the first article on any given topic represented (at that time) no special achievement since there was so much unoccupied intellectual space and so few publications. It can be seen that no one journal in our sample was consistently more innovative than the others. At first the *J.P.E.* led (followed by the *E.J.*); later the *Q.J.E.* took over (with the *A.E.R.* a close second); and by period III, when the *A.E.R.* enjoyed a slight lead together with the *A.E.R./S.*, the differences were negligible.[38]

Table 2 Number of 'firsts'

Period	A.E.R.	A.E.R./S.	Q.J.E.	J.P.E.	E.J.	Eca.
Ib	12 (16)	11 (12)	16 (19)	26 (40)	21 (29)	2 (3)
II	11 (19)	2 (8)	14 (18)	8 (16)	7 (13)	5 (5)
III	5 (11)	5 (9)	1 (6)	2 (8)	2 (5)	2 (5)
IV	2 (7)	1 (6)	1 (1)	1 (1)	1 (1)	0 (2)
V	1 (1)	0 (3)	1 (1)	1 (1)	0 (0)	0 (0)

Note: Unbracketed figures refer to 'firsts' in the entire *Index*. Bracketed figures refer to 'firsts' within the selected group of journals.

Innovativeness is by no means the only conceivable statistical measure of the success of a scholarly or scientific journal. Another is the frequency with which its articles are cited in other publications, a criterion utilized by students of the sociology of science. Unfortunately, unlike the natural sciences, there are no published citation indexes in economics. However, there are two kinds of indirect but comparatively authoritative sources which can be used for this purpose – namely the thirteen volumes of officially sponsored AEA collections of *Readings*, and the five volumes of *Surveys* of recent developments in economics.[39] Admittedly, the contents of these publications reflect the subjective judgements of their respective authors and editors (or editorial committees). Yet, taken as a whole, they

165

provide a basis for evaluating the relative success of our selected journals in publishing important articles.

Examination of the *Readings* volumes reveals that more articles were selected from the *A.E.R.* than any other journal in our sample (see Table 3), and analysis by date shows that this was largely due to the publication of significant articles during Homan's editorship.[40]

Table 3 Articles reprinted in AEA readings

	I	II	III	IV	V	VI	Total
A.E.R.	–	2	25	5	2	3	37
A.E.R./S.	1	5	5	1	–	2	14
Q.J.E.	3	15	10	4	–	–	32
J.P.E.	1	11	12	1	2	2	29
E.J.	4	13	3	5	4	1	30
Eca.	–	15	6	2	–	1	24

Somewhat different impressions emerge when we aggregate the article and essay citations in the five survey volumes (see Table 4).

Table 4 Citations in the survey volumes

	2 surveys of contemporary economics	3 surveys of economic theory	Total
A.E.R.	157	117	274
A.E.R./S.	46	35	81
Q.J.E.	76	73	149
J.P.E.	91	100	191
E.J.	84	163	247
Eca.	45	60	105
R.E. Stud.	52	152	204
Ecom.	87	102	189
R.E. Stat.	89	112	201
O.E.P.	10	40	50

Note: R.E. Stud. = *Review of Economic Studies*; Ecom. = *Econometrica*; R.E. Stat. = *Review of Economics and Statistics*; O.E.P. = *Oxford Economic Papers*.

These totals do not, of course, provide a reliable index of the quality of material published, for outstandingly bad articles might conceivably be cited repeatedly! Nevertheless, they provide some indication of the intensity of use, and therefore the value, of different journals to leading members of the economics profession. And it will be seen that here, as in the previous case, the *A.E.R.* takes pride of place – although this is mainly due to its lead in 1948–52, whereas it fell behind the *E.J.* and the *Review of Economic Studies* in the 1965–6 surveys.

This data can also provide a basis for some tentative comparisons of the citation habits of economists with those of other scientists. It has long been recognized that in physics and chemistry, for example, the great majority of citations at any time refer to scientific papers published in the very recent past; the chances of any given paper being cited fall off very rapidly in subsequent years. In these circumstances it is noteworthy that in both groups of the *Surveys* volumes half of all citations of essays and articles referred to publications 6.5 years old or less, as compared with earlier estimates of a 'half-life' of eight years in chemistry and five in physics [Fussler, 1949 and 1950; Price, 1963, p. 79]. The constancy of this figure over the period 1948–52 to 1965–6 is a matter of surprise, since it is in marked contrast with the falling trend in the half-life of natural science articles. It would, of course, be premature to draw any sweeping conclusions from this contrast, for the age-distribution of citations is affected by a subtle combination of influences, including: the size and rate of growth of the relevant literature;[41] the rate of obsolescence of current knowledge; time lags in the diffusion of scientific knowledge; the nature of the subject matter; and the prevailing scholarly and scientific conventions.[42] Nevertheless, this is obviously a matter on which further research would provide significant indications of the changing character of the economics profession.

VI CONCLUSIONS

The literature of economics is so vast that it invites statistical analysis. The present article is merely designed to indicate some of the constructive uses of the *A.E.A. Index*, and its very limitations may encourage others to undertake more ambitious and sophisticated studies. In economics we are still far from the bibliographical network diagrams and citation indices which have been devised to reveal 'historical dependencies' in the natural sciences. It would therefore be presumptuous to herald the dawn of a new quantitative historiography parallel to the so-called 'new' economic history. And yet, as stated earlier, the scope for research in this field is virtually unlimited. In addition to analysis of short- and long-term changes in content distribution – which can be undertaken for more recent periods than those selected here – the structural and organizational characteristics of both general and specialized journals can be studied, and geographical and chronological patterns of innovation and diffusion of economic techniques, ideas, and policy proposals can be traced.[43] And if the present generation of journal editors will co-operate, it may eventually be possible to reveal some of the more esoteric aspects of their contribution to the advancement of science.

APPENDIX

Any statistical analysis of the *A.E.A. Index* must necessarily take account of three major limitations: 1) each of the 23 principal categories contains a heterogeneous collection of individual items, the number and range of which differ substantially from one volume to another; 2) many of the 700 or so sub-categories contain very few entries, especially in the earlier years, while '15 to 20 percent of the items have been classified in two or, occasionally, three or more sub-classes' (Introduction to vols. I–V, p. ix); 3) the classification system has been designed for bibliographical purposes, not for the sake of historical research, and, as the editorial committee notes, the schedule employed is, 'in some respects a compromise between principle and practice'.

The first of these limitations seriously diminishes the value of any time-series analysis of content distribution (e.g., by decennial or five-year moving averages) and explains why, in the present case, the *Index* volume periodic system has been retained in the discussion of general trends. Time series analysis could, of course, be applied to individual sub-categories or groups of sub-categories, but in view of the small numbers involved in the majority of cases (since our study is confined to only five journals) most of the significant features can be seen by direct inspection. Moreover, it will be recalled that the present exercise is designed to reveal research possibilities, not to present definitive or comprehensive findings.

In principle, the arbitrary character of the classification system (e.g., with bridge or portmanteau articles, and in those fields where the substance has changed more radically than the nomenclature) poses the most serious problems, especially in view of the significant element of duplication (or even triplication). Emphasis has therefore been placed on the need for careful inspection of individual articles before drawing any precise conclusions (e.g., with respect to leads and lags, innovativeness, or other short-term characteristics; cf. Introduction, pp. ix–xi, xiii–xiv, for further comments on problems of classification).

It will also be helpful to define the notion of an 'article' as used in this study. In most respects the *Index* definition has been adopted (cf. ibid. p. vii) except that review articles and obituaries have been excluded, and each part of a multi-part article has been counted separately. Even here, however, as the *Index* committee acknowledges, some arbitrariness is unavoidable, for the practice of individual journals has varied over time (e.g., in recording 'communications').

NOTES

* In preparing this article I have been assisted by a grant from the American Economic Association. My wife, Sonia E. Coats, performed most of the statistical

drudgery; I have also benefited from critical comments and advice from Diana Crane, André Gabor, A. O. Hughes, Mark Perlman, and George Stigler.

1 It appears that the periodical literature in economics has been growing exponentially at an even faster rate than that in some branches of natural science [Holt and Schrank, 1968]. I owe this reference to Professor Diana Crane.

2 This study was undertaken as a by-product of research on the history of the American Economic Association. See Coats 1969.

3 To be more exact, the additional precision obtainable from more sophisticated techniques seemed unlikely to be sufficient to justify the considerable effort involved in processing the raw data in the *Index* volumes. For a discussion of these data problems see the Appendix at the end of this article.

4 The journals are *The Quarterly Journal of Economics* (October, 1886), published by Harvard; *The Economic Journal* (March, 1891), published by the British Economic Association (later the Royal Economic Society); *The Journal of Political Economy* (December, 1892), published by the University of Chicago; *The American Economic Review* (March, 1911), published by the American Economic Association; *Economica* (January, 1921), published by the London School of Economics. Subsequently the journals will be cited respectively as: *Q.J.E., E.J., J.P.E., A.E.R., Eca.. The Papers and Proceedings of the A.E.A.* will be referred to as *A.E.R./S.*

For a general survey of the range and variety of social science journals see the articles by Daniel Bell and Donald MacRae on American and British periodicals [Bell, 1967 and MacRae, 1967].

5 For example, each of the following served as editor for more than twenty years: F. W. Taussig, *Q.J.E.*; J. L. Laughlin, *J.P.E.*; D. R. Dewey, *A.E.R.*; F. Y. Edgeworth and J. M. Keynes, *E.J.*

6 Compare, for example, the articles by Pan A. Yotopoulos [1961] and F. R. Cleary and D. J. Edwards [1960].

7 In only two of our five cases, the *A.E.R.* and *E.J.*, both organization journals, is there any substantial surviving body of editorial correspondence, and in the latter case it is not yet available to scholars. For an analysis of the AEA papers see Coats [1969]. In order to judge the nature and quality of editorial decision-making it would be necessary to have access to a file of articles rejected as well as those accepted for publication, and in no case known to me does this exist. Indeed, even now few editors of economic journals retain their correspondence, ostensibly owing to lack of office space, but also perhaps in self-defence!

8 Of course, the *Index* periods (I: 1886–1924; II: 1925–39; III: 1940–9; IV: 1950–4; V: 1955–9) are essentially arbitrary. They have neither historical nor scientific significance. Yet it is not worth analysing the data by decade or five-year moving averages because the units are non-homogeneous, and the character and range of periodical publication in economics has changed so rapidly during the period under review. Moreover, in analysing short-term movements the boundaries between the successive volumes have been ignored.

9 It was fully appreciated at the time that the inauguration of the *A.E.R.* might prove embarrassing to its chief American rivals, the *Q.J.E.* and *J.P.E.* It will therefore be of interest to compare the pre- and post-1910 periods in order to discover whether these two periodicals changed their content distribution after the new competitor appeared. See pp. 158–9, n 18.

For the background to this episode see my earlier article [Coats 1969, pp. 57–62].

10 This is contrary to my earlier [Coats, 1969, pp. 61–2] premature, conclusion; the distribution of contents was more evenly spread over the whole range of categories in period III than in earlier or later periods.

11 For example, *Eca.*, cat. 2, periods III–IV, IV–V; *J.P.E.*, cat. 11, periods III–IV, IV–V; *J.P.E.*, cat. 14, periods Ia–Ib, Ib–II; *Q.J.E.*, cat. 19, periods II–III, III–IV.

Another indication of growing conformity, or perhaps editorial inertia, is the fact that the number of significant inter-period changes in the allocation of space to individual categories tended to diminish with the passage of time, both in individual journals and within the group as a whole.

12 The comparative percentages are:

Category	All journals (Bronfenbrenner)		Selected journals (Coats)	
	I	V	I	V
2	8.42	16.77	10.3	36.0
4	5.10	2.78	3.0	6.8
5	1.21	1.47	1.45	1.0
7	1.25	2.87	0.75	1.3
8	2.16	3.55	0.73	2.5
9	10.11	5.89	12.0	6.0
11	7.50	9.64	8.0	10.4
14	3.26	6.27	2.5	2.4
15	17.75	11.73	20.0	8.8
19	11.55	8.05	11.4	4.6

13 See my previously mentioned article [Coats, 1969, pp. 59–61]. 'Theory' is not, of course, confined to Category 2. The comparative figures are:

	Number of articles		
Category 2	Ia	Ib	II
A.E.R.	–	9	22
Q.J.E.	20	16	29
J.P.E.	57	6	15
E.J.	6	8	28
Eca.	–	–	29

14 See J. L. Laughlin to F. W. Fetter in the AEA Papers. [American Economic Association], November 26, 1902. The answer, of course turns on the definition of 'practical'. The *Q.J.E.* was certainly publishing far more in category 2: Ia, *Q.J.E.* 20 per cent; *J.P.E.* 7 per cent; *E.J.* 6 per cent; Ib, *A.E.R.* 9 per cent; *Q.J.E.* 16 per cent; *J.P.E.* 6 per cent; *E.J.* 8 per cent. However, an examination of 'policy' topics designated as such in the *Index* yields the following results for Ia: *J.P.E.* 13.75 per cent; *Q.J.E.* 14.5 per cent; *E.J.* 24 per cent. This, too, is largely a matter of definition.

15 The percentages of articles in the leading categories in the *A.E.R./S.* were as follows:

Category	Ib	II	III	IV	V
2	7.0	13	8.0	23	22
4	3.0	3	2.0	1	6
9	7.0	11	8.0	3	4
11	6.5	9	14.0	12	7
13	9.5	0	15.0	7	2
15	17.5	19	14.0	11	18
19	10.5	6	0.2	5	3
All other	39.0	39	38.0	38	38

16 Generally speaking the President usually selects the topic and an organizer for each session at the annual meeting, and the organizer then selects the individual speakers (in consultation with the President).

17 For background material see my article [Coats, 1969, pp. 61–5]. A comparison of Homan's regime (1941–51) with the last decade of Dewey's editorship (1911–40) reveals that while the long-term trends in categories 2, 4, 9, 15, and 19 continued, the only other marked changes were the increase in category 13, War and Defence Economics (which was attributable to the war) and an increase in category 1, Scope and Method, from 4.5 per cent to 7 per cent. Considering that Homan consciously exerted his editorial initiative during the unusual circumstances of the war period, the changes were surprisingly small.

18 Of the other significant categories, 9 moved with the long-run trend in the *Q.J.E.* and *J.P.E.*, but against it in the *E.J.*; category 11 moved with the trend in the *Q.J.E.* but showed no significant change elsewhere; and 19 moved with the trend in the *E.J.* but changed little elsewhere. The comparative percentages for the categories showing significant changes are:

	A.E.R.		Q.J.E.		J.P.E.		E.J.	
	Ia	*Ib*	*Ia*	*Ib*	*Ia*	*Ib*	*Ia*	*Ib*
2	–	9	20	16	7	6	6	50
4	–	1	6	3	2	2	4	2
9	–	16	12	5	18	10	9	14
11	–	6	6	11	8	7	11	10
13	–	5	0.5	7	1	8	1	13
14	–	3	1	3	1	8	1	0.5
15	–	20	18	26	24	20	17	13
19	–	12	7	8	13	14	15	11

19 Apart from the *A.E.R.* and *A.E.R./S.*, the *Index* lists only six other economics journals in the USA in period I, two of which first appeared in 1919, and one in 1922. However, a number of periodicals which published academic articles on economics are missing from the list.

20 For example, Taussig to Dewey, November 1, 1911; Dewey to Taussig, May 16, 1913; Taussig to Dewey, May 20, 1913; Charles Bullock to Dewey, January 10, 1917; in AEA papers [American Economic Association]. There are other examples, but in this matter the editorial correspondence may be an unreliable guide to the extent of collaboration.

21 This may, of course, be simply another example of the editorial inertia referred to *supra*, note 11.

22 The *Index* classification is a substantial revision and amplification of Homan's method of classifying books and articles in the *A.E.R.*, which was introduced soon after he became its editor in 1941. The compiler's remark that it was developed 'after many discussions and consultations with various specialists' (cf. *Index*, p. ix), is a masterpiece of understatement, as the Association's files abundantly testify. Obviously a classification compiled in the early 1900s would be very different, but the precise implications for our content analysis are difficult to specify. Of the seven hundred odd categories and sub-divisions, articles had appeared in approximately 70 per cent by the end of period I, and 80 per cent by the end of period II.

23 Taking Stigler's two examples: (a) 'the cycle of interest in Monopolistic competition in the 1930's', and (b) 'the sweep of linear programming . . . in the 1950's', we find:

Row	Category	Number of articles						
		Ia	Ib	II	III	IV	V	VI
a1	2.133: Competition and Monopoly	17	15	67	89	56	42	31
a2	2.1332: Competition: Pure, Monopolistic, Imperfect. Entry	3	2	22	16	3	11	3
a3	2.1333: Oligopoly: Bilateral Monopoly	1	0	10	19	14	10	6
b1	7.11: Linear Equations and Inequalities, etc.	–	–	–	–	16	19	18
b2	7.121: Mathematical Programming	–	–	–	4	22	37	36
b3	14.339: Operations Research	–	–	–	–	11	21	17

Note: Rows a1, a2, and a3 refer only to the five selected journals. The remainder cover all journals in the *Index* volumes. As might be expected, our selected journals were slow to introduce mathematical articles of the type included in rows b1, b2, and b3.

24 The totals for sub-category 2.34: Growth and Development Theory are: I: 5; II: 17; III: 39; IV: 83; V: 146. Especially marked increases occurred in the following sub-categories: 2.3401: growth models; 2.3405: underdeveloped economies, general; 2.3420: capital formation and growth, general; 2.3423: underdeveloped areas, capital formation; 2.3440: technological change and adaptation, general.

25 The distinction between endogenous and exogenous movements corresponds to that employed by Bronfenbrenner in classifying economic 'fads'. In the former category the literature is 'feeding upon itself'; in the latter, it is dominated by influences originating outside the academic community.

26 As follows:

Category	Number of articles					
	Ia	Ib	II	III	IV	V
15.8: Transportation	173	166	89	45	26	32
15.82: Railroads	117	109	45	13	6	6

In this case, Laughlin's professed concern with 'practical questions' (cf. *supra*, p. 158) is borne out by the figures.

Journal	Category 15.8 (Transportation), number of articles					
	Ia	Ib	II	III	IV	V
A.E.R.	–	30	8	5	3	5
A.E.R./S.	–	22	23	23	16	19
Q.J.E.	60	39	14	6	0	2
J.P.E.	71	57	29	4	2	2
E.J.	42	18	11	4	2	2
Eca.	–	–	4	3	3	1

27 This group sought formal status as a constituent body within the AEA, but the matter was not finally settled until the constitutional implications of the problem had been fully explored. Cf. *A.E.R./S.*, 1949, *39*, p. 487, and 1953, *43*, p. 558.

28 The principal figures in category 1.3 are as follows:

172

Journal	Number of articles					
	Ia	Ib	II	III	IV	V
A.E.R.	–	7	10	23	2	2
A.E.R./S.	–*	4	4	11	12	5
Q.J.E.	4	1	1	1	–	–
J.P.E.	16	22	5	1	–	–
E.J.	7	4	–	–	–	3
Eca.	–	–	–	1	1	–

* The pre-1911 annual proceedings have not been included; but there were several sessions on the teaching of economics at the early meetings of the Association. By contrast, the *E.J.* displayed virtually no interest in this subject, publishing seven articles in 1.3 before 1911 and only seven more in the whole period 1911–59.

For evidence that Dewey recognized the *J.P.E.*'s 'corner' in this field, see Dewey to E. N. Tucker, October 17, 1913, in the AEA papers [American Economic Association].

29 Category 2.2: Factors of Production and Distributive Shares. The figures in brackets refer to sub-section 'general': 2.20.

Journal	Number of articles					
	Ia	Ib	II	III	IV	V
A.E.R.	– (–)	14 (1)	43 (5)	43 (–)	18 (1)	15 (1)
Q.J.E.	107 (29)	25 (2)	31 (1)	19 (–)	7 (–)	11 (1)
J.P.E.	18 (8)	10 (–)	21 (2)	15 (–)	7 (–)	6 (–)
E.J.	20 (4)	12 (1)	25 (3)	4 (–)	8 (1)	16 (–)
Eca.	– (–)	– (–)	15 (3)	15 (–)	2 (–)	9 (1)

30 Within our sample, the *E.J.* led in sub-category 2.3401 with two articles in 1939, two in 1949, and one in 1950; the *A.E.R.* followed with one in 1943, and one in 1947. In 1952 six more appeared, and by 1963 the cumulated total was *A.E.R.* 14; *A.E.R./S.* 7; *Q.J.E.* 7; *J.P.E.* 2; *E.J.* 32; *Eca.* 6.

31 Some of these hypotheses could be framed as quiz questions for historians of economics. For example, to choose at random: How far did AEA policy determine the exceptionally heavy concentration on category 13 (War and Defence Economics) in the *A.E.R.* and *A.E.R./S.* in period III? Why did *Eca.* print so much in category 8.2 (National Income and Wealth) during the 1940s, a category dominated at other times by the *E.J.*; and why did the American journals usually publish so little in this category? Why did the *E.J.* publish so many articles in category 6 (Contemporary Economic Conditions, Policy and Planning) between 1927 and 1933? Why did category 11 (International Economics) drop sharply in the *J.P.E.* in the 1950s when it expanded rapidly in the other four journals?

32 This applies in the cases of *The Economic History Review* (1927), *The Journal of Business* (1928), *The Journal of Marketing* (1936), *National Tax Journal* (1948), *Proceedings of the Industrial Relations Research Association* (1948).

33 In period I the *E.J.* served in part as a Commonwealth periodical. Its international coverage was more pronounced than that of the *A.E.R.*, *Q.J.E.*, or *J.P.E.* After the founding of the regional journals referred to in the text, the number of *E.J.* articles on the areas concerned tended to fall, but not dramatically.

34 I am indebted to Professor Piero Barucci of the University of Florence for

stimulating comments on this point. On some of the general issues involved, see Joseph J. Spengler [1970] and the references cited therein.

35 The concept of 'tacit knowledge' is developed in Polanyi [1958, pp. 87ff, 207ff].

36 For example, see Crane [1967]. The term 'gatekeepers' is derived from Alfred de Grazia [1963].

37 This impression is reinforced by other cases, *e.g.*, in the same period: 2.3404 (Developed Economies, Stagnation). The debate about 'economic maturity' or stagnation effectively began in 1937 in the *A.E.R.* and *A.E.R./S.* but the first articles in this sub-category appeared in 1929 in *Eca.* and *The Journal of the Royal Statistical Society*.

In studying priorities, the links between the *A.E.R.* and *A.E.R./S.* should be examined, for at times these two publications seem to have been in collaboration even though they were, in principle, independent.

38 These results are expressed in absolute terms, as the computation of relative figures (taking into account variations in the number of articles per journal per volume) does not affect the order of precedence.

39 Volumes of *Readings* were published on the following dates: 1942; 1944; 1946; 1949; 1951 (two); 1952; 1953; 1955; 1958; 1959; 1966; 1968.

A *Survey of Contemporary Economics*, vols. I and II appeared in 1948 and 1952, respectively. The three *Surveys of Economic Theory* (1965–6) contained articles originally published in the *A.E.R.* and *E.J.* between 1959 and 1965.

40 Several articles were also selected from the following journals: *Review of Economics and Statistics*: 14; *Review of Economic Studies*: 8; *Econometrica*: 7. The relative positions of individual journals are unaffected by taking account of variations in the number of articles per journal per volume.

41 On this point cf. *supra*, note 1.

42 See Price [1963, pp. 79–81] and MacRae [1969]. I owe this reference to Professor Crane.

43 The *Index* can also be used to study the trend (if, indeed, there is one) towards multiple authorship in economics, a movement which has been termed 'one of the most violent transitions that can be measured in recent trends of scientific manpower and literature' [Price, 1963, p. 89].

REFERENCES

American Economic Association. Correspondence in the AEA files, Northwestern University Library and Secretary's office, Vanderbilt University.

Bell, D. 'Social Science Press in the United States', *Int. Soc. Sci. J.*, 1967, *19*, pp. 245–54.

Bronfenbrenner, M. 'Trends, Cycles, and Fads in Economic Writing', *Amer. Econ. Rev. Papers and Proceedings*, May 1966, *56*, pp. 538–52.

Cleary, F. R. and Edwards, D. J. 'The Origins of the Contributors to the American Economic Review during the 'Fifties', *Amer. Econ. Rev.*, Dec. 1960, *50*, pp. 1011–14.

Coats, A. W. 'The American Economic Association's Publications: An Historical Perspective', *J. Econ. Lit.*, Mar. 1969, *7*(1), pp. 57–68. Reprinted in this volume, pp. 264–79.

Crane, D. 'The Gatekeepers of Science: Some Factors Affecting the Selection of Articles for Scientific Journals', *Amer. Sociologist*, Nov. 1967, *2*, pp. 195–201.

Fussler, H. H. 'Characteristics of Research Literature Used by Chemists and Physicists in the United States', *Library Quarterly*, 1949, *19*, pp. 19–35; 1950, *20*, pp. 119–43.

de Grazia, A. 'The Scientific Reception System and Dr Velikovsky', *Amer. Behavioral Scientist*, 1963, *7*, pp. 38–56.

Hagstrom, W. O. *The Scientific Community*. New York, 1965.

Holt, C. C. and Schrank, W. E. 'Growth of the Professional Literature in Economics and Other Fields, and Some Implications', *Amer. Documentation*, Jan. 1968, *19*, pp. 17–26.

Kuhn, T. S. *The Structure of Scientific Revolutions*. Chicago: University of Chicago Press, 1962.

MacRae, D. 'Social Science Press in the United Kingdom', *Int. Soc. Sci. J.*, 1967, *19*, pp. 236–44.

MacRae, D., Jr. 'Growth and Decay Curves in Scientific Citations', *Amer. Sociological Rev.*, Oct. 1969, *34*(5), pp. 631–5.

Polanyi, M. *Personal Knowledge: Towards a Post-critical Philosophy*. Chicago, 1958.

Price, D. J. de S. *Little Science, Big Science*. Columbia, 1963.

Spengler, J. J. 'Notes on the International Transmission of Economic Ideas', *Hist. Polit. Econ.*, Spring 1970, *2*, pp. 133–51.

Stigler, G. J. 'Statistical Studies in the History of Economic Thought', in his *Essays in the History of Economics*. Chicago, 1965, pp. 44–50.

Yotopoulos, P. A. 'Institutional Affiliation of the Contributors to Three Professional Journals', *Amer. Econ. Rev.*, Sept. 1961, *51*, pp. 665–70.

10

THE LEARNED JOURNALS IN THE DEVELOPMENT OF ECONOMICS AND THE ECONOMICS PROFESSION

The British case

I INTRODUCTION

The first recognizably modern learned economics periodical published in Britain, *The Economic Journal*, was inaugurated exactly a century ago, in 1891. The organ of the newly formed British Economic Association (BEA), later the Royal Economic Society (RES) (Coats, 1968; Kadish and Freeman, 1990; Winch, 1990), it soon acquired a distinguished reputation in its field, which it has retained ever since. Together with the appearance of the first edition of Alfred Marshall's magisterial *Principles of Economics* in the previous year, the early 1890s truly constitute a watershed in the history of British economics. Yet, given the high reputation British nineteenth-century economists enjoyed within the international scholarly community, the surprising thing about the advent of the *Economic Journal* is not its timing – for in the last quarter of the century new scholarly organizations and publications were proliferating in many countries – but the fact that its sponsors were so hesitant, tardy, and unadventurous in approaching the desired consummation. The absence of strong leadership from Alfred Marshall, unquestionably the most influential single British economist of the period, was a retarding factor. But, more generally, by comparison with the situation on the European continent and, especially in the USA, the slow growth of British higher education and the delayed academic institutionalization of political economy constitute more important explanations (Larson, 1978; Coats, 1980). For it is generally acknowledged that the expansion of modern social science periodical literature has not solely, or perhaps even mainly, been determined by intellectual forces (Lengyel, 1967; Macrae, 1967; Bell, 1967).

By comparison with the USA, where the study of the numbers and significance of economic journals has become a minor growth industry during the past two decades or so, British economic journals have been largely ignored by historians and sociologists. The difference is not simply quantitative, for there have been enough British publications since the 1960s to constitute a valuable data source for those who, like their American counterparts, wish to enhance their knowledge and understanding of the structure and functioning of the economics profession. The difference is, broadly speaking, sociological or cultural, and one of the aims of the present paper is to suggest the reasons for this state of affairs, and to propose research topics deserving of exploration. The first, and more modest, task however is to provide an outline history of the development of British learned economic journals.

Chronologically speaking the subject falls into four distinct phases:

(i) pre-history, prior to the foundation of the *Economic Journal*;
(ii) 1891 to World War I, when that periodical had only a single rival, the *Economic Review*;
(iii) the inter-war years, when a handful of new journals appeared, especially in the 1930s; and
(iv) the post-1945 era, which eventually witnessed an explosive growth roughly comparable to that occurring earlier or contemporaneously in many other countries.

II PRE-HISTORY

As in any other scholarly or scientific discipline the emergence of specialist learned or professional journals in economics has been determined by a combination of supply and demand factors, such as: the growth of knowledge in the field; the availability of a sufficient number of willing authors deemed competent by the cognoscenti or intellectual group involved; and the existence of an audience for their effusions. Since the publications have often been subsidized by educational bodies, private sponsors, or even government agencies, market forces may not have been a preponderant influence. Indeed, some recent commentators have suggested that the interests of editors and authors have frequently taken preference over the interests of the readership! (Lengyel, 1967, p. 147; Sczepanski, 1967, pp. 234–5). In Britain, or more particularly in England, the necessary preconditions for economic periodicals were present at least by 1820, in the heyday of Ricardian economics. Yet political economy was apparently not yet sufficiently clearly differentiated from cognate subjects to suggest the need for a specialized periodical. Instead, authors of economic articles turned mainly to that great literary organ, *The Edinburgh Review*, which was followed at a distance (both qualitatively and quantitatively) by its Tory rival *The Quarterly Review*, *The Westminster Review* (a Benthamite product) and, more distantly still by *Blackwood's Magazine* and *Fraser's Magazine* (Fetter, 1953, 1958, 1960, 1962, 1965). By mid-century over one thousand economic articles had appeared in these periodicals (Stigler, 1965, p. 41). Yet despite the subject's growing intellectual authority and scientific prestige – albeit with some setbacks – by the time W. S. Jevons and Marshall embarked on their careers the supply of suitable outlets had changed little since the 1820s. The National Association for the Promotion of Social Science was too ephemeral, and the proceedings of the London, Manchester, and Dublin Statistical Societies were too narrowly quantitative, descriptive, and miscellaneous in content to satisfy the economists' needs. So up to the 1890s, and indeed for some time thereafter, they were obliged to rely on the various reviews: *Edinburgh, Fortnightly, Contemporary, National,* or other miscellaneous publications such as the *Academy, Macmillan's Magazine,* or the *Pall Mall Gazette.*

The movement to rectify the situation gathered momentum in the second half of the 1880s, about the time when Marshall began his long and influential tenure of the Cambridge chair, and it was undoubtedly encouraged by the founding of the American Economic Association, in 1885, and the inauguration of Harvard's *Quarterly Journal of Economics (Q.J.E.)* the following year. In 1887, a lively article in the *Q.J.E.* by H. S. Foxwell (Foxwell, 1887), Marshall's Cambridge colleague, correctly foreshadowed things to come in England, although the possibility of working through or even taking over the *Journal of the Royal* (from 1887) *Statistical Society* was still under consideration into the mid 1890s.[1] It was, however, deemed unsatisfactory for a variety of reasons (Coats, 1968), and so, following the transatlantic lead, the first open British learned society cum professional organization of economists was launched, with the publication of the *Economic Journal (E.J.)* as one of its primary objectives.

III 1891–1921

Any late-twentieth-century professional economist who peruses the early numbers of the *Economic Journal* cannot fail to observe its marked, if superficial resemblance to recent issues in respect of its typeface, layout, and contents (apart from the leading articles), including such matters as extended book reviews, economic notes and memoranda, current topics, and periodicals and book listings. Indeed, from its very beginnings the new periodical (initially 840 pages in the first year) provided invaluable services to the expanding national and international community of professional economists. Yet it must not be supposed that all was plain sailing, for shortly before the first (unintentionally delayed) issue was in print a rival periodical, *The Economic Review,* edited in Oxford by a group of social reformist clerical dons, appeared on the scene. This publication, the organ of the Oxford branch of the Christian Social Union, has too frequently been dismissed or overlooked by historians of economics, although it was symptomatic of the state of British economics at the time, and the source

178

of considerable concern and embarrassment to Marshall and the *Economic Journal*'s sponsors. To some, like Marshall's contentious Cambridge colleague, the economic historian William Cunningham (who relished Marshall's discomfort), the two publications reflected the basic differences in aims and spirit between Oxford and Cambridge (Cunningham, 1891). In the terminology of Foxwell's *Q.J.E.* article mentioned earlier (Foxwell, 1887), the *Review* was a product of the moral/humanistic wing of the so-called 'new' movement in British economics, which was traceable in part to Marshall's Balliol predecessor, Arnold Toynbee (Kadish, 1986); while to a late-twentieth-century observer the two ventures demonstrate how blurred was the demarcation between amateurs and professionals in British economics at the time.

Limitations of space preclude a full account of this fascinating episode, which has been carefully examined by recent historians of economics, most notably Alon Kadish (1982, especially chapter 6). The Oxford plan to launch an *Economic Monthly Review* was conceived as early as 1885, the year Marshall took up the Cambridge chair, four years before the Oxford Branch of the Christian Social Union was founded; nevertheless the scheme took the BEA's sponsors completely by surprise (Coats, 1968, p. 355). At the Association's inaugural meeting Marshall put on a brave face, saying that had their proposed *Economic Journal* 'been started a little time ago' (incidentally, a move he had opposed), the announcement of the *Economic Review* 'would have caused them some dismay. But, as things were, he thought they were strong enough to support both journals.' Nevertheless, a few days earlier he had confided to L. R. Phelps, of Oriel College, one of the *Review*'s three editors:

> I desire the success of your journal, as you originally described the aims to me, almost as much as that with which I am more directly concerned. But undoubtedly the way would have been easier for us if you had been able to adopt a title which suggested that the two journals were designed to meet different needs, to supplement one another and not to compete with one another.
>
> (Marshall to Phelps, 31 October, 1890,
> quoted in Kadish, 1982, p. 187)

In particular Marshall regretted the choice of the term *Review*, which was to have been the title of the BEA's organ, suggesting that some such title as *The Journal of Social Reform* would have been more appropriate. But the Oxford dons were not intentionally making life difficult for Marshall and his colleagues. Indeed, they deliberately postponed publication of the *Review*'s first issue from October 1890 to January 1891, the date scheduled for the *Economic Journal*'s inauguration; but owing to the economists' procrastination the latter did not actually appear until March of that year.

Beyond this, the *Review*'s editors revised their original announcement that 'The *Review* will be concerned chiefly with modern economic difficulties as they bear on the whole of life', substituting the slightly narrower statement that it would concentrate mainly on 'the moral and social bearings of economic problems'. This was broadly compatible with Marshall's description of the *Review* as designed 'for the purpose of dealing with problems in which ethical and religious questions took the first place, but which had a kernel of economic difficulty' (cited Coats, 1968, p. 356). The issue was sensitive, for the relationship between ethics and economics was being actively debated at the time by the economists (Maloney, 1985, chapter 9), the clergy, and the laity. The *Review*'s inaugural editorial statement (*Economic Review*, vol. 1, pp. 1–3) flatly denied the possibility of drawing a sharp line between 'the spheres of the Economic Moralist and the scientific Economist', a position directly contrary to Marshall's campaign to establish economics as a science independent of the Cambridge Moral Sciences Tripos. In practice, of course, Marshall repeatedly slipped back and forth between the two 'spheres', while paying lip service to the distinction between the economist's roles, *qua* scientist and *qua* private citizen (Coats, 1990; Maloney, 1985).

Although the *Review*'s inaugural editorial denied that it was 'the organ of those who lean to historical method', there were clear echoes of the English *Methodenstreit* in the statement that: 'Though the fight between the two [sic] schools still rages somewhat fiercely' there were signs of reconciliation pointing to 'a new and larger Economics, using history and not abusing theory' (a statement Marshall might have approved). The *Review* was designed to help 'adherents of the two schools' to reach 'a common meeting-ground' and thereby 'understand one another better'. The *Economic Journal*, too, adopted a consciously conciliatory policy, undertaking to open its pages to representatives of all schools 'doing genuine work', and tactfully refraining from defining genuineness. Curiously enough, this eclecticism was reflected in the contents of the early issues, which were not nearly as clearly distinguishable from the *Review* as might have been expected. Of course the latter devoted much more space to topics like: 'The Moral Factor in Economic Law'; 'Some Aspects of Game-preserving'; 'A Social Policy for Churchmen'; 'The Social Doctrines of the Sermon on the Mount'; and 'Commercial Morality'. Yet it also included many articles on strikes and other labour problems; bimetallism; the incidence of urban rates; the distribution of wealth; graduated taxation; co-operation; and other matters of the kind treated (albeit usually somewhat differently) by the *E.J.* For its part, during its early years the *E.J.* printed comparatively few purely theoretical articles, a disproportionate number of which were written by its principal editor, F. Y. Edgeworth (Kadish and Freeman, 1990, p. 42), and numerous articles on topics that might have seemed more suitable for the *Review*, such as: 'Women's Work in Leeds'; 'The Difficulties of Individualism'; 'Co-operation and Profit Sharing'; 'The Wife's Contribution to Family Income'; 'The Industrial Residuum'; 'The Relativity of Economic Doctrine'; 'Patriarchal and Socialist Remedies'; and 'Ethics and Economics'.[2] With occasional contributions by W. J. Ashley, E. Cannan, Cunningham, Foxwell, J. A. Hobson, D. H. MacGregor, and L. L. Price (but not Marshall), it is clear that the economists did not entirely shun it. The *Review*'s economic articles were regularly listed in the *E.J.*'s bibliography and abstracts of current periodicals, together with a curious miscellany of other publications, and it continued publication right up to 1914, when the war evidently killed it off.

IV 1921–45

This phase properly begins with the first appearance of *Economica*, the publication of the London School of Economics (LSE), the principal institutional rival to Cambridge economics. Until 1933 *Economica* was subtitled *A Journal of the Social Sciences*, and this accurately reflected its contents, which ranged widely across the social sciences including demography, law, international relations, and public administration. By the early 1930s however, soon after Lionel Robbins's return from Oxford and Friedrich von Hayek's arrival from Vienna, marked changes in the curriculum and growth of the teaching and research personnel in economics led to the inauguration of a new journal *Politica*, to cover 'Political Science, Sociology, and International Relations and allied subjects', leaving the new series of *Economica*, from 1934, free to specialize on economics and economic history.

This is but one among several indicators of the growth of specialization in British economics during the interwar years, for in 1926 two new scholarly organizations were founded, the Economic History Society and the Agricultural Economics Society, each of which proceeded to issue its own periodical. The case of the *Economic History Review*, which first appeared in 1927, is curious, for a year earlier the editor of the *Economic Journal*, J. M. Keynes, had announced his intention to publish a series of annual supplements to the *Journal* under the title *Economic History*, which would be issued free of charge to RES members. Although his motives are still unclear, it seems likely that he wished either to forestall the publication of a separate economic history periodical, a project that had been under active consideration for some time, or simply to assert the *Economic Journal*'s claim to economic history as part of its territory (Barker, 1977, pp. 11–12). As the principal proponent of an independent economic history publication was the Reader in Economic History at Oxford, Ephraim Lipson, it is tempting to interpret Keynes's action either as another manifestation of the long-standing rivalry between the Oxford and Cambridge approaches to economics, as in the 1890s, or even as a legacy of deeper methodological disagreements between orthodox neo-classical economists and the proponents of an alternative historico-inductive conception of economics (Koot,

1987). As is well known, Keynes took for granted the superiority of Cambridge economics (Coats, 1967, p. 708); but his challenge to the new Economic History Society, if such it was, proved to be transitory, for the *Economic History* supplement to the *Economic Journal* ceased publication in World War II. Perhaps the market, even at a zero price, could not sustain this addition to the literature, substantial though it was.[3]

The second example of specialization is somewhat different, for the antecedents of the post-1945 *Journal of Agricultural Economics* took the form of a periodical *Report of the Proceedings of a Conference of the Society* (i.e. the Agricultural Economics Society), a journal differing in content and organization from the others considered here. It deserves attention, however, as evidence of the vigour of the agricultural economics profession, a species of economics that has had a distinctive history on both sides of the Atlantic (Coats, 1976; Hawley, 1990). For although mainstream economists have generally looked down on their agricultural brethren, the latter have had a pioneering role in government economic policy and research; and in Britain, as in the USA, there was little overlap or interchange between agricultural and other economists until well after World War II.

Of the other three principal economic periodicals launched in Britain during the 1930s the *Manchester School of Social Studies* most clearly exemplified the institutional urge to provide a publication outlet for its economists. Despite its title, the *School* has always been primarily an economic journal; and in the initial editorial the need for its services was justified by the claim that:

> Each University develops in time a technique of thought, a method of approach, and a convention of economic understanding peculiarly its own. Everyone passing through a University assimilates to some extent its mode of thought. In Manchester this outlook has been necessarily influenced by the industrial activities congregated around us, and by the special problems with which these activities have been brought face to face.... This journal is not the organ of the University staff alone, but the body of the Manchester School as a whole.
>
> (M. S. 1930, vol. 1, pp. 1–2)

This body was not simply confined to the propagandist free trade descendants of Cobden and Bright, for it covered those members of the university (and presumably ex-members) 'engaged in industrial or commercial undertakings'. Whether the Manchester 'mode of thought' was sufficiently different from that in other universities located in industrial cities, such as Sheffield, Leeds, or Liverpool, was not argued. The editorial manifesto, presumably written by the editor, G. W. Daniels, went further than the editorial statements in any other British journal since the *Economic Review* in advocating a distinctive conception of economics. The *Manchester School*'s version was, however, innocuously eclectic, combining 'pure economics' with 'the consideration of realistic data'. Economics, it declared, was 'an art of industrial navigation' requiring both theoretical research and practical verification and deduction; and in its early years the *School* printed a number of general articles examining the nature of economics as a science and its relationships with other disciplines.

Somewhat less self-consciously, but with a roughly comparable mixture of theory and applied economics, *Oxford Economic Papers*, first published in 1938, also identified itself as a single university publication, though the initial editorial statement (repeated until 1947) somewhat half-heartedly added that submissions from outside Oxford would be considered. Needless to say, few such contributions appeared in its pages, which contained a smaller proportion of articles by non-British authors than the other journals considered here.

By far the most cosmopolitan of the interwar British periodicals, however, was the *Review of Economic Studies*, disparagingly known in Cambridge as 'the children's magazine' or, alternatively, 'the green publication of the LSE' (Moggridge, 1973, vol. 13, p. 326; vol. 14, p. 299). Drawing most of its material from the younger generation of economists or graduate students, and with its managing editors based, respectively, in London (Abba Lerner), Cambridge, Mass. (Paul Sweezy), and Oxford and London (Ursula Webb, later Ursula Hicks), the early issues contained papers by authors from Switzerland, Austria, France, Denmark, and Egypt, as well as North America. It was conspicuously more devoted to theoretical and technical refinements than any of its peers, including the *E.J.*, and there were numerous short articles or discussions of such arcane theoretical topics as: the elasticity of substitution; arc elasticity of demand; the determinateness of equilibrium; and the measurement of monopoly power. There was also some predilection for methodology, as in the later 1930s issues of *Economica*; but the *Review* also published a number of solidly empirical and applied articles, though proportionately fewer than the other British journals.

As might be expected, during World War II most of the periodicals drastically reduced the number of pages they produced, whether as an economy measure or because so many of their potential contributors were otherwise engaged, either on government work or in the armed forces. Yet curiously enough, a new academic economic journal appeared during this period, initially (in December 1939) in typescript as a monthly diary on current economic affairs, but subsequently (from 1940) as a printed periodical, variously named as, in particular, the *Institute of Statistics (Oxford) Bulletin*. In this form it included a number of substantial articles on wartime economic problems and policies by well-known academics such as M. Kalecki, P. W. S. Andrews, and T. Balogh; and of course it has continued to appear ever since.

One tricky problem in this study is the decision where to draw the line between academic and non-academic publications, a matter that is most pertinent in the case of the various bank publications. In the pre-1939 British situation it seems appropriate to consider only two: the *Banker* and *Lloyds Bank Monthly Review*, which, from 1926 and 1930 respectively, fairly regularly printed named articles by well-known economists, including Balogh, A. L. Bowley, H. Clay, T. E. Gregory, R. Harrod, Hayek, N. Kaldor, Keynes, MacGregor, Robbins, and R. S. Sayers, as well as the Americans J. M. Clark and H. Parker Willis. The total number of such articles was small by comparison with those appearing in the regular academic journals; but after 1945 these periodicals reappeared, together with the *Midland Bank Review* and the *Three Banks Review*, providing valuable fora in which leading academic economists could reach a significant audience for their views on past, present, and future economic problems and policies.

V POST-1945

According to a recent *Analytical Guide to Economics Journals and Serials* (Sichel and Sichel, 1986) confined to English-language publications, some sixty-five periodicals currently have a British base.[4] Needless to say, this figure is somewhat arbitrary. In compiling an inventory of this kind difficult editorial decisions are unavoidable, and on close inspection about seventeen of the British items seem decidedly of minor or only marginal interest. Even so, the remaining forty-eight constitute an enormous increase over the number appearing before 1939, and it is worth noting that irregular serial publications have been excluded here, although many of them contain significant research contributions. The most rapid growth of numbers has occurred since the mid-sixties, and there was evidently a demonstration effect at work. The great expansion of higher education at the time was obviously important, with the concomitant increase of academic staff and degree-granting institutions – universities and polytechnics. But it is also noteworthy that commercial sponsorship of reputable academic publications has become accepted, some of which are managed by learned societies or specialist groups. The falling real costs and increasing efficiency of publishing have played a part in the ever-growing volume of new titles, notwithstanding the recent cuts in university and polytechnic library budgets.

It is obviously impossible to describe adequately the range and variety of titles and contents of the new British postwar economic periodicals. The period has been one of rapidly expanding technique and increasing specialization, both of which are reflected in the list. But there has also been a significant growth in the number of 'applied' and policy-oriented periodicals, which find a market in government, business, and banking as well as academe. Of the regional journals the *Scottish Journal of Political*

Economy (from 1954 – a surprisingly late date) is pre-eminent, and also well known is the former *Yorkshire Bulletin of Economic Research* (1949; from 1971 renamed the *Bulletin of Economic Research*). Cambridge, once the unquestioned centre of British academic economics, now publishes two additional journals, the *Cambridge Economic Policy Review* (1975) prepared by members of the Cambridge Economic Policy Group for the Department of Applied Economics at Cambridge, whereas the *Cambridge Journal of Economics* (1977), adopting an approach 'rooted in the traditions of Marx, Kalecki and Keynes', is the organ of the Cambridge Political Economy Society. More recently a new *Review of Political Economy* (1988, and therefore not included in the above guide) is designed primarily as an outlet for the post-Keynesian and institutionalist viewpoints.

VI GENERAL REFLECTIONS

(a) The cultural context

Like other social science periodicals, economic journals broadly reflect the general cultural as well as the institutional structures of the societies in which they appear, and the present case is no exception. It is appropriate that for so much of its existence the *Economic Journal* has been not only the most venerable but also the most prestigious British publication in its field, for age and status have so often been associated in British life. The organ of the most important organization of British economists, the *E.J.*, was for long edited from Cambridge, generally acknowledged as the leading centre of the discipline. Admittedly the founding editor, F. Y. Edgeworth, was based in Oxford; but he never put a strong personal stamp on the *Journal*. (However, see Newman, 1990; and Kadish and Freeman, 1990, p. 42.) Indeed, he seems to have been inefficient, reluctant to make editorial decisions, and decidedly deferential to Marshall's authority. (Harrod, 1952, pp. 159–60; Price, n.d., pp. 32, 34, 60; Coats, 1968, p. 362 n.) In 1911 the twenty-eight-year-old Maynard Keynes, quintessentially a Cambridge man, took over and efficiently dominated the *E.J.* for most of the next thirty years. With him, as with his long-serving assistant editor and eventual successor, E. A. G. Robinson, the vast majority of British economists and many others abroad regarded the *E.J.*–Cambridge link as a central feature of British economics. Whether that was desirable, or not, is another matter (see *infra*, p. 192ff.).

Before examining the nature and implications of that state of affairs it will be helpful to provide some background comments on the professional situation.

During the modernization process of the later nineteenth and twentieth centuries British higher education adapted itself slowly, and in retrospect remarkably painlessly, to the growing demand for new categories of trained specialized personnel. The rise of professionalism in the academic community, as in society at large, involved the effort by new specialist groups to acquire social status and market power; nevertheless there was a clear difference between the assertive competitiveness prevalent in the USA and the 'controlled selection' evident in the UK, where social differentiation was well understood and widely accepted. The slowly expanding corps of academic professionals experienced a combination of co-option and segregation into the intellectual élite, especially at Oxford and Cambridge, where the universities were gradually adjusting to the pressures of the time, endeavouring to reconcile the traditional values and vested interests of the educational establishment with the emergent class structure and commercial motivations of industrial capitalism (Larson, 1978; Coats, 1980).

To suggest that the academic economists were in the vanguard of this movement would be to credit them with more energy and imagination than they demonstrated, if only because of the extraordinary influence of Alfred Marshall, who largely set the tone and shaped the direction of British economics for almost half a century. A leader who invariably played down intellectual novelties, including his own, repeatedly insisted on the continuity of economic ideas (especially British ideas), and emphasized the duty of respect for one's elders and betters, he provided in his monumental *Principles* an architectonic structure (or paradigm) capacious and flexible enough to accommodate economists and laymen of very varied views, skills, interests, and methodological predilections. Three years before his *magnum opus* appeared his Cambridge colleague, Foxwell, testified to Marshall's influence on British academic appointments in economics, commenting perceptively that for generations British economists had been 'men of one book'. Part of Marshall's achievement was to displace J. S. Mill's *Principles* and reign virtually uncontested, at the pedagogical level, even for some time after the appearance of Keynes's *General Theory*. Against this background the assumption of Cambridge pre-eminence was almost unchallenged, at least until after World War II.

(b) Editorial influence and policies

Long-serving editorships are not uncommon in economics. Davis R. Dewey managed the *American Economic Review* from 1911 to 1940; Frank W. Taussig edited or was directly associated with the *Q.J.E.* from the early 1890s to 1938; and Lionel Robbins was either joint editor or a member of the Editorial Board of *Economica* from 1930 to the mid-1970s, though in the later years his connection seems to have been only nominal. Keynes, however, virtually dominated the *E.J.* from his appointment in 1911 until 1945, shortly before he died.

Unlike Dewey's papers, Keynes's editorial papers are not yet officially open, but fortunately we have Donald Moggridge's invaluable essay on

'Keynes as Editor' to confirm that despite the remarkable extent and variety of his ideas and activities Keynes found the time to play 'the central role in the development of the *Journal*'s character and reputation' (Moggridge, 1990, p. 143). Unlike most other editors of major journals for whom we have evidence or gossip, Keynes 'had few inhibitions in placing his own articles in his own *Journal*', sometimes even 'using his position as editor to reply to articles by others in the same issue in which they appeared, going so far as to place his own comments immediately after the piece that had irked him' (ibid., p. 145). Nor does he seem to have submitted any of his own contributions to an external referee – thereby exemplifying the personalization which, according to Richard Whitley, has been characteristic of British social science journals (Whitley, 1970).

Of course, during the 1930s Keynes's ideas became so important a part of British economics that he could scarcely have avoided some participation in the debate; and where his area of interest was concerned 'he consulted extensively, initially with Dennis Robertson and subsequently with A. C. Pigou' (Moggridge, 1990, p. 146). He periodically solicited contributions, in one instance even helping to arrange finance for a research project that eventually yielded three articles in the *Journal*; and despite his practice of making quick decisions, he sometimes took 'immense pains and trouble' helping an author to get his material into an acceptable publishable form (ibid., p. 147).

One of Moggridge's most surprising disclosures is what he terms Keynes's 'occasional zenophobia', an attitude which, however extreme, did not prevent the percentage of articles by non-British, especially American, contributors from rising significantly during his regime, as it did in other British economic journals. Possibly Keynes was merely following the RES Council's suggestion, of March 1925, that in order to limit the *Journal*'s size 'the editors be requested to exercise at their discretion some discrimination against the insertion of articles from foreign contributors except in the case of special interest or importance' (ibid., pp. 144, 151).

So much for British insularity! But what of Cambridge insularity? Inevitably there were leaders and followers, insiders and outsiders in British economics, as elsewhere, but few critics would have been willing to go as far, especially publicly, as Harry Johnson, a wide-ranging international economist of Canadian origin who spent six years as a Fellow at King's College, the very heart of the Keynesian establishment. Writing in 1977 of the post-World War II years, he protested that:

> Qualified economists in other British universities never became resigned to the impression that Cambridge economists seemed assured of publication of everything they wrote in *The Economic Journal*, that often unfamiliar Cambridge names dominated the reviews section of the *Journal*, and that unknowns from Cambridge and its hinterlands

were frequently chosen over acknowledged experts from elsewhere for the British contingent at the Round Tables of the International Economic Association, which Austin Robinson dominated through his dominance of the Royal Economic Society.

(Johnson, 1978, p. 154)

This is a sweeping, even sensational charge by a strategically placed critic who, incidentally, published more economic articles than any other economist of his time. His claim obviously cannot be fully investigated here, even as far as it concerns the *Journal*, for to do so would require a careful analysis and judgement based on a complete list of articles submitted to and accepted or rejected by its editors. No such list exists. However, it is clear that although for most of its existence (except 1934–45), the *E.J.* had two editors (or one editor and an assistant), one of whom came from outside Cambridge, the chief figure in Johnson's demonology is Austin (E.A.G.) Robinson, who was assistant editor to Keynes from 1934 to 1945 and subsequently joint editor with Roy Harrod (1945–61) of Oxford, and Charles Carter (1961–70). But before considering Robinson's defence of his stewardship, it is appropriate to look at some relevant statistics although, needless to say, they require careful interpretation.

Table 1 clearly shows the extent to which Cambridge-based authors dominated the *Economic Journal* (the data represent numbers of articles, not pages) throughout the period, though their preponderance was diminishing after 1939. Up to 1949, Oxford authors were less prominent than those from London, whereas thereafter these proportions were reversed, but not dramatically. The tremendous preponderance of London authors (not necessarily all from LSE) in *Economica* is only to be expected of a department or 'house' journal, albeit not necessarily to that extent; similar patterns have been found in the USA with the *Q.J.E.* and the *Journal of Political Economy* (*J.P.E.*). Indeed, one of the complaints levelled at Cambridge was that the *E.J.* was treated more like a house journal than the organ of a national scholarly society. On the whole, Cambridge authors appeared in *Economica* less frequently than might have been expected, possibly because they regarded it as inferior. Authors from other British universities occupied a growing share of both periodicals, a trend reflecting the expansion of numbers outside the big three; while the decline of non-university authors in both publications is evidence of the growing 'academicization' of British economics. Table 2 provides a more detailed breakdown of articles in both periodicals from 'other' UK universities, while Table 3 compares the proportions of British and non-British authors. Striking features are the irregularly growing percentage of American authors in both periodicals, and the much higher share of non-American overseas authors in the *E.J.* than in *Economica*. The former's role as a Commonwealth-oriented publication, in respect of both its contents and its authorships, has already been mentioned.

Table 1 Institutional affiliations of British-based authors of articles in *Economic Journal* and *Economica*, 1920–69

	Oxford			Cambridge			London			Other universities			Non-university authors		
	(1) E.J. %	(2) Eca. %	(3) (1)–(2)	(4) E.J. %	(5) Eca. %	(6) (4)–(5)	(7) E.J. %	(8) Eca. %	(9) (7)–(8)	(10) E.J. %	(11) Eca. %	(12) (10)–(11)	(13) E.J. %	(14) Eca. %	(15) (13)–(14)
1920–9	12.1	3.6	+ 8.5	32.1	6.6	+ 25.5	17.3	70.3	−53.0	12.5	10.5	+ 2.5	26.0	9.0	+ 15.0
1930–9	10.2	6.3	+ 3.9	33.8	4.2	+ 29.6	19.3	70.7	−51.4	17.2	7.7	+ 9.5	19.5	11.1	+ 8.4
1940–9	12.2	5.4	+ 6.8	26.3	8.2	+ 18.1	15.7	55.9	−40.2	18.8	13.5	+ 5.3	27.0	17.0	+ 10.0
1950–9	20.5	3.9	+ 16.6	23.9	10.7	+ 12.2	18.2	51.4	−33.2	26.9	26.0	+ 0.9	10.5	8.0	+ 2.5
1960–9	17.4	7.2	+ 10.2	23.1	3.7	+ 19.4	13.8	58.0	−44.2	32.7	23.1	+ 9.6	13.0	10.0	+ 3.0

Table 2 Geographical distribution of articles in *Economic Journal* and *Economica*, 1920–69, contributed by British academic authors outside Oxford, Cambridge, and London

| | English 'other' | | | | Scottish | | | | Welsh | | | | Irish | | | |
| | E.J. | | Eca. | | E.J. | | Eca. | | E.J. | | Eca. | | E.J. | | Eca. | |
	No.	%	No.	%	No.	%	No.	%	No.	%	No.	%	No.	%	No.	%
1920-9	15	9.1	9	5.5	2	1.2	2	1.2	–	–	6	3.6	4	2.4	–	–
1930-9	22	11.5	7	4.2	7	3.6	4	2.4	1	0.4	2	1.2	3	1.8	–	–
1940-9	18.5	12.1	10	3.4	6	3.9	1	0.7	1	0.6	6	4.1	2	1.2	2	1.4
1950-9	35	16.3	28	15.0	12	5.6	8	4.3	6.5	3.0	10	5.3	4	1.8	1	0.5
1960-9	36	23.7	32	18.0	6.5	4.3	6	3.4	3.5	2.3	1	0.6	4	2.6	–	–

Note: Percentages show proportions of British articles contributed to each periodical in each period.

In commenting on these statistics it is vital at the outset not to exaggerate the extent of British economics editors' control over the supply of publishable material during the greater part of the period under scrutiny. Up to, say, the 1960s, there was nothing approaching the familiar recent situation of the editor of the *American Economic Review*, who regularly receives nine hundred or one thousand or more submissions a year. Under such circumstances, given unlimited support, time, and energy he can, in principle, exercise considerable influence over the type of subject matter as well as the quality of material published. Yet even here, an editor is to some extent a captive, a passive recipient of material sent to him unsolicited; and as authors send articles to journals which they hope will publish them any editor tends to get more of the same – i.e. having printed material of a certain type or on a specific topic prospective authors will expect him to more or less continue in the same vein. This practice may well restrict the range of his choice.

Table 3 Geographical origins of contributors of articles to *Economic Journal* and *Economica*, 1920–69

	British		American		Others	
	E.J. %	Eca. %	E.J. %	Eca. %	E.J. %	Eca. %
1920–9	70.8	88.8	8.2	3.2	21.0	8.0
1930–9	74.2	79.0	7.0	11.1	16.9	9.9
1940–9	85.0	78.5	8.9	12.0	6.1	9.5
1950–9	66.3	79.2	22.1	9.6	11.6	11.2
1960–9	49.6	53.4	32.2	32.9	18.2	13.7

In the British situation, until quite recently, there were occasional pressures on space, for example, for financial reasons (as with the *E.J.* in the mid-1890s) or because of wartime restrictions, or more likely because of a long-run tendency for the book review section to get out of control (in the extreme case leading, as with the *Journal of Economic Literature*, to the inauguration of a new publication). Of course editors can solicit material, or make requests for particular articles, lectures, or conference papers which they know to be as yet uncommitted. However, soliciting can be a risky, time-consuming, and frustrating business involving an unacceptable surrender of editorial independence or conflict with prospective authors who fail to deliver material of acceptable quality.

All this suggests that had the *E.J.*'s editors wished to change drastically the type of material they published, or the sources from which it emanated, their power to do so would have been quite limited. Such a conclusion is compatible with the results of a study of long-term trends in the contents of general economics journals published two decades ago.[5] However, somewhat different results might emerge from a more detailed study of British economics journals since, say, the late 1930s.

In Moggridge's above-quoted article he makes no attempt to show how far, if at all, Keynes tried to influence the distribution of contents of the *E.J.* However, Austin Robinson, reflecting on his long experience with the *E.J.*,[6] recalled that the two main objectives were to publish: (i) important new thinking in economic theory, and (ii) good applied economics; and on the whole they were more critical of the latter than the former.[7] They constantly bore in mind the *Journal*'s non-academic audience,[8] and therefore tried to avoid loading it with esoteric, particularly mathematical, theory. But this was seldom an acute problem in Keynes's time, for most of the issues arising in connection with the *General Theory* were matters the layman could comprehend.

From a notebook that Keynes kept from 1911 to 1915, and during the 1930s, it is evident that the *E.J.*'s editors were accepting more articles than they were rejecting – a state of affairs very different from the present time, when ten or twenty times the number of articles published are rejected. On the whole they had a slight preference for British articles, *ceteris paribus*, because they felt a special responsibility to the British economics community. During the 1930s American articles tended to consist largely of pedestrian exercises in applied economics or minor extrapolations of theory; but by Carter's time, in the 1960s, the competition from the USA created acute editorial pressures. On the whole, Robinson concluded, little worthwhile work was rejected. The RES was glad to see other journals started. Although frequently unfinished work failed to materialize, much that was submitted to the *E.J.* was 'half baked', and the relatively low proportion of contributions from 'Redbrick' (i.e. provincial) universities was due to the fact that many of their economists did not write articles.

An important point added by later *E.J.* editors, Charles Carter and Brian Reddaway (of Cambridge), was that:

> in recent years, as a mater of principle, no article has ever been accepted or rejected by an editor on his own responsibility if it came from someone in his own university. Reddaway has told me of one case at least in which both he and Champernowne would have published an article by a Cambridge author but rejected it (against their beter judgement) on advice from a reader from outside Cambridge. In these days I feel sure there is no preference for people from one's own university.[9]

With respect to the supply of high-quality material, at least up to the 1960s, Lionel Robbins, from *Economica*'s perspective, essentially endorsed Robinson's view:

> Looking back I cannot think that, during my lifetime, much worth-

while stuff has failed to be published because of the institutional or even ideological prepossession of the publishers or editor concerned. I daresay you could find isolated incidents where editors have failed to see excellence or thought-provoking qualities which they should have seen. But I certainly cannot believe that there has been enough of this to have greatly influenced the general evolution of economic thought in this country.[10]

Robbins considered there was nothing surprising in the above-quoted figures showing the proportion of *E.J.* articles published by Cambridge economists, given Cambridge's pre-eminence in the discipline. He did, however, acknowledge that the *E.J.*–Cambridge relationship might have given cause for concern in some quarters.

I do not think that it is unnatural that, since the editorship was for a long time located at Cambridge, there may have been a tendency for reviewing and so on to drift into the hands of Cambridge reviewers or people connected with Cambridge; and doubtless as flourishing departments of economics arose elsewhere than at London and Manchester, there may have been in the past some cause for feeling that the changes which have recently taken place were necessary. But I do not myself feel that anything was very badly wrong; and on the whole I think that the history of the *E.J.* is something which our profession can reasonably be proud of.

(Ibid.)

Obviously Robbins was commenting here on the situation which subsequently provoked Johnson's outburst, cited earlier; and the mildness of his tone may well conceal some genuine grounds for complaint, for he wrote as an elderly pillar of the establishment, like Robinson; and his *Autobiography of an Economist* gives an account of the development of British economics in his lifetime which, many observers would say, significantly understates the extent of divisions and controversies in the profession (Robbins, 1971).

The 'changes' to which Robbins refers are of direct interest here, for they include the gradual shift of control of the *E.J.* away from Cambridge until, by the late 1970s, it had passed out of Cambridge hands to a greatly enlarged editorial board composed of economists from provincial universities. Robinson remained as a co-editor until 1970 (ending a thirty-six-year editorial involvement, even three years longer than Keynes's reign), and the first non-Oxbridge-based editor, Charles Carter (of Manchester, later of Lancaster, where he was Vice Chancellor) did not assume office until 1961, and then served until 1970. From 1971 to 1975 there was a reversion to exclusive Cambridge control of the *E.J.* by a three-person editorial team, but by this time the Royal Economic Society had been severely weakened, and had experienced an acute financial crisis. It had become increasingly out of touch with the rapidly expanding profession in the older provincial and newly established universities, while a rival organization, the Association of University Teachers of Economics (AUTE) (which had been founded, with some Cambridge support, as far back as the late 1920s) was growing apace, and holding conferences which aroused considerable anti-establishment enthusiasm. The AUTE did not, however, attempt to publish a journal.

In response, the RES introduced a more regular rotation of its Council, in 1968; established an Editorial Advisory Board for the *E.J.* in 1971; and allowed the editorship to shift away from Oxbridge to the provincial universities, especially after 1975. The RES also sponsored both regular and occasional Conferences either alone, or in conjunction with the AUTE. Thus, at last, a glacial shift in the composition and structure of the British economics profession had occurred.[11]

What of *Economica* and the LSE, the acknowledged second leading centre of British economics? Undoubtedly, as Robbins observed, and the statistics clearly show, its journal was

> regarded as a special vehicle for papers produced by the School or by close Associates of the School . . . [yet] it was never intended in any way to be a reflection of one school of thought. . . . Moreover, as time went on, and the position of the Economics department at the School became consolidated on a broad basis, we certainly tried to make it more of a learned journal in its own right and less of a house journal. But as Hicks has pointed out to you, the *E.J.* paid far more than we did per page and, although by 1934 or thereabouts this objective began to dominate, I would still feel obliged in conscience to tell lecturers at the School who brought me articles that, if they were hard up, they had better go first to the *E.J.* because it paid better.[12]

And he added that the bank journals paid much better still!

In his response to the statistics in Tables 1, 2, and 3, Hicks, who had been a junior member of the staff at LSE in the early thirties, remarked that:

> Looking back over my own articles, I would say that one naturally began by trying to get something published in the *E.J.*, as that was a source of prestige (I suppose I got what the Americans call 'tenure' as a result of my first *E.J.* article). But after that it was natural to publish in the place where discussions on the matter [one] was writing [on] were going on. There was a great deal that came out of LSE seminars and that naturally went in *Economica* until it got too bulky and then *R.E.S.* [*Review of Economic Studies*] came in as an overflow.[13]

During the thirties, he added, societies and conferences became more important.

> Things written for the London Economic Club naturally went into *Economica*; for Econometric Society meetings into *Econometrica*; and so on. If however one wrote a paper to be given in a country which did not have an English language journal, it didn't belong anywhere in particular, so one tried it out on the *E.J.* Two of my own articles, in 1939 and 1947, are to be accounted for in that way.
>
> (Ibid.)

(c) Prestige and quality

That the *E.J.* for much of its career enjoyed a reputation as the leading British economics journal seems clear enough from the preceding account. But what of its quality?

Recently two respectable commentators have, quite independently, given a derogatory evaluation describing it in one case as 'dull' in its early years and, in the second instance, seemingly 'to modern eyes a dull and second-rate quarterly' prior to 1936 (Collard, 1990, p. 173; cf. Maloney 1990, pp. 1, 11). The qualifying phrase here is crucial, for present-day readers tend to look mainly for theoretical contributions which seem significant to later generations even if, incidentally, they were incomprehensible or of no interest to the author's immediate audience. From this standpoint it is relevant that before Keynes became assistant editor in 1911 Edgeworth seemed reluctant to publish purely theoretical articles other than his own; whereas thereafter the proportion of space devoted to theory (according to the *A.E.A. Index of Economic Journals* classification) rose steadily, as in other leading Anglo-American economic journals (Coats, 1971, p. 31). The underlying problem here is how to evaluate contributions to 'applied' economics. If it is automatically assumed that applied work is only of passing interest and cannot be evaluated according to any agreed criteria, then it is easy to understand how the history of economics tends to be interpreted mainly or exclusively as the history of economic theory.

Incidentally, the agreement between Collard and Maloney on the *E.J.*'s dullness is more apparent than real, for the latter concludes his assessment with the remarkably confident claim that the post-1918 *Journal* is 'the most indispensable and exciting place for the exchange of economic ideas anywhere in the world' (Maloney, 1990, p. 24). One wonders how many non-British historians of economics would agree provided, of course, that one is not concentrating solely on a relatively brief period in the 1930s.

There are, unfortunately, no reliable indexes of scholarly or scientific quality, although some significant evidence (calling for cautious interpretation) can be derived from citations. There are no published citation indexes in economics for most of the period covered here, but some useful data can be derived from the thirteen volumes of officially sponsored AEA collections of *Readings* and the five volumes of *Surveys* of recent developments in economics which clearly reveal that the *E.J.* was significantly more heavily cited than the *Review of Economic Studies* (which came second among the British journals), *Economica*, or *Oxford Economic Papers* (*O.E.P.*). In fact the *E.J.* was much more heavily cited than the *Q.J.E.* or *J.P.E.* (Coats, 1971, p. 42).

A further indication of 'scientific importance', which is presumably fairly closely correlated with quality, is innovativeness, and here too the *E.J.* ranks more highly than *Economica* according to the evidence contained in the first five volumes of the *A.E.A. Index* (ibid., pp. 39–41). Its record compares very favourably with the leading American journals. It should, however, be noted that, given the fixed *A.E.A. Index* categories, the scope for 'firsts' diminished significantly with the passage of time, so that *Economica* could not hope to compete with the *E.J.* on equal terms (ibid.).

VII CONCLUSIONS

As noted at the outset, in sharp contrast to the American situation, systematic study of the growth, contents, and significance of the British economics journal literature is still in its infancy. So far as I have been able to discover, there is only one short published article specifically devoted to the subject.[14]

The reasons for this state of affairs are unclear: but it seems to reflect British economists' comparative lack of interest in the sociology and professionalization of their discipline. This attitude may be changing, however, as suggested by the recent RES-sponsored study by Ruth Towse and Mark Blaug.[15]

As a result of past neglect, the scope for research into this area is virtually unlimited. American researchers, mainly but not exclusively economists, have examined such matters as: the numbers and types of economic journals; editorial functions and policies; the changing contents of the literature – fads, fashions, cycles, the rise and fall of specific topics and sub-disciplines; the gap between actual research practices and the 'written up' published accounts of research; conventional styles, citation practices, etc.; the output of 'star' economists; the relationships between academic productivity and earnings; authorship patterns and affiliations; the ranking of journals and departments; national styles; and the diffusion of economic ideas and techniques. Needless to say, not all of these matters have been exhaustively explored or are of equal interest to British economists. But it is worth noting that in various studies of journals rankings undertaken among American economists in the 1970s and (one) in 1990, the *E.J.*, *Economica*, and *Review of Economic Studies* have been designated as 'highly rated', within a small élite group, while *O.E.P.*, the *Scottish Journal, Manchester School*, and *Yorkshire Bulletin* have also attained respectable positions in the lists. However, some of these studies cannot be taken very seriously for in one instance respondents gave quite favourable ratings to two non-existent 'dummy' periodicals!

One point of interest not previously considered here is the changing relative importance of books, monographs, and articles as the discipline has become more theoretical, mathematical, quantitative, and (?) scientific. It is a current commonplace that books are less 'important' than articles, whether as contributions to the advance of scientific knowledge or as a source of data on the state of the subject and the profession. There may, however, be some danger of overstating the value of the kind of research undertaken and proposed here, as suggested by the comments of that distinguished sceptic and pioneering contributor to the field, George Stigler, who has observed that the economics journal output

> is a literature that no person could possibly read – the limits imposed by sanity are stricter than those imposed by time. Indeed, it is a literature that perhaps is read by a number of economists only moderately larger than the number of writers. The best memories can recall only a tiny fraction of this literature, and if the literature were irrevocably destroyed, most of it would utterly perish from human knowledge.
>
> (Stigler, 1982, p. 223)

Nevertheless, the flood continues to grow, although as far back as the 1890s there were already complaints that readers were being swamped.

NOTES

A bibliography of scholarly articles on economic journals appeared in the same issue of *Economic Notes by Monte dei Paschi di Siena* (vol. 20 no. 1, 1991, pp. 181–8).

1 The establishment of the BEA and the *E.J.* caused some concern to leading members of the Royal Statistical Society, who thought that a 'combined effort' might be 'more successful in attracting public favour' (Farrar, 1894, p. 609). The following year there was a reference to the shortage of good papers at their meetings.

2 For more detailed analysis of the contents of the *E.J.* during its earlier years see Jha (1963) and the chapters by John Maloney, Ian Steedman, Philip L. Williams, and Peter Newman, in Hey and Winch (1990).

3 After the *Economic History* supplement to the *Economic Journal* ceased publication the RES provided a subvention to the Economic History Society to permit the expansion of the *Economic History Review* (Barker, 1977, p. 2).

4 Valuable regular listings of economic periodicals can be found especially in the American Economic Association's *Journal of Economic Literature* and, less ambitiously, in the UK government's Department of Trade and Industry weekly abstracts of current economic journals.

5 'Despite significant initial differences in the range and distribution of their

contents, not to mention differences in sponsorship, location, and longevity, they all tended to concentrate their attention on the same few principal [subject] categories. Moreover, with the passage of time their content distribution tended to become more alike . . . the largest changes in the distribution of contents within any single journal between successive periods have been those which brought abnormally large or small categories closer to the general average; in the few instances when a particular journal diverged from the general trend in any period, such a movement proved to be temporary.' Thus there is some evidence to suggest that for the general journals in the sample, 'their editors were subject to forces beyond their control: that far from being dynamic entre-preneurs of the Schumpeterian type, they were merely passive recipients of a changing flow of manuscripts over which they exercised little or no editorial influence'. (Coats, 1971, p. 32.)

6 In a private communication to the author, 'on Economic Journal Editorial Policy', dated 1 November 1973. This paragraph and the next is based on this source.

7 '[O]ur criteria regarding applied economics were two: First, was the article providing some new approach to the methods of analysis of a problem or a group of problems? Second, did the article throw interesting and important light on the orders of magnitude of some elements of the economic situation which were of current or permanent interest and importance?' The editors were more inclined to reject applied work if it was due to appear in a book or some 'less professionally economic journal'. (Ibid.)

8 However, to judge by the RES's official records this problem never aroused the concern that was so apparent in the American Economic Association during Davis Dewey's regime as editor of the *American Economic Review* (cf. Coats, 1969, 1964).

9 From the covering letter, E. A. G. Robinson to A. W. Coats, 1 November 1973, Professor Reddaway subsequently added that he did not know how far back this practice went. 'Charles Carter was using it in relation to Lancaster articles when he was the main editor for articles in the period before we took over.' W. B. Reddaway to A. W. Coats, 24 July 1973. (The period in question was 1961–70.)

10 Lord Robbins to A. W. Coats, 26 July 1973.

11 Since this paper was presented in Siena I have had access to the invaluable 'inside' account of the operations of the Royal Economic Society in Robinson, 1990, which is fully compatible with the interpretation offered herein, although Robinson denies that the Society was 'Oxbridge dominated' (p. 179). He recalls that management of the RES and the *E.J.* was 'more efficient' when both were effectively under Keynes's control, and admits, that the Society was 'undemo-cratic' prior to 1954, becoming somewhat more representative from 1960. The *E.J.* had no editorial board until 1971, eighty years after its foundation, when for the first time there were at least 'two independent viewpoints' on *E.J.* policy. The whole story is an eloquent testimony to the extraordinary continuity of British institutions. (op. cit., pp. 166, 168, 170, 173, 179, 180.)

12 Robbins to Coats (1973).

13 John Hicks to A. W. Coats, 5 July 1973.

14 K. J. Button and D. W. Pearce, 'What British Economists Think of their Journals', *International Journal of Social Economics* vol. 4 (1977), pp. 150–8.

15 R. Towse and M. Blaug, *The Current State of the British Economics Profession* (London: Royal Economic Society, 1988).

REFERENCES

T. C. Barker, 'The Beginnings of the Economic History Society', *Economic History Review*, 2nd Series, vol. 30, 1977, pp. 1–19.

D. Bell, 'The United States of America', *International Social Science Journal*, vol. XIX no. 2, 1967, pp. 245–54.

A. W. Coats, 'The American Economic Association, 1904–1929', *American Economic Review*, vol. 54 (June 1964), pp. 261–85. Reprinted in this volume, pp. 239–63.

——, 'Sociological Aspects of British Economic Thought (ca. 1880–1930)', *Journal of Political Economy*, vol. 75 (October 1967), pp. 706–29. Reprinted in this volume, pp. 105–33.

——, 'The Origins and Early Development of the Royal Economic Society', *Economic Journal*, vol. 78 (June 1968), pp. 349–71. Reprinted in this volume, pp. 313–37.

——, 'The American Economic Association's Publications: An Historical Perspective', *Journal of Economic Literature*, vol. VII. (March 1969), pp. 57–68. Reprinted in this volume, pp. 264–79.

——, 'The Role of Scholarly Journals in Economics: An Essay', *Journal of Economic Literature*, vol. IX, (March 1971), pp. 29–44. Reprinted in this volume, pp. 155–75.

——, 'The Development of the Agricultural Economics Profession in England', *Journal of Agricultural Economics*, vol. 27 (September 1976), pp. 381–92. Reprinted in this volume, pp. 419–32.

——, 'The Culture and the Economists: Some Reflections on Anglo-American Differences' *History of Political Economy*, vol. 12 (Spring 1980), pp. 588–609. Reprinted in this volume, pp. 134–54.

——, 'The Distinctive LSE Ethos in the Inter-war Years', *Atlantic Economic Journal*, vol. X (March 1982), pp. 18–30. Reprinted in this volume, pp. 372–92.

——, 'Marshall and Ethics', in Rita McWilliams Tullberg ed., *Alfred Marshall in Retrospect* (Aldershot: Edward Elgar, 1990), pp. 153–78. Reprinted in vol. I in this series.

D. Collard, 'Cambridge after Marshall', in J. K. Whitaker, *Centenary Essays on Alfred Marshall* (Cambridge: Cambridge University Press, 1990), pp. 164–92.

W. Cunningham, 'Nationalism and Cosmopolitanism in Economics' (Presidential Address to Section F of the British Association for the Advancement of Science), *Journal of the Royal Statistical Society*, vol. LIV (1891), pp. 164–662.

Lord Farrer, 'The Relations Between Morals, Economics and Statistics', *Journal of the Royal Statistical Society*, vol. 57 (December 1894), pp. 595–608.

F. A. Fetter, 'The Authorship of Economic Articles in the *Edinburgh Review*, 1802–47', *Journal of Political Economy* (June 1953), vol. 61, pp. 232–59.

——, 'The Economic Articles in the *Quarterly Review* and their Authors 1809–1852 Parts I and II', *Journal of Political Economy* (February, April 1958), 66: pp. 47–64, 154–70.

——, 'The Economic Articles in *Blackwood's Edinburgh Magazine* and their Authors, 1824–1853, Parts I and II', *Scottish Journal of Political Economy* (June, November 1960), vol. 7: pp. 85–107, 218–30.

——, 'Economic Articles in the *Westminster Review* and their Authors, 1824–1851', *Journal of Political Economy* (December 1962), 70: pp. 570–96.

——, 'Economic Controversy in the British Reviews, 1802–1850', *Economica*, N.S. (November 1965), vol. 32, pp. 424–37.

H. S. Foxwell, 'The Economic Movement in England', *Quarterly Journal of Economics* (October 1887), 2: pp. 84–103.

R. F. Harrod, *The Life of John Maynard Keynes* (London, Macmillan, 1952).

E. W. Hawley, 'Economic Inquiry and the State in New Era America: Antistatist

Corporatism and Positive Statism in Uneasy Coexistence', in M. O. Furner and B. Supple (eds.), *The State and Economic Knowledge. The American and British Experiences* (Cambridge, Woodrow Wilson Centre and Cambridge University Press, 1990), pp. 287–324.

J. D. Hey and D. Winch (eds.), *A Century of Economics. 100 Years of the Royal Economic Society and the Economic Journal* (Oxford, Basil Blackwell, 1990).

N. Jha, *The Age of Marshall* (Ashoda Rajpath, Patna, Novelty and Co., 1963).

E. S. Johnson and H. Johnson, *The Shadow of Keynes* (Oxford, Basil Blackwell, 1978).

A. Kadish, *The Oxford Economists in the late Nineteenth Century* (Oxford, Clarendon Press, 1982).

——, *Apostle Arnold. The Life and Death of Arnold Toynbee, 1852–1883* (Durham, N.C., Duke University Press, 1986).

A. Kadish and R. D. Freeman, 'Foundation and Early Years', in Hey and Winch, op. cit., pp. 22–48.

G. M. Koot, *English Historical Economics, 1870–1926. The Rise of Economic History and Neomercantilism* (Cambridge, Cambridge University Press, 1987).

M. S. Larson, *The Rise of Professionalism: A Sociological Analysis* (Berkeley, University of California Press, 1978).

P. Lengyel, 'The Social Science Press: Introduction', *International Social Science Journal*, vol. 19, no. 2. 1967, pp. 145–61.

D. G. Macrae, 'Social Science Press in the United Kingdom', *International Social Science Journal*, vol. 19, no. 2, 1967, pp. 236–44.

J. Maloney, *Marshall, Orthodoxy and the Professionalization of Economics* (Cambridge, Cambridge University Press, 1985).

——, 'Gentlemen Versus Players, 1891–1914', in Hey and Winch, op. cit., pp. 49–64.

D. E. Moggridge (ed.), *The Collected Writings of John Maynard Keynes. The General Theory and After. Parts I and II* (London, Macmillan, St. Martin's Press, 1973), vols. 13 and 14.

D. E. Moggridge, 'Keynes as Editor', in Hey and Winch, op. cit., pp. 143–57.

P. Newman, 'Reviews by Edgeworth', in Hey and Winch, op. cit., pp. 109–41.

L. L. Price, *Memories and Notes of British Economists 1881–1947*, chapter 30, 'Oxford Economists and Others', pp. 32–4, 60. Unpublished, Brotherton Library, Leeds University.

Lord L. Robbins, *Autobiography of an Economist* (London, Macmillan, St. Martin's Press, 1971).

A. Robinson, 'Fifty Five Years on the Royal Economic Society Council', in Hey and Winch, op. cit., pp. 161–92.

J. Sczepanski, 'Poland', *International Social Science Journal*, vol. 19, no. 2. 1967, pp. 227–35.

B. Sichel and W. Sichel, *Economics Journals and Serials. An Analytical Guide* (New York, Greenwood Press, 1986).

R. Skidelsky, *John Maynard Keynes, Hopes Betrayed 1883–1920* (London, Macmillan, 1983).

I. Steedman, 'The *Economic Journal* and Socialism, 1890–1920', in Hey and Winch, op. cit., pp. 65–91.

G. J. Stigler, 'Statistical Studies in the History of Economic Thought' (1964), reprinted in his *Essays in the History of Economics* (Chicago, University of Chicago, 1965), pp. 31–50.

——, *The Economist as Preacher* (Chicago, University of Chicago, 1984).

R. D. Whitley, 'The Formal Communication System of Science: A Study of the Organization of British Social Science Journals', in P. Holmos (ed.), *The Sociology of Sociology, The Sociological Review Monograph*, Keele University (September 1970), pp. 163–79.

———, 'The Operation of Social Science Journals: Two Case Studies in British Social Science', *Sociological Review*, vol. 18 (July 1970), pp. 241–58.

P. L. Williams, 'The Attitudes of the Economics Professions in Britain and the United States to the Trust Movement, 1890–1914', in Hey and Winch, op. cit., pp. 92–108.

D. Winch, 'A Century of Economics', in Hey and Winch, op. cit., pp. 3–21.

Part II

INSTITUTIONS, THEIR HISTORY AND ACTIVITIES

11

THE FIRST TWO DECADES OF
THE AMERICAN ECONOMIC
ASSOCIATION*

As this month marks the 75th anniversary of the formation of the American
Economic Association it is an appropriate moment to recall the state of
American economics in 1885 and to reassess the changing character and
fortunes of the organization in its formative years. Earlier accounts have
emphasized the theoretical and policy issues that divided the so-called 'old'
and 'new' schools of economics [15] [16] [17] [18] [9, Ch. 9] and have
unduly neglected other, less obtrusive, aspects of the story. The following
pages are designed to supplement the published record and to place the
Association's early history in a wider intellectual and social context.

I THE INAUGURATION

The American Economic Association was officially inaugurated on September 9, 1885 in the Bethesda Parish building at Saratoga Springs, New York,
following discussions among a miscellaneous group of scholars, ministers
and social reformers who were attending the second meeting of the American Historical Association. The initiator of this venture, Richard T. Ely,
a vigorous young member of the Johns Hopkins University faculty, was
following the lead of his senior colleague in the history department of that
institution, Herbert Baxter Adams, who was the founder and secretary of
the older association. The dramatis personae and the location reveal the
character of the enterprise,[1] for there was at that time no independent
academic discipline of economics with a recognized corps of practitioners;
and religious inspiration and reformist zeal were to play a major role in
the organization's early history. The personal link between Ely and Adams
symbolizes the connection between the rising tide of economic thought and
the contemporary movement towards genuine 'university' education in the
USA. Both men had embraced the Germanic conception of higher education and scholarship which formed the intellectual core of this movement;
and they had received encouragement and advice from D. C. Gilman, the
distinguished first president of Johns Hopkins, so that the two associations

illustrate the exuberant activity of the institution at the head of the 'academic procession'.

Just as the process of adapting the German university to American needs and conditions required the cooperation of established scholars, administrators and trustees, so the process of launching a professional association of economists would have failed if Ely had relied exclusively on the support of the young men who had recently completed their studies in Germany. The idea of an economic association was undoubtedly German in origin; but an earlier attempt to form an association in 1883–4 had foundered because it had been modelled too closely on the *Verein für Sozialpolitik* and because its sponsors had placed too much emphasis on the role of the state in economic affairs [17, pp. 133–5, 296–9]. The programme of this abortive Society for the Study of National Economy had met with a chilly reception not only because its provisions entailed too specific and radical a break with the past but also, one suspects, because its progenitors, E. J. James and S. N. Patten, represented the University of Pennyslvania, an institution that was out of touch with the contemporary 'university' movement and had long been regarded with suspicion as the home of protectionism and the centre of opposition to orthodox political economy.[2]

Ely had formulated a plan for an association of 'economists who repudiate *laissez-faire* as a scientific doctrine' as early as 1884, but he deferred his proposal until it was clear that the James–Patten scheme had failed [14, F. A. Walker to Ely, Apr 30 1884] [15, p. 55 n]. When he drafted his platform for the American Economic Association in the following year, Ely toned down his references to the role of government in economic and social life; the names of James and Patten did not appear among the signatories of the 'call' to Saratoga, although they were among the founder-members of the new body; and the prestige of Johns Hopkins probably added weight to his appeal. But whatever the reasons, Ely's call met with a warm response not only from the young scholars who had been impressed by the reigning German school of historical economics but also from leading historians, prominent past, present and future university presidents like Gilman, Andrew White, C. K. Adams, W. W. Folwell and Francis A. Walker (who was also a distinguished representative of the older generation of economists), such outstanding liberal ministers as Lyman Abbott and Washington Gladden, and officers of the American Social Science Association.[3]

II SOCIAL SCIENCE VERSUS SOCIAL REFORM

Notwithstanding its broad and influential support, the American Economic Association was fully established only after a struggle for recognition and support that continued intermittently throughout a seven-year probationary period. These initial difficulties cannot be explained merely by reference to the dispute between the old and new schools of economics over questions of scientific method, economic theory and public policy that were debated at length in *Science* magazine in 1885-6 and discussed in many other learned and popular journals and newspapers.[4] Certainly this dispute had an important bearing on subsequent doctrinal developments; but there was a deeper question of principle involved, namely: how far was the Christian impulse to social reform compatible with the scholarly impartiality deemed appropriate to a scientific body? The effort to reconcile these two aspects of the Association's original purpose came to be the constant preoccupation of its officers, and had a marked impact on its character and early development. Since both the public and the academic reputation of the organization were at stake, neither of which could safely be ignored by its members in view of their peculiar and sometimes uncomfortable involvement in contemporary social issues, this matter merits careful examination.

The difficulties involved in the task of reconciling scholarly impartiality with reformist zeal were largely responsible for the gradual attenuation of the original platform or statement of principles. Ely's initial draft was significantly 'modified in the direction of conservatism' [16, p. 144] at the inaugural meeting, before it was incorporated in the Association's constitution, and was published with the proviso that it was not to be regarded as binding upon individual members. Nevertheless it still contained references to the positive role of the church, the state and science in the solution of social problems by the 'development of legislative policy'; and these references provoked the hostility of those defenders of the received tradition by whom, as Francis A. Walker later recalled, *laissez faire* 'was not made the test of economic orthodoxy, merely. It was used to decide whether a man were an economist at all.'[5]

To regard this hostility simply as an expression of opposition to the proposal to increase the functions of the state would, however, be a mistake, for there were some who doubted whether it was proper for a supposedly impartial scientific body to subscribe to any policy recommendations whatsoever. Ely himself had acknowledged the dangers of partisanship when he complained, in his original draft, that 'economists have been too ready to assert themselves as advocates', although he defended the platform somewhat inconsistently on the grounds that 'it is not easy to arouse interest in an association that professes nothing' [18, pp. 7, 19]. Simon Newcomb, an early opponent, may have been unduly caustic when he remarked that in Ely's view the Association was 'intended to be a sort of church, requiring for admission to its full communion a renunciation of ancient errors, and an adhesion to the supposed new creed' [31, p. 106]; but his comment reveals the attitude of one influential section of orthodox opinion.

Thus it soon became apparent to the Association's officers that the statement of principles might prove to be a liability, for there was ample evidence that it acted as a deterrent to some of the more conservative economists.[6] With the disappearance of the initial attitude of exclusiveness,[7] which had been inspired by the fear that the organization might be captured by orthodox doctrinaires, there was a growing desire to enrol the Harvard, Princeton and Yale economists, who had hitherto held aloof more because of their suspicion of the platform than because of their uncompromising adherence to classical doctrine. By 1887 the proposal to modify or abandon the platform was under discussion, and John Bates Clark wrote to Henry Carter Adams [1, May 4 1887]:

> I had better tell you what I suggested to Dr. Ely as a compromise policy in the matter of [the] platform. I understand Pres't Walker wishes to drop the platform wholly. I had not anticipated quite so radical a move, though I have from the first thought that the platform would ultimately cease to be necessary. It does a certain work by giving character to the association during its earlier years. My proposal was that we agree not to oppose the abolition of the platform a year hence, provided the measure be not pushed this year. The friends of the measure will ask 'why not now if ever'? My idea is that the work of the platform is essentially temporary, and that two (practically three) years will prove long enough to retain it.

In fact events closely followed Clark's proposal, for the decision to drop the statement of principles was approved by the Association's council in December 1887, and ratified at the third annual meeting twelve months later [4, p. 86]. But although some prominent members insisted that no change of principle was involved, the vehemence of their denials suggests the importance they attached to this change of policy.[8]

In this connection Ely's position is of particular interest, for despite the danger of overestimating the role of a single individual in the life of an organization, it is no exaggeration to say that in the early years of its history, the public response to the American Economic Association was largely determined by the various reactions to his work. As academic economists at that time, whether employed by state or private universities, repeatedly felt the pressure of public opinion [29, part 2], this response could hardly be a matter of indifference to the rising economics profession. Apart from acting as the organization's initiator, first secretary (for seven years), promoter-in-chief and most ardent defender, Ely was a prolific writer whose studies of current labour, taxation and monopoly problems made him the most widely discussed economist in the country in the late 1880s and 1890s. As the most outspoken critic of the old school of American political economy, Ely drew the full fire of the diehard exponents of that doctrine; and even his closest friends among the younger generation of economists, J. B. Clark and H. C. Adams, warned that certain features of his work lent support to the repeated accusations that he was a socialist and a sentimentalist.[9] Their concern for Ely's security of tenure at Johns

Hopkins was doubtless reinforced by their desire to protect the reputation of the American Economic Association and its adherents.

Of these two accusations, the former has been stressed by subsequent historians, and was undoubtedly a most serious matter at the time. Ely's boldly sympathetic study of the labour movement appeared shortly after the Haymarket bomb incident in Chicago had aroused widespread public alarm, and the story of Newcomb's damaging unsigned review in the *Nation*, the most influential journal of the day, which described Ely as a socialist and a man 'seriously out of place in a university chair', has often been told.[10] In the event, although this attack undoubtedly enhanced the suspicion of the Association in some quarters, it shocked economists of various shades of opinion, who rallied to Ely's support; and by persuading F. W. Taussig of Harvard to apply for membership, the first representative of the old school to do so, it directly strengthened the organization's representation among the 'younger traditionalists'. Indeed this proved to be but the first of many occasions on which the economists overcame personal and doctrinal differences in order to display their professional *esprit de corps* on behalf of one of their number who was threatened by outside interference.

In retrospect, however, the charge of 'emotionalism' or 'sentimentalism' resulting from Ely's religious fervour and his persistent stress on the inseparability of economics and ethics was more important in the long run; for it caused greater concern to his fellow economists and it contributed directly to his temporary break with the Association in 1892, a move which seriously threatened the unity of the organization. This matter has been unduly neglected by earlier commentators, although it sheds considerable light on the development of the economics profession and on the changing character of the Association, from that of an agency of social reform – a function that was dear to the hearts of the founder-members – to a more strictly scientific and scholarly body.

In order to explain the issues involved it is necessary to recall the state of American economic and social thought in the 1880s. At the centenary of the Declaration of Independence Charles Dunbar of Harvard had confessed that 'the United States have, thus far, done nothing towards developing the theory of political economy' which had become a body of rigid dogma as expounded both by its acknowledged leaders and by the numerous popularizers [12, p. 140]. Political economy had been assigned a subordinate role in the college curriculum, as a branch of mental and moral philosophy; its teachers, usually doctors of divinity, lacked interest and training in it, and the resulting doctrines comprised a blend of vulgarized Ricardianism and New England theology that offered little of relevance to contemporary life [32]. The intellectual (and financial) poverty of most American colleges had forced many able students to seek their advanced training abroad – in Germany rather than in England, not only because German academic life was flourishing, but also because religious influence was still strong in the best-known English colleges. As J. Dorfman has shown [10], German historical ideas had already met with a favourable reception in the USA in the 1870s, well before the flood of returning graduates had reached its peak. The flexibility of these ideas – in marked contrast to the received tradition – made them readily adaptable to domestic conditions and encouraged the hope that they might help to solve contemporary economic and social problems. Moreover they blended with the popular currents of scientific and evolutionary thought that were undermining the pedagogical foundations of the established economic and social creed and challenging the prevailing theological control of the college curriculum [28] [11, pp. 43–4].

In these circumstances it was inevitable that hostile critics should interpret the strong religious and ethical tone adopted by some of the new-school economists as a sign of soft-headedness and a return to less scientific thought.[11] Ely was indubitably the chief offender; but the early works of J. B. Clark and H. C. Adams (whose names were frequently linked with Ely's by the critics), E. B. Andrews, C. D. Wright, and other prominent members of the American Economic Association also bore the indelible imprint of their religious convictions and moral purpose; and by the late 1880s it was a commonplace of popular literature that economics must, or indeed had already, become an 'ethical science'.

It is therefore no coincidence that the Association attracted considerable support among the liberal clergy,[12] for liberal theology and a progressive attitude to social policy were often found in conjunction with one another. Some of Ely's correspondents praised his 'brotherly sentimental' economics and likened the work of the American Economic Association to that of the Home Missionary Society;[13] but it is understandable that orthodox economists like Laughlin, Taussig and Hadley wondered whether the organization was merely substituting one brand of partisan advocacy for another, more pernicious one.

When Hadley protested that the 'so-called moral reaction' against orthodox economics was really an 'emotional' one, he was not only expressing his irritation at the arrogant assumption of 'a superior moral purpose' on the part of those 'trying to right visible wrongs by direct state action', and his belief that 'the harm which has been done by laws based on unemotional reasoning is but a drop in the bucket compared with that which has been done by laws based on unreasoning emotion'; he was also endeavouring to defend the economist's scientific reputation.[14] Like his less conservative colleagues, Hadley was only too familiar with the poverty, insecurity and vulnerability of the little band of professional economists [15, pp. 94–5], and he was convinced that prestige and influence could be earned only by exercising sound scholarship and wise statesmanship. When he asserted that the 'economists as a body . . . strongly disapprove the attempt to "popularise" economics by giving too much weight to the conclusions of uninstructed public sentiment' [26, p. 191] he was voicing an opinion that was then (i.e., 1894) shared by most of his fellow members. Since the mid-1880s there had been a noticeable shift in the prevailing tone of American economics, and this shift cannot be fully understood without a close examination of the circumstances underlying the change of leadership in 1892.

III THE ASCENDANCY OF SCIENCE

During the first seven years of its existence, the leadership of the American Economic Association rested continuously in the hands of Walker as president and Ely as secretary; and the election of Dunbar[15] to the presidency has usually been regarded as a turning point in the organization's development. The transfer of leadership not only indicated that the original fear of capture by the forces of reaction had diminished; as a conciliatory gesture to a prominent representative of the old school it also constituted an armistice that marked the end of hostilities between the two warring schools and the beginning of a period of broad consensus on fundamentals and renewed emphasis on theoretical work.

Although correct in its essentials, this version tells only part – and, from the present point of view, not the most important part – of the story. Ely's resignation as secretary in 1892 was the immediate outcome of a dispute which marked the effective repudiation of the Association's original commitment to quasi-religious social reform; it was accompanied by his decision to move to the University of Wisconsin, a change that symbolized the westward shift in the centre of gravity of American economics; and it was followed, later in the decade, by undercurrents of discontent in the academic ranks which threatened the unity and stability of the American Economic Association. These are matters of more than parochial interest, for they enable us to discern hitherto undisclosed links between the new, German-inspired, school of economics and the progressive reform elements in American institutionalism. Cf. [22] [21, ch. 7].

As we have seen, there was nothing novel about the desire to widen the Association's representation among the more orthodox economists. There had been a steady if slow influx of such members from 1887 on, due both to individual decisions and to collective efforts at recruitment.[16] The initial sense of insecurity had soon passed, and as early as 1887 Walker had declared his willingness to stand down from the presidency if it would serve the cause, although Ely privately expressed his fears of the continued danger of control by the Yale and Princeton men in 1888, when he sought to persuade H. C. Adams to take over some of the secretarial duties.[17] The dispute of 1891–2 was, however, only indirectly connected with this process, for it was occasioned by Ely's decision to hold the next annual meeting at the Methodist summer camp site at Chautauqua, New York, a decision which brought a chorus of protest from some of the leading members.

There were various reasons for this reaction: the belief that Ely had acted unconstitutionally in forcing his decision on an unwilling executive committee; the suspicion that he was putting his personal interest in Chautauqua before the welfare of the organization, since it was feared that the Association's scientific reputation might be endangered if it became too closely associated with a popular religious educational movement;[18] and finally, the prospect that it would deter the leading representatives of the old school, several of whom had joined but had not yet participated in the Association's activities [19, Seligman to Farnam, June 2 1892]. In the event, the dispute was patched up. Although it was too late to alter the venue of the meeting, which had already been announced in the press,[19] opposition to it was moderated by the knowledge that a public row would harm everybody, and by the fact that Ely, who had at first threatened to resign instantly if the decision were overruled, had agreed to submit his resignation at the next meeting.[20]

Some members of the Association undoubtedly interpreted this outcome as a victory for the old school rather than a sign of the achievement of unity. Nor was this interpretation confined to those dissatisfied with the change. In a final, unsuccessful effort to persuade W. G. Sumner to join, his Yale colleague H. W. Farnam gave a vivid glimpse of the Chautauqua meeting:

> This is the first time Yale has been represented at one of these meetings by one of its professors and I think that it created a good impression to have one of them here. At any rate they made me one of the Vice-Presidents.
>
> . . . .
>
> There was in general quite a new deal in the officers. Dunbar was made President; a young man by the name of Ross of Cornell was made Secretary and though Ely was consoled by the office of Vice-President, this means practically the end of his régime in the association. In fact it was rather amusing to see on how many occasions he found himself in a minority of one.
>
> . . . .
>
> In view of these changes do you not think that you would like to join? . . . I think that you would find yourself quite in sympathy with the present spirit of the society.
>
> [19, Sep 5 1892]

There was indeed some justification for the dissatisfaction of such men as Ely, E. W. Bemis and J. R. Commons, to whom the adoption of a more scholarly and 'scientific' stance entailed a withdrawal from active participation in economic and social reform, and a growing emphasis on theoretical problems.[21] Yet there is no reason to conclude that the change of leadership, and the subtle shift of policy implied therein, was the outcome of the sinister machinations of a few diehard reactionaries, for it evidently reflected the prevailing tone of professional opinion. When the trend of American economics is seen in its social context, it becomes clear that the preoccupation with marginal utility and marginal productivity analysis in the 1890s did not merely reflect the dissatisfaction with the unfruitful methodological and doctrinal controversies of the previous decade; it also reflected the economists' yearning for scientific status and prestige. This they sought to attain by dissociating themselves from the past, and by establishing economics as an independent scholarly discipline, free from theological, ethical, historical and sociological connotations and, above all, free from the taint of missionary zeal and political partisanship.

One of the by-products of this broader process was the emergence of sociology and economic history as separate disciplines both in the USA and Europe, a process to which such prominent members of the American Economic Association as F. H. Giddings, E. A. Ross, A. W. Small and W. J. Ashley made notable contributions. On a sociological plane, the change in the character of the Association constitutes one element in what has recently been called the 'status revolution' [27, pp. 149–55] – a movement that brought with it a rise in the prestige of the professors and a decline in the status of the clergy. By facilitating the secularization of their discipline the economists were also – not always unwittingly [34] – seeking to enhance their professional status.

IV MIDWESTERN ACADEMIC DISCONTENT

Yet beneath the superficial harmony resulting from the collective desire to minimize controversy on methodological and policy questions there were significant notes of discord. By far the most interesting and the most neglected aspect of this situation is the emergence of a distinct regional pattern of opinion reflecting contemporary political, social and intellectual tensions which was aided by the expansion of economic training in the middle west. It is obviously impossible to consider here the problems of analysing regional variations in social and cultural conditions and of tracing their effects upon the work in particular university disciplines.[22] But as the economists could hardly avoid discussing such contemporary issues as free silver, the trusts and the tariff, matters on which there were certain clearly marked regional differences of interest, it is no surprise to find that their attitudes sometimes reflected the pressure of public opinion. The selection of faculty was influenced by local prejudices, and the number of summary dismissals and 'academic freedom' cases in the 1890s made the penalties of a defiance of local sensibilities painfully clear [29, pp. 413–45].

Of course these incidents reveal that at least some economists openly resisted local prejudices, and others were doubtless protected by their own tact or by the courage and good will of their university authorities. But as the opinion spread that the American Economic Association had become more conservative, there was a swelling chorus of dissatisfaction from various midwestern centres at a time when radicalism was rife in that region, and this dissatisfaction gave considerable concern to the organization's officials, especially when the threat of a rival body appeared in 1895 with the formation of the Political Science Association of the Central States.

The proposal to form this association appears to have originated with John R. Commons and his colleagues at the University of Indiana during the summer of 1894,[23] and it undoubtedly reflected a fairly widespread feeling that the existing national organizations of economists and historians were indifferent to the needs of middle-western scholars. The fear that the new body might become a serious rival to the American Economic Association seems to have been inspired less by the danger that it would be dominated by the 'Ely–Commons faction'[24] than by the possibility that it might be captured by the predatory powers of the University of Chicago, an institution which was expanding rapidly with the aid of John D. Rockefeller's fortune and which was widely regarded as a hostile and ruthless rival to the established leaders of the academic world.[25] However, the determined efforts of J. L. Laughlin and H. E. von Holst failed, and the new organization was launched under the leadership of men whose first act was to pass a resolution 'distinctly affirming it as the policy of the Political Science Association to arrange its future meetings so as to avoid conflict with the two national organizations in which we are all vitally interested'.[26]

Although the new body did not prove to be a serious rival of the American Economic Association, it had a direct impact on the latter's policies; and the purposes behind its formation merit consideration partly because they have apparently not been published previously, and also because they reveal the difficulties facing the officers of the national economic association in their efforts to retain its hold over the profession. G. W. Knight outlined the purposes of the organization in a letter to H. C. Adams: to bring together four groups of scholars who could 'get together' in no existing association; to cater for many 'poor fellows' in the 'western region . . . who as college instructors are trying to work and do their best in two or more of these fields, and who are only partially at home in any other one Association'; to discuss the 'many questions of pedagogy and methodology in connection with these fields, and *peculiar to the institutions of this section of the country*, or at least away from the sea-board'; and to give opportunities to men who would not or could not shine at the national meetings [1, Jan 8 1895].

It is clear that the new body succeeded in focusing attention on the westerners' grievances. Although J. B. Clark and J. W. Jenks, as president and secretary of the American Economic Association, did not at first regard it as a serious rival of their own organization,[27] H. C. Adams, who was invited to head the economics section of the Political Science Association, was much less sanguine. Influenced both by his position as head of the economics department in what was widely regarded as the leading state university, and by his scepticism towards recent theoretical tendencies,[28] he sympathized with the motives behind the new venture, and in a letter to J. B. Clark he frankly criticized the economic association's handling of the situation.

> You ask what I think of the plan of holding in alternate years sectional meetings of the Association. To answer definitely, I do not think it would do at all, that is, it would not serve the purpose we of the West had in mind when insisting that the American Economic Association should meet West of the Allegheny mountains. Perhaps the thing we aim at cannot be attained, that is to keep the A.E.A. to represent the economists of the U.S. This is a very big country and travelling is of course burdensome. But I think the men in the East show altogether too much disinclination to come West. Certainly if it is impossible to have good meetings in any of the western cities, at which a great majority of the members of the East shall be in attendance, we might as well face the issue at once and allow that there shall be three or four economic associations in the country. Of course I shall go with my section if anything of this sort seems to be inevitable.
>
> . . . .
>
> [The Political Science Association] . . . need not be a rival of the A.E.A. . . . I am quite confident, however, although I have no direct evidence of the fact, that it was intended by those who have been responsible for starting it, to break off from the A.E.A.
>
> [1, Jan 7 1895]

Some weeks later, after considerable discussion, it was decided to hold a joint meeting of the two associations at Indianapolis. The location is significant, not only because of its proximity to the birthplace of the Political Science Association, but also because the University of Indiana, and Commons in particular, were under severe attack in the state legislature, and it was felt desirable to show 'the people of Indianapolis and of the state the determination of the economists of America, no matter what their opinions, to insist upon the freedom of instruction and investigation'.[29] At this meeting H. C. Adams was elected president of the American Economic Association, a move that, while fully justified by his standing in the profession, was no doubt influenced by the desire to conciliate the westerners.[30]

V RECESSION, REVIVAL, AND THE ATTAINMENT OF UNITY

Thus the crisis passed, and the American Economic Association records contain no further evidence of rivalry with the Political Science Association.

But despite continued efforts to meet the needs of western members,[31] the organization was hardly thriving, and its failure to expand caused serious concern between 1894 and 1899, the period immediately preceding Ely's presidency.[32] There was a significant shift of emphasis which may have reflected the belief that 'political economy is swinging back to a renewed attention to practical or business affairs'.[33] Although there appears to have been no serious effort to recruit new members until 1899, the 1896 *Handbook* made a general appeal for recruits, and from 1894 onwards the introductory description of the Association's character and purpose increasingly emphasized the width of its support among business and professional men.[34] In 1899, as an outcome of this tendency, there was a serious examination of the desirability of electing a businessman as president in succession to A. T. Hadley; but this proposal was rejected, partly because it would have represented too sharp a reversal of the former emphasis on the scholarly character of the Association. As J. B. Clark put it,

> we should remain a scientific body. . . . At bottom even the philistines will have more respect for such a body than they would for one that should put a man of affairs at its head. I may be wrong, but I dread any yielding to the view that economic wisdom resides outside of the schools and inside of the counting house.
>
> [3, Clark to C. Hull, Dec 23 1899]

As it transpired, Ely's long-delayed return to the fold, followed by his unexpected election to the presidency,[35] provided a happy, if temporary, solution to the dilemma. Whatever the estimate of Ely's scholarship, his inexhaustible energies and remarkable administrative gifts were enlisted at a most opportune time. Under his businesslike guidance and largely owing to his personal efforts, membership expanded sharply,[36] interest revived, and the Association prospered.

Yet complete unity was not attained until 1904 when, following a University of Chicago decision to invite the historical and economic associations to a joint meeting in their city, J. L. Laughlin at last applied for membership.[37] Trivial as this incident may now appear, it seemed a matter of some importance to the officials of the American Economic Association. It dispelled the fear that Laughlin might use his considerable influence as head of the Chicago department of economics to spread distrust and hostility towards the Association,[38] and by adding the support of the only contemporary economist of note who had hitherto held aloof, it enabled the economists to present a united front in their efforts to enhance the public prestige and influence of their professional discipline. In retrospect it is clear that Laughlin's action marked the final disappearance of the suspicion the organization had encountered in varying degrees since its inception, and betokened its permanent establishment as a strictly scientific and scholarly body.

216

NOTES

* This paper incorporates research initially undertaken for a Johns Hopkins Ph.D. thesis (1953) and continued in 1958–9 with the aid of a Rockefeller Foundation fellowship.

1 Apart from the religious element in the setting, Saratoga Springs was the regular meeting place of the American Social Science Association, under whose auspices the AEA was created [5, p. 548].

2 Some years later E. J. James recalled his efforts to form an association and remarked that some of the academic economists he consulted believed that no new body was needed since the ASSA, which had been founded in 1865, 'practically performed the only available function of such an organization' [15, p. 109].

3 It has been suggested that the more conservative members of the ASSA joined the AEA [5, p. 520]. For a full account of the inaugural meeting see [18].

4 The argument began with E. J. James' hostile review of Simon Newcomb's *Principles of Political Economy* in *Science, 6* (1885) pp. 470–1, which brought replies and rejoinders ibid., pp. 495–6, 517–18, 538, 563 and was formally continued in the ensuing two volumes with articles by many of the leading contemporary economists.

5 [40, p. 254]. It is significant that Walker was no young upstart seeking to overthrow the ruling doctrines, but a mature and highly respected innovator working within the received tradition. His difficulties were strikingly revealed in a letter to Ely dated April 30, 1884: 'Perhaps no one has had more occasion than myself to feel the need of such moral support from fellow workers in political economy as might come from formal association and concerted action. When I first started out in 1874, I suffered an amount of supercilious patronage and toplofty criticism which was almost more than I could bear. Downright abuse would have been a luxury . . .' [15, p. 78].

6 E. W. Bemis, reporting to Ely a conversation with J. L. Laughlin of Harvard, wrote: 'He refuses to join the A.E.A. because it has any constitution save love of truth, for he does not know what he will believe five years hence and hence cannot belong to any class of disciples. Then too he took occasion to pour out his disapproval of an association which seemed desirous of excluding Prof. Sumner, if no one else, for though he claimed to dislike his evident dogmatism he preferred to be associated with men of opposite views and did not believe Prof. Sumner would make trouble.

. . . .

All this and much more he professed to say from a love of science and a dislike to divide its force' [14, Sep 29, 1886].

Similarly, E. R. A. Seligman wrote to Ely: 'I met Hadley [of Yale] at the Political Economy Club last Monday. When he heard that the "confession of faith" had been dropped, he said he would join the Association gladly, and that he proposed to take a warm interest in us, and lend an active hand whenever possible. Put him down as a member' [3, Jan 2 1889].

One branch association, of which there were six by the end of 1888 [4, pp. 87–91], applied for membership without the statement of principles [14, Seligman to Ely, Jan 29 1888].

7 In his autobiography Ely frankly disclosed this attitude. Although 'we were anxious to win the great body of economists . . . [we] aimed to gather like-minded men, congenial men who it was supposed could profitably work together. Not every economist was at first asked to join, although no economist who expressed a desire to join was refused enrollment' [17, pp. 141–2].

8 Thus Seligman, the treasurer, wrote to Ely: 'In answer to Dr. [Albert] Shaw's letter, I would say that in my opinion the change was not made in deference to any coterie – least of all the New York Nation coterie. . . . At the New York meeting President Walker stated that he was in favor of a change and had never favored the original platform because [it was] a platform. . . . None of the members present in the least desired any "back down" but it was thought that the portions omitted were not essential, [and] might be misinterpreted . . . I do not think, nor did anyone suppose that the change could possibly be interpreted as denoting a change in the sentiment which dominates the Association. It was simply held that the welfare of the Society would best be promoted thereby . . .' [14, Jan 29 1888]. Shaw, of Minneapolis, a former student of Ely at Johns Hopkins, subsequently became editor of the *Review of Reviews*.

9 For instance, in reply to Ely's request for comments on his work, Clark, a very mild-mannered man, asked: 'Does this passage justify the accusation brought against us of confusing the boundaries of economics and ethics? . . . is political economy ever hortatory?' and again: 'Is the impression when the essay is in print heightened or diminished by the use of such strong expressions? Is not the rhetoric of restrained statement, if not of understatement, better?' H. C. Adams wrote: 'The political economy of Mill does not "glorify selfishness". The expression is unscientific. A good deal of this part of your paper seems to me to be polemic rather than critical' [14, vol. 18, Miscel. Scrap Books, Nov 1887].

10 [9, p. 163]. Newcomb was then professor of mathematics at Johns Hopkins, and to the end of his life Ely believed that there was a local plot to expel him from the university [16, p. 146]. For contemporary references see [6, Ely to Clark, Dec 1 1886; H. C. Adams to Clark, Dec 16 1886; A. Johnston to Clark, Dec 17 1886; W. Gladden to Clark, Dec 25 1886].

In fact the current terminological confusion made it difficult to determine a writer's attitude to socialism. For example [7, pp. 566–7, 570, 577]. About this time H. C. Adams wrote in his personal diary: 'I am a socialist – to tell the truth – with the very characteristic exception of accepting their plan of reconstruction' [1]. It is, therefore, hardly surprising that H. W. Farnam remarked, in a review of *The Labor Movement in America*: 'Dr. Ely says – and he certainly ought to know – that he is no socialist. Yet much that he says sounds so much like what a good many of the socialists say, that he ought hardly to complain, if people occasionally mistake him for one' [20, p. 686].

11 W. G. Sumner's characteristically outspoken reference to 'the whimsical people who have hobbies of one sort or another, and who cluster around the Social Science Association, come forward with projects which are the result of a strong impression, an individual misfortune, or an unregulated benevolent desire, and which are therefore the product of a facile emotion, not of a laborious investigation' [39, p. 305] may have been typical of the hard-headed conservative viewpoint. Cf. *infra*, n. 14.

12 The Association's first published membership list, dated March 1886, included the names of 23 clergymen in a total of 181 members. The number rose to a peak of 39 by 1894 (when the total had reached 800). This is far below the 60 claimed by W. D. P. Bliss in 1892 [36, p. 9], but it may not be possible to identify all the clergy in the membership list.

13 [14, H. F. Craven to Ely, Nov 11 1902; J. B. Sewell to Ely, Dec 30 1890]. The Ely papers include many such eulogistic references to his moral and religious influence. For a modern opinion see [8, ch. 4].

14 [26, pp. 186–7]. For other conservative reactions to 'emotionalism' see [13, p. 24] [30, p. 2]. It was then, and indeed still is, a central tenet of orthodox

methodology that analysis and prescription should be rigidly separated, and this was one of the points of difference between the old and new schools. But it is risky to generalize about their respective attitudes to science. Walker and Patten, for example, repeatedly emphasized the distinction between analysis and policy recommendations, whereas Clark, who steadily became more conservative, was always criticized for his failure to make this distinction. There was a key debate on this issue, and on the general question of the social role of the scholar, following Hadley's presidential address in 1899 [25, pp. 62–88].

15 Dunbar had written a moderate critique of the new school in the opening number of the *Quarterly Journal of Economics* [13], of which he was the editor. He had been invited to join the AEA by Walker and Ely [37, Ely to Seligman, Apr 25 1887] and at a council meeting the next month it was agreed that a deputation should confer with Dunbar about his enrolment. Dunbar (and Hadley) had been present at the Boston meeting in May 1887 and he joined a year later [3, Seligman to Ely, Nov 21 1888; Dunbar to Ely, Dec 12 1888].

16 Hadley and Laughlin did not accept early invitations to join the council [37, James to Ely (copy), Apr 27 1887]. Subsequently Taussig wrote to Seligman that Laughlin 'intimates that he will come in if Ely goes out' [37, May 30 1892]. In fact Laughlin did not join until 1904, although as late as 1898 efforts were still being made to persuade him [3, Horace White to W. Willcox, May 25 1898].

There had been several attempts to include 'the Yale circle' [37, Clark, and Ely to Seligman, Apr 25 1887]. Sumner, the most dogmatic exponent of orthodoxy, presented the most delicate problem. It would be 'unworthy of us' Clark wrote to Ely, either 'continuing on "a platform of opposition to Sumner" as one of his close friends called it in conversation with me . . . [or] making undue overtures to him. This would also be making too much of him. He is a prominent man; but if he is a great man I have never done him justice. He seems to me to be chiefly what Pres't Walker once called him, a cantankerous man . . . A few could assure him that he would be welcomed – provided that the fact is that he would be; – but for the executive committee in their official capacity to invite him seems to me to be too far to go . . . I know, of course, that he feels excluded, and would not join without some unusual encouragement. That encouragement had better limit itself to private assurances; and these would have to be preceded by some mutual expressions of view. The case of Professor Dunbar is not in favor of more official invitations' [14, May 30 1889].

17 'Some seem to think that all things considered, I ought to keep the place and that the division of the office as I wanted is not desirable just now. I have heard a hint, I may tell you in confidence, about a combination of Yale, Harvard and Columbia to capture the thing and run it, but that would mean ruin. The West and the South would never submit. Apart from that, a large proportion of our members support us because they suppose we stand for something positive; and were [word illegible] a little because we dropped our "Statement of Principles". Now if the choice of Secretary should seem to indicate a further reaction, there are intimations of a split. This would be a great pity' [14, Ely to Adams, Dec 17 1888]. Ely's fears might be dismissed as wildly exaggerated but for the fact that his prophecy almost came true six years later. See *supra*, pp. 213–5.

18 For Ely's Chautauqua activities see [17, pp. 79–87]. Among those who opposed Chautauqua George Gunton complained that 'it is very much like having it held at some spiritualist camp-meeting' [37, Gunton to Seligman, Dec 26 1891]. Similarly Davis R. Dewey wrote that the objectors felt that 'Chautauqua is not

associated with the highest academic scholarship' [14, Dewey to Ely, Jan 10 1892]. Walker, in referring to a 'serious and determined protest' from F. H. Giddings, Taussig and Seligman [and later H. C. Adams], added that he personally would like to visit 'the great intellectual camp meeting of the country' [14, Walker to Ely, Dec 18 1891].

19 There is evidence that Ely had 'jumped the gun' [37, Walker to Seligman, Dec 10 and Dec 19 1891] [14, Giddings to Ely, Jan 1892].

20 'To my request for a call to the Executive committee or of the council,' Walker wrote to Seligman 'he replies that this can only mean a purpose to humiliate and insult him and that he will straightway resign.

. . . .

'Small loss, you say; and I don't disagree with you. The time passed, three years ago, when Ely had anything to give to the Association. Since then he has been a drag on the Association. But he promises to resign peacefully in August, whereas if he goes out now there will be a specious row. All the Socialist and semi-Socialist papers will join in attacking the Association and raising Ely to the rank of a martyr. The whole Chautauqua influence will be invoked against us. The newspapers will take the affair as "another row among the political economists" ' [37, Dec 23 1891].

Clark agreed: 'President Walker is right in deprecating the row I am sure. It would mean a fight with all that would, in that event, range itself on Dr. Ely's side, and that would be a great deal' [37, Clark to Seligman, Dec 30 1891].

21 In part the development of a more detached and cautious approach reflected the growing awareness of the complexity of current problems and the inadequacy of simplified solutions. Yet this had usually been the 'conservative' attitude [cf. 39, p. 306]. For a recent comment on this see [38].

22 For one interpretation of the differences between eastern colleges and midwestern state universities see [33, pp. 108–17] [cf. 23, pp. 21–7].

23 [1, Commons to Adams, Jan 9 1895]. G. W. Knight, the secretary, assured Adams that, 'It is not in any way a University of Chicago organization or machine, nor did the call for the conference originate with them' [Jan 8 1895, italics in original]. J. H. Canfield, Chancellor of the University of Nebraska, also claimed authorship of the scheme [3, Canfield to J. W. Jenks, Jan 21 1895].

24 [1, Adams to Jenks, Jan 7 1895]. Commons assured Adams that he had no hostile intentions towards the AEA [1, Jan 9 1895]. In a letter to Ely, however, Commons had spoken of an 'organization of Western economists' who 'would be mainly your students', at least initially. There was a need, he added, for such meetings of sympathizers, 'especially now that these forces of opposition seem to be marshalling together' [14, Sep 17 1894].

In a brief but revealing letter to Ely the President, Jesse Macy of Grinnell, Iowa, remarked that the Political Science Association was founded on ideas similar to those prevailing when the AEA was started, adding that the new body must not be 'swallowed' by the AEA [14, Apr 19 1895].

25 Among the economists this attitude was based partly on the current suspicion of business influence and, more specifically, on Laughlin's unwillingness to join the AEA and his independent establishment of the *Journal of Political Economy* at a time when strenuous efforts were being made to consolidate and reduce the number of periodical publications on economics. Taussig, for instance, referred to his and Dunbar's 'disgust at this intrusion [i.e., the *JPE*] into the field. It is a clear case of not having the interests of science at heart; though it may be a question whether this interest is pure and undefiled in the breast of any of us.

We all have a concern for our own institutions' [37, Taussig to Seligman, Mar 17 1892]. Similarly [19, Seligman to Farnam, Jun 2 1892].

26 [1, Jan 8 1895]. Yet the reports diverged somewhat. Whereas Knight claimed that 'no one was more solicitous that it should not be or even seem to be run by the Chicago men than those men themselves; especially was this true of Professor Small who, by the by, is a prince of good fellows', Bemis reported that the resolution encountered fierce opposition from Laughlin and von Holst (professor of history at Chicago) and three or four others [3, Jenks to Adams, Jan 8 1895].

The officers of the new association were president: Jesse Macy, Grinnell College, Iowa; vice-presidents: A. Small (Chicago, sociology), C. H. Haskins (Wisconsin, history), Adams (Michigan, economics) and J. Woodburn (Indiana, political science); treasurer: F. W Blackmar (Kansas, economics); secretary: G. W. Knight (Ohio, economics).

27 [1, Jenks to Adams, Jan 8 1895; Clark to Adams, Jan 10 1895] [3, Clark to Jenks, Jan 12 and Jan 21 1895]. Yet Clark's initial response was 'The West is stirred up. . . . One thing is clear: – we must make our association so good, and so fair in its policy, that there can be no ground for leaving it, however many rivals enter the field' [3, Clark to Jenks, Jan 10 1895].

28 Adams was at the University of Michigan, and was also Chief Statistician to the Interstate Commerce Commission. There are many examples of his attitude to theory: 'To my mind the Austrian School has already exhausted itself and I am wondering whether so clear a man as Clark will be able, after committing himself to the mechanical reasoning of the School, [to overcome] its limitations' [1, Adams to Seligman, Jun 1 1896]. Also [1, Adams to Seligman, May 14 1902; Adams to K. Coman, Feb 6 1897]. However Adams recognized his own limitations as a theorist. Of Clark he admitted: 'I hardly feel competent to follow him in his later development, but so far as I can understand him, I am obliged to dissent from many of the conclusions that he thinks so pertinent' [1, Adams to C. P. Emerick, Feb 5 1897].

29 [1, Commons to Adams, Apr 6 1895]. Also [3, Clark to Jenks, Jan 21 1895]. Commons was subsequently forced to resign [9, p. 285] although Adams had strongly defended him in a letter to President J. Swain of the University of Indiana [1, Aug 22 1894].

30 The selection committee comprised Taussig (Chairman), Farnam, R. P. Falkner (Pennsylvania), Ross (Stanford) and W. A. Scott (Wisconsin).

Recent research has tended to enhance Adams' reputation [2, pp. 3–55] [35, ch. 7].

31 From 1898 the annual meetings were recommended in the *A.E.A. Handbook* partly because they 'counteract any tendency to particularism which geographical separation and the diverse traditions of American colleges might be deemed to foster'. In this issue a geographical distribution of members was included for the first time.

32 In 1894 the treasurer complained that membership was far below that of the American Statistical Association [3, F. B. Hawley to Jenks, Nov 5 1894]; and five years later Seligman (then treasurer) informed Willcox (then secretary) that the membership of the American Historical Association was both higher (1200) than that of the AEA, and increasing, adding that 'if we once cease to advance the crisis is not far off' [3, Feb 15 1899]. Other letters of 1899 refer to the 'crisis' and the need for 'careful attention and nursing'. Membership had fallen from 781 in 1893 to 661 in 1894; and had only risen to 685 by 1898 and 745 by late 1899.

33 [24, p. 55]. Giddings called on members 'to take a more prominent stand on questions of public policy' and 'to make the A.E.A. an increasingly powerful influence upon public opinion . . . we must not impose upon ourselves a creed, or promulgate dogmas; but we should make it clear that there is a vital difference between scientific and unscientific views of those great subjects' [24, p. 56 sentence order altered].

34 Early in 1899 a circular was drafted for prospective members including the following phrases from Hadley's 1898 presidential address: 'If we fail in our influence in public life we fail in what is the most important application of our studies. . . . The largest opportunity of our economists in the immediate future lies not with students but with statesmen. . . . [In future the Association] will be of interest to thoughtful businessmen, newspaper men and holders of public office' [1, Willcox to Adams, Feb 16 1899]. Somewhat bluntly it was added that the limits of college membership had been reached!

35 Although Ely had presided at the 1893 meeting in Chicago, he had subsequently held himself aloof until 1899, when he offered a paper. Indeed, he even allowed his membership dues to lapse for '5 or 6 years' [3, Willcox to Giddings, Dec 2 1897]. At the 1899 meeting Hadley, the president, selected him as chairman of the nominating committee on the assumption that in view of his recent absences he would hardly be a candidate for office. But, to the secretary's surprise, he was elected president [3, Willcox to S. M. Lindsay, Jan 2 1900; Willcox to Hull, Jan 6 1900].

36 Membership rose from 745 in Dec 1900 to 950 in Dec 1901 during Ely's term of office, and to a peak of 1011 in 1902. Thereafter it remained at about this level until 1909, when the then secretary T. N. Carver conducted another membership campaign.

Of Ely's presidency Hull, the treasurer, wrote to Taussig: 'I think that Ely, too, has the idea of distinguishing his adminstration by adding to the membership of the Association, and to judge from his initial success as Secretary, I fancy his design is not altogether hopeless of execution' [3, Mar 8 1900]. At the conclusion of Ely's term of office Hull wrote: 'I feel that we really owe more as an organization to you than to any other President whom we have had since I have known anything about our affairs' (i.e., since 1893) [14, Hull to Ely, Nov 22 1901]. Similarly [14, Fetter to Ely, Jan 11 1902].

37 [14, Small to Ely, Jan 10 1904]. Jameson, secretary of the American Historical Association and professor of history at Chicago, spoke of Laughlin's genuine cordiality towards the AEA and the difficulty 'of persuading several scores or hundreds of members that his attitude is and would be a cordial one' [3, Jameson to Seligman, Nov 29 1902].

38 However unjust to Laughlin, this feeling was real enough. Wesley Mitchell, then a promising young man, was especially invited to read a paper in 1902 in an effort to protect him from 'bad influences' at Chicago [3, Fetter to Seligman, Oct 18 1902; Willcox to Hull, July 23 and 27 1900].

The abolition of the council, proposed in 1904 and effected in 1905, was a final explicit acknowledgement of the disappearance of the possibility of domination by a sect or group of reformers [15, p. 8].

REFERENCES

1 H. C. Adams, *Papers*, by kind permission of Mrs H. C. Adams, Ann Arbor, Michigan. (Now housed in the Michigan Historical Collections, at Ann Arbor.)

2 ——, *Relation of the State to Industrial Action*, ed. J. Dorfman. New York 1954.

3 American Economic Association, *Papers*, Secretary's Office, Northwestern University. (Now housed at Northwestern University library.)

4 ——, *Report of Third Annual Meeting*, Pub. A.E.A., Proc., First Ser., July 1889, 4, 229–323.

5 L.L. and J. Bernard, *Origins of American Sociology, The Social Science Movement in the United States*. New York 1943.

6 J. B. Clark, *Papers*, Columbia University Library.

7 ——, 'The Nature and Progress of True Socialism', *The New Englander*, July 1879, *151*, 565–81.

8 J. Dombrowski, *The Early Days of Christian Socialism in America*. New York 1936.

9 J. Dorfman, *The Economic Mind in American Civilization*, III. New York 1939.

10 ——, 'The Role of the German Historical School in American Economic Thought', *Am. Econ. Rev.*, Proc., May 1955, *45*, 17–28.

11 ——, *Thorstein Veblen and his America*. New York 1934.

12 C. Dunbar, 'Economic Science in America', *North Am. Rev.*, Jan 1876, *122*, 124–54.

13 ——, 'The Reaction in Political Economy', *Quart. Journ. Econ.*, Oct. 1886, *1*, 1–27.

14 R. T. Ely, *Papers*, Wisconsin State Historical Society, Madison, Wis.

15 ——, 'The American Economic Association 1885–1909', *Pub. A.E.A., Papers*, Third Ser., Apr. 1910, *11*, 47–93.

16 ——, 'The Founding and Early History of the American Economic Association', *Am. Econ. Rev.*, Mar. 1936, *26*, 141–50.

17 ——, *Ground Under Our Feet*. New York 1938.

18 ——, 'Report of the Organization of the American Economic Association', *Pub. A.E.A.*, First Ser., Mar. 1887, *1*, 5–46.

19 H. W. Farnam, *Papers*, Yale University Library.

20 ——, Review of R. T. Ely, 'The Labor Movement in America', *Pol. Sci. Quart.*, Dec. 1886, *1*, 683–7.

21 S. Fine, *Laissez-Faire and the General-Welfare State; A Study of Conflict in American Thought*. Ann Arbor 1956.

22 ——, 'Richard T. Ely, Forerunner of Progressivism', *Miss. Val. Hist. Rev.*, Mar. 1951, *37*, 599–624.

23 N. Foerster, *The American State University, Its Relation to Democracy*. Chapel Hill 1937.

24 F. H. Giddings, Vice-Presidential Address of Welcome, *Handbook A.E.A.*, 1898, pp. 55–6.

25 A. T. Hadley, 'Economic Theory and Political Morality', *Pub. A.E.A., Proc.*, Third Ser., Feb. 1900, *1*, 62–88.

26 ——, Review of Ely's 'Socialism and Social Reform', *The Forum*, Oct. 1894, *18*, 184–91.

27 R. Hofstadter, *The Age of Reform*. New York 1955.

28 ——, *Social Darwinism in American Thought*. Boston 1955.

29 —— and W. Metzger, *The Development of Academic Freedom in the United States*. New York 1955.

30 J. L. Laughlin, 'The Study of Political Economy in the United States', *Jour. Pol. Econ.*, Dec. 1892, *1*, 1–19.

31 S. Newcomb, Review of Ely's 'Outlines of Economics', *Jour. Pol. Econ.*, Dec. 1894, *3*, 106–11.

32 M. J. L. O'Connor, *Origins of Academic Economics in the United States*. New York 1944.

33 H. W. Odum, 'The Social Sciences', *A State University Surveys the Humanities*. ed. L. C. Mackinney, N. B. Adams, H. K. Russell. Chapel Hill 1945.
34 S. N. Patten, 'The Place of University Extension', *University Extension*, Feb. 1894, 1–36.
35 M. Perlman, *Labor Union Theories in America*. Evanston 1958.
36 W. Rauschenbusch, *Christianizing the Social Order*. New York 1912.
37 E. R. A. Seligman, *Papers*, Columbia University Library.
38 G. J. Stigler, 'The Politics of Political Economists', *Quart. Jour. Econ.*, Nov. 1959, *73*, 522–32.
39 W. G. Sumner, 'Sociology', *Princeton Rev.*, Nov. 1881, *57*, 303–23.
40 F. A. Walker, 'Recent Progress of Political Economy in the United States', *Pub. A.E.A., Proc.*, First Ser., July 1889, *4*, 17–40.

12

THE POLITICAL ECONOMY CLUB

A neglected episode in American economic thought[1]

During the decade of the 1880s, more striking new departures occurred in American economics than in any other comparable period. At that time the conflict between the established Ricardian *laissez-faire* orthodoxy and the newly imported German historical ideas reached its climax; a wave of public interest in economic problems provided the opportunity for several able young men – who came to dominate American economics for the next three or four decades – to obtain their first professorial appointments; the academic economists, as a body, slowly but surely were divesting themselves of the accumulated propaganda and theological trappings of their subject, and securing its recognition as the leading independent social science discipline; the first professional economic journals appeared, and the foundation of the American Economic Association on September 9, 1885, approximately the mid-point of the decade, symbolized the birth of an indigenous national tradition of economic scholarship.[2]

Although the concluding stages of this long period of gestation have repeatedly been subjected to close scrutiny, the process is intrinsically so interesting that it would be unwise to neglect any new evidence bearing on it. Earlier students have examined in detail the American Economic Association and its immediate precursor, the abortive Society for the Study of National Economy.[3] But the Political Economy Club, which constituted the nucleus of orthodox opposition to the AEA during its precarious formative stage, has hitherto been shrouded in mystery owing to the paucity of significant evidence. Even now, although it is possible to fill in some of the details from surviving correspondence, there is much that remains to be explained.

There were many precedents to guide the founders of a loose, semiformal social body like the (American) Political Economy Club, for it was an organization appropriate to a period when there were but a few full-time economists mainly located on or near the Eastern seaboard, many of whom already knew each other personally. As English economic ideas still dominated the American scene, the venerable Political Economy Club of

London, founded in 1821, afforded an obvious model. At least two members of the American group, Horace White and Hugh McCulloch, had attended its meetings in London, and the latter had been a member from 1874 to 1879.[4] Moreover, the similarity between the two groups was more than superficial. In each case the founders were 'men with distinct opinions which they desired to see prevail. They wanted to overthrow laws which they believed to be mischievous. They desired freedom of trade. The object of the Club was not purely scientific or critical. It had distinctly practical aims. . . . Not that they were by any means all of one mind.'[5] No existing organization could effectively meet the members' needs for closer contact and mutual stimulus. The American Statistical Association was too specialized, while the American Social Science Association and the American Association for the Advancement of Science were too diffuse and unwieldy. And there was, as yet, no precedent for an economic organization such as the American Economic Association which ostensibly had professional and scholarly objectives and yet was neither a closed society of scholars nor a private club. Hence the Political Economy Club might have proved to be the seed from which the American Economic Association grew, for there is evidence that two members of the club, F. A. Walker and R. T. Ely, who subsequently became the first President and Secretary of the new Association, entertained the idea of 'asserting ourselves aggressively' within the Political Economy Club as an alternative to launching an entirely new organization.[6] It is, therefore, worth examining the Club's history not only because it sheds additional light on the difference between the 'old' and 'new' schools of economics, but also because its failure helps to explain why the AEA succeeded.

The earliest reference to the proposal to form an economists' club appears in a letter, dated April 11, 1882,[7] from J. L. Laughlin, then instructor in political economy at Harvard, to Edward Atkinson, the prominent Boston businessman and popular writer on economic subjects. The project did not, however, begin to take shape until the following year, for on January 29, 1883, Laughlin again wrote to Atkinson[4]:

The matter of the 'American Society of Political Economy' (?) has been simmering in my mind, and I have now thought it worth proposing some plan. As you say, 'bores' must be excluded. So, it seems best to approach a few of the leading economists first, taking a small number, and then their collective wisdom can be used in regard to further elections. It ought to be made a dignified body, for it can be authoritative and useful in many ways. It could encourage economic studies by offering prizes, as in France, for work which deserves it well, and propose many subjects affecting our own country for which it offers honorable rewards. There is danger that it may engender the spirit of a clique; but this can be avoided largely by the selection of men.

I venture to mention some such names as the following, to start with: 1. Simon Newcomb, Washington [Professor of Mathematics in the US Navy]; 2. Chas. F. Dunbar, Cambridge [Professor of Political Economy, Harvard]; 3. Edward Atkinson, Boston; 4. Francis A. Walker, Boston [President of MIT]; 5. J. Laurence Laughlin, Cambridge; 6. William G. Sumner, New Haven [Professor of Political and Social Science at Yale]; 7. Arthur Latham Perry, Williamstown [Professor of Political Economy and History at Williams]; 8. David A. Wells, Norwich, Conn. [economist, businessman]; 9. Carl Schurz, New York [statesman, journalist and political philosopher]; 10. Andrew D. White, Ithaca, New York [President of Cornell, lately Minister to Germany].

How does this list strike you? It is capable of extension, but perhaps that had better be deferred. If it seems good, why not yourself mention the matter to Gen. Walker – or, if you prefer, I can. Then I suggest the printing of a small statement with your name, Gen. Walker's, and my own, to be sent to the others here mentioned asking for their co-operation. I am willing to draw up a sketch for the approval of yourself and Gen. Walker, before being sent out. You and he are both busy men, and I can relieve you of the correspondence, at present at least. As soon as answers are received, a date can be fixed for a meeting and organization.

The 'bogus' economists in Washington headed by John C. New[8] who organized as 'The American Association of Economists' suggested that we were none too early in thinking of such a scheme. Then, too, with some unity of action and support, it might be possible to establish a decent journal devoted to economic and financial subjects – some time in the future, perhaps. We need to be stimulated and to get an interchange of ideas, as much as any other body of scholars, and our meetings ought to bring out good work.

If you and Gen. Walker approve, let me know – or any new plan – and I will go on to prepare a statement.

A marginal note at the top of this letter indicates that it was forwarded to Walker; but no further developments occurred until November 1883, when definite plans were made to hold the inaugural meeting in New York, at the home of Horace White, editor of the *New York Evening Post*. Laughlin described the objectives of the Club more explicitly in his invitation to Simon Newcomb:

A few of us have suggested the plan of an organization of the political Economists of the country for conference, for discussion, for mutual stimulus, for encouragement of the study in the proper scientific spirit by others, and for various objects easily recognized as the aims of such a body. No plan as yet exists, but it is proposed to gather around a dinner table in New York or Boston about the 30th inst. to discuss the question, and, if we think best, to bring the young infant into the world.

We want your presence and cooperation, and should be greatly disappointed if the time was an inconvenient one for you. Please name another date when you might come, in case of a disagreement on the 30th.[9]

When Newcomb indicated his readiness to attend and participate in the Club, Laughlin despatched a list of members containing two significant additions: 'Two protectionists have been invited,' he observed, 'Thompson and Hamlin, so that it shall not be regarded as a meeting of a clique from the beginning. It should have a scientific object, and not be the tone of any one set, I take it.'[10] But despite Laughlin's good intentions, most members of the public regarded economists as advocates of either free trade or protection, and the Political Economy Club, like its predecessor in London, rapidly acquired the reputation of being a free trade clique. Nor was this reputation wholly undeserved. There is no evidence that either Thompson or Hamlin ever attended;[11] several prominent members were actively engaged in free trade propaganda; and the majority supported the Cleveland ticket in 1884 and the tariff reform movement of 1886.[12] With this bias in its membership, Laughlin's hope that the Club would be scientific and nonpartisan was unlikely to be fulfilled, and an indication of the kind of difficulties he encountered is provided by the correspondence relating to the selection of a topic for the December 1884 meeting.

This correspondence opens with a letter to Laughlin from Horace White stating that he and Wells had selected as the topic for the next discussion:

What ought to be the policy of the Democratic Party with regard to the tariff? This is not the question tentatively considered at the last meeting, but both Wells and myself consider it far better than an academic discussion of the effect of machinery on wages.

[16, Nov. 25, 1884]

At this, Laughlin, the secretary of the Club, forwarded White's letter to Newcomb, the president, with the following comment:

There are two things I do not like in it. First, White's letter seems to imply that a topic was chosen by the Club, viz.: 'Effect of machinery on wages,' but that Wells and he chose to over-rule the Club by making another choice. Second, it seems to me that the word 'academic' in the letter has a good deal of meaning as touching the future of our Club. The one who regards a discussion of principles as 'academic' will not further the progress of our science. And as economists we ought to meet this tendency at once, gently but firmly. We certainly do not intend our Club for a political organ in the sole interest of free trade. I think it would be very undignified for a Club of professed economists to talk at their dinner of the policy of the Democratic party. Free trade is not the whole of P. E. by any means, however much it may now interest us as a political question.

It seems to me, therefore, we ought to gently repress the tendency to make our Club a body for free trade agitation as (I think) Wells and White would have it; and point it steadily to discuss the really difficult and unsettled question[s] in P. E. wh. all recognize as important in their effect on the whole fabric of our science. I do not mean that we should never talk politics informally; but I object to any such formal declaration in a fixed subject, as a deflection of the trust reposed in us for the furtherance of the study of P. E.

[20, Nov. 30, 1884]

Newcomb's reply disclosed his sympathy towards Laughlin's view, and also revealed some of the personal factors involved. Recalling his impression that all the members but Sumner had agreed to the 'effect of modern improvements upon the economic interests of the labouring classes' as the topic for debate, he added: 'I also perfectly remember Professor Sumner's objection to it which was that there was nothing to say about it except that if any class of men were not able to adapt themselves to the advance of the age they would get left.' Newcomb conceded that White and Wells might possibly have been asked to select a subject, and commented, with reference to it, that he

would hesitate to criticize the conclusions of men so much better acquainted with the world than I am were it not that persons with very little knowledge can sometimes make valuable suggestions. Now it strikes me that if it should get into public prints that our Club has undertaken to discuss the proper policy of the Democratic party the unholy paragrapher would poke fun at us over the whole land and Messrs. Randall, Carlisle and Co. would enjoy the fun of seeing him do it.[13]

[20, Dec. 1, 1884]

In his reply to Laughlin, White explained that the original topic had been changed because

there was a great deal of opposition to it, chiefly in the part of Prof. Sumner. It was this opposition as well as the indefiniteness of the proposed topic which led me to think of putting up a question having more relation to the current dissensions of the press and of Congress. The English and French societies of economists take up questions

229

relating to party politics, and I don't see why we may not. If we exclude all such questions we shall narrow our field very much.

However, I am not tenacious. You might put both questions in the paper . . . and then leave the society to take one or the other or both.

[20, Dec. 4, 1884]

In fact, the combined influence of the secretary and president prevailed, and White was advised to propose his topic for debate on a subsequent occasion. But despite its temporary ascendancy, the academic interpretation of the Club's role did not remain unchallenged. Edward Atkinson, who occasionally entertained the members at his home with a dinner cooked in his beloved Alladin oven, also hoped that their activities would not be confined to scholarly disputation, and in 1888 he informed Laughlin that, in reply to some circulars he had despatched, 'very pleasant responses' had been received 'from some of our members on the proposition to make the Political Economy Club a little more of a force' [4, Nov. 15, 1888].[14] Atkinson's exact intention is unknown; but it is unlikely that he proposed to make the Club an organ of doctrinaire free trade opinion, for he regarded himself as one of the 'lawless, outside, free lances on Economic Questions. . . . I don't like the "Socialists of the Chair" or the "Economists of the Closet" ',[15] and had withdrawn from the free trade clubs in 1887 in order to promote moderate tariff reform, partly because of his position in the business community and partly 'because I dislike and disapprove of the methods of the *doctrinaire* free traders as much as I do those of the intolerant protectionists'.[16]

Atkinson's scheme was probably rejected, for the control of the Club's affairs remained in the hands of the academic members. As early as December 1884 Newcomb expressed the opinion that the president should be elected annually by ballot, adding that 'I feel a great deal of diffidence in presiding in the presence of such men as Wells, White and Sumner';[17] yet three years later his proposal to resign was unanimously rejected because, as Laughlin put it, 'we are only too glad to have a double star at the head of our constellation to give up the chance so easily. Your reign is undisputed.'[18]

Laughlin's desire to preserve the Club's original character and function also explains his action in January 1888 when, as a result of the breakdown of his health and his sudden departure for Santo Domingo, he unceremoniously unloaded the secretarial duties on H. W. Farnam of Yale.[19] Farnam shared Laughlin's sentiments, and consequently when Atkinson suggested that the Club should engage in publication Farnam demurred, on the grounds that its purpose was 'mainly social' and that most of its members were relieved to belong to a body which did not exact that toll.[20] Laughlin's illness was only temporary, and he appears to have resumed his secretaryship in 1889, when Farnam went on an extended trip abroad.

This effort to preserve the Club's character by maintaining the continuity of its management is curiously reminiscent of the early history of its chief rival, the American Economic Association, whose first president and secretary, F. A. Walker and R. T. Ely respectively, were retained in office for seven years. In the latter instance the principal motive was fear of outside intervention which might lead to control by the 'old school' economists; whereas, in the case of a closed society like the Political Economy Club, the threat necessarily came from within. Yet the very diversity of the Club's membership, which was at first almost evenly divided among professors, businessmen and journalists, proved to be the main safeguard, for once it had been launched as a private dining club no single group was strong enough to divert it into another channel. Admittedly, the older generation of economists consisted mainly of 'practical' men who demonstrated comparatively little interest in theoretical problems, and who believed that their principles were directly applicable to current practice. But there was a variety of organizations especially designed and better equipped to engage in politico-economic propaganda; and by December 1884 the Political Economy Club's membership included a strong contingent of young scholars whose divergent views on policy matters may have combined with their interest in broad questions of principle to keep it on the straight and narrow path of informal debate.[21]

The most significant feature of this expanded membership is the inclusion of such outspoken critics of the older generation of economists as H. C. Adams, R. T. Ely and E. J. James, who were instrumental in forming the association that eventually supplanted Laughlin's club and caused its decline. The presence of these up-and-coming young radicals in a body that has usually been regarded as the last bastion of the doctrinal establishment is eloquent testimony to the genuineness of Laughlin's professed desire to form a representative, scientific organization. It also provides an early example of the catholicity that subsequently impelled him, despite his own extreme conservatism, to include in his department at the University of Chicago such unorthodox colleagues as Davenport, Hoxie, Mitchell and Veblen.[22] Unfortunately there is little available information concerning the relations between members of the 'old' and 'new' schools of economics in the Political Economy Club, for it seems that the leading spokesmen for the younger generation only infrequently attended its meetings. Henry Carter Adams, for example, attended but once in April 1888 and again in April 1890, although the second occasion appears to have been convivial, for he told his mother:

I had a headache most all day yesterday, perhaps it was on account of a dinner I went to of the 'Economy Club' at Prof. Simon Newcomb's. . . . I cared most to see the Hon. Hugh McCulloch; who was at the heart of the banking system during the war, and who has twice been Secretary of the Treasury. He is not a *great* man in the sense that he is a great fighter; but he has been a very useful public servant, one that has been and is an honor to the country.[23]

By this time Adams was at the outset of his long and fruitful career as Chief Statistician to the Interstate Commerce Commission; moreover his even-tempered disposition, as well as his experience, must have helped him to enjoy and profit from the company of his elders. The inclusion of Ely, however, is particularly surprising, for he was the most hostile critic of economic orthodoxy, who subsequently became Laughlin's bête noire and he was profoundly suspicious of some members of the older generation. It is, however, doubtful whether he ever appeared at the Club's gatherings before 1892, for Farnam, who attended regularly and sometimes acted as host, did not meet Ely until the crucial Chautauqua meeting of the American Economic Association in that year.[24] E. J. James, also, repeatedly clashed with his fellow clubmen in print, and probably in person; and when F. A. Walker invited Newcomb to a meeting at his house in 1888 he took the precaution of adding that 'Dr. James is *not* to be here; so there will be no danger of a riot.'[25] Walker, himself, occupied a somewhat uneasy intermediate position between the two contending parties, for he was both a distinguished representative of the older generation and the leader and sympathetic supporter of the 'new school'. His heterodox monetary views brought him into conflict with other Club members over the question of bimetallism, and the following complaint to Farnam indicates that his arguments with his more orthodox clubmates were sometimes frustrating:

> I wish that half a dozen of us, representing different views of the subject, could get together sometime, without an Atkinson, without a Laughlin, and without a Horace White! and see exactly how far we agree and in precisely what we differ. Qualitatively, I think we should differ but little; and I am disposed to think that we could reach something like a rude approximation to quantitative statements of the elements involved.[26]

This letter suggests how difficult it was to get an impartial, scientific discussion of technical and contentious policy questions in a small, close-knit body like the Political Economy Club. Its gatherings were so intimate and personal that it was easy for men of forceful character and decided opinions, like Sumner, Wells and White, to dominate its proceedings. Although Laughlin managed to prevent the Club from degenerating into a mere propaganda agency, his attempt to confine its attention to questions of principle proved unsuccessful.[27] The older generation of economists were, for the most part, practical men, who were experienced in public affairs but who usually lacked sound professional training in economics. They were 'commanding men' – as A. T. Hadley, a conservative member of the younger generation, once admiringly remarked – who regarded economics as a body of concrete propositions from which definite, explicit policy conclusions could be drawn.[28]

By contrast, the AEA marked the emergence of a more mature, more complex, and more scholarly approach to economic thought. Although the Association's founders were bold and even defiant in their hostility to the ruling orthodoxy, they were flexible and open-minded in their positive views. They differed indeed among themselves on basic questions of method, theory and policy; but they shared a common desire to encourage scholarly investigation and the exchange of information, and they soon moderated their initial aggressive tone. As the Association's membership expanded and it lost its reputation as an organ of a particular school or sect, its annual meetings provided an open forum in which any inclinations toward dogmatism were inhibited by the conventions of scientific procedure and the etiquette of formal debate. One wonders whether the same restraints existed in the meetings of the Political Economy Club.

At the silver jubilee meeting of the AEA in 1909, Laughlin maintained that the Political Economy Club had failed to become the representative organ of American economics because it was 'not comprehensive enough for a country with an area as wide and with economic interests as diversified as those of the United States'.[29] Yet this is an unsatisfactory explanation, for the Club included in its membership representatives of all but the most radical economic opinions even *before* the AEA came into existence, and it continued to be more comprehensive – at least in its nominal membership – until 1888. Nor is it true to say that the older body was more restricted in its sphere of operations, for both groups met in Eastern seaboard centres until 1893, when they both met in Chicago during the World's Fair.

The most important difference between the two organizations lay neither in the range of their membership nor in the location of their meetings but in their readiness to accept new members and new ideas. Whereas the Political Economy Club continued to be a closed private club, many of whose members regarded themselves as custodians of 'sound' economic doctrine, the AEA from its inception aimed to recruit as many fee-paying members as possible, whether scholarly or not, and was almost equally acquisitive in its attitude to intellectual innovations. At first, it is true, the Association's membership was small and many of its adherents were clergymen and reformers notable for their moral enthusiasm rather than for their scholarship. But before long its membership policy was vindicated; the initial distrust of the so-called 'new' school of economics was gradually overcome, and the AEA gained adherents from the ranks of the Political Economy Club as its more broad-minded members were reassured by their colleagues, such as Seligman, Mayo-Smith and Walker, who already belonged to both societies.[30] By the end of the 1880s the AEA was already beginning to assume the role of leadership among American economists which it has occupied ever since; and when the British Economic Association (later the Royal Economic Society) was founded in 1890, the English 'learned' society model was consciously rejected in favour of the open plan of the AEA.[31]

Thus the future lay with the AEA; and the Political Economy Club, like its English counterpart, preserved its original form and function. Until 1892, when Laughlin, the secretary, became head of the department of economics at Chicago, the Club continued to meet regularly – usually three times a year in April, June and December – at the house of one of its members in New York, New Haven, Boston or some intermediate or adjacent point. In April 1890 its meeting was held at Newcomb's house in Washington, and in April 1893 at the home of Stuart Wood in Philadelphia. With Laughlin's move to the Middle West, however, the established pattern was disrupted, and although Laughlin periodically extended invitations to some of his former colleagues in the East, a surviving membership list for the mid-1890s indicates that its support came entirely from Chicago and a few leading midwestern university centres.[32] The Political Economy Club still included a sizable proportion of businessmen; and as late as 1899 even the AEA was still making a strong appeal to the business community and serious consideration was given to a proposal to elect a man of affairs, C. S. Fairchild, who had been Secretary of the Treasury under Cleveland, as its president.[33] But the proposal was defeated, and the AEA steadily became more national in its representation while remaining academic in its outlook, and the Political Economy Club dwindled into insignificance.[34]

APPENDIX

In a letter to Farnam dated Jan. 12, 1895 (Farnam papers) Laughlin remarked that there had been 26 meetings of the Club up to that time. He was then 'getting the proceedings ready for the printer' (ibid., Jan. 7, 1895); but if printed, no copy seems to have survived. The following is a list of meetings, topics and speakers mentioned in surviving correspondence.

Nov. 30, 1883	Inaugural meeting [at H. White's?], New York.
Jun. 11, 1884	No details.
Dec. 30, 1884	New York, 'The effect of machinery upon the economic interests of the labouring classes'.
Apr. 20 [?], 1885	No details.
Oct. 10, 1885	At Farnam's, New Haven.
Dec. 27, 1887	At C. F. Adams', Boston, 'The Treasury Surplus'.
Apr. 3, 1888	At Hewitt's, New York, 'The New Tariff Bills'.
Jun. 23, 1888	At Tuxedo Park, 'The Repercussions of Taxes'.
Dec. 29, 1888	At Walker's, Boston. [Hugh McCulloch on 'Paper Money'?]

Apr. 23, 1889	'Trusts'.
Jun. 10 [?], 1889	At Atkinson's, Brookline, Mass., 'The Single Tax', introduced by White.
Dec. 28, 1889	New York, 'The Silver Question in Great Britain and the USA'.
Apr. 13, 1890	At Newcomb's, Washington.
Dec. 26, 1890	No details.
Mar. 31, 1891	No details.
Dec. 10, 1892	No details.
Apr. 8, 1893	At Stuart Wood's, Philadelphia, 'Has the gold standard of value appreciated any since the demonetization of silver?' introduced by Newcomb.
Sept. 16, 1893	At Laughlin's, Chicago.
Dec. 31, 1895 May 1902 May 1903	All in Chicago.

NOTES

1 This article is a by-product of research into the history of American economic thought undertaken in 1958–9 with the aid of a Rockefeller Foundation fellowship. I am indebted to Joseph Dorfman of Columbia University for his criticism and correction of an earlier draft, and to various other persons, too numerous to specify, who have responded to requests for information.

2 The principal sources on these matters are cited in Coats [6]. Among those who attained full-time professional status as economists in the 1880s were: H. C. Adams, E. B. Andrews, R. T. Ely, H. W. Farnam, A. T. Hadley, E. J. James, J. L. Laughlin, S. N. Patten, E. R. A. Seligman and F. W. Taussig.

3 See especially [9, ch. 2] [11, pp. 133–5, 296–9].

4 See [21, p. 311 and n.]. For 18th century economic clubs see [15, p. x].

5 From reminiscences by Sir J. MacDonnell [21, pp. 338–9].

6 Unfortunately only one passing reference to this possibility has survived. See F. A. Walker to R. T. Ely [12, April 30, 1884].

7 After commenting on one of Atkinson's papers, Laughlin remarked [4]: 'It has often occurred to me that we ought to have a Congress of American economists at least once a year for discussion of such questions. There is Gen. Walker, Prof. Sumner, Prof. Dunbar, Prof. Perry, Simon Newcomb, etc., etc. – a very good band of immortals to begin with. We might, too, have some influence as a body on economic questions in this country. How does the idea strike you?'

8 John C. New, Indiana lawyer, banker, newspaper editor and prominent Republican, had been US Treasurer from 1875–6, and was Assistant Secretary of the Treasury from 1882–4. Cf. [3, v. 4, p. 500]. There seems to be no record of his 'American Association of Economists'.

9 [20, Nov. 11, 1883]. Newcomb was one of America's foremost scientists and a prominent writer on economics. See also Laughlin to Atkinson, Nov. 11, 1883 [4].

10 [20, Nov. 26, 1883]. Robert Ellis Thompson, Professor of Social Science at the

University of Pennsylvania and first Dean of the Wharton School of Finance and Commerce, was one of the best-known disciples of Henry C. Carey. Cyrus Hamlin, President of Middlebury College, Vermont, sometimes lectured on free trade and protection [3, v. 3, p. 66]. At this time neither Thompson nor Hamlin had indicated his willingness to attend. Cf. Laughlin to Atkinson, Nov. 23, 1883 [4].

11 Thompson may have attended, for his name appears on a printed list of members dated 1887 in the Ely papers, a list which includes the name of his University of Pennsylvania colleague, E. J. James. Moreover, as late as March 28, 1888, Thompson wrote to H. W. Farnam of Yale expressing regret at his inability to attend a forthcoming meeting [13].

12 David A. Wells, the most active proponent of free trade in the Club, has been called 'the man who would gladly have played the role of Richard Cobden in America'. See [17, p. 203]. Wells had joined with White and Atkinson to form the American Free Trade League in 1869, and he played the leading role in the League's offspring, the Society for Political Education, formed in 1879, whose members included Sumner, C. F. Adams and White. (By this time Atkinson had dropped out.) Wells' *Primer of Tariff Reform* [23] may have played a decisive part in the campaign of 1884. See [17, pp. 117–18, 142, 147–8. Cf. 19, pp. 156–8, 280–2].

13 Newcomb was evidently referring to Samuel J. Randall, leader of the Democratic protectionists in the House of Representatives, and John G. Carlisle, Speaker of the House, who was a mild, low-tariff reformer. See Nevins [19, ch. 17]. His reference suggests that the Club's activities might already have been known in political circles.

14 His Alladin oven is described in Harold F. Williamson's book [24, pp. 231–4].

15 Atkinson to Richmond Mayo-Smith [4, June 16, 1890].

16 Atkinson to Charles Nordhoff [4, June 1, 1885]. On another occasion he wrote to David A. Wells: 'I think that the method adopted, of which Professors Perry and Sumner are the chief exponents, has done more to perpetuate a high tariff than have all the advocates of that system put together. When they lead people to think there is a profit in protection in excess of freedom they excite every unreasoning man to try to get a share of this profit' [4, Aug. 5, 1886]. Cf. [24, pp. 91–3, 135].

17 Newcomb to Laughlin [20, Dec. 1, 1884].

18 Laughlin to Newcomb [20, Dec. 31, 1887].

19 Laughlin to Farnam, Jan. 31, 1888, and Mar. 28, 1888 [13]. On Feb. 29, 1888 Farnam informed Horace White of Laughlin's sudden departure and referred to Laughlin's note 'which may be taken, I presume, to be his last will and testament, and in which he constituted me his sole heir and legatee in the Secretaryship of the Political Economy Club'. Farnam added that this seemed inconsistent with the Club's principles and with the members' belief that 'public office is a public trust', but that in the emergency he was prepared to act 'ultra vires'. In his letter of March 28th Laughlin apologized for his precipitate action saying that without Farnam the Club 'would have been dinnerless and abandoned to the storm of tariff discussion without a guide'.

20 Farnam to Atkinson [13, Jan. 9, 1889].

21 A list of members dated Dec. 30, 1884 included the following additional academic representatives: H. C. Adams, J. H. Canfield, R. T. Ely, H. W. Farnam, A. T. Hadley, E. J. James, A. L. Perry, R. Mayo-Smith. By 1887, A. L. Chapin, J. F. Colby and S. Macvane were also members, and E. R. A. Seligman joined early in 1888. (In some cases, e.g., Canfield, membership was purely nominal.)

The 1887 list included the following non-academic members: M. B. Anderson (President, University of Rochester); H. C. Burchard (Director of the Mint); W. C. Ford (Chief of Statistics Bureau, Department of State); E. L. Godkin (Editor of the NY Nation); A. S. Hewitt (ironmaster, later Mayor of New York); J. J. Knox (banker, former Comptroller of the Currency); M. Marble (newspaper editor); W. Minot, Jr; and H. Villard (railroad promoter, financier).

22 Cf. [5, p. 94]. It is doubtful whether the seminal influence of this conflict of views and personalities has been fully recognized. Not only was Chicago the battleground, both literally and figuratively, between the contending forces of Eastern conservatism and Midwestern radicalism; but in addition, Laughlin was the original of the caricature of the typical orthodox economist at whom the young 'institutionalists' directed their shafts. See Coats [7].

23 H. C. Adams to Mrs E. D. Adams [1, Apr. 14, 1890].

24 Farnam to E. R. A. Seligman [13, June 5, 1892].

25 Walker to Newcomb [20, Dec. 22, 1888]. For James' clash with Newcomb, see [6]. These exchanges initiated the *Science* economic discussion in the following year. For a later clash between James and Atkinson, see Atkinson to James [4, Sept. 30, Oct. 14, and Oct. 20, 1887].

26 Walker to Farnam [13, Sept. 17, 1896]. Laughlin may have been referring to the same kind of difficulty when he pressed Newcomb to attend a meeting at New Haven. 'The new organization at Saratoga [i.e., the AEA] will no doubt be discussed in our Club, and our objects may be defined. Be sure and come. We need your "scientific method".' Laughlin to Newcomb [20, Sept. 26, 1885].

27 A list of topics and dates of known meetings, is provided in the Appendix to this article. It was, however, the approach rather than the nature of the topic that determined the character of the Club's proceedings.

28 Cf. A. T. Hadley [4, p. 70]. This passage from his presidential address to the AEA in 1898, 'The Relation Between Economics and Ethics', clearly exemplifies the differences between the older and the younger economists. Broadly speaking, Hadley preferred the wrong but consistent and explicit advice of the older group to the more cautious and vague approach of the younger generation. In place of 'a presumptuous claim of knowledge', he asserted, the new political economy 'substitutes either controversies or confessions of ignorance'. For an excellent example of the merits and limitations of the older, more practical approach, see the admirable book by J. R. W. Leiby [18].

29 See discussion following [10].

30 One example of contact in the Club which benefited the AEA is afforded by the following letter from Seligman to Ely dated Jan. 2, 1889: 'I met Hadley at the Political Economy Club last Monday. When he heard that the "confession of faith" had been dropped, he said he would join the Association gladly and that he proposed to take a warm interest in us and lend an active hand whenever possible. Put him down as a member' [2]. The 'confession of faith' referred to is the Association's 'Statement of Principles'.

31 See Albert Shaw [22].

32 This undated list in vol. III of the Scrap Books in the Ely Papers [12], includes the following university members: H. C. Adams and F. M. Taylor (Michigan); J. Cummings, H. R. Hatfield, J. L. Laughlin, T. B. Veblen (Chicago); R. T. Ely, B. H. Meyer, M. H. Robinson, W. A. Scott (Wisconsin); G. M. Fiske, D. Kinley (Illinois); W. W. Folwell, F. McVey (Minnesota); J. H. Gray (Northwestern). There were also nine members representing manufacturing, railroading or banking.

33 See, for example, W. Willcox to C. Hull, Dec. 12, 1899, and J. B. Clark to

Hull, Dec. 15 and 23, 1899, AEA papers [2]. The original suggestion came from F. W. Taussig of Harvard.

34 I have been unable to trace the exact date of the Club's demise. The last recorded meeting I have discovered is May 1903. The Western Economic Society, founded in 1911, performed similar functions in the Chicago area until the 1920s. (For this information I am indebted to Harold G. Moulton, who was its executive secretary until 1922.) Some additional details about the Club appear in Dorfman [8].

REFERENCES

1 H. C. Adams, *Papers*, Ann Arbor, Michigan.
2 American Economic Association, *Papers*, Secretary's Office, Northwestern University.
3 *Appletons' Cyclopaedia of American Biography*, vols. 3 and 4. New York 1888.
4 E. Atkinson, *Papers*, Massachusetts Historical Society, Boston, Mass.
5 A. Bornemann, *J. Laurence Laughlin: Chapters in the Career of an Economist*. Washington 1940.
6 A. W. Coats, 'The First Two Decades of the American Economic Association', *Am. Econ. Rev.*, Sept. 1960, *50*, 555–74. Reprinted in this volume, pp. 205–24.
7 J. Dorfman, *The Economic Mind in American Civilization*, vol. III. New York 1949.
8 R. T. Ely, 'The American Economic Association 1885–1909', Publications of the American Economic Association, Third Ser., *Papers*, Apr. 1910, *11*, 47–93.
9 ——, *Ground Under Our Feet*. New York 1938.
10 ——, *Papers*, Wisconsin State Historical Society, Madison, Wis.
11 H. W. Farnam, *Papers*, Yale University Library, New Haven, Conn.
12 A. T. Hadley, *The Education of the American Citizen*. New York 1901.
13 H. Higgs, *Bibliography of Economics 1751–75*. Cambridge, 1935.
14 E. J. James, 'Newcomb's Political Economy', *Science*, Nov. 27, 1885, *6*, 470–1. Letters to editor, reply by S. Newcomb, and by F. Franklin, ibid., 495–6; letter to editor, rejoinder, by E. J. James, ibid., Dec. 11, 1885, 517–18.
15 F. B. Joyner, *David Ames Wells, Champion of Free Trade*. Cedar Rapids 1939.
16 J. R. W. Leiby, *Statistics and the Labor Problem: A Biography of Carroll D. Wright*. Cambridge, Mass. 1960.
17 A. Nevins, *Grover Cleveland, A Study in Courage*. New York 1938.
18 S. Newcomb, *Papers*, Nov. 11, 1883. Library of Congress, Washington, D.C.
19 *Political Economy Club, Founded in London, 1821*. London 1921.
20 A. Shaw, 'Report of the Organization of the British Economic Association', Publications of the AEA, first ser., Jan. and Mar. 1891, *6*, 163–74.
21 D. A. Wells, *A Primer of Tariff Reform*. New York 1884.
22 H. F. Williamson, *Edward Atkinson, the Biography of an American Liberal 1827–1905*. Boston 1934.

13

THE AMERICAN ECONOMIC
ASSOCIATION, 1904–29*

PROLOGUE

At its birth in 1885 the American Economic Association was a healthy infant whose lusty cries for attention and nourishment soon attracted enough interest and support to ensure that it would enjoy a vigorous and effective life. Yet even the most auspicious beginnings could not entirely counteract the effects of heredity. The offspring of mixed parentage – European scholarship and Yankee social reform – the Association revealed even before its seventh year those schizoid tendencies which were to continue in evidence throughout its adolescence and early adulthood. The inherited tensions resulting from the conflicting attractions of pure science and public service were, admittedly, reinforced by environmental influences. But even when the environment became more favourable, when the internal divisions among its members had faded into the mists of memory, and when the foundations of a long and fruitful career had been securely laid, there still remained doubts – not only about the most effective methods of achieving the Association's purposes, but also about the very nature of those purposes.

I INTRODUCTION: SCHOLARSHIP OR SURVIVAL?

It is often difficult to discern clearly demarcated turning-points in the life of an individual or the development of an organization, and there are no compelling reasons why the second instalment of the history of the American Economic Association should begin in 1904 [6]. However, that year witnessed the formal burying of a hatchet and the inauguration of what the Secretary called an 'era of good feelings' [1, F. A. Fetter to E. R. A. Seligman, Apr 4 1904] for, after delicate and protracted negotiations, it was decided that the next annual meeting should be held at the University of Chicago, whereupon J. L. Laughlin, Head of the Department of Economics at Chicago and the only prominent survivor of the 'old school' opposition to the American Economic Association, graciously accepted the inevitable and at last became a member. This happy event[1] did not, of course, mark the complete disappearance of 'the petty and ridiculous politics that seem to be inseparable from the conduct of all American associations'.[2] The wide variety of interests and the geographical dispersion of the Association's membership were themselves sufficient to ensure the persistence of disagreements about its policy – as, for example, in the perennial problem of choosing a suitable location for the annual meeting. Nevertheless, from the early years of this century, personal, doctrinal, and institutional rivalries played a subordinate role in the organization's history, and under its benevolent and enlightened leadership the unity of the American economists was assured.

In a sense, 1904 marks the end of the parochial phase of the AEA's history, and in subsequent years its officers were free to devote more of their time and energy to the task of establishing and enhancing its position on the national stage. This does not mean that their trials and tribulations were over: for although the Association's position as the leading organization of American economists was rarely questioned, its precise character and purpose remained in doubt, and from time to time financial difficulties threatened its very existence. In this case, as so often occurs, ends and means were interdependent, and in times of crisis the future of the organization seemed to hang on the outcome of a struggle between scholarship and survival. This struggle was not solely or even mainly attributable to financial difficulties; nor was it an unusual experience for a scholarly organization in the USA, since it reflected the basic insecurity of the intellectual's position in American society. Nevertheless, the problem presented itself to the economists in an especially acute form because the scientific status of their discipline was open to question, and they were torn between the conflicting claims of scholarship and public service. Both as individuals and as an organized body, the American economists sought to enhance their public prestige and influence, especially with the business community, without at the same time jeopardizing their reputation as detached, impartial scientists. To the individual economist the problem of deciding how to divide his time and energy between the groves of academe and the market place was a subjective one, to be resolved by a personal decision which, even if conscious, was seldom irrevocable; and for many economists the outcome must have been largely determined by the chance availability of employment opportunities. To the officers of the American Economic Association, on the other hand, this problem necessarily assumed a more overt, institutional form, and the solutions adopted are revealed in the membership campaigns, in the effort to avoid public policy commitments, in the conduct of the Association's annual meetings, and in the form and content of its publications. In view of the wider issues concerning the position of the professional economist in American society, an examination of these mudane affairs possesses an interest which transcends the parochial or the antiquarian. If, for example, we find that by the end of the 1920s the American Economic Association had solved its internal, organizational problems and had come to terms with its environment, we may thereby obtain some indication of the progress (or perhaps the corruption) of American scholarship.[3] If, however, these problems were still unsolved, we are automatically provided with a number of pertinent questions about the subsequent development of American economic thought.

II THE SIZE AND CHARACTER OF MEMBERSHIP

If one may judge an organization by its membership, the American Economic Association has never been a purely scholarly and scientific body, and in this respect its policy has consistently adhered to the wishes of the young rebels who founded it in the 1880s partly in protest against the domination of American economic thought by what they conceived to be an exclusively orthodox 'school' [6] [7] [8]. In its initial, reformist phase, when the first Secretary, Richard T. Ely, was largely responsible for these matters, determined efforts were made to enlist the support of a wide variety of nonacademic persons, and the early membership lists included a high proportion of clergymen (some of whom were also college professors). Yet even at that stage there were some members who wondered whether the desire for comprehensiveness and catholicity was being pushed too far, and this doubt recurred from time to time in later years.

During the late 1890s, a conscious effort was made to arouse the support of business and professional men [6, p. 571], and the first systematic membership campaign was undertaken by Ely, almost single-handed, in 1900–2, while he was President of the Association. The timing of this campaign was no coincidence, for Ely not only possessed the requisite combination of character, skill, and outlook; he was also seeking to demonstrate his indispensability to an organization which he regarded, with only partial justification, as his own offspring. It was, however, a coincidence that the second membership campaign, launched in 1909, was conducted by a man of similar qualities, Thomas Nixon Carver. Like Ely, Carver possessed dynamic energy, considerable administrative skill, a taste and a talent for popularization, and a firm belief that the Association should play an active part in disseminating 'sound' economic ideas and shaping public policy. His attitude towards the AEA was, of course, less possessive than Ely's; but neither man displayed any hesitation in impressing his own forceful personality on the organization.

Both of these campaigns were prompted by a desire to increase the Association's activities at a time when its membership revenue was expanding slowly. The finances were, it is true, much stronger in 1909 than they had been ten years earlier; but the need for revenue was even greater because of the decision to begin publishing the *American Economic Review*.

When Carver was elected Secretary, at the 1908 annual meeting, a membership committee was also appointed; but although the ensuing campaign gathered momentum the prospects of eventual success seemed poor for, as Carver showed in a lucid economic analysis of the problem incorporated in his Secretary's report for 1911, a very large increase in membership would be needed to make a significant addition to the Association's income. The campaign expenses were so high that each new member added a net marginal income of only $1.40, and the rate of growth of income was far too slow to cover the expected rise of expenditure [3, pp. 132–7]. However, this analysis attracted the attention of a New York lawyer, Albert de Roode, one of Carver's former Harvard students, and he and a group of his business colleagues offered to provide a special fund of $1,000 for the campaign. As he explained in a letter to Carver:

> Our interest in the work is because we understand that the Association wishes to extend its scope and influence among the non-academic members of the community – in other words, the propagation of sound economic doctrine among the unenlightened and the stimulation of discussion on economic subjects among those not professionally interested in it.[4]

Carver readily accepted these terms of reference because they were in complete harmony with his own conception of the Association's functions, and de Roode's plan involved no change in either the character or the direction of the campaign. The most active person on the membership committee was Roger W. Babson, a professional statistical forecaster who became Chairman of the Committee in 1912, and he too was anxious to strengthen the Association's links with the business community. As it transpired, despite a considerable expenditure of time and money, the last stage of the membership campaign yielded disappointing results for, as Carver pointed out, a condition of diminishing returns had been reached, and a high proportion of the nonacademic recruits retained their interest for only a year or so and were sometimes aggrieved when they were subsequently asked to pay up their outstanding dues![5]

In the present context, the numerical and financial details of the membership campaign are less interesting than its implications for the character and functions of the American Economic Association. Some members favoured the 'open' membership plan because it was 'democratic', and when a Council member attended the inaugural meeting of the British Economic Association (later the Royal Economic Society) in 1890, he reported with evident satisfaction that the British economists had followed the American example in rejecting all proposals designed to restrict membership [11, p. 166]. Others, however, objected to the policy of 'going into the far-flung highways for mere neophytes' [1, O. F. Boucke to Secretary, May 1 1925], and when one circular called upon members to solicit subscriptions from local organizations and suggested that they might 'take out membership for some friend as a Christmas present',[6] there were grounds for thinking that the limits of scholarly and scientific dignity had been exceeded. Some of those invited to join accepted the honour with alacrity, remarking that they had only held back because they had assumed that they lacked the necessary qualifications;[7] but occasionally those who refused took the opportunity of expressing their opinion of academic economists and current economic policy in no uncertain terms![8] The *reductio ad absurdum* of this promiscuous membership policy was the businessman who, having accepted Babson's invitation to join, wrote to the Secretary asking him to outline 'a course of study that would not be too heavy, and to which a business man could give attention day by day with the hope of a fair mastery of this subject'; and Carver seems to have accepted this pedagogical function as a normal part of his secretarial duties.[9]

Another corollary of the Association's purely pecuniary criterion of membership was its unwillingness to be held responsible for either the personal character or the views of its members. For example, when the Secretary of the New York Reform Club offered to extend its facilities to members of the American Economic Association, he was warned:

> there is no test for membership in the Association. . . . The payment of annual dues is in itself prima facie evidence of an interest in economic questions, but our membership includes people of very different political opinions and social walks of life. There is a remote danger that if membership offers the additional privileges of your library, some might join for that purpose.[10]

Similarly, when Richard T. Ely's Institute for Research in Land Economics and Public Utilities was attacked in 1926 as 'a cunning propaganda institute in disguise',[11] the Association's officers resisted the demand for an investigation, not only because Ely was a distinguished officer of the Association and the source of the complaint was prejudiced, but also because 'such an investigation would be outside the functions of this organization'.[12] A somewhat similar sentiment had been expressed earlier by the Secretary, Allyn A. Young, in 1915 when the American Association of University Professors was founded, and some prominent members of the AEA were heartily relieved at the prospect that the difficult and inconclusive business of investigating complaints of violations of academic freedom would be taken over by another organization.[13]

Unlike the governing bodies of the Royal Economic Society and the Scottish Economic Society,[14] the Executive Committee of the AEA had no power to request the resignation of any member whose conduct was held to be prejudicial to the interests of the organization; nor is there any evidence either that such power was sought or that the economists ever even contemplated the establishment of any procedure for dealing with cases of unprofessional conduct. In this matter, fear of destroying the 'open' character of the Association was reinforced by an acute awareness of the virtual impossibility of obtaining agreement about the nature and tests of professional work in economics.

III THE PROBLEM OF PROFESSIONAL IDENTITY AND STANDARDS

Like many of its individual members, the American Economic Association had a foot in two distinct worlds, the world of learning and the world of business, and it has never been easy to serve two masters simultaneously. The 'open' membership policy, the question of professional standards in economics, and the problem of deciding how far the Association should cater to the needs and interests of businessmen were all interrelated, and while Carver and Babson were proponents of an activist policy which emphasized the Association's links with and responsibilities to the business community,[15] Carver's successor, Allyn Young, who was Secretary from 1913 to 1920, adopted a quite different standpoint. Emphasizing the scholarly and scientific objects of the organization, Young admitted his 'reluctance to try to extend our membership among business men except in so far as they thoroughly understand our work'; and to Davis R. Dewey, the managing editor of the *American Economic Review*, he confided:

> I believe that we can make a sounder and more effective appeal to business men by putting the matter squarely on that basis (i.e. that they feel it an honor to be associated with us rather than merely getting their money's worth) than by attempting to cater in the slightest degree to their special interests as contrasted with those of the professional economists.
>
> [1, Feb 18 1915; cf. Young to E. A. Pratt, Nov 11 1915]

The crux of the problem, however, lay hidden in that portmanteau term 'professional', and this definitional difficulty assumed concrete form as Young went on to criticize the *Review* for printing too many merely 'practical' and 'topical' leading articles.

> Such considerations as those of timeliness and of practical interest should be made distinctly subordinate in the selection of leading articles. Of course we ought to have at least one timely article in each number, but I do not think it should be necessary to go beyond that. Let me say frankly that this seems to be the opinion of a very large majority of members of the Association whom I have heard talk about the Review. They are satisfied with it in every way except the leading articles, and these they feel have not in general a sufficiently professional quality.
>
> [Ibid.]

These remarks not only raised questions about the precise meaning of the terms 'practical' and 'timely', 'scholarly' and 'professional'; they also suggested that academic and nonacademic members of the Association possessed distinct and contrasting interests – a notion that was not confirmed by the discussion evoked by Young's comments. To deny 'professional' calibre to practical and timely articles was, *ipso facto*, to condemn them, for it clearly implied that the *Review* was failing to maintain the standards appropriate to a scholarly and scientific organization. Yet Young himself, when pressed, found it difficult to define the term 'professional' in a satisfactory way. In a subsequent letter to Dewey he explained:

By articles of a distinctly professional or technical nature I meant articles which were shaped with primary reference to the interests and needs of economists, whether dealing with theory or with other matters. I would not put a merely descriptive article, written without reference to its bearing on fundamental questions of principle, under this head.

[1, Apr 12 1915]

This sweeping reference to the 'needs of economists' represented a serious oversimplification of the problem, as is shown by the responses of members of the editorial board of the *Review*. The most decisive repudiation of Young's views came from H. E. Mills, who protested that his use of the expression 'professional quality' was too vague and conveyed 'a certain impression of desire for other worldliness'. Mills continued:

Economics in America suffered because it was so professional and apart from real life. That time has happily gone because economists have come to study in a scholarly and professional way topics that are timely and have practical interest. College and university teaching deals more and more with concrete subjects in a professional and scholarly way. . . . I do not think we should 'cater' to business men members; but on the other hand to separate from them is unwise and the Review may render a great service by showing to the business man the scientific and professional methods of approaching and handling concrete, practical questions. . . . It must be remembered that a large proportion of the trained and able economists of the country are now working upon and primarily interested in matters of practical significance, and hence articles of such character are likely to predominate.[16]

The reactions of other members of the editorial board, while on the whole supporting Mills rather than Young, also reveal the impossibility of drawing any sharp line between the categories 'professional and scholarly' on the one hand, and 'practical and timely' on the other. Herbert Davenport, for example, endorsed Young's opinion that few businessmen read the *Review* – a view that is confirmed by other correspondence in the Association's files – and added that most businessmen 'would find what we call practical articles about as unusable as the very distinctly theoretical ones'. But while opposing a policy of 'going out for' more theoretical articles, he nevertheless considered that 'if good stuff of the theoretical emphasis offers, we might wisely adopt a working presumption in its favour'. Henry B. Gardner and Clive Day contended that the so-called 'practical' articles not only helped professors to keep up with current questions of the day but had also proved to be of great value in teaching; and for most of the respondents the crucial question was not 'balance' but 'quality'. Frank Fetter, for example, himself an economic theorist, considered that one good theoretical article was worth several concrete and descriptive ones; but he believed that few good theoretical articles were available:

> Economic theory should be the product of the ripest and maturest economists, but most of them are interested in specific practical issues. It is the young men, hardly fully fledged, working for their doctor's degrees or little past that point who offer the major part of the manuscripts in theory, is it not, to say nothing of the rank amateur businessman or engineer who has lately discovered that 'the earth do move.'

[Ibid.]

There was no deliberate change of editorial policy as a result of this discussion. Some economists believed that there was a tacit division of the market between the *American Economic Review* and its long-established rival, the *Quarterly Journal of Economics*, and on the basis of this supposition there may have been some tendency for authors to submit their more theoretical articles to the Harvard journal. But whatever the grounds for this belief, criticism of the *Review* was endemic, for it was impossible to please all the members of its heterogeneous and widely scattered audience. As late as 1928 Dewey (who continued to be managing editor until 1940) was still patiently explaining that:

> The range of interest of our constituency is appalling; and it has been assumed that the Review must meet all of these varied interests. No single individual partakes of all the items on the menu of a large hotel. He selects only a few; but the hotel apparently thinks it necessary to provide this wide selection.

[1, Dewey to Deibler, Mar 30 1928]

From time to time dissatisfied members proposed changes in the policy or composition of the Association, and these proposals clearly reveal the variety of interests involved. It was sometimes suggested that a professional association of nonacademic economists should be formed in affiliation with the American Economic Association, and on one occasion this suggestion was made by a business economist who was on the point of returning to a full-time academic post.[17] In 1915, shortly after the discussion of the *Review*'s policy, a similar proposal was advanced by Dr A. M. Sakolski, who was employed in the valuation office of the Delaware and Hudson Company, Albany, New York. Sakolski wrote to Allyn Young complaining that Roger Babson was taking unfair advantage of his connection with the Association, and suggesting 'Isn't it time that a genuine scientias society of American economists should be formed, separate though not in opposition to the American Economic Society [sic]?' [1, n.d. (probably May 1915)]. Subsequently he elaborated his proposal which, he said, had been initiated by Dana Durand, Head of the Bureau of the Census, and his letter reveals the underlying motives:

> The membership of a scientific society could be limited to members of the AEA having several years standing in the organization and also possessing the training, the qualifications and the activities of scientific economists. This arrangement would create an alliance without a definite corporate relationship. . . . Perhaps I feel more keenly about the matter than you, because I lack an academic connection and have no standing in a recognized profession. In spite of my official title, I am, after all, nothing but a clerk and cannot well claim the respect that is given lawyers, engineers and physicians in their duties. Only recently the American Society of Civil Engineers raised the qualifications for membership to their organization. If this policy were followed by the 'scientific' group of the AEA it would, in my opinion, shut out the pseudo economists, statisticians, 'industrial engineers,' efficiency experts, etc. etc. who advertize their membership in the AEA as recognition of their scientific standing. Certainly teachers among economists, and especially those training men to follow this line of work, ought to favor the formation of a strictly professional society.
>
> [1, Sep 23 1915]

While Sakolski's letter discloses some of the difficulties encountered by the would-be scientific economist in business, Young's sympathetic replies reveal the dilemma of his academic counterpart:

> I do feel that the Economic Association has gone too far in catering to the interests of businessmen and to the outside public generally, but I cannot believe that it would be wise to attempt to start another organization.
>
> [1, May 24 1915]

At one time, Young admitted, he had believed in the desirability of a purely scientific society of economists; but he now considered that if a limited society were to be formed it should be entirely separate from the American Economic Association, since the latter required at least 2,500 members in order to sustain its current activities and could not, therefore, afford to be selective. Recently, Young continued, he had accepted an invitation to be a 'Fellow' of the American Statistical Association, supposedly 'a small and select body of statisticians of established reputation', but he doubted the advisability of such a category in economics.

A body like the Institute of Actuaries of Great Britain, or like the American Actuarial Society can set up definite standards for membership, and can even set rigorous entrance examinations. In such a Society a fellowship means something, and has deservedly a real professional value. I doubt very much whether in our field it is possible to set up standards so definite and exact that we can create an organization membership which will in itself be a mark of definite standing and attainments. That seems to be the most substantial difficulty in the way of your plans.[18]

By a curious coincidence, about a month after his correspondence with Sakolski (which apparently bore no tangible organizational fruits), Young received a letter from E. A. Pratt, Chief of the Bureau of Foreign and Domestic Commerce of the Federal Department of Commerce, who represented the opposite point of view. Complaining that the *Review* contained little of interest to businessmen and nonacademic readers, Pratt added:

The difficulty is, of course, that the Association is really trying to do
Please do not interpret this to mean that I discount in any way the value of the university professor and what he has to say, but if you expect to draw business men to your organization, it seems to me absolutely necessary that you have them among your officers, that you put them on the program of your annual meetings and that you publish in your economic review things which would be of interest to them, written by men whose names will carry weight among them, and that you do not absolutely worship the strictly academic.

[1, Nov 8 1915]

In his reply Young granted the justice of some of Pratt's criticisms and explained:

The difficulty is, of course, that the Association is really trying to do two things at once, that is, to stand as the representative scientific organization of the professional economists, and more especially, the academic economists of the country, and at the same time to gather into its membership men from all walks of life who are interested in any way in practical economic problems. . . . The Association was in its beginnings primarily an academic organization, and I am inclined to think that probably it was wiser that it should remain so. If it should break away from its academic moorings, another Association would probably be formed to take its place. At the same time we do not want to sail under false pretences. This explains my reluctance to try to extend our membership among business men except in so far as they themselves understand our work.

[1, Nov 11 1915]

To Dewey, Young confided:

I am inclined to think that sooner or later we shall have to face the question of just what kind of an association we want to be. My own efforts, as you know, have been devoted to strengthening our hold upon those persons who might be counted upon to support a strictly professional and scientific association. I do not believe that Babson's efforts among business men have done us any good, for few of his nominees remain members for more than one year.

[1, n.d. (probably Nov 1915)]

Dewey's reply raised a question of central importance:

I have wondered whether it would be better to have two classes of members, one class for the most part composed of academic members who should pay the full fee of five dollars on the basis of professional interest and loyalty and the other class of cooperative members who would perhaps pay a smaller fee and would connect themselves rather from public interest, very much as they subscribe for their other objects which are regarded to be for social welfare.

[1, Nov 15 1915]

The fundamental question of professional identity and standards could not, however, be disposed of so easily, and there is no reason to think that any such modification of the existing egalitarian membership policy would have been accepted at an annual meeting. Too many economists objected strongly to the creation of any special fellowship or other membership hierarchy, because it smacked of oligarchy and might lead to the domination of the organization by one of its constituent groups, such as the nonacademic economists or an Eastern academic élite.[19] In the event, a genuine problem of classification according to professional qualifications and expertise was forced upon the economists by the war, when the AEA committee was asked by the Federal Civil Service Commission to examine 900 cards filled in by economists and statisticians who had expressed their willingness to serve the government. As the President of the Commission wrote:

It is understood that your committee will discard the names of persons who do not properly come within the category of economic expert, will classify under proper headings those who are trained along economic lines, and will make such comment in individual cases as you consider advisable.

[1, President, US Civil Service Commission to Secretary, Oct 8 1917]

Like certain other delicate constitutional matters that arose during the wartime emergency, the question of the classification of economists did not come to a head, largely because of the speedy and successful termination of the war. In 1919 Abram Berglund of the Tariff Commission sent a report on classification to Young, but by this time the question had become somewhat academic, in the pejorative sense of the term.[20] During the 1920s the problem recurred again from time to time, but no action was taken. By 1924, as the result of another systematic membership campaign, a five-fold classification of members was introduced, but like the conventional distinctions between 'honorary', 'life', and 'ordinary' members, this, too, was based exclusively on financial considerations.[21]

IV PUBLIC RESPONSIBILITY AND NONPARTISANSHIP

In addition to questions arising from the size and character of its membership and its responsibilities to both academic and nonacademic economists, the officers of the Association were always conscious of their relationship to the general public. The original constitution had stated that, 'In the study of the industrial and commercial policy of government we take no partisan attitude', and throughout the period under review serious efforts were made to adhere to this general principle, for nonpartisanship was usually held to be the *sine qua non* of a scholarly and scientific approach to economic questions. In practice, however, this policy was more difficult to execute than might be supposed at first sight, for the organization's officers received many inquiries, invitations, and appeals which made it exceedingly difficult for them to maintain their pose of olympian detachment. If they occasionally strayed from the narrow path of righteousness, it was mainly because they were anxious to demonstrate the economist's importance to the business community and to the general public, for as Ely had frankly admitted when he presented his 'Statement of Principles' at the inaugural meeting in 1885, 'it is not easy to arouse interest in an association which professes nothing' [10]. These deviations were, of course, especially liable to occur under the leadership of activists like Ely, Carver, and Irving Fisher (who was President of the Association for a time during World War I), and the variety of forms which this deviationism assumed are worth noting because they reveal how varied were the temptations and pressures to which the economists were subjected.

Given the persistent differences of opinion as to what the Association should do, it is hardly surprising to find that there were corresponding differences about what it should not do, and the task of interpreting the 'nonpartisanship' clause of the constitution was one to gladden the heart of the most devious of constitutional lawyers. Even Young, who so strenuously upheld the cause of scholarship, proudly proclaimed that the Association had 'done as much as any one influence to disseminate sound ideas on many economic problems',[22] but he would hardly have agreed with Carver that its 'main purpose' was 'to run the affairs of the country in an economical and progressive way' [1, Carver to J. E. Woodbridge, Jan 30 1912]. In some cases, of course, there was no difficulty in deciding on the appropriate course of action. The Secretary merely refused to assist those inquirers who wanted to know how to organize birth control education and research, or how to use Fuller's Earth, and he flatly told one correspondent that the AEA took no official position on either the tariff question or the forthcoming presidential election.[23] On other occasions a request that the Association should 'probe a little into the alcohol problem' from the standpoint of 'pure scholarship' was rejected, and an invitation to join the opposition to a law which would have permitted the importation and dissemination of literature on contraception was refused;[24] but some problems could not be dealt with so easily.

One group of problems arose in connection with the appointment of official representatives to attend conferences or meetings sponsored by other organizations, and here the policies of the Executive Committee demonstrated remarkable inconsistencies. As the Secretary explained to a member on one occasion,

> In 1907 . . . [Jeremiah W.] Jenks, then President, by authority of the Executive Committee, appointed delegates to the National Peace Conference. At this very same meeting of the Executive Committee it was voted impossible to cooperate as an Association with the Anti-Child Labor movement. I have also been informed that at a preliminary meeting of those interested in the Conservation of National Resources our Association was represented. If so the representatives were appointed by the President on his own responsibility. At the November meeting last year of the Executive Committee this very Association requested us to appoint representatives to cooperate with that movement. The explicit request for cooperation caused the Committee to decline the request. At that time Professor J. B. Clark argued that if our appointment of representatives were confined to their appearance in the role of interested inquirers merely, we might legitimately appoint delegates. To this view Judge Dill [a Vice-President of the AEA] replied that the appointment of delegates, no matter what the intention, would be construed as sympathetic cooperation. The vote seemed to imply that Judge Dill's opinion was the prevailing one.[25]

Apart from the immediate question whether a delegate might be regarded

251

as a passive observer or an active participant in the proceedings of the sponsoring body, there was the question whether an individual member or group of members could, under any circumstances, be held to commit the Association, *as an Association*, to support or oppose any policy position. In 1928, Fred M. Taylor, then President of the Association, turned down an invitation to become a Vice-President of the Stable Money Association mainly on the grounds that 'I have for many years been an almost fanatical supporter of the doctrine that professors as such should keep out of all propaganda work',[26] and this decision was fully consistent with the action taken by the Executive Committee a year earlier, when it had refused to hold a joint session with the Stable Money Association because the latter 'was carrying on a campaign of education or propaganda, rather than constituting a scientific body, like other allied associations'.[27] But although Young had informed a critic in 1916 that the AEA was 'debarred by its constitution from taking any position on any *disputed* economic problem',[28] this did not mean, as some cynics might suppose, that the Association was thereby required to remain totally inactive in the field of policy. Among 'safe' issues there were such matters as opposition to a rise in postal rates on the publications of scientific societies[29] and periodic demands for federal aid to American scholars participating in international scholarly and scientific conferences;[30] and during World War I the economists went far beyond the strict constructionist position adopted by Secretary Ray B. Westerfield who, in 1925, replied to a seemingly innocuous Department of Commerce request for an official comment on 'the values of simplification in our present industrial and commercial situation' by stating that the AEA was 'not interested in propaganda'.[31]

During the war, the Association endeavoured to do its bit by assisting in the classification of economists who offered to work for the federal government, by inaugurating a scheme designed to coordinate research activities, and by publishing a number of bulletins and special studies of current economic problems. These were but natural responses to the needs of the time, but under the exuberant leadership of Irving Fisher and others, the Association took a number of steps which might, in the long run, have seriously undermined its customary policy of impartiality and detachment. Of these one of the most interesting was Fisher's appeal on behalf of the Thrift Campaign sponsored by the War Savings Committee of the US Treasury, under the chairmanship of Frank A. Vanderlip. According to a circular signed by Fisher which was distributed to all members:

At the Philadelphia meeting a Committee on the Purchasing Power of Money in Relation to the War was appointed. In accordance with the vote at that meeting, this committee, with the authority of the Executive Committee, *but without committing the Association as such*, is publishing a series of bulletins. A copy of the first of these is enclosed.

This bulletin was issued through Mr. Vanderlip's Committee, which prepared the introductory statement. It was sent to 20,000 newspapers but was not widely utilized, one reason being that many newspapers could not afford to antagonize advertisers of non-essentials. This obstacle emphasizes the very real need of the intelligent and patriotic help of economists.

. . . Any suggestions as to further committees which might be appointed or as to activities in which the Association or its members might engage which would be of value to the country in the present crisis, would be greatly appreciated.[32]

From the constitutional point of view, the crux of the matter was the almost scholastic distinction contained in Fisher's introductory observation: 'As you know, the Association, *as such*, does not engage in propaganda. The appeal is to the members individually',[33] for this rubric could be used to cover a multitude of sins. The best example of the dangers of this distinction is provided by the postwar enthusiasm for the peace movement. Although the executive committee was reluctant to give an open vote in favour of the League of Nations' Resolutions, it recommended the incoming President (H. B. Gardner) to 'submit them to each individual member with any recommendation he might care to make'.[34] In response to this request, a circular signed by Gardner was dispatched to all members stating:

In accordance with established precedent no action in the name of the Association was taken by the Association or its Executive Committee, but there was a general feeling that the matter was of such great importance that it should be brought to the attention of the individual members of the Association. Fully concurring, as I do, in this feeling, I herewith transmit the resolutions and urge each member of the Association to immediately express his convictions on the question to the congressmen and senators from his state.

While action in the name of the Association is open to objection, there is no question that the membership of the Association should make its influence felt in the decision of a question of such tremendous importance not only for our own nation but for the future of the world.[35]

Presumably, when the future of the world was at stake, it was permissible to stretch the AEA constitution to its limit; but it has been well said that of all constitutional arguments the most damnable is that of emergency, and, in taking such liberties with its customary practices, the Association was running a considerable risk. Apparently the gamble was successful, for there were no protests and this proved to be an isolated incident. There were, however, some who doubted the advisability of the activist policy undertaken during the war itself.

One of these cautious spirits was Frank A. Fetter, an erstwhile Secretary and President, who was always sensitive to the scholarly and scientific proprieties. Even at the height of the wartime enthusiasm he wrote:

> I hope that the committee on prices will be restricted to the field which, as I understand it, the Executive Committee meant to author-ize it to survey – viz. the problem of price inflation in this war. It will be *ultra vires* and will involve the Association in activities contrary to our constitution if it tries to wander over all creation and to direct the general economic policies of the nation in this whole war.
>
> [1, Fetter to Young (n.d.), 1918]

The kind of danger that Fetter envisaged was revealed in a statement published by one AEA committee which announced that its work was

> intended to put into popular language some of the simple economic principles or *precepts* connected with the Purchasing Power of Money, and particularly to emphasize the importance of saving money with which to buy Liberty Bonds and pay taxes instead of lending to the Government merely what we borrow of the banks, which procedure is apt indirectly to raise commodity prices.[36]

To those members who feared that such publications would commit the Association, *as an association*, to any given policy recommendations there was, of course, a standard reply, namely that the reports of AEA committees did not constitute official policy positions, but merely the views of the authors. This position was consistently maintained, as for example in the Secretary's report of 1900, which stated rather vaguely that 'the Association vouches for [a report] as far, and no further, than for the works of other authors which it issues',[37] or, as in a secretarial letter of 1926, that

> The responsibility for the ideas contained therein rests entirely with the individuals who draft these reports and cannot, in fact, be said to express the attitude of the Association, as an organization. Any expressions of opinion contained in such reports must stand on their own merits.[38]

Nevertheless, as Judge Dill remarked in connection with the appointment of representatives as observers of or delegates to other organizations,[39] despite the Association's good intentions it seems likely that most readers attached much more weight to an authorized report signed by a number of leading economists, especially when it was circulated by a government department, than to a regular leading article in the *Review*.

During and after the war, on the crest of a wave of enthusiasm for empirical research, there was a lengthy discussion of various prospects to establish links between the American Economic Association and the Institute for Economic Research (usually known as the Brookings Institute). Initially there was some possibility that the Association might sponsor or even found such an institution;[40] but long after the Institute had been inaugurated with the aid of funds provided by Robert S. Brookings it was suggested that the AEA should establish its permanent office in the Institute's building in Washington [1, cf. H. Seager (President of the AEA) to Westerfield, Nov 10 1922]. Even in the 1890s, the desirability of such an office and a paid secretary (on the lines of the American Historical Association) had been debated, but although the matter was still under consideration as late as 1928, no action was taken,[41] and the Secretary's office has retained its present location at Northwestern University since 1925. As always, one of the main reasons for the Association's reluctance to identify itself with another body, even a reputable independent research organization, was the fear that this might in some sense commit the American Economic Association to support of the findings of the Institute's publications. This concern was fully revealed in 1925, when a proposal to launch a large-scale investigation of 'the present method of industrial price fixing and price quotation in relation to economic theory' was advanced by H. Parker Willis.[42] This was not the first proposal of its kind; and during the war clear precedents in favour of such a scheme had been established. Nevertheless, many prominent members were opposed to it for a variety of reasons. Allyn Young (then President of the AEA), for example, considered that 'there are a hundred other questions of equal importance. I believe it to be particularly unwise that the Association should have any direct connection with the investigation of any one economic problem, no matter how important.' Carl R. Plehn held that the Association 'should not lend our name and become morally responsible without control', and considered that the wartime undertakings were 'exceptional'. And even Thomas W. Page, who was President of the Institute for Economic Research and a long-standing member of the Association, expressed his inability to understand 'how such an investigation could be undertaken by an independent agency subject to the approval and under the direction of a special committee of the Economic Association. I see no harm in conferring with such agencies as may be deemed competent, but I gravely doubt whether any satisfactory arrangement for cooperation can be made.'[43]

As it transpired, no investigation was undertaken, mainly because neither the Institute nor any other suitable research body was able to provide the requisite services on terms within the Association's financial means. Here, as elsewhere, the outcome of long deliberation was dictated as much by fortuitous circumstances as by sensitivity to fundamental questions of principle; but there seems little reason to doubt that the strong opposition to any active AEA intervention in questions of current economic importance was a significant factor in the situation.

Finally, under the general heading of policy questions, the conduct and content of the annual meetings of the Association were occasionally the subject of heated controversy. According to the activist view propounded by Carver and others, the selection of topics and speakers assumed almost legislative proportions for, as he informed one US Senator, 'all sorts of public measures are discussed, and we try in that way to influence public opinion, but not by officially endorsing a measure by any formal vote' [1, Carver to C. S. Page, Oct. 2 1912]. Obviously the programme of the annual meeting does afford some guide to the subjects deemed worthy of engaging the members' time and attention, and it is incumbent upon the organizers to secure competent and representative speakers. But in the period under consideration highly topical and controversial matters were sometimes discussed by spokesmen of various interest groups or by economists engaged in studying these questions, and there were inevitably some occasions when critics complained that the organizers had failed to provide a properly balanced treatment of the issues at stake.[44] The planning of the annual meetings, therefore, came to be regarded as yet another matter in which it was vital that the Association should adhere to a policy of strict neutrality.[45]

V THE ATTAINMENT OF FINANCIAL INDEPENDENCE

The final episode of this story exemplifies the perennial interaction of the forces of continuity and change in historical narrative. Like other scholarly associations in the USA and elsewhere, the war brought a serious setback in the Association's finances owing to a fall in membership income and a sharp rise in costs, and consequently in the early 1920s a third, and what has proved to be a final, membership campaign was undertaken. Once again the funds were provided by a group of businessmen who, as earlier, had been persuaded by a few wealthy academic economists to come to the Association's rescue.[46] Once again a Membership Committee was established (which included Roger W. Babson), and energetic solicitation among nonacademic as well as academic groups produced a large crop of new recruits.[47] This time, however, the American Economic Association was incorporated in Washington in 1923; a permanent endowment fund was raised with the aid of established members and interested outsiders; and the investment of these funds subsequently formed the basis of the Association's now almost indecently healthy capital position.[48]

There were, of course, favourable external conditions that contributed to this happy solution of the Association's bread and butter problems – especially the contemporary prosperity of business, and the growing number of full-time economists employed by universities, colleges (especially Schools of Business), business enterprises, government agencies, and independent research institutions. By the second half of the 1920s the organized economists had, in effect, succeeded in raising themselves by the businessmen's bootstraps to an enviable position of independence, a position which their predecessors had for so long unsuccessfully striven to attain. Naturally there were still some delicate policy problems to be decided, and, as previous paragraphs have indicated, the variety of needs and interests of the Association's membership meant that its officers were never able to satisfy all of their constituents all of the time.

Nevertheless, in the years before the impact of the Great Depression was felt, the American Economic Association finally managed to consolidate and husband its resources and had at last reached its long-delayed maturity.

NOTES

* This article is a sequel to one published earlier in the *American Economic Review* [6], and the author wishes to thank the Secretary of the Association, Harold F. Williamson, and his Research Assistant, Richard Buth, for their help in finding and photocopying source materials. See also [6].

1 'Laughlin's paper alone . . . was quite enough for the entire session, and I felt much sympathy with his exclamation at the close that he wished we had three hours to debate this subject. . . . Certainly the meeting in Chicago must be counted a very successful one from the point of view of attendance, spirit and interest' [1, Fetter to F. W. Taussig, Jan 6 1905].

2 [1, F. H. Giddings to Fetter, May 3 1902]. This remark was made in the course of the interminable debate over the question of an AEA journal, a topic which was first raised in the early 1890s and finally settled with the publication of the *American Economic Review* in 1911. An account of this debate must be postponed until a subsequent occasion. See below pp. 257–79.

3 The question 'Are the Economists a Bunch of Kept Cats?' was (not too seriously) discussed at the 1963 meeting of the Mid-Western Economic Association at St Louis. For comments on the problem of professional ethics in the 1920s, see [9, pp. 208–11].

4 [1, de Roode to Carver, Apr 9 1912. Also de Roode to Carver, Mar 18 1912; Sep 24 1912; Carver to de Roode, Apr 13 1912]. De Roode's name was at first unknown even to members of the membership committee. [Cf. 1, R. Babson to Carver, Apr 16 1912; Carver to Babson, May 6 1912; Fetter to Carver, Apr 12 1912; Carver to Fetter, May 21 1912].

5 [4, p. 202]. During the period 1909–13 a net increase in membership of 1,483 was claimed, and by December, 1915 Carver's successor, A. A. Young, considered that a state of 'normal equilibrium' had been reached [5, p. 221]. However, the annual secretary's reports give somewhat different total membership figures, e.g., 1900 – 774; 1902 – 1,111 (during Ely's campaign); 1908 – 1,030; 1909 – 1,360; 1913 – 2,513; 1915 – 2,422. The totals were continually being 'pruned' by removing the names of delinquents. For subsequent figures, see *infra*, note 47.

One nonacademic member who had asked by what authority the Secretary proposed to cut him off on the grounds of nonpayment of his subscription eventually enclosed a cheque in settlement 'of all claims of every kind and description, scientific, commercial or otherwise' [1, H. Stewart to Secretary, Mar 8 1919].

6 This is taken from an undated circular, probably drafted in November, 1911, which may not have been actually sent out to members.

7 In a letter reminiscent of the responses to Ely's appeals in the early days of the AEA, the Pastor of the Congregational Church at Northbridge Center (Mass.?) expressed his appreciation of the nomination for membership and hoped soon to be able to send the Treasurer the proper credentials so as to ensure his enrolment. 'In view of present world conditions I believe it is important that leaders of the new World Order [sic] such as leading economists either in actual business life or associated with it should unite to study the problems involved' [1, W. W. Evans to Secretary, May 23 1921]. (*Plus ça change, plus c'est la même chose.*)

Another respondent was pleased that he was not considered too radical to be a member but asked to see the Constitution in order to reassure himself that the AEA was not like such other organizations as the New Haven Railroad, the International Motor Co., etc. 'in each of which the membership has been ignored by the management and finds itself without recourse' [1, H. F. Stimpson to Secretary, Oct 18 1913; Nov 14 1913].

8 One respondent sent a curt telegram stating 'Make your publications worth the money' [1, E. A. MacClean, New York City, Feb 4 1914]. Another associated the work of the AEA with 'the attempts of half-educated writers to direct and lead public thought', which had helped to feed the 'mad ambition and lust of power by the reckless demagogue who once brought this country during the most prosperous period of its existence to the verge of ruin' [1, J. H. Moore, San Francisco, May 9 1912]. (He was presumably referring to Theodore Roosevelt.) However, the correspondent who described the economists as equivalent to 'intellectual prostitutes' apparently had not been invited to join the AEA [1, S. O. Gordon to Secretary, Apr 5 1922].

9 [1, E. C. Miller to Carver, Mar 18 1912; Carver to Miller, Mar 26 1912]. Roger W. Babson had invited Miller to join the Association.

Another insight into the character of the membership was provided by the correspondent who, when asked to renew his subscription, replied, 'Our subscription has been made to you from year to year for the purpose of being helpful to you, and not with a view to our own improvement. We never asked for your literature, nor did we expect to receive any . . . if it has been received we have been so unfortunate as not to have perused it' [1, F. Beidler to Secretary, Jun 11 1914]. Nevertheless, he paid his bill in full!

10 [1, Fetter to M. R. Maltbie, Oct 29 1904]. Maltbie had assumed he could 'take it that the fact that they are members of the AEA is sufficient guarantee of their character, and that no improper advantage will be taken of the library privileges'. Fetter was not so sure, for he recalled how people had unsuccessfully sought membership in the AEA in order to obtain free sets of the Census volumes which had been offered to members.

11 E. O. Jorgenson, a representative of the Manufacturers' and Merchants' Federal Tax League, protested that the Institute 'has laid down its conclusions in advance of its investigations' and 'has, before any of its facts have been gathered, condemned certain far-reaching measures which an increasing number of scholars believe to be beneficial to the people and approved certain other far-reaching measures which many scholars also believe to be detrimental to the people', thereby completely disregarding 'the principles of fairness and impartiality'. Moreover, the Institute's conclusions 'harmonise exactly with the views of the corporations and special privilege groups which are financing it'. Although the Institute's host institution, 'Northwestern University, strange to say, has ignored our protests entirely', Jorgenson enclosed a copy of his book, *False Education in our Colleges and Universities*, and demanded 'prompt and rigid investigation' by

a committee of the AEA [1, Jorgenson to E. W. Kemmerer (President of the AEA), Jul 31 1926].

12 [1, Kemmerer to Jorgenson, Dec 30 1926]. This letter was written after a meeting of the Executive Committee of the AEA. Cf. Young to F. C. Deibler (Secretary): 'The request that the Association institute an investigation of the Institute for Land Economics will be turned down flatly, I hope. This is not only because it is not the business of the Association to make such investigations, but also because the proposal is an insult to Professor Ely and his associates. It comes from an irresponsible and prejudiced source' [1, Dec 11 1926].

13 [1, H. C. Adams to Young, Apr 26 1915; Young to Adams, May 5 1915].

14 According to the by-laws of the Royal Economic Society, 'if any Fellow or Honorary Fellow shall so conduct himself that, in the opinion of the Council, it would not be for the credit and advantage of the Society that he should longer continue to be a Fellow or Honorary Fellow thereof, the Council shall take the matter into consideration at a meeting convened for the purpose.' The Council of the Scottish Society of Economists, in the early years of this century, could delete the name of any member 'at their discretion, and thereupon such member shall forfeit all rights and interest in the Society without the right of appeal'. Cf. *infra*, note 18.

In response to a specific enquiry as to 'what may be regarded as the proper standards of practice in the line of business which you represent', Deibler replied, almost facetiously: 'You should know that our middle name is "Ethics", but we have no particular code' [1, R. A. Clemen, Chicago, to Secretary, Nov 15 1929; Deibler to Clemen, Nov 19 1929].

15 Although on one occasion Carver wrote that 'the main purpose' of the AEA was 'to run the affairs of the country in an economical and progressive way', he was aware of the duality of interests. 'I hope the Association will never forget that it exists primarily in the interests of scholarship. Nevertheless, I think we have another important function, namely to act as a leaven to the whole national lump, and to do what we can to spread the habit of sound economic thinking among the business and professional classes, who have so much to do with the determination of national policies. Just how to maintain a proper balance between the interests of pure scholarship and those of popularisation must always be a difficult problem' [1, Carver to J. E. Woodbridge, Jan 20 1912; Carver to Prof. B. H. Putnam, Mount Holyoke College, Jan 24 1912].

16 Mills' comments, together with those of J. E. Coulter, H. Davenport, C. Day, F. A. Fetter, and H. B. Gardner, are preserved in the AEA files.

17 [1, G. J. Eberle to J. H. Hollander, Jun 6 1921; Eberle to Westerfield, Dec 21 1921]. On Dec 15 1921 the Secretary dispatched a circular to members of the Executive Committee which referred to Eberle's proposal that the Association should establish 'certain minimum qualifications for persons who call themselves professional economists' with the aim of protecting 'the science and the professors, and to assure clients and prospective clients a certain standard of services'. No action was taken.

18 [1, Young to Sakolski, Sep 25 1915]. It may be noted that although the Royal Statistical Society and the British Economic Association both had a constitutional procedure for dealing with the expulsion of undesirable members (which seems never to have been implemented), neither the American Statistical Association nor the American Economic Association had a comparable procedure.

19 Although the danger of a regional split within the AEA had apparently disappeared by the early 1900s, echoes of the earlier difficulties were occasionally heard, especially in connection with the perennial problem of the location of

annual meetings. For example, H. Davenport wrote to Young on May 11, 1914, 'it has largely been on the basis of these non-professional members that the large majority of eastern men in the Association has existed, and the right or claim built thereon to have most of the Association meetings take place in the East'. In a judiciously impartial reply, Young wrote that the 1914 Handbook 'will contain for the first time a geographical index of our membership. This should furnish ammunition for one side or the other' [6, pp. 567–70].

20 [1, Berglund to Young, Dec 24 1919]. Under each of three broad headings, 'Economist', 'Agricultural Economist', and 'Social Economist', there were five subcategories based on age, academic qualifications, and experience.

21 [1, for example, Westerfield to T. W. Page, Mar 26 1924 and Page to Wester-field, Dec 24 1924]. Also the circular to members of May 3, 1924, which was followed by a change in article III of the Constitution. The new categories were 'subscribing' and 'contributing' members.

See also [1, T. W. Page to Deibler, Dec 7 1925; Managing Director of the Taylor Society to Secretary, Jun 23 1926].

22 [1, Young to A. Belmont, Mar 25 1915]. Young argued that the AEA had made especially valuable contributions to the subjects of money, credit, and banking.

23 [1, W. S. Reynolds to Secretary, Dec 13 1928; Secretary to Reynolds, Dec 20 1928; A. E. Carfman to Secretary, Dec 3 1928; H. Clews to Secretary, Sep 24 1912; Secretary to Clews, Sep 20 and 30 1912]. Mr Clews, a New York banker, had been asked if he would allow his name to be used on a circular letter to be sent to prospective members.

24 [1, W. E. Johnson (editor of the *Standard Encyclopedia of the Alcohol Problem*) to Secretary, Jan 16 1905; Secretary of the National Catholic Welfare Conference to Deibler, Nov 18 1925]. In his reply of Nov 23, 1925, Deibler offered to bring the matter before the Executive Committee but predicted that they would refuse to act.

25 [1, Acting Secretary of the AEA to Dewey, Jan 23 1909]. (Dewey was then President of the Association.)

26 [1, F. M. Taylor to N. Lombard, Jan 14 1928]. The leaders of the Stable Money Association included such prominent economists as I. Fisher and J. R. Commons.

27 [1, Deibler to H. G. Moulton (Director of the Brookings Institute of Economics), Dec 3 1927; T. S. Adams (President of the AEA) to Lombard, Nov 10 1927; Moulton to Adams, Dec 8 1927].

A similar problem arose in connection with other policy-oriented associations, such as the American Association for Labor Legislation, but, as Adams explained to Moulton, the AALL had begun as an offshoot of the AEA and its place on the latter's programmes had been established by an 'old precedent' [1, cf. Ely to Fisher, Jan 24 1919]. An account of the relationships between the AEA and other associations must be deferred until another occasion.

28 [1, Young to S. H. Pomeroy, Oct 23 1916, italics supplied]. Pomeroy had responded to an invitation to become a member by inquiring 'I would ask why you bob up at Election times with your solicitation when your support of levelling wages is so antagonistic to our general welfare. Drop ambiguities and tell me how this country can thrive without a tariff to be made high or low to correspond with the differences in wages in this country and abroad' [1, Pomeroy to Secretary, Oct 18 1916].

On one occasion Young went even further, asserting that 'the AEA is prohibited by its constitution from taking any attitude whatsoever on any public question' [1, Young to A. B. Parker, Feb 13 1920].

29 [1, Editor-in-Chief of *Engineering News* to Secretary, Dec 21 1916]. Young replied on Jan 24 1917, 'if a protest will be of any avail at this time I should be glad to enter one for myself *and for the Association* and to ask others to co-operate'. (Italics supplied.)

It is amusing to note that the Association's determined effort to be regarded as a scientific society bore unexpected fruit when its members were denied the standard reduction of railroad fares accorded to members of 'educational' organizations.

30 A resolution to this effect was passed at the Minneapolis meeting in 1913 and again at the 1924 annual meeting.

On another occasion the Secretary suggested that although the Association could not 'take a stand' on the question of changes in the copyright law, he could insert a statement in the *Review* advising interested members to exert pressure on their Congressman [1, Westerfield to M. L. Rainey, Jan 9 1923].

31 [1, Secretary, Department of Commerce, to Westerfield, Apr 4 1925; Westerfield to Dept of Comm., Apr 14 1925]. Westerfield's response was somewhat surprising in view of the Association's earlier cooperation with federal departments, especially in connection with the Census.

32 [1, Fisher to members, Mar 9 1918, italics supplied.]

33 Ibid. (Italics supplied.)

34 [1, Fisher to Gardner, Jan 21 1919]. On Jan 2 1919, Fisher had explained to Gardner, in a letter informing him of his election to the Presidency of the AEA, 'it was thought best by the Executive Committee not to pass it, partly because of our precedents and partly because we did not think the resolution would be as effective as individual letters'. Gardner could, if he wished, express his own opinion. 'In any case, it would not commit the Association as such.'

35 [1, Gardner to members, Feb 11 1919]. The resolutions advocated the establishment of a 'League of Nations to enforce Peace and Justice throughout the world', and asserted that 'we favor the entrance of the United States into such a League of Nations as may be adequate to safeguard peace'. As a sequel to this incident, in January, 1921, the AEA received urgent requests from William Howard Taft, President of the League to Enforce Peace, asking them to send two representatives to a national meeting in Washington, but there is no evidence that this request was granted. Possibly by this time the sense of emergency had passed and strict constitutionalism reigned once more. In 1923 the Association refused to allow the American Peace Award to ballot its members in connection with a national referendum on the question of a plan for international peace. [1, Secretary to American Peace Award, Jan 3 1924].

36 [1, italics supplied]. A copy of this statement approved by the Committee on the Purchasing Power of Money is in the 1918 file.

37 [2, pp. 47–8]. The occasion was the publication of a volume of *Essays in Colonial Finance*, with the aid of funds subscribed by W. E. Dodge, T. Marburg, I. N. Seligman, S. Wood, and the late T. G. Shearman. From time to time other businessmen provided funds for similar purposes.

38 [1, Secretary to R. C. Reusch, Dec 7 1926]. He explained that the publications of the War Finance Committee (1919) were 'the only expression of opinion [on the subject of the issuance of war bonds] that could be regarded as the attitude of the A.E.A.'.

39 *Supra*, p. 251.

40 [1, see the report by E. D. Jones submitted to Young, dated Dec 9 1919. Also W. H. Hamilton to Jones, Nov 18 1919; Fisher to Gardner, Jun 4 1919].

41 [1, see, for example, Deibler to T. S. Adams, Jan 7 1928, and Oct 12 1928;

Deibler to Dewey, May 8 1928; Dewey to Deibler, May 21 1928; E. C. Day to Deibler, May 28 1928].

42 [1]. This is cited from Willis' motion, as amended by J. R. Commons, and submitted to the Executive Committee in December, 1925.

43 See Young's handwritten comment on the back of a circular dispatched to members of the Executive Committee [1, Jan 23 1925; also Young to Westerfield, Feb 18 1925; Plehn to Westerfield, Feb 16 1925; also Page to Westerfield, Jan 29 1925]. Plehn also added: 'The subject is hot with controversy. Hence any advisory committee should see that its proceedings are of record in such a manner as to clearly show how far it took responsibility, if at all. That "if at all" means that in my own opinion a *competent* bureau would prefer to assume full responsibility.' (Italics in original.) Some members of the Committee either expressed no opinion or raised no objections to the proposal. For the final outcome, see Young's undated circular to members of the Executive Committee [1, (*c.* Oct 1925) and Deibler to Young, Oct 29 1925].

44 See, for example, J. D. Hubbard, a Chicago employer, who appeared on a 'Closed and Open Shop' panel discussion in 1904, and subsequently complained bitterly that most speakers were biased against employers: 'As a fair and open discussion, the Symposium must be deemed an absolute failure' [1, Hubbard to Taussig, Dec 31 1904]. Similarly, with reference to the representativeness of H. C. Adams' views on public utility corporations see [1, H. T. Newcomb to Dewey, Sep 7 1909].

45 As in very recent years, there were periodic complaints that the same names appeared too often on the annual programmes and that young men and lesser-known (especially midwestern) institutions were underrepresented [1, Cf. Fetter to Taussig, Aug 28 1905; J. H. Raymond to Carver, May 1 1912; Deibler to H. H. Burbank, Oct 12 1925].

46 [1]. In January, 1919, the Association received $5,000,the outstanding balance of a sum of $20,000 which had been provided to support the publication of studies in war finance, and in September, 1922, a special finances subcommittee was set up under the chairmanship of E. R. A. Seligman. In May, 1921, this committee included H. W. Farnam, W. F. Gephart, H. R. Hatfield, J. Hollander, J. T. Holdsworth, E. Johnson, L. C. Marshall, and F. W. Taussig, several of whom had given sums of money to the Association on more than one previous occasion. By the following year $10,000 had been raised from a group of 'thirty gentlemen', and by January, 1923, Seligman was hoping to raise a further $3,000 a year for three years by means of members' contributions to a permanent endowment fund.

47 [1]. In January, 1925, it was estimated that the campaign had brought in 629 permanent new members during the period 1922–4. The Secretary's reports show the following total membership figures: 1917 – 2,602; 1920 – 2,866; 1924 – 3,547; 1925 – 3,746; 1927 – 3,507; 1929 – 3,748. For earlier figures see *supra*, note 5.

48 [1]. On February 29, 1928, the Secretary wrote to H. C. Freeman that the Association now had an accumulated balance of $30,000. Mr Freeman accepted an invitation to become a subscribing member.

REFERENCES

1 American Economic Association, *Papers*, Secretary's Office, Northwestern University.

2 ——, *Secretary's Report*, in *Thirteenth Annual Meeting, Pub. A.E.A., Proc.* Third Ser., ii, 43 (1901).

3 ——, *Secretary's Report, Twenty-fourth Annual Meeting, Am. Econ. Rev., Proc.*, March 1912, *2*, 132–4.

4 ——, *Secretary's Report, Twenty-sixth Annual Meeting, Am. Econ. Rev., Proc.*, March 1914, *4*, 201–3.

5 ——, *Secretary's Report, Twenty-eighth Annual Meeting, Am. Econ. Rev., Proc.*, March 1916, *6*, 220–3.

6 A. W. Coats, 'The First Two Decades of the American Economic Association', *Am. Econ. Rev.*, Sept. 1960, *50*, 555–74. Reprinted in this volume, pp. 205–24.

7 ——, 'The Political Economy Club: A Neglected Episode in American Economic Thought', *Am. Econ. Rev.*, Sept. 1961, *51*, 624–37. Reprinted in this volume, pp. 225–38.

8 J. Dorfman, *The Economic Mind in American Civilization*, vol. III. New York 1949.

9 ——, *The Economic Mind in American Civilization*, vol. IV. New York 1959.

10 R. T. Ely, 'Report of the Organization of the American Economic Association', *Pub. A.E.A.*, First Ser., March 1887, *1*, 5–46.

11 A. W. Shaw, 'Report of the Organization of the British Economic Association', *Pub. A.E.A.*, First Ser., vi, 163 (1891).

14

THE AMERICAN ECONOMIC
ASSOCIATION'S
PUBLICATIONS
An historical perspective*

The birth of the *Journal of Economic Literature* marks a new phase of the American Economic Association's publication policies. The *Journal*'s parents are, to say the least, unevenly matched: the *American Economic Review* is in its fifty-eighth year, whereas the *Journal of Economic Abstracts* is only five years old; and the sponsoring organization can trace its history over eighty-three years.

Since limitation of space precludes an exhaustive examination of the Association's publication record, the following account will concentrate on the principal serials. Only brief references will be made to the annual *Papers and Proceedings*. The innumerable surveys of 'contemporary' and 'recent' economic thought, collections of readings, occasional reports, supplements, directories, handbooks, and other miscellaneous contributions to the literature of economics will be entirely ignored. Within these stringent limitations, the main story conveniently falls into two parts: first, the protracted pre-history of the *American Economic Review*, dominated by the *Publications*; and second, the Dewey, Homan, and Haley editorial regimes of the *A.E.R.*, 1911–62.

THE EARLY PERIOD

By present day standards, the quantity of economic publications was minute when the Association was founded in 1885. In the following year it began to issue an irregular series of monographs, conference proceedings, annual reports, and handbooks, under the rubric *Publications of the American Economic Association*. However, before long there was serious competition from other scholarly publications. During the Association's first year, Harvard launched the *Quarterly Journal of Economics* and Columbia the *Political Science Quarterly*, which was devoted to economics only in part. By the mid-1890s the *Journal of Political Economy* had made its appearance, in company with two more partly economic periodicals – the *Yale Review* and the *Annals of the American Academy*. Even more direct competition came from various university monograph series, and it soon appeared that the Association was becoming dependent on studies in economic history and the history of economic thought, not to mention highly specialized doctoral theses from universities lacking publication outlets – or, even worse, theses rejected by other publishers.[1] H. H. Powers, then chairman of the Publication Committee,[2] commented 'we shall run the Association into the ground if we make it too much of an archaeological society' [1, Powers to E. D. Durand, November 4, 1895]. During the same anxious period F. W. Taussig questioned

> whether our whole traditional system of regular monographs may not need to be remodelled. The Association certainly is not now securing the prestige which it ought to have from its publications. . . . I fear it is the old story: each Institution and each set of Professors thinks most of its own corner.
>
> [1, Taussig to J. W. Jenks, October 18, 1895]

In the next few years various attempts were made to increase the Association's membership and sales. Shorter monographs, articles, reviews, annual proceedings, and membership lists were printed in a variety of combinations that confused members and exasperated librarians, and between 1896 and 1899 four volumes of separate *Economic Studies* were issued in addition to the monographs.[3]

Policy vacillated between the desire to produce 'a series in which practical questions shall be scientifically discussed' and more scholarly works of the kind which would be unattractive to commercial publishers. Many of the monographs were designed to provide a scholarly background to current economic and social questions, such as municipal ownership, child labour, and the silver question, and although Secretary Ely was probably right in thinking that the demand was inelastic [10, p. 108],[4] the desire to add to the membership acted as a check upon price increases. Some monographs sold well; for example, E. R. A. Seligman's *Progressive Taxation in Theory and Practice* (1894), and Irving Fisher's *Appreciation and Interest* (1896). However, as it was felt that the author should derive some return from reprints and reissues, the Association's finances did not benefit substantially.

By far the most interesting, ambitious, and exhaustively debated proposal was a scheme to consolidate all or most of the existing economic periodicals into an Association journal. First mooted in the early 1890s, this idea was examined privately by several of the interested editorial bodies in 1896, openly discussed at the annual meetings in 1898 and 1899, and systematically investigated by the Chairman of the Publication Committee (Jacob Hollander) in 1902.[5] Opinion was deeply divided, but after protracted discussion and under vigorous prompting from Hollander's committee the Executive Committee eventually declared its support for a

Quarterly Bulletin to be in the nature of a professional Journal for economic and social students, to contain personal notes and current professional news, and to be given mainly to bibliography of current literature.[6]

[2, p. 39]

The new periodical, entitled the *Economic Bulletin*, first appeared in 1908, but even before the first volume was completed, a new committee had been appointed to consider the possibility of converting it into an Association journal, and eventually the die was cast at the twenty-fifth anniversary celebration in New York, in December, 1909 [4, p. 77] [3, pp. 57–8].

In the end, the *American Economic Review* was launched in 1911 mainly because a substantial body of rank and file members was determined to assert the Association's right to its own journal. Nevertheless, in 1910 a last minute attempt to effect a consolidation was made when the editorship of the *A.E.R.* was offered first to F. W. Taussig, of Harvard, partly because of the high reputation he had earned as editor of the *Quarterly Journal of Economics*, but also because the thought lingered that the *Q.J.E.* could be converted to an 'official' Association periodical. However, Taussig, who was motivated by institutional loyalty, graciously declined the invitation, and the choice then fell upon Davis R. Dewey, of the Massachusetts Institute of Technology.

THE AMERICAN ECONOMIC REVIEW

Dewey's editorship

Dewey's name is unfamiliar to present day readers (apart from economic historians, who remember his *Financial History of the United States*), but as a past member of the Publication Committee, an ex-President of the Association, and a former Secretary and editor of the American Statistical Association's publications – a post he had held for fifteen years – he was well qualified to be editor of the *A.E.R.* He accepted the appointment reluctantly, for he did not consider himself a 'thoroughbred economist' and thought Taussig was the right man for the job.[7] Nevertheless, Dewey was to continue as Managing Director of the *A.E.R.* for nearly thirty years.[8]

Dewey was largely content to follow the policies laid down by the Publication Committee and by Edwin Kemmerer, the *Economic Bulletin*'s young editor, and the transition to the new regime was effected smoothly and amicably. Dewey aimed to publish about 200 pages an issue, of which 75 would be devoted to leading articles while the remainder would cover abstracts and lists of books, periodical articles, and public documents, personal notes, and announcements of the kind deemed appropriate to an association journal.

Dewey's policies

Dewey was determined to make the *A.E.R.* 'the organ of the members of the Association rather than the organ of the editors . . . a working tool for the hundreds of graduate students who were on their way to becoming teachers of economics' [9, p. ix]. His conception of his editorial function called for continuous compromise between the claims of the various segments of the community of economists, and he was well aware that balance, like impartiality, is often achieved at the expense of liveliness. While he agreed that the standards of the *A.E.R.* should not be so high as 'to exclude the work of all but the recognized leaders of the profession' [1, M. Watkins to P. T. Homan, May 24, 1933], he nevertheless aimed to edit it 'for the professional portion of our membership', rather than laymen [1, Dewey to L. Haney, November 4, 1935].

By training and predilection Dewey was a statistician and historian rather than an economist, and he made no effort to conceal the limitations of his theoretical equipment. While not hostile to theory, he assigned it a subordinate role, believing that priority should be accorded to the economist's 'sacred obligation to handle facts with respect' [1, Dewey to H. G. Moulton, March 8, 1924]. His contention that 'we have been living too much on theoretical hypotheses in the past, and there is a vast amount of testing to be done before we are going to make substantial progress in understanding the economic structure' [1, Dewey to ? Wadsworth, n.d. (1925)] has a distinctly up-to-date ring, and during the New Deal period he argued that economists should educate the layman, expose the fallacies in popular reform proposals, and devote less time to 'the pursuit of an elaborate research study which undoubtedly has value, but is not as much needed at the present time as public education' [1, Dewey to L. Haney, November 4, 1935]. In policy matters Dewey was conservative, less because he favoured the status quo than because he was sceptical of panaceas; and he was always conscious of the gap between promise and performance.

At the outset Dewey aimed to publish leading articles on 'subjects of immediate and widespread interest . . . treated by seasoned minds in a scholarly way' which would capture and hold the attention of both academic and non-academic readers [1, Dewey to D. Kinley, November 3, 1910], and at first he solicited articles from a variety of sources. To one potential contributor he explained that the editorial board did not

> intend to make a popular magazine, but we believe that current economic questions must be treated by scholarly men and not left to the sensational magazine writer, familiarly known as the muck-raker. If our students of economics had investigated economic conditions a little more diligently some ten years ago our magazines would not have had the opportunity to distort the truth.[9]
>
> [1, Dewey to W. J. Ashley, January 9, 1911]

The early volumes of the *Review* now seem dull and heavy, for bibliographical material is rarely exciting and many of the articles were concerned with current problems and descriptive materials now of interest only to historians of the period. In subsequent years, Dewey's effort to please academic and non-academic readers by combining practical relevance and topicality while simultaneously maintaining scholarly standards, proved to be a continual headache.

Developments during Dewey's period

The *A.E.R.*'s contents reflected the collective judgement of an ever-changing combination of economists drawn from an ever-widening circle of institutions. At first, when the Managing Editor's constitutional position was obscure, Dewey selected the panel of editorial advisers, but from 1914 on he preferred to leave it to the Nominating Committee. When he received conflicting advice Dewey invited the editors concerned to reconcile their differences. If this proved impossible, the final judgement was his and neither his decisions nor his ultimate responsibility as Managing Editor seem to have ever been questioned.

An important discussion of editorial policy occurred in 1915, when Secretary Allyn Young complained that the *A.E.R.* contained too many 'practical' and 'topical' articles and that too little effort was being made to cater to the special interests of 'professional economists'; but members of the Editorial Board disagreed [1, Young to Dewey, February 18, 1915].[10] Consequently there was no perceptible change in editorial practice, and, to judge by the editorial correspondence, there was no serious examination of editorial policy during the remaining twenty-five years of Dewey's editorship. The annual meetings of the board seem to have been concerned with tactical, rather than strategic issues, and on the whole Dewey received less continuous and detailed advice that he had hoped for at the outset, when he had budgeted for three editorial meetings a year.

During the early years the space devoted to leading articles increased somewhat, and the *Review* thereby became more competitive with other journals. The proportion of space allotted to reviews, abstracts, and bibliography decreased, and a new section on Documents, Public Reports, and Legislation was added, but it dwindled to insignificance during the 1920s. Dewey was at first reluctant to undertake the bibliographical work, preferring to leave this to the *Journal of Political Economy*, which already printed a substantial bibliography. However, Kinley, E. R. A. Seligman, and Kemmerer were insistent, the latter maintaining that it would be a 'serious mistake . . . for the economists of this country to be made dependent upon . . . a private concern' [1, Kemmerer to Dewey, August 1, 1910].[11] Here, as elsewhere, the constitution and Dewey's responsibility to the large and heterogeneous Association audience precluded his expressing his own views on public policy questions. In retrospect his approach seems colour-less and lacking in enterprise or initiative, and he deliberately chose to remain unobtrusive. Nevertheless, the voluminous editorial papers reveal that his task demanded impartiality, good judgement, and the ability to mollify the aggrieved and strike a balance between conflicting opinions and interests.

As an organization journal the *A.E.R.* inevitably tended to be a general rather than a specialized publication. In accordance with his desire to avoid duplicating the work of other journals, Dewey deliberately refrained from publishing articles on sociology and political science, and he also restricted the number of theoretical articles because the *Quarterly Journal of Economics* was 'devoting itself to theory – I suppose with considerable success' [1, Dewey to W. J. Ashley, January 9, 1911]. Furthermore, Dewey undoubtedly discouraged technical and specialized articles by asking the authors to simplify or adapt them for non-specialist readers, and he some-times advised them to re-submit their contributions to the *Q.J.E.*, the *Journal of the American Statistical Association* or, in the 1930s, *Econometrica*. However, in view of his own lack of interest in economic theory, it is noteworthy that the proportion of technical articles rose in the *A.E.R.* (as in the *Q.J.E.* and *J.P.E.*) with the passage of time, and it would hardly be surprising if the average quality fell, especially as it became known that the *A.E.R.* was reluctant to publish esoteric or *avant garde* items.[12]

Judgements of quality are, of course, notoriously subjective. However, if a more objective criterion is sought, for example by analysing the contents of the *A.E.R., Q.J.E.*, and *J.P.E.* during the period of Dewey's editorship, one finds fewer differences than might have been expected. The *A.E.A. Index* lists twenty-one subject categories and in only five of these were there any significant differences in the proportions of space allocated by the *A.E.R.* and *Q.J.E.* during the period 1911–24, and four categories in the 1925–39 period. During the same periods the *A.E.R.* and *J.P.E.* differed in only one and four categories respectively, while in the *Q.J.E.* and *J.P.E.* the corresponding figures are five and two. However, there was no marked *general* tendency for the leading American economic journals to become more alike with respect to the distribution of contents, and if the *Economic Journal* (another organization periodical) is taken into account this general impression is reinforced.[13] The main changes in the *A.E.R.* during Dewey's regime included a substantial rise in the proportion of theoretical articles (mentioned above) and a substantial fall in the proportion of articles on Industrial Organization and Public Policy (Category 15) and Labor Eco-nomics (Category 19).[14]

Whatever may be the judgement of Dewey's contribution to the *A.E.R.*, the ceremonial transfer of his editorial blue pencil to Paul Homan in December, 1940, was generally welcome. Dissatisfaction with the character and contents of the *A.E.R.* had been growing for some time, and as Dewey was eighty-two when he retired, it is hardly surprising that his efficiency had declined and that he was out of touch with the ideas and needs of the younger generation of economists. The responsibility for his protracted stay must rest with the Executive Committee and the Presidents, rather than Dewey himself. In 1922 he had welcomed a proposal to establish the Association headquarters in Washington, at the Brookings Institute – a scheme involving the consolidation of the editor's, secretary's, and treasurer's functions, and one which would have undoubtedly entailed his retirement, and in 1930 he had expressed a desire to resign. It seems clear that during the late 1930s successive Executive Committees shirked the difficult task of choosing a new editor, partly from regard for Dewey's feelings, but also because they wished to avoid controversy. It is no coincidence that when the decision was eventually taken, the editorial mantle fell upon a man whose suitability for the office had been recognized five years earlier, when Dewey's resignation first seemed likely.

Homan's editorship

Paul Homan professed to be 'bursting with ideas' [13] when he took up the reins of office of Managing Editor at the age of forty-seven, and there is no doubt that he transformed the *A.E.R.* during his eleven-year tenure. From the outset he introduced a personal note which had hitherto been lacking, addressing himself directly to his readers in occasional editorial notes and in the annual reports, inviting advice and criticism, and disclosing his plans for improving the content and format of the journal. Circumstances were difficult owing to the outbreak of the war, which inevitably disrupted academic life, and to the fact that he moved several times between Ithaca, Washington, and London before settling in Los Angeles in 1950. The first of these moves aroused some misgivings in the minds of his Association colleagues, who feared that the *A.E.R.* would be neglected; and his work in London necessitated the appointment of Fritz Machlup (who, like Homan, was then working in Washington) as Acting Managing Editor from July, 1944 to August, 1945.

The supply of manuscripts 'diminished alarmingly' towards the end of 1943, when it seemed likely that the size of the *A.E.R.* would have to be reduced 'severely' in order to maintain its quality [16, p. 411] [21, p. 469].[15] But after a further deterioration, the situation improved during Machlup's tenure and the supply of manuscripts continued to increase after the war.[16]

It is never easy to give a precise estimate of an editor's achievement, and in Homan's case the problem is exacerbated by the acute transitional difficulties of the war period followed by the rapid post-war growth and rising standards of the economics profession. However, there is no denying the importance of his enterprise, energy, and enthusiasm, and his ability to seize the opportunities presented by the wartime emergency. Like Dewey, he was a middle-of-the-road economist, with a well-developed sense of historical perspective, and he combined a good command of theory with an appreciation of the relevance of economics to public policy.[17] Homan's ability to command the respect of his fellow economists also contributed to his success, for in addition to their willingness to submit manuscripts and write reviews he was able to enlist the services of some of 'the most gifted younger economists' as members of his editorial board.[18]

No doubt there were definite advantages in having the editor in the nation's capital, which was the hub of the economics profession during those years. The Washington location enabled Homan to raise the quality of the *A.E.R.* by bringing it into closer touch with the ideas and activities of the leading economists in the USA, especially the younger and more active men. Through what would nowadays be termed the 'invisible college', Homan learned of the issues in the forefront of discussion (and, even more important, those that were likely to occupy this position in the foreseeable future) and he exercised his editorial initiative in securing discussions of 'timely topics' such as rationing, the 'inflationary gap', and the economic aspects of the defence programme.[19] For example, in 1942, as the result of his initiative, a special supplement was published on the work of the Temporary National Economic Committee in an effort to raise the prestige of the *A.E.R.*, and two years later a similar volume appeared (partly as an outgrowth of the annual meetings) on *Implemental Aspects of Public Finance*.

It would be misleading to paint too rosy a picture of the condition of the *A.E.R.* in the 1940s. In his annual reports Homan commented on the general quality of the articles in engagingly frank terms, and by 1950 he had evidently accustomed himself to the fact that

> simple competence is all that is to be expected in journal articles and that in any case distinguished intellectual performance is rare. Taken in conjunction with the contents of other journals, the contents of the *Review* demonstrate that there is throughout the profession a state of active and intelligent discussion of important problems of analysis and policy, and that little space is devoted to barren discussion.
>
> [18]

Doubtless the *Review* suffered from Homan's repeated moves, and he confessed that he was not invariably 'meticulous in the performance of his editorial duties', partly owing to the pressure of other duties, but also because he treated the editorship as 'approximately a quarter-time job added on to a full-time job' [1, Homan to H. Ellis, October 5, 1950]. Despite rapidly rising costs and prices during Homan's regime, the editor's salary remained at the 1929 level; and financial constraints also explain why some of his ambitious schemes for changing the format, style, and typography failed to materialize. Even so, the present cover, size, and internal layout owe more to Homan than to any of his successors.

If the official correspondence and reports can be taken as a guide, there were more serious complaints about editorial policy during Homan's regime than at any other time in the *Review*'s history; but it is far from easy to determine the extent of the Managing Editor's responsibility for this state of affairs. Controversy among American economists was becoming more intense during the latter half of the 1930s, and the *Review* was one of the principal battlegrounds on which current methodological, doctrinal, and policy disagreements were fought out.[20] Disputes among contributors, including demands for replies and rejoinders, were by no means new, for Dewey had more often been troubled by complaints about reviews than any other matter – a point to be noted by the new editor of this journal.[21] But as the 'Communications' section of the *Review* indicates, complaints were more frequent and bitter as the Keynesian 'revolution' and the New Deal progressed, and dissatisfaction continued to mount during the war until President Joseph S. Davis felt obliged to establish a subcommittee on book reviews, to examine several complaints about editorial policy and a number of other 'festering grievances [which] have been affecting the morale of the Association in more than one quarter' [1, Davis to J. W. Bell, July 6, 1944].

However, the subcommittee made no startling recommendations, either because the more novel proposals put to them were not practicable, or because they accepted the views of those who, like the Acting Managing Editor, expressed

> serious misgivings about any attempt at standardization of literary products. A codification of standards may result in improvements in one or two directions. We may get fairer reviews, and we may get duller reviews. I, for one, feel that dullness would be too high a price for fairness.[22]
>
> [1, Fritz Machlup to Davis, July 26, 1944]

But although the outcome of the investigation was slight, it is important to note that the Executive Committee made no attempt to restrict the editor's freedom of action, thereby adhering to its established non-interventionist policy. Nor is there any evidence that either Homan or his successors attempted to restrain reviewers or print rejoinders except in cases where a reviewer was 'seriously negligent or has in a very important way distorted the author's meaning' [1, B. F. Haley to H. Hazlitt, August 1, 1960]. Naturally complaints continued, though at a somewhat diminished rate; but this cannot be directly attributed to editorial policy, for as the most recent editor remarked, it is generally true that 'any respectable journal, as a matter of policy, must accord complete freedom to reviewers' [1, J. Gurley to A. Lauterbach, August 27, 1965].

Haley's editorship

In December, 1949, Homan expressed his desire to resign. A committee was duly appointed to select his successor, and in this instance, unlike the two previous cases, the process of deliberation is fairly well documented. It would, of course, be invidious to mention names in a situation which President F. H. Knight termed 'worse than making a major appointment to a faculty, and that's bad enough' [1, Knight to Homan, September 29, 1950]. But the statement of requirements of a successful editor drafted by one of the selectors may be quoted:

> [He] should be someone who has already made something of a repu-
> tation; he should neither be too young nor too old (say 40 to 55); he
> should have a good background in theory (which after all is the
> common meeting ground of all the special fields of economics). He
> should command respect for character and judgment, as well as
> proficiency in some of the more decent parts of economics; he should
> have some enthusiasm for the job of editor; and he should have good
> prospects of *lasting* (from the age [*sic.* angle?] of age, health, and
> stability of character, for a decade or so). A journal stands to gain a
> good deal from continuity in its direction. To these two qualifications,
> I would add one or two more or less *ad hoc* considerations. First,
> Harvard should be ruled out because two journals are already edited
> there. Second, I would prefer an Academic to a civil servant editor.[23]

Bernard Haley fulfilled these requirements. He had published comparatively little, but his standing as an economic theorist had been recognized
by his selection as author of the chapter on 'Value and Distribution' in
the Association's first *Survey of Contemporary Economics* (1948), and his editorial ability had been revealed both when he took charge of the second
Survey volume (1952) and earlier when he had served on Dewey's editorial
board from 1938 to 1940. Indeed, it is a curious testimony to the Association's consistency (or conservatism) that he had then been mentioned as
a possible successor to Dewey. And, as Homan remarked recently, Haley
and he were 'intellectual twins'!

Haley's editorship marked a less dramatic break with the past than
Homan's. The Managing Editor's reports became less personal and colour-
ful, but the approach was more matter-of-fact and businesslike, and the
editorial work more meticulous. During Haley's editorship there was a
striking increase in the flow of manuscripts (from an average of 206 per
annum in the last three years of Homan's tenure to 285 in the corresponding
phase of Haley's regime, and 534 in 1967). The editorial board was
increased from seven to nine members and there was a remarkable increase
in the number of specialist readers whose advice was sought.[24] The increasing supply of manuscripts not only added to the editor's work load, it also

enhanced his responsibility for the make-up of the journal. Toward the end of Haley's term, if not earlier, many more manuscripts were passed by his editorial advisers than could possibly be printed, so that having initially sifted the wheat from the chaff before consulting them, he ultimately had considerable freedom in deciding which varieties of wheat to offer his readers. Hence, while the need for editorial initiative diminished, the need for sound editorial judgement increased markedly.

Under Haley's management the *Review* advanced along the lines laid down by his predecessors. There were no striking changes in format, character, or objectives; but the swelling tide of reviewable books soon put increasing pressure on space. In general the book review section provided the most direct evidence of the *Review*'s leading responsibility for international economic scholarship, for notwithstanding the rapid growth in the number of economic periodicals, no other American journal approached it with respect to the number and range of book reviews. Despite the precedent established under Dewey, periodical listing and abstracting was not undertaken, partly because the *Economic Journal* already provided a valuable service of this kind, and there was considerable hesitation before the *Journal of Economic Abstracts* was launched in 1963.[25] In 1956, following a discussion with various editors of economic journals, the size of the section devoted to leading articles in the *Review* was deliberately held down, partly because it was feared that expansion 'would lead to a definite deterioration in the quality of articles published by the allied quarterlies' [1, Harold Fraine, editor of the *Journal of Finance*, to Haley, January 30, 1956]. Now, however, the decision to expand this section by transferring the reviews to a new *Journal of Economic Literature* indicates that the pressure on space has at last become irresistible.

From the historian's standpoint, perhaps the most interesting by-product of Haley's editorship was a survey of opinion about the *Review*, which was published in the *Papers and Proceedings* of May, 1958 [12]. As might have been expected, it gave abundant testimony to the *Review*'s value to the profession, and to its high standing by comparison with other economic periodicals. Respondents were generally less satisfied with the range and quality of leading articles than with the book review and 'service' sections (e.g., professional notes, bibliography, dissertation lists, and announcements), but this reaction seems to have been as much a reflection of the divergences of interests and tastes within the profession as a judgement of the quality of editorial performance. The heaviest concentrations of opinion revealed a desire for papers to be less technical and theoretical, for a decrease in the use of mathematical techniques, and for more articles dealing with current policy problems. Curiously enough, this division of opinion recalls the earlier problems raised by the heterogeneous character of the Association's membership, for there was already some deliberate editorial limitation of esoteric contributions. Hence the poll tended to confirm the wisdom of the *Review*'s long-established policy toward the profession at large.[26]

CONCLUSION

The foregoing account is merely a sketch of certain aspects of the Association's publication record, and it gives only a hint of the richness of the available evidence, especially on the period from about 1910 to the mid-1940s. Comparatively little correspondence has survived from more recent times (although the annual reports of the Managing Editor constitute a valuable source), and the Secretary's papers add little, mainly because the Executive Committee has always treated the *Review* as an autonomous undertaking, apart from the general question of finance. In this, as in other 'structural' features apart from its large circulation, the *Review* is a fairly typical American social science journal, if one can judge from a recent survey of the literature [5]. However, another recent student has argued that the *Review* has been generally less receptive than the *American Sociological Review* to publications produced by authors in 'low minor' universities, a difference which is attributed to the fact that a much higher proportion of the *Review*'s editors have been selected from 'major' universities [8]. If this were so, it would support the oft-heard complaint that the *Review*, like the Association itself, is dominated by an 'establishment' – whatever that vague term connotes.[27] Unfortunately the statistical basis of this argument is suspect, and it also depends on a somewhat superficial analysis of the differences between the two disciplines.[28] Nevertheless it is cited as an example of the kind of study which may shed new light on the role of the *Review*, and the Association itself, in the development of American economics.

NOTES

* I would like to thank two past editors of the *American Economic Review*, Paul Homan and Bernard F. Haley, for their comments on an earlier version.
1 The list of Publications printed annually in the *Papers and Proceedings* of the Association does not specify each item, and as the contents of the Publications were excluded from the *A.E.A Index of Economic Journals*, a number of important papers and Presidential Addresses have been virtually consigned to oblivion.
2 At first the Secretary was in sole charge of the selection and issuance of the *Publications*. In the early 1890s, after Richard T. Ely's resignation, the Publication Committee was established.
3 This series was discontinued because the returns did not justify the outlay. 'For four years the average monthly sales have been steadily and rapidly falling while the receipts from members and subscribers have remained about constant' [23, p. 46].
4 I owe this reference to Professor G. J. Stigler, who commented, 'See, we were born in monopoly.'

5 These discussions have left a fascinating legacy of documents in the Association's files which afford unrivalled insights into the conditions of scholarly publication in economics and the obstacles to interuniversity cooperation at the turn of the century.

6 It was believed that a periodical of this kind would be less likely to compete with existing publications than a regular journal.

7 Both he and David Kinley, the chairman of the appointing committee, contemplated the possibility of a merger with the American Statistical Society's publications.

8 An excellent impression of the man and his ideas can be obtained from the proceedings of the testimonial dinner held on the occasion of his retirement [9].

9 In soliciting a contribution from a Boston lawyer, he advised him to 'write such n article as you would for the Atlantic Monthly, omitting possibly some of the more elementary considerations in regard to which you can take it for granted that this constituency is more or less familiar' [1, Dewey to G. W. Anderson, November 28, 1910].

10 Some extracts from the ensuing correspondence are quoted in my article on the American Economic Association [6, pp. 269–71]. See *supra* pp. 239–63.

11 Opposition to Chicago and the *J.P.E.* was still widespread [7]. Moreover, Kemmerer had been involved in a dispute with L. C. Marshall about the beginnings of the *J.P.E.*'s bibliography [20] [22]. In fact, Kemmerer's fears proved to be exaggerated. See J. L. Laughlin to Dewey, August 10, and September 7, 1910 [1].

12 The following figures indicate the percentage of articles published during Dewey's regime in Economic Theory Including Monetary Theory (Category 2 in the *A.E.A. Index* classification):

	A.E.R.	Q.J.E.	J.P.E.
1911–24	9%	16%	6%
1925–39	22%	29%	15%

The change of emphasis under Dewey's successor, Paul Homan, is suggested by the following letter from a potential contributor: 'I do not think that I should have dared to send a work of its character to the old *A.E.R.*, but this issue containing articles by Slichter, Ezekiel, Niesser, Hardy and others emboldens me to make the attempt' [1, P. A. Samuelson to Homan, April 9, 1942]. In fact, the article was not published!

13 'Significant' differences represent cases where there is a divergence of 4 per cent or more between two different journals in the proportion of space devoted to a given category. Needless to say, the individual categories are too broad to form the basis of a precise analysis; nor is this an appropriate place to print the figures on which my comments are based. Subsequently, I hope to publish a study of the contents of the leading American and British journals during the period 1886–1960, which has been supported by a grant from the American Economic Association. I would like to thank my wife, Sonia E. Coats, who has performed most of the drudgery involved in compiling the figures.

14

Category	1911–24	1925–39
2	9%	22%
15	20%	11%
19	12%	7%

The fall in Category 15 appears to be directly connected with the beginning of the *Journal of Business* in 1928. Similar trends in these three categories were evident in the *Q.J.E.*, *J.P.E.*, and *E.J.* during this period. In 1940–9 these trends continued, apart from a sharp fall in Category 2 in the *E.J.* and a significant rise in Category 19 in the *Q.J.E.*

15 During this period other economic journals experienced serious difficulties in retaining subscribers (e.g., *The Review of Economic Studies* and *Econometrica*) and maintaining size and standards (e.g. *J.P.E.* and *Review of Economics and Statistics*).

16 Early in 1944 Machlup declared: 'The *Review* is practically upon its uppers due to the great decline in the flow of publishable manuscripts. In fact the flow has so diminished that I do not even have the pleasure of refusing many unpublishable manuscripts' [1, Machlup to D. Yoder, January 18, 1944]. However, ten months later he reported: 'The drought of manuscripts of which Homan complained seems to be over. We are getting manuscripts by the dozens, indeed, so many that I can reject the worst ones without bothering the members of the editorial board' [1, Machlup to N. Buchanan, October 23, 1944]. Unfortunately there are no figures for the supply of manuscripts at this time, and the volume of surviving editorial correspondence is much smaller than in Dewey's period.

17 For his comments on the need for a proper balance between theoretical and policy-oriented articles see his report [15, p. 788]. He was sceptical toward some of 'the new tricks in theory'. Cf. Homan to Fritz Machlup, January 28, 1941 [1].

   Professor Homan was surprised to find that during his editorship the proportion of space allocated to the History of Economic Thought (Category 4) had risen significantly – from 2.75 per cent in 1925–39 to 7.5 per cent in 1940–9. His own major contribution to this field, *Contemporary Economic Thought* (1928), has stood the test of time remarkably well.

18 Homan acknowledged their assistance in his farewell report [19, p. 744]. It was not only the younger men who rallied round. A distinguished middle-aged scholar, accepting an invitation to join the board, wrote: 'Frankly I should have refused to allow my name to be submitted under the old regime, whose ideals and practices I disapproved of in almost every conceivable respect. But there have been so many signs of real understanding and proper ideals since you took over the editorship that I have no hesitancy' [1, A. W. Marget to Homan, Oct. 7, 1942].

19 The proportion of space devoted to Category 13, War and Defence Economics, rose more sharply in the *A.E.R.* during the period 1940–9 than in the *Q.J.E.*, *J.P.E.*, or *E.J.* However, as might be expected, it rose more sharply still in the *Papers and Proceedings*, which even more directly reflected the current interests of the profession.

   Like Dewey, however, Homan sometimes felt uncertain about the 'degree of editorial enterprise' appropriate to a 'members' journal' [17, p. 900].

20 The editorial correspondence provides abundant evidence of the division of opinion. By contrast – if one can judge by the official correspondence and the reminiscences of numerous members – the Executive Committee seems to have remained comparatively peaceful. This can only partly be explained by saying that there was no point in struggling to capture the Executive because it possessed comparatively little power – an idea first suggested to me by Professor John Perry Miller. The turbulent history of other scholarly organizations with similar powers and responsibilities belies this explanation. Moreover, since 1945 the Executive's wealth and power have grown rapidly, without any corresponding increase of factionalism.

21 Limitations of space make it impossible to provide satisfactory examples of these

complaints, not only because the most spectacular instances were complex and protracted, but also because it is necessary in each case to provide a background and explanation of the motives of the participants.

22 Taken out of context, Machlup's remark may appear more cynical than he intended. Nevertheless both he and Homan favoured fewer, longer, and more critical reviews, and Homan believed there was greater scope for improvement in the book review section than elsewhere in the *Review*. Cf. [13, p. 212] and [14, p. 931]. On his retirement Dewey had enjoined his successor to: 'Publish at least one review in each issue which will arouse the animosity of the author. There is nothing more stimulating than controversy' [9, p. x].

23 Other members of the Committee agreed that the editor should be affiliated to an institution which did not already publish an economic journal, and Secretary Bell considered that he need not be a 'highly productive' scholar or a specialist in theory, but added that theory was important, otherwise 'the journal may gravitate to the level of a nonprofessional magazine on current economic topics' [1, J. W. Bell to Knight, June 30, 1950].

24 The proportion of manuscripts published fluctuated between 27 per cent in 1949–50 and 14 per cent in 1965–6 [11, p. 699]. The practice of calling on editorial readers apparently began under Haley. But the number of names printed grew from 46 in 1953 to 169 in 1968. Other indications of the change of scale of the *Review*'s operations include a fall in the percentage of articles accepted; an increase in the number of pages per issue, and the number of copies printed; and a sharp increase in the total budget and the editor's salary.

25 The publication of abstracts ceased in 1929 when the ill-fated *Social Science Abstracts* appeared, and despite considerable discussion they were not resumed when that venture failed in 1932.

26 As Haley observed, many of the innovations proposed by respondents would have involved a more active policy of 'selecting subjects and authors' [12, p. 648]. No such policy has been implemented, apart from the 'Survey' articles published during the period, which were the outcome of an Association decision rather than editorial initiative.

27 There have been recurrent complaints about the reappearance of the same names at the annual meetings, and about the limited range of institutions from which the authors of articles in the *A.E.R.* have been drawn. The whole question of the representativeness of the Association needs to be studied systematically.

28 I am indebted to my colleague, A. O. Hughes, for his comments on the technical aspects of this paper.

REFERENCES

1 American Economic Association. Correspondence in the AEA files, Northwestern University library.

2 *American Economic Association, Publications*, Third Series, Nineteenth Annual Meeting, 1907, *8*, 39.

3 *American Economic Association, Publications*, Third Series, Twenty-first Annual Meeting, 1909, *10*, 57–8.

4 *American Economic Association Quarterly*, Handbook, 1910, 77.

5 D. Bell, 'United States of America', *Int. Soc. Sci. J.*, 1967, *19*, 244–54.

6 A. W. Coats, 'The American Economic Association, 1904–29', *Amer. Econ. Rev.*, June 1964, *54*, 261–85. Reprinted in this volume, pp. 239–63.

7 ——, 'The Origins of the "Chicago School(s)"?', *J. Polit. Econ.*, 1963, *71*, 487–93. Reprinted in this volume, pp. 280–8.

8 D. Crane, 'The Gatekeepers of Science: Some Factors Affecting the Selection of Articles for Scientific Journals', *Amer. Sociol.*, Nov. 1967, *2*, 195–201.

9 D. R. Dewey, 'Remarks of Davis Rich Dewey at Testimonial Dinner', *Amer. Econ. Rev.*, Proc., Feb. 1941, *30*, vii–xi.

10 R. T. Ely, *Monopolies and Trusts*. New York 1906.

11 J. G. Gurley, 'Report of the Managing Editor for the Year Ending December, 1967', *Amer. Econ. Rev.*, May 1968, *58*, 699–704.

12 B. F. Haley, 'Report of Survey of Membership with Regard to *American Economic Review*', *Amer. Econ. Rev.*, Proc., May 1958, *48*, 643–9.

13 P. T. Homan, 'Editorial Note', *Amer. Econ. Rev.*, Mar. 1941, *31*, 212.

14 ——, 'Editorial Note', *Amer. Econ. Rev.*, Dec. 1941, *31*, 931.

15 ——, 'Editorial Note', *Amer. Econ. Rev.*, Sept. 1945, *35*, 788.

16 ——, 'Report of the Managing Editor of the American Economic Review for the Year Ended December 1943', *Amer. Econ. Rev.*, Proc., March 1944, *34*, 411–13.

17 ——, 'Report of the Managing Editor for the Year Ending December, 1945', *Amer. Econ. Rev.*, Proc., May 1946, *36*, 900–3.

18 ——, 'Report of the Managing Editor for the Year Ending December, 1950', *Amer. Econ. Rev.*, Proc., May 1951, *41*, 788–91.

19 ——, 'Report of the Managing Editor for the Year Ending December, 1951', *Amer. Econ. Rev.*, Proc., May 1952, *42*, 744–6.

20 E. W. Kemmerer, 'The Bibliography of Economics in the United States', *Bibliogr. Soc. Amer., Pap.*, 1909, *4*, 83–91.

21 F. Machlup, 'Report of the Acting Managing Editor of the American Economic Review for the Year Ending December, 1944', *Amer. Econ. Rev.*, Proc., May 1945, *35*, 469–71.

22 L. C. Marshall, 'The Bibliography of Economics in the United States', *Bibliogr. Soc. Amer., Pap.*, 1909, *4*, 73–82.

23 W. F. Willcox, 'Report of the Secretary', *Econ. Stud.*, April 1899, *4*, 43–8.

15

THE ORIGINS OF THE 'CHICAGO SCHOOL(S)'?

It would, no doubt, be both tactless and improper for a foreigner to meddle in the domestic dispute provoked by Mr Miller's contention that there is a distinct and recognizable 'Chicago School' of economics,[1] even on the pretext of offering his services as an impartial, self-appointed arbitrator. Nevertheless, as one not unfamiliar with the current academic scene and the history of American economics, I cannot forbear to comment on certain curious parallels between the present situation and the 1890s and early 1900s, when the Department of Economics at the new University of Chicago first made an impact on the higher learning in the USA. In an effort to minimize the inevitable misunderstandings, let me emphasize that, apart from a few noncommittal concluding remarks, I am primarily concerned with the past, not with the present; that, although this note was prompted by Miller's paper, it refers only indirectly to the substantive issues raised by him and by his commentators; and that, as far as I am aware, there is no doctrinal continuity between the initial period – which, at the very latest, terminates with J. L. Laughlin's retirement as head of the department in 1916 – and more recent circumstances.

I

The opening of the University of Chicago in October, 1892, was the most significant event in the late-nineteenth-century 'revolution' in American higher education since the inauguration of the Johns Hopkins graduate school in 1876, and a variety of circumstances – such as endowment, leadership, timing, and location – combined to ensure that the new fledgling would have a vigorous and controversial infancy.[2] The well-publicized birth announcements appeared as the 'Populist revolt' was approaching its climax, and the first birthday celebration was held in the midst of one of the worst depressions in the nation's history. At that time of seething agrarian discontent there were some who speculated about the possibility of open conflict between the industrial East and the rural West, and it was in Chicago, the principal storm centre of this turbulent era, that William Jennings Bryan delivered his rousing 'cross of gold' speech in 1896.

Recent historical research has demonstrated that contemporary fears were exaggerated. Despite repeated efforts to consolidate farmer–labour alliances, the Populists gained comparatively few votes in any of the urban areas, and few members of the educated and professional classes endorsed the agrarian demagogues' campaign against the eastern industrialists and financiers.[3] There was, however, among the intellectuals a mounting distrust of big business, and within a few short years a group of moderate social reformers, urban middle-class politicians, and members of the New England élite (who despised the vulgar *nouveaux riches*) were to combine forces in the Progressive movement that virtually dominated the American political scene during the first two decades of this century.

In these circumstances the new university inevitably encountered widespread suspicion and hostility. Even intelligent and well-informed commentators occasionally wondered whether John D. Rockefeller's munificent donations meant that the corrupting influence of business wealth would soon be felt within the ivory towers, while radical journalists and politicians had no hesitation in bestowing upon the new institution the opprobrious title of 'the Standard Oil University'. Unfortunately, the driving ambition of its first president, William Rainey Harper, merely served to strengthen the analogy. As a former Yale biblical scholar, his academic credentials were sound enough; but his methods appeared to resemble those formerly employed by the university's notorious benefactor. His most spectacular coup, 'Harper's raid' on the new graduate faculty of Clark University, was generally deplored in academic circles.[4] Few underpaid professionals could resist the pecuniary inducements offered by this 'captain of erudition', as Thorstein Veblen so aptly dubbed him; but the heads of established departments feared that their own forces would, in turn, be decimated, while those engaged in building up new graduate schools, especially in the Middle West, resented the vast resources of Chicago in the competition for the limited supply of talented faculty and students.

In this setting the leadership of the Chicago Department of Economics was especially important, in relation both to the public 'image' of the university and to its place in the economics profession at large. As noted elsewhere,[5] there was a marked westward shift in the centre of gravity of American economics in the early 1890s, as important new ventures were initiated at Wisconsin, Chicago, and Michigan; and it is a curious fact that at one stage Harper seriously considered offering the headship of the Department of Economics to Richard T. Ely, who had been his colleague in the Methodist Summer Camp at Chautauqua and who was one of the most prominent academic spokesmen for economic and social reform. Although Ely assiduously preserved his personal records, the exact details of their negotiations may never be revealed. Harper was evidently planning a 'raid' on the Johns Hopkins faculty in which both Ely and the historian Herbert Baxter Adams were to be carried off to his lair; but his interest in Ely may have diminished once it became clear that Adams was unwilling to move. Alternatively, Ely may have accepted the advice of those who warned that he might encounter bitter controversy, since 'the chasm between capital and labour is deeper and broader in Chicago than anywhere else in the country',[6] or have agreed with the correspondent who feared 'the seductive influence of a powerful capitalist backing to the institution, drawing all its departments as by a moral gravitation into an apologetic attitude for its own existence'.[7] Whatever the explanation, Harper turned to the opposite end of the professorial spectrum and offered the post to J. Laurence Laughlin, of Cornell, one of the most conservative economists in the country.

Had Harper deliberately set out to confirm the suspicions of those who regarded the University of Chicago as a tool of the business interests, he could hardly have made a better choice. An erstwhile member of the Harvard faculty, Laughlin was a dogmatic theorist and vigorous controversialist whose insistence upon the need to separate 'what is' from 'what ought to be' did not prevent him from engaging in downright partisan advocacy of his favourite policy proposals.[8] Soon after his arrival in Chicago, Laughlin became notorious throughout the Middle West as the foremost academic proponent of gold monometallism. He strenuously attacked the free silverites in several signed editorials in the *Chicago Times-Herald* and was eventually forced to engage in a public debate with one of his leading antagonists, William 'Coin' Harvey, who, in one of his best-known pamphlets, had depicted Laughlin as one of his converts. And in view of the bitterness of the current monetary controversy, it is hardly surprising to find that Laughlin was described by one midwestern editor as 'the overzealous gold-bug teacher of the Oil Trust seat of economic ignorance'.[9]

Laughlin's uninhibited participation in public controversy affords but one of several examples of his lack of harmony with the prevailing mood of the American economics profession. Leaders of the older generation had often been readily identifiable as spokesmen for free trade, protection, or laissez faire; but, in the 1890s, conscious efforts were being made to consolidate the profession, to avoid unseemly partisanship, and to enhance the scientific reputation of the discipline.[10] Had Laughlin been a less uncooperative, less isolated individual, the pro-silver press attacks on him might have aroused the sympathy of his professional colleagues, for during this decade several well-known economists lost their jobs or suffered in other ways from extramural pressures. Yet, in retrospect, it seems likely that the trend of professional opinion was growing more impatient of Laughlin, for both moderately conservative and reform-minded economists had grounds for complaint. Laughlin's action in founding the *Journal of Political Economy* at a time when serious efforts were being made to consolidate existing publication outlets into one major American economic journal was viewed as a typical example of his unwillingness to co-operate and of Chicago's brash academic imperialism.[11] His consistent refusal to join the American Economic Association, deliver a paper, or even attend its meetings helped to reinforce this feeling; and there was more than a suspicion that Laughlin had attempted to capture the Political Science Association of the Central States when it was founded in 1895, with the aim of making it a Chicago satellite and a midwestern rival of the American Economic Association.[12] In addition, Laughlin's policy pronouncements were hardly calculated to endear him to the reformist elements in the economics profession, and when a Chicago economist, E. W. Bemis, loudly protested in 1895 that he had been dropped from the university because he had attacked business corruption and law-breaking, there were many who uncritically accepted this explanation and concluded that Laughlin and Harper were willing tools of the business interests.[13]

Thus a variety of circumstances conspired to give the Department of Economics at Chicago an unenviable reputation in the 1890s and early 1900s as a centre of doctrinal orthodoxy and extreme conservatism in matters of policy. Laughlin did not finally capitulate and join the American Economic Association until 1904, and as late as 1902 Frank Fetter (the secretary of the association) explained that he had invited one of Laughlin's able young colleagues, Wesley Mitchell, to give a paper at the annual meeting in order to bring him into the community of economists and thereby protect him from 'bad influences' at Chicago.[14] Laughlin's reputation probably enhanced his difficulties in recruiting and retaining faculty and students, although there is no direct evidence on this point. However, there is corroborative evidence in the case of the closely related Department of Sociology. After the Bemis affair, at least one person refused to subscribe to the department's publication, the *American Journal of Sociology*, in protest,[15] and Albion Small, the professor of sociology, subsequently informed Harper that 'persistent and malignant prejudice against the University of Chicago on grounds which affect principally the departments of Economics and Sociology' had kept down the numbers of students. Accordingly, after the former economist E. A. Ross had been summarily dismissed from Stanford University in another widely publicized affair, Small urged Harper to appoint him for a summer session as a means of enhancing the university's reputation as a bastion of academic freedom, even though he believed 'Ross deserved everything that he got'.[16]

Whatever the effects of Chicago's unfavourable public 'image' may have been, the belief that the Department of Economics was solidly conservative, or unduly under Laughlin's influence, undoubtedly represented a gross distortion of the facts. This example may therefore serve as a warning to those who make the mistake of judging an entire department by the reputation of its best-known member. Laughlin was, indeed, a rigid thinker, an uncompromising and sometimes unfair polemicist, and an extreme conservative. Nevertheless, during his twenty-four years at Chicago his department became a leading centre and breeding ground of economic heterodoxy. Laughlin's action in taking Thorstein Veblen with him to Chicago from Cornell in 1892 has often been recounted; but it was no aberration. He tried to protect and promote Veblen, despite Harper's disapproval, and he behaved in a similar manner toward other able but unconventional subordinates, such as Herbert Davenport, Robert Hoxie, Wesley Mitchell, Walton Hamilton, and J. M. Clark.[17] Laughlin was an unrelenting individualist who genuinely respected the independence of his colleagues, and he was as outspoken in his resistance to Harper's encroachments upon his departmental independence as he was toward the encroachments of government upon individual freedom in public affairs.[18] His initial refusal to join the American Economic Association, because of his distaste for 'Elyism' during its early years, illustrates both his conservatism amd his stubbornness, and, once having adopted this position, he was loath to change his mind, even though the circumstances had altered.[19] His role in the Bemis affair is obscure, though he cannot be absolved from all responsibility.[20] It must, however, be emphasized that Bemis had been appointed by Harper, not by Laughlin himself, and was employed in the Extension Division, not in the Department of Economics. Laughlin disliked and disapproved of Bemis and refused to take him into the department; but, unlike Albion Small, Laughlin did not attack Bemis publicly, and his attitude toward Harper could never be called sycophantic.

II

By the time Laughlin retired in 1916, his department had lost most of its original distinguishing features, and Chicago had become widely recognized as one of the nation's leading centres of academic economics. Laughlin's successor, Leon C. Marshall, was neither immoderate nor doctrinaire, and, although Jacob Viner's arrival in Chicago in 1916 establishes some continuity of personnel between the beginnings and the Frank Knight–Henry Simons era in the 1930s, it cannot seriously be argued that there was any significant doctrinal continuity. Furthermore, whatever may be said of the present, there was in Laughlin's day nothing resembling either Miller's or Bronfenbrenner's conceptions of the 'Chicago School'.

In retrospect, it appears that the dominant intellectual influences upon Chicago economics in the 1890s and early 1900s were Veblen and John Dewey rather than Laughlin; and, although Laughlin himself contributed to the rigorous training of many able young scholars, especially by compelling them to exercise their logic against his forceful arguments, in the long run his influence may have been negative rather than positive. Laughlin's young heterodox colleagues probably found in him the original from which they fashioned their stereotype of the rigidly orthodox doctrinaire, which became a veritable straw man during the institutionalist heyday of the 1920s. And it was doubtless with Laughlin in mind that Herbert Davenport once jokingly protested that, on the Judgement Day, Veblen would be accountable to his Maker for having spoiled so many promising theorists.[21]

Nevertheless, even in the USA, echoes of the past sometimes linger on, and it is conceivable that traces of Chicago's early reputation as a centre of economic conservatism have survived until recent times. As one of Chicago's most illustrious figures has remarked in a somewhat different context, 'we know little of how traditions get established, while it seems clear that once established, a tradition does not get changed through calling attention to its absurdity, or that of the factual assumptions upon which it rests'.[22]

It is surely no coincidence that the young Bronfenbrenner encountered such unfavourable attitudes toward the 'Chicago School' on the shores of Lake Mendota, the home of a rival politicoeconomic school. The Wisconsin tradition was far more coherent and continuous than its Chicago counterpart, and it owed much more to Ely and to the 1890s than the admirers of John R. Commons are willing to concede.[23] The Wisconsin Progressives' conviction that the control of universities by businessmen was a threat to academic freedom and, possibly, to democracy was by no means unique. But in Madison this general suspicion was reinforced by the struggle for midwestern academic supremacy, by the long-standing rivalry between state and private universities, and by the nature and extent of the University of Wisconsin's unique involvement in state politics.

Bronfenbrenner's negative 'visceral reaction' toward those who included him in the 'Chicago School' was both natural and characteristically American in its anti-authoritarianism. Yet, in a country so vast and varied as the USA, schools of economics or other doctrine may contribute a welcome measure of coherence and stability to an otherwise bewilderingly chaotic intellectual scene – provided, of course, that they are not too sharply differentiated, too rigid, or too hostile toward one another. The members of such schools may, indeed, gain in depth and strength what they lose in breadth, and there is little likelihood of the emergence of anything comparable to the Cambridge or German historical schools of economics, both of which inhibited new scientific developments and (though the evidence is incomplete) probably exerted undue influence over university appointments. Alfred Marshall was surely *too* deferential to the past, whereas Laughlin was wholly justified in protesting, during the early years of this century, that his countrymen were overeager to reconstruct the basic theories of economics *ab initio*.[24] In the USA at that time there was a pressing need to distinguish between G (the Good Economists) and non-G, since the qualifications for appointment to faculty positions varied enormously; and there was a growing desire to consolidate existing gains and to define

285

and raise professional standards in an effort to enhance the status, influence, and pecuniary rewards of the profession.

These reflections suggest that the importance of Miller's courageous effort to define the 'Chicago School' transcends the immediate point of issue. It may never be possible to provide precise definitions of such notions as 'schools', 'good economists', or 'professional standards'; but attempts to do so are neither unnecessary nor worthless. Economists cannot understand the nature and development of their discipline if they confine themselves to the history of economic analysis,[25] and Bronfenbrenner's attempt to classify economists in terms of the hypotheses they employ, the results they seek, and the policy positions they favour may prove to be a lasting addition to the historian's critical apparatus.

NOTES

1 H. Laurence Miller, Jr, 'On the "Chicago School of Economics" ', *Journal of Political Economy*, LXX (February, 1962), 64–9. See also in the same issue, 'Comment' by George J. Stigler, pp. 70–1, and 'Observations on the "Chicago School(s)" ', by M. Bronfenbrenner, pp. 72–5.

2 For general background on the matters discussed in this and the next two paragraphs see J. S. Brubacher and Willis Rudy, *Higher Education in Transition: An American History, 1636–1956* (New York, 1958); Thomas W. Godspeed, *A History of the University of Chicago* (Chicago, 1916); John D. Hicks, *The Populist Revolt* (Minneapolis, 1931); Allan Nevins, *Grover Cleveland: A Study in Courage* (New York, 1938), esp. pp. 589–629, 649–713; and Joseph Dorfman, *The Economic Mind in American Civilization* (New York, 1949), vol. III, chaps. x–xii.

3 For example, see Eric F. Goldman, *Rendezvous with Destiny* (New York, 1953), pp. 58–60; also Hicks, op. cit., pp. 243, 269.

4 For a vivid, though hardly impartial, account of this incident see G. Stanley Hall's autobiography, *Life and Confessions of a Psychologist* (New York, 1923), pp. 295–7. Hall, who was president of Clark, refused an offer from Harper and 'told him that his action was like that of the eagle who robbed the fishhawk of his prey. . . . It was an act of wreckage comparable to anything that the worst trust had ever attempted against its competitors.' Hall subsequently regarded this incident as the turning point in Harper's efforts to acquire a distinguished faculty and a guaranty that Chicago would not be 'Chautauquaean'.

5 A. W. Coats, 'The First Two Decades of the American Economic Association', *American Economic Review*, L (September, 1960), 564 (reprinted in this volume, pp. 205–24).

6 However this correspondent, the reformist clergyman Lyman Abbott, considered Harper's appointment as president and his invitation to Ely to take the chair as strong indications that the men behind the University are thoroughly progressive men' and concluded that 'the atmosphere of Chicago would be more favourable to free investigation and to a freedom of teaching on sociological topics than the atmosphere of Baltimore' (Abbott to Ely, March 20, 1891, in Ely Papers, Wisconsin State Historical Society).

7 Reverend Leighton Williams to Ely, April 11, 1891, Ely Papers. This letter suggests that Ely had already rejected Harper's call.

Four years later, at the height of the Bemis affair (see above, p. 283), Ely's negotiations with Harper were discussed in the national press. One newspaper stated that Ely had refused a chair because of Standard Oil influence; a subsequent report quoted Harper as denying that the post had ever been offered to Ely, whereupon Ely indignantly demanded that Harper publish a retraction. Harper refused, however, on the grounds that the question of Ely's appointment had never been brought before the Board of Trustees (see Bemis to Ely, August 13, 16, and 18, 1895; Ely to Harper, August 17, 1895; Harper to Ely, August 20, 1895, all in Ely Papers).

8 Alfred Bornemann, *J. Laurence Laughlin: Chapters in the Career of an Economist* (Washington, 1940), esp. chaps. i, iii–v. Many of the statements about Laughlin in subsequent paragraphs are based on this source (see also Dorfman, op. cit., pp. 271–5, and Lucy Sprague Mitchell, *Two Lives: The Story of Wesley Clair Mitchell and Myself* [New York, 1953], pp. 85–6).

9 Thomas F. Bryson, editor of the *Farmer's Tribune* (Des Moines), May 8, 1895 (a cutting is in the Laughlin Collection, University of Chicago Library). For the debate with Harvey see Bornemann, op. cit., pp. 41–2. The expressions 'Oil Trust University' and 'Standard Oil University' appear from time to time in the correspondence of contemporary economists, and as late as 1906 the Chicago economists still suffered occasionally from this taunt (see Laughlin, 'Academic Liberty', *Journal of Political Economy*, XIV [January, 1906], 41–3).

10 As Henry Farnam wrote to Francis Walker: 'In view of the amount of ignorance and misinformation which is constantly being displayed on economic subjects, I think it especially important that those who study questions without any prejudice, but solely with a view to ascertaining the truth, should not scandalize the profane and diminish the authority of scholars by unnecessary controversy' (November 6, 1896, in Farnam Papers, Yale University Library). Farnam was not, of course, specifically referring to Laughlin.

11 F. W. Taussig, for example, referred to his and Charles Dunbar's 'disgust at this intrusion into the field. It is a clear case of not having the interests of science at heart; though it may be a question whether this interest is pure and undefiled in the breast of any of us. We all have a concern for our own institutions' (Taussig to E. R. A. Seligman, March 17, 1892, in Seligman Papers, Columbia University Library).

12 On these matters see Coats, op. cit., pp. 214–6. In a draft letter to Harper dated August 15, 1902, Laughlin blamed his Chicago colleagues for having 'allowed the organization to slip out of our hands. Ely and others finally throttled the scheme when they held the offices' (cf. n. 14 below).

13 The best account of this affair appears in Richard Hofstadter and Walter P. Metzger, *The Development of Academic Freedom in America* (New York, 1955), chap. ix.

14 Frank A. Fetter to Seligman, October 18, 1902, in American Economic Association Papers, Secretary's Office, Northwestern University (hereinafter cited as 'AEA Papers'). A few weeks earlier Laughlin and Harper had exchanged letters on the subject of Mitchell's intended departure from Chicago, in the course of which Harper remarked: 'There is a strong feeling that the Department of Political Economy in our University is isolated from the work of Political Economy throughout the country.' In his reply Laughlin hotly denied this contention and gave a lengthy review of the difficulties he had encountered over the *Journal of Political Economy*, the Political Science Association of the Central States, and the Bemis case (Harper to Laughlin and Laughlin to Harper [draft], both dated August 15, 1902, in Department of Political Economy file, University of Chicago Library).

15 See Joseph Dorfman, *Thorstein Veblen and His America* (New York, 1934), pp. 122–3.

16 'Nothing that he [Ross] could say could hurt us; but on the other hand his engagement would spike the guns of [those who] claim that the "proprietary institutions" are afraid of the things that such men can say' (Small to Harper, January 31, 1901; also Small to Harper, December 21, 1898, both in Albion W. Small file, University of Chicago Library). Small was undoubtedly more sensitive to outside opinion than Laughlin; hence his insistence in 1895 that the Chicago men wished to avoid the impression of trying to run the new Political Science Association.

17 Sometimes even those who knew the facts could not overcome their dislike of Laughlin. Thus Fetter, in an undated letter to Seligman (probably written late in 1902), rejected Chicago as a suitable place for an American Economic Association meeting because of 'the irreconcilable head of the department'. Although he admitted that 'the younger men are *all right*, we must not forget', he concluded, that Nashville was a better 'place for missionary work' (AEA Papers).

18 Several of Laughlin's letters to Harper contain frank criticisms of Harper's autocratic and high-handed methods.

19 Two years before Laughlin finally joined the AEA, his colleague, J. Franklin Jameson, wrote to Seligman mentioning Laughlin's 'genuine cordiality' toward the association and the difficulty 'of persuading several scores or hundreds of members that his attitude is and would be a cordial one' (November 29, 1902, AEA Papers).

20 In a letter to Harper, dated August 6, 1894, Laughlin complained that Bemis' one-sided public statements on the railway question were 'making very hard the establishment of a great railway interest in the university. . . . At every turn in Chicago, in July, I heard indignant remarks about Bemis . . . [and] in my opinion, the duty to the good name of the University now transcends any soft heartedness to an individual' (J. L. Laughlin file, University of Chicago Library).

21 Dorfman, *Thorstein Veblen*, p. 311. It is worth noting that 'Freddie' Taylor, of Michigan, one of Laughlin's contemporaries, occupied a similar role, for it was said that much of the careful drilling in 'orthodox' principles which students obtained in Taylor's famous introductory course was subverted by his junior colleagues in their own courses or in Taylor's sections (Dorfman, *Economic Mind*, p. 401).

22 Frank H. Knight, 'Schumpeter's History of Economic Analysis', *Southern Economic Journal*, XXI (January, 1955), 272.

23 Obviously this statement cannot be adequately documented here. But Commons' personal and doctrinal links with Ely (and with Bemis) in the 1890s, especially his Christian Socialism, and the early formulations of his ideas on law and economics, sovereignty, and the representation of interests, provide positive examples. On the negative side, the Wisconsin 'school' of the 1920s and 1930s owed far more to Ely's crude 'look-and-see' method than to Commons' obscure though penetrating theories of 'reasonable value'.

24 See my 'Alfred Marshall and Richard T. Ely: Some Unpublished Letters,' *Economica*, XXVIII (new ser.; May, 1961), 191–4 (reprinted in vol. I in this series).

25 For some welcome recent comments on this point see D. Winch, 'What Price the History of Economic Thought?' *Scottish Journal of Political Economy*, IX (November, 1962), 193–204. This title is calculated to appeal to Chicagoans!

16

JOHN ELLIOTSON SYMES, HENRY GEORGE AND ACADEMIC FREEDOM IN NOTTINGHAM DURING THE 1880s*

I

In his admirable brief history of University College, Nottingham, Professor A. C. Wood provided far more illuminating glimpses of the trials and tribulations of late-nineteenth-century British academic life than are usually to be found in works of this genre. This partly reflects the circumstances of the case, for the relationships between town, gown, and administration were unique, and 'indifference, political prejudice, class consciousness and misguided suspicion' played an unusually prominent role in the institution's early years.[1] But in addition, full credit must be accorded to the author, who successfully 'humanized' his narrative by emphasizing personalities rather than the tedious factual details which so often overburden official histories, and to the university authorities, who wisely refrained from censoring the record of their predecessors' indiscretions.

To recount the events described in Professor Wood's volume would be a work of supererogation, and it would be difficult to match his elegant style and his fund of anecdotes. Nevertheless, at the present time of rapid change in higher education, when new universities are springing up and extra-mural pressures on the academic community are growing, the early struggles of University College, Nottingham, have a peculiar fascination, and this article is designed to provide some new information and a re-interpretation of the existing record. The available evidence suggests that there have been fewer violations of academic freedom in Britain than in many other countries: fortunately we had no Adolf Hitler to put us to the test in the 1930s, and no Senator Joe McCarthy to shock us into academic introspection during the 1950s. But, as a result of these and other circumstances – such as the generally retarded state of sociological studies in Britain, and an uneasy feeling that a detached investigation of our more honorific institutions is liable to degenerate into unseemly muckraking –

we have tended to take our universities for granted, and the sociology of British academic life remains a wholly uncharted field. Even in the USA, the home of muckraking journalism and Parsonian obscurantism, the subject has flourished only recently.[2] Yet when it eventually attains some measure of intellectual respectability in Britain, as it undoubtedly should and will, the early history of University College, Nottingham, will surely occupy a prominent and distinctive place in the record.

There are many resemblances between nineteenth-century British provincial university colleges and publicly supported institutions of higher education in the USA, and the similarities are especially marked in the case of Nottingham, the only university college to be financed and controlled by its local authority.[3] This is especially pertinent to the present subject, for the prevalence of academic freedom 'cases' in the history of American higher education bears eloquent testimony to the American scholar's dependence on his society. The primary function of an ivory tower is to afford a peaceful haven for those engaged in intellectual pursuits; but it may also serve as a shield, to protect them from outside attacks. Transatlantic ivory towers have, however, been notoriously insecure and ill-defended, for most American academics have been acutely aware that a democratic community tends to regard the scholar as a public servant, whose status and emoluments should closely reflect the 'practical' value of his services to society. With the professionalization of higher learning during the past century, many American scholars have gone out of their way to pass this anti-intellectual test of scholarly performance and have eagerly sought parity of esteem with other professional groups, such as lawyers, doctors, and engineers. Professional prestige and academic independence have been directly, though not perfectly, correlated, and while abuses of academic freedom have not been unknown in private universities and colleges, they have probably been more frequent and certainly more flagrant in publicly supported institutions. It is here that we encounter the problems created by the scholar's proximity to the extra-mural world; and it is against this background that the early history of University College, Nottingham, can best be viewed.

The late-nineteenth-century transformation of British higher education, from a collegiate to a university-dominated pattern, was inevitably slower and more sedate than its American counterpart, and the influence of German ideas and experience was correspondingly less marked. There was no large-scale migration of young, impressionable British students to continental universities comparable to that from the USA during the post Civil War period, and, with the exception of a few farsighted natural scientists, those who ventured abroad seem not to have been unduly critical of conditions at home. The collegiate tradition was more successful and more deeply rooted in Britain than in the USA, mainly because it was adapted to the educational prejudices of a comparatively hierarchical and inegalitarian society. Consequently, German academic standards and ideals of *Lehrfreiheit* and *Lernfreiheit* had less appeal in Britain,[4] where academic independence seems to have been the rule rather than the exception.

Nevertheless, conditions were changing in Britain. University reform was under discussion from the mid-century, and there were distinct similarities between the provincial university colleges of the 1880s and their American equivalents – the urban universities and land-grant colleges.[5] The former began, admittedly, under the benevolent auspices of Oxford and Cambridge, and it was hopefully suggested at Nottingham in 1879 that the local college should 'as far as practicable' be a detached portion of the University of Cambridge, 'rather than an isolated provincial institution'.[6] This proposal was rejected, but the founders endeavoured to meet local needs by drawing upon the intellectual resources and prestige of the ancient foundations. At the same time, however, the provincial colleges were attempting to fill a yawning gap in the national educational system by providing opportunities for vocational training and social and cultural advancement, and their direct dependence on local financial and student support made them highly sensitive to local interests. The official histories contain abundant evidence of the university administrators' preoccupation with these matters, and those quantitative criteria which have long been the bane of American educational institutions – such as size of enrolment, numbers and variety of courses, tangible academic 'results' (both from faculty and from students), and financial strength – figured prominently in their early struggles. The ambivalence of their educational objectives must also have had a profound influence on the daily lives and attitudes of the academic staff, but, with the notable exception of Nottingham, the official histories provide only tantalizing hints of this aspect of the story. Evidence of outside interference with appointments, dismissals, teaching, and research duties is usually vague and scanty. The provincial dons were, however, well aware of the inferiority of their position *vis-à-vis* their Oxbridge colleagues, with respect to both educational standards and security of tenure; and this sense of inferiority must occasionally have made them feel aloof, indifferent, and even disdainful towards their students and the local townspeople.

II

The significance of these Anglo-American comparisons becomes clearer when we consider the case of the Reverend John Elliotson Symes (1847–1921), one of the four original Professors appointed at University College, Nottingham, in 1881. The occupant of a chair of English Language and Literature, Symes was responsible for the entire Arts department, and he also taught History and Political Economy. In addition, he participated in a variety of current social reform movements at a time when economic depression, the land question, and socialism were topics of intense public controversy, and these activities earned him a somewhat mixed reputation among the local citizenry. As Professor Wood has shown,[7] he was under threat of dismissal during the municipal financial crisis of 1887, and he was often the subject of vigorous public criticism of a kind more frequently encountered in the USA than in Britain. Indeed he had numerous counterparts across the Atlantic, where even more turbulent social conditions prevailed.

At this time the American academic world was becoming professionalized, and the modern research-oriented specialist was beginning to supplant the traditional college teacher, who had usually been a clergyman engaged in teaching a miscellaneous group of subjects. During the 1880s, a number of young reform-minded economists and social scientists were challenging the dominant body of orthodox, *laissez-faire*, economic and social doctrine, and as systematic studies of academic freedom have demonstrated, economic heresy was beginning to outstrip religious heresy as the most frequent cause of excommunication from academic life.[8] Symes would have been entirely at home among the 'new school' economic heretics in the USA, where he would have been an even more obvious candidate for martyrdom than he was in Nottingham. The fact that he not only retained his post, but even became Principal of the college in 1890, must therefore be interpreted as a victory for the cause of academic freedom. But as we shall see, it proved to be almost a Pyrrhic victory.

Symes, who had obtained his BA degree at Downing College, Cambridge, in 1871, was an obvious candidate for a professorship at Nottingham, since the University College was a direct outgrowth of a series of Cambridge University Extension lectures in which he had played a prominent part. The university extension movement was, of course, designed to cater to the needs of the lower-middle- and working-class people who were in practice, if not in principle, excluded from the older universities, and, like many other successful extension lecturers, Symes was a clear and forceful speaker (he had been President of the Union while at Cambridge) and a man of markedly humanitarian social sympathies. Professor Wood has correctly described him as a Christian Socialist; but the term is too imprecise for our purposes, for in the 1880s Christian Socialism extended from the middle almost to the extreme left of the political spectrum, and by the mid-1890s a speaker at the Church Congress could declare, without undue exaggeration: 'We are all Christian Socialists now.'

The exact nature of Symes's views is a matter of vital importance to the present investigation. Was it true, as local newspaper editors and correspondents complained, that he was a socialist, an uncritical disciple of Henry George, and a partisan opponent of the government's Irish policy? Were his views extreme enough to justify dismissing him from his chair, as some of the complainants maintained? And, above all, is there any evidence that he modified his views or his public pronouncements in face of extra-mural pressure?

The primary purpose of this article is to provide answers to the first and third of these questions, both of which involve matters of fact. However, before turning to these matters it seems advisable to offer a few preliminary observations on the second question, which concerns the principle of academic freedom. The ideal of academic freedom – the professor's right to complete independence of thought and expression, his right to teach, investigate, and publish the results of his investigations without restraint – has become a major issue only during the past century, and its recent importance reflects both the expanding role of universities in our complex modern society and the growing public interest in university affairs. Although academic freedom may, at first sight, appear to be simply one limited aspect of a more general principle of free speech, the two freedoms have not invariably been co-existent; indeed, the modern interest in academic freedom derives from nineteenth-century Germany, where it conferred a privileged status on the professor precisely because universal freedom of speech was lacking. Even there it was largely confined to intramural freedom, and the professor's right to make extra-mural statements on political matters, for example, was either denied or hedged around with various qualifications. By contrast, in the USA, where general freedom of speech was regarded as an inalienable constitutional right, the professors naturally sought to extend the Germanic concept to include both extra- and intra-mural freedom of expression; but in a democratic community which valued thought less highly than action, and which had traditionally accorded a low status to public school teachers, this ideal was not easily attainable. It is here that we can see the pertinence of our Anglo-American comparisons, for however desirable extra-mural freedom may have seemed in principle, most American public and privately supported educational establishments were directly dependent on outside financial aid, and were therefore peculiarly sensitive to public criticism which might conceivably jeopardize their survival. In such circumstances as these, which applied with equal force to University College, Nottingham, the absolutist position that no professional utterance should be deemed censurable, however blasphemous, obscene, treasonable, radical, or partisan, could hardly be regarded as defensible. And once the general principle was qualified, it became no easy matter to determine exactly where the boundaries of discretion should be drawn, at least without some reference to local conditions. Possibly some set of principles akin to those enunciated by the American Association of University Professors in 1915 would have been appropriate to Nottingham in the 1880s.[9] But there was no comparable organization in Britain, partly because the academic community was dominated by the Oxford and Cambridge colleges, most of which were well-established, autonomous corporations governed by the teaching fellows themselves. The need for an academic freedom 'code' is, of course, a proof of the existence of intolerance, and it is all too easy to adopt a complacent attitude of superiority towards the American situation, based upon our long-cherished tradition of toleration, and the fact that our stable, hierarchical society has usually accorded the scholar a considerable measure of prestige and independence. Yet the following pages reveal that such a code, if recognized by the college authorities and the public, would have been both appropriate and desirable in Nottingham during the 1880s. And a reading of other official histories of provincial colleges suggests that only our customary reticence in dealing with such unsavoury matters has prevented historians from recognizing the importance of this problem in late-nineteenth-century British academic life.

III

These considerations are especially relevant to the case of Nottingham, for the problem of academic freedom tends to be acute in situations where a close relationship exists between the university or college and the public. The most important single feature of the early history of University College, Nottingham, was its direct dependence on the city corporation. From this unique fact stemmed most of its strengths and weaknesses. The Victorian corporation generally lacked what would nowadays be termed a favourable public 'image', and there is no reason why the average councillor should have possessed any grasp of university needs and potentialities. The initial proposal (aided by an anonymous donation of £10,000) to construct a building to accommodate the university extension lecture programme, quickly grew into a far more ambitious and costly project, and Professor Wood is surely right in supposing that the municipal authorities would never have supported the scheme had they recognized its full implications.

Like its counterparts in the USA, the embryonic Nottingham University suffered from the absence of good secondary educational facilities, and despite the earnest efforts of its teaching staff, comparatively little advanced work could be offered during the early years. Consequently, partisan critics inevitably made derogatory comparisons between the college and the local Mundella school,[10] and in 1882, when Oxford and Cambridge agreed to permit qualified Nottingham students of three years' standing to forego one year's residence for their own BA degree, nobody could deny that there was a wide gulf between the local college and the ancient foundations.

However, University College, Nottingham, made slower progress than other provincial colleges which encountered similar problems, and it seems clear that the primary obstacles were political and social rather than educational. On the basis of superficial comparisons, Nottingham might stand condemned as one of the less generous, public-spirited, and education-conscious of Victorian cities, for its university college was starved of local financial support, to say nothing of good will, until well into the present century.[11] Admittedly the lace industry was in difficulties during the depression of the 1880s, and the town contained many small businessmen rather than a few large-scale, wealthy entrepreneurs; but the same was true of Birmingham, whose college blossomed into a full university in 1900 with the aid of lavish local donations soon after the return of prosperity in the mid-1890s. Part of the explanation for Nottingham's backwardness undoubtedly lies in the reluctance of local worthies to support an institution maintained out of the rates, and thus, in a sense, to pay twice while subsidizing a municipal enterprise. But a more direct deterrent to potential donors was the consistent hostility and scepticism expressed by the *Nottingham Daily Guardian* (a Tory newspaper), the Liberal MP Colonel Seely (a prominent local coalowner), and by other local people.

Throughout the early years of the university's life, the corporation was dominated by a liberal–radical caucus, and the college unavoidably became identified with this viewpoint. Its activities as well as its reputation may have been decisively shaped by this connection, for in 1896–7, as well as in 1901–2, government inspectors praised it as 'the most democratic institution' and 'the nearest approach of all the colleges which we visited to a people's university'.[12] On one occasion, the editor of the radical *Nottingham Daily Express* explicitly rejected the notion that the college should prepare students for Oxford and Cambridge. Its principal function, he declared, should be to give 'the masses' opportunities for advanced technical training so that the ratepayers' initial outlay would ultimately be recompensed by an improvement in the quality and an increase in the sales of local manufactures![13] Symes himself recommended that class fees be fixed at the lowest possible level even at the expense of his own salary;[14] and there was an almost irresistible tendency to judge the success of any instructional venture by the numbers in attendance rather than by the quality of the work performed.

In accordance with the founder's wishes, the new buildings on Shakespeare Street housed a variety of day and evening classes of very diverse standards. But while fully utilizing the educational overhead, this practice inevitably blurred the distinction between the university college and other local educational institutions such as its predecessor, The Mechanics Institute, the local secondary schools, and the People's College. Moreover, the diversity of functions undoubtedly constituted one important source of friction between the c   on, the corporation-dominated committee of management, and the   ic staff. The corporation could not overlook the ratepayers' complaint that the enterprise did not 'pay'. The college was often described as 'a white elephant', and one memorable letter published during a municipal financial crisis angrily proposed that the land and buildings should be sold to fulfil the urgent need for a central railway station.[15] Another free enterpriser, who may indeed have known his Adam

Smith, suggested that the college should be let to the professors at a reasonable rent, whereupon – if their defenders were to be believed – they could soon 'retire with ample fortunes' derived from the proceeds of their public lectures. Everyone would then be pleased, for 'by allowing the college tub to sit on its own bottom' the ratepayers would be relieved of their financial burden.[16]

Needless to say, the academic staff took a very different view of the situation, and proposed quite different remedies. They felt aggrieved when the college was attacked during corporation meetings, especially when the newspapers printed adverse comments attributed to members of the committee of management, and although the Town Clerk had promised to withdraw from the committee and allow the professors to have 'full swing' before the college began its first classes, they lacked independence. From the outset 'the four professors had no official corporate capacity' and each took charge in turn on an informal basis. Even when a Board of Professors was created in 1887, with a Principal elected annually by the members, the position remained virtually unchanged, for the Board's powers were strictly limited and 'everything had to be submitted to the committee for its approval'.[17] Under more favourable circumstances these constitutional arrangements might have been matters of secondary importance. But as things were, the contentious Professor of Natural Sciences, the Rev. J. F. Blake, was probably justified in claiming that the lack of confidence in the Principal, and the unwillingness to grant him adequate powers, was a major reason for the institution's difficulties.[18] Similarly, the fact that the committee could cancel any appointment by giving six months' notice or paying six months' salary in lieu thereof 'without giving any specific reason for their action' was hardly calculated to enhance the professor's sense of security, and Symes cannot have failed to notice that on one occasion a hostile local editor remarked, in the course of a diatribe against his 'extreme socialistic opinions', that such 'mischievous nonsense' received attention only because of 'the *temporary* position held by the writer'.[19]

IV

It is now time to outline the nature and development of Symes's religious, economic, and social ideas, all of which became matters of public interest during the 1880s. Although this may appear to be a comparatively straight-forward task, the evidence is scanty, and both Symes's opinions and his allegiances were changing. His published statements were invariably couched in temperate, scholarly language; but his views were frequently unclear as he was inclined to sacrifice consistency in an effort to provide a fair statement of both sides of controversial questions. Thus, while he acquired a reputation for impartiality among his supporters, his moderate standpoint inevitably made him a target of attacks by extremists in both camps. It is impossible to say how far a prudent regard for the penalties of outspokenness, rather than conviction, temperament, or training may have dictated his approach. His daughter recalls that 'he had a deep distrust of rhetoric, and of purely emotional appeals',[20] and there was a marked contrast between Symes's measured detachment and the eager partisanship of his intimate friend, Stewart Headlam, whose courageous but reckless attacks upon established authority made him totally unacceptable to most orthodox churchmen and respectable members of society.

We must not, however, too readily dismiss Symes as a conventional academic figure. He openly supported various prominent radical organizations, occasionally becoming a vice-president or member of the executive council; his allegiances appeared to be shifting towards the socialists and extreme radicals during the 1880s; and for those who were content to rely on the principle of guilt by association, Symes's personal links with such notorious public figures as Headlam (a socialist clergyman), Charles Bradlaugh (the prominent atheist radical), and Henry George (the American land reformer), were sufficient to condemn him. At the very least, Symes's personal connections appear somewhat incongruous in one so detached and scholarly; and George Bernard Shaw, himself a militant socialist, brilliantly characterized Symes when, as he recalled, 'in my youthful Marxite bumptiousness I told him that he was in the position of the chaplain of a pirate ship'.[21]

During the late 1870s, when Symes was a curate at Stepney, he attended secularist meetings in company with his brother-in-law, George Sarson, and Headlam, and the three prepared and distributed heterodox pamphlets at the Church Congresses of 1877 and 1880.[22] On the latter occasion, Symes, who was then a schoolmaster at Newcastle-upon-Tyne, attracted considerable praise from a variety of quarters for his courageous speech in a discussion of 'Existing Forms of Unbelief'. It would be folly, Symes warned, to underestimate the strength and influence of the secularists, whose 'religion' by no means ignored 'the emotional or spiritual role of humanity. I speak from experience, having attended frequently at secularist meetings, having the honour of some slight acquaintance with Mr. Bradlaugh, Mrs. Besant, and other leaders of the movement. You will scarcely ever hear a lecture from them in which some appeal is not made to those emotions which we recognize as among the noblest of our nature.'[23]

Naturally enough, Symes's unexpected tribute was welcomed by Bradlaugh's weekly paper, *The National Reformer*, and within a month he had accepted an invitation to become a Vice-President of Bradlaugh's Land Law Reform League.[24] Symes was, of course, no atheist; he was only a mildly heterodox 'broad churchman', and his support for Bradlaugh's organization was probably little more than nominal. Yet his harmless gestures towards the secularists were sometimes misinterpreted, for he lectured periodically at secularist meeting houses, and on at least one occasion his concessions to the infidels were roundly attacked by a pamphleteer.[25] In this post-Darwinian period many believers were seriously disturbed by any signs of doctrinal laxity, especially on the part of clergymen, and there were doubtless some who reacted to Symes's views in a manner similar to a local lady who objected strongly when copies of the *Christian Socialist* were sent to her in error.[26]

Symes's involvement in the land reform agitation and the socialist movements of the 1880s was, however, far more important than his periodic efforts to instruct or to convert the secularists. His support for Bradlaugh's Land Law Reform League seems to have been purely nominal; indeed, the organization had only a short effective life, for public interest soon shifted from English to Irish land problems, while Bradlaugh himself became involved in a bitter, six-year struggle to gain admission to the House of Commons following his election victory at Northampton in 1880. Moreover the tide of reform opinion was shifting against him, for according to the leading Marxist socialist, Henry M. Hyndman, Bradlaugh was 'an individualist among individualists' who 'never lost a chance of speaking against socialism',[27] whereas within the next few years socialism was in full flood. Against this background, Symes's resignation from the Land Law Reform League in January 1884, on the grounds that his views had 'considerably altered',[28] appears to be symptomatic of a more general change of opinion, and it raises the question whether Symes should be classified as a socialist.

The term socialist had a far more vague and sinister connotation in the 1880s than it does today, and the central clues to Symes's position lie in his relationship with Henry George, a relationship which aroused the hostility of several of his most outspoken local critics. George, whose book *Progress and Poverty* exerted an enormous influence on British radical opinion at that time, was no socialist himself, but as one modern historian has aptly remarked, he 'furnished an intellectual bridge over which many people passed from individualism to socialism'.[29] Characteristically, Symes began the crossing but did not complete it, so that in this, as in so many other matters, his commitment was less than wholehearted.

Henry George's son, who wrote his father's official biography, declared that Symes's *Short Text Book of Political Economy* (which began its successful career in 1888 and eventually went into ten or eleven editions) was 'written from the single tax point of view' and he accordingly hailed its appearance as a 'striking sign' of the progress of the master's ideas among English economists.[30] This was an over-enthusiastic judgement, as George's latest biographer recognizes, for Symes was never an uncritical admirer.[31] Nevertheless, like many of his contemporaries, Symes was undoubtedly captivated by George's peculiar combination of religion, social radicalism, and Ricardian rent theory, and George's influence was probably the determining intellectual factor in shaping his economic ideas.

Symes met Henry George in London during the latter's first visit to these shores, probably through Headlam, who was an enthusiastic Georgite. When the Land Reform Union was founded in 1883 to propagate George's ideas, Symes became a member of the general executive committee, retaining that capacity after the organization was captured by the more dedicated Georgites in 1884, and renamed the English Land Restoration League.[32] Yet Symes was never an ardent proselytizer, despite his resignation from Bradlaugh's organization about the time of George's second coming, and it is worth noting that Nottingham lagged far behind Liverpool, Birmingham, Hull, and Newcastle as a provincial centre of Georgist agitation. We can only conjecture whether Symes's restraint is mainly attributable to his retiring, scholarly disposition, his reluctance to flaunt his allegiance before his local critics, or his serious reservations about George's proposals. These reservations are revealed in a letter written to George in November 1883, offering him hospitality should he decide to visit Nottingham during his forthcoming lecture tour, which was to be sponsored and financed by the Land Reform Union. *Progress and Poverty*, Symes remarked, had already made 'hundreds of converts', and yet its impact on amateur and scientific economists had been blunted because 'the general proposition of the tendency of rent to monopolize the limit of all advances seems too flagrantly opposed to the facts we see'.[33] In other words, while Symes defended George's proposal to tax land 'almost up to its full value as an ideal to be aimed at', he was fully aware of the difficulties of attaining this ideal, especially if the Georgist plan to introduce a sudden increase of land taxes were to be adopted. Such a policy would cause great hardship to landlords; it would discourage industry and thrift by undermining the security of property, and it would disrupt the prevailing pattern of demand for commodities and bring about great losses of previously invested skill and capital.[34] In his text book, which presumably reflected his mature deliberations on the subject, he claimed that although a land tax was in many respects the best form of taxation, and a tax on the 'unearned increment' of land would raise sufficient revenue 'to defray all the expenses of government', it would not be expedient in present circumstances. 'One of the hardest problems of statesmanship is to reconcile the legal rights established in the past, with the rights and interests of successive generations. To ignore the former would certainly involve serious economic evils, apart from the terrible hardships it would inflict on individuals.'[35]

This is the nub of the matter. Symes was both temperamentally and intellectually incapable of regarding land value taxation as a panacea. He advocated taxing the *annual* value of land, but not the *capitalized* value,[36] and he also advocated a progressively graduated income tax. Like Alfred Russell Wallace, the proponent of land nationalization,[37] Symes disapproved of George's unwillingness to compensate the landlords, and on this point his views resembled those of Alfred Marshall, the influential leader of the 'orthodox' Cambridge school of economics, who had attacked George at a famous meeting at Oxford University. Unlike Wallace, however, Symes opposed State ownership of landed property – that is, land nationalization in the strict sense of the term.

Thus, in respect of his attitude towards land taxes, Symes adopted a position which differed in degree, rather than in kind, from the central radical tradition of nineteenth-century English political economy, enunciating views which are directly traceable to James Mill in the 1820s. Broadly speaking, this was also true of his views on socialism. He went further than his contemporary, W. Stanley Jevons, towards the socialist position; yet he fell far short of Hyndman, Headlam, and William Morris. The theoretical basis of his objections to pure socialism were revealed in an extended comment on an article by the Fabian, Sydney Webb, entitled 'Henry George and Socialism', in which Symes denied that George was inconsistent because he refused to declare himself a socialist. The essential difference, Symes explained, was that the supply of land was fixed, whereas the supply of capital was not, so that there was an asymmetry between the 'law of rent' (the income from land) and the 'law of interest' (the income from capital). Taxation of land values would not reduce the effective supply of land, whereas a tax on capital would lead to a fall in the national capital stock and a flight of capital abroad.[38] Symes consistently adhered to this position throughout the 1880s, and it is easy to see why socialists regarded his radicalism as half-hearted, for even moderate reformers thought it unjust that land should be subjected to a growing burden while capital escaped scot free. One intelligent Nottingham newspaper critic complained, with partial justification, that 'Professor Symes's socialism is not the real thing at all, but only an impulsive sympathy with the theory', adding that Symes's 'vain attempts to reconcile socialism with political economy' led him to popularize socialist ideals while repudiating their doctrines.[39] More than twenty years later Symes himself conceded that the 'broad churchmen', in whose ranks he should be numbered, included both supporters and opponents of socialism, and claimed that the first test of any socialistic proposals should be their effect upon human character, whereas the material question of whether they would 'promote a juster distribution of wealth without unduly encroaching upon the total wealth that has to be distributed' was a secondary consideration.[40]

These remarks undoubtedly reflected Symes's deepest convictions, for he was shocked by the widespread poverty of the 1880s, and he regarded his proposals merely as an extension of existing government intervention, such as that embodied in the Factory Acts, the Education Acts, and the Poor Law. His most far-reaching recommendations were contained in a paper 'Socialism by Taxation', delivered before Headlam's clerical–socialist group, The Guild of St Matthew, of which Symes was, from time to time, a member of the executive council. On this occasion Symes considered various methods of raising revenue to finance social reforms (e.g. slowly rising land taxes and progressive income taxes), but his most novel suggestions concerned methods of relieving the hardships of the poor by public expenditures. Taxes on the value of working-class dwellings should be abolished, in order to reduce rents, and public money should be spent on improving these dwellings (which should then be let at competitive rents) and on providing one free meal a day for poor children from the ages of 5 to 12 years. Most drastic of all, however, he favoured the establishment of government workshops, on the lines of Louis Blanc's *Ateliers Nationaux* 'to mitigate the uncertainties of modern industrialism'. Under such a system, he admitted, 'the expense might *on the average* be greater than the waste involved in the existing industrialism', but averages were irrelevant, for the average income per capita in England was already supposed to be rising, despite the prevalence of abject poverty among 2 or 3 millions.[41]

From a theoretical viewpoint Symes's advocacy of government workshops contrasted strangely with his 'orthodox' rejection of the socialist case for taxes on capital. Of more immediate importance, however, was the local outburst provoked by reports of his views.[42] In subsequent years he never repeated his more radical proposals. But on more than one occasion he declared that the case for socialism became stronger as educational standards rose – a somewhat tendentious observation, coming from a prominent leader of local education; and he continued to advocate a redistribution of income in favour of the poor, and did not conceal his belief in the desirability of a growing measure of state interference in economic and social life. In the mid-1890s he made an ingenious and systematic effort to reconcile individualism and socialism by means of the formula: 'socialism for the young and old, individualism for the mature', arguing that aid to the young would reduce the inequality of opportunity and provide a firm foundation for competitive individualism among the mature. He offered this formula as a general basis for future policy rather than a rigidly enforceable plan, claiming that it would not necessarily imply 'an abandonment of either Individualism or Socialism as an ultimate ideal'.[43] Thus, once again, Symes offered a compromise which exposed him to criticism from both extremes.

V

What were the public reactions to Symes's views, and what were the effects of these reactions upon Symes himself, his colleagues, and the reputation and progress of the college?

Although the official history presents Symes as a somewhat unworldly character, he evidently realized on more than one occasion that his future was in jeopardy, and he can hardly have been indifferent to the repercussions of his public statements on the local attitude towards the college. In January 1884, his paper 'Socialism by Taxation' was the subject of a scathing editorial in the *Nottingham Journal*, a strong rebuke from a local

MP at the annual meeting of the Nottingham Chamber of Commerce, and a substantial newspaper correspondence.[44] In self-defence Symes wrote to the press and subsequently to the chairman of the Committee of Management, Leonard Lindley, claiming that he had carefully shown his students 'what I considered to be the chief fallacies' in *Progress and Poverty*, and pointing out that the Cambridge University examiner's report had given 'no hint of having discovered any trace of heretical opinions' in his lectures or among his students. Before taking any action, he concluded, the committee should consult the experts 'and not be influenced by the judgement of newspapers or the irresponsible talk of such people as Col. Seely'.[45]

This incident can hardly have enhanced the reputation of the college among local businessmen, and the same is true of a similar occurrence six months later, when the newspapers published reports of a sermon in which Symes deplored the low wage rates and evil working conditions endured by women employees in the frilling process, a branch of the Nottingham lace trade. On this occasion too, Symes considered it advisable to defend himself in print, remarking that although some employers were guiltless, 'the tremendous power which modern industrialism gives them is one which ought not to be left uncontrolled'.[46] As the government-appointed factory inspectors were overworked, and some employees were reluctant to report offences for fear of reprisals, he proposed that an unofficial Vigilance Committee should be established to maintain decent minimum working conditions. In the course of the ensuing discussion Symes's proposals met with a mixed reception. But it seems likely that his ideas were distasteful to employers in the lace industry, and Symes himself was held up to ridicule by a reporter in the *Nottingham Guardian*.[47]

Three years later Symes unintentionally became involved in a political issue when he delivered three public lectures on the Irish problem, which had been the subject of bitter controversy for several years. In the light of contemporary circumstances his criticisms of British government policy in Ireland seem extraordinarily restrained, and the published reports of his lectures give no indication of bias. Nevertheless, there was a violent protest from the editor of the Tory *Nottingham Guardian*. 'It is to be regretted,' he thundered, 'that Professor Symes should be permitted to use the University College for political purposes. The lectures he has delivered there have evidently been designed for the purpose of propagating Home Rule doctrines, and the statements in them have been grossly misleading, and in some cases positively inaccurate . . . in fact his whole statement is so discoloured as to be utterly misleading. It is only right that a protest should be raised against the use of University College for the purpose of political and party propaganda.'[48]

Once again a considerable discussion ensued in the local press, in the course of which the editor denied that he was accusing Symes of propagating Home Rule doctrines – despite the above-quoted passage! Nevertheless, the damage was done; and by arousing in turn the Chamber of Commerce, the lace employers, and the Tory voters Symes may, single-handedly, have checked the potential flow of donations into the college coffers. And as Professor Wood has shown, the lack of local generosity seriously impaired the chances of obtaining full university status in the early 1900s.

What were the effects of these experiences upon Symes himself? We can only conjecture; but it may be significant that by the time his textbook appeared in 1888, his tone had become more impartial and detached, and his policy proposals less startling, even though his organizational affiliations had become more radical. In part, of course, this is attributable to the fact that his book and his paper on socialism were designed for entirely different audiences; it was appropriate to exclude controversial questions which did not admit of a 'scientific treatment' when addressing elementary students, whereas the paper 'Socialism by Taxation' was presented to the members of Headlam's socialistic Guild of St Matthew. On the other hand, there is a distinct possibility that Symes consciously or instinctively reverted to a scholarly attitude in self-defence.

Early in 1887 he delivered three public lectures and conducted three separate discussion periods at the university on the subject of the current economic depression, and the press reports indicate that he carefully avoided the most contentious issues. On more than one occasion when highly controversial questions were raised, he retreated behind the shelter of his professional robes, refusing to discuss 'revolutionary proposals' or related issues 'except where political economy seemed to him to speak with some certainty'. It would obviously be unwise to attach too much significance to these remarks. But when there were complaints in the correspondence columns that the discussion following the first lecture 'was not a free one' Symes was reported, at the next meeting, as denying this charge, but admitting that 'he claimed the liberty of silence when he thought good for himself (Laughter and Applause)'.[49] Is it too much to detect, behind this casual remark, a certain sensitivity born of bitter experience, and even a prescient foreboding of the wrath to come? It is, indeed, arguable that Symes was mentally prepared for martyrdom, for in his first book he had written: 'The champion of an unpopular cause knows what it is to be sneered at, to be pointed out as a dangerous person, to be implored by friends and relations not to risk his position or his reputation, and to be suspected of mean and unworthy motives, even if the cry of "stone him" or "crucify him" be not raised for his destruction. And, do not suppose it is weakness which makes such a man shrink from abuse and misunderstanding, or which renders calumny and contempt more endurable than physical pain. Some of the greatest heroes have been also among the most sensitive men.'[50] Six months later he was under threat of dismissal, and in a letter to Mr Lindley he protested that his departure would neither 'tend to popularize the College' nor add to the enrolment, since 'the number of

students in classes *taught by me* is larger than that in all other three departments put together (excluding Government Science classes)'.[51] Yet there
was an element of irony in this argument, for we have Lord Snell's testimony that he and the Reverend C. H. Grinling (who had criticized from
his pulpit the prevailing level of wages in the local lace trade) had conspired
to swell Symes's classes by bringing in 'as many as possible of the young
political thinkers of the town' whose 'character must at times have caused
him some embarrassment'.[52] Here too a mere counting of heads could be
misleading.

As it transpired, Symes weathered the storm of public criticism, not only
retaining his chair, but becoming Principal in 1890. This constituted a less
dramatic transformation of his position than might appear on the surface,
for the Principal was at first merely the chairman of the Board of Professors
– a body possessing very limited powers.[53] Symes had always had his
defenders on the Committee of Management, but unfortunately, the available records give no clear indication of the reasons why he survived,[54] and
the fact that some of his colleagues were less fortunate only serves to deepen
the mystery.

In the official history, Professor Wood dealt at some length with several
disputes which occurred between members of the academic staff and the
committee of management during the 1880s – incidents which he regarded
as 'trivial in themselves', though they revealed an understandable *'gaucherie'*
on the part of the authorities.[55] Although they form part of the background
to the present study, these incidents need not be recounted here, for it is
hardly surprising to find that a group of local councillors lacked experience
in dealing with academic men. On the other hand, the case of William
Thompson, another victim of the 1887 financial crisis, whose name is absent
from the official history, is worth considering because it has an indirect
bearing on the Symes affair. Thompson was Symes's appointee; it was an
enquiry about Symes's duties which began the process that culminated in
Thompson's dismissal; and Symes's opinions and reputation may well have
had some influence on Thompson's fate.

Thompson's position was somewhat obscure.[56] From January 1883, until
the decision to 'dispense with his services' in July 1887, Symes had apparently engaged him annually as a 'volunteer lecturer' in English Language
and Literature, and although he had not been appointed by the Committee
of Management, Thompson's activities had been officially recognized in
the college calendar, in advertisements, and by the Cambridge University
authorities under whom he had served as a local extension lecturer.
Thompson's name was mentioned by the chairman of the Committee of
Management during a town council meeting in April 1887, in reply to a
questioner who enquired whether it was true that Professor Symes 'gave
only 4½ hours a week to his duties at the college';[57] and despite the
chairman's defence, the published report of the enquiry must have

prompted the question whether so under-employed a professor required any assistance! In July, Thompson suddenly learned of his fate from Symes, who wrote: 'I consider that you are entitled to be informed of the grounds of this decision. But I can only say that the committee were influenced by rumours that have reached them of the opinions you have expressed. No one disputed your competency as a teacher.'[58]

In an effort to exonerate himself, Thompson despatched a series of letters to the Mayor, the Town Clerk, and the chairman of the Committee of Management seeking a clear statement of the charges against him. These letters reveal the extraordinary anomalies of his position. According to the Town Clerk, his *locus standi* was merely that of 'a professor's friend'; no motion concerning him had been carried in the committee, and apparently nothing would prevent him from lecturing during the coming session, provided he were re-engaged.[59] This interpretation, Thompson protested, was 'diametrically opposed' to the situation as understood by Symes (who was then in Switzerland), and even if correct, it would represent an insufficient basis from which to plan his commitments for the ensuing year. 'The question is not a legal one, it is simply a question of dealing fairly and honourably'; the fact that the town council had reduced the college grant 'cannot be a reason for dismissing an unpaid lecturer, much less for dismissing him in such a way as to stigmatize him, making it difficult for him to get employment in his profession'. Thompson also objected strongly to the suggestion that he 'find a place more suitable than the college for the propagandism' of his views, maintaining that the only 'colouring' in his lectures came, unavoidably, from his basic 'mental attitude'. While making no secret of his own opinions, Thompson concluded, he held 'very strongly (with regard to colleges supported by national or local taxes) that those who are on the staff ought not to be questioned on such matters by the college authorities, excepting insofar as their opinions may affect (1) teaching (2) conduct, in matters of ordinary morality'.[60]

It was natural enough for Thompson to interpret his dismissal as a matter of principle, but it is not clear that the principle at stake was one of academic freedom. As in the case of Mr Solomon in Classics, the most glaring weakness lay in the absence of precise terms of appointment. He was evidently close to Symes, if not as close as may be suggested by the expression 'professor's friend', and there is little reason to doubt that the attacks on Symes initiated the inquiry which eventually sealed Thompson's fate. There is little evidence as to Thompson's opinions, although one of his contributions to the *Church Reformer* reveals that he shared Symes's concern for the hardships of the poor and his desire for reform.[61] On the other hand, the Committee was under great pressure to reduce the cost of running the college, and they naturally sought to economize by removing the marginal men.

In any event, Thompson's protests proved unavailing. The Town Clerk denied him the right to publish both sides of the correspondence and, possibly for the same reason, the local newspaper editors also denied him an outlet in their columns. There is no evidence that the Committee of Management granted Thompson's request that the case be investigated in the presence of representatives from Oxford and Cambridge, who were official members of the Committee. Some friends helped him to publish his own side of the correspondence privately, and the affair was mentioned in the *Leeds Mercury*.[62] But in view of local censorship, that was as far as the matter went.

VI

This has, inevitably, been a somewhat inconclusive story, for it is rarely possible to provide a wholly satisfactory explanation of an affair of this kind. Even in the most fully documented cases there are gaps in the evidence, unfathomable motives, and conflicts of testimony. Nevertheless, it is possible to give definite answers to two of the questions raised above, and there need be little doubt about the answer to the third, even though we cannot be certain.

The foregoing review of Symes's ideas and published expressions of opinion demonstrates that he was certainly no extremist, and there is no legitimate definition of academic freedom which could have justified his dismissal. On the other hand, it seems very likely that he moderated his public statements, if not his personal opinions, as a result of external pressure, and doubtless he was as much concerned for the welfare of the college as for his personal security. In Thompson's case there is more than a suspicion that his association with Symes, as well as his opinions, made him a suitable victim of the economy axe, and if this is so it means that there were limitations on intra-mural as well as extra-mural freedom of expression. In any case, one is safe in concluding that in an institution so precariously situated and so closely linked with the community as University College, Nottingham, in the early 1880s, a professor like Symes, whose duties required him to give public lectures on topics of intense public interest at a time of bitter social and political conflict, could hardly expect to enjoy that inner peace of mind which is the indispensable prerequisite of genuine academic freedom.

NOTES

* I am indebted to my wife, Sonia E. Coats, who undertook extensive preliminary research in the University records and Nottingham newspapers; to Ann Fro-shaug, who discovered and examined additional source materials, and made several valuable suggestions; to the University and City of Nottingham library staffs; and to several other persons who either read an earlier version of this article or responded to inquiries.

1 A. C. Wood, *A History of the University College, Nottingham, 1881–1948* (Oxford, 1953), p. 51. In view of my heavy reliance on this volume, I have made few detailed citations.

2 R. Hofstadter and W. Metzger, *The Development of Academic Freedom in the United States* (New York, 1955) and R. McIver, *Academic Freedom in Our Time* (New York, 1955) are especially relevant to the present study. See also P. F. Lazarsfeld and W. Thielens, Jr, *The Academic Mind: Social Scientists in a Time of Crisis* (Glencoe, Ill., 1958); T. Caplow and R. J. McGee, *The Academic Marketplace* (New York, 1961); and the post-1945 volumes of the *Bulletin of the American Association of University Professors*.

3 Cf. W. H. G. Armytage, *Civic Universities* (London, 1955), p. 226.

4 Briefly, *Lehrfreiheit* referred to the professor's freedom of teaching and inquiry, and *Lernfreiheit* to the student's freedom to study what and where he chose, without administrative control. Cf. Hofstadter and Metzger, op. cit., pp. 383ff. In the following pages I have drawn freely upon this valuable source.

5 R. H. Kolbe, *Urban Influences on Higher Education in England and the United States* (Macmillan, 1928) contains some suggestive comparisons.

6 From a Memorial to the University of Cambridge, dated 10 June, 1879, reproduced in the University College Minute Book, vol. 1. It also was suggested that the teaching staff should hold office in Cambridge or should freely circulate between the two centres.

7 Apart from the character sketch on pp. 37–40 of Professor Wood's study, valuable glimpses of Symes's personality and career can be found in Lord (Henry) Snell, *Men, Movements and Myself* (London, 1938), and in F. G. Bettany, *Stewart Headlam: A Biography* (London, 1926). None of Symes's personal papers or correspondence has survived, and local inquiries have proved fruitless.

8 Hoftstadter and Metzger, op. cit., pp. 423ff.

9 Among other provisions, this code stated that the professor should refrain from indoctrinating immature minds; he should 'present scientific truth with discretion'; his conclusions should be 'gained by a scholar's method and held in a scholar's spirit', and they should be set forth with 'dignity, courtesy and temperateness of language'. While extra-mural freedom of speech was demanded, it was pointed out that 'academic teachers are under a peculiar obligation to avoid hasty or unverified or exaggerated statements, and to refrain from intemperate or sensational modes of expression'. In contrast to the German view that political partisanship was incompatible with objective inquiry, the American code remained non-committal. Hofstadter and Metzger, op. cit., pp. 407–12.

10 Examples of this can be found in the local press as late as January, 1911.

11 In 1910 a new wave of controversy arose, in the course of which many earlier arguments were re-hashed. One frequent correspondent, 'Civis', declared that because of the expenditures involved 'The college will do well to drop the proposal to turn itself into a university. It is a wild chimerical idea.' He added that 'Nottingham comes out miserably' by comparison with other cities, since both the college and the Castle Museum had 'completely failed to appeal to the generosity of Nottingham's richest citizens'. *Nottingham Guardian*, 18 and 11 Jan., 1911. Also Wood, op. cit., pp. 47–61.

12 Wood, op. cit., p. 42.

13 *Nottingham Daily Express*, 27 Oct., 1884.

14 See Symes's 'Report on the Scheme of Instruction', 11 June, 1881, in the University Manuscripts; see also the slightly different reports by Professors Blake and Fleming for 1881–2.

15 'There is no town in the Midlands, probably not in England, which is so much in need of a central railway station as Nottingham. . . . By all means pay back to the mistaken donor his £10,000, although he richly deserves to lose it. The "University" has been a miserable failure from the beginning, and moreover, like all other folly it has been, is, and will be costly – abominably and unfairly costly – to the already overburdened ratepayers of this town. Let the building and site be devoted to a purpose which shall be to the increased convenience and profit of the community, not an elephantine burden and crushing nightmare.' 'Civis', in the *Nottingham Guardian*, 19 July, 1887.

16 'Senex' in *Nottingham Guardian*, (?) July, 1887. (This letter is included in a book of press cuttings in the University Mss.) This writer cited Alderman Cropper's description of the college as 'A fraud upon public credulity', claimed that Councillor Sands 'feels very uneasy at being on the College Committee' and cited a local machine builder's opinion that the workshop teaching in the college was 'worse than useless'.

17 Wood, op. cit., p. 34. The Town Clerk's proposal appears in a letter to Symes dated 8 Aug., 1881, in a letter book in the University Mss.

18 *Nottingham Daily Express*, 20 Dec., 1887. Blake, who was then under threat of dismissal, claimed that Symes endorsed this opinion.

19 *Nottingham Journal*, 19 Jan., 1884. Italics supplied. The terms of appointment were set out in a report to the Town Council, dated 7 Feb., 1881, in University Mss.

20 In a private communication from Miss Eleanor Symes dated 16 Jan., 1963.

21 Bettany, op. cit., p. 54. Slightly different versions of this anecdote appear in Archibald Henderson, *George Bernard Shaw: His Life and Works* (Cincinnati, 1911), p. 48, and in the later edition, *George Bernard Shaw: Man of the Century* (New York, 1956), p. 800.

22 Bettany, op. cit., pp. 39, 52–4, 84–5.

23 *The Official Report of the Church Congress Held at Leicester*, 1880, p. 325. There is a striking contrast between Symes's tactful refusal to speak about certain burning theological questions, and Headlam's blunt statement of his radical views on these same issues. Ibid., pp. 650–1. The President of the Congress, the Lord Bishop of Peterborough, praised Symes's 'able and manly speech', p. 355, whereas other discussants objected to Headlam's remarks.

24 *The National Reformer*, XXXV (1880), 276–7, 327. For criticism of Symes's views, and his reply, Ibid., 307–8, 364. As *The National Reformer* misprinted Symes's name as 'the Rev. H. Symes', and 'the Rev. J. E. Syme' (on 31 Oct. and 7 Nov., 1880, respectively), there is some danger of confusing him with his contemporaries, the prominent Birmingham secularist contributor to that journal, Joseph Symes, and the economist David Syme. H. M. Lynd's excellent study *England in the 1880's* (London, 1945), p. 143, makes confusion worse confounded by referring to him as the Rev. J. E. Tymes.

25 H. Sulley, *The Bible Defended from Religious Unbelief* (1884). This pamphlet discusses four lectures, one delivered by the 'Rev.' Professor Symes MA, at St Mary's Church, Nottingham. Complaining that Symes conceded so much to the secularists that he pleased them as much as Bradlaugh, the reviewer cited one commentator who remarked, somewhat ambiguously, that 'if all Christians were noble characters like Professor Symes, secularism would have won the day, and they would never have to fight against Christianity'. Symes's own views were subsequently stated in his volume, *Broad Church* (London, 1913).

26 'In answer to the enclosed post card, Mrs. Davidson begs to say she never ordered the Christian Socialist to be sent to her, whoever ordered it must pay

for it – Mrs. Davidson was much annoyed at such a publication being sent to her, and had she known from whence it came she would have written to forbid it. After looking at the first number the succeeding ones were put into the fire without being opened. She considers such a publication being sent to her is a very great liberty, and that such disgraceful writings being disseminated among the people by those who ought to know better, is enough to bring a judgment on England, and no doubt to those who work such evil, evil will be meted out in full measure, if not in this world, certainly in the next.' This letter, from Sneinton Manor House, Nottingham, was reprinted in *The Christian Socialist*, III (Oct., 1885), 75. Symes occasionally contributed to this journal, and his lectures and books were reviewed in its pages.

27 H. M. Hyndman, *The Record of an Adventurous Life* (London, 1911), pp. 309–10. For details of Bradlaugh's career see H. B. Bonner, *Charles Bradlaugh* (London, 1908). (This is the seventh edition.)

28 *The National Reformer*, XLIII (1884), 58.

29 Lynd, op. cit., p. 143. See also Elwood P. Lawrence, 'Uneasy Alliance: The Reception of Henry George by British Socialists in the Eighties', *American Journal of Economics and Sociology*, XI (1951), 61–74, also his book *Henry George in the British Isles* (East Lansing, 1957).

30 Henry George, Jr, *The Life of Henry George* (New York, 1900), p. 513.

31 Charles A. Barker, *Henry George* (Oxford, 1955), pp. 524, 673.

32 The best contemporary source of information on these two organizations is Headlam's journal, *The Christian Socialist*, espec. I (June, 1883), Supplement; and II (June, 1884), 12–13.

33 This letter, dated 22 Nov., 1883, is in the Henry George collection in the New York Public Library. The collection contains scarcely any references to the activities of Nottingham Georgists.

34 J. E. Symes, 'Socialism by Taxation', *The Church Reformer*, III (Jan., 1884), 2–6.

35 J. E. Symes, *A Short Textbook of Political Economy* (London, 1888), pp. 187–8. Neither Henry George nor his book was mentioned in this volume.

36 Symes, *Nottingham Daily Express*, 24 Jan., 1884; 'Socialism by Taxation', op. cit., p. 5; he also advocated compensation in a lecture on 'Socialism', see *Nottingham Daily Express*, 12 Dec., 1887.

37 For Wallace's views, see his *Land Nationalization: Its Necessity and Aims* (London, 1892), chap. VIII.

38 Symes, letter on 'Henry George and Socialism', *The Church Reformer*, VIII (Feb., 1889), 40. For another Symes–Webb exchange, in which the latter criticized the 'orthodoxy' of Symes's textbook, Ibid., VIII (July, 1889), 156–7.

39 Richard Simon, *Nottingham Daily Express*, 14 Dec., 1887. Simon who wrote several moderately critical letters, found it difficult to reconcile Symes's condemnation of land confiscation with his advocacy of increasing land taxes 'finally absorbing the whole'. However, the central dilemma was posed by Goddard Orpen in his translation of Emile de Laveleye's *The Socialism of Today* (London, 1885), pp. 299–300, when he observed that 'without compensation, nationalization of the land is flagrantly unjust and quite hopeless; with compensation, its benefits are remote and doubtful'.

40 Symes, *Broad Church*, pp. 115–16.

41 An analysis of this paper appeared in Laveleye, op. cit., pp. 367–9. For local reports and comments, mostly hostile, see *Nottingham Journal*, 18, 19, 21, 22, 23, 24, 26, 29 Jan., 1884; also *Nottingham Daily Express*, 22, 23, 24 Jan., 1884.

42 See below, section V.

43 Symes, 'An Eirenikon to Socialists and Individualists', *The Westminster Review* CXLII (1894), 644–9.

44 The editor deplored Symes's 'extreme Socialistic opinions', his ardent support of Henry George, and his 'extreme hatred of the middle and upper classes', especially property owners. Teachers and clergymen who attacked property, he warned, 'must be prepared to sustain all the well-directed blows which will fall on their heads in the heat of socialistic controversy', *Nottingham Journal*, 19 Jan., 1884. A few days later Col Seely MP, with reference to Symes, spoke of the 'iniquity' of property taxes, and declared that Symes's employment plan was 'the most fatal and dangerous step which could be taken by any nation', Ibid., 23 Jan., 1884; and the ensuing correspondence, especially J. Fletcher, 29 Jan., 1884. The *Nottingham Daily Express* also reported Col Seely's remarks, but without editorial comment. On 25 Jan., 1884, *The Church Times* commented that Symes's 'formula of taking from the rich and giving to the poor' was 'a plagiarism from R[obin] Hood, who, after all, was a thief'.

45 Symes to Lindley, 5 Feb., 1884, in University Mss. On 24 Jan., 1884, Symes had protested, in letters to the *Nottingham Journal* and the *Nottingham Daily Express*, that Seely had misrepresented him, and also claimed, on the authority of Henry Sidgwick's *Principles of Political Economy*, that 'a gradual advance in the direction of the Socialist ideal is not opposed to the principle of distributive justice, or of sound political economy'. A subsequent correspondent to the *Nottingham Journal*, writing under the pseudonym 'Anti-Spoilation', on 26 Jan., 1884, questioned both the accuracy and the legitimacy of Symes's citation. It is noteworthy that a controversy about the inclusion of George's *Progress and Poverty* in the list of political economy text books in use at the City of London College was then in progress. Earl Fortescue, a Vice-Patron of the college, resigned in protest, and shortly thereafter the Principal (whose name, appropriately enough, was Richard Whittington) declared that the book was included with the aim of exposing its fallacies, and thereby reducing its harmful effects upon the students. But, he conceded: 'It may, however, in future, to avoid misunderstanding of the subject, be deemed advisable to exclude the book from the list of textbooks.' See *The Times*, 29 Jan., 5 and 12 Feb., 1884.

46 *Nottingham Journal*, 4 June, 1884. Also Ibid., 6, 11 June, 1884; and *Nottingham Daily Express*, 6 June 1884.

47 On 7 June, 1884, the *Nottingham Guardian*'s 'Special Commissioner', who announced that 'the soul of the professor is in revolt', toured various factories and found no evidence of the evils described in Symes's sermons. Moreover, after recording that one employee threatened to give any Vigilance Committee 'the length of her tongue', he concluded that it was 'not an edifying sight' to contemplate this academic 'champion of the ladies . . . who should be dignified and practical, ignobly tilting at windmills'.

48 *Nottingham Guardian*, 26 Nov., 1887; also Ibid., 25, 26, 29, 30 Nov., and the defence of Symes in the *Nottingham Daily Express*, 1 Dec., 1887, under 'Current Topics'.

49 This remark was reported in the *Nottingham Guardian*, 5 Feb., 1887. On 1 Feb., in the course of discussion of the first lecture, he was reported as saying that 'he wishes to disclaim the idea that a professor of political economy was bound to answer every question (Applause)'; on 9 Feb., that 'it would not take much courage to denounce the drink traffic, but this is not the place to discuss that question'; and on 12 Feb., that 'he had tried to keep clear of controversy except where political economy seemed to him to speak with some certainty'.

About this time, 'orthodox' economists were placing more emphasis on the methodological dictum that economics, as a science, is concerned with 'what is', not with 'what ought to be'. Nevertheless, many ethical value judgements appeared in Symes's *Short Text Book*. For example, although he could not consider the pros and cons of the existing provisions for the poor, 'at least it ought to be acknowledged as a blot on our civilization that we do not see our way clear to doing anything in these directions by State action' (p. 177). Statements of this kind, which abound in his writings, testify to the difficulties of reconciling humanitarianism and scientific detachment.

50 *Newcastle Sermons on Theology and Life* (London, 1882), p. 70.

51 Symes to Lindley, 2 July, 1887, in University Mss.

52 Lord Snell, op. cit., pp. 66–7.

53 Wood, op. cit., p. 34. Professor Wood has suggested that 'Symes' political indiscretions' may help to explain why he was 'passed over' when the Principalship was established in 1887. Ibid., p. 39.

54 Unfortunately neither the records of the Town Council, the Committee of Management, nor the Minutes of the Board of Professors shed any light on this question, and as far as can be ascertained, none of the leading participants left any significant collection of unpublished papers.

55 Wood, op. cit., p. 41. Also pp. 35–41 where the cases of Professor J. F. Blake and Mr J. Solomon are discussed. Several of Blake's letters, which severely criticized the management of the college and made gloomy prognostications about its future, appeared in the press. Mr Solomon's official status in Classics was akin to that of William Thompson in English.

56 The evidence in this case is limited and somewhat onesided – though what there is is plausible and entirely consistent with other, well-documented observations about the contemporary situation. The evidence consists of (a) press reports of the Town Council meetings; (b) two letters from Thompson to Leonard Lindley, Chairman of the Committee of Management; a draft letter (probably from Lindley to Thompson); and copies of University advertisements bearing Thompson's name, etc., all in the University Mss; (c) Thompson's fifteen-page printed leaflet, containing copies of eight of his communications addressed to the Mayor, Town Clerk, and University Registrar. This is in the Local Collection, City Library, Nottingham. There is, therefore, little direct evidence from the official side.

57 *Nottingham Journal*, 5 Apr., 1887.

58 This letter, dated 16 July, 1887, is reproduced in Thompson's leaflet in Nottingham City Library.

59 Thompson to Lindley, 19 Sept., 1887, University Mss. Also Thompson to S. G. Johnson (Town Clerk), 24 Aug., 1887, in Thompson's leaflet.

60 Thompson to Johnson, 26 Aug., and 23 July, 1887, in Thompson's leaflet. It should be noted that Thompson was not entirely correct in rejecting the explanation that his dismissal was an economy measure. Although he received no direct payment from the college he collected class fees which, after his dismissal, could have been added to the college income provided that his class was conducted by a salaried professor (e.g. Symes) whose income remained constant.

61 W. Thompson, 'The Plumage and the Bird', *The Church Reformer*, IV (Nov., 1885), 241. In this note, Thompson commented on the currently sensational child prostitution case, involving Eliza Armstrong and the reformist editor of the *Pall Mall Gazette*, W. T. Stead. Thompson blamed society in general for

permitting the poverty, luxury, and idleness which produced such evils. Cf. Frederic Whyte, *The Life of W. T. Stead* (New York, 1925), i, chap. viii.

62 On 9 Sept., 1887, according to Thompson. See his letter to Lindley, 19 Sept., 1887, in University Mss.

17

THE ORIGINS AND EARLY DEVELOPMENT OF THE ROYAL ECONOMIC SOCIETY

I

The year 1890 has long been acknowledged as an important turning-point in the history of British economic thought because it witnessed the publication of Marshall's epoch-making *Principles of Economics*, a volume that quickly gained international recognition as a major contribution to the subject, and which was rightly regarded as marking the recovery of British economics from the stultifying influence of Mill's *Principles* and the debilitating methodological controversies of the 1870s and 1880s. Yet, if one attaches importance to the activities as well as the ideas of economists, the inauguration of the British Economic Association (later the Royal Economic Society) at University College London on November 20 – a few days after the climax of the Baring financial crisis – demands recognition as a more significant indication of the state of the subject.

The founding of the BEA obviously met a long-felt need, for the organization rapidly acquired a sizeable and impressive membership, and its publication, the *Economic Journal*, soon became established as the leading British organ of professional economic opinion. Several accounts of its beginnings and early development have appeared in this *Journal*,[1] and the present essay supplements the published record by drawing on the Association's archives and some unpublished letters, and re-examines its role in late-nineteenth- and early-twentieth-century British economics.

II

The story begins well before the inaugural meeting, for Herbert Somerton Foxwell, one of the founder-members, had already announced in the Harvard *Quarterly Journal of Economics* in 1887 that an 'economic society' was to be formed 'with the hearty co-operation of the leading English economists' and a quarterly 'economic journal' that would be issued and probably edited from Cambridge under the direction of Professor Marshall. The project was 'well advanced', though not definitely assured; and as it had

313

been 'mature in the minds of the projectors for some time' it was 'scarcely doubtful that we shall shortly follow the lead so ably set us on your side of the Atlantic' (i.e., by the founding of the American Economic Association in September 1885).[2] Foxwell added that the projectors proposed to 'undertake a series of reprints and translations, and compile a dictionary' in addition to the journal, and these comments provide clues to the authorship of the scheme, enabling us to trace its origins back to 1885.

Foxwell's correspondence with R. H. Inglis Palgrave, which has recently come to light, reveals that the proposed 'economic society' was an outgrowth of Palgrave's plan for a Reprint Society which would publish translations and reprints of scarce economic works.[3] Foxwell strenuously advocated the more ambitious scheme because it would permit them to 'fraternize with the American [Economic] Association' in their publishing ventures,[4] and after protracted discussions this course was adopted. Why was it thought necessary to launch a new society, when any one of three existing bodies could conceivably have formed the nucleus of a scholarly economic organization comparable to the American Economic Association: the Political Economy Club of London; Section F (Economics and Statistics) of the British Association for the Advancement of Science; and the London (from 1887, the Royal) Statistical Society? Of these, only the last seems to have been seriously considered, presumably because the first was a long-established private club with fixed traditions and a pro-free-trade reputation, and the second was too amorphous and occasional – meeting as it did only annually, in widely scattered places, before miscellaneous audiences composed largely of members of the general public.[5] The Statistical Society presented a more attractive prospect: it had long been associated with economic and social inquiries; both Foxwell and Palgrave were members of its council; and many prominent economic writers were already members. Moreover, as Foxwell pointed out, the Society had already declared its intention, once the number of Fellows increased, 'to publish standard works on Economic Science and Statistics, especially such as are out of print or scarce'.[6]

In his first letter to Palgrave Foxwell had remarked that Marshall favoured the idea of transforming the Statistical Society into a 'Society for Economic Science and Statistics', and a number of unsuccessful moves were made in this direction during the next two years. In November 1885 Mr Hyde Clarke, a member of the Council, had proposed that the Statistical Society should hold periodical Economic meetings, and Foxwell reported that

> many of us have wanted this for a long time. It would double the public interest in the Society. I suppose the objection will be that too much prominence may be given to the speculative as opposed to the positive element. I don't think this impossible to be avoided.[7]

314

Yet Foxwell himself had doubts about the wisdom of any proposal to work through the Statistical Society as an alternative to founding a new body, although he added that Marshall and others were anxious that the Society

> should develop the Economic side of its operations. It would be good for Statistics, as giving them the theoretic basis they require, if they are to be intelligent; and it would be good for economics as encouraging the use of the inductive and historical methods.

His main objection, however, was that

> the idea of a Society which takes as its province any investigations carried on by a statistical or numerical method is absurd and anomalous. If logically carried out; it should include those researches in Astronomy, Physics, Meteorology, Physiology, Chemistry, etc ad infinitum – which happen to make use of this method . . . what we should certainly aim at is the ultimate approach to some rational consistent conception of the Society's province. It must be confined to economic and social science. . . . Is there any parallel in the whole range of the sciences, for the selection of some special method of treatment? We shall be having an Electric measurement Society next: or a Spectroscopic Society, or a Drum Tracer Society. . . .
>
> Practically it is still a greater mistake – for it alienates from the Statistical Society a large number of educated persons interested in economic and social science: and on the other hand the Society is filled with mere men of figures, a large number of whom, as the Council has lately observed with concern, use their membership simply as a trade advertisement, and seriously endanger the reputation of the Society.
>
> The remedy for this seems to me to be that the Society should revert more nearly to its original ideal. Its first object was the study of the condition of the people: and its first papers were almost wholly economic.

Unless the Statistical Society's membership could be broadened, to accommodate the extension of its economic activities, Foxwell believed that it could not serve as a substitute for a proper economic association.

> It is very cliquey, and too full of business men: I mean of mere men of business of course, for a businessman may be as educated as anyone else. It is extremely difficult to obtain a hearing for anything new; even for the scientific handling of the idolized method itself: and the Society seems likely to perish from sheer dulness.[8]

There is no way of knowing whether Foxwell's views were typical, but they vividly convey one informed opinion of the problem. As it transpired, there was resistance from within the Society itself, for although Mr Hyde Clarke's motion in favour of holding a monthly economic meeting was passed, it provoked such opposition that Foxwell termed it 'rather a Pyrrhic victory'.

> I was I confess surprised at the temper and the ignorance shown in the discussion. The majority of members seem to make the question personal, though what interest they had in it was hard to discover: and I found that the prevailing idea of Political Economy was that it was made up of tabular statistics and party politics! It was almost hopeless to discuss the question before such an audience. I merely pointed out that Jevons, who was so far from being a partisan that I never gathered for which party he would vote, and who is generally regarded as our most scientific economist, was driven to the Monthlies or to private arrangements for the publication of three fourths of his work. The answer given was two fold.
>
> (1) The Society is already economic and would publish anything good.
>
> (2) It isn't and oughtn't to be economic, because political economy is mere a priori partisan disputation.[9]

Unfortunately at this point the flow of Foxwell's long and entertaining letters temporarily dried up, and the hope of converting the Statistical Society appears to have been abandoned – although there were periodic negotiations during the 1890s. The decision to form an economic society may have been taken late in 1886 when J. N. Keynes, who had participated in the earlier discussions, reported that the Cambridge Syndics were unlikely to undertake the reprints, and concluded that it was essential to form a society – adding that he was personally much less interested in the publication of reprints than Foxwell or Palgrave. The movement for an association soon gained momentum, for in January 1887 Foxwell informed Palgrave that John Biddulph Martin, a partner in the well-known banking family, had written

> of his own accord to say that he thinks there is room for an Economic Society alongside of our Statistical Society, and that he is ready to do what he can to assist its formation. He has been reading the account of the American Economic Association.[10]

Martin's suggestion is noteworthy, because he was on the councils of the Statistical Society and the British Association, and could therefore act as a go-between, and he eventually became the first Treasurer of the British Economic Association.

At this point it seemed that the stage was set for the new organization, but in fact three more years were to elapse before the decisive action was taken in the spring of 1890. Unfortunately the reasons for this delay are still obscure, for the available evidence is inconclusive and in part conflicting;

nevertheless, a number of possible explanations can be offered. One was the difficulty of obtaining a suitable editor, for as Foxwell informed Palgrave:

> If Keynes could have seen his way to edit it, we should have started it here last December [i.e. 1887?]. Now, they seem to be on the verge of starting it in Oxford. But we don't find it so easy to get an Editor – any number of men with strong views will volunteer, but these are just the persons we don't want. We want cool heads, keen brains, and impartial judgment. With these are required scholarship, information, and if possible knowledge of German. It seems to me a most difficult and delicate post.[11]

Another factor was Marshall's hesitancy, and his influence was important, since he was the acknowledged leader among the academic economists. Admittedly Marshall drafted the formal letter of invitation to the inaugural meeting and took the lead on that occasion; but this was mainly because he was acting under a sense of duty as President of Section F of the BAAS, an office which he held by virtue of his intellectual eminence rather than his energy and constructive leadership,[12] and he then confessed that

> He was not one of those who thought that they should have started this movement very long ago. . . . He had been rather in the position of an old fogey, and he had doubted whether it would be possible to maintain a journal at a high level of excellence.[13]

Even after the Association was formed, he continued to favour an amalgamation with the Statistical Society, and it would be peculiarly appropriate if the two most memorable economic events of 1890 – the founding of the BEA and the first appearance of Marshall's *Principles* – occurred in that year largely because of his excessive caution.

George Bernard Shaw offered an interesting clue to the problem when he recalled that

> For some years I attended the Hampstead Historic Club once a fortnight, and spent a night in the alternate weeks at a private circle of economists which has since blossomed into the British Economic Association – a circle where the social question was left out, and the work kept on abstract scientific lines.[14]

But this reminiscence merely complicates matters. The so-called 'Economic Circle', which met at the house of the stockbroker Henry Raimé Beeton, who was a close personal friend of such economists as Phillip Wicksteed and Foxwell, played an important part in the formation of Fabian economic ideas; and at its meetings, Shaw recalls 'the conditions were practically university conditions', and Jevons' theory of utility was one of the principal topics of debate. Its members included Wicksteed, Foxwell, Edgeworth, G. Armitage Smith and, less frequently, Marshall and William Cunningham, in addition to the Fabians Shaw, Sidney Webb and Graham Wallas; and we are told that its meetings led to the formation of the Economic Club in 1889, which was 'organized mainly at the instance of Alfred Marshall'.[15]

It may never be possible either to prove a direct connection between Henry Beeton's 'Economic Circle' and the foundation of the BEA or to explain fully the reasons for the delay in forming the latter. Indeed, this delay may appear trivial now, but at the time it might well have proved fatal, for while Marshall (and possibly others) hesitated, a group of clergymen at Oxford went ahead with their plans to produce a quarterly *Economic Review* under the auspices of the Christian Social Union, which first appeared in print only two months before the *Economic Journal* began its career. As early as November 10, 1885, Foxwell had mentioned to Palgrave that 'from Oxford a proposal is made to start an Economic Monthly Review', and later that month he disclosed that three such proposals were under discussion, adding 'I am not sure that Cunningham may not spring a first number on us by surprise some fine day.'[16] Even so, when the *Economic Review* eventually materialized it apparently took the founder-members of the BEA completely by surprise, for as Martin wrote to Palgrave on July 14, 1890:

> Cunningham dined with us last week, and astonished me by telling me of the proposed Economic Journal, of which he sent me his circular the next day. I very much wonder how it was that Marshall and the rest of us have never heard of it. I had formed the same idea as yourself that not much good will come of mixing religion and economic subjects and I did not notice among the promoters any name of which I know much.[17]

At the inaugural meeting of the BEA Marshall put up a brave front, saying that had their own *Economic Journal*

> been started a little time ago, the announcement that the Oxford University branch of the Christian Union [*sic*] was going to bring out an *Economic Review* would have caused them some dismay. But, as things now were, he thought they were strong enough to support both journals.[18]

However, a few days earlier, in a private letter to L. R. Phelps of Oriel College, Oxford, one of the *Review*'s three editors, he had confided:

> I desire the success of your journal, as you originally described the aims to me, almost as much as that with which I am more directly concerned. But undoubtedly the way would have been easier for us if you had been able to adopt a title which suggested that the two journals were designed to meet different wants, to supplement one another and not to compete with one another.[19]

On the whole, Marshall described the *Review* accurately when he said it was started 'for the purpose of dealing with problems in which ethical and religious questions took the first place, but which had a kernel of economic difficulty in the background',[20] so that it assumed a broad, somewhat amorphous character throughout its twenty-five years. Yet a layman who examined the early numbers of these two journals would not detect any great differences: their style and format were similar; there were fewer theoretical and technical articles in the early issues of the *Journal*; and its initial policy was to welcome contributions from representatives of all 'schools' of thought.[21]

III

Whatever the reasons for the delay between 1887 and 1890, the final stages in the gestation of the BEA are amply documented. In April 1890 Committee members of Section F of the BAAS were invited to approve the scheme for an *Economic Journal* and/or an English Economic Association, the latter to undertake 'the encouragement of research and discussion, the publication of monographs, the translation of Foreign works and the republication of English works that are out of print'. They were also asked whether the journal should be published and edited by a sub-committee of the Association, and whether the organization should adopt the English 'learned society' form or copy 'the American Economic Association, which holds meetings only at rare intervals, and the membership of which does not profess to confer any sort of diploma'.[22] At the BAAS Committee meeting the date of the 'semi-public' inaugural gathering of the BEA was initially fixed as July 23, but it was subsequently postponed until the autumn, because Courtney and Goschen, who had been asked to preside, could not attend. Another reason, as Marshall explained to Bonar,[23] was that after the inauguration several executive committee meetings would be needed in order to choose an editor and prepare the first issue of the journal, and if this period fell in the summer there might be an inordinate delay and a consequent loss of interest in the journal. However, the intervening months were not wasted. At least four drafts of Marshall's letter of invitation to the inauguration were circulated and discussed, and the minor changes of wording they contain reveal how painstakingly the ground was prepared and what points the founder-members regarded as especially worthy of attention. Nothing was left to chance: the official resolutions were carefully phrased, and the proposers and seconders were selected in advance, presumably in order to create an impression of harmony and unanimity. In fact, the only controversial note was struck by George Bernard Shaw, who questioned the wisdom of having 'as the head of the Association ... a gentleman who was identified with any political party in the State', but this intervention was handled with such tact and good humour as to enhance rather than diminish the general sense of well-being. In reply, Marshall declared:

> I am one of those who am not a political supporter of Mr. Goschen. I believe all agree with me that since we cannot have an economist who has no political opinions at all, we could not have a better President than Mr. Goschen.

However, the nominee, with becoming modesty, demurred on the ground that

> there is some force in Mr. Shaw's remarks. For my part there is nothing that would attract me more in this Association than the power it may give of bringing together those who take the extreme views of some economic questions with those who take just the opposite. I think the Council might well reflect before deciding upon my nomination.[24]

In the event, Goschen's suggestion was approved, and his nomination was subsequently confirmed by the Council; but the incident illustrates the general sense of the public character of the occasion. There was a striking contrast between the calm and serenity of this inaugural meeting and the current reputation of political economy, for the editor of *The Times* was only mildly exaggerating when he described the period as one 'when all is controverted, when axioms and elementary truths are in dispute, when political economy is a cluster of furiously conducted controversies, and the heretics outnumber the orthodox'. Reading between the lines of the official report, one can sense that some of the non-academic economists present at University College probably shared his opinion that the academics were leaning over backwards in an effort to be fair to all parties. 'To what pass has political economy come,' he declared, 'when the only test in use among the disciples is that which might suit Oddfellows or Freemasons.' There was, he conceded, an urgent need for frank and open discussion, and a search for unity of opinion on fundamentals; but there was an equal need to establish high intellectual standards 'to which all men must conform on pain of being refused a hearing'. Above all, the formation of a body of 'educated opinion' should be one of the Association's responsibilities, for 'at present no doctrine is too crude or monstrous if it falls in with someone's interest'.[25]

These remarks provide a background to those questions which seemed especially important to the founder-members, namely: what should be the functions of the new organization; what, if any, conditions of membership should be imposed; and how could they ensure that the Association's journal would represent 'all shades of opinion'? As J. B. Martin observed, in supporting a resolution at the inaugural meeting:

320

We are starting an organization of a hybrid nature, for which there is little precedent, and the rules and regulations therefore, call for most careful consideration . . . when this paper was put into my hands this evening I noticed that almost all the resolutions were to be proposed by some gent who has made a mark in parliamentary life, and who has studied economics from the point of view of a public man, while they were supported by gentlemen of the professional type. . . . We are here not only to start a magazine; we are starting also a Scientific Society, although it has perhaps little in common with other scientific societies except the subscription of £1 annually.[26]

The hybrid character of the BEA reflects the mixed composition and motives of its founder-members; more important still, it reflects the condition of the subject in the 1890s. Admittedly, serious academic training in economics was still in its infancy, and there were few full-time university and college teachers of the discipline. Nevertheless, there was a nucleus sufficient to constitute a select body like the Psychological Society, founded in 1901, whose membership was carefully restricted to 'those who were recognized teachers in some branch' of the subject, or 'who had published work of recognized value';[27] but the economists were unwilling to assume the responsibility of drawing invidious distinctions between those considered eligible for membership and those who were not.[28] They realized there were no easily definable criteria of expertise in economics, and the professors – on whom the task of determining 'professional competence' would presumably have fallen – were, on the whole, more reluctant than the laymen to impose any membership requirements whatsoever, other than the payment of a nominal subscription. Undoubtedly they recognized the importance of the contributions already made by non-academic economists to the development of British economics; and they feared that without a considerable body of members, the Association's funds would be insufficient to support a regular journal of high scholarly merit. Above all, they were extremely anxious to avoid the impression of establishing a new economic 'orthodoxy', similar to that which had prevailed in the mid-Victorian era, and they knew that any move to exclude the exponents of a particular doctrine or method would be likely to reopen the controversies of the two preceding decades, which had seriously weakened the scientific reputation of the subject. By enlisting the support and membership of prominent statesmen and public men, the BEA would be in a better position to exert an influence on the public attitude to economic questions than any purely academic or otherwise highly selective body. But there was a delicate problem of deciding where scientific and scholarly influence ended and practical, policy-making influence began – a problem of which the founder-members were only too well-aware. Marshall, like his fellow academics, appreciated the situation when he warned against the dangers of trying to exert a 'wholesome influence', and he expressed the hope that their membership would include 'every school of economists which was doing *genuine work*'.[29]

In the end, a compromise solution was adopted. The BEA followed the example of its American precursor and became an 'open' society rather than a strictly 'learned' body.[30] Prospective members were to be approved by the Council in addition to paying a small subscription; but soon after the inaugural ceremony thousands of letters of invitation were despatched to potential members and to an extremely miscellaneous list of organizations. Towards the end of the year a small group of officers met repeatedly at J. B. Martin's house to frame the Association's rules,[31] and they included a curious provision whereby

> If any Member or Honorary Member so demean himself that it would be for the dishonour of the Association that he longer continue to be a Member or Honorary Member thereof, the Council shall take the matter into consideration at a Meeting convened for the purpose.

This rule was, of course, simply an echo of an almost identical clause in the Royal Statistical Society's regulations; it had no practical consequences, for the records contain no evidence of any formal attempts to discipline existing members or impose restrictions on entry.[32] Yet it has no counterpart in the regulations of the AEA, and its mere existence, to say nothing of its wording, conveys undertones of the 'gentleman's club' tradition. Considering the unwillingness to differentiate between 'qualified' and 'unqualified' applicants, and the absence of any concept of professional ethics, such a rule could only provide the vaguest indication of what conduct was liable to 'dishonour' the organization. An examination of the early membership lists reveals, as might have been expected, a preponderance of academic, business and professional men, and a notable lack of working-class or trade-union members;[33] and, again, predictably, a substantial proportion also belonged to the Royal Statistical Society.[34]

IV

The results of all this activity were conspicuously successful, despite the competition provided by the *Economic Review*. Some two hundred persons attended the inaugural meeting; when the first issue of the *Economic Journal* appeared in March 1891 the membership was approaching 500, and a total of 710 was achieved by the end of that year. As this figure included more than fifty life members, the subscription income was sufficient to support the *Journal*, but in order to tide over the initial period when expenditures were made in anticipation of income, the Council organized a Guarantee Fund, which, as Edgeworth stated in his appeal for aid, was 'needed to enable the Council to deal at once with publishers and printers. It is proposed to make the fund £500 for the first year, and in the event of any call upon it subscribers are only to pay *pro rata*.'[35] The appeal was successful, and the required sum was guaranteed annually for a period of three years by some thirty contributors, none of whom contributed more than £25 per annum.[36] The initial period of financial stringency passed without a real crisis, despite the fact that the income from life memberships was being used to meet current expenditures, and the Association continued to pay nominal salaries to its Editor and Secretary and fees to the contributors to the *Journal*. But in subsequent years, although its investments were worth more than £800 from 1893 onwards, the income position remained unsatisfactory; the membership reached a peak of around 750 in 1893–4 and diminished thereafter, and of course the number of annual subscriptions fell faster still. In 1896 the Council felt obliged to reduce the size of the *Journal* and to reduce the number of copies printed 'so far as prudent' in an effort to economize, but neither the decision to authorize the Secretary to pay 'a bonus of 1/- to the clerk for each new member obtained through his efforts' nor the earnest appeal to members 'to do all they can to induce suitable persons to join' had much effect.[37] Some members of the public were apparently uncertain whether any special membership qualifications were required, and William Smart considered that existing members could easily obtain new recruits if they knew there was a need for them. 'There is eno [*sic*] of a halo round the BEA to make the ordinary man think that he is honoured by being asked to join: that at least is my experience', he wrote; but Higgs was more sceptical, underlining the word 'experience' and adding 'not mine' – and the evidence suggests that he was right.[38] The membership total hovered around the 500 mark throughout the late nineties and early 1900s and did not reach the 1893 total (750) again until 1915. The Annual deficits or surpluses were small throughout the pre-Charter years, and in the early 1900s the Association's capital assets were not much over £900. It supported the publication of two reprints of the kind planned by its original founder-members,[39] but the situation was always somewhat precarious, and it was not until World War I that any substantial current surpluses were earned.

Once the Association had been launched, there were still some doubts as to its precise nature and functions. Its principal task, the management of the *Economic Journal*, was assigned to Edgeworth, who was soon to be assisted by Higgs,[40] and the publication was well received. Such strenuous efforts were made to ensure the representation of 'all shades of economic opinion' that the early numbers contained a variety of statements from individualistic, socialistic and Ruskinian standpoints, and comparatively few strictly technical or theoretical articles were printed. As regards its other activities, however, there seems to have been some indecision stemming, perhaps, from the fact that the Association was a semi-public scientific and scholarly body with a large contingent of non-academic members.

Unlike the American Economic Association in its early days, there was no conscious commitment to social reform; but the Executive Committee demonstrated a curious reluctance to hold periodic meetings or conferences with formal papers and discussions, whether annually, like the AEA or more frequently, like the Royal Statistical Society. At the outset there was even some unwillingness to make the annual meeting a semi-social occasion by holding a dinner, probably because it was feared that such occasions might be marred either by unseemly methodological wrangles or by statements that appeared to commit the Association to a specific position on some question of public policy.[41] In these circumstances there was inevitably some doubt as to the exact purpose of the annual address to the Association, as revealed in correspondence about the 1894 meeting. In February A. J. Balfour, one of the four Vice-Presidents, responded to Goschen's invitation by asking whether it would help the Society if he were to address them.

> They are, or ought to be, a strictly scientific body, and I have always felt that there is a certain absurdity in a layman addressing experts upon their own subject. It is many years now since I have been able to devote any time to strictly economic investigations, and even if it had been otherwise, I could hardly have expected men like Marshall, Edgeworth, and Sidgwick, to gather economic wisdom from my lips.
>
> It is perfectly true that economic theory touches political practice; and that I might be supposed to have something to say to you upon this border-region. But you have already dealt, in your own admirable address, with the only topic which, as it seems to me, is worth discussing in this connection.[42]

Balfour offered to take the Chair, and Goschen, who appreciated the force of Balfour's remarks, accepted his recommendation that Sidgwick should be approached. However, Sidgwick declined on the grounds that:

> I am not a 'real economist' in an *academic* sense: I studied the subject a good deal in earlier years – especially between 1878 and 1883; and wrote a book on it; but since I was appointed to the Chair of Moral Philosophy here in 1883, I have felt it my duty to make Political Economy a mere πάρεργον. . . .
>
> Now I think the Council are perhaps right in desiring to *alternate*, in their annual addresses, between eminent statesmen and academic persons, although the addresses of the former are aways likely to be more interesting to the general public: but then I think the academic person should be a 'real economist', a student who is making economic science his main business, and is therefore duly acquainted with recent work in the subject – an economist 'up-to-date', in short.[43]

Sidgwick suggested that if no academic person could be persuaded to speak, Courtney or Giffen 'or some other eminent person with practical knowledge or experience' should be invited; but another academic, Foxwell, was the next to be approached. However, this suggestion also proved unfruitful. Higgs reported that Foxwell had declared himself too busy and added:

> Besides I am so full of the money question I could talk of nothing else – in fact I feel it is trifling to go into academic questions while so big a practical problem remains unsettled. On the other hand, if I were to speak on the Monetary Question I should probably give offence. Feeling is too high on this matter.[44]

In response to this, the Executive Committee instructed Higgs to ask Goschen whether Foxwell should be invited to speak on this subject 'on the understanding that the Association is not made responsible for any particular views upon the currency', but Goschen demurred. 'I am averse to accepting Professor Foxwell on the topic he suggests,' he replied. 'A bimetallic address would not help the Association coming after the bimetallic conference and exciting as it would do much hostility.' If the alternatives, Leon Say, F. W. Taussig and J. S. Nicholson, were not available, he concluded that they must either postpone the address or hold it only bi-annually.[45]

This was not the end of the matter, however, for Nicholson, who at first agreed to act, subsequently attempted to withdraw under protest:

> I most strongly object to Mr. Goschen laying down limits as to the choice of a subject. I think it would be very bad policy for the Council to try to get addresses of a certain pattern. As a matter of fact I am tired of writing on currency and am busy with other things, but as a matter of principle I object to what seems an attempt to fetter opinion. Perhaps I have misread your letter.[46]

Higgs naturally hastened to assure him that this was so, and gave some account of the background to the invitation.

> The Council has adopted the policy of making the Annual meeting an 'attraction' by adding to our brief and formal business an address from some eminent statesman or economist . . . and in the opinion of the Council (which has adopted Mr. Goschen's view) the currency question would not just now be sufficiently attractive to members generally to make the meeting a success; and on this account it was hoped that out of the fulness of your store you would give us something else, as I quite expected you would prefer to do.
>
> I trust after this explanation, and the knowledge that the Economic Journal keeps open house, you will not think that there has been any attempt to fetter opinion; and I earnestly hope that you will see your way to help us out of the difficulty into which we have got apparently through the fault of
>
> Yours sincerely,[47]

Eventually, Nicholson agreed to address the Association on the subject of 'Political Economy and Journalism', but the outcome as such is less interesting than the tortuous preliminaries.

Throughout its first decade, the Association's business seems to have been conducted in a fairly casual and informal manner – apart from its financial affairs and the management of the journal (for which, unfortunately, no editorial records have survived). When the rules were being reconsidered at the time of the application for a Royal Charter, Edgeworth wryly commented that if they had previously enforced the rule requiring five fellows to constitute a quorum, a good many of the earlier meetings would have been ruled unofficial; and the Council members' reluctance to interfere in the organization's affairs is suggested by Marshall's desire for less frequent Council meetings, 'so excellently has the work of the organization been done by the faithful few who have done the real work, especially Edgeworth and yourself'.[48] There were, however, disadvantages from the faithful's viewpoint, for as Higgs had earlier complained to Goschen:

> Our business suffers very much owing to the small attendances at the meetings. Taking the last 12 meetings the average attendance is under 3 persons including the Treasurer, Editor, and myself. Two or three times during the last year only one person was in the Council room, the result is that the business is referred from Council to Council, and any matter of importance (which so small a meeting hesitates to decide) drags on w'out a settlement. The 'particular' request addressed to members last week was responded to only by Mr. Martin and Mr. Hoare, and the latter gentleman (who had never attended before) left after a few minutes . . . some means are needed to change this if possible.[49]

Nevertheless, two years later the Council accepted the inevitable, and decided that Executive Committee meetings would henceforth be merged with the quarterly Council meetings, and the Association continued to be effectively managed by a handful of principal officers.

Whether other administrative or constitutional arrangements would have yielded different results it is impossible to say, but throughout the early years of its existence the Association's activities remained limited. The Minutes contain periodic references to the possibility of holding discussions, but nothing was done about this until 1906, when a proposal to hold an 'Annual Congress' was approved. In 1892 it was suggested that a joint conference should be held in conjunction with the RSS, and several leading members, including Marshall and Bonar, hoped that the two bodies would eventually join forces. If a successful joint meeting could be arranged, Marshall believed:

The younger and more enterprising members of the B.E.A. would be brought into contact with the older and more steady-going members of the R.S.S. . . . But as things are the younger men could not expect to have the new joint body managed sufficiently on their own lines to satisfy their wants; and I fear that, if they did not actually leave the Association, they would be inclined to start a new journal and a new set of meetings; or else to develop existing ones that would for a time run parallel to, and afterwards surpass in public interest, the heavier and more old fashioned society.[50]

However, nothing came of these proposals, although the possibility that the two organizations might have a joint President and Governing Body was also considered.[51]

A combination of apathy and fear of establishing a new doctrinal orthodoxy or controlling authority may have restricted the activities of the BEA, but the Council did occasionally act as the spokesman for British economics. It refused to accept local economic and philosophical groups as affiliates, to provide speakers for the Cardiff Impartial Society, or to lend support to the Decimal Association. But in support of a BAAS Committee report on 'The Methods of Economic Training in this and Other Countries',[52] which severely criticized the weak and disorganized state of economics teaching in British institutions of higher education, the Council endeavoured to persuade the Civil Service Commissioners, the Council for Legal Education, and the University of Wales to give political economy a larger place in their examinations. No record of formal contact with the first of these bodies has survived; but a number of exchanges took place with the other two, although with somewhat inconclusive results. The Court of the University of Wales 'expected' that political economy would form an integral part of a new curriculum which was being planned, but the newly appointed Professor of Philosophy, J. S. Mackenzie, pointed out that no improvement was likely until independent lectureships were founded and inquired whether any members of the BEA might be willing to provide the necessary funds.[53] In 1901 the Council's official action helped to prevent Foxwell's first great economic library from going to the USA, for the Secretary's letter attracted the attention of Sir Walter Prideaux of the Goldsmith's Company, who purchased the collection; but thirteen years later the Council tried in vain to support Foxwell in his stormy dealings with the University of London Senate.[54]

During the Association's early years only a few minor incidents ruffled its placid course. It refused to be drawn into a dispute between its printer and the London Society of Compositors, but it threatened legal action when the *Bradford Observer* printed extracts from an *Economic Journal* article without permission.[55] In 1894 the Council investigated a dispute between Edgeworth and a regular contributor, John Rae, who had accused the editor of general

327

inefficiency and failure to pay the sums due to him; but the Council acquitted Edgeworth of discourtesy.[56]

V

In December 1902 the BEA obtained a Royal Charter, changing its name to the Royal Economic Society, by which it is now known throughout the world. A proposal favouring this course had been made as early as January 1896, but the process was not initiated until March 1901. Three months later King Edward VII agreed to become the Association's Patron, and during the ensuing two years the movement towards a Royal Charter was brought to a successful conclusion, though not without a considerable investment of time, energy and funds.[57] The effect of the new dispensation on the organization's character, rules and functions was so slight that one is prompted to inquire why the whole venture was considered worth while; and the question provides a peg on which to hang some general comments on the BEA and the social and professional position of the British economists at the beginning of this century.

Comparison with the history of other learned and professional bodies suggests that the BEA's application for a Charter was primarily motivated by the desire for additional prestige – for parity of esteem with the older, more securely established Royal Statistical Society – rather than more specifically professional considerations.[58] In 1872 that body had persuaded the Prince of Wales to act as its Honorary President, and in the ensuing year it had managed to increase its membership by a figure greater than any year since its foundation.[59] No doubt the economists hoped to reap a similar harvest; at least they displayed no interest in the possibility of extending the range of their activities – for example, by establishing a code of professional ethics, adopting measures designed to protect the profession or the public, acting as a pressure group or providing welfare benefits for members. Like the RSS, the RES remained a 'study association', making no attempt to set examinations or tests of professional competence of the type normally adopted by 'qualifying associations'. The acquisition of a Royal Charter and the change of designation from 'member' to 'Fellow' presumably brought some additional prestige to the individual adherent, but the possibility of framing more selective conditions of membership, such as those adopted by the Royal Society or the recently formed British Academy, seems never to have been considered; and in explaining why this was so some additional light can be shed on the composition of the organization, the motives of its leading members and the contemporary view of economics as an academic discipline and a professional pursuit.

As we have seen, the economists demonstrated some signs of growing professional self-consciousness, for example, in complaining that they lacked influence, that the public did not value their subject, and that the existing provisions for instruction and examination in political economy were lamentably deficient. But after summoning the energy necessary to launch an organization they were evidently unwilling to take more active steps to enhance their influence, raise occupational standards or consolidate their professional and occupational position. To say this does not necessarily imply any criticism; indeed, given the circumstances of the time, it is doubtful whether much more could have been achieved. The prevailing disagreements about the nature and scope of economics precluded any attempt to establish a uniform scheme of qualifying examinations or a professional code;[60] the leading universities were only just beginning to establish degree courses in economics; and the bureaucratic impulse towards uniformity was much weaker in the core group of university teachers, who were already acquiring a growing share of the management of the Association,[61] than among other professional groups, such as local and central government employees, school teachers or medical men. The BEA's primary object was to increase the flow of publications by establishing a scholarly and scientific periodical, and the *Economic Journal* might have been run as a private venture had there not been the fear that it would be regarded as the spearhead of a new doctrinal orthodoxy. As it transpired, the founders provided an impartial outlet for work of recognized quality, and their 'open' membership plan was so successful that even in a field where cranks, quacks, heretics and outsiders flourished, they enlisted the active support of all those with serious claims to specialist economic knowledge without either forming a select coterie or unduly diluting the initial scholarly purpose.

Yet the BEA failed to advance as rapidly as might have been expected from its auspicious start. Its membership stagnated, despite the Royal patronage, for the number of full-time economists did not expand rapidly enough to offset the reaction following the initial burst of enthusiasm; and the opportunities for formal discussions remained unduly limited owing to the excessive fear of controversy (although there are some indications from the size of the attendance at the annual meetings that a bolder policy would have borne considerable fruit). For a surprisingly long period the non-academic members played a more prominent part than might have been desirable in the interests of pure scholarship,[62] but this was due to the diminutive proportions of the academic body of economists and the remarkable persistence of the amateur non-specialist tradition of British political economy. In retrospect, it even seems surprising that the RES maintained its independence, for amalgamation with the RSS was still being mooted after World War I. But although the corpus of economic specialists remained small and undifferentiated, a sufficient loyalty and *esprit de corps* was aroused to enable the organization to overcome its early growing pains. And as most economists were practitioners of an individualistic discipline, it is fitting to conclude with the observation of a mid-nineteenth-century commentator, that:

> The most effectual method which any class of men can adopt for securing their political rights, and advancing their professional standing, consists not in disputation and warm argument, but in a steady and persevering attention to individual improvement, and the establishment of such regulations as are calculated to ensure collective privileges by increasing the amount of individual merit.[63]

APPENDIX: I MEMBERSHIP OF BRITISH ECONOMIC ASSOCIATION (DECEMBER 31, 1891)

Of the 710 members, 115 had foreign addresses and 94 have not been identified. The remaining 501 members fall within the following categories:

Accounting	16
Administration	29
Army	8
Bankers	48
Business	113
Civil Service	44
Church	16
Government	12
Insurance	7
Journalism	16
Landowners, etc.	22
Law	51
Medicine	6
Teachers (non-university)	13
Teachers (university)	86
Miscellaneous	14

The following points should be noted. First, there are, of course, various problems of classification, especially those arising in cases where a person held more than one occupation. Retired persons have been listed under their former occupations. *Civil Service* includes central and local government. *Government* includes current and past statesmen, Cabinet Ministers, colonial governors, etc. *Administration* includes secretaries of non-business organizations such as charity societies, JPs and members of public bodies. *Landowners* includes persons of independent means with no specific profession or occupation, eleven of whom were members of the House of Commons. MPs with known occupations have been placed in the appropriate occupational category.

Second, this information forms part of a long-term study of the composition of the 'economics profession' in the UK, which has been partly financed by the University of Nottingham and the Institute of Economic and Social Research at the University of York. I wish to thank the many local librarians who responded to inquiries, and also Paul Wiles, Rita McWilliams and, especially, Sonia E. Coats, who compiled the occupational data.

NOTES

1 See 'The British Economic Association', *Economic Journal*, vol. 1, 1891, pp. 1–14; 'After Seven Years', ibid., vol. 8, 1898, pp. 1–2; 'The Society's Jubilee 1890–1940', and 'Obituary, Henry Higgs', ibid., vol. 50, 1940, pp. 401–9, 546–61.

2 H. S. Foxwell, 'The Economic Movement in England', *Quarterly Journal of Economics*, vol. 2, 1887, pp. 84–103 (dated September 1887); also the note, ibid., p. 64, dated October 1887. Cf. A. W. Coats, 'The First Two Decades of the American Economic Association', *American Economic Review*, vol. 50, 1960, pp. 555–74 (reprinted in this volume, pp. 205–24).

3 Foxwell and Palgrave were keen bibliographers and students of contemporary monetary questions. Their correspondence is currently in the possession of Major Geoffrey Barker, who proposes to deposit them in King's College Library, Cambridge. He has generously given access to, and permission to quote from, these letters. (Unless otherwise stated, all footnote references up to and including note 17 are from this source.) Palgrave had discussed with Jevons a plan to publish a translation of Roscher's *Political Economy*. See Jevons to Palgrave, March 5 and April 7, 1875, in King's College Library, Cambridge. I am indebted to Professor R. D. Collison Black of Queen's University, Belfast, for this reference.

4 'The Americans do these things in first rate style (see their reprint of Utopia), and the strong Anglomania and 18th-century revival which has set up in New York, Boston and Montreal would be in our favour.' Foxwell to Palgrave, October 28, 1885. As a connoisseur, Foxwell had misgivings about a Reprint Society under the influence of the Banker's Institute, as Palgrave had proposed. Efforts to secure financial guarantees from the Syndics of the Cambridge University Press proved abortive.

5 Economics had been in bad odour with the BAAS in 1878 when it was suggested that Section F should be abandoned, as economics was not a 'science'; and Henry Sidgwick once noted in his diary that despite some good papers, it seemed impossible to have a good discussion owing to time limits and the presence of 'certain familiar bores'.

James Mavor, the economic historian, complained that the Economic section of the British Association was 'of little or no account', for like the Social Science Association, its discussions linked economics and sanitation; 'the result is that discussion is upon drains rather than industrial relations.' The American Economic Association, he added, had beneficially influenced the Glasgow University 'economic Association', and he wished a comparable body could be established in Britain. Mavor to Richard T. Ely, April 13, 1888. In Ely papers, Wisconsin

331

State Historical Society, Madison, Wisconsin.

For a defence of Section F see William Cunningham, 'Nationalism and Cosmopolitanism in Economics', *Journal of the Royal Statistical Society*, vol. 54, 1891, pp. 644–6.

6 Foxwell to Palgrave, November 25, 1885, quoting an announcement on the cover of the Society's Journal.

7 Foxwell to Palgrave, November 10, 1885. For the reference to Marshall's views see the letter of October 28, 1885.

8 Foxwell to Palgrave, November 25, 1885. Italics in original. Cf. the reference to advertising by members in the *Journal of the Royal Statistical Society*, vol. 50, 1887, p. 453.

9 Foxwell to Palgrave, December 13, 1885.

10 Foxwell to Palgrave, January 7, 1887. See also J. N. Keynes to Palgrave, November 28, 1886, and December 9, 1886.

11 Foxwell to Palgrave, undated (probably early 1888). Foxwell had hoped to start the new society in Queen Victoria's Jubilee year, enlisting the support of James Goschen, the Chancellor of the Exchequer, who eventually became the first President of the BEA. Cf. Foxwell to Palgrave, January 7, 1887.

Two years later E. C. K. Gonner complained of the lack of an economic review. 'It does make study in England rather hopeless as far as progress and influence go when everyone is engaged in working in isolation. . . . The only branch which has of very late years progressed in any [word illegible] degree is that of statistics, and I cannot but think that that progress is in part at least due to the Statistical Society.' Gonner to Sir Robert Giffen, June 18, 1889, in Giffen collection, London School of Economics.

12 Martin considered that Marshall would never be a 'working president', but that he would give a good paper. He would personally have preferred William Cunningham, the economic historian, as President. Marshall had apparently refused earlier invitations. Cf. Martin to Palgrave, November 7, 1889, and November 14, 1889.

13 See the report of the inaugural meeting in *The Times*, November 21, 1890. These phrases do not appear in the version published in the *Economic Journal*.

In 1891 Marshall pressed Edgeworth to become Secretary of the Royal Statistical Society, in addition to his editorial duties, so that he could 'have a regular office [in London] and work the two Associations in harmony'. Marshall to Edgeworth, February 16, 1891; also September 4, 1892. In Marshall Library, Cambridge.

14 George Bernard Shaw, *The Fabian Society: Its Early History* (Fabian Tract no. 41), 1892, p. 16. For a good account of Fabian economics see A. M. MacBriar, *Fabian Socialism and English Politics* (1962), chap. 2.

15 On these matters see Archibald Henderson, *George Bernard Shaw: His Life and Works* (1911), pp. 130, 157–9; also the careful analysis in Ralph Howey, *The Rise of the Marginal Utility School* (1960), pp. 118–30. However, Shaw may have been thinking of the Junior Economic Club formed at University College in July 1890, a body which its first Secretary and Treasurer, Henry Higgs, declared had 'neither common aims nor membership' with the British Economic Association. Higgs to Foxwell, June 20, 1896. This is one of an important collection of letters in the possession of Miss Audrey Foxwell, who has kindly given me permission to quote from them. I owe my knowledge of them to Professor R. D. Collison Black.

16 Foxwell to Palgrave, November 10, 1885, and November 21, 1885. It should be

noted that the Christian Social Union was not founded until 1889. Foxwell was therefore referring to different proposals.

17 Martin to Palgrave, July 14, 1890.

18 *Economic Journal*, vol. 1, p. 4.

19 Marshall to Phelps, November 5, 1890. In Oriel College, Oxford. Phelps was one of the original members of the BEA Council. The other editors were John Carter, Exeter College, and W. H. J. Campion, Keble College. The Presidents and Vice-Presidents of the Oxford Branch of the CSU were prominent young clergymen, but the list of prospective contributors to the *Review* included W. J. Ashley, W. Cunningham, Richard T. Ely (of Wisconsin), Sydney Ball, L. T. Hobhouse, H. de B. Gibbins and W. A. S. Hewins. Shortly thereafter the list was extended to include Sidney Buxton, Edwin Cannan, T. Kirkup, Sydney Olivier, H. Llewellyn Smith and Sidney Webb. Despite extensive inquiries, I have unfortunately been unable to trace any editorial papers.

Despite the friendly overtures to Marshall in the editorial introduction to vol. I of the *Economic Review* the editors observed that the 'fight between the two schoools [of economics] still rages somewhat fiercely', and Carter informed Richard T. Ely, the leading American spokesman for the 'ethical and historical' approach to economics, that 'our relations with Professor Marshall are a little strained. He is rather sore that we have started before him', and suggested that Ely's proposed article on Marshall should not be too outspoken. 'We do not object to printing a criticism of Prof. Marshall. But the title "Prof. Marshall's Utopia" might appear rather too hostile.' Carter to Ely, April 3, 1891, in Ely Papers, University of Wisconsin. In fact, the article, though announced, was never published.

20 *Economic Journal*, vol. 1. The circular soliciting support for the *Review* stated that it would 'be chiefly concerned with modern economic difficulties as they bear upon the whole of life, but it will also include more technical articles dealing with special aspects of our industrial system, or treating the historical condition and development of some particular period'.

21 In his Presidential address to Section F of the BAAS, 1891, 'Nationalism and Cosmopolitanism in Economics', Cunningham observed that the *Economic Review* and the *Economic Journal* exemplified the Oxford and Cambridge 'spirit' respectively. Their subsequent development, however, reflects the growing gap between the clergy and the academic economists, a matter that deserves systematic investigation. In the 1890s Marshall was rightly regarded as a thinker who bridged the narrow gap between economics and ethics, religion, and social reform. Cf. K. Inglis, *Churches and the Working Classes in the Nineteenth Century* (1963), pp. 257–9. On the Oxford background see Melvin Richter, *The Politics of Conscience, T. H. Green and His Age* (1964).

22 Cf. the draft and preliminary Agenda for the 1890 BAAS meeting sent by Marshall to James Bonar on April 10, 1890. Royal Economic Society Archives, Marshall Library, Cambridge. Unless otherwise stated, all subsequent references are from this source. It stated that 'some consultation' with Professor Foxwell and Mr Palgrave had already taken place, and suggested that those invited to the inaugural meeting should include members of the Council of the Royal Statistical Society, the Political Economy Club and all past or present lecturers in economics 'in any University or Public College in the U.K.'. Subsequently members of the Councils of the Manchester and Dublin Statistical Societies were also included.

23 Marshall to Bonar, April 5, 1890.

24 *Economic Journal*, vol. 1, pp. 13–14. Another potentially controversial aspect of

333

the initial proposals seems to have passed unnoticed. Up to and including the report in *The Times*, on November 21, 1890, the organization was described as the English Economic Association, but by the time the *Economic Journal* appeared it had become British!

25 *The Times*, November 21, 1890.

26 These remarks, from an unpublished draft, have been slightly rearranged.

27 Cf. Beatrice Edgell, 'The British Psychological Society 1901–41', *Bulletin of the British Psychological Society*, Supplement (1961) p. 5. The society began with ten members and still only had thirteen at the end of its first year. *The British Journal of Psychology* first appeared in 1904, but the society did not assume financial responsibility for it until 1914. The American Psychological Association began on exactly the same basis as its British counterpart.

28 The next three paragraphs are based mainly on the report in vol. 1 of the *Economic Journal*. For further comments on the significance of these matters see my article 'The Role of Authority in the Development of British Economics', *Journal of Law and Economics*, vol. 7, October 1964, esp. pp. 95–8 (reprinted in this volume, pp. 82–104). It is, however, worth noting that the Junior Economic Club's membership was confined to 'Those who can furnish satisfactory evidence of economic training', partly with the aim of excluding the Fabians. Cf. Higgs to Foxwell, July 18 and September 23, 1890. In Miss Foxwell's possession. Cf. Higgs' obituary, *Economic Journal*, vol. 50, pp. 546–51.

29 *Economic Journal*, vol. 1, pp. 5–6. Italics in original.

30 See Albert Shaw's 'Report of the Organization of the British Economic Association', *Publications of the American Economic Association*, 1st Ser, vol. 6, 1891.

31 The drafting committee comprised Martin, Foxwell and T. H. Elliot (of the Board of Agriculture), and of course Edgeworth and Higgs also participated.

32 On October 5, 1891, the BEA Council minutes record the following item: The Secretary having read a letter from the President's Private Secretary as to unfit persons being nominated members in America, it was decided that a reply be sent saying that the Council regret to hear that exception has been taken with regard to the election of any members of the Association, and they hope that by the appointment of the Corresponding Members in Foreign Countries and the Colonies it will be possible to prevent the recurrence of any 'similar complaints'. There are no subsequent references to this problem.

33 While members of Chambers of Commerce and Employers' Associations were invited to join, no circulars were sent to Trade Unions, presumably because it was assumed that their members would not be interested. On December 5, 1890, Henry Higgs wrote to Edgeworth: 'No to Ambassadors and the Primrose League. Of the latter we shall catch all worth catching in other ways. Clubs we shall have to secure as subscribers to the journal.' A speaker at the 1892 Annual General Meeting, commenting on the report, said that 'members of the Industrial classes had hoped that more would have been done to disseminate information on Economics', but although the Council took note of this in their Minutes, no action was taken.

34 See the Appendix for an analysis of the early members of the BEA.

35 Printed letter dated February 1891. The guarantee-fund idea antedated the formation of the Association, and originated in the proposal 'to issue the journal as a private concern'. However, it was subsequently agreed that the publication would be more likely to 'represent all shades of economic opinion, and be the organ of not one school of English economists, but of all schools' if it was published 'under the authority of an Economic Association'. Second draft of the proposal for the inaugural meeting, dated June 1890. The *Economic Review* also

began with the aid of a guarantee fund, and though it was occasionally subsidized by the Oxford branch of the CSU, it was run independently of that body.

36 Following a deficit in 1891, a call of 10*s.* in the £ was made on the guarantors, despite Marshall's objection that it was 'not absolutely required to save the Association from failure'. He felt that they should consider 'those guarantors for whom the advancement of science does not hold the same predominant and absorbing position as it does for most of the members of the executive committee'. Later that month the Council 'negatived' his proposal to give them the option of a refund; but no further calls were made on the guarantors. Marshall to Higgs, March 27, April 3 and 5, 1893. Council Minute of April 11, 1893, in BEA Minute Book.

37 Council Minute of November 11, 1897; *Economic Journal*, vol. 8, March 1898, p. 2.

38 Smart to Higgs, July 10, 1896.

39 The Association distributed Quesney's *Tableau Œconomique* to members and provided a grant to aid the publication of Petty's *Of Taxes and Contributions*.

40 In his reminiscences of Marshall, Edgeworth recalled that after his appointment as editor: 'I wrote to Marshall asking advice on every small difficulty which arose, until he protested that, if the correspondence was to go on at that rate, he would have to use envelopes with my address printed on them.' Cf. A. C. Pigou (ed.), *Memorials of Alfred Marshall* (1925), p. 69. Unfortunately, like most of their correspondence, these letters have not survived.

41 At the inaugural meeting Marshall observed that 'the question as to the desirability of holding meetings for discussion had been long and frequently debated in private . . . [and] they had almost unanimously come to the conclusion that it would be better not to hold them at present. For such discussions, unless conducted by a very strong Association, might do harm: they might be attended chiefly by people whose time was not very valuable. And, partly because many of their members lived very great distances from London, they thought it unwise to start public discussions. Opportunities for discussion were given by the British Association and the Statistical Association. The Economic Club was already doing, in a quiet way, the kind of work which could be done by means of meetings.' *Economic Journal*, vol. 1, p. 8. The 'Economic Club' Marshall mentioned is referred to *supra*, notes 15 and 28.

42 Balfour to Goschen, February 27, 1894.

43 Sidgwick to Goschen, March 21, 1894. Italics in original.

44 Foxwell to Higgs, April 30, 1894. Foxwell was then the most prominent academic spokesman for the Bimetallic League.

45 Higgs to Goschen, May 2, 1894; Goschen to Higgs of the same date.

46 Nicholson to Higgs, 13 May, 1894. Nicholson had accepted the invitation on May 4, 1894.

47 Higgs to Nicholson, May 17, 1894. Higgs quoted Goschen as saying, 'I would not suggest Dr. Giffen because he is not sufficiently well known as an economist *to draw a large meeting.*' Italics in original. In 1893 Goschen had described himself as one of the 'oi polloi', adding that he had been rash in agreeing to become President, and rasher still in giving the address. *Economic Journal*, vol. 3, September 1893, p. 377.

48 Edgeworth to Chairman, March 8, 1903; Marshall to Higgs, December 5, 1896.

49 Higgs to Goschen, January 7, 1895. An analysis of the attendance at Executive Committee and Council meetings reveals that the condition described by Higgs persisted up to 1903. Apart from the principal officers, Edgeworth and Higgs, by far the most regular attenders were James Bonar (who became Chairman of

the Council in 1896), T. H. Elliott, J. B. Martin and L. L. Price. On one occasion Higgs asked Lord Farrer whether, if re-elected to the Council, he would be able to attend meetings, but otherwise little or no effort seems to have been made to ensure participation. When the new bye-laws were discussed at the time of the Charter, Price observed that if Council members were not to be eligible for immediate re-election there might not be enough of them to continue the society's business. Higgs to Farrer, May 14, 1895; Price to Edgeworth, March 7, 1903.

50 Marshall to Edgeworth, September 4, 1892.

51 Cf. the remarks by Lord Farrer in the *Journal of the Royal Statistical Society*, vol. 57, 1894, pp. 608–10.

52 See the annual reports of the BAAS for 1893, pp. 571–2, and 1894, pp. 365–91. The reports were edited by E. C. K. Gonner, and the other committee members were Cunningham (Chairman), Edgeworth, Foxwell, Higgs and J. N. Keynes.

53 Mackenzie to Higgs, January 13, 1895; also January 16, 1895, and Higgs to Lord Aberdare, August 14, 1894. About this time the Council for Legal Education was approached via Goschen and Professor J. E. C. Munro (a BEA Council Member), but though there was considerable correspondence, and that organization appointed a sub-committee on the matter, no action was taken.

54 For Foxwell's account of the sale see his letter to Sir T. Larmor, St John's College, Cambridge. Also BEA minutes June 2 and December 6, 1901.

On November 30, 1915, the Council complained to the Chancellor of the University of London of the Senate's 'act of gross discourtesy to a distinguished economist' in demanding the immediate delivery of the remainder of the library. See the University's reply, March 25, 1915, and BEA minutes July 27 and November 3, 1914; February 17, April 24 and May 5, 1915.

55 BEA minutes April 18, 1891, and April 4, 1894, and correspondence. As a result of this incident the Association's copyright was vested in the Trustees, a practice already adopted by the Statistical Society.

56 BEA minutes, July 13, 1896, and correspondence, including a long printed memorandum from Rae.

57 Minute Books, January 20, 1896; March 15, 1903; June 21, 1901; October 10, 1902; February 6, 1903. The cost of the charter was put at £111 0s. 6d.; and as a result the organization had to acquire an overdraft which was paid off by the sale of stock early in 1903.

Higgs, as Secretary, who had access to high government circles, initiated the Charter proceedings which were completed largely by Bonar, who was acting Secretary while Higgs was on government service abroad.

58 In the remainder of this article I have drawn heavily on the analysis and illustrations contained in Geoffrey Millerson, *The Qualifying Associations, A Study in Professionalization* (1964). He emphasizes the time, trouble, expense and uncertainty involved in a petition for a Royal Charter, and the extensive data in his appendix 1 shows how unusual it has been for a non-examining institution to acquire a Royal Charter since 1890. Ibid., pp. 254–8.

59 *Annals of the Royal Statistical Society* (1934), p. 105.

60 As Millerson observes, the British have been generally reluctant to establish written codes of professional ethics, and a 'written code might cast doubts on the very claim of the occupation to describe itself as a profession'. Op. cit., p. 160. Marshall's emphasis, at the inaugural meeting, on the duty to be restrained in criticizing one's brother economists was a significant comment on the prevailing lack of professional self-confidence.

61 In 1903 there was one professor (i.e., Marshall) out of five Vice-Presidents, as

against none in 1891, and the percentage of full-time academics among the officers and council members rose from 35 to 45 per cent in the same period.

62 This is, of course, debatable, depending on the relative importance attached to scholarly as against other activities, and the respective weights assigned to theory, applied economics and influence on public policy. Whereas the President of the BEA (and RES) was, until 1928, a non-academic figurehead, Marshall having refused the honour in 1906, the President of the American Economic Association has always been a full-time professor or ex-economist University President (e.g., F. A. Walker, A. Hadley, E. J. James).

63 Jacob Bell (1842) quoted by Millerson, op. cit., p. 53.

18

THE CHANGING SOCIAL COMPOSITION OF THE ROYAL ECONOMIC SOCIETY 1890–1960 AND THE PROFESSIONALIZATION OF BRITISH ECONOMICS

I

In an earlier article we presented data on the social composition of the Royal Economic Society in the period 1890–1915, a period we then characterized as 'a water-shed dividing the predominantly amateur tradition of the eighteenth and nineteenth centuries from World War I, when the professionalization of economics began to gather momentum'.[1] We now proceed to extend our study to 1960, the date of the most recently published RES membership list, by analysing a 10 per cent sample of home-based members in selected years throughout the period since the society's foundation, in 1890.[2] In the concluding paragraphs we shall comment on the significance of this data for students of the British economics profession.

As we explained in the first instalment of this study, the RES membership lists include the names of many subscribers who possess no serious claims to be regarded as 'professional economists' by any normal definition of those terms. Nevertheless, throughout its long life the society's ranks have included the great majority of British professional economists, as well as many serious amateur students of the subject, and our occupational statistics (in Table 4, *infra*) provide some basis for judging the relative importance of the two categories. The Society's periodical, *The Economic Journal*, has always been scholarly in content and impartial in outlook, and its editors have never attempted to cater for the general public. Admittedly some subscribers may have been attracted by the opportunity to style themselves 'Fellow of the Royal Economic Society', a title available to all members from the early years of this century until 1968; but there is no evidence that this motive was sufficiently strong to affect the results of our study.

Table 1 Growth of Royal Economic Society membership

Membership category	1891 No.	%	1915 No.	%	1925 No.	%	1939 No.	%	1950 No.	%	1960 No.	%	1969 No.	%
Institutions	5	(0.7)	50	(6.7)	230	(9.9)	513	(11.4)	622	(10.4)	803	(14.2)	1307	(17.4)
Foreign	112	(15.8)	195	(26.1)	764	(32.7)	1580	(35.1)	1955	(32.7)	2381	(42.0)	6195	(82.6)
Home	594	(83.5)	502	(67.2)	1340	(57.4)	2409	(53.5)	3406	(56.9)	2483	(43.8)		
Total	711		747	(+5)	2334	(+212)	4502	(+93)	5983	(+33)	5667	(−5)	7502	(+32)

Sources: 1891–1960 from published RES membership lists; 1969 from *Annual Report*, 31 December, 1969
Note: Home members are those with addresses in the British Isles, some of which may, of course, be forwarding addresses.

Table 1 summarizes the long-term growth of the society's membership. Despite the apparent stability of the total, in the first, pre-World War I phase, there was actually a sharp decline to around 500 members in the late 1890s after the initial wave of enthusiasm had died away, and even in 1915 the home membership had not recovered to the 1891 level. Following the 1914–18 war slump, membership recovered rapidly and continued to expand in a healthy manner until 1939; but after another substantial post-war recovery in the late 1940s the story was very different. During the 1950s the RES's home membership actually fell (by nearly 27 per cent), a trend that is all the more surprising in view of the growing public interest in economic questions at the time.[3] There was also, of course, a steady expansion in the study and teaching of economics and related subjects in institutions of higher education during the 1950s, part of which is shown in Table 2. But as Table 4 (*infra*) indicates, university teachers and students have always comprised a small proportion of the organization's subscribers, so there is no *a priori* reason to expect a significant correlation between academic expansion and RES membership.[4]

Table 2 Growth of academic appointments in economics and related subjects in British universities 1891–1969

	1891	1915	1925	1939	1950	1960	1969
Total	20	85	180	286	446	679	1802
% growth	–	+ 325	+ 119	+ 59	+ 56	+ 52	+ 165.4

Sources: Except for 1891, data derived from Commonwealth Universities Year Book (various titles). 1891 data derived from official publications and correspondence with university and college libraries.
Notes: Wherever possible, temporary and part-time appointments have been excluded, and persons known to have held two or more appointments in the same college or university have been counted only once. During the 1960s a number of new universities were opened and several existing institutions were transferred into the university category.

Two other features of Table 1 deserve comment, namely, the continued expansion in the institutional (i.e. mainly library) subscribers, and the initially high and subsequently rising number of foreign members of the RES. Both these trends reflect the scholarly reputation of *The Economic Journal* which has long been more cosmopolitan in its coverage than the other leading academic economic journals published in English.[5]

Before presenting the results of the study, some general comments on the extent and quality of the sample data may be in order. As will be seen from Table 3, there are considerable gaps in the available biographical information. Of the three characteristics required, father's occupation proved by far the most elusive – sometimes surprisingly so, even in the case of quite eminent persons. The methods of enquiry and sources used necessarily varied somewhat from period to period owing to the distant date of publication of some major sources (notably *Alumni Cantabridgienses* and *Alumni Oxonienses*) and to gaps and discontinuities in others (e.g. the records of professional bodies). Direct enquiries were made in the case of individuals with known educational or professional affiliations, and letters were sent to the addresses of members in the 1950 and 1960 samples. As might be expected, in any given instance rapidly diminishing returns usually set in at a fairly early stage; but it is hoped that the sheer volume of data compensates in part for its unavoidable shortcomings.

Changes in the occupational distribution of RES members over the seventy-year period are indicated in Table 4,[6] which reveals that three categories of members predominated throughout, namely: businessmen, university teachers, and civil servants, in descending order of importance. Apart from 1925, when the proportion of businessmen in the sample was unusually low, the first two together comprised more than one-third of the total membership; and their combined share rose after World War II to more than 57 per cent in 1960. Despite the fall from the initial high figure of 22 per cent, the business contingent rose to a surprisingly high level in the last two selected years, and would have been slightly higher still if the journalists and insurance employees had been included in the same category. The proportion of university teachers fell somewhat during the interwar years; but the post-1939 recovery continued through the 1950s, whereas the proportion of civil servants remained fairly stable from 1915 through 1950, falling off sharply thereafter. Over the period as a whole accounting and banking constituted the fourth and fifth categories in order of size, although in each case the proportions fluctuated sharply in a manner that defies explanation. Of the remaining categories, administration, law, and non-university teaching occasionally rose to significant levels; but the others were never important.

Considering that the RES was a learned society publishing a purely scholarly journal, the size of the business contingent in the membership is most surprising, for British businessmen have not usually been noted either for their command of scientific and technical expertise or for their interest in academic subjects. The relative increase in businessmen's participation since 1925 may reflect the influence of increasing numbers of graduate entrants into business and the growing support for commercial and business education, especially since the mid-1930s.[7] The presence of accountants and bankers in the society is less remarkable, given the nature of their professional training and their concern with fiscal and financial problems, but it is less easy to explain the comparative stability of the civil service element, or the sharp decline in that category in the 1950s when the number of economists in government employment was growing (though perhaps slowly). During the nineteenth century a number of leading economists participated in government while certain government officials and civil servants made important contributions to the development of economic ideas.[8] Moreover, civil servants appear to have played a prominent role in

Table 3 RES samples and proportions of information known at various dates

| | 1891 | | 1915 | | 1925 | | 1939 | | 1950 | | 1960 | |
	No.	% known	No.	% known	No.	% known	No.	% known	No.	% known	No.	% known
Size of sample	60		51		134		242		340		249	
Member's occupation	55	92.0	44	86.0	86	64.0	171	71.0	183	54.0	167	67.0
Member's education	36	65.5	19	44.2	38	44.2	73	42.7	101	55.2	114	68.3
Father's occupation	32	58.2	14	32.6	27	31.4	62	36.3	91	49.7	111	66.5

Sources: General biographical and reference volumes; school and university records (especially *Alumni Cantabrigienses* and *Alumni Oxonienses*); *Times* obituaries; correspondence with local libraries and, for the post-1939 samples, with members and their relatives.

Table 4 Occupational distribution of RES members

Occupations	1891 No.	1891 %	1915 No.	1915 %	1925 No.	1925 %	1939 No.	1939 %	1950 No.	1950 %	1960 No.	1960 %
Accounting	5	(9.1)	2	(4.5)	8	(9.3)	23	(13.5)	29	(15.8)	17	(10.2)
Administration	3	(5.5)	8	(18.2)	6	(7.0)	11	(6.4)	3	(1.6)	5	(3.0)
Army	1	(1.8)	–	–	2	(2.3)	1	(0.6)	–	–	2	(1.2)
Banking	4	(7.3)	3	(6.8)	16	(18.6)	14	(8.2)	11	(6.0)	9	(5.4)
Business	12	(21.8)	8	(18.2)	7	(8.1)	34	(19.8)	52	(28.4)	55	(32.9)
Church	1	(1.8)	1	(2.3)	1	(1.2)	5	(2.9)	1	(0.6)	–	–
Civil Service	6	(10.9)	6	(13.6)	14	(16.3)	28	(16.4)	29	(15.8)	14	(8.4)
Government	1	(1.8)	2	(4.5)	–	–	1	(0.6)	1	(0.6)	–	–
Insurance	1	(1.8)	–	–	1	(1.2)	3	(1.8)	3	(1.6)	–	–
Journalism	3	(5.5)	–	–	2	(2.3)	–	–	3	(1.6)	1	(0.6)
Landowners	2	(3.6)	–	–	–	–	3	(1.8)	–	–	2	(1.2)
Law	2	(3.6)	3	(6.8)	6	(7.0)	2	(1.2)	3	(1.6)	3	(1.8)
Students	–	–	–	–	–	–	2	(1.2)	1	(0.6)	–	–
Teaching (non-university)	2	(3.6)	–	–	6	(7.0)	16	(9.4)	13	(7.1)	18	(10.8)
University teaching	10	(18.2)	10	(22.7)	17	(19.8)	26	(15.2)	32	(17.5)	41	(24.6)
Miscellaneous	2	(3.6)	1	(2.3)	–	–	2	(1.2)	2	(1.1)	–	–
Total known	55		44		86		171		183		167	
Occupation unknown	5		7		48		71		157		82	
Size of sample	60		51		134		242		340		249	

Sources: General biographical volumes; school and university records (especially *Alumni Cantabridgienses* and *Alumni Oxonienses*); records of professional bodies; *Times* obituaries; correspondence with individuals and institutions.

Note: These occupational statistics represent a 10 per cent sample of RES home membership at the dates selected. *Classification of occupations:* Wherever possible individuals are listed under their main occupation at the time. MPs are listed under their occupations or, if no occupation, as landowners. Retired persons are listed under their former occupation. *Administration* comprises members of public bodies, JPs, secretaries of non-business organizations, etc. *Civil Service* includes both central and local government officers. *Government* includes past and present statesmen, cabinet ministers, colonial governors, etc. *Landowners* includes persons of independent means with no designated profession or occupation.

the Royal Statistical Society (founded in 1834), and it may be conjectured that this tradition was inherited by the RES.

Table 5 presents the occupational distribution of RES members' fathers. However, before comparing these statistics with the distribution of members' occupations in Table 4 readers should be reminded that the actual numbers involved are often too small to form a reliable basis for generalization. Even so, some of the more striking inter-generational differences are worth noting. There was, for example, a consistently higher proportion of fathers in the older professions (i.e. church, law, medicine, armed services) despite the fact that the percentage of fathers in this occupational group fell sharply after 1925, mainly due to the declining number of clergyman fathers. Parallel features are evident in the category of landowners (which includes gentlemen of leisure and MPs with no other known occupations) although the proportion of fathers under this heading fell dramatically after 1915 and remained low. Opposite trends are apparent in the cases of civil service and university teaching; that is, the proportion of sons was consistently higher (and by a very large margin in the latter instance) and the percentage of sons remained roughly constant or rose while the percentage of fathers remained roughly constant or fell. Yet, once again, it is in the business category that we encounter the most unexpected results. Table 5 indicates that the proportion of businessmen fathers of RES members was remarkably high, was tending to increase, and was consistently higher throughout than the percentage of businessmen members.

The significance of these findings can be shown by comparing the data in Tables 4 and 5 with the results of the well-known study of Cambridge alumni published by Hester Jenkins and D. Caradog Jones.[9] Table 6, columns (1) to (2), reveals that in 1891 the RES membership contained a far lower proportion in the older professions (5.4 per cent as against 59 per cent, mainly owing to the large number of Cambridge alumni clergymen), and a correspondingly higher proportion engaged in administration (+ 14 per cent); business, finance, and banking (+ 38.5 per cent); and teaching (+ 9.8 per cent). Somewhat less striking, though still significant, differences emerge when we compare the 1891 fathers of Cambridge alumni with the fathers of RES members – i.e. Table 6, columns (3) and (4) – for among the latter there was, once again, a significantly lower percentage in the older professions (25.1 per cent as against 50 per cent) and a significantly higher percentage in administration (+ 14.1 per cent) and in business, finance, and banking (+ 17.7 per cent). There was, however, a lower percentage of RES members' fathers than of Cambridge alumni fathers in teaching (− 4 per cent).

By the late 1930s the occupational composition of the Cambridge alumni had changed in response to the needs of a modern industrial society, but there were still significant differences between that group and the RES members. Table 6, columns (5) to (6), reveals that the proportion of RES

Table 5 Father's occupation

Occupations	1891 No.	1891 % known	1915 No.	1915 % known	1925 No.	1925 % known	1939 No.	1939 % known	1950 No.	1950 % known	1960 No.	1960 % known
Accounting	–		–		–		2	3.2	1	1.1	3	2.7
Administration	–		–		1	3.7	–		–		–	
Army (Armed services)	1	3.1	–		–		1	1.6	5	5.5	2	1.8
Banking	–		–		1	3.7	1	1.6	–		4	3.6
Business	8	25.0	6	42.9	7	25.9	23.5	37.9	45	49.5	51	45.9
Church	6	18.8	1	7.1	5	18.5	5	8.1	5	5.5	4	3.6
Civil Service	3.5	10.9	1	7.1	2	7.4	6.5	10.5	6	6.6	8	7.2
Government	1	3.1	–		–		–		–		–	
Insurance	1	3.1	–		–		–		–		2	1.8
Journalism	1.5	4.7	–		–		1	1.6	1	1.1	–	
Landowners	6	18.8	2	14.3	–		2	3.2	–		2	1.8
Law	–		1.5	10.7	3	11.1	1	1.6	5	5.5	6	5.4
Medicine	2	6.3	–		1	3.7	2	3.2	2	2.2	2	1.8
Teachers, non-university	–		0.5	3.6	2	7.4	5	8.1	3	3.3	4	3.6
University teachers	–		1	7.1	3	11.1	3	4.8	1	1.1	3	2.7
Miscellaneous	2	6.2	1	7.1	2	7.4	9	14.5	17	18.7	20	18.0
Total												
'Known' members	32	58.2	14	32.6	27	31.4	62	36.3	91	49.7	111	66.5
'Not known'	28		37		107		180		249		138	
Size of sample	60		51		134		242		340		249	

Sources: See Table 4.

Table 6 Occupational distribution of RES members[a] and Alumni Cantabridgienses[b]

Occupations	1891				1939			
	Members % (1)	Al. Cant. % (2)	Members' fathers % (3)	Al. Cant. fathers % (4)	Members % (5)	Al. Cant. % (6)	Members' fathers % (7)	Al. Cant. fathers % (8)
Administration	20	6	17.1	3	25.8	10	12.1	8
Bank, etc.	18.2	2	3.1	3	25.8 } 43.3		4.8 } 44.3	
Business	27.3	5	29.7	12	17.5	31	39.5	46
Church	1.8	38	18.8	31	2.9	6	8.1	7
Landowners	3.6	7	18.8	19	1.8	0	3.2	2
Law	3.6	14	–	9	1.2	11	1.6	7
Medicine	–	7	6.3	10	–	12	3.2	8
Teaching	21.8	12	–	4	22.8	16	12.9	7
Miscellaneous	3.6	9	6.2	9	2.4	14	14.5	15

Sources:

a. RES membership, as in Table 1.

b. Alumni Cantabridgienses, as in Hester Jenkins and D. Caradog Jones, 'Social Class of Cambridge University Alumni of the 18th and 19th Centuries', Brit. J. Sociol., vol. 1 (June 1950), pp. 93–116.

Classification of occupations: As above, except for categories combined as in Jenkins and Caradog Jones, i.e. Administration includes civil service, government, Army, and public administration; Banking includes accounting, insurance, and stockbroking; Business includes journalism; Teaching combines university and non-university.

members in the older professions was still much lower than Cambridge alumni (− 25.1 per cent, and mainly due to law and medicine, rather than the church), whereas the proportion of RES members was significantly higher in the cases of administration (+ 15.8 per cent), banking and business (+ 12.3 per cent), and teaching (+ 6.8 per cent). Comparisons between the fathers of the two groups, Table 6, columns (7) to (8), indicates that the proportion of RES fathers was lower in the older professions (− 9.1 per cent) and, surprisingly enough, in business and banking (− 1.7 per cent); but the percentage was, once again, higher in administration (+ 4.1 per cent) and teaching (+ 5.9 per cent).

Table 7 presents the main differences between the occupational characteristics of the RES members and the Cambridge alumni members within each sample. It shows that ex-Cambridge men were far more likely to be in teaching or in business, but slightly less likely to be in administrative or governmental posts than other RES members. The proportions in all these three occupational categories were high, but they fluctuated sharply, despite a generally rising percentage in administration until 1950.

Jenkins and Caradog Jones interpreted the changes among the Cambridge alumni in the period from the late nineteenth century to the late 1930s as evidence of a 'new attitude' towards education on the part of those engaged in business and commerce, and a corresponding growth of undergraduate interest in the employment opportunities in these fields. If this is so, the RES members appear to have been in the vanguard of this movement and they were more 'advanced' than their fathers and the general run of Cambridge alumni. On the average they were far more likely to be administrators, businessmen, bankers, or teachers, and less likely to be men of leisure, clergymen, lawyers, or doctors. These differences reflected – to some extent, if not completely – their fathers' occupational characteristics, and this point leads us to an examination of the RES members' educational background, particularly schooling, which Jenkins and Caradog Jones regard as a 'more reliable index of social class than university'.[10]

Table 8 shows the results of a statistical analysis of the schools attended by RES members, and although it is again necessary to recommend caution in interpreting the data there can be no doubt as to the significance of the general trend. Despite the small numbers involved and the difficulties of classifying individual schools at such widely spaced intervals of time, there was a remarkable increase in the proportion of members from grammar and state schools. The first three categories (public + private + tutor) together accounted for almost 95 per cent of the 1891 sample and thereafter declined to around 50 per cent in 1960, and this trend is compatible with the decline in the proportion of members employed in or descended from the landowning and older professional groups.

Table 7 Occupational distribution of RES members and Alumni Cantabridgienses (percentage)

Occupations	1891 RES	1891 Alumni Cant.	1915 RES	1915 Alumni Cant.	1925 RES	1925 Alumni Cant.	1939 RES	1939 Alumni Cant.	1950 RES	1950 Alumni Cant.	1960 RES	1960 Alumni Cant.
Administration	20.0	18.2	36.3	18.2	25.6	33.3	25.8	27.3	19.1	21.7	12.6	3.4
Bank, etc.	18.2	–	13.6	–	29.1	6.7	25.8	9.1	23.9	–	17.4	10.3
Business	27.3	45.5	15.9	18.2	10.4	23.3	17.5	13.6	29.5	34.8	31.7	37.9
Church	1.8	–	2.3	–	1.2	–	2.9	–	0.6	–	–	–
Landowners	3.6	9.0	–	–	–	–	1.8	4.5	–	–	1.2	–
Law	3.6	–	6.8	9.1	7.0	10.0	1.2	–	1.6	–	1.8	–
Medicine	–	–	–	–	–	–	–	–	–	4.3	–	–
Teaching	21.8	27.3	22.7	54.5	26.8	26.7	22.8	40.9	23.5	39.2	35.4	48.4
Miscellaneous	3.6	–	2.3	–	–	–	2.4	4.5	1.7	–	–	–
Number in sample	55	11	44	11	86	15	171	22	183	23	167	29

Sources: See Table 4.

Table 8 Educational background of RES members, 1891–1960

Schools	1891		1915		1925		1939		1950		1960	
	No.	% known	No.	% known	No.	% known	No.	% known	No.	% known	No.	% known
Public	21	58.3	7	36.8	13	34.2	26	35.6	32	31.7	34	29.8
Private	11	30.6	6	31.6	18	47.4	19	26.0	29	28.7	25	21.9
Tutor	2	5.6	–	–	1	2.6	1	1.4	–	–	1	0.9
Grammar	–	–	5	26.3	2	5.3	23	31.5	35	34.7	44	38.6
State (elementary)	2	5.6	1	5.3	4	10.5	4	5.5	5	4.9	10	8.8
Total known	36	65.5	19	44.2	38	44.2	73	42.7	101	55.2	114	68.3
Size of sample	60		51		134		242		340		249	

Table 9(a) **RES members' undergraduate degrees (sample)**

	1891		1915		1925		1939		1950		1960	
	No.	*%*	*No.*	*%*	*No.*	*%*	*No.*	*%*	*No.*	*%*	*No.*	*%*
Arts	18	69.23	14	70.00	23	51.11	35	41.17	34	33.33	37	38.95
Law	7	26.92	4	20.00	6	13.33	12	14.12	15	14.71	5	5.26
Science	1	3.85	–		3	6.67	14	16.47	8	7.84	7	7.37
Social science	–		2	10.00	13	28.89	24	28.24	45	44.12	46	48.42
Total	26	100	20	100	45	100	85	100	102	100	95	100
Size of sample	60		51		134		242		340		249	
No. of known members	55		43		86		171		183		167	
% known with degrees	47		46.5		52		50		55.5		57	

Note: Each figure represents a separate degree, and some members had more than one undergraduate degree.

Table 9(b) RES members' doctoral degrees

Type of degree	1891	1915	1925	1939	1950	1960
Ph.D.s	–	1	3	4	13	16
Other doctorates	8	8	7	8	6	2
Total	8	9	10	12	19	18
% of sample known		4.5	21	11.5	7	10.4	11

Note: Some 'other doctorates' may have been honorary degrees.

Further evidence of the educational background of RES members appears in Table 9 (a) and (b), the first of which shows that approximately half of those whose occupations are known had obtained an undergraduate degree, a proportion that rose somewhat (from 47 per cent to 57 per cent) over time. As might be expected, the percentage of members with social science degrees (mainly in economics and commerce) rose sharply, especially after World War II, and it may be presumed that many of the arts degrees listed included a sizeable component of political economy. On the other hand, a declining percentage of members had degrees in law or a natural science. Table 9 (b) demonstrates that on the average only about 11 per cent of RES members possessed any kind of doctorate, and that this percentage did not rise over time. As the Ph.D. is nowadays often thought of as the ticket of entry to the academic profession this result may seem somewhat surprising; but it must be recalled that academics comprised only a small proportion of the total membership. A slightly different index of professional competence appears in Table 10, which shows the number of RES members in our lists (the whole list, not merely the 10 per cent sample) who have published one or more articles in a recognized scholarly economic journal. These figures probably underestimate the number of identifiable economic writers in the organization, for no account has been taken of books, monographs, newspapers, or other species of economic literature. Nevertheless, it seems safe to assume that the proportion of members with economic writings to their credit rarely rose above 20 or at most 25 per cent, which constitutes another index of the predominantly non-professional character of the society.

Tables 11(a) and (b) indicate the occupational characteristics and educational backgrounds of the society's governing body: its council and officers (e.g. President, Secretary, Treasurer, etc.). As might be expected of a learned society, university teachers always constituted the overwhelming proportion, and their relative importance increased over time. Until 1915 a significant number of men in government were included among the council and officers, probably owing to the policy of enlisting the support of eminent persons whose names would add lustre to the organization; but this category contributed only an insignificant proportion thereafter. Civil

Table 10 Number of RES members who have published articles in economic journals

Number of articles	1891		1915		1925		1939		1950		1960	
	No. of members	% of total	No. of members	% of total	No. of members	% of total	No. of members	% of total	No. of members	% of total	No. of members	% of total
One or two	103	17.3	166	33.1	259	19.3	384	15.9	491	14.4	436	17.6
Three or more	38	6.4	90	17.9	133	9.9	210	8.7	262	7.7	248	10.0
No. of home members	594		502		1340		2409		3406		2480	

Source: Based on the American Economic Association Index of Economic Journals, vols. I–VI (1886–1963).
Note: These tables cover all listed RES members, not merely those in the samples.

Table 11(a) RES officers and council members

Occupations	1891 Members	1891 Fathers	1915 Members	1915 Fathers	1925 Members	1925 Fathers	1939 Members	1939 Fathers	1950 Members	1950 Fathers	1960 Members	1960 Fathers
Accounting				1		1		1		1		
Administration	1½		4		1		1	1½		1		2½
Army	3	3		2		2		1		2	4	1
Banking	1	6	4	5	4	1	3	1	2	1	1	
Business		8		6		8		6	½	3		9
Church	⅓			7		7½		8½		6½		4
Civil Service	4	1	7	3	6	2	4	2	4	2	4	5
Government	5½		6		2	1		1		1		1
Insurance												
Journalism	1⅓	½	1		2		1	1	1½	1	2	1
Landowners	1	3		3	1	2	1			1		1
Law		1½		4		2						1
Medicine		2		2								
Teachers, non-university						½				2½		3½
University teachers	13⅓		19	1	20	1	27	1	32	3	31	3
Miscellaneous		2		1		4		5		4		6
Unknown		4		7		5		8		11		4
Total	31	31	42	42	37	37	38	38	40	40	42	42

Note: Fractions indicate that an individual had more than one occupation.

servants and businessmen-plus-bankers were the only other noteworthy elements, each of which usually comprised 10–15 per cent. The known occupations of council members' fathers are limited in number, but sufficient to draw attention to the consistently high percentage of businessmen-plus-bankers (as among members' fathers, in Table 5), a group which usually represented between 23 and 33 per cent of the total. There was also a sizeable, but diminishing percentage of clergyman fathers of RES council members and officers. Table 9(b) conveys the available information about the educational background of council members, who appear to have been on the whole more highly educated and from a higher social class than the majority of members. The very low percentage who attended grammar or state schools is noteworthy, and surprisingly enough the proportion in these categories showed no tendency to increase over time.

Table 11(b) RES officers and council members: educational background

Schools	1891	1915	1925	1939	1950	1960
Public	13	19	21	26	26	30
Private and Tutor	10	22	15	8	7	5
Grammar	4	1	1	3	7	6
State	3	–	–	–	–	–
Unknown	1	–	–	1	–	1
Total	31	42	37	38	40	42

II

Before attempting to draw some conclusions from our RES data it is worth attempting some comparisons with the pre-1890 era. We shall confine our attention to occupational characteristics as the most reliable single index of social composition; but even so, we can form only rough and ready impressions owing to the difficulties of compiling and interpreting occupational data about pre-1890 economic writers and policy makers. There are formidable problems of definition, for some occupations have retained their names but altered their character radically, while others familiar today have no counterpart in earlier epochs. Another difficulty arises from the growth of specialization. Many economic writers of earlier generations were leisured men who had no regular occupation but who dabbled in several. Moreover, in the course of a lifetime a man could change his occupation several times (a problem that is eliminated from the RES study by the selection of a separate sample for each date), and in such cases appropriate fractions have been imputed to each of several different occupational categories.

Table 12 Occupational distribution of British 'economists' prior to 1890

	(1) Pre-1750		(2) 1750–1890		(3) Political Economy Club	
Occupations	No.	%	No.	%	No.	%
Accounting	–	–	6	(1.75)	–	–
Administration	6	(5.0)	9	(3.0)	1	(0.6)
Army	2½	(2.0)	2½	(1.0)	5	(3.2)
Banking	5	(4.0)	12	(5.5)	16	(10.4)
Business	38½	(32.0)	31	(12.5)	24	(15.6)
Business, stockbroking	–	–	3	(1.0)	2½	(1.6)
Church	13½	(11.5)	18	(7.25)	2½	(1.6)
Civil Service	19½	(16.0)	25	(8.5)	27	(17.5)
Government	6	(5.0)	19½	(6.5)	27½	(17.9)
Insurance	1	(1.0)	2	(0.5)	–	–
Journalism	6½	(5.5)	28	(11.0)	9	(5.8)
Landowners	11	(9.0)	22	(8.5)	9	(5.8)
Law	7	(6.0)	24	(9.0)	13½	(8.8)
Medicine	1	(1.0)	4	(1.0)	–	–
Teachers, non-university	1	(1.0)	3	(1.0)	1	(0.6)
University teachers	2½	(2.0)	50	(22.0)	16	(10.4)
Total	121		259		154	

Sources: Data in cols (1) and (2) drawn from *Palgrave's Dictionary of Political Economy* (ed. H. Higgs) 3 vols (London, 1923–6). Additional names drawn from J.A. Schumpeter, *History of Economic Analysis* (Oxford, 1954); M. Blaug, *Economic Theory in Retrospect*, 2nd ed. (Homewood, Ill., 1968); G. J. Stigler, *Essays in the History of Economics*, (Chicago, 1965), ch. 3. Data in col. (3) drawn from H. Higgs (ed.) *Political Economy Club of London* (London, 1921).

Notes: A pre-1750 economist is one who died or whose major works were written before that date. A similar principle was employed in selecting economists of the 1750–1890 period. Of course, some Political Economy Club members are included in the figures in col. (2) as well as in col. (3). Fractions indicate that an individual had more that one occupation. *Classification of occupation*: As far as possible, the same as in Table 9.

Table 12 represents a summary of the results of a biographical analysis of the careers of important British economic writers in the years before the inauguration of the RES. The names have been selected from a few readily accessible reference works,[11] and a division has been introduced at 1750 because this roughly approximates the dividing line between the pre-classical (or pre-Adamite) period and the beginnings of 'modern' systematic theory. Prior to that date, it is usually supposed, economic writers were usually either merchants, government officials, or partisan pamphleteers (including journalistic hacks like Daniel Defoe), whereas in later generations academic authors were increasingly prominent. The Political Economy Club of London founded in 1821, has been analysed separately in column (3) because this was a private club containing many committed free traders and a proportion of leading government figures and professors.

Generally speaking, Table 12 confirms the impressions derived from 'history of economic thought' textbooks, but adds precision to them. Among pre-1750 economists, businessmen (especially merchants) predominated, while civil servants (or their contemporary equivalents, many of whom had ample spare time for literary activities) occupied second place. Next in order were clergymen and landowners (a category including MPs and persons of independent means without a regular occupation), which is hardly surprising considering that they comprised a substantial proportion of the educated classes; while other pre-1750 groups are distributed in a manner that hardly merits specific comment. Matters differ strikingly, however, when we turn to the period 1750–1890. Although political economy played a minor part in most academic institutions until the late nineteenth century, academics comprised a surprisingly high proportion of the post-1750 'economists' – a fact that may indicate the increasingly specialist and scientific character of their discipline. The percentage of businessmen economists fell markedly from the earlier period, as did also the percentage of clergymen and civil servants; but there was a notable increase in the number of journalists, a broadly defined category which included various persons who supplemented their incomes by writing books and articles in popular magazines, such as the *Edinburgh Review*. These men were the forerunners of the present day financial and economic journalists, and their activities reflect the growing nineteenth-century interest in economic ideas and policy – a factor that may partially account for the increasing prominence of lawyer-economists. Civil service economists, on the other hand, are comparatively less important than before 1750, possibly because they were more preoccupied with their official duties than their leisured predecessors.

Comparison of the 1750–1890 economists with the Political Economy Club's membership list strikingly displays the distinctive characteristics of that private body. As its founders aimed to influence the course of legislation they deliberately included cabinet ministers within their ranks (some of whom, like the Chancellor of the Exchequer, were *ex-officio* members) and the fact that more than one-third of all the club's members were either employees or members of the government is a remarkable testimony to the closeness of the connections between orthodox free trade economics and public policy. A glance at columns (2) and (3) also indicates that the club had no monopoly of the academic economists; and indeed, the number of its professorial adherents would doubtless have been lower still but for the fact that the holders of certain leading chairs were also, like some ministers, *ex-officio* members. Businessmen and bankers played an important role in the club, as in the wider community of economists, for it was a 'practical' organization whose members were chiefly concerned with theoretical questions in so far as they bore on current and future policy issues. Bankers were among the leading supporters of free trade and minimal government interference; but while the club was a social and intellectual élite, its narrowness was one of the principal reasons why it proved necessary to establish the RES in 1890.

The occupational distribution of the early RES members cannot be directly compared with that of the 1790–1850 economists for several obvious reasons. Apart from the wide differences in time span, the earlier group is confined to persons who have achieved some recognition as 'economists', whereas the RES included many members who had only a casual interest in the subject. Nevertheless, it may be noted that the first RES list (Table 4) contained a significantly higher percentage of businessmen (+ 8.3) and accountants and a lower percentage of journalists (− 5.5), churchmen (− 5.45), lawyers (− 5.4), landowners (− 4.9), and men in government (− 4.7). The proportion of university teachers in the RES was also slightly lower than in the pre-1890 group, where the percentage was remarkably close to the average RES proportion throughout the 1890–1960 period.

III

What light does the foregoing material shed on the professionalization of British economics since the 1890s? As the RES was more a learned society than a guild-type professional organization or qualifying association, the occupationally diffuse character of its membership comes as no surprise. Indeed, the economist's functions have never been precise and restricted. His expertise equips him to compile, analyse, interpret, and disseminate information about economic affairs and to forecast economic trends, but he can perform these tasks equally well in a wide variety of occupational contexts. Moreover, while our data would permit a much finer breakdown of occupations (e.g. in the general category business) than we have provided in the foregoing tables, it would not furnish the kind of detailed job descriptions required to trace the economist's changing functions since the 1890s. We can, however, provide a general profile of the 'typical' RES member of 1960, who was far more likely to be a teacher (whether in a university or elsewhere) or a businessman than his 1891 counterpart, and far more likely to be the son of a businessman than of a clergyman or landowner. He was far more likely to have attended a grammar or state school than his predecessor, and somewhat more likely to have obtained an undergraduate degree, especially in the social sciences. If he was an officer or council member he was more probably a university teacher than his 1891 equivalent, and his father was much less likely to be a member of the older professions. By comparison with the general run of Cambridge graduates both he and his father were more likely to be teachers or businessmen, and less likely to be members of the older professions; and if he was himself a Cambridge man (whether in 1891 or 1960) he was more likely than other RES members to be a teacher or businessman (but not a banker) − a fact which may reflect the strength and continuity of the Cambridge tradition in economics.

Whether or not these differences reveal the increasing professionalization of British economics inevitably depends in large measure on one's definition of a 'profession', which is unfortunately one of the more elusive terms in the current social science vocabulary. If, for example, attention is focused on the overt institutional manifestations of professionalism – such as control of entry, establishment and enforcement of professional standards, formulation of a code of ethics, etc. – then the economists clearly have a long way to go. But if, on the other hand,[12] emphasis is placed on the existence of a corporate sense of identity and shared values, the command of a recognized corpus of knowledge, possession of a common language which is imperfectly comprehended by outsiders, reliance on formalized university training, and the capacity to reproduce the next generation socially by influencing the qualifications of professional trainees, then there has obviously been substantial progress towards the emergence of an economics profession in Britain since the beginning of this century and, more especially, since 1945.[13] Thus economics may be regarded as fairly typical of the 'newer type of profession now emerging, the application of a scientific speciality to practical problems', a species which 'remains closer to the academic traditions of proof' than to the older guild type of profession (e.g. law, medicine). In economics, as in the other newer professions 'the allegiance of members is primarily to the substantive field, not the guild. Their professional behaviour is guided far more by the ethic of science than by the ethic of the client–professional relationship. Their academic counterpart is the professor who does consulting work.'[14]

The RES data provided in this paper provides only limited and indirect evidence of this newer type of professionalization, though it is compatible with it. The strongest common link among Fellows of the Society was their subscription to *The Economic Journal*, a periodical which was certainly far more technical in content and specialized in coverage in 1960 than in the 1890s; and although subscribers are not necessarily readers, the subscription (i.e. membership) lists obviously provide important insights into the journal's audience.[15] But if, as sociologists have recently suggested,[16] the crucial index of professional status is public recognition rather than more precise objectively discriminable differentia, then we must perhaps seek evidence for the existence of an economics profession in everyday usage, and in the advertising columns of our leading newspapers,[17] rather than in the membership lists of the Royal Economic Society.

NOTES

* Co-written with S. E. Coats.

1 A. W. Coats and S. E. Coats, 'The Social Composition of the Royal Economic Society and the Beginnings of the British Economics "Profession" 1890–1915', *Brit. J. Sociol.*, vol. 21 (March 1970), p. 75. (Reprinted in this volume pp. 338–60.)

2 The research was initially financed by the Institute of Economic and Social Research at the University of York and by the University of Nottingham; and was completed with the aid of funds from the Houblon–Norman Fund of the Bank of England. In addition to those persons whose help was acknowledged in the previous article, we would especially like to thank Mrs E. Harper, who undertook much of the data collection and computation.

3 However the society undertook no membership campaigns and, as already noted, its officers made no conscious effort to arouse the interest of the general public.

4 Nevertheless, in the strictly academic sphere opportunities were missed. The society held no annual conferences, nor did it seek to promote or organize research. The small but significantly growing attendance at annual meetings of the Association of University Teachers of Economics during the 1950s reveals that there was a constituency waiting to be led. This growth accelerated rapidly in the 1960s, and the RES has just recently adopted a more active policy of supporting these conventional scholarly gatherings.

5 See my article 'The Role of Scholarly Journals in the History of Economics: An Essay', *J. Econ. Lit.*, vol. 9 (March 1971), pp. 29–44 (reprinted in this volume, pp. 155–75). The rise of overseas membership to 112 within a year of the society's foundation (as the British Economic Association) bears witness to the existence of an international network of economists.

6 The figures in Table 3 represent a 10 per cent sample of RES home membership at successive dates, and therefore vary from the figures presented in the earlier article, which were based on the total membership at those dates. Discrepancies of more than 2 per cent between the two results occurred in the following cases (quoting the earlier percentages):

1891: Accounting 9.1; Banking 9.5; Journalism 3; Law 10.

1915: Administration 9; Government 2; Journalism 2.5; Landowners 3; Non-university teaching 3; University teaching 26.

7 However Dr Michael Sanderson's careful researches reveal that there were no dramatic changes in these background conditions during the interwar years. Cf. his *The Universities and British Industry 1850–1970* (London 1972), chapters 9–11.

8 James Mill, N. W. Senior, J. R. McCulloch, and J. S. Mill represent obvious examples of economists participating in government, while Sir Robert Giffen and Lord Goschen are outstanding examples of civil servants who made significant contributions to economics. There were also a number of economists and near-economists in government departments, especially the Treasury and the Board of Trade.

9 'Social Class of Cambridge University Alumni of the 18th and 19th Centuries', *Brit. J. Sociol.*, vol. 1 (June 1950), pp 93–116. Cf. Coats and Coats, op. cit., p. 77. As noted earlier, the figures in the text differ from those in our earlier study as we are now dealing with a 10 per cent sample.

10 Op. cit., p. 108.

11 The sources are listed at the foot of Table 12, and have been selected because

of their representative or comprehensive character. It is unlikely that the incorporation of other sources of this kind would have affected the outcome significantly.

12 Cf. William J. Goode, 'Community Within a Community: The Professions', *Amer. Sociol. Rev.*, vol. 22 (April 1957), p. 194.

13 One important manifestation has been the steady, if slow growth of the economist's role in the Civil Service, especially since the establishment of the Government Economic Service in 1965.

14 William J. Goode, 'Encroachment, Charlatanism and the Emerging Profession: Psychology, Sociology and Medicine', *Amer. Sociol. Rev.*, vol. 25 (December 1960), pp. 912–13, 906.

15 It is noteworthy that the proportion of RES members who contributed articles to scholarly economic journals remained roughly constant (Table 10) although the percentage of university teachers in the sample rose from 18.2 in 1891 to 24.6 in 1960 (Table 4).

16 Cf. Howard Becker, *Sociological Work, Method and Substance* (London, 1971), ch. 6: 'The Nature of a Profession' (originally published in 1962). Also Geoffrey Millerson, *The Qualifying Associations, A Study in Professionalization* (London 1964), p. 9: 'an occupation does not have to be organized to be a profession.' However, 'subjectively, members of the occupation must be conscious of themselves as professionals. Objectively, those using the services, and the general public, must be willing to recognize and accept the occupation as a profession.'

17 For example recent Civil Service Commission advertisements informing honours graduates how to become 'a professional economist'.

19

ALFRED MARSHALL AND THE EARLY DEVELOPMENT OF THE LONDON SCHOOL OF ECONOMICS

Some unpublished letters

The founding and early history of the London School of Economics has repeatedly attracted the attention of historians, but its place in the development of British economics has hitherto been unduly neglected. As is well known, the Webbs and their co-founders were not seeking to establish a new centre of socialist propaganda, for, as Fabians, they believed that 'it only needed patient explanation of facts to persuade others of the truths of Socialism and the desirability of socialistic reforms'.[1] Nevertheless, they undoubtedly intended to encourage the ideas of schools of thought other than 'the theoretical and individualist economics of Ricardo and Mill',[2] and to this end they chose as the first Director a young Oxford scholar, W. A. S. Hewins. Hewins' undergraduate studies had reinforced his initial prejudices against orthodox economics, and he became an active member of an important group of young Oxford dissidents whose number included the economic historian W. J. Ashley; the clergyman-editor of the *Economic Review*, John Carter; the economist and journalist, J. A. Hobson; the geographer (and subsequently, second Director of the LSE), Halford J. Mackinder; and the educationalist, Michael E. Sadler. Despite friendly warnings from the Oxford economic historian, J. E. Thorold Rogers, that he would jeopardize his career if he adopted too radical an approach, Hewins went ahead with his plans to reorganize the teaching of economics, and these proposals formed the basis of the scheme for the new institution which he submitted to Sidney Webb in 1894.[3]

In view of the precarious financial position of the LSE and the inevitable suspicions aroused by its links with the Fabian society, Hewins launched a vigorous publicity campaign designed to emphasize the novelty and the importance of this new educational venture. Naturally enough, he drew heavily upon the report of an authoritative subcommittee of the British Association for the Advancement of Science, published in 1894, which had stressed the urgent need to improve the facilities for teaching and examining economics in British universities and colleges,[4] and in so doing he offended Alfred Marshall, who was not only the leading contemporary British economist, but also one of the principal defenders of the received tradition of British economic thought.

In his autobiography Hewins mentioned W. J. Ashley's report that Marshall

> was very angry with me on account of an official report published by the Education Department on the London School of Economics. Ashley said to him, 'Why, what is there wrong in it?' and Marshall replied, 'There is nothing wrong in it, it is the devilish subtlety of it.'[5]

This disclosure is, to say the least, enigmatic. However, the substance of Marshall's objection can now be revealed, for some of his letters to Hewins have recently come to light.[6] They are of interest for three distinct reasons: they disclose Marshall's conception of economics as a science and as a practical study; they explain his objections to Hewins' report on the LSE; and they contain significant remarks on the state of economics teaching and study at Cambridge shortly before Marshall began his campaign for an Economics Tripos – a campaign that was crowned with success in 1903. Marshall evidently considered that Hewins' account of the LSE, which appeared in a government publication in 1898,[7] did less than justice to the situation at Cambridge; and he probably felt that Hewins had painted far too gloomy a picture of the state of British economics prior to 1895. At that time, according to Hewins, scarcely any branch of English higher education was so ill provided for as economics. Scientific work had usually been subordinated to the study of practical questions, and economics had been neglected by existing educational institutions and starved of both state and private funds. The leading British economic writers had rarely derived their inspiration or their preparatory training from elementary economics; the number of academic economists was small; professorships were few and poorly paid; and consequently talented men turned to other matters, refusing to embark upon a scholarly and scientific career 'in which bare subsistence is uncertain'. It was, admittedly, 'just possible to earn enough to live with extreme economy by combining together several different economic sources of income. But this requires unusual ability, perfect health, and unremitting toil'; and the associated activities might well prove detrimental to scientific work.

In commenting on conditions outside London, Hewins spoke more severely of Oxford than of Cambridge, where 'economic studies have been organized up to a certain point with energy and success . . . and the teaching at Cambridge is more systematic and continuous'. Even so, Marshall may have regarded this concession as patronizing, for although Hewins had acknowledged the LSE's debt to its precursors, he had proudly claimed that the School's performance already showed 'that the problem of organizing higher economic teaching in England is not insoluble' – a matter that had presumably remained in doubt up to 1895.

Unfortunately Hewins' letters to Marshall have not survived. Earlier correspondence in the Hewins papers indicates that the two men were on friendly though not intimate terms, but the first reference to the LSE occurs in the following.

Balliol Croft, 12.10.99.

My dear Hewins,

It seems strange to me to be asked my views as to the study of pure economic theory; as tho' that were a subject on wh I were fit to speak. For indeed I was never a partisan of it; and for more than a quarter of a century I have set my face away from it. As early as 1873 (I think that was the year) Walras pressed me to publish something about it; and I declined with emphasis.[8]

The fact is I am the dull mean man, who holds Economics to be an organic whole, and has as little respect for pure theory (otherwise than as a branch of mathematics or the science of numbers), as for that crude collection and interpretation of facts without the aid of high analysis which sometimes claims to be a part of economic history.

In the next two paragraphs, Marshall made some unfavourable remarks on Wilhelm Launhardt's *Die Betriebskosten der Eisenbahnen* (1877), arguing that the author had gone to work by a 'wrong route':

My route would be parallel to his – or what I believe to be his, but turned round through 180°. I would not let students look at Launhardt, till they had attained enough of railway instinct to know beforehand whether passenger rates would be high or low relating to goods rates in America, and in what parts of the world the quickest trains speed would bear the lowest ratio to (I mean be the least in excess of) the average passenger train speed and so on. Then I would give them several concrete books such as Hadley's,[9] and tell them to put into mathematical phrase (if they happened to like mathematics) but anyhow into precise quantitative phrases, such parts of their reasoning as were capable of it; *not* throwing away the rest, but keeping it formulated by side of the mathematics. Next they should try to find the general mathematical proposition of wh that proposition was a special case: next they should try to interpret that general proposition into English, and not lightly take a denial: that should be their main effort to wh they should give most weeks and months of work; and when they had done it they might throw away their mathematics;

unless indeed they cared to keep a few specimens of such work in an old curiosity shop.

When they had got that proposition they might turn round again thro' 180°; and starting from it take the various special problems as illustrations. Having discovered the One in the Many, they might set forth afresh the Many in the One. I repeat I regard the use of mathematics on the way as a gain when convenient, but not as of the essence of the work. In my view the *Many* is the ground of study; the *One* is the Holy Grail to be sought by the pious and laborious pilgrim; and the One where so found is to help as a guide through life over the broken ground of the Many. Launhardt's plan *seems* to me (I have not read him) that of standing where he happens to be, and jumping in the air and jumping again, in hopes that the Holy Grail will come floating past and stick in his fingers as he jumps.

This prolix exposition of what I conceive to be *the* method of economics would be of absurd length, if it were really an answer to your question. But really it is evoked by your remark as to the Church Congress.

The plain fact is that I have felt rather sore since I read your account of 'the position of Economics in England' in Sadlers Educational Blue Book. Some newspaper reports of public speeches by you had fretted me a little before: but when I read that I felt that I must make a protest, in public or private, sooner or later.

I think it is certain there are virtues in the London School wh I do not know of, and you do; and I think it is probable that you know more about its shortcomings than I do. Nor do I blame you in the least for setting forth its merits, and leaving others to find out the deficiencies; some of wh are perhaps inseparable from those merits, while others will be removed as the School grows stronger with time.

But while impelled to lay stress on one side of the case as to London, it seems rather hard that you should have laid stress on the other side as regards Cambridge. I gather that you really do not know what is being done here, nor how it is being done. Taking the least important point of all, the number of lectures given, I think you would be astonished if you counted up the number that are given in the year here on subjects of the same order as those treated in the London School: I believe you would find that our number is not less than yours; though of course the proportion of them that are elementary is large; because the average age of our students is low.[10]

But the main point is that Cambridge has an idea of its own which asserts itself in spite of the partially non-Cambridge idiosyncrasies of one or two members of the staff. The incidental work wh we do not advertise, but should be compelled to advertise if we were starting a new place like the London School (or to quote my own experience

Bristol University College in 1879, where my duties as advertiser in chief were specially onerous) – this incidental work is very great. I regard it as the most important half of my own work; and it is governed vy much by a central idea, Cambridge born.

You will say – why then not write a separate and peculiar panegyric of Cambridge? I have sometimes thought that that is what I ought to have done when Sadlers blue book appeared. But my personal disinclination for such work, my loathing for it is beyond conception. What I had to do of it at Bristol nearly killed me. And it would have been difficult to keep quite clear of controversy, by implication if not explicitly. For one thing I could hardly have fully admitted that Cambridge has the faults that attach to its virtues (as well as others), without implying that in my opinion London also has those faults which attach to *its* virtues.

So I have tried to indicate what I mean by the guiding principle of those Cambridge men who are – in my view most truly Cambridge men – the Search of the One in the Many and the Many in the One.

For I hope that in the address, wh I am delighted that you are to give at the Church Congress,[11] your text will be 'Economics should be studied, and it can be studied in London', and that you will *stop there*; that you will *not* add as you did, I think in the blue book: – 'and it cannot be studied anywhere else in England! So down with the cash please, for without the London School there would be no true economic study at least on this side of salt water.'

Yours very heartily

Alfred Marshall.

Returning to Launhardt. I have been looking at him again. I see he is not quite so wooden as I thought. But he still seems to talk of Betriebs-Kosten as tho experts had not agreed to deny the existence of such a thing. As perhaps you know, I think experts overstate the case. But to ignore the difficulty, is the work of a 'pure' theorist in the dyslogistic sense of the term.

You know that I have begged of Berry's[12] Goodness – he is not paid save by microscopic fees – to lecture on 'The Diagrammatic treatment of Pure Economic Theory' (mathematics being added for mathematicians): but these are really lectures on method and language: aimed at strengthening grasp, not inculcating doctrine.

I think lectures on Cournot for the same purpose would be useful to some persons.

A few days later Marshall added a further explanation.

Balliol Croft, 17.10.99.

My dear Hewins,

Many thanks for your friendly letter, and for your particularly kind remarks about myself. But of course it is for Cambridge that I am jealous. I did not see why the scope of your paper required you to make implicit comparisons between London and other centres of instruction. Had you stuck to your subject: which, I understand, was the London School of Economics, no one could have blamed you: for it is obviously a good subject and one on all fours with those of many other articles in the Report. But you took your subject to be the London School in its relation to other schools; and, you must forgive me for saying, that, whatever your intention, the effect of your words was to give people a wrong impression of that relation, both as regards the methods and the volume of teaching, and of initiating original work.

I say this the more freely, because I know from experience how difficult it is to give to others a correct impression of one's own feelings in matters of proportion. I often find that one half of my remarks, especially on controversial and personal matters, gets home, and the other half does not: so that 'the taste left in the mouth' is different from what I had designed, and from what I believed it had been, till informed to the contrary. In speaking thus frankly, I am but doing as I would be done by in all such cases. I know well that newspaper reports are misleading as regards the general tendency of speeches as well as their details.

Again thanking you. I am Yours sincerely, Alfred Marshall.

I thought your paper at the Church Congress was excellent in every way.

This postscript suggests that Hewins may have accepted Marshall's advice about his address to the Church Congress, but Marshall's interest in the LSE did not end here, for seven months later (by which time the School had been incorporated into the University of London) he raised a semantic issue that obviously seemed to him of some importance.

Balliol Croft 29/5/00

My dear Hewins,

I have just looked at the London University Calendar. I find that the subject wh you had described as economic *science* is officially called 'pure theory'. I knew that that had been assigned some place: but I am rather indifferent about it. Much of 'pure theory' seems to me to be elegant toying: I habitually describe my own pure theory of international trade as a 'toy'. I understand economic science to be the application of powerful analytical methods to unravelling the actions of economic and social causes, to assigning each its part, to tracing mutual interactions and modifications; and above all to laying bare the hidden *causas causantes*.

The M.A. Scheme in the hands of good examiners may conceivably promote the scientific study of past facts to a very limited extent. But it seems to me to have no room for the scientific study of those facts which are of the most importance and most fully alive [?].

In the hands of second-rate examiners it will I think foster sciolism as regards facts, and frivolity as regards reasoning.

Marshall's interest in matters of terminology and curriculae probably stemmed from his involvement in Cambridge academic politics, for sometime during the ensuing year he was appointed to a committee of the Historical Board whose task was to report on methods of extending the study of modern economics and politics in the university,[13] and his next letter to Hewins directly reflects this activity.

6.6.01

My dear Hewins,

I hear little of what is going on; especially just now. But an accident brought to my ears a rumour that rapid progress is being made with the scheme for the new London University course in Economics, and that it pays a scant honour to the Scientific as distinguished from the technical aspects of economics: while it finds room for Ancient history – an important subject in itself, but one to wh English youth already give a disproportionate amount of time, and one wh already has far more than its proper share of endowment direct and indirect.

The whole rumour may be based on a mistake: for, in the form in wh it reached me, it represented this policy as having been carried to a grotesque extreme. And if there is *no* truth in it, just drop me a card to put me out of my anxiety; and trouble no more about it.

In any case you will perhaps be so good as to excuse me from a discussion of details. I know you are extremely busy. I am never fit for correspondence; and I am specially unfit just now.

But this reminds me that I cannot recollect whether I have ever sent you of the scheme, now inclosed,[14] wh I drew up a few weeks ago for a Tripos here. It may interest you possibly: though it is laid on the shelf for the present. It is based on long discussions wh were held here some years back: but the titles of the papers on politics are new; and Dickinson is responsible for them. He may perhaps have shown you the paper.

The only distinct trend of opinion as to it – outside of vague polite phrases – is characteristic. It is a restive suspicion that Commercial Law is not a good subject for undergraduate study.

I never thought it was by itself: and I am not at all sure that it is even as subsidiary to economic analysis. Perhaps it will disappear from the next draft.

Forgive my bluntness and abruptness.

From yr sincerely

Alfred Marshall

P.T.O. I inclose also a short list of books supplementary to the Tripos lists, wh I am giving to people who are carrying the study of economics even that vy little way for wh alone present Cambridge arrangements makes provision.

I think a Faculty of Economic and Political Science is unworthy of its name unless it makes it to the examination-interest of students to give time enough for reading those books (in addition to the Tripos books); or other books of equivalent substance.

Rumours about London University affairs seem to have been rife in Cambridge about this time, as shown by the following communication, written four months earlier than the one quoted immediately above, which raised a matter that subsequently became the subject of public controversy.[15]

19.2.1901

My dear Hewins,

I did not answer your letter, because I thought I might meet you at the Political Economy Club, to which, by rare exception I went last Friday week. Failing that, I again delayed till I should have seen Acworth.[16] He came here yesterday, delighted the young men's Club beyond measure by his talk about railways, and has just left. I had heard rumours that led me to think there was some danger that the economic department of the London University might be 'captured' by people acting more or less in alliance with the Fabians. I am more in accord with some Fabian opinions and aims than are many academic economists: but I could not contemplate such a danger without grave anxiety. I have spoken without reserve on this subject to Miss Brooke and to Bowley: and I think you may have heard something of my views on it. So I write at once to say that Acworth has convinced me that my fears were based on a misapprehension.

You and I are busy, and it is difficult to arrange for a talk about anything. Also, both because I am ignorant of the resources and difficulties of London education, and for other reasons, I think it most unlikely that I could contribute anything useful to the solution of those difficult problems of organization in which you are immersed. But those problems are of vital importance for the economic wellbeing of England: London and Cambridge have in many respects a closer kinship with one another than with any other economic schools on this side of the Atlantic; and, if at any time you would like to arrange a talk, I would gladly try to hit it off with you.

Yours sincerely,

Alfred Marshall.

These letters require no detailed commentary. They reveal something of the uncertainties and conflicts of loyalty resulting from the founding of a new centre of economics teaching and research, and, appropriately enough, the two correspondents exemplified the outspokenness and impetuosity of youth and the cautious conservatism of age (Hewins was 34, Marhsall 57). As the acknowledged leader of British academic economics, Marshall felt obliged to apply some paternal restraint to the new foundling, though his motives were not wholly disinterested given his ambitions for Cambridge economics. The correspondence suggests that his well-known distaste for controversy dates back to his period as Principal and Professor of Political Economy at the new University College, Bristol, from 1877 to 1883 – though it evidently did not deter him from engaging in a famous public debate with Henry George, in 1883.[17]

Marshall's references to 'pure' economic theory and the distinction between the 'scientific' and 'technical' aspects of economics are explicable when viewed against the background of his campaign to promote economics at Cambridge. Here it was academic prejudices and vested interests that chiefly concerned him; whereas his earlier objections to the phrase 'empirical study' in the above-mentioned report of the British Association for the Advancement of Science[18] must be seen in the context of the public debate about the respective merits of the historical and deductive methods, which had plagued British academic economists during the 1870s and 1880s. By the turn of the century the subject was on the point of achieving full academic recognition, and Marshall was naturally anxious that its twentieth-century development should be based on solid foundations. While discouraging the study of pure theory for its own sake, he believed that the discipline should be based on systematic economic analysis which would constitute a 'centre of intense intellectual activity',[19] and the student would then need to acquire skill in the application of principles to actual problems. All these matters were the subject of intense interest to the leading professional economists of the day, and although there were deeper undercurrents of personal, methodological and policy disagreements, the discussion seems on the whole to have been conducted in a commendably calm and rational manner.

NOTES

1 Margaret Cole, *The Story of Fabian Socialism*, 1961, p. 32, and ch. VIII. See also Janet Beveridge, *An Epic of Clare Market, Birth and Early Days of the London School*

of Economics, 1960; Sir Sidney Caine, *The History of the Founding of The London School of Economics and Political Science,* 1963.

2 F. A. H[ayek], 'The London School of Economics, 1895–1945', *Economica,* vol. XIII (1946), p. 5.

3 W. A. S. Hewins, *The Apologia of an Imperialist,* 1929, vol. 1, pp. 15, 19, 20.

4 'The Methods of Economic Training adopted in this and other Countries', *Report of the British Association for the Advancement of Science* (1894), pp. 365–91. The Committee consisted of W. Cunningham. E. C. K. Gonner, F. Y. Edgeworth, J. N. Keynes and H. Higgs.

5 Hewins, op. cit., pp. 26–7.

6 They form part of a substantial collection of Hewins' papers, which are now in the possession of his grandson, Mr Richard Hewins. I am most grateful for Mr Hewins' permission to publish them.

7 W. A. S. Hewins, 'The London School of Economics and Political Science', *Special Reports on Educational Subjects* (ed. Michael E. Sadler), C.8943 (1898), pp. 76–98. The following quotations are on pp. 80, 80–1, 77.

Hewins' accounts of the obstacles to a scientific career in economics were at least partly based on personal experiences, for his father had gone bankrupt shortly before he went to Oxford, and he subsequently lived modestly and worked assiduously, giving University Extension lectures and writing numerous articles for the *Dictionary of National Biography,* Palgrave's *Dictionary of Political Economy,* and so on.

8 There is no record of this. The first known contact between Marshall and Walras was in March 1883. See W. Jaffe (ed.), *The Correspondence of Léon Walras and Related Papers,* 3 vols., 1965.

For some revealing evidence of Marshall's reluctance to discuss theoretical questions, see his correspondence with Wicksell, reproduced in T. Gardlund, *The Life of Knut Wicksell,* 1958, pp. 339–45.

9 Presumably A. T. Hadley's *Railroad Transportation,* 1885, a leading American work on the subject.

10 Hewins' account of the LSE included details of lectures and attendances, which reveal that audiences were much larger in 'practical' subjects like Railway Economics and Law of Accident Insurance than in more conventional topics like economic theory, economic history and statistics. However, substantial numbers attended a lecture on the Measurement of Economic Quantities and two lectures on the Theory of Bimetallism, the latter being then a subject of popular controversy.

11 'The Relations of Economic Knowledge to Christian Charity', *Report of the Church Congress,* 1899. The paper contained no explicit references to economics at London or Cambridge.

12 Arthur Berry, of King's College, Cambridge.

13 The other members of the Committee were Goldsworthy Lowes Dickinson of King's College, Cambridge, who also taught politics at LSE, and A. W. Ward, the Master of Peterhouse. See Marshall to H. S. Foxwell, May 8, 1901, in Marshall Library, Cambridge: 'At the meeting before last, I urged that if our studies were made to give no room for what business men want, we must expect their money to go to new Universities; and we should continue money-starved. I find that some thought that I was going for a "commercial school".'

About this time new universities were being started or planned in Birmingham, Sheffield, Leeds, and elsewhere, and the LSE had obtained some financial support from the London Chamber of Commerce. Two days later Marshall informed Foxwell of an abortive attempt to obtain money from the American steel magnate, Andrew Carnegie, who had recently made a substantial gift to the University of Glasgow.

14 Unfortunately Marshall's 'scheme' is not attached to his letter. Various proposals were under discussion among the Cambridge economists during the 1890s, and after 1900 the controversy about the future of economics became vigorous and sometimes heated. A useful collection of fly sheets can be seen in a Guard Book on Economics and Associated Branches of Political Sciences, in the Cambridge University Archives.

15 On this occasion the leading economist-critics were Clara Collett and Henry Higgs, who were members of the London Economic Club (based at University College, London) and close associates of the Cambridge economist, H. S. Foxwell. In addition to the normal complexities of London University politics, there was also the question of housing Foxwell's great economic library which had recently been purchased by the Goldsmiths' Company. See, for example, Beveridge, op. cit., p. 51, and Hewins to S. Webb, Jan. 14 and 26, 1903, in Passfield Papers, British Library of Political and Economic Science.

16 W. Acworth, who lectured in Railway Economics at the LSE. The other persons referred to in this letter are A. L. Bowley, the statistician, and Miss Brooke, who is still unidentified. (Emma Brooke, the Fabian and Suffragist, and Gertrude Mary Brooke, BA, London, 1892, are possible candidates.)

17 See, for example, E. P. Lawrence, *Henry George in the British Isles*, 1957, p. 70; C. A. Barker, *Henry George*, 1955, pp. 403–4.

18 Marshall to J. N. Keynes, June 10, 1894, in Marshall Library, Cambridge: 'I think Edgeworth has spoken to you about the objectionable phrase "empirical study" in the last report of the Committee of the British Association of which you are a member. In these cases there is always a danger that one or two men of ardent, polemical zeal will arrange between them a report, so worded as to commit more moderate men to phrases which they would not themselves have chosen; and thus do a great deal of harm by publishing in a report, having high authority, opinions which would have been harmless if published only in the names of those who have been most active in formulating them . . . those very few students of economics whom we get at our English universities are taught to use the inductive method in a scientific way. I believe that scarcely any of the great German Economists of the historical School could endorse the suggestion that the "empirical method" should be encouraged; . . . Given the number of our students I think we make the most of them; because we encourage specialized inductive study only after and not before the B.A. degree. . . . And should we make any arrangements of a more formal kind for post-graduate study, we shall, I have no doubt, include aid and guidance in the investigation by trained students of special points in economic history.'

19 The quotation is from Marshall's brochure, *The New Cambridge Curriculum in Economics*, 1903, which, with its citation of the opinions of leading businessmen and public officials and its references to the importance of the 'professional study' of economics and the 'national interest in the supply of trained economists', has a curiously up-to-date ring.

20

THE DISTINCTIVE LSE ETHOS IN THE INTER-WAR YEARS

In the history of British economics between the world wars, Keynes and Cambridge have, doubtless inevitably, attracted a disproportionate share of attention. Nevertheless, this is only part of a larger and more complex story, and one of the main functions of this session is to redress the balance somewhat. There are still serious gaps in our knowledge, and detailed research on certain aspects indicated later would yield rich dividends. But the field is by no means untilled, and this paper draws heavily on four invaluable published sources[1] and (to a lesser extent) unpublished research by Charles Blitch, Elizabeth Durbin, Alon Kadish, and Gerard Koot.

Given the time constraints this account is necessarily selective and impressionistic, and the title is designed to focus attention on certain distinctive features of the LSE situation of the kind liable to be wholly ignored, or at least underemphasized in conventional histories of economics. The paper is concerned less with the history of economic theory and policy than with the interaction of personalities and ideas in a specific, but rapidly changing institutional setting – that is, with the climate of opinion, the 'atmosphere' (a term used by a number of the *dramatis personae*), and what Henry Johnson has called the 'social geography' of the subject.[2] The aim is to provoke discussion that will provide stimulating leads for future researchers.

Although at this time and place the question may appear unnecessary if not unseemly, it is useful to begin by asking: Why explore the development of economics at LSE during the inter-war years? Arguably, if the ideas and issues involved are still worth considering up to 60 years later, does it matter whether their proponents were at LSE, Cambridge, Oxford, or elsewhere?

Without becoming heavily involved in counterfactuals, the appropriate response, is, surely, that – as Professor Koot has observed – from its inception, Sidney and Beatrice Webb designed LSE partly, even largely, as a counterweight to Cambridge economics. Its success or failure in this respect is obviously of interest in the intellectual history of a country whose academic life was still largely dominated by the ancient universities. In a

372

talk with the school's director in 1932, Sidney Webb recalled that 'he and his friends wanted to have a centre of economics teaching that would not be dominated by individualists', adding: 'I was in revolt against one Professor of Economics: I wanted a lot of Professors' so that the subject could be treated from various angles.[3]

Ironically enough, by 1932, LSE economics itself appeared to many observers to be dominated by individualists – but that is another matter, to be considered later. Of course, to regard LSE, whether in economics alone or more generally, merely as a reaction against ideas and conditions elsewhere, involves a serious distortion of perspective. Nevertheless, it is useful to record some of the basic facts that reveal its distinctiveness as an institution.

Between the wars, especially under William Beveridge's directorship, from 1919 to 1937 LSE changed dramatically,[4] not least in respect of the student body, a constituency seldom considered seriously by historians of economics. Admittedly, after a brief postwar hiatus, the total number of students remained roughly constant at around 3,000, but the composition was transformed. The Webbs had always sought to emphasize practical work, especially public administration, and from the outset evening studies were encouraged; special courses were provided for civil servants, army officers, colonial administrators, businessmen, etc.; and considerable efforts were made – for a time with only limited success – to develop Higher Commercial Education.

Throughout the period there were many mature 'full course' students taking degree, diploma, or certificate courses who were not full-time, for many were working in or around London during the day and studying in the evenings and at weekends. Beyond this, in 1919 two-thirds of all LSE students were 'occasional' – i.e., attending odd lectures or seminars – and one-third were 'full course', whereas by 1937 these proportions had been almost exactly reversed.

There was also in this period a four-fold increase in the number of inter-collegiate students, mainly from King's College or University College, London, and a two-and-one-half-fold increase in the number of overseas students (from 291 in 1919–20 to 717 in 1936–7). The number of first degree students little more than doubled (1919–20, to 827 in 1936–7, or just over 50 per cent from 1920–1 to 1936–7) while the number of higher degree students increased much faster – by nine-fold (from 32 in 1919–20 to 293 in 1936–7, or just over six-fold from 1920–1).

Another significant difference from the ancient universities lay in the sexual balance. Over the whole period, it was approximately 3:1 in favour of males, with the proportions varying between 6:1 and 8:1 in the evenings and a correspondingly higher ratio of female daytime students. The environment was far more conducive to sexual equality and equal social intercourse than in Oxbridge, and while the proportion of female teaching staff was not high, the fact that Professor Lillian Knowles, the economic historian, was Director of the Faculty of Economics from 1922 to 1924 suggests that women's opportunities were not as restricted as elsewhere.

This state of affairs constituted the basis for a more healthy social as well as intellectual environment than at Oxbridge, making LSE in some respects more like a provincial than an ancient university, notwithstanding its metropolitan location. Curiously enough, Beveridge himself, with his Oxford background, displayed a certain ambivalence towards this state of affairs. While claiming that: 'We set ourselves to prove that a full University life did not depend upon living together in a medieval building', he found grounds for self-congratulation in the fact that under his guidance the LSE had approached 'assimilation to older universities' with respect to both its student body and its staff–student relationships.[5]

The latter point is of some importance, especially considering LSE's occasionally turbulent post-1945 history. In the 1920s, LSE students had very little personal contact with members of the teaching staff, many of whom were themselves part-timers. While this may have helped or obliged them to develop qualities of independence, especially as so many were mature or from overseas, it necessarily created an environment very different from the traditional Oxbridge college-based tutorial system. It may also have facilitated specialization among the academic staff, a point to be considered later.

Beveridge was surely right in emphasizing the LSE's cosmopolitanism – not only in the origins of its student body, particularly its graduates, but also in the teaching staff – especially in the 1930s. There was a constant flow of distinguished visitors, many of whom gave occasional lectures or courses, or attended seminars. Of course, this was due to the combination of the school's growing academic reputation and its metropolitan location. Its proximity to the hub of the nation's life, and its focus on the whole range of the social sciences, made it considerably different from the conventional ivory tower image. That 'the world is too much with us' was undoubtedly at times a source of tension, even conflict, and it is important to note that this world included Fleet Street as well as the City, Parliament, and Whitehall.

George L. Schwarz and Graham Hutton are only two of the better-known examples of the ease with which LSE teachers and students could make the transition from academic life to financial journalism; and as is well known, at times the links between LSE and politics, especially in the case of Harold Laski, could be an acute source of embarrassment both to the individuals concerned and to the school's authorities.[6]

Unfortunately, the political dimension cannot be adequately explored here, though it affected the relations between individuals and departments within LSE and, of course, the school's public reputation. However, some reference to its relevance to economics – especially economic policy, ideology, and the conception of the proper role of the economist as a professional – will appear below.

Against this background, it is hardly surprising that to contemporaries it was usually the differences, rather than the similarities between LSE and Oxbridge that loomed large, both socially and intellectually. There appear to be no reliable comparative data on the social composition of the London and Oxbridge student body and teaching staff, though there is fairly clear evidence that British economists in general came from a somewhat broader social spectrum than other Oxford and Cambridge alumni, and the same is probably true of other social scientists – who, of course, constituted the vast majority of LSE students and teachers.[7] Given the national, ethnic, and religious variety of their backgrounds, this aspect would repay systematic investigation.

It would, of course, be foolish to generalize about these differences on the basis of a single example, but Lionel Robbins figures so prominently in the story, and has written so revealingly about his experiences, that it is difficult to resist quoting him. A grammar school boy who became a full-time LSE student after his World War I army service, he was the first of its graduates to break into what he termed 'the charmed circle of Oxford'.

After two brief spells of teaching at New College, Oxford, which he depicted in glowing terms, he nevertheless admitted that he had never 'felt completely at home', in Oxford University, partly owing to 'a certain inner insecurity *vis-à-vis* an atmosphere at once highly individual and very different from anything to which I had been accustomed', and partly because he 'found it peculiarly difficult to harmonize with . . . the curious combination of worldliness and insularity of so much of the Oxford conversation of those days'. More particularly,

> little suspicion of any sort of inadequacy disturbed the supreme self-confidence of the dominant majority, although in fact there was much both in organization and intellectual tradition that was open to criticism.[8]

During the inter-war years, there were major changes in the LSE's teaching staff. The number of full-time teachers rose from 17 to 79 in the period 1919–37, and during the 1920s many of the older pre-war staff departed. In its earliest days the school had necessarily recruited its staff from outside, having few if any home-grown products, and there was some warrant for Marshall's reputed comment that the teaching programme 'was compiled to suit the lecturers that were available, not on a systematic organization of subjects'.[9] Indeed, many of the numerous 'occasional' lecturers had appeared only for one or two years in the school's *Calendar*.

However, between the wars an increasing number of appointments to the school's economics staff were made from among its own graduates, several of whom had spent periods of teaching in the Commonwealth before

375

returning to London.[10] The possibility of in-breeding was counteracted by the influx of influential outsiders, initially Allyn Young and, thereafter, economists from the European continent, for example, Ludwig Lachmann, Fritz Machlup, and most notably, Fritz Hayek – of whom more anon.

With the growth of scale and increase in the numbers of full-time staff came internal organizational developments which justify the generalization that LSE was the first modern British university institution, so far as the social sciences are concerned. What does this mean in practice?

The growth of specialization and the compartmentalization of knowledge have been among the most conspicuous trends in twentieth-century university development, and, in organizational terms, compartmentalization has entailed the creation of specialized courses and degrees run by academic departments. The emergence and significance of academic departments has hitherto been unduly neglected by intellectual historians. But as the American historian, J. H. Hexter, once observed, given the inherent tendency towards the growth and sub-division of knowledge into academic disciplines and sub-disciplines, one might have expected a corresponding indefinite proliferation of academic departments.[11] The fact that this has not occurred fully suggests that there must have been some measure of academic contraception to prevent it!

The history of academic departments at the LSE is as yet unwritten, but in considering the role of economics in the institution it must be remembered that it was a School of Economics and Political Science. Unlike Oxford and Cambridge, where teaching was divided between a weak university organization and a number of colleges of widely differing academic prestige and resources, there was scope at LSE for a more centralized and coordinated structure.

However, during much of the 1920s this was inhibited by certain personalities – notably Edwin Cannan, whose conception of economics will be referred to later – and the paucity of full-time teaching staff. As Robbins has recorded in his *Autobiography*, when Cannan retired in 1926:

> There was adequate coverage of the specialisms: Banking and Currency, Commerce, Transport, and Accounting including Business Administration. But Economics, Analytical and Descriptive, including Public Finance, was under-staffed at the junior level; and the Chair itself in Cannan's time had been on a half-time basis. This clearly was very unsatisfactory especially at an institution where Economics was part of the title.[12]

When he became Professor, in 1929, after the brief interlude under Allyn Young (whose initial three-year tenure may not have been extended even had he wished to stay permanently),[13] Robbins fully recognized his reponsibilities and the opportunity open to him. Although he was still only 30 years old, he had had experience of LSE as an undergraduate, research assistant, and lecturer, and had maintained his LSE contacts during his periods at New College. His dissatisfaction with the Oxford situation has already been indicated, and must have influenced his conception of the appropriate organization of economic studies.

During the 1930s, the scope for specialization at LSE in economics increased markedly, but it is not clear that the barriers to migration increased.[14] However, under Robbins economics undoubtedly became a much more active and influential force in shaping the school's intellectual climate, especially as the intense controversies of the early 1930s were not confined to technical matters but also extended to methodology, policy, political, and ideological issues.

It is impossible to grasp the significance of the differences in LSE economics between the 1920s and the 1930s without reference to the position and views of William Beveridge, the Director. As José Harris has shown, although he was deeply immersed in his administrative duties, Beveridge never ceased to regard himself primarily as a scholar and researcher, and several times tried to exchange his Directorship for a Professorship at the school.[15]

Beyond this, he had ambitious plans to provide a secure natural science foundation for the social sciences, believing that in so doing he was carrying out the Webbs's original intention of basing

> economics, politics and all the other social sciences on collection and examination of facts rather than on analysis of concepts.[16]

This objective underlay his successful application for funds from the Rockefeller Foundation in the mid-1920s and the creation of a Chair of Social Biology, occupied from 1929 by Lancelot Hogben, a development that provoked considerable controversy. On occupying his chair Robbins, notwithstanding his youth and comparative inexperience, was 'very confident that I knew what was needed so far as organization and administration were concerned'.[17] Moreover, he soon expressed views, both in his Inaugural Lecture and in his *Nature and Significance of Economic Science* [1932], in flat contradiction with those of both Beveridge and Cannan who, as Hayek has recorded, had 'created the tradition which, more than anything else, determined the intellectual climate in the central department of the School'.[18]

Cannan is nowadays remembered chiefly as an outstanding historian of economics; a fierce critic of classical economics; and a remarkably effective teacher whose iconoclastic treatment of Cambridge economics endeared him to all who, like the Webbs and Beveridge, wished to emancipate English economics from the dominant Marshallian tradition.

Cannan's debunking of esoteric language and his advocacy of an unpretentious 'common sense' approach to economic problems – for which he has been praised by no less an authority than Joseph Schumpeter[19] – led his former student and colleague, T. E. Gregory, to remark that 'No man . . . was ever less "professional" in his manners or his way of life.'[20] The precise meaning of this compliment becomes less obscure when it is set against Cannan's Presidential Address to the Royal Economic Society in 1933, which was undoubtedly directed in part against Robbins, whose claims to the chair he had supported.

Under the title 'The Need for a Simpler Economics', Cannan complained that

> the almost complete absorption of the younger teachers in making what they rightly or wrongly believe to be important advances in the higher branches of theory is leaving the public at the mercy of quacks

and he appealed to them

> to assist common sense to grasp the basic elements of economic science. . . . The mind of the public is an Augean stable

he declared, in characteristically blunt terms, and it was the economists' job to cleanse it:

> Do not let them (i.e., the young teachers of economics) avert their eyes from the disgusting mess and run back to find contentment in neat equations and elegant equilibria.[21]

These remarks represent an unusually full and explicit statement of views Cannan had long held, and they gained force against the background of recent developments at LSE and the depression, which had brought a crisis in the relations between the economics profession and the public.

The contrast with Robbins and, of course, with Hayek, could hardly have been clearer. In his Inaugural, 'The Present Position of Economic Science', delivered in January 1930, Robbins had referred to the current 'boom in economic theory' and called for a re-examination of fundamental theoretical questions.

He repudiated the notion that the emerging discipline of economics would be 'a body of knowledge accessible to everyone' and flatly denied that it was the economist's duty 'to make plain to everyone the main doctrines of their science'. On the contrary, while 'economists might be more intelligible than they are', it was 'no service to knowledge to make things simpler than they are'. Indeed, if economists devoted themselves to popularization they would diminish their subject's beneficial influence.

> The sort of Economics which the Press and the public would like is an Economics which is bound to be wrong or misapprehended. Surely it is better to push ahead with our analysis, embrace technicality with open arms if technicality will help us, and come to be so frequently

378

right that we acquire the respect now given without question to the practitioners of the natural sciences.[22]

These passages have been cited at length because they reveal striking underlying differences of professional style and objectives. Despite his Oxford background, Cannan was broadly in harmony with the Webbs's conception of the functional role and status of the 'expert', a role which, to Gregory at least, was very different from that of the 'professional'.

By contrast, Robbins represented the emergence of a more academic type of professionalism, though this did not necessarily entail either a denial of responsibility towards the public or, as Alfred Marshall had believed, an avoidance of vigorous participation in public debate on contentious policy issues. These issues became far more important at LSE in the 1930s than even in Cambridge, because of its metropolitan location, its less secure reputation and status, and Harold Laski's notorious political activities.

In discussing the relations between the London and Cambridge economists during the 1930s Robbins has noted that

the historian of the future . . . should be warned that any generalizations he may wish to make must fit facts of considerable complexity if they are not seriously to misrepresent the situation.[23]

The same is true of internal relationships, both personal and intellectual, within the LSE. Beveridge's 'insensate hostility to pure theory' and his 'positive antipathy to economics as it was developing in the 1930's'[24] as Robbins described it, were not diminished by Robbins's flat rejection of the claim that

By the application of the methods of higher statistical analysis to dense masses of statistical analysis, laws of 'economic behaviour' are to be discovered which will put Economic Science on a basis of equality with the Natural Sciences.[25]

Beveridge's reaction may have been influenced by disappointed expectations, for after his graduation Robbins had worked for a year as Beveridge's assistant on the second edition of his *Unemployment: A Problem of Industry*,[26] and he may have assumed that Robbins would promote similar empirical work during his Professorship. Nevertheless, these differences did not prevent the two men from cooperating against Keynes's apostasy over the free trade issue in 1930–1, and, unlike Hugh Dalton, one of Robbins's strongest supporters before he was appointed to the Chair, Beveridge had no objections at that time to Robbins's individualism.[27]

As José Harris has shown, Beveridge was a deeply unhappy man subject to serious emotional fluctuations, intellectual vacillations and inconsistencies, but he was converted to free market economics during the early 1930s. Indeed:

In 1931 C. M. Lloyd, the head of LSE's Social Science department, told the Webbs that 'owing to Beveridge's powerful personality the dominant tone among the younger economics lecturers at the School of Economics is almost violently anti-labour, against socialistic services and in favour of the whip of starvation being applied all round, to force the manual workers to accept lower wages and to work longer hours'.[28]

Harris adds that this was 'perhaps an exaggeration of Beveridge's views', yet

in many respects it is difficult to conceive of a more striking contrast than that between the optimistic young social reformer of the 1900's and the implacable free marketeer of 1929–32.[29]

During the running battle between Laski and Robbins, when each was accusing the other of being a propagandist,

what had previously been a forum for the mutual exchange of ideas became for a time an embattled institution polarized into two hostile and non-communicating ideological camps.

Beveridge, with what Harris terms his 'anti-Marxist obsession', was aligned against the socialists, whereas Dalton ascribed 'the possibility of intellectual friction' primarily to Robbins.[30]

Three years later, at the end of 1935, another distinguished left-wing LSE scholar, R. H. Tawney, considered it was no longer possible for LSE staff to study 'present day problems'. He believed Beveridge's concern at student Marxism and the hostile reaction of the school's city governors were creating such a restrictive environment that there was 'far more freedom of expression in Oxford today than at the London School of Economics'.[31]

It would take considerable research to determine how far these impressionistic remarks can be relied on, and how far this atmosphere permeated the discussion of economics at LSE. But it should be noted that the role of government in the depression, the need for deflation or inflation, and the role of planning, were highly contentious and sensitive issues during the 1930s. For some these were largely matters of purely intellectual interest; but for others they were highly political issues.

In assessing Robbins's influence on the tone and content of LSE economics in the 1930s, his emphasis on the value of pure theory and the deductive method is only one of a number of factors. Of more general importance, especially as affecting the relations between some of the London and Cambridge economists, was his knowledge of and enthusiasm for the works of American and continental European economists, especially the Austrians, an enthusiasm he successfully communicated to his students and colleagues. In this respect, he was continuing the LSE tradition of providing an alternative to Cambridge economics, a more sophisticated and cosmopolitan one than Cannan's.

As Robbins has revealed in his *Autobiography*, he came under the spell of his 'love-affair with Vienna, its setting, and its culture', during his undergraduate days in the early 1920s.[32] This attachment was evidently shared in some measure by his colleagues, Gregory and Plant.[33] Contrary to the impression of poise and urbanity familiar to those who have known him only in later years, the youthful Robbins was a highly emotional individual[34] who, after leaving the army, had gone through a period of Guild Socialist revolutionary fervour, followed by some disillusionment, before attending the LSE. There, as he recalls, his beliefs

> underwent a process of considerable change . . . [and] the picture of the economic system as presented by Dalton and Cannan was gradually influencing me in directions diametrically opposed to my earlier convictions.[35]

During the 1920s, Robbins arrived at Austrian economics via Gustav Cassel, Irving Fisher, and Frank A. Fetter, and, as in Plant's case, meetings with Ludwig von Mises in Vienna opened the way to stimulating

> contacts with members of the Swedish, Swiss and Italian schools of economics who, because of the absence of linguistic impediments, already enjoyed much closer collaboration and amicable debate with Austrian economists.[36]

On Robbins's invitation, Hayek gave a series of lectures at LSE early in 1931, and accepted a permanent chair later the same year. From that time, Robbins's seminar became, like its precursor, the Vienna seminar of Menger and von Mises,

> the forum for timeless discussion of Hayek's ideas on monetary influences on the structure of production and industrial fluctuations, and their many-sided implications throughout the field of economic, social, and political policy.[37]

So swift was the translation of the LSE ethos in economics that Plant was not surprised, on visiting Kiel in 1933, to find LSE described as 'ein Vovort von Wien' (i.e., a suburb of Vienna).[38] J. R. Hicks has reported that when Robbins stimulated his interest in economic theory, from 1929, he was encouraged to read Cassel, Walras, Pareto, Edgeworth, Taussig, Wicksell, and the Austrians

> with all of whom I was much more at home at that stage than I was with Marshall and Pigou (we were such good 'Europeans' in London that it was Cambridge that seemed 'foreign'). I was so out of tune

with Cambridge economics that the 'cost controversy' (the beginnings of the 'theory of the firm') made little impression on me. I did not see what relevance it had to what I was doing. Still less did I perceive the relevance of the Cambridge work on monetary theory.[39]

Here, in the formative development of one of our most distinguished economic theorists, can be seen both the strengths and the limitations of Robbins's, and, subsequently, Hayek's influence.

A brief glance at the scene as it appeared later from the Cambridge standpoint may be helpful here, especially as it comes from D. H. Robertson, who was not fully in harmony with Keynes and his followers as they proceeded along the road from the *Treatise* to the *General Theory*. As he wrote to Keynes, in October 1931:

> This 3-cornered debate, all of us talking different dialects, has become so complicated that I hesitate to say whether you are representing me aright. For if I haven't learnt to talk the 'savings and investment' tongue, neither have I learnt to talk 'the goods of higher and lower orders' tongue of Vienna. . . . I suspect that Hayek, in his pp. 45 ff. and 70 ff., though I can't make sense of them as they stand, has got hold of something real, which needs to be synthesized with your and my 'wasted savings'.[40]

Another, again pro-Cambridge but not blindly pro-Keynes, interpretation is that of H. O. Meredith, the economist–economic historian, who wrote to Keynes several weeks later:

> It is unfortunately true, I think, of the last fifty years that Austria has had an elaborate analysis but no machine and Cambridge a machine but an insufficiently formulated analysis.[41]

He found it difficult to excuse what he called Hayek's misunderstandings of Keynes's *Treatise* and added, a fortnight later, with reference to Hayek's August *Economica* article:

> I took him . . . to be a pedant trained in Austrian economics and eager to show (not without some encouragement from London) . . . that your work was spoiled by being cast in the mould of Marshall instead of that of Böhm-Bawerk.
>
> There is this much excuse for him that Cambridge has always underrated the intellectual quality of Austrian economics, and this much excuse for Cambridge that Austrian economics have always been *pre judice* more interesting than important. Where he fails (apart from general mental limitations) is that he doesn't understand the method you are working for. You would not, I guess, find Schumpeter teaching such nonsense, because he was at pains in his youth to understand Marshall.[42]

These passages reveal both the novelty of Hayek's approach and some of the mental confusion engendered by the clash of incompatible intellectual frameworks – for it may be too much to speak, in Kuhnian natural science terms, of incommensurable paradigms. It is impossible to endorse Meredith's view that in 1931 Austrian economics was less important than interesting, for quite apart from the theoretical stimulus, confusion, and conflict it generated, Hayek's view of economic fluctuations had profound policy implications in the midst of an unprecedentedly severe depression.

Here, too, it may be appropriate to cite Robbins, who subsequently acknowledged that his own diagnosis and policy recommendations had been seriously misguided. In his bitter conflict with Keynes in the Economic Advisory Council's Committee of Economists he continued, as he says, 'to maintain my intransigence' on the question of the desirability of increased public expenditure during the slump.

> I signed a report whose anti-expansionist recommendations I had certainly played a part in shaping. I also played a part in the initiation of a letter to *The Times*, signed by others who shared my opinion, opposing recommendations for relaxation which had been put forward by Keynes and his friends. It would be unjust to have called me a deflationist: I have never believed in deliberate contraction of expenditure (public *plus* private) as a whole. But I was certainly an antiexpansionist where public expenditure was concerned, at a time when, as I now think, I should have been on the other side.[43]

In seeking an answer to the question: 'How had I got myself into this state of mind?' which led him to commit 'the greatest mistake of my professional career', Robbins explicitly blamed the influence of von Mises and Hayek.

> The trouble was intellectual. I had become the slave of intellectual constructions which, if not intrinsically invalid as regards logical consistency, were inappropriate to the total situation which had then developed and which therefore misled my judgement. I realized that these constructions led to conclusions which were highly unpalatable as regards practical action. But I was convinced that they were valid and that therefore it was my duty to base recommendations as regards policy upon them. There was a touch of the Nonconformist conscience here.[44]

Subsequent commentators have disagreed widely in their assessments of the intensity, duration, and significance of the conflict between LSE and Cambridge in the 1930s,[45] and it would be pointless to try to provide a definitive evaluation here. The range of issues involved was broad, including methodology, theory, policy, ideology, the role of the economist in public life, and the proper code of professional conduct.[46]

The situation was both complex and transitional. Individuals' views were changing, in some cases rapidly and dramatically, for as Donald Winch has observed, during such an episode,

> Those advocating changes cannot depict with clarity all the features of the new world they wish to enter; the old and the new do not face each other over the same terrain.[47]

Moreover, throughout there was the overriding presence of Keynes, whose fertility, energy, mercurial disposition, and rapid shifts of opinion and interest were hardly calculated to facilitate harmony and orderly progress towards consensus.[48]

Nevertheless, a few tentative conclusions may be helpful to subsequent investigators.

First, it is important not to exaggerate the homogeneity of opinion either in Cambridge or in London. The differences between Keynes, Robertson, and Pigou are now familiar from Keynes's *Collected Writings* (and one could also add M. H. Dobb as evidence of diversity on the Cam). In London, Cannan no doubt exaggerated characteristically when he expostulated: 'That fellow Hayek has corrupted them all and ought to be deported.'[49] But as already suggested, the organization and structure of LSE teaching made it easier for Robbins and Hayek to dominate theoretical discussion than for Keynes (or earlier for Marshall) at Cambridge.

There appears to have been considerable agreement among the senior LSE economists: Robbins, Hayek, Gregory, Plant, Benham, on both doctrinal and policy matters.[50] The most intensive phase of debate and hostility between London and Cambridge occurred in the years 1930–2 (or 1933), whereas during the second half of the decade there was a period of stability within LSE and, as Robbins has maintained, the difference between the two 'had greatly diminished by the later 1930's', though it was still noticeable.[51] What remain to be fully investigated, however, are the precise nature and timing of the changes that occurred among LSE economists during that decade.

Second, as much of the controversy centred around Hayek, it is worth noting his retreat from direct confrontation with Keynes by the mid-1930s. Apart from his distaste for controversy and desire to develop his theory of capital and his studies of the methodological basis of the social sciences, he had found his exchanges with Keynes unhelpful.

As he reported many years later, with reference to the first phase of controversy over Keynes's *Treatise*:

> Great was my disappointment when . . . after the second part of my article he told me that he had in the meantime changed his mind and no longer believed what he had said in that work. This was one of the reasons why I did not return to the attack when he published

his *General Theory* – a fact for which I later much blamed myself. But I feared that before I had completed my analysis he would have again changed his mind. Though he called it a 'general' theory, it was to me too obviously another tract for the times, conditioned by what he thought were the monetary needs of policy.[52]

There could hardly be a clearer revelation of the differences of professional style between the two protagonists – the one restless, constantly modifying his position, and always sensitive to the direct policy relevance of even the most abstruse theoretical discussion; the other more characteristic of the pure scholar, continually working away at fundamental theoretical problems in a more 'roundabout' process of knowledge production.

One crucial factor here, as a young colleague of Hayek's has recalled, is that Hayek's work was not 'English Economics' because of its reliance on Böhm-Bawerk, who was difficult for more pragmatic British empiricist economists to swallow.[53] In response to Hayek's criticism, Keynes himself conceded that English economists had unduly neglected the works of Wicksell and Böhm-Bawerk.[54] As Hicks subsequently put it:

We absorbed Hayekian ideas (there are Hayekian influences not only on Robbins and Robertson, but even on Harrod and Kaldor, for instance, if one looks for them). It is not so much that it [i.e. Hayek's economics] was rejected; it slipped through our fingers.[55]

This is not the place to survey the subsequent development of Hicks's ideas under the influence of Pareto and Walras through the 'neo-classical synthesis' to a position which has recently been termed neo-Austrian,[56] though his retrospective comment on the policy aspects of Hayek's work is worth noting:

It is in its application to deflationary slumps that Hayek's theory is at its worst; it is a terrible fact that it was in just such conditions – in 1931–2 – that it was first propounded. In such conditions its diagnosis was wrong, and its prescription could not have been worse.[57]

Hicks has recorded his indebtedness to Swedish as well as Austrian economics, and another distinguished LSE graduate economic theorist of the 1930s, G. L. S. Shackle, was also greatly influenced by the Swedes, especially Gunnar Myrdal, to whose ideas he had been introduced by a young LSE lecturer, Brinley Thomas.[58] This again reveals the range of sources accessible to young LSE economists at the time and is attributable both to its generally cosmopolitan tone,[59] and to the serious attention paid to the history of economic thought.

Robbins's and Hayek's major contributions to scholarship in this field constituted both another major difference from Cambridge, and a continuation of the LSE tradition initiated by Cannan, Gregory, and H. S. Foxwell (a Cambridge economist critical of Marshall, who for many years lectured on monetary topics at LSE). Pigou's indifference to doctrinal history, and Keynes's stimulating but rather casual treatment of his predecessors, are well known.

During the 1930s, Robbins's (and Hayek's) seminar was the central focus of intense debate on theoretical matters, and opposition to the professors' opinions and susceptibility to Keynes's ideas gathered momentum, even before the *General Theory* appeared. There is clear evidence of the type of generation gap usually encountered in periods of intellectual crisis and revolution, though in this case the leading revolutionary, Keynes, was himself middle-aged, and some of his supporters at LSE were not much younger than his opponents.

Undoubtedly, the leading LSE figures in the transfer of allegiance from Hayek to Keynes were Nicholas Kaldor and Abba Lerner, and in the later 1930s others joined with them, sometimes for brief periods, such as Tibor Scitovsky, Harold Barger (who was teaching Statistics at University College), and Michael Kalecki.[60] This is an intensely interesting, as yet unwritten, chapter of doctrinal history which merits systematic investigation.

As explained at the outset, doctrinal history is not the primary theme of this paper. Nevertheless, it would be inappropriate to conclude without reference to two interrelated topics nowadays especially associated with LSE in the 1930s.

The first is the great debate over economic calculation under socialism, and the wider problem of the nature and functioning of the market economy, issues that revealed the complexity of the personal and doctrinal alignments among the school's economists.

For while Hayek, Robbins, Plant, and Gregory were all defenders of the market and critics of socialist economic planning, there was sharp disagreement in 1936–8 between two of the younger interventionists – Evan Durbin, the socialist, and Abba Lerner, the Keynesian.[61] This debate raised matters of fundamental technical importance still recognized as such today – e.g., the nature of market adjustment processes, and the problems of decentralized and incomplete information, especially associated with von Mises and Hayek. Needless to say, these questions were of direct policy and political, as well as theoretical, significance.

The second and final topic is that of cost – the emergence of a subjectivist approach that has come to be known as the LSE concept of cost, largely as the result of James M. Buchanan's historical investigations.[62] For present purposes it is sufficient to note the influence of Wicksteed, Robbins, von Mises, and Hayek on the evolution of this doctrine, and the manner in which it was applied to business decisions by Plant's students, R. H. Coase, G. F. Thirlby (an LSE graduate, colleague of W. H. Hutt at Cape Town, and subsequently a member of staff at LSE), and their colleagues R. S. Edwards, R. F. Fowler, and David Solomons.

The development of this approach to cost, which bears a close affinity to the penetrating work of yet another LSE graduate, G. L. S. Shackle, provides further evidence of the distinctively non-Marshallian, neo-classical approach to economics at LSE during the inter-war years.

NOTES

1 F. A. Hayek, 'The LSE 1895–1914', *Economica*, N. S., vol. 13, February 1946, pp. 1–31; Donald Winch, *Economics and Policy. A Historical Study*, London: Hodder & Stoughton, 1969, espec. part two: Lord Robbins, *Autobiography of an Economist*, London: Macmillan, 1971; José Harris, *William Beveridge. A Biography*, Oxford: Clarendon Press, 1977.

2 Harry Johnson and Elizabeth S. Johnson, *The Shadow of Keynes. Understanding Keynes, Cambridge and Keynesian Economics*, Oxford: Basil Blackwell, 1978, espec. pp. 84–8. It is doubtful whether social geography can be fully and accurately depicted other than by an 'insider'.

3 *London School of Economics Reminiscences of Former Students, Members of Staff and Governors, with other material relating to the History of the School 1922–1947*. (British Library of Political Science, Archives Department R(SR) 1101.) I owe this reference to Dr Alon Kadish.

4 This and the next paragraph is based on Lord Beveridge, *The London School of Economics and its Problems 1919–1937*, London: Allen & Unwin, 1960, pp. 30–3, and appendices.

5 Ibid., pp. 33, 96. For evidence of Beveridge's relief on his return to Oxford in the late 1930s see Harris, op. cit., pp. 362–3.

6 Cf. Beveridge, op. cit., pp. 55–6; Harris, op. cit., pp. 292ff.

7 A. W. Coats and S. E. Coats, 'The Changing Social Composition of the Royal Economic Society 1890–1960 and the Professionalization of British Economics', *British Journal of Sociology*, vol. XXIV, June 1973, pp. 165–87 (reprinted in this volume, pp. 338–60).

8 Robbins, op. cit., p. 110. Robbins also turned down a Cambridge University lectureship because it carried no 'guarantee of a college fellowship and I did not want to find myself fluttering on the periphery of even so distinguished a community as Cambridge', p. 109.

9 *LSE Reminiscences*, op. cit., p. 39.

10 The roster included R. G. D. Allen, F. C. Benham, R. H. Coase, H. Dalton, R. Edwards, J. C. Gilbert, T. E. Gregory, D. G. Hutton, N. Kaldor, A. Lerner, W. A. Lewis, A. Plant, G. Schwarz, G. Thirlby, B. Thomas.

11 J. H. Hexter, *Reappraisals in History*, London: Longmans, 1961, p. 197.

12 Robbins, op. cit., p. 119. Even a casual perusal of the school's annual Calendar from 1928–9 through to the early 1930s reveals the dramatic change that occurred in the size and importance of economics. By 1931–2 Economics, Analytical and Applied, now included: I General Economic Theory; II Applied Economics, incorporating (a) General and (b) Banking and Currency; III Regional and Particular Studies; IV Business Administration, including Accounting. By 1939–40 III and IV appeared as subsections of II, together with Estate Management and Transport. In the 1920s, Banking and Currency, Commerce and Industry, and Transport, had been listed separately from Economics.

13 According to some accounts, Beveridge was unwilling to renew Young's initial three-year tenure because he was not a good teacher for the average under-

graduate. Other versions suggest that he never intended to stay, but planned either to return to Harvard or to go to Chicago, whence he had received a very attractive offer. It is interesting to speculate on the possible effects on the 'Chicago School' of Young's being there until the early 1940s, for he was only 52 when he died, in 1929.

14 This is not the place to review departmental rivalries and boundaries at LSE which are discussed in Robbins, op. cit., and Harris, op. cit. See also Gregory's 'Edwin Cannan: A Personal Impression', *Economica*, N. S., vol. 2, November 1935, p. 372, where he refers to a 'running battle' between the economists and the geographers in the 1920s. Of more direct interest to the historian of economics is J. R. Hicks's recollection that he thought of himself as a labour economist until Robbins encouraged him to develop his ability in advanced economic theory. Even then, he recalls, 'I was entirely a victim of the traditional "division" between real and monetary economics; monetary economics was not my concern, for was it not organized (at the London School) in a different department from that in which I was teaching?' Cf. *The Theory of Wages*, London 1963, p. 307. Within the general field of economics during the 1930s, the most important division was probably that between Economics and Commerce, the latter under the leadership of Robbins's friend and fellow LSE undergraduate, Arnold Plant, who became Professor of Commerce in 1930 and Head of the Department of Business Administration.

One significant indicator of the growth of scale, specialization, and compartmentalization of social studies at LSE is the founding of the periodical *Politica*, in 1931, as a result of Robbins's desire that *Economica*, launched a decade earlier, should focus more exclusively on economic subjects.

15 Harris, op. cit., for example p. 267.

16 Beveridge, op. cit., p. 83.

17 Robbins, op. cit., p. 122.

18 Hayek, op. cit., p. 6.

19 J. A. Schumpeter, *History of Economic Analysis*, London, 1954, p. 832. See also Hugh Dalton, 'Professor Cannan's General Contribution' in T. E. Gregory and Hugh Dalton, *London Essays in Economics in Honour of Edwin Cannan*, London, 1927: To Cannan, economic science 'is rather a bluff common sense, non-mathematical, without humbug or pretentiousness, and practising a strict economy of those technical terms which so easily degenerate into clumsy and aesthetically repulsive jargon. . . . Compared with some economists of the Cambridge School he is apt to appear relatively unsystematic and to judge questions more on their particular merits and less as special illustrations of far-reaching general propositions', p. 8.

20 Gregory, 'Edwin Cannan', op. cit., p. 371.

21 Edwin Cannan, 'The Need for Simpler Economics', *Economic Journal*, vol. XLIV, September 1933, pp. 367–9, 378. Curiously enough, Robbins's self-denying ordinance did not deter him from writing to *The Times*, for example against Keynes's heretical lapse from free trade. As he told Cannan, 'Beveridge, Clay, Plant, Layton and myself and one or two others have formed a sort of Committee of Public Safety and are getting out a book on the question which we hope will check the landslide of public opinion and if necessary to counteract the Report' of the Committee of the Economic Advisory Council. Cf. Harris, op. cit., p. 317. The book was *Tariffs. The Case Examined*, London, 1931, edited by Beveridge. On the Report see Susan Howson and Donald Winch, *The Economic Advisory Council 1930–1939. A Study in Economic Advice during Depression and Recovery*, London: Cambridge University Press, 1977, espec. pp. 57ff.

22 Lionel Robbins, 'The Present Position of Economic Science', *Economica*, vol. 10, March 1930, pp. 23–4. F. A. Hayek, 'The Trend in Economic Thinking', *Economica*, vol. 13, May 1933, p. 127.

23 Robbins, *Autobiography*, p. 135.

24 Ibid., pp. 129, 136.

25 Robbins, 'The Present Position of Economic Science', p. 20. Also his *An Essay on the Nature and Significance of Economic Science*, London: Macmillan, 1932, chapter 5.

26 Harris, op. cit., p. 322; Robbins, *Autobiography*, pp. 96–7. Robbins had had a considerable influence on the published version of the book, and had been Beveridge's examiner when it was submitted for a London D.Sc. degree – yet another indication of Beveridge's desire to be recognized as a scholar.

27 Hugh Dalton, *Call Back Yesterday, Memoirs 1887–1931*, London, 1953. Dalton had actively campaigned for, and he and Cannan had initially welcomed Robbins's appointment, as an individualist who would add variety to the teaching staff. But Dalton subsequently complained that 'there has been a tendency since then for this variety to disappear and for the School to teach a much more uniform brand of right wing economics – and politics too'. Robbins was 'apt to hold opinions with an excess of emotional fervour. He has a phobia about State action, except in wartime. He is apt to ignore the realities of politics and public opinion', pp. 115–16. Even more strongly worded complaints are to be found in Dalton's diaries and correspondence – a point for which I am indebted to Elizabeth Durbin.

28 Harris, op. cit., pp. 322–3; cf. pp. 324–5.

29 Ibid., p. 323.

30 Ibid., pp. 296, 303.

31 Ibid., p. 303.

32 Robbins, *Autobiography*, op. cit., p. 91.

33 Cf. Arnold Plant, 'Homage to Hayek' in his *Selected Essays and Addresses*, London, 1974, pp. 168–9.

34 Robbins, op. cit., pp. 67–8, 90–1, 95, 97–8, 152–3. Several of these passages reveal the interdependence of emotional and intellectual considerations in the formation and changes of his views. Also Dalton, as quoted above, note 27.

35 Ibid., op. cit., p. 93.

36 Plant, op. cit., p. 169. Another important non-Marshallian influence on Robbins was the English economist, Philip Wicksteed.

37 Ibid.

38 Ibid., p. 170.

39 Hicks, op. cit., p. 306.

40 D. H. Robertson to J. M. Keynes, 4 October 1931, in *The Collected Writings of John Maynard Keynes*, ed. D. Moggridge, London: Macmillan, for the Royal Economic Society, 1979, vol. XXIX, p. 271. The reference is to Hayek's *Prices and Production*, 1931.

41 H. O. Meredith to J. M. Keynes, 22 November 1931, ibid., pp. 266–7.

42 *Idem*, 8 December 1931, ibid., pp. 267–8.

43 Robbins, op. cit., pp. 152–3. Cf. Howson and Winch, op. cit., pp. 46–81, especially p. 64 n. The letter Robbins referred to was also signed by Gregory, Plant, and Hayek.

44 Robbins, op. cit., pp. 153–4. Robbins also acknowledges that his reaction against the Cambridge dictum that it's 'all in Marshall' was excessive, and that in his response to the works of non-British economists 'I now suspect that I found more novelty or relevance than there really was', ibid., pp. 105, 128.

45 For example, Donald Winch, *Economics and Policy*, op. cit., chapters 8 and 9, especially 'Keynes versus the London School of Economics', pp. 189ff. Bernard Corry, in his introduction to a reprint of Edwin Cannan's *Review of Economic Theory*, London, 1964 refers to 'rivalry, if not open warfare' between London and Cambridge. Among topics not previously mentioned here are the Keynes–Beveridge controversy over population growth in the 1920s and Keynes's severe critique of Cannan's monetary theory in the same period.

On the other hand Robbins, as already indicated, and Austin Robinson, play down both the conflicts and the differences; likewise Elizabeth Durbin, basing her contention on her father's archives and extensive interviews, broadly agrees, emphasizing the smallness of the academic community and the repeated contacts between the two centres. Cf. Elizabeth Durbin, *The Fabians, Mr. Keynes, and the Economics of Democratic Socialism*, chapter 2, unpublished typescript (subsequently published as *New Jerusalems. The Labour Party and the Economics of Democratic Socialism*, London: Routledge & Kegan Paul, 1985).

A study of articles in *Economica* and the *Economic Journal* reveals a strong tendency for London authors to publish in the former and Cambridge authors in the latter. There were, however, some exceptions, and it should be noted that in addition to the *Economic Journal*'s greater prestige it paid its contributors, a factor of some significance to young teachers during the depression. While the *London and Cambridge Economic Service* was a joint publication with Harvard, from 1922, the *Review of Economic Studies*, which first appeared in 1933 and was distinctly more London- than Oxbridge-based, was commonly referred to in Cambridge as 'the children's magazine'. Cf. Keynes's *Collected Writings*, op. cit., vol. III, 1973, p. 326, vol. XIV, 1973, p. 299. See also pp. 183 in this volume.

46 There is a fascinating discussion of professional authority and the appropriate code of conduct in W. H. Hutt, *The Economists and the Public. A Study of Competition and Opinion*, London, 1936, espec. chapter 14, which includes an appendix on Keynes's attack on orthodox economics. Hutt was an LSE graduate and Professor of Commerce at Cape Town. He spent several summers at LSE during the 1930s. LSE economists were undoubtedly more concerned about the problems of professionalization than their Cambridge counterparts.

47 Winch, op. cit., pp. 181–2.

48 Keynes's *Collected Writings*, vol. XIII, reveals that some of his most loyal supporters regretted, and unsuccessfully sought to discourage, his exaggeration of the differences between himself and the 'classical' economists.

49 Cited by C. R. Fay, 'Edwin Cannan: A Tribute to a Friend', *The Economic Record*, vol. 13, June 1937, quoted in Alon Kadish, *Oxford's Young Economists During the 1880's and Early 1890's* (unpublished D.Phil. thesis, Oxford, 1979), p. 275.

50 Especially on free trade, deflation, and economic planning. It is noteworthy that Dalton, a socialist who was still a Reader in the early 1930s although only a part-time lecturer, was also a free trader. Evan Durbin, who was also a socialist, was a Hayekian in theoretical matters.

51 Robbins, op. cit., p. 133.

52 'Personal Recollections of Keynes and the "Keynesian Revolution" ', originally published in *The Oriental Economist*, January 1966 and reprinted in his *New Studies in Philosophy, Politics, Economics, and the History of Ideas*, London 1978, p. 284. It has been suggested that this was an *ex post facto* rationalization.

53 J. R. Hicks, 'The Hayek Story', *Critical Essays in Monetary Theory*, Oxford 1967, pp. 204–5.

54 J. M. Keynes, 'The Pure Theory of Money', *Economica*, vol. 11, November 1931,

p. 394, in response to Hayek's review of his *Treatise on Money*: 'Reflections on the Pure Theory of Money of Mr. Keynes, Part I', *Economica*, vol. 11, August 1931, pp. 277–80. Keynes had actually made this admission earlier, and acknowledged the limitations of his command of German, in a footnote to the *Treatise on Money*. Cf. the *Collected Writings*, op. cit., vol. V, 1971, p. 178 n. Curiously enough, the tone of the correspondence between Keynes and Hayek remained polite, even friendly, although in his review of *Prices and Production*, Keynes had remarked that it 'seems to me one of the most frightful muddles I have ever read, with scarcely a sound proposition in it beginning with page 45, and yet it remains a book of some interest which is likely to leave its mark on the mind of the reader. It is an extraordinary example of how, starting with a mistake, a remorseless logician can end up in Bedlam', 'Pure Theory of Money', op. cit., p. 394. For a somewhat similar Cambridge response, see Piero Sraffa, 'Dr Hayek on Money and Capital', *Economic Journal*, vol. 42, March 1932, p. 45.

55 Hicks, op. cit., pp. 204–5.

56 Cf. Ludwig M. Lachmann, 'Sir John Hicks as a Neo-Austrian', *South African Journal of Economics*, vol. 41, 1973, pp. 195–207.

57 Hicks, op. cit., p. 214.

58 Apparently Shackle originally intended to write his dissertation on Hayekian lines but continued under Hayek's supervision after he encountered the Swedish literature and Keynes's ideas. His first article, on Hayek, was 'Some Notes on Monetary Theories of the Trade Cycle', *Review of Economic Studies*, vol. 1, October 1933, pp. 27–38. For his retrospective assessment of the period see his *The Years of High Theory*, London: Cambridge University Press, 1967, which has barely any reference to Hayek.

59 An odd but significant instance of Robbins's tendency to resort to the works of foreign economists for guidance was his effort to persuade his colleagues on the EAC's Committee of Economists to consult Hayek, W. Röpke, and B. Ohlin, as a counterweight to Keynes's influence. His fellow committee members did not agree. Cf. Howson and Winch, op. cit., p. 60. Also Colin Clark, 'The "Golden" Age of the Great Economists. Keynes, Robbins et al in 1930', *Encounter*, vol. XLVIII, January–June 1977, p. 88. According to Clark, who was on the staff of the EAC, Robbins stated 'menacingly', 'They will soon tell you what's wrong.' Clark describes the Keynes–Robbins encounter as a 'bitter clash leading to a complete breach', and specifically refers to Robbins's 'emotional' defence of free trade. Cf. pp. 82, 89. Robbins's idealism is clear in his minority report and in his moral stand against Keynes. Cf. Howson and Winch, pp. 230–1, 161.

60 On 13 November 1936, Joan Robinson informed Keynes that the younger generation of economists at LSE discussing his theories included Lerner, Sol Adler, Ralph Arakie, and Aaron Emanuel. *Collected Writings*, op. cit., vol. XIV, p. 148 n. Lerner apparently switched allegiance from Hayek to Keynes after spending the winter of 1935–6 in Cambridge. 'After that there was a joint London, Cambridge, and Oxford seminar . . . of the research students at these three universities. Anyone from another university who was interested could join, of course, and it would meet one Sunday a month in one of the three towns, and discuss more or less Keynesian economics.' The *General Theory* was a big and immediate success. 'Naturally there was some discussion, not everybody understood the whole thing at once . . . we in London had some advantage – because we had Lerner explaining what it all meant. And this was very good teaching indeed.' From 'An Interview with Ludwig Lachmann', *Austrian Economics Newsletter*, vol. I, Fall 1978, p. 2. Lachmann, who had received his original

training in Germany, studied under Hayek at LSE and subsequently became a leading proponent of Austrian economics.

61 The literature on this topic is extensive. For example, E. F. M. Durbin, 'Economic Calculus in a Planned Economy', *Economic Journal*, vol. 46, December 1936; Abba Lerner, 'Statics and Dynamics in Socialist Economics', ibid., vol. 47, June 1937; F. A. Hayek, ed., *Collectivist Economic Planning*, London: George Routledge, 1935; Hayek, *Individualism and Economic Order*, Chicago: University of Chicago Press, 1948. More recently, Karen I. Vaughn 'Economic Calculation under Socialism: The Austrian Contribution', *Economic Inquiry*, vol. 18, October 1980, pp. 535–54 and the work of Elizabeth Durbin, referred to in note 45 above.

62 See Buchanan's excellent brief review of the subject in *Cost and Choice. An Inquiry in Economic Theory*, Chicago: Markham Publishing Co., 1969, especially chapter 2: 'The Origins and Development of a London Tradition'. Also his 'Introduction: LSE cost theory in retrospect' in J. M. Buchanan and G. F. Thirlby, eds, *LSE Essays on Cost*, London: London School of Economics and Political Science and Weidenfeld & Nicolson, 1973. The subjectivist approach to decision-making, and indeed to economics generally, is currently enjoying a revival. It is, for example, the theme of Section F of the British Association for the Advancement of Science, September 1981, under the Presidency of Jack Wiseman, a postwar exponent of the LSE cost concept. See J. Wiseman, ed., *Beyond Positive Economics*, London: Macmillan, 1983. See also my essay "The Revival of Subjectivism in Economics", in this collection reprinted in vol I in this series.

Part III

THE ECONOMICS PROFESSION AND THE ROLE OF ECONOMISTS IN GOVERNMENT

21

ECONOMICS AS A PROFESSION

Every profession lives in a world of its own. The language spoken by
its inhabitants, the landmarks familiar to them, their customs and
conventions can only be learnt by those who reside there.

(Carr-Saunders and Wilson 1933: iii)

I INTRODUCTION

Most economists see themselves, and wish to be seen by others, as professionals, although if pressed many would find it difficult to say precisely
what that designation means. This is understandable, for the terms 'profession' and 'professionalization' have long been the subject of dispute
among specialists, most of whom are sociologists and therefore not taken
seriously by economists. Moreover, as noted later, there are specific reasons
why the economics profession is difficult to define and identify. What is
less understandable, indeed inexcusable, is the dearth of serious research
on the nature, historical evolution and significance of the professionalization
of economics, whether by economists or by other scholars. Of course, there
has been considerable discussion of the profession's problems, especially
during and since the so-called 'crisis' of the late 1960s and early 1970s
(e.g. Heller 1975; Coats 1977; Bell and Kristol 1981 among others), but
most of this has been either occasional, personal partisan or mainly methodological. There is no full-scale published study of the growth of the
economics profession in the UK or the USA, the two leading countries in
the development of modern economics; and comparative work on the subject is still in its infancy[1] – although there has been some promising, but
essentially preliminary, research on the role of economists in government
that is referred to below. Consequently, given the current state of our
knowledge, the following account must perforce be sketchy and impressionistic.

Some things, however, are indisputable. During the past half-century or
so the number of trained economists has increased remarkably by comparison with the rest of the period since Adam Smith published *The Wealth of*

395

Nations, and this is attributable to both supply and demand forces. Prior to the late nineteenth century in the UK and the USA, and much later still in most other countries, there was little or no formal training in economics as we know it today. When the social sciences eventually emerged as a group of identifiable specialized disciplines, ecomomics was in the vanguard, partly because it was a subject of obvious public interest and significance, but mainly because it was based on a well-developed and recognizable corpus of theoretical knowledge. The latter feature is nowadays seen as the *sine qua non* of a 'modern' science-based profession, as contrasted with such traditional professions as the church, the law and the military.

In the extraordinary global expansion of higher education after World War II economics was by no means the least of the disciplinary beneficiaries, and naturally enough this process called for a rapid growth in the numbers of academic teachers and researchers. However, this was but an extension of a much earlier and broader process of economic and social change – namely, the growth of specialization and division of labour in modern urban industrial communities. As one thoughtful sociologist has pithily observed: 'an industrializing society is a professionalizing society' (Goode 1960: 902). Another has claimed that:

> The development and strategic importance of the professions probably constitutes the most important change that has occurred in the occupational structure of modern societies. The growth of the professions has brought to prominence a set of occupations which never figured prominently in the ideological thinking that, after having crystallized in the late nineteenth century, has tended to dominate public discussion in the twentieth.
>
> (Parsons 1968: 536)

The weasel word 'ideological' is pertinent here in at least two distinct but interrelated senses. The first and more obvious of these is political. Thus radical, Marxist, institutionalist and other dissenting economists have argued that orthodox mainstream neoclassical doctrine explicitly or implicitly involves an acceptance of the socio-economic status quo. For example, marginal analysis focuses attention on small-scale incremental adjustments of present discontents, thereby discouraging more fundamental questioning of the existing order, and it is certainly true that when marginalism was gaining acceptance among academic economists around the turn of the century there was a concomitant narrowing of the discipline's scope (symbolized by the terminological shift from 'political economy' to 'economics'), a move that enabled economists to delegate to other social science specialists such troublesome issues as the distribution of income and wealth, the power structure and social justice. Such a contraction of scope is a familiar feature of the professionalization process. Of course, some critics strenuously resisted this constriction of their subject matter.

However, the change was facilitated by the practice of distinguishing sharply between the 'science' (i.e. theory or analysis, sometimes referred to as economics 'proper') and the 'art' of political economy (i.e. the discussion of current economic problems and policies), so that the adept economist could both have her cake and eat it, i.e. she could participate as a detached impartial expert in public policy debates without thereby compromising her scientific purity.[2] How far the laity acknowledged this differentiation of roles is another matter.

More recently, with the growth of non-academic employment opportunities in business, banking, local, regional and national government, and international agencies, an increasing number of economists have entered policy-making positions, and the consequent politicization of the subject has made the distinction between the science and the art more and more difficult to sustain in practice. Especially during and since World War II – although the process was already well under way in some countries from the Great Depression of the early 1930s – professionally trained economists have occupied prominent positions as heads of state, cabinet ministers, principal official advisers to government, chief executives of large corporations and so on. They have been outspoken in public debates on contentious policy issues in many different fora at a variety of levels, and they played a major part in the construction and operation of the international economic organizations that have become so integral a part of the post-war world.

All this makes it difficult to maintain that economics is an essentially technocratic and apolitical subject. Indeed, one perceptive economist critic has persuasively argued that there are not one but three distinct professional economic ideologies or world views – the conservative, liberal and radical versions – each with its own ideological assumptions, theories and policy preferences, and that by his definition the majority of academic economists are liberals (Ward 1979). This seems entirely appropriate, given the discipline's eighteenth-century liberal moral philosophical antecedents.

However, there is a second meaning of the word ideological that is particularly relevant here. This is the concept of professional ideology – the set of ideas, beliefs, values, standards and behaviour patterns that differentiates one category of professionals from others. As noted in the opening epigraph, a professional ideology is an integral part of the common culture shared by the workers in any reasonably well-defined field. It is circumscribed by the group's accepted aims, conventions and methodological rules; it is reinforced by the development of an esoteric language inaccessible to laymen; and it also usually embodies elements of 'tacit' knowledge which even experienced practitioners find difficult to articulate fully. In the economist's case a central tenet of this ideology is the conception of the neutral objective scientific expert which underlies the above-mentioned distinction between 'science' and 'art', or between 'positive' and 'normative' economics, to use the current jargon (Hutchinson 1964). In the economics community the academic ideal, namely that of the pure research truth-seeker, the detached non-partisan expert, outweighs any more pragmatic conception of professionalism or public service; and when this ideal is transported into the non-academic realm it often takes the form of partisan advocacy of efficiency and market methods (Nelson 1987) which, according to some critics, are given unwarranted priority over considerations of equity – an emphasis facilitated by the efforts at the turn of the century to sever the links between political economy and ethics. These professional values are deep rooted, firmly stressed in the standard textbooks and inculcated, both tacitly and explicitly, in the initiation, training and socialization of new recruits to the field. And however remote from reality the conception of professional neutrality may seem, it has exercised a potent force in the creation and maintenance of the economists' collective professional identity.[3]

Of course, the subjective components of professional ideology count for little without the external dimension of public recognition of the occupation's cultural status, which takes the form of specialized appointments, above-average remuneration, the delegation of responsibility and authority, and social esteem. Command of esoteric knowledge and skills is usually certified by the award of degrees, diplomas and other qualifications, for which a lengthy period of training is required; and controls over entry, whether through the training process or direct regulation by a body issuing credentials, or both, serve to limit the supply of new recruits and thereby to maintain the profession's privileged status.

A profession is not a static phenomenon, identifiable simply by a fixed list of traits.[4] Professions grow and develop over time, and professionalization is a dynamic process that involves

> an attempt to translate one order of scarce resources – specialized knowledge and skills – into another – social and economic rewards. To maintain scarcity implies a tendency to monopoly: monopoly of expertise in the market, monopoly of status in the system of stratification.
>
> (Larson 1978: xvii)

Against the cynical view that the essence of professionalism is power – a species of conspiracy against the laity – there is the contrasting belief that the professional has a distinctive moral obligation to his or her clients, or to society at large – for instance in the obligation to use expertise responsibly in the service of others.[5] Whichever of these standpoints is preferred, it is clear that economists have not attained full professional status; indeed, they may not have seriously tried to do so. They have traditionally been ideologically opposed to monopoly, and this has led them to question the merits of professionalism more openly and persistently than other social scientists (Johnson 1972: 15).[6] How far they have sought detachment from the market-place, another characteristic associated with the professions, is a nice question (Herman 1982).

Although academic economists necessarily influence entry into the profession through their control of the degree process, they have consistently opposed any kind of formal professional accreditation. The leading British and American learned societies or professional organizations rely solely on the economic criterion, for they are open to anyone willing to pay the requisite membership fee, and economists have made no collective effort to prescribe standards of professional conduct, whether in universities or elsewhere. Even now, when the level of technical sophistication of Ph.D. students from so-called élite graduate departments has reached heights that to older professionals seem dizzyingly abstract, there is often still no clear occupational discrimination in the non-academic world between (a) those with advanced as well as undergraduate degrees, (b) those with joint or mixed rather than single honours undergraduate degrees (Towse and Blaug 1988) and (c) those in higher management or civil service positions with no formal training whatsoever in economics. Sceptics may argue that it is not ideological distaste grounded in an inherited liberal moral philosophy that explains the reluctance to enforce strict controls over entry, a code of professional ethics or procedures for excommunicating those who fail to maintain acceptable standards of behaviour or performance. Rather, it is the wisdom of recognizing that that species of professionalism is simply unenforceable, perhaps even undefinable, in economics.[7]

Underlying this situation is a troublesome epistemological question: exactly what do economists 'know' (i.e. that other professionals do not)? Of course, trained economists can be expected to 'know' the corpus of economic analysis enshrined in innumerable conventional textbooks (which, incidentally, display a remarkable degree of uniformity). Presumably, they understand the nature and operations of the price mechanism far better than non-economists do; and also the functioning and interdependence of markets at home and abroad, the significance of scarcity and opportunity costs, the nature and functions of money, banking, finance, etc., and so on. Yet many of the economist's fundamental ideas are elementary and very general, albeit with wide applicability. Do they suffice as a foundation for claims to expertise in non-academic settings?

Judging by half a century's experience of economists' employment in government the question can confidently be answered in the affirmative. After all, despite the well-publicized conflicts and disagreements within the profession, the demand for economists in the public service has been remarkably sustained, and although much less is known about their successes and failures in the private sector, no doubt the same answer applies there also. However, there are important reservations to be made which cannot be fully explained and justified here.

399

With respect to government employment, attention has usually been focused on the economists' role in the higher-level advisory or decision-making positions, whereas in demand terms activities within the bureaucratic machine are obviously more significant, albeit less glamorous. These activities vary enormously, and sweeping generalizations must therefore be suspect. Nevertheless, the nature, extent and effectiveness of the economists' work will obviously depend on such factors as the range and variety of the government's economic and social policies (*laissez-faire* is not good for the profession), the political climate (a degree of stability is essential), the character of the bureaucracy (corruption, politicization and inefficiency are obvious impediments) and the readiness to acknowledge the authority of the economist's expertise (which is dependent on the society's culture, the educational system and the degree of consensus within the economics community) (cf. Coats 1981, 1986; Pechman 1989). Economists can perform many different functions in many different contexts, but they are usually more effective in departments or agencies with a relatively clear economic purpose and responsibility. They may be temporary or permanent employees, working either in segregated specialist units (for example, as model-builders and forecasters) or as isolated free-floating individuals in close day-to-day contact with generalist administrators or with other specialists or professionals (and in such cases conflicts of professional values and ideologies may become significant). Much of the lower-level work consists of routine data collection, presentation and analysis, calling for little or no input of the economist's specialist knowledge and equipment. And as government work, like economics itself, has become more and more quantitative, partly in response to the almost insatiable demand for economic and social statistics, economists often find themselves working alongside other numerate specialists such as statisticians, mathematicians, operations researchers or accountants. It is in these situations that the economists' product can and must be differentiated, for in addition to their quantitative, technical and mathematical abilities they also possess a distinctive intellectual apparatus or 'way of thinking' that is unfamiliar to most (but not all) non-economists.[8] The value of this basic, seemingly elementary, mental equipment has repeatedly been stressed by senior professional practitioners reflecting on their experience in government. They have frequently been agreeably surprised by their ability to pose penetrating and effective questions that others were either unable or unwilling to ask. In this context, overemphasis on quantitative methods can be professionally as well as intellectually debilitating, for the solutions to complex policy problems can rarely be reduced to quantitative terms.

As is clear from comparative studies of national governments and international agencies, the tasks performed by a government economist will largely depend on the scale, structure and responsibilities of the organization in which he or she works. Many are employed within the several levels between the top official advisers and policy-makers and the humbler toilers in the bureaucratic vineyard, many of whom are mere number-crunchers. Policy proposals may originate anywhere within the government machine, or from outside, but much of the essential policy formulation and implementation occurs in the middle levels. Proposals are usually modified, refined and reshaped repeatedly – i.e. if they are not abandoned – while moving through the official channels; and once a firm decision has been made, implementation often necessitates its adaptation and interpretation to fit specific circumstances that were not envisaged by the original drafters and decision-makers. Economists contribute to all these activities.

Experienced government economists have learnt that if they are to be effective they must accept the facts of bureaucratic and political life. As Robert Nelson has observed in a valuable recent survey of a large literature, they cannot function simply as undeviating partisan advocates for efficiency. In practice they

> must also tailor their advocacy of market methods, efficient resource use, and other economic approaches to the political environment . . . modify proposals to make them attractive in terms of equity, or to avoid infringing on real or perceived 'rights' . . . recognize that they are members of an organization with which they must conform to some degree . . . [and] develop and exercise skills in bureaucratic and political tactics, which are necessarily interwoven with their exercise of economic experience.
>
> (Nelson 1987: 50)

In official life personality, intuition, imagination, communication skills, speed and stamina may count for more than logic and technique, and the implications of these requirements for graduate training in economics will be considered later. What is clear at this point is that adherence to a strict form of professionalism, which tends to assume the omnipresence of rationality, may be positively harmful.[9] There are many complaints that much of the trained economist's hard-earned professional capital is useless or actively misleading in government work, while the academic emphasis on the value of originality is out of place in an organizational setting where teamwork is essential. Some prominent economists, like the late Harry G. Johnson, have claimed that good economists do not go into government, or, if they do they do not stay good for long, since they rapidly suffer from professional obsolescence. Others believe that government work is necessarily corrupting, even if only mildly so, because of the unavoidable compromises involved.

II PASSAGES IN THE HISTORICAL DEVELOPMENT OF THE ECONOMICS PROFESSION

Given the difficulties of definition, the history of the economics profession has no unambiguous starting point.[10] While the French Physiocrats may be seen as the first modern 'school' of economists in the intellectual rather than the sociological sense of that term, it is convenient to begin with the Ricardians, the first group of British economists to regard themselves, and to be recognized by important segments of the public, as experts in economic affairs. To a remarkable extent this status was attributable to the personal influence of David Ricardo himself, a retired stockbroker, the very epitome of the scientific intellectual, whose work drew upon and developed Adam Smith's ideas. Ricardo became widely acknowledged as the leading economic authority of the day because of the skill, lucidity and disinterestedness with which he analysed the hotly contested technical and policy problems of the currency, banking and international trade, both in his published writings and in his House of Commons speeches. At that time 'economist' was not yet a recognizable occupational category, and although scholars have suggested that either T. R. Malthus or J. R. McCulloch should be described as the first British professional economist, since each derived most of his income from economic teachings or writings, there was no clear demarcation between those who were qualified to write on economic subjects and those who were not. Despite Thomas Carlyle's familiar jibe about 'the gloomy professors of the dismal science', most of the leading economists spent a limited proportion, if indeed any, of their time in academic employment, and as academic instruction in political economy was woefully inadequate there was no reliable source of prospective new recruits. The Political Economy Club of London, founded in 1821, provided an organizational centre for the discussion and propagation of 'sound' doctrines, particularly free trade. However, it was but one of many such private clubs at home and abroad, and the other prerequisites of professionalization were lacking. The Ricardians' influence derived from their claim to scientific authority which they strenuously asserted in books, pamphlets, magazines, newspapers, official enquiries and parliamentary debates. For the present purpose, however, the most distinctive feature was their effort to distance themselves, as experts, from the amateurs, especially the despised 'practical' men. As Ricardo's ally, James Mill, confidently proclaimed: 'a reasoner must be hard pressed when he is driven to quote practical men in aid of his conclusions. There cannot be a worse authority, in any branch of political science, than that of mere practical men' (Mill 1824, cited by Coats 1964: 90). Mill insisted that: 'Among those who have so much knowledge on the subject as to entitle their opinion to any weight, there is wonderful agreement', despite some disputation 'on the minor questions involved' (Mill 1836, cited by Coats 1964: 90), while a few years later Robert Torrens, a fringe member of the Ricardian group, was confident enough to assert that an economist should be appointed to the Board of Trade because

> it partakes of the nature of a professional appointment, requiring a peculiar course of study, and knowledge of an almost technical nature. . . . Though the time may not have actually arrived, yet it is rapidly approaching, when it will be deemed as necessary to select the members of the Board of Trade from the Economists, as it is to take the Bishops from the Church, or the Law Officers from the Bar.
>
> (Torrens 1826, cited by O'Brien 1965: 32)

Needless to say, this forecast was wildly overoptimistic. Yet it illustrates the trend of opinion among the spokesmen for classical economics, which soon hardened into a rigid orthodoxy in the hands of popularizers and propagandists. Conceivably the intellectual groundwork for professionalization had been laid, but until the late nineteenth century the academic preconditions were insufficient to provide a significant supply of trained economists clearly differentiated from the many amateur practitioners, some of whom carried considerable weight with both the public and the professors.

The marginal revolution of the 1870s was a watershed in the development of the modern economics profession, a complex process that involved changes both within the discipline itself (for example, the shift from political economy to economics noted earlier) and in the higher educational system, which became the principal source of new recruits. In the late nineteenth and early twentieth centuries the essential institutional conditions for academic specialization were being established, such as degree courses, the shift of emphasis away from teaching towards research, the launching of new journals devoted exclusively to economics and the founding of new learned societies that eventually acquired quasi-professional status, even though they were open to all comers.[11] Among these organizations, the American Economic Association (1885) and the British Economic Association (1891, later the Royal Economic Society) were particularly significant (Coats 1960, 1968b). Both had a very heterogeneous membership, especially initially; both were effectively dominated by academics; and both served as models for similar bodies in other countries.

In an original and penetrating book, John Maloney (1985) has examined the influence of the Marshallian paradigm on the professionalization process in the UK. He distinguishes between a primary professional orthodoxy 'based on a theoretical paradigm capable of supporting a programme of research, uniting economists who have its partisanship, regular use and comparative mastery', and secondary professional orthodoxies that

> though dependent for their effect on the primary ones, feature a

consensus on some policy question which, because it involves non-economic arguments, admits of a distinctively limited 'professional view'. This implies that the purely technical questions of economic policy, because they impose the same strictly economic terms of discourse on everyone, have less power to create genuine professional orthodoxies.

(Maloney 1985: 230–1)

In the USA the primary professional orthodoxy was slower to emerge and to attain hegemonic status for a variety of reasons including the sheer size and diversity of the territory; the far greater number, heterogeneity and competitiveness of the higher educational institutions; the persistence of heterodox economic ideas, in part a legacy of the German historical school; and a culture far less deferential to intellectual and scientific authority than its British counterpart (Coats 1980). In both countries there was an influential secondary professional orthodoxy based on free trade ideas, which serves as a reminder of the intimate interdependence of theory and practice in the development of professional economics.

This interdependence was strikingly revealed in the UK during the intense public controversy over tariff reform in the early years of this century. In 1903 fourteen leading economists signed a letter to *The Times* opposing Joseph Chamberlain's reform proposals and voicing their concern at 'the prevalence of certain erroneous opinions' in favour of protection, a doctrine which, they asserted, had been discredited 'partly for reasons of the same kind as those which, as now universally admitted, justified the adoption of free trade' (*The Times*, 15 August 1903, cited by Coats 1964: 100). Here is a prime example of orthodoxy at work: presumably the 'sound' doctrine propagated earlier by the Political Economy Club and subsequently 'universally admitted' should have been sufficient to counter the resurgence of protectionism, despite markedly changed historical conditions.

Unfortunately, the letter from the fourteen professors not only brought predictable howls of protest from Chamberlain's supporters, but also provoked a number of dissenting letters to *The Times* from reputable academic economists who either opposed or were not fully committed to free trade, whether as a scientific doctrine or as a policy. Some of them firmly objected to the attempt to bring the weight of scientific authority to bear on this controversial political issue (Coats 1964: 100–3).[12] Alfred Marshall, the most influential British economist of the day, soon bitterly regretted his participation, which breached his customary practice of cautious detachment from contentious public issues, and undoubtedly the public's reaction taught other economists the need to exercise individual and collective discretion, and to avoid exposing their deeper disagreements to the laity.

In the USA during this formative period the prevalence of serious threats to academic freedom provided an additional powerful incentive to self-restraint, and in due course, after considerable heart-searching, a kind of professional consensus emerged among the leading economists with respect to the proper forms and limits of professional participation in public affairs (Furner 1975). In neither country was there any concerted effort to devise a formal code of professional behaviour designed to protect the disciplinary practitioner. Yet in both cases, and especially in the USA, there was a growing sense of professional community born of the desire to combine the scientist's intellectual prestige and occupational security with the reforming urge to make a constructive impact on the discussion and solution of contemporary economic problems.

The Keynesian revolution of the late 1930s and 1940s was another major watershed in the professionalization of economics, as it was in the development of economic ideas and policy. Although both Keynes's ideas and his policy proposals proved to be deeply controversial, the conjunction of macroeconomic analysis and major advances in the supply of official statistics gave economists the wherewithal to demonstrate their potential value to society, and on this basis the expansion of the non-academic, especially government, economics profession gained substantial momentum. There had, of course, been many earlier examples of governments, public commissions, banks and businesses employing expert economic advisers, usually on an occasional or even personal basis, but sometimes more formally and permanently. Had the American participation in World War I been more lasting, the number of economists in the federal service would surely had continued to grow apace, and the permanent complement of peacetime civilian service economists might well have remained high. Indeed, it was in the early 1920s that American agricultural economists first became established in the federal administration, and it is no coincidence that their transatlantic counterparts became the first group of permanent economic specialists in British government, roughly a decade later (Coats 1976; McDean 1983). The Great Depression marked a new low in the profession's public esteem, for the economists' response to the urgent and widespread demand for explanations and solutions to the crisis proved to be confusing, often contradictory and therefore deeply disappointing to politicians and the general public alike. But the recovery and approach of war radically changed the climate of opinion.

During the 1940s the global centre of economics, both as a science and as a profession, shifted decisively and permanently from Europe, especially the UK, to the USA, and within that country in wartime Washington became the intellectual as well as the governmental centre of economists' ideas and activities (including, temporarily, the editorship of the leading professional journal, the *American Economic Review*). Keynes's theoretical ideas and policies dominated academic economics during the first two post-war decades, although never to the same degree in the USA as in the UK, and, indeed, the multi-centred distribution of academic resources in the USA and the challenge of dissenting orthodox and heterodox doctrines combined to sustain the subject's intellectual vitality.

In retrospect it appears that the USA's post-war leadership was inevitable, in economics as in many other academic disciplines, given the country's overwhelming superiority in material and human resources – the latter's having been disproportionately strengthened by the influx of European émigrés, many of whom had crossed the Atlantic to escape Nazi persecution. The list of Presidents of the American Economic Association provides evidence of the recognition that some of these individuals evidently earned, and the presence of Paul Samuelson, Milton Friedman and George Stigler in the roster of Nobel Prizewinners testifies to the emergence of a cohort of distinguished Americans trained in their native universities during the 1930s who came to professional maturity in the ensuing decade.

This is not the place to examine post-1945 developments in economic doctrines. In the present context the most important consequences of the Americanization of economics (and, gradually, its internationalization also) has been that American methods of advanced training, theories and techniques, intellectual values and professional standards have become increasingly acknowledged and adopted throughout the world, obviously with varying time lags and degrees of resistance.[13] This process was enormously facilitated by a number of factors including the growth and acceleration of global communications; the movement of large numbers of foreign students who studied and obtained their professional credentials in the USA and, to a lesser extent, in the UK and Western Europe; the veritable army of American and British professors who have taught, studied and undertaken research or advisory work in foreign countries, the proliferation of international conferences, scholarly organizations and study groups; and, less conspicuously, the emergence of small but influential global networks of economic specialists (for example, in development economics, international trade and monetary affairs) and a cadre of economists employed by foreign governments, international agencies and other para-statal bodies. Another major force in the internationalization of economics, as in some other disciplines, has been the increasingly widespread and efficient distribution of research monographs, professional journals, official reports and, especially, relatively standardized elementary and advanced teaching texts and related materials. Of course, the flow of ideas, methods, techniques and various species of hardware and software has by no means been all one way, and there is some danger of overstating the extent of uniformity, especially if we focus on the conventional contents of the standard macroeconomics and microeconomics curriculum. However, as noted at the beginning of this study, in the present state of our knowledge we have embarrassingly little systematic data on the precise nature and differences of national 'styles' in training, research and publication (Johnson 1973).

III RECENT DEVELOPMENTS AND CONCERNS

For a variety of historical and cultural reasons that cannot be explored adequately here, Americans have long been more fascinated (and worried) than their European counterparts by the nature, growth and influence of the professions. Consequently, matters of this kind have attracted more controversy and research in the USA than elsewhere.

Needless to say, much of the activity in this area stems from dissatisfaction with the status quo, and in the case of economics it is hardly surprising that the euphoria of the Keynesian era (c. 1945–65) was followed by a reaction both within and outside the economics community. The doctrinal challenges to Keynesian ideas from monetarists, post-Keynesians, Marxists, radicals, institutionalists and neo-Austrians were reinforced by the manifest inability of mainstream 'neoclassical' economists to cope with the problems associated with 'stagflation'. But the most distinctive feature of this particular 'crisis' was the extent to which it exposed the widspread and deep-seated loss of professional self-confidence. This was manifested in a veritable orgy of public self-flagellation led by some of the profession's most respected figures in a series of presidential addresses and invited public lectures (Heller 1975; Coats 1977). The critics focused on some of the familiar negative features of professionalism, such as rigidity, conformity, resistance to innovations (other than those of an approved species), the maintenance of tight disciplinary boundaries, the exclusion and/or denigration of dissenters, and excessively centralized control over access to resources, training and employment opportunities.

It is pertinent to note that professional standards, like methodological rules, have prescriptive and regulative as well as cognitive functions, and the quest for scientific truth or community service can easily be sacrificed to the interests of maintaining and advancing special privileges, securing higher remuneration, and protecting the field from enroachments by charlatans and those operating in closely related or overlapping disciplines or occupations.

These and many other features of the sociology of economics have been analysed and documented in a large, contentious, and often entertaining and insightful body of literature that is far too large to be cited extensively here. Not all of this outpouring can be dismissed, as some critics have been wont to do, as the work of cranks, dissidents and incompetents; some of it emanates from acknowledged leaders of the profession.[14] Some, indeed, regard these criticisms not as pathological, but rather as evidence of vigorous health (Heller 1975). Nevertheless, there is general recognition that too much well-publicized disagreement, especially with respect to fundamentals, may undermine the discipline's scientific status in the public's eyes.

Many of the most outspoken critics of the state of economics complain that the profession is too hierarchical and élitist, and that it is dominated by a relatively small contingent of orthodox neoclassical economists centred in a few leading departments. As one President of the American Economic Association has declared, there is nowadays

> a new despotism. That consists in defining scientific excellence as whatever is closest in belief and method to the scholarly tendency of those who are already there. This is a pervasive and oppressive thing not the less dangerous for being, in the frequent case, both righteous and unconscious.
>
> (Galbraith 1973)

The professional establishment is said to control directly or indirectly the selection of officers of the American Economic Association, the editors and editorial boards of the Association's publications and other leading professional journals, the winners of the principal honours and awards, and the allocation of major research funds through the peer review system employed by the National Science Foundation and the principal private grant-giving agencies. Members of this élite also determine the basic requirements of core courses in the élite graduate schools, thereby controlling the means of certification, the entry of new recruits into the profession, and their career prospects through both the informal communications network that influences most appointments and the publication process that so heavily shapes the individual's subsequent career. There are, of course, many specialist subgroups, invisible colleges, schools and networks, and occasionally an exceptional individual who has had the misfortune to be trained or appointed at one of the lesser institutions is spotted, like a star athlete, and recruited by a major league team. But for the most part the students of the leading graduate schools remain within the élite circuit if they can, and in due course produce their own progeny who help to perpetuate the system.

Various useful studies have been undertaken to document this state of affairs. In particular, the journals network, which reveals both the core of the profession's reputational system and the processes whereby new ideas are generated and disseminated, has been extensively examined. Among the topics covered are the use of citation indexes to trace the institutional affiliations of authors of articles in the leading periodicals in an effort to determine how far there is a closed community of the élite; the prestige ratings of various journals; the earnings and career implications of publication in a leading journal; the mathematical and technical content of articles; the extent to which authors seriously endeavour to refute and/or empirically test their findings; the number of publications by 'star' economists; fashions, trends and cycles in the literature; and so on.[15]

Of course, every human organization, not least every academic discipline, necessarily has its leaders and followers, its superior performers and its mediocrities, and disputed scientific findings, evaluations and decisions cannot be settled by conventional democratic processes, even within the community of the competent. Moreover, it is natural for those in the establishment who have already achieved success to approve of the system in which they have attained their eminence, since their own virtues and abilities have been so fittingly recognized and rewarded. A telling example of this perspective is the complacent analysis of the process whereby private foundation grant allocations purportedly facilitate the concentration of research and talent in the already acknowledged 'best' university departments, thereby reinforcing their members' existing ability to attract able colleagues, hire research assistants, obtain any requisite equipment and produce more successful work, thus enhancing their department's visibility and prestige rating in the economics community (Stigler 1967).

Whether this system works well or badly depends on the alternative possibilities – a matter rarely considered, since it involves a massive counterfactual that not even the most ambitious exponent of the new cliometric history would undertake lightly. In practice professional inertia is likely to preclude any dramatic changes: most scientists are reformers, not radicals. Unfortunately both critics and defenders of the status quo too often base their assessments on personal experience and hearsay rather than reliable evidence, and there are underlying differences of professional values and standards, if not incommensurable paradigms.

Rather than elaborating on this subject by citing individual economists' views, which are hardly detached, it is more illuminating to turn to an impartial sociologist of science, Richard Whitley, who has reviewed modern economics from the standpoint of his ambitious comprehensive typology of the natural and social sciences. Whitley treats scientific fields as reputational systems of work organization and control in terms of specific key variables deriving from their individual histories and subject content. Against this background, Anglo-Saxon economics emerges as a unique case (Whitley 1984, 1986).[16]

As in physics, the theoretical core of economics dominates textbooks, training programmes, the communication system and academic posts and honours, but economics is distinct from other fields in that, unlike physics, there is a marked division between theoretical and empirical work. This is partly due to the lack of technical control over empirical work which limits the applied economist's dependence on the theorist (unlike the situation in physics), and also because of the existence of other audiences outside the theoretical establishment and the scientific or professional community. Competition by producers within the central core, although intense, is restricted to technical refinements and extensions of the analytical scheme to novel problems that can be tackled with existing techniques. The dominance of the established theoretical goals, and the degree of impersonality and formalization of coordination and control procedures, vary as between empirical specialisms because the relatively intractable and unpredictable nature of empirical phenomena restricts the extent to which systematic comparison and validation of task outcomes can be accomplished through the formal communication system. The heterogeneity of applied fields is limited by 'rigid delimination' of the types of problems deemed legitimate and important; on the other hand, deviations on the periphery can be largely ignored by the intellectual élite who control the dominant communications media and training programmes.

This analysis is compatible with many of the familiar complaints from those dissatisfied with the state of the discipline, especially the excessive emphasis on a high level of abstraction, mathematization and formalization in advanced training programmes (cf. Bauer and Walters 1975; Hutchison 1977; Blatt 1983; Morishima 1984; Grubel and Boland 1986; Woo 1986) and the irrelevance of much of this work to contemporary problems and especially policy issues. The fact that one major school of economists based in Chicago has endeavoured to extend its 'imperialistic' sway (Stigler 1984) by applying a standardized analysis to a whole range of problems formerly thought to lie outside the economist's domain merely confirms the arguments of those who complain of the tendency towards uniformity in the discipline.

There are, of course, other contending approaches within mainstream economics that challenge the Chicagoans' approach. But this does not necessarily reflect a happy state of affairs, as suggested by the distinguished ex-Chicago economist who reported, sadly:

What generates in me a great deal of scepticism about the state of our discipline is the high positive correlation between the policy views of a researcher (or, what is worse, his thesis director) and his empirical findings. I will begin to believe in economics as a science when out of Yale there comes an empirical thesis demonstrating the supremacy of monetary policy in some historical episode – and out of Chicago, one demonstrating the supremacy of fiscal policy.

(Patinkin 1972: 142, cited by Hutchison 1977: 61)

Another recent critic, also with strong earlier Chicago associations, has outspokenly protested at the exaggeration of internal divisions within the discipline:

The typical economist, alas, is harshly if unreflectively dogmatic, demanding that students or colleagues be members in good standing of this or that church. Sales people for university textbooks in the United States complain that an economics professor simply will not look at a text that does not come from the right church: he asks, shamefully, is the book monetarist or neo-classical or Marxist or Keynesian? . . . the extent of real disagreement among economists . . .

is in fact exaggerated ... [this] makes all the more puzzling the venom they bring to minor disputes.

(McCloskey 1985: 184)

What this discloses about the character of textbooks, the extent of disagreements among economists, and their values – professional or other – cannot be further explored here.

Continuing concern about the state of economics as a discipline and a profession has led to recent official investigations sponsored by the Royal Economic Society and the American Economic Association – inspired in the latter instance by a disturbing study of graduate training in élite departments (Colander and Klamer 1987; Klamer and Colander 1989). The British study is complete, and can be considered more briefly because the major findings appeared in the March 1990 issue of *The Economic Journal*. It is broader in scope than its American counterpart for it focuses on the stock, supply, demand and patterns of employment of British economists, as well as some characteristics of economics departments in British universities and polytechnics (Dolton and Makepeace 1990; Towse and Blaug 1990). To a historian, the surprising thing is that no previous study of this kind has been undertaken (but cf. Booth and Coats 1978), whereas studies of the market for economists, their salaries and employment opportunities have quite frequently appeared in the USA, usually in reports initiated by or papers presented to the American Economic Association at the annual meetings. American labour economists have often taken an interest in these matters.

Among the findings of the Towse–Blaug study, the most striking are the limited size of the total flow demand for economists and the prediction that it will decline in the foreseeable future. Despite the loss of university posts (especially professorships) since the 1981 university cuts there is apparently still an excess supply of professional economists, so that reports of the 'dire straits' of economics departments have been exaggerated. The spectacularly high salaries attached to certain posts in the City of London are untypical, and there has been no mass exodus of academic economists to that centre. Unlike the USA, many non-academic economists in the UK have only an undergraduate degree, often of a non-specialized kind, although the reporters firmly insist that 'there is no warrant whatever for thinking that an undergraduate course in economics is a vocational preparation for a world of work in which the graduate will normally be called upon to use his economic expertise' (Towse and Blaug 1990: 98). On the other hand there are conclusions that would certainly strike a responsive chord across the Atlantic. For example, 'the constant complaint of virtually every employer of professional economists that new recruits lack familiarity with data sources, and have never been taught national income accounting' (Towse and Blaug 1990: 98), and the view widely held both inside and

411

outside higher education that 'economics degrees are too theoretical, too impractical, too unrelated to the possible uses of economics in business and government . . . [and that] teaching is indifferent to the actual pattern of employment of economics graduates' (Towse and Blaug 1990: 99).

Given the scale of the economics profession in the USA, the investigation conducted by the American Economic Association's Commission on Graduate Education in Economics is necessarily much larger than its British counterpart, although its terms of reference are narrower.[17] Of particular interest is the fact that the Commission has surveyed not only the six so-called élite departments but also other tiers of departments covering nine, fifteen, twenty and forty-two additional Ph.D. programmes. No such systematic comparison has ever been undertaken previously.

Despite the loud and persistent chorus of complaints about the state of contemporary American economics, some of which have already been noted, and the general desire for changes in economics Ph.D. programmes expressed by faculty, graduate students and recent Ph.D.s in response to the survey, there was a large consensus in favour of the weights currently attached to various types of knowledge in the curriculum, according to which economic theory is given priority followed by econometrics, empirical economics, applications, institutions, history and literature. With respect to skills, it was generally acknowledged that the following were currently emphasized in Ph.D. programmes, in descending order of importance: analytics, mathematics, critical judgement, applications, computation, creativity and communications. However, there was much less agreement that this was the way things should be. In agreement with many of the profession's public critics, it was felt that mathematics and computation were overrated and creativity was undervalued, and when recent Ph.D.s were asked about the importance of various skills in their current jobs, whether in graduate economics programmes, business or government, they again ranked mathematics lower and communications skills and creativity higher than the weights assigned to them in current graduate teaching. Thus, as is probably the case in the UK, 'both faculty members and graduate students' sense that 'the mix of needed skills differs from the skills being developed in graduate training' (Hansen 1990). Departments offering Ph.D. programmes tend to continue to appoint new recruits with much the same skills as already emphasized, rather than those more highly valued by prospective employers, but whether this is evidence of professional inertia or *faute de mieux* (the absence of suitable alternatives) is unclear. As Robert Solow argued in his comments, the results display more satisfaction with what is taught and the teachers' ability to teach it than what should be taught in a better, if not an ideal, world: 'If I knew how to teach creativity and critical judgment, I guess I would do it. I know how to recognize them [i.e. like pornography?], and can even offer examples, but

412

that is very far from being able to teach them' (Hansen 1990: 448–50). On the whole, he felt, the survey results were 'predictably bland'.

Of course, by any standards the Commission's members constitute part of the profession's élite, so that radical proposals for change are hardly to be expected, especially given the strong practical sense that such ideas are hardly likely to be implemented. It is much too early to predict the outcome of this investigation, other than the Commission's recommendations, which will no doubt be vigorously discussed with a wide variety of reactions. The supplementary studies to appear later will undoubtedly add substantially to the accumulating, although uneven, body of data on the economics profession in the USA. And, in line with the opening paragraph of this study, we may conclude with the hope that other organizations and scholars will be encouraged to undertake serious research on the history, current condition and future prospects of the profession.

NOTES

1 In their classic volume Carr Saunders and Wilson (1933: 2) observe that: 'An adequate study of the rise of one of the great professions with its roots deep in the past would be the work of a lifetime.'

2 Furner (1975) provides a valuable analysis of this issue in which the economists figure prominently. Unfortunately there is no comparable study for a more recent period, or for the UK.

3 Professional ideology can, of course, be defined narrowly, as in Joseph Schumpeter's pertinent distinction between the ideology of the mathematical mind and that of the mind allergic to mathematics (Schumpeter 1949: 351). This particular ideological divide is nowadays much more significant in economics than it was forty years ago, for mathematical competence is now virtually a precondition of entry into the economics profession and an indispensable weapon in the early stages of a career. This is serious, notwithstanding jocular references to the 'spiralling "arms race" ' in econometrics and the intergenerational 'balance of terror' between established incumbents and their technically sophisticated young colleagues (Wiles 1984: 292). From a huge relevant literature the following citations must suffice: Bauer and Walters (1975) and Woo (1986). There are valuable remarks on the professionalization–mathematization link in other disciplines in Whitley (1977, 1984).

4 Many such listings have been proposed. One multivariate analysis identified six elements and twenty-one sub-elements (Jenkins 1970: 59).

5 Some analysts regard the service or fiduciary ideal as a middle-class rationale reflecting the professionals' self-deception, rather than any deliberate effort to deceive the lay public. Much of the literature vacillates between viewing professions as a broad educational and cultural stratum or as a distinctive species of occupational organization. Historically, the former is more applicable to the continental European so-called 'public' professions and the latter to the Anglo-American 'free' professions, although with the development of bureaucracy and the welfare state the distinction between them has become blurred.

6 The literature on professions and professionalism is vast, conflicting and sometimes even sensational. In a fascinating survey, a leading expert in the field, Walter Metzger, has coined the term 'professionism' to cover 'all systematic

attempts to attribute historical trends – especially undesirable ones – to the rise of the professions or to the foibles of professionals' (Metzger 1987: 13). No doubt the economists too have suffered from the general decline of deference towards expertise.

7 There may indeed be some consolation in the Victorian dictum that a gentleman needs no code of ethics, whereas no such code will make a gentleman out of a crook!

8 Rhoads (1985) gives a perceptive political scientist's conception of the strength and limitations of the professional economist's intellectual apparatus.

9 Commenting on the irrational elements in policy-making, a very experienced British ex-government economist remarked that 'the atmosphere of a large Government department is frequently almost indistinguishable from that of the loony bin. I use the term in no pejorative sense; it is simply one of the facts of official life' (Cairncross 1970). For fascinating and illuminating stories of American economists' experiences in government service see Allen (1977). See also Coats (1987).

10 According to one scholarly historian of economics the Sophists were the first 'professional instructors' in the subject (Gordon 1975: 2, 15).

11 Broadly speaking professional organization preceded doctrinal consolidation in American economics, whereas the opposite was true in the UK.

12 The editor of *The Times*, which supported Chamberlain's proposals, poked fun at 'the spectacle of these fourteen dervishes emerging from their caves and chanting their venerable incantations against the rising tide of inquiry . . . the day has gone by when the professors of political economy can impose opinions upon the country by the weight of authority. . . . A more scientific conception of their own science, which pretends to be, but never is, an experimental science, would save the professors from the painful discovery that they convince nobody who stands in need of conviction' (*The Times*, 18 August 1903, cited by Coats 1964: 101). Coats (1968a) gives a more extended account.

13 There is a perceptive, and at times amusing, analysis of the Americanness of American economics in a neglected article by Johnson (1977b).

14 The critics include J. K. Galbraith, N. Georgescu-Roegen, H. G. Johnson, T. Koopmans and W. Leontief in the USA, and P. Bauer, P. Deane, F. Hahn, T. W. Hutchison, E. H. Phelps Brown, G. D. Worswick and A. A. Walters in the UK. For examples of the sociologically oriented critical literature see Leontief (1971, 1982), Ward (1972), Leijonhufvud (1973), Johnson (1977a, b), Stanfield (1979), Katouzian (1980), Canterbery and Burkhardt (1983), Earl (1983, 1988), Wiles (1984), Coats (1985), Burkhardt and Canterbery (1986) and Tarascio (1986).

15 From a large output the following items must suffice: Bronfenbrenner (1966), Siegfried (1972), Lovell (1973), Eagly (1974), Stigler (1982a, b) and Liebowitz and Palmer (1984).

16 According to Whitley the key variables in any scientific field are the degrees of functional and strategic mutual dependence among scientists and the degrees of technical and strategic task uncertainty.

17 I am most grateful to my colleague, Anne Krueger, the Commission's Chairman, and Lee Hansen, its Executive Director, for making available the main and supplementary reports prior to publication, and also the additional comments by Commission members Alan S. Blinder, Claudia Goldin and T. Paul Schultz, and by Robert Solow. The final report and some supplementary reports have now been published in the *Journal of Economic Literature*.

REFERENCES

Allen, W. R. (1977) 'Economics and Economic Policy: Modern American Experiences', *History of Political Economy* 9: 48–88.

Bauer, P. T. and Walters, A. (1975) 'The State of Economics', *Journal of Law and Economics* 8: 1–23.

Bell, D. and Kristol, I. (eds) (1981) *The Crisis in Economic Theory*, New York: Basic Books.

Blatt, J. (1983) 'How Economists Misuse Mathematics', in A. S. Eichner (ed.) *Why Economics is Not Yet a Science*, Armonk, NY: M. E. Sharpe. pp. 166–86.

Booth, A. and Coats, A. W. (1978) 'The Market for Economists in Britain, 1945–75: A Preliminary Survey', *Economic Journal* 88: 436–54. Reprinted in this volume, pp. 474–95.

Bronfenbrenner, M. (1966) 'Trends, Cycles, and Fads in Economic Writing', *American Economic Review* 56: 538–52.

Burkhardt, J. and Canterbery, E. R. (1986) 'The Orthodoxy and Legitimacy: Toward a Critical Sociology of Economics', in W. J. Samuels (ed.) *Research in the History and Methodology of Economics* 4: 229–50.

Cairncross, A. K. (1970) 'Writing the History of Recent Economic Policy', unpublished, quoted by permission.

Canterbery, E. R. and Burkhardt, J. (1983) 'What do We Mean by Asking Whether Economics is a Science?', in A. S. Eichner (ed.) *Why Economics is Not Yet a Science*, Armonk, NY: M. E. Sharpe. pp. 15–40.

Carr Saunders, A. M. and Wilson, P. A. (1933) *The Professions*, Oxford: Clarendon Press.

Coats, A. W. (1960) 'The First Two Decades of the American Economic Association', *American Economic Review* 50: 555–74. Reprinted in this volume, pp. 205–24.

—— (1964) 'The Role of Authority in the Development of British Economics', *Journal of Law and Economics* 7: 85–106. Reprinted in this volume, pp. 82–104.

—— (1968a) 'Political Economy and the Tariff Reform Campaign of 1903', *Journal of Law and Economics* 11: 181–229. Reprinted in vol. I in this series.

—— (1968b) 'The Origins and Early Development of the Royal Economic Society', *Economic Journal* 78: 349–71. Reprinted in this volume, pp. 313–37.

—— (1976) 'The Development of the Agricultural Economics Profession in England', *Journal of Agricultural Economics* 27: 381–92. Reprinted in this volume, pp. 419–32.

—— (1977) 'The Current Crisis in Economics in Historical Perspective', *Nebraska Journal of Economics and Business* 16: 3–16. Reprinted in vol. I in this series.

—— (1980) 'The Culture and the Economists: Some Reflections on Anglo-American Differences', *History of Political Economy* 10: 298–314. Reprinted in this volume, pp. 134–54.

—— (ed.) (1981) *Economists in Government: An International Comparative Study*, Durham, NC: Duke University Press.

—— (1985) 'The American Economic Association and the Economics Profession', *Journal of Economic Literature* 23: 1697–727. Reprinted in this volume, pp. 433–73.

—— (ed.) (1986) *Economists in International Agencies. An Exploratory Study*, New York: Praeger.

—— (1987) 'Economists in Government: An Historical and Comparative Perspective', *Canberra Bulletin of Public Administration* 53: 45–55. Reprinted in this volume, pp. 606–29.

Colander, D. C. and Klamer, A. (1987) 'The Making of an Economist', *Journal of Economic Perspectives* 1: 95–111.

Dolton, P. J. and Makepeace, G. H. (1990) 'The Earnings of Economics Graduates', *Economic Journal* 100: 237–50.

Eagly, R. V. (1974) 'Contemporary Profile of Conventional Economists', *History of Political Economy* 6: 76–91.

Earl, P. E. (1983) 'A Behavioral Theory of Economists' Behavior', in A. S. Eichner (ed.) *Why Economics is Not Yet a Science*, Armonk, NY: M. E. Sharpe. pp. 90–125.

—— (1988) 'On Being a Psychological Economist and Winning the Games Economists Play', in P. E. Earl (ed.) *Psychological Economics. Development, Tensions, Prospects*, pp. 227–42, Boston, MA: Kluwer.

Furner, M. O. (1975) *Advocacy and Objectivity: A Crisis in the Professionalization of American Social Science 1865–1905*, Lexington, KY: University of Kentucky Press.

Galbraith, J. K. (1973) 'Power and the Useful Economist', *American Economic Review* 63: 1–11.

Goode, W. (1960) 'Encroachment, Charlatanism, and the Emerging Professions: Psychology, Sociology, Medicine', *American Sociological Review* 25: 902–14.

Gordon, B. S. (1975) *Economic Analysis Before Adam Smith. Hesiod to Lessius*, London: Macmillan.

Grubel, H. G. and Boland, L. A. (1986) 'On the Efficient Role of Mathematics in Economics: Some Theory, Facts and Results of an Opinion Survey', *Kyklos* 39: 419–42.

Hansen, W. L. (1990) 'Educating and Training New Economics Ph.D.'s: How Good a Job are We Doing?', Commission on Graduate Education in Economics, Preliminary Report, *American Economic Review, Papers and Proceedings* 80: 431–50.

—— (1991) 'Education and Training of Economics Doctorates: Major Findings of the American Economic Association's Commission on Graduate Education in Economics', *Journal of Economic Literature* 29: 1054–87.

Heller, W. W. (1975) 'What's Right With Economics?', *American Economic Review* 65: 1–26.

Herman, E. S. (1982) 'The Institutionalization of Bias in Economics', *Media, Culture and Society* 4: 275–91.

Hutchison, T. W. (1964) *Positive Economics and 'Policy' Objectives*, London: Allen & Unwin.

—— (1977) *Knowledge and Ignorance in Economics*, Oxford: Basil Blackwell.

Jenkins, H. G. (1970) 'Professional Organizations', in J. A. Jackson (ed.) *Professions and Professionalization*, pp. 53–107, Cambridge: Cambridge University Press.

Johnson, H. G. (1973) 'National Styles in Economic Research: the United States, the United Kingdom, Canada, and Various European Countries', *Daedalus* 102: 65–74. Reprinted in H. G. Johnson, *On Economics and Society*, Chicago, IL: University of Chicago Press, 1975.

—— (1977a) 'Methodologies of Economics', in M. Perlman (ed.) *The Organization and Retrieval of Economic Knowledge*, pp. 496–509, Boulder, CO: Westview Press.

—— (1977b) 'The American Tradition in Economics', *Nebraska Journal of Economics and Business* 16: 17–26.

Johnson, T. J. (1972) *Professions and Power*, London: Macmillan.

Katouzian, H. (1980) *Ideology and Method in Economics*, London: Macmillan.

Klamer, A. and Colander, D. C. (1989) *The Making of an Economist*, Boulder, CO: Westview Press.

Krueger, A. O. et al., (1991) 'Report of the Commission on Graduate Education in Economics', *Journal of Economic Literature*, 29: 1035–53.

Larson, M. S. (1978) *The Rise of Professionalism: A Sociological Analysis*, Berkeley, CA: University of California Press.

Leijonhufvud, A. (1973) 'Life among the Econ', *Western Economic Journal* 11: 327–37.

Leontief, W. (1971) 'Theoretical Assumptions and Non-observed Facts', *American Economic Review* 71: 1–17.

—— (1982) 'Academic Economics', *Science* 217: 104–5. Reprinted in A. S. Eichner, (ed.) *Why Economics is Not Yet a Science*, Armonk, NY: M. E. Sharpe, 1983, pp. vi–xi.

Liebowitz, S. J. and Palmer, J. P. (1984) 'Assessing the Relative Impacts of Economic Journals', *Journal of Economic Literature* 22: 77–88.

Lovell, M. C. (1973) 'The Production of Economic Literature: An Interpretation', *Journal of Economic Literature* 11: 27–55.

McCloskey, D. (1985) *The Rhetoric of Economics*, Madison, WI: University of Wisconsin Press.

McDean, H. C. (1983) 'Professionalism, Policy, and Farm Economists in the Early Bureau of Agricultural Economics', *Agricultural History* 37: 64–82, 83–9.

Maloney, J. (1985) *Marshall, Orthodoxy and the Professionalization of Economics*, Cambridge: Cambridge University Press.

Metzger, W. P. (1987) 'A Spectre is Haunting American Scholars: The Spectre of "Professionism" ', *Educational Researcher* 16: 10–19.

Mill, J. (1824) 'War Expenditure,' *Westminster Review* 2: 45.

Morishima, M. (1984) 'The Good and Bad Uses of Mathematics', in P. Wiles and G. Routh (eds) *Economics in Disarray*, Oxford: Basil Blackwell, pp. 51–77,

Nelson, R. H. (1987) 'The Economics Profession and the Making of Public Policy', *Journal of Economic Literature* 25: 49–91.

O'Brien, D. (1965) 'The Transition in Torrens' Monetary Thought', *Economica (N.S.)* 32: 269–301.

Parsons, T. (1968) 'Professions', in D. Sills (ed.) *The International Encyclopedia of the Social Sciences*, vol. 12, New York: Macmillan, pp. 536–47.

Patinkin, D. (1972) 'Keynesian Monetary Theory and the Cambridge School', *Banca Nationale del Lavoro Quarterly Review* 25: 138–58.

Pechman, J. A. (1989) *The Role of the Economist in Government: An International Perspective*, Washington, DC: Brookings Institution.

Rhoads, S. E. (1985) *The Economist's View of the World. Government, Markets, and Public Policy*, Cambridge: Cambridge University Press.

Schumpeter, J. (1949) 'Science and Ideology', *American Economic Review* 39: 345–59.

Siegfried, J. J. (1972) 'The Publishing of Economic Papers and Its Impact on Graduate Faculty Ratings, 1960–1969', *Journal of Economic Literature* 10: 31–49.

Stanfield, R. J. (1979) 'The Social Structure of the Economics Community', in R. J. Stanfield, *Economic Thought and Social Change*, Carbondale, IL: Southern Illinois University Press.

Stigler, G. J. (1967) 'The Foundations and Economics', in W. Weaver (ed.) *U.S. Philanthropic Foundations, Their History, Structure, Management and Record*, New York: Harper, pp. 276–86.

—— (1984) 'Economics: the Imperial Science?', *Scandinavian Journal of Economics* 86: 301–13.

—— and Friedland, C. (1982a) 'The Pattern of Citation Practices in Economics', in G. J. Stigler (ed.) *The Economist as Preacher and Other Essays*, Chicago, IL: University of Chicago Press, pp. 173–91.

—— and —— (1982b) 'The Citation Practices of Doctorates in Economics', in G. J. Stigler (ed.) *The Economist as Preacher and Other Essays*, pp. 192–222, Chicago, IL: University of Chicago Press.

Tarascio, V. J. (1986) 'The Crisis in Economic Theory: A Sociological Perspective', in W. J. Samuels (ed.) *Research in the History of Economic Thought and Methodology* 4: 283–95.

Torrens, R. (1826) Letter to Wilmot Horton, 7 November.

Towse, R. and Blaug, M. (1988) *The Current State of the British Economics Profession*, London: Royal Economic Society.

—— and —— (1990) 'The Current State of the British Economics Profession', *Economic Journal* 100: 227–36.

Ward, B. (1972) *What's Wrong With Economics?*, London: Macmillan.

—— (1979) *The Ideal Worlds of Economics. Liberal, Radical, and Conservative Economic World Views*, New York: Basic Books.

Whitley, R. (1977) 'Changes in the Social and Intellectual Organization of the Sciences: Professionalization and the Arithmetic Ideal', in E. Mendelsohn, P. Weingart and R. Whitley (eds) *The Social Production of Scientific Knowledge*, Dordrecht: Reidel, pp. 143–69

—— (1984) *The Intellectual and Social Organization of the Sciences*, Oxford: Clarendon Press.

—— (1986) 'The Structure and Context of Economics as a Scientific Field', in W. J. Samuels (ed.) *Research in the History of Economic Thought and Methodology* 4: 179–209.

Wiles, P. (1984) 'Epilogue: The Role of Theory', in P. Wiles and G. Routh (eds) *Economics in Disarray*, pp. 293–325, Oxford: Basil Blackwell.

Woo, H. K. H. (1986) *What's Wrong With Formalization – in Economics? – An Epistemological Critique*, Newark, CA: Victoria Press.

22

THE DEVELOPMENT OF THE AGRICULTURAL ECONOMICS PROFESSION IN ENGLAND

I

If the members of a profession fail to produce their own historians they must take the consequences when outsiders rush into the breach. This, I trust, is sufficient justification for this paper, which is designed to arouse interest in an unduly neglected aspect of the development of agricultural economics. It is a by-product of a larger study of the changing role of economists, statisticians and agricultural economists in Whitehall, especially since 1945,[1] and it is necessarily somewhat biased by my preoccupation with the government sector. However, this background has certain advantages, as well as limitations. Some valuable work has already been done on the history of this Society, the Provincial Agricultural Economics Advisory Service, and the Agricultural Economics Research Institute at Oxford, and I have drawn freely upon these sources without making detailed acknowledgements (Thomas, 1954; Murray, 1960). But the development of the agricultural economics profession within the Civil Service has, I believe, largely been overlooked, even though government has played a larger part in this subject than in the case of any of the other social science disciplines. In the following paragraphs, subject to limitations of space and my knowledge, I shall try to provide a modest corrective to the previous imbalance, while at the same time offering a perspective which I hope will strike you as both unfamiliar and fruitful. There is obviously no single correct standpoint from which to treat a topic of this kind. As with my own subject, economic history, agricultural economics is the uneasy offspring of a liaison between two mature parent disciplines, and it can legitimately be approached from either side. If I appear to slight the agricultural sciences it is simply an unavoidable consequence of my ignorance, and the fact that I have a special interest in the history of economics and the sociology of the professions. However I must add, in self-defence, that an approach from the side of economics, rather than agriculture, is more appropriate now than it would have been in pre-war days.

419

II

The concept of a profession is one of the most elusive in the social scientist's vocabulary, and I am reluctant to confront you with the definitional problems involved. But as it is central to my theme, I must note that any acceptable definition must have both static and dynamic elements: that is, it must combine a list of characteristics or 'traits' which differentiate the professionals from laymen with an account of the process by which this differentiation was achieved and sustained (Elliott, 1972; Johnson, 1972). Any profession has both an internal and an external dimension: its members must be subjectively aware of themselves as professionals, and objectively acknowledged as such by those who use their services, and by the public at large. Recognition must be based on the possession of degrees, diplomas and qualifications which are not readily accessible to laymen, and it may take the form of specialized appointments, high remuneration, delegation of responsibility or authority, or social esteem. Moreover, workers in any reasonably well-defined field share a common culture which is circumscribed by accepted conventions and methodological rules, and it may also contain important elements of 'tacit knowledge' which cannot be obtained from published sources. As a result it is said that 'every profession lives (at least to some extent) in a world of its own. The language spoken by its inhabitants, the landmarks familiar to them, their customs and conventions can only be thoroughly learned by those who reside there' (Carr Saunders and Wilson, 1933).

I have deliberately quoted this passage from a standard study of the professions to show that I know my place – that as an outsider I cannot presume to penetrate fully into the arcane mysteries of your secular order. Nevertheless, it is clear even to an outsider that agricultural economics has been undergoing a recognizable process of professionalization during the past half century or so, and that it conforms broadly to the newer type of profession based on the command of a specialized body of knowledge, intellectual skill or technique acquired by means of a protracted period of training or apprenticeship. Unlike the older type of so-called 'status' professions such as law or medicine, whose practitioners exercise considerable control over membership and occupational conditions, the newer type of profession 'remains closer to the academic conditions of proof... gives less protection to the individual member... [and] concerns itself less with official certificates of competence than the traditional profession'. Its members' organizations are 'learned societies', and their allegiance is primarily to the substantive field, not the guild. Although their functions may be performed largely in a bureaucratic context, 'the science, not the bureaucracy, defines employment standards, and because the work is largely science, not art, it can be evaluated with some precision. Competence can be tested, and thus there is less need for either certification or licensure or guild protection' (Goode, 1960; also Millerson, 1964).

As is well known, the crucial formative phase of British agricultural economics occurred during the inter-war years. This was not, of course, the true beginning of the subject, even in institutional terms, for the first academic department was established at Oxford, in 1913, as the Agricultural Economics Research Institute. Under its Director, C. S. Orwin, it subsequently became the leading research organization in the field, but it necessarily made only a limited impact in wartime. Official research into agricultural economics dates from the Agricultural Costings Committee of 1920 (Whetham, 1972), and three years later the Provincial Agricultural Economics Advisory Service (PAES) was established, and a Committee on Agricultural Economics was created at the instigation of the Ministry of Agriculture, 'to co-ordinate research and advisory work in agricultural economics in England and Wales'. Orwin, who had played an important part in the formation of the PAES, became the first Chairman of the Committee, and in 1924 another major landmark was passed when his former research student, A. W. Ashby, moved to Aberystwyth and became the first holder of a Chair in Agricultural Economics in 1929. There he launched the first honours undergraduate course in the subject, and this marked a significant stage in the provision of adequate training facilities. The Oxford Institute provided no formal instruction, but as Ashby's career indicates, it became a major focus for young research workers, and in time produced a stream of influential recruits to the profession. In 1923 another major academic tradition in agricultural economics was inaugurated at Reading, and in March 1926, largely as the result of Ashby's initiative, the Agricultural Economics Society was formed at Oxford.

Enough has been said to show that the foundations for the self-sustained growth of the agricultural economics profession were laid in the mid-1920s. But one further aspect of the story needs to be recounted in some detail, as it has hitherto been unduly neglected. Once again Ashby figures, though indirectly, as a catalyst. For a short time he had served as a temporary economic adviser to the Ministry of Agriculture, and on his departure in 1924 the decision was taken to appoint R. R. (later Sir Ralph) Enfield as an 'economic student and investigator', thereby converting him from a conventional administrative Principal to an economic specialist.[2] Prior to that time the Ministry's Finance and Economic Department had included an Economics Division responsible for routine administrative work on economic matters, and by 1924 the need for expert economic knowledge and advice on a continuing basis had obviously been recognized. Enfield's qualifications had been demonstrated by the success of his book on the *Agricultural Crisis of 1920–23*, and he became the spearhead of the corps of Ministry officials who have played so significant a role in the development of the profession. In 1929 Enfield was accorded the official title of Economic

Investigator, and four years later an influential panel of experts reported on the need for additional qualified staff to enable him to 'build up a body of organised economic knowledge available for the guidance of the Ministry even on selected subjects which are likely at any moment to become of immediate importance', in addition to his regular day-to-day duties. Moreover, they added, 'if adequate weight is to be attached to economic advice' Enfield must be accorded 'a sufficient status' so that he could 'discuss with Heads of Divisions on an equal footing the economic aspects of any project before it reaches the stage of definite Ministerial decision'. He should be 'available for direct consultation with the Minister' and be required 'to accept responsibility for the advice which he gives of a specialised economic character'. (From the Addendum – signed by A. D. Hall, H. E. Dale, H. L. French and A. W. Street – to an Official Report on The Economic Work of the Ministry of Agriculture and Fisheries, 1933. The full report was also signed by Enfield and the Secretary to the Committee, H. C. Cotsell.)

As it transpired, Enfield's subsequent status was probably less elevated than these terms envisaged, and it has been said that his influence on Ministry affairs was less weighty than that of A. W. Street, head of the Markets division, which had been set up to administer the Agricultural Marketing Acts. Nevertheless, the recommendation that he be provided with 'three qualified assistants' plus a clerical staff was duly implemented, and in 1934, A. Jones, J. H. Kirk and E. F. Nash joined the Ministry, all three of whom have subsequently had distinguished careers in agricultural economics.

It is tempting to dwell on this episode, which constitutes the beginnings of systematic full-time employment of professional economists in the English Civil Service. It occurred first in agriculture because the government adopted a more active and detailed interventionist policy in that sector than elsewhere in the inter-war period. The new posts were created, it was said at the time, 'on the assumption that there will be increasing government intervention and guidance in industry, including agriculture – instead of allowing commercial evolution to take its course'; and, as the recipient of this memorandum confided to his superior: 'Admittedly it is experimental, but I am sure that in the centre of the Economics Division of the Ministry there is a need for a small but well-equipped section of advisers systematically engaged and regularly consulted.' Ten years later very similar terms were employed in the 1944 *White Paper on Employment Policy*, a document which signalized the government's commitment to post-war Keynesian-type macroeconomic policies. It announced the intention 'to establish on a permanent basis a small central staff qualified to measure and analyse economic trends and submit appreciations of them to the Ministries concerned'. This staff, in the Economic Section of the Cabinet Office under the leadership of Professor (now Lord) Robbins, had proved its value in wartime (Robbins, 1971). But the possibility of a peacetime continuation of the experiment had been approached very cautiously, partly because of ideological objections to the concept of an economic planning staff and detailed government interference in the economy. But by this time the special relationship between the Government and Agriculture had become fully accepted, and wartime and post-war developments in this field were directly built upon the foundations established in pre-war days. Interestingly enough, it was not until 1953, when the Economic Section of the Cabinet Office was transferred to the Treasury, that the situation of any other group of economists in Whitehall approximated at all closely to the pioneering role of their counterparts in agriculture; and even then the Economic Section functioned as a somewhat isolated unit within the Treasury, its members often being regarded by administrators as a collection of bright academics on leave from the universities rather than as regular Civil Servants. And it was not until after the Treasury reorganization of 1962 that the Economic Section staff gradually became more fully integrated into the department's day-to-day operations.

During the remainder of the 1930s the position of the professional economists in the Ministry was gradually consolidated, but their presence in a fundamentally non-specialist bureaucracy gave the Treasury's establishments officers considerable difficulties of definition and grading – e.g. whether to classify them as administrative or specialist/technical personnel. Salaries and career prospects were poor, and it proved difficult to retain them permanently; but from the point of view of the agricultural economics profession as a whole this was no disadvantage as it helped to establish close personal relations between ex-government economists in universities or business and their official counterparts. This has been an important factor in the formation of a coherent profession, especially in the post-war years. Enfield's position was gradually enhanced as he became increasingly involved with outside bodies, both at home and abroad, and towards the end of the war he was transferred from the post of Principal Assistant Secretary in charge of the Economics and Statistics Division to become Chief Economic Adviser to the Ministry. However, this was evidently regarded as a personal appointment concerned especially with international matters such as the United Nations Food and Agriculture Organization, and the title lapsed after his retirement in 1952. A few years later the possibility of reviving the post of Chief Economic Adviser was considered, a move which would have been appropriate given the continually increasing range of the agricultural economists' activities, but the proposal was not implemented.

III

When Enfield became Chief Economic Adviser his successor was J. H. Kirk, who was officially described as 'not only an Assistant Secretary but also an economist', terms which again reveal the bureaucratic inhibitions concerning the position of professionals within the hierarchy. In his Presidential address to this Society, in 1964, Professor Kirk described himself somewhat unflatteringly as the 'paymaster and slave-driver' of the PAES (Kirk, 1964–5), and it is this aspect of the relationship between the Ministry's officials and the agricultural economics profession which has hitherto attracted the most attention – for example in Lord Murray's Presidential Address (Murray, 1960).

To most members of the emerging profession the Ministry inevitably appeared both as an indispensable source of finance and employment opportunities and as a threat to their academic status and scientific independence. Here, as elsewhere, patronage did not ensure gratitude, but it is worth noting that the shared suspicion or hostility towards the Ministry may have served to foster a sense of professional solidarity. Certainly in no other branch of economics was there a counterpart to the Committee on Agricultural Economics or its successor, from 1930, the Conference of Advisory Economists, both of which provided regular occasions for personal and operational contacts between Ministry economists and outsiders. Lord Murray has admirably portrayed the difficulties and achievements of this relationship, but in noting that only 16 per cent of the Committee's discussions were devoted to 'professional' matters he unwittingly played down the role of these institutional arrangements in developing the agricultural economists' common interests and professional self-awareness. The co-ordination and consolidation of the advisory work proceeded slowly, partly because there were genuine differences of interest among the parties involved. Naturally enough, Ministry officials were primarily concerned to obtain an adequate and continuing supply of data relevant to their policy functions, whereas the advisory economists were preoccupied with the burden of routine data collection and with the desirability of establishing a satisfactory division of labour between this 'required' work, the provision of advice to farmers, teaching, and the production of independent scientific research in accordance with the recognized standards of the academic community. Cause and effect were inextricably linked here, for while the required work constituted the *raison d'être* for essential government support, as long as it was seen as an oppressive burden it inevitably exacerbated the difficulties of attracting and retaining recruits of high calibre capable of developing the intellectual and scientific potentialities of the subject. No doubt some of the advisory workers were content with their humble, undemanding lot, even though they pretended to aspire to higher things. But the more active and creative spirits resented their position as 'tame economists', or what Americans would call 'a bunch of kept cats'. As Maxton put it, in the paper summarized below, the contrasting motives included 'authority as against independence; routine as against variety; concentration as against dispersion of resources; the collective as against the individual task. Inevitably there was an ebb and flow of emphasis on one or the other. In recent years there has been a very definite movement towards the collective routine policy.' Salaries, conditions of work, and career prospects were poor; there were the conflicting pulls of local and national responsibilities; the commitment to mundane practical tasks of merely short-run interest, the results of which were not seen by workers in the field, served as a check to the production of more analytical or purely scientific research of potentially greater long-run significance; and the conflict between the Ministry's desire for order and control and the academics' desire for independence was personified in the unfortunate clash of personalities between Enfield and Orwin.

As the Ministry's activities expanded during the later 1930s the conditions became ripe for an open confrontation, which might well have occurred but for the war. Many of the tensions involved can be grasped by considering John P. Maxton's remarkably powerful, if somewhat discursive and repetitive paper, 'Professional Stocktaking' (Maxton, 1940). No doubt his views were untypical; he was an unusually perceptive and forceful critic. Moreover, the fact that they were published in wartime, and not delivered at a regular conference as originally intended, must have diminished their immediate impact. Nevertheless, his contribution is a major landmark in the profession's awareness of its problems and prospects.

Agricultural economics, Maxton declared, was still in its childhood. Its condition was basically healthy but uncertain, for while there was a definite demand for its practitioners' services, they were subject to great but undefined expectations. There was a serious danger that they would respond too literally to the demand for the narrow and inhibiting functions for which they were paid. 'We are in danger,' he said, 'of mistaking the fertiliser for the crop.' Echoing familiar recent complaints, he deplored the excessive involvement in accounting procedures and the mistaken belief that practical experience and direct fact-gathering were uniquely valuable as ends in themselves. While by no means denying the value of facts, he insisted that 'amassing facts for the purpose of making piles of them is not the real purpose of agricultural economics'. There had been an excessive investment of resources in patchy and spasmodic 'special' studies; the profession had been dominated by the theory of the 'set enquiry' or the 'planned project'; and there had been a corresponding failure to develop a clear diagnosis of problems and to formulate coherent and systematic analysis to bridge the gap between data and policy. As a remedy for this situation Maxton aimed to provide a philosophical and methodological framework which could serve as 'the basis of a positive background policy for the

425

profession of agricultural economics'. As things stood the profession lacked 'a definite assured existence, although no doubt there is a certain satisfaction in the fact that the authorities provide salaries for agricultural economists as such without being too clear about what they are paying for'. Agricultural economics was not recognized as a distinct speciality. Its practitioners lacked a clear sense of professional identity and purpose, and 'there was an absence of any common distinguishing factor which at once linked [their] distinct jobs together and at the same time clearly differentiated agricultural economics from other professions'. It was essential that they should comprehend the relationship between their own task and that of others, if only to protect the profession from encroachment by cranks and amateurs. The paramount need was to grasp that 'since ours is not a manual craft, it is in the realm of specialised and trained facility of the intellect that the profession has to seek its distinction', and it was essential to organize the profession's resources so as to achieve this end.

IV

Since 1945 there has been substantial progress towards the professionalization of agricultural economics in the manner envisaged by Maxton. During the war there was a healthy growth in the spirit of co-operation among the constituent members, notwithstanding a serious dispute about the status and functions of the Oxford Institute, and the government's sustained interest in the agricultural sector of the economy in the post-war years ensured the continued importance of both the Ministry of Agriculture's corps of professional economists and the Provincial Agricultural Economics Service. While the other agricultural advisory services were absorbed into the government machine the economists remained outside, for theirs was regarded as the most politically sensitive branch, and it was thought that continued association with the universities would guarantee their reputation for impartiality and objectivity, maintain their good relations with the farming community which supplied the essential data, and reduce the Ministry's embarrassments in the event of conflicts over policy decisions. In due course, after protracted negotiations which have been outlined in Lord Murray's Presidential Address, those members of the PAES with the requisite academic qualifications were fully assimilated into the university system, thus reducing one of the significant obstacles to academic recognition and diminishing, though by no means entirely eliminating, the occasions for friction with official authority. By 1950 it was recognized that the PAES had become an integral part of the government's price-determining machinery; but from the university standpoint it was a 'foreign body', a 'cell of Civil Servants' in the academic community, whereas from an official standpoint it was 'an exceptionally intractable body to try to regulate on even quasi-Civil Service lines', partly because the individual universities' attitudes and practices varied considerably. There were, for example, discrepancies between academic and Civil Service salaries which at one stage imperilled the future of the PAES; but in terms of professional status academic legitimation was essential. It is, however, interesting to speculate what the present position of agricultural economics would be if the economic advisory service had been fully absorbed into the Ministry in the early post-war years.

The assimilation of the PAES into the universities during the 1950s did not immediately obliterate the stigma of inferiority resulting from the agricultural economists' reputation as mere data-collectors and their status as 'kept cats' on the periphery of the academic community. No other branch of the social sciences has had such intimate associations with the government, which has not only influenced the character and volume of research and investigation in the field – so that the goal of complete scientific independence has not been attained – but has also directly affected the creation and filling of academic appointments. It is surely significant that in an era of unparalleled university expansion agricultural economics has fared less well than other social sciences, such as economics and economic history, possibly because the universities have been reluctant to allocate funds to a field which they hope will be financed by direct government grants. Moreover, the growth of agricultural economics in terms of appointments, departments, and courses has not been irreversible. At my own University of Nottingham, for example, a Chair was created in 1960 but not re-filled ten years later, when the well-established department was divided between the School of Agriculture and the Department of Economics. A more unusual case was that of Leeds, where a Chair of Agricultural Economics was authorized in 1968, but never filled, and the decision to create an independent department, also in 1968, was implemented and then reversed five years later. The causes of this unspectacular and intermittent progress of agricultural economics would repay investigation. But it must not be thought that the relationship with the government was always disadvantageous. Quite apart from the fact that official support has been indispensable during the first half century, it has been said that a skilful operator in the advisory service could get the best of both worlds, by playing the university and the Ministry against each other!

Learned societies have usually made significant contributions to the professionalization of the social sciences, but their size, composition, and range of activities have varied considerably from one discipline to another. Some merely concentrate on the publication of scholarly papers and the provision of facilities for conferences and discussions, while others become deeply involved in the organization and management of research projects, the provision of studentships and fellowships, and even propaganda designed to enhance their members' standing with the public and with official bodies. The Agricultural Economics Society has, on the whole,

427

adopted a less active policy than might have been expected given the members' collective interests and concerns. Leading members were certainly active in defence of the Oxford Institute in 1944, but the Conference of Advisory Economists took the lead in dealing with the government both in narrowly technical matters and on broader questions of a professional character. Membership of the Society has always been mixed, as might be expected in an applied discipline, though probably not more so than in the case of the Royal Economic Society, which has always been dominated by academic personnel even though these have constituted only a small proportion of the membership (Coats and Coats, 1973). By contrast, the Presidents of this Society have included a significant number of non-academics and Civil Servants, somewhat akin to the Royal Statistical Society, a body which has frequently petitioned the government on matters affecting the provision of statistical data or the professional interests of its constituents. In his Presidential sketch of this organization's history, in 1953, Edgar Thomas declared that 'it cannot be overemphasised that our Society is not a Society of *professional* agricultural economists, and it is to be hoped that it will never be allowed to become one', a sentiment that doubtless reflected the profession's long-standing association with the farming community. The Society had, he added, a dual role, 'as a *non-professional society* to provide a common meeting ground for the intelligent layman and the professional economist interested in the factual, economic and social problems of agriculture and rural life; [and] as a *scientific society* to strengthen the scientific basis of the approach of its members to the study of these problems'. Yet he appeared to define the profession somewhat narrowly, as confined to members of the PAES, Other Research Workers in Agricultural Economics, and Lecturers in the subject – who then constituted some 40 per cent of the membership. But the percentage of professionals would have been significantly higher had he also included the *bona fide* agricultural economists among the Officers of Government Departments, Co-operative Organizations, Business and International Organizations also listed as members.

V

Looking at recent issues of the Society's journal one wonders whether Professor Thomas still considers that its pages are 'refreshingly free from the self-conscious technical virtuosity and the contrived terminological *éclat* which mar so much specialist literature in the social sciences' (Thomas, 1954). During the past two or three decades agricultural economics has become increasingly technical and specialized and has moved some distance from its earlier 'muddy boots' association with farm management towards 'black coated' academic economics. If its university growth has perhaps been somewhat chequered, its record in government has been one of solid achievement.[3]

For a number of years the Ministry of Agriculture economists' major task was – to use Maxton's terms – the 'sifting, weighing and analysis of evidence' for the Annual Price Review, which has been a central feature of the government's policy since the Agriculture Act of 1947.[4] This review guaranteed the economists' indispensability to government, but may also have limited their opportunities within the bureaucratic hierarchy, for by Civil Service standards it was a lower level activity than the advisory work undertaken by members of the Economic Section of the Cabinet Office (later the Treasury). Soon after the war, with the concurrence of senior departmental officials, the MAF's agricultural economists were defined as a Departmental Class of Civil Servants with their pay linked to that of the Scientific Officer Class, and were consequently eligible for membership of the Institution of Professional Civil Servants, whereas the Economic Section's members, like the statisticians, were accorded parity with the more prestigious Administrative Class, and were consequently admitted into the First Division Association. Ironically enough, given the pre-war aspirations mentioned earlier, being 'scientific' and 'professional' carried less weight in Whitehall than being a generalist administrator! Doubtless some senior officials regarded the agricultural economists as inferior in quality to the 'economist-administrators' of the Economic Section, and this impression may have been reinforced by their involvement in the Annual Review, a task which recalled the pre-war days of routine data collection. Yet oddly enough, the agricultural economists worked very closely with statisticians who enjoyed Administrative Class status, and this sometimes produced anomalies disconcerting to the bureaucratic mind.

Early in 1965, at a time when the number of Whitehall economists was increasing rapidly, the Government Economic Service was created, but the agricultural economists were refused admission even though by this time their case was strongly supported by senior officials in their Ministry. The main reason given for their exclusion was that they were by qualifications and experience narrow specialists, and therefore unsuited for the wider ranging work of the GES, which called for personnel who were basically general economists. This may have been true of some, but by no means all, for the range of their activities had greatly expanded since the late 1950s – for example in the international field, where the demand for their services accelerated markedly with the prospect of entry into the EEC. Moreover, by the mid-1960s the general character of government economists' employment was changing in a manner that significantly diminished the differences between the functions of agricultural and other economists. From the early 1960s the renewed interest in economic planning both at the national and at the local levels generated a demand for microeconomists whose work called for a more detailed empirical knowledge of particular sectors and aspects of the economy and closer integration into day-to-day departmental activities than had been required in the Economic Section.

Also the sheer growth in the number of economists and statisticians in government led to a more complex division of their labour and an enhanced need for specialists, such as transport, industrial, or development economists. Consequently the earlier dividing line between general and specialist economists became blurred, a process accentuated by the arrival of a younger generation of agricultural economists with a more theoretical and quantitative training in economics. Hence, during recent years, there has been a growing official recognition of the desirability of a closer integration between the functions of the agricultural economists and economists in other departments, and an appreciation of the advantages to be derived from an interchange and more flexible deployment of the various species. After a 1971 arbitration award for Civil Service scientists the pay of the principal agricultural economist grade fell behind that of the economic adviser, but towards the end of 1974 a systematic comparison of posts held by agricultural and other economists demonstrated that there was sufficient comparability between the two hierarchies as regards work content and responsibility to justify a merger. Accordingly, the pay scales were aligned with effect from 1st January, 1975, and the agricultural economists were regraded into the economist group on 1st September, 1975.

VI

Members of the audience may be forgiven, especially on this commemorative occasion, if they view this happy ending as part of a moral tale of Virtue Rewarded. Yet may it not suggest that in the future agricultural economists may suffer some loss of collective professional identity as their discipline increases its ties with general economics? In this connection I may perhaps be pardoned if I disclose that while one distinguished ex-government economist advised me to exclude the agricultural economists from my research on the grounds that they were a quite separate breed, a leading member of your Society expressed surprise that I considered it necessary to draw any distinction whatever between the two, since both were, after all, 'economists'.

During the last half century the status of agricultural economics has suffered partly because it has been an applied discipline, whereas the highest prestige in the intellectual pecking order is generally accorded to theoretical subjects. However, comparisons between agricultural economics and general economics seem a good deal less invidious now than a few years ago, for theoretical economics is currently in a state of depression, some competent observers believing that there is a serious 'cognitive crisis' in the discipline.[5] The reasons for this sorry state of affairs are too varied and complex to be considered here, for they include methodological, doctrinal, and policy issues. One important focus of criticism has been the proliferation of those elaborate and sophisticated mathematical and econometric models which have little or no relation to reality, and which are dismissed as useless or positively misleading by the growing army of economists outside academic employment, and by some academics too. Nor is this merely a reiteration of the traditional crude backwoods empiricists' repudiation of 'theory', for the critics have included outstanding theorists as well as more practical-minded individuals. Generally speaking this reappraisal has been healthy, even though it may cause a temporary decline of morale in the economics profession as a whole. Yet it also reflects a major shift of emphasis in the discipline, as economics in government, business, and other non-academic organizations absorbs a higher proportion of the profession's talent than ever before. Economists employed outside universities are no longer confined to the lower level types of computation, analysis, and interpretation of empirical data; they are also making significant conceptual innovations directly relevant to the practical problems they encounter, and in so doing they are helping to narrow the traditional gap between 'pure' and 'applied' economics, to the benefit of both sides.

In these circumstances agricultural economists have less reason to be on the defensive than hitherto. They can look forward to the future with confidence, taking comfort from the words of a Nobel Laureate in Economics, Wassily Leontief of Harvard who, in his Presidential Address to the American Economic Association, described the development of agricultural economics in the USA as 'An exceptional example of a healthy balance between theoretical and empirical analysis and of the readiness of professional economists to co-operate with experts in the neighbouring disciplines' (Leontief, 1971). Whether the same can be said of agricultural economics in Britain I must leave you to judge. But it has obviously come a long way since the foundation of this Society.

POSTSCRIPT

Several valuable comments and criticisms were offered by members of the audience at Newcastle. It was noted that while the title should have included Wales, Scottish developments had been ignored, and would repay further study. Mr Wynne, of Leeds, maintained that agricultural economics had been taught there in the first decade of this century and that A. G. Ruston had held the first full-time lectureship in the subject from 1919. Additional information about early developments in teaching will be welcome. Several speakers emphasized the exceptionally close collaboration between agricultural economists and administrators in MAF, based on their shared empiricial knowledge, and argued that other government economists could not match the agricultural economists' command of their subject matter. Treasury economists, for example, did not need to know one end of a cow from the other!

The constructive collaboration between Ministry officials and the advisory economists was acknowledged and the relationship was not regarded as unduly inhibiting. Professor Kirk wondered whether the growth of numbers and specialization, and the trend towards economics, were undermining the profession's collective identity. However, no one thought the Society could or should have been used as a means of promoting professional interests. In any case, Professor Thomas, as the ruling spirit, would not have allowed them to convert their learned organization into a trade union.

NOTES

1 This research has been financed by a grant from the Social Science Research Council. I am greatly indebted to the many government officials who have traced documents and given me the benefit of their advice and experience. I have also had a number of valuable interviews with senior agricultural economists in Whitehall and in the universities.
2 The remainder of this section is based largely on official files.
3 This is but part of a more complex story which cannot be fully recounted here.
4 For a more comprehensive account of their activities see Kirk (1964–5) and Napolitan (1975).
5 For a review of the main issues and defensive replies by two leading ex-government economists see Leontief (1971), MacDougall (1974), and Heller (1975).

REFERENCES

Carr Saunders, A. N. and Wilson, P. A. (1933). *The Professions* Oxford: Clarendon Press.
Coats, A. W. and Coats, S. E. (1973). The Changing Social Composition of the Royal Economic Society 1890–1960 and the Professionalization of British Economics, *Br. J. Sociol.* **24**, 165–87. Reprinted in this volume, pp. 338–60.
Elliott, P. (1972). *Sociology of the Professions*. London.
Goode, W. T. (1960). Encroachment, Charlatanism and the Emerging Profession: Psychology, Sociology, Medicine, *Am. Sociol. Rev.* **25**, 902–14.
Heller, W. W. (1975). What's Right with Economics?, *Am. Econ. Rev.* **65**, 1–16.
Kirk, J. H. (1964–5). The Economic Activities of the Ministry of Agriculture, Fisheries and Food, *J. Agric. Econ.* **16**, 164–84.
Leontief, W. (1971). Theoretical Assumptions and Nonobserved Facts, *Am. Econ. Rev.* **61**, 1–7.
MacDougall, D. (1974). In Praise of Economics, *Econ. J.* **84**, 773–86.
Maxton, J. P. (1940). Professional Stock-Taking, *J. Agric. Econ.* **6**, 142–80.
Millerson, G. (1964). *The Qualifying Association. A Study in Professionalization*. London: Routledge & Kegan Paul.
Murray, Sir K. A. H. (1960). Agricultural Economics in Retrospect, *J. Agric. Econ.* **13**, 374–92.
Napolitan, L. (1975). The Statistical Activities of the Ministry of Agriculture, Fisheries and Food, *J. Agric. Econ.* **26**, 1–17.
Robbins, Lord (1971). *Autobiography of an Economist*. London: Macmillan Ltd.
Thomas, E. (1954). On the History of the Society, *J. Agric. Econ.* **10**, 278–92.
Whetham, E. H. (1972). The Search for the Cost of Production, 1914–30, *J. Agric. Econ.* **23**, 201–11.

23

THE AMERICAN ECONOMIC ASSOCIATION AND THE ECONOMICS PROFESSION*

The centenary of the American Economic Association (AEA) in September 1985 is an appropriate occasion for a brief review of some aspects of the professionalization of economics in the USA, as revealed in the organization's voluminous archives and numerous publications.

In a mood of centennial euphoria there is admittedly some danger of exaggerating the importance of this event, for some of its critics would argue that the AEA has consistently demonstrated a singular reluctance to assume a role of active leadership on the economics profession's behalf. But whatever the merits of this contention – a matter on which the following pages will shed some light – the now traditional policy of concentrating on the promotion of scholarly and scientific activities while studiously avoiding partisanship on policy issues was hammered out painfully during the first decade of its existence. Like the Association itself, this policy reflected the attitudes and aims of its leading members and their response to the intellectual and social conditions of the time.

In order to avoid misunderstanding, it is necessary to emphasize the limited scope of this essay. Despite its chronological sweep it is neither a potted history of the AEA nor a comprehensive survey of the organization's services to its members and its relationships to the economics profession as a whole and the general public. It is primarily focused on certain problems arising in the professionalization process.

Part I reviews some general features of the professionalization of the social sciences in the USA and the background circumstances and influences affecting the AEA's birth and early development. Parts II to IV consider some of the principal professional issues dealt with by its officers and executive committee, especially during and since World War II, for in that period the Association's scale, resources, and activities expanded considerably, and matters of professional interest and concern became increasingly pressing. Part V contains some concluding (and apparently provocative) reflections on past experience, with special reference to the 'proper' scope and functions of a social science association.

433

I

The emergence of the economics profession in the USA cannot be dated precisely. As applied to the social sciences the concept of a profession is both fuzzy and controversial, for unlike the traditional or 'status' professions such as law and medicine, the social scientists have lacked clear legal recognition, strict controls over entry, a formal code of ethics, and effective means of disciplining their errant members.[1] In the late-nineteenth-century USA even the traditional professions lacked the status and powers enjoyed by their European counterparts, and as the economists' ingrained distaste for monopoly has led them to question the merits of professionalism more consistently than other social scientists,[2] it is hardly surprising that the professionalization of their discipline has been a slow and at times uncertain process.

For the present purpose it is convenient to distinguish between the internal and the external dimensions of the economics profession. From an intraprofessional standpoint the essential prerequisite is the existence of a group of individuals subjectively aware of themselves as professionals, with shared knowledge, interests, skills, and standards of conduct and perform- ance – although these standards may be neither explicit nor precisely defined. The extraprofessional requirement is public recognition of their command of specialized knowledge, usually in the form of academic degrees or qualifications not readily accessible to the layperson. This recognition leads to especially designated appointments, differential and higher re- muneration derived from the inelasticity of supply, delegation of responsi- bility or authority, and a measure of social esteem.

A profession is not a static phenomenon. The professionalization of the social sciences has involved

> a three-part process by which a community of inquirers is established, distinguishes itself from other groups and from the society at large, and enhances communication among its members, organizing and disciplining them, and heightening their credibility in the eyes of the public. Any act which contributes to these functions, which streng- thens the intellectual solidarity of this very special kind of community, is a step towards professionalization.
>
> [Haskell 1977, p. 19]

Although the AEA was but one among some two hundred new learned societies established in the USA during the 1870s and 1880s, its formation was a landmark in the development of economics for it manifested the collective self-consciousness of a small but ambitious, energetic, and soon to be influential band of aspiring scholars, who were supported by a miscellaneous group of university presidents, reform clergymen, and other public-spirited individuals (Dorfman 1949; Coats 1960). As with other modern science-based occupations, the emergence of an economics profession in the USA was crucially dependent on the available knowledge-producing institutions, and were the term not so barbarous it would be more fitting to speak of the *academicization* of nineteenth-century economics rather than its professionalization.[3]

The Young Turks who founded the AEA were the opportunistic beneficiaries of a remarkable late-nineteenth-century transformation of American higher education which, in its scale and speed of change, far outstripped contemporary developments abroad. From the 1870s there was a significant increase in the number of genuine American universities – some brand new, others modified versions of older foundations, as well as a rapid expansion in the number of students, professorships, specialized courses for graduates, Ph.D. degrees,[4] and other indispensable concomitants of twentieth-century academic life such as library and laboratory resources, and opportunities for research, publication, and attendance at academic gatherings. There were also a number of other changes: a noticeable shift in the academic reward system away from elementary teaching toward advanced training and research; a significant enhancement of academic salaries owing to the highly competitive educational environment; and a striking increase in the scale, organization, and bureaucratization of university life. Not all those involved welcomed these changes. And given the growing resemblances between the larger academic institutions and business corporations, both of which reflected the general 'trend towards nationally oriented, impersonal, hierarchical organizations' (Oleson and Voss 1979, p. xix), it is no wonder that the most penetrating contemporary critic of American society depicted the new breed of college and university presidents as 'captains of erudition' (Veblen 1918, p. 73).

No group of academic disciplines was more profoundly affected by the educational revolution than the social sciences, for they can hardly be said to have existed in the 1860s (Ross 1979). Within that group economics undoubtedly occupied the strategic position, not simply because its intellectual structure was stronger and more fully developed on the basis of the classical tradition from Adam Smith through to John Stuart Mill, but also because its subject matter was so integral to the processes of industrialization, urbanization, and modernization that were currently advancing apace. As society became more complex and the social division of labour more minute and interdependent there was a growing demand for experts and specialists of all kinds, and it has been aptly remarked that 'an industrializing society is a professionalizing society' (Goode 1960). The changes in American higher education in the late nineteenth century have been acutely summarized as involving a simultaneous broadening of the base and a narrowing at the top, both of which directly benefited the economists. At the lower level, the disintegration of the traditional liberal arts curriculum (consisting primarily of classical languages, literature, mathematics, and moral philosophy) was hastened by the introduction of the elective system, which enabled students to express their effective demand for more 'modern' subjects, including political economy. At the upper level there was a discernible shift of emphasis toward more advanced instruction, specialization, and research, largely following German precedents, but adapting German practices to suit American cultural interests and democratic prejudices.[5]

The effect of these changes on the career prospects for economic specialists was dramatic (Parrish 1967). At this distance in time it is difficult to appreciate how primitive the academic situation was in the early post-Civil-War years. Political economy was usually taught from rudimentary textbooks by clergymen as a minor adjunct to the standard college course in moral philosophy; but at least it existed, whereas the other social sciences had no place whatever in the curriculum. There were practically no openings for full-time professors of political economy, as it was then called, and no clear demarcation existed between amateurs and professionals or between popularization and scientific or scholarly work. Any economics writer who ventured an opinion on current economic affairs was liable to be branded – usually not without justification – as a partisan spokesman for free trade, protection, or some other popular nostrum. By the end of the century, however, the pattern of future development was already clear.

> In the 1870s only three institutions awarded a total of three Ph.D.'s in political economy. In the 1880s, five institutions awarded a total of eleven. In the 1890s, twelve institutions awarded 95 degrees. . . . [Moreover] dissertations became longer, more sophisticated and more specialized, i.e., they were no longer the mark of a cultured gentleman but the demonstration of professional skill.
>
> [Parrish 1967, p. 11]

Whereas in 1880 only three men in the 28 leading schools 'devoted most of their time to political economy', by 1890 there were 20 chairs in the subject, and 51 by 1900. 'If nothing else, the "pioneer" economists had created full employment for themselves' (ibid.) and the comparative advantages of the trek to Europe for advanced study in the field had diminished markedly.

The AEA was directly modelled on its immediate predecessor, the American Historical Association (AHA) founded in 1884, and both organizations were by-products of the vigorous academic entrepreneurship of Daniel Coit Gilman, president of Johns Hopkins, the university then at the forefront of the American academic procession (Hawkins 1960). Gilman was one of the brilliant band of captains of erudition who set out to raise the standards and extend the influence of American scholarship. The founding of national learned and scientific societies was one of the means to achieve this end, and it is no coincidence that two of his more ambitious and energetic young professors, Herbert Baxter Adams and Richard T. Ely, became, respectively, the first secretaries and principal promoters of the AHA and AEA. Although the two associations had many features in common, there were revealing differences. Unlike the AHA, the AEA was a direct offshoot of an earlier, more comprehensive body, the American Social Science Association (ASSA), which had been founded in 1865 by a group of public-spirited citizens who were concerned about the growing social and economic problems of the northeastern cities (Haskell 1977; Bernard and Bernard 1943). Whereas there had been no explicitly historical component in the ASSA, there had been an economic section – variously known as Economy, Trade and Finance, or Social Economy, and several of its active members were among the AEA's founders.

The establishment of an independent association of economists represented the writing on the wall for the parent-body, which could not compete either in intellectual quality or support with the new generation of academic specialists. Though as yet small in numbers and limited in influence, these founding fathers of the modern social sciences in the USA constituted the wave of the future. They were better educated, and more single-mindedly dedicated to science and to reformist public service than their amateur generalist predecessors. After their defection the ASSA slowly disintegrated and sank into oblivion in 1912, not long after the founding of the American Political Science Association (APSA) in 1903 and the American Sociological Society (ASS) two years later, both of which were offspring of the AEA.

Throughout this period the AEA and AHA periodically held joint annual meetings, and the range of topics discussed often reflected the fact that many academic economists still taught subjects that would nowadays be regarded as outside their proper domain. Indeed, many social scientists had joint titles – it was said that they occupied settees rather than chairs – and it was by no means uncommon for a professor to switch from one discipline to another.[6] Nevertheless, the trend toward subdivision and concentration of intellectual activities was irresistible. As a Johns Hopkins graduate remarked as early as 1882, 'vive la spécialisation. Go to, let us centrifugate' (Higham 1979, p. 7).

The social composition and management of the AEA differed markedly from that of its sister organization, the AHA, which was dominated by an older cadre of patrician leisured amateurs until the early years of this century. Like their economist counterparts, the AHA's founder members (several of whom also joined the AEA) decided to be independent of the ASSA despite overtures from that body. But although there were already 15 full-time professors of history, 5 full-time assistant professors, and about 30 graduate students in the mid-1880s it was not until 1907 that a 'purely and exclusively' professional historian was elected president of the AHA.[7] Two other features of this formative period reveal instructive differences between the AHA and the AEA. In 1889 the AHA obtained a federal charter from Congress and therewith the government provided free office space and paid the expenses of printing the AHA's annual reports, which not surprisingly soon became substantial. However, Adams' efforts to secure congressional support for an historical manuscripts commission and unified management of the national archives proved unsuccessful. Secondly, there was a partial split in the historians' ranks in 1895 owing to dissatisfaction with the practice of repeatedly holding annual meetings in Washington, DC,[8] when a group of Ivy League professors launched the *American Historical Review* independently of the AHA in a determined effort to establish and maintain professional scholarly standards. The reasons for this breach between the old style intellectuals and the academic historians – which was not finally repaired until 1915, when the AHA took full control of the *Review* – are too complex to be examined here. Nevertheless, the historians' experiences provide an instructive contrast with the development of the economists' collective solidarity under academic leadership[9] and their subsequent reluctance to base either their administrative or their editorial functions in the nation's capital. Proposals to establish a Washington headquarters were under consideration almost continuously from the late 1920s until World War II,[10] and have recurred periodically since that time. But the desire to limit the AEA's functions, avoid creating a cumbersome bureaucracy like those of other national scholarly organizations, and, above all, to keep clear of political entanglements, has prevented such schemes from coming to fruition.

The origin of the AEA's central and consistently maintained tradition of nonpartisanship and avoidance of official commitments on practical economic questions and political issues is directly traceable to its foundation and early development. The professionalization of the social sciences has seldom been either painless or rapid, and during the Association's first three decades a peculiar combination of internal and external circumstances exacerbated the difficulties of achieving a reasonable consensus among American economists with respect to their communal aims, procedures, and standards of professional conduct. This early phase admirably illustrates the intimate connections between methodology, doctrine, policy, and professionalism in economics, connections still largely underestimated by practising economists and by the discipline's historians.

The core group of AEA founder members – Henry Carter Adams, John Bates Clark, Ely, Edmund Janes James, Simon Nelson Patten, and Edwin R. A. Seligman – are usually viewed as a 'new' school of economists trained in Germany, imbued with ideas and methods derived from the German Historical School, and determined both to overthrow the entrenched 'Clerical Ricardian' orthodoxy, which had hitherto dominated college textbooks, and to challenge the laissez-faire policy views propagated by journalists like Edwin L. Godkin and Horace C. White, and academics like Lyman Atwater, Arthur Latham Perry, Amasa Walker, and, above all, William

Graham Sumner, the leading American disciple of Herbert Spencer (Dorfman 1949; Fine 1964; Hofstadter 1955). But their constructive aims were at least equally important. Study in Germany at an impressionable age had sensitized the new school economists to the need for a body of ideas, techniques, data, and policy proposals relevant to the rapidly changing American situation. Neither purely German ideas nor a watered down version of English classical economics would suffice. For example, they regarded the Malthusian theory of population and the Ricardian concern with land shortages as irrelevant to American circumstances, emphasized the lack of adequate empirical and statistical studies of contemporary economic problems, and sought a middle way in policy matters between German state intervention and English laissez-faire doctrine. However, in order to achieve their objectives they first had to establish their claims to intellectual authority and public recognition, and despite the generally receptive climate of opinion there were serious constraints to be overcome. Neither the academic establishment nor the general public was ready to grant the new professionals the prestige, deference, and occupational security accorded to the leading continental European professors; and even those who had never actually studied abroad were frustrated when they left the new graduate schools to take up appointments in impecunious colleges where they were overburdened with heavy, broad-ranging teaching duties, low salaries, poor library facilities, and limited or nonexistent research opportunities and resources. Then, as now, there was a substantial gap between the leading academic institutions and the also-rans, and this gap fostered a corresponding dissonance between professional expectations and their attainment. The creation of a national association helped to develop a network of professional communications and a growing awareness of collective interests. But it also contributed to the emergence of a national scholarly élite, and may have reinforced some professors' sense of alienation from local communities whose members were reluctant to acknowledge the novel and growing claims of scholarship and scientific expertise.[11]

If 'a professor is a man who thinks otherwise', as the historian Carl Becker reputedly said, then it is easy to understand why the shift of emphasis from the teaching of established truths to the advancement of knowledge and the investigation of current problems was liable to generate frictions between the social scientists and certain segments of their audience. Americans had never been willing to defer to intellectuals or experts (Hofstadter 1969), and although being an investigator did not necessarily entail social criticism, at least not in any radical sense, there were obvious reasons why the two were liable to be associated. The late nineteenth century was a time of disturbing economic, social, and political tensions, and the fact that the business community was generally getting a bad press when the economists were undertaking more thorough studies of their activities increased the likelihood that even the most objective and impartial enquiries would furnish ammunition for the innumerable critics of contemporary capitalism, among whom the new social scientists were becoming increasingly visible. There were also ideological sources of conflict. Laissez-faire and conservative social Darwinism were still the ruling beliefs among members of the social and business élites (Fine 1964; Hofstadter 1955), whereas many of the younger social scientists were reformers who regarded uninhibited individualism and unfettered competition as the cause of many, if not most, current economic and social evils. In some cases they adopted a species of Christian Socialism, sympathizing with the principal socialist criticisms of capitalism without necessarily endorsing the socialists' analysis or proposed remedies (Everett 1946; Ross 1977–8; Coats 1968). As might be expected, in some quarters such views were regarded as dangerously radical, and tensions mounted within the academic community as businessmen increasingly replaced clergymen on college and university boards of trustees.

During the 1880s and 1890s the reputation of the emerging economics profession and the degree of consensus among its members were disproportionately affected by the writings and other activities of the AEA's ambitious and controversial first secretary, Ely, whose career exemplifies the close interdependence of the internal and external dimensions of the professionalization process (Rader 1966; Ely 1938). Ely's enthusiastic advocacy of German economic ideas, methods, and policies, his outspoken attack on classical economics, his emotional support for the organized labour movement, and his sympathetic treatment of socialism widened the gulf between the 'old' and 'new' schools, created dissension among the Association's members, and alienated some of its potential allies within the academic community. Ely's initial conception of the organization's objectives and functions, as embodied in his original Statement of Principles, was too assertive, interventionist, and Germanic to be generally acceptable; consequently it was toned down, modified in the direction of conservatism, and eventually abandoned in 1888.[12] Behind these changes and the disagreements about the nature and methods of economics, there were conflicting views about the most effective strategy for improving economists' professional standing and their influence on contemporary affairs. Ely's combination of religious inspiration and uninhibited reformist zeal, as well as his prolific oversimplified popularizations of complex economic and social questions, seemed incompatible with professional behaviour and the tone and style appropriate to scholarly and scientific work.[13] Several of the new school's members were no less Christian than Ely, and no less concerned to advance the cause of social reform. But in addition to blurring the distinction between the old style of moralizing propaganda and the emerging conception of an impartial, detached scientific analysis of contemporary affairs Ely's approach also aroused unnecessary opposition from influential sections of the laity.

While the AEA's internal problems were resolved by 1892, when Ely resigned as secretary together with the Association's distinguished first president, Francis A. Walker,[14] the remaining disagreements within the profession on methodological, doctrinal, and policy issues might have generated greater controversy had it not been for the mounting external threats to academic freedom and security of tenure. This trend had serious implications for the AEA and the entire academic profession as well as the individuals actually and prospectively involved. What formal action, if any, should the Association take on behalf of any member who suffered or was threatened with dismissal for expressing views unacceptable to donors, trustees, university presidents, or – in the case of public institutions – state legislatures or voters? To refrain from open partisanship on controversial public policy questions was one thing; to refrain from criticizing actions that jeopardized the Association's primary goal – the promotion and dissemination of scholarly and scientific work – was quite another.

For the present purpose it is unnecessary to provide yet another review of the sequence of academic freedom cases involving economists, from Henry Carter Adams at Cornell in the 1880s, through Edward W. Bemis at Chicago, Richard T. Ely at Wisconsin, John R. Commons at Indiana and Syracuse, Elisha B. Andrews at Brown, to Edward A. Ross at Stanford at the turn of the century.[15] In each instance the outcome was determined by a complex interaction of intra- and extraprofessional factors, including the individual's institutional location, ideological position, professional standing, and the behaviour of the university authorities. For the present purpose, it is sufficient to cite Mary Furner's conclusion that by 1905

> the academic freedom cases helped to establish the dominance of a small, highly professionalized elite which determined a model for younger, less self-conscious academics to follow. In perilous times it was imperative to be able to count on the support of one's colleagues. . . . Out of all the cases emerged a rudimentary discipline which identified the degree and type of advocacy that was entitled to collective security. Within the limits where agreement could be reached on goals and tactics, the economists had exchanged the capricious discipline provided by powerful external opponents for the more steady influence of national professional control.
>
> [Furner 1975, p. 257]

However, this control was strictly informal. It operated through an extensive communications and placement network in which the AEA was a central component, even though the organization as such undertook no explicit functions or responsibilities in these matters. The annual meeting provided ample opportunities for discussion and the planning of collective action.

On one notable occasion at the Detroit annual conference in 1901, soon after the Ross case at Stanford, the AEA came very close to direct participation in academic freedom issues when a three-man committee of prominent members was established to investigate the affair. However, the committee had no official status; its *Report* was printed privately, rather than in the Association's *Publications*, and although it was signed by fifteen prominent economists and social scientists from leading institutions, including the then current president (Ely) and two past AEA presidents, the secretary, Charles H. Hull, did so only in his individual capacity. The reasons for this circumspection are too complex to be explained in detail here.[16] Opinions differed as to the propriety of Ross's conduct at Stanford. There was an understandable reluctance to commit the AEA in a matter on which most members had not been consulted; and it was thought that indirect pressure on the Stanford authorities would be more effective than an open attack. The proposal to publish an official AEA resolution on the matter seems not to have been seriously considered, and an informal attempt to organize a boycott of Stanford appointments proved ineffectual. The historians, incidentally, took no collective action whatsoever even though several of their disciplinary colleagues had been dismissed or had resigned in protest, together with several Stanford economists.

Subsequent historians have disagreed as to whether the Association and the economists as a group adopted the wisest or most efficacious course of action in this case. Yet there is no denying its crucial importance in the development of professional self-consciousness among American social scientists and in the formation of AEA policy in such matters prior to World War II. A further step was taken in 1913 following the publication in the *American Economic Review* of letters bearing on Willard Fisher's enforced resignation from Wesleyan. Once again, the economists organized an investigation,[17] headed by Seligman, and although it proved abortive it encouraged them to contribute their share to the report of an interim Joint Committee on Academic Freedom and Academic Tenure composed of members of the AEA, APSA, and ASS, which was published in full in the *American Economic Review* (Mar. 1915, pp. 316–23). This report paved the way for the formation of the American Association of University Professors (AAUP) two years later,[18] an event subsequently regarded as a landmark in the development of the academic profession in the USA. It was also a turning point in the AEA's involvement in academic freedom and certain other narrowly professional issues. For although many economists have supported the AAUP, and several have served it as president or in other important capacities, the AEA's officers were obviously relieved to let these matters pass into the AAUP's hands. Indeed, they took no formal interest in such issues until the late 1940s, under very different circumstances.

II

By the end of its third decade the AEA was firmly established, albeit on a modest scale. The more conservative economists' initial suspicions that the AEA was dominated by a group of radicals had been successfully dispelled; the climate of public opinion in the so-called progressive era was more favourable to moderate economic, social, and political reform; American economists were gaining more respect from their foreign counterparts and were enjoying increased opportunities to serve as experts on various public bodies at home (Church 1974); and the challenges to academic freedom had helped to generate a sense of professional solidarity and *esprit de corps*, at least partially diverting attention from continuing disagreements on intellectual and policy issues. The launching of the Association's own periodical, the *American Economic Review* (*AER*), in 1911 – after considerable dissatisfaction with the original monograph *Publications* series, and the short-lived experiments with the *Economic Studies* (1896–9) and the *Economic Bulletin* (1908–10) – demonstrated its members' determination to assert the Association's independence vis-à-vis the academic élite.[19] It brought an end to what one leading member termed 'the petty and ridiculous politics that seem to be inseparable from the conduct of all American associations' (Giddings to Secretary Frank A. Fetter, 3 May 1902, AEA Papers), for there had been deep heart searchings and indecision about the advisability of adding yet another journal to what seemed (amazingly from a present day perspective) an already overcrowded scholarly publication market. Admittedly the Association's finances were still shaky, and efforts to increase funds by campaigning for subscriptions from interested nonacademic persons, especially businessmen, left a legacy of problems for the *Review*'s editor, Davis R. Dewey, who endeavoured to cater to nonacademic interests without compromising scholarly and scientific standards. Despite occasional complaints, Dewey's policy[20] remained essentially unchanged right up to his retirement in 1940, at the age of 82 – at least ten years after he first expressed a desire to resign!

During the 1920s the Association's finances were put on a secure footing (Coats 1964) not long before the onset of the USA's greatest depression, which left remarkably few traces in the organization's records. In that bleak era some members resigned or failed to maintain their subscriptions either because they were unemployed or suffering from reduced income or local bank failure, or because their state institution was paying salaries in warrants uncashable elsewhere in the country. But the annual meetings and publications continued unchecked, and of course both provide ample evidence of the economists' preoccupation with the nature, causes, and remedies for current discontents. There were various appeals to the secretary from members and outsiders hopeful that he or the profession could provide a cure for the depression, and periodic offers of advice and assistance came from those convinced they already knew the solution. Throughout this time of trial, when many economists proposed schemes to promote economic recovery and sizeable groups signed petitions in protest against certain government actions (Dorfman 1959), the AEA's officers studiously avoided the temptation to make policy recommendations, and the Association as such remained strictly neutral and nonpartisan.

Nevertheless, in the interwar years there were distinct signs of change in the organization's procedures and in its members' attitudes. Of special interest here is the growing concern with certain professional issues that had occasionally surfaced in earlier years and were to become increasingly insistent during and after World War II. Four such issues can be mentioned briefly: efforts to persuade the Association's officers to classify economists, for a variety of reasons;[21] concern about professional standards; proposals favouring the establishment of a code of professional ethics; and an increasingly general recognition of the Association's responsibilities to the profession and to the general public. All these matters reflected the economists' response to changing external circumstances, especially increasing opportunities for employment in business and government and participation in public policymaking; but the connections are complex and indirect.

The idea of classifying economists was an obvious by-product of the AEA's heterogeneous membership and the desire to preserve the Association's scholarly and scientific character. The early membership had been highly miscellaneous, partly owing to Ely's promiscuous quest for supporters. Pressure for the formal classification of economists had arisen in World War I, when federal officials sought AEA help in selecting economists for government employment as part of the effort to mobilize skilled manpower, but little came of this effort owing to the brevity of the USA's active participation in the hostilities. In the mid-1920s the matter arose again when civil servants approached the AEA for assistance in defining economists under the Classification Act of 1923, but the issue presented no significant problems until the early 1930s, when the introduction of a new and more democratic procedure for electing officers inspired proposals to restrict voting rights to 'properly qualified' members, for example, Ph.D.s.[22] However, there was no serious attempt to implement such a scheme. In addition to the obvious difficulty of drawing an appropriate line between those granted such privileges and the general membership, and strong protests from those who feared disenfranchisement, there had been recurrent complaints that the Association was already controlled by an élite, mainly from the leading eastern universities. Curiously enough, while some members favoured the creation of a limited category of Fellows, on the lines of the British Royal Statistical Society, or the formation of an independent organization of 'scientific' economists, which would obviously have threatened the AEA's hegemony, the idea of a professional association of nonacademic economists had been mooted as far back as 1921, thereby anticipating the eventual formation of societies for business and government economists.

The classification issue arose again in World War II, and could no longer be ignored. James Washington Bell, who occupied the office of Secretary from 1936 to 1961, drafted the first official AEA definition of the economics profession for the National Roster of Scientific and Specialized Personnel in 1945. He was a conservative man, who usually resisted efforts to persuade the AEA to take a more active role in matters of professional concern. In this instance, however, he reluctantly assumed the responsibility knowing that if he refused, a Washington bureaucrat would concoct a definition; and several years later a revised official version was formulated by three leading AEA members. In 1949 one member protested that the National Roster definition was 'pitched so high that only giraffes can reach it. We need a description low enough that some of the calves can get in' (Jules Backman to Bell, 27 July 1949, also 25 May 1949; AEA Papers), and his concern is understandable when we appreciate that he was in dispute with the New York State Tax Department which had questioned whether economics was in fact a 'profession'. As it transpired, he lost his case!

It is not entirely clear why proposals to introduce the certification of economists or the accreditation of college courses in economics were more frequent during the 1930s than in previous decades. Although neither of these ideas seems to have reflected widespread feelings among the AEA's members, or to have been treated very seriously by its officers, they revealed genuine concern both about the economist's role and responsibilities in public affairs and the absence of any recognizable professional standards. There appears to have been a general movement to establish more formal restrictions on entry on behalf of professionals suffering from or threatened with unemployment, while among the economists, those employed in business and government clearly felt that they lacked adequate recognition as specialists or experts in their field. As with the question of the AEA's electoral procedure, the desire for certification can be interpreted either as a sign of underconfidence or, alternatively, simply as a response to the growth in the number of economists regarding themselves as bona fide professionals entitled to more recognition and autonomy in the workplace. With respect to the accreditation of college courses, economic education at various levels has been on the AEA's agenda intermittently throughout its history in connection with the market for economists (supply as well as demand), salary levels, career prospects, and the quality and content of teaching in high schools, colleges, and universities. But accreditation would have been a new and ambitious departure, calling for a substantial extension of the AEA's customary activities and a considerable expansion of its staff and budget, even if a consensus could have been reached on the appropriate standards to be applied. It is not difficult to understand why the executive committee, and especially the secretary, proved to be unresponsive to any such scheme.

During the 1920s the relationships between the economists and the business community appear to have been noticeably more harmonious than around the turn of the century, and a number of leading economists began to express concern that the profession was becoming too deeply involved with business interest groups (Dorfman 1959; Fetter 1925). The economists' interest in professional ethics at this time centred on three distinct matters: their responsibilities as advisers to government bodies and private organizations – a matter of obviously growing importance; the direct or indirect involvement of some economists in stock exchange speculation; and the issues of principle and practice arising from the acceptance of continuing research grants or retainers from private sources and vested interest groups. Only the last of these directly impinged on the AEA, and this issue is of special piquancy from an historical standpoint for there were sustained and widely publicized attacks on Ely's Institute for Research in Land Economics and Public Utilities beginning in the mid-1920s. Thirty years earlier Ely's position at the University of Wisconsin had been seriously jeopardized by critics who had denounced him as a dangerous radical or socialist. But, as is not unusual, the ageing process had tempered his youthful exuberance, bringing a greater caution and a more conservative attitude on policy issues, including the reversal of his earlier endorsement of public ownership of 'natural monopolies'. Needless to say, the AEA's executive committee refused to give way to the single taxers' organized demand for a formal investigation of Ely's Institute. But the attacks were of sufficient weight, in combination with the Progressives' recent recapture of the Wisconsin state government, to induce Ely to move his institute from Madison to Northwestern, a private university. Beyond this, the wider implications of the economists' increasing involvement with the business community led the AAUP to establish a subcommittee headed by Seligman (a former AEA president and renowned champion of academic freedom) 'to investigate the subject of academic obligations and public-utility propaganda'. In the course of preparing their report the subcommittee prescribed a code of ethics in connection with grants from private industry, with special reference to economists and engineers, commenting that 'in the past there have been some sad instances of loss of standing on the part of hitherto distinguished scholars' (Dorfman 1959, p. 209, quoting 'Academic Obligations: A Report on the Public Utility Propaganda', *Bulletin of the AAUP*, May 1930). However, no reference to this report appeared in the *AER*.

In the 1930s the AEA's secretary received an increasing number of enquiries about the Association's code of ethics, some of which emanated from students whose teachers encouraged them to investigate the practices and principles of various learned societies and professional organizations. Needless to say, the AEA had no such code, nor had the officers any sanctions or means of enforcement, and the executive committee, when pressed, viewed the investigation of such matters as beyond the range of its proper functions. Of course, some matters of professional behaviour could not be ignored, but wherever possible these were dealt with on an individual basis, without involving the executive committee or the membership at large.

Throughout the Association's history no subjects have been more contentious than book reviews and the refereeing (and rejection!) of articles submitted for publication. In numerous instances wounded or irate authors have questioned individual referees' and reviewers' competence, integrity, and even sanity, and overworked editors have had to decide whether the aggrieved party had a case sufficiently strong to justify a second review or reconsideration of a manuscript. During the 1940s, for example, there were such persistent and heated protests over certain book reviews in the *AER*, probably reflecting deep divisions over Keynesian economics, that in 1945 the executive committee decided to establish a committee of enquiry that would prescribe acceptable principles for reviewers (Proceedings, May 1946, pp. 904–6). Occasionally editors have been threatened with libel; but the only one who spent time in jail during his incumbency did so for conscientious political reasons, not for incompetence or malpractice!

In the late 1950s a charge of plagiarism was levelled against certain leading economists which could not be ignored because the frustrated complainant had circularized his accusations among a large number of AEA members. In the event this too was handled by a small subcommittee appointed by the executive committee, which performed its task discreetly without a formal hearing, much to the plaintiff's dissatisfaction when it concluded that there was no case to answer.[23] As with the issue of academic freedom, the AEA's officers and executive committee were naturally reluctant to be involved in such matters. The usual response to enquirers was that the AEA needed no special code of ethics because the canons of correct professional practice were too obvious to require specification. However, as we shall see, neither this issue nor the problem of academic freedom, could be dismissed so easily after 1945.

III

During World War II the centre of American economics shifted decisively towards Washington, DC. Unprecedented numbers of professional economists entered public service, including the armed forces, where they performed valuable research and executive as well as combatant functions. A large proportion of college and university teachers were in absentia; consequently graduate instruction and research virtually ceased, and the lower level teaching of economics was severely curtailed (Homan 1946). However, the dramatic changes of the period and the inevitable diversion

447

of professional energies from peacetime academic work have tended to obscure the extent to which the foundations of the country's subsequent world leadership in the discipline had already been securely laid in the interwar years. In addition to the emergence in the 1930s of a generation of brilliant young native economists carefully nurtured and stimulated by the presence of an outstanding group of older European émigrés,[24] a firm empirical and conceptual base was provided for the development of national income analysis and the other statistical requirements for wartime and postwar economic management. And of course the flowering of Keynesian economics in the late 1930s was yet another element bridging the gap between the pre- and postwar eras.

Despite its customary determinedly aloof and detached posture, the AEA could hardly remain unaffected by the war. Constraints on transportation led to the serious constriction, and in one year the cancellation, of the annual meeting, and when the *AER*'s energetic and youthful editor, Paul Homan, decided to join the Washington throng and take the journal with him, the move had symbolic as well as practical significance. As in World War I, many economists believed that the Association should make a collective contribution to the war effort. In retrospect, the most interesting manifestation of this desire was the executive committee's decision, inspired by Frank Graham of Princeton, to establish a Committee on the Focusing of Informed Opinion, in January 1943, to circularize questionnaires to some (but not all) AEA members in an attempt to discover how far there was a consensus on various issues, and to consider making 'the informed opinion of our members more effective in matters of political importance; for example, the rubber inquiry, rationing, price control, etc.' (Proceedings, Mar. 1943, p. 473). This decision gave birth to a Committee on Association-Sponsored Consensus Reports the following spring, which in turn spawned several 'ad hoc independent committees' to report on specific questions of public policy without, of course, implying any formal commitments on the part of the Association as a whole. Even so, Secretary Bell predictably had considerable misgivings, since the scheme 'raised many questions involving the expansion of the scope of the Association's activities' (Secretary's Report, Proceedings 1945, p. 453).

This was neither the first nor, indeed, the last attempt by American economists to explore the extent and constructive potential of any consensus within the profession. One of the first committees created under AEA auspices in the 1880s had been designed to secure agreement on the definition of standard economic terms, and in 1934 the statistician Wilford I. King tried to persuade Dewey to publish a provisional statement by his Committee on Economic Accord, which aimed to reach agreement on matters of definition and fundamental principle.[25] Neither effort had any detectable impact; but the experiment of the 1940s was potentially of much greater significance. Graham believed the AEA 'should assume responsibility for organizing a recognized corps of experts capable of formulating the collective judgment of students of social, economic, and political problems whose reports would represent professional judgment with regard to public policy in these matters' (Proceedings, 1943, p. 423). Whether such quasi-authoritative judgements were compatible with the Association's traditional nonpartisanship seems not to have aroused serious misgivings among executive committee members. Here, as elsewhere, considerations of constitutionality were overriden, under emergency conditions, by the economists' desire to educate the public and influence the course of policy-making.

After much debate, two initial consensus committees were established concerned, respectively, with 'Agricultural Price Supports and their Consequences', and 'The Functions of Government in the Post War Economy'. It was soon clear that the latter topic was 'too vague and broad to elicit answers of a sufficiently explicit character to determine areas of agreement and disagreement among the economists consulted' (Proceedings 1945, p. 423). Nevertheless both committees produced reports in 1945, and during the ensuing decade a series of other reports designed to bring 'the wisdom of economists to bear on public issues' appeared in the Proceedings under the general auspices of the variously titled committees on Association-Sponsored Consensus Reports, public issues, and so on. A proposal to produce a pamphlet series containing the results of these investigations and, like a similar scheme mooted in World War I, designed to educate the public, did not bear fruit. However, the reports that were eventually printed in the *AER* should not be lightly dismissed. Some bore the names of very distinguished economists, such as the 1950 Report on Economic Stability which, it was suggested, might be published by the Joint Economic Committee of Congress. Moreover the efforts at consensus are of lasting interest to students of wartime and postwar American economic thought, quite aside from their value as evidence on the perennial question whether any group of professional economists can be persuaded to agree on anything!

Another recurrent issue that gained an added impetus in wartime was the matter of the Association's responsibility, if any, for the recruitment, training, and utilization of economists in the public service. Assistance to the Civil Service Commissioners had been under serious consideration in the later 1920s, at the same time as the scheme to consolidate the AEA administrative and editorial offices in Washington, possibly at the Brookings Institution – which was, of course, heavily involved in public policy questions. The economists' increasingly prominent involvement in Washington during the New Deal inevitably brought both warm support and deep antagonism from opposite ends of the political spectrum, making 'the Economics Profession and Government' a matter of intense professional concern.[26] In 1935, there was another appeal for support, this time on behalf of a Commission of Inquiry on Public Service Personnel appointed by the Social Science Research Council, designed to improve the quality of government employees. Even Secretary Bell conceded that this might be one cause meriting the Association's wholehearted and open endorsement, although this scheme too had its controversial aspects, for it contemplated certification of individuals 'by accredited professional associations and by legally established professional bodies for all professional and technical positions' (Luther Gulick to Bell, 17 Jan. 1935; Bell to Gulick, 28 Jan. 1934, AEA papers). This led to a joint session with the American Statistical Association and further discussion. In a powerful paper summarized in the Proceedings and printed in full in the *AER* in 1941, Copeland proposed that

> a certificate of professional competence be established for economists, but on a voluntary, not a mandatory basis. If something like Gresham's law is not to operate in the field of economic research, we should find ways and means to overcome the difficulties involved and introduce the equivalent of coinage for research workers who conform to a suitable minimum standard.
>
> [Proceedings 1940, part 5, p. 413]

As might have been expected, the executive committee's initial response on the main issue was negative, for the committee argued that an open society like the AEA, with virtually unrestricted membership, was 'not suitably constituted to undertake the responsibility of certifying the competency of its members as economists'. However, they offered to assist public authorities with civil service examinations 'where possible' and with the solution of other classification problems 'when called upon to do so' (Secretary's Report, Proceedings 1940, part 5, p. 494). Moreover, on this occasion the matter did not end there, for Copeland was invited to submit suggestions for implementing his ideas and evidently he did so to some purpose, for a Committee on Standards for Economists in the Public Service was established in 1941 and continued for several years. Nevertheless, the question of 'competency' soon receded into the background as the committee became increasingly involved with other social science bodies and government agencies, and the focus of interest shifted to the question of the kinds of training needed in government (Proceedings 1944, pp. 404, 407–8). This shift in interest constituted part of the background to the postwar AEA-sponsored studies of undergraduate and graduate education in economics.[27]

Questions of professional standards and certification continued to interest AEA members throughout the 1950s (although they tended to be overshadowed by a more immediately urgent, related issue, academic freedom, which will be considered below). In 1953, in response to a number of petitions calling for AEA action, an Exploratory Committee on the Status of the Profession was established and undertook an investigation of the subject. However, in practice, as one respondent observed, although the certification of economists was not implausible in the abstract, any effort to implement such a scheme

> would be hopelessly bogged down in complex problems of interpretation. Unless the standard were made very elastic indeed the Ph.D.'s from some schools would complain bitterly of discrimination. Some persons who do not have doctoral degrees are probably well qualified as economists, but what kind of certifying agency would conduct examinations etc. to determine whether they have the minimum professional training? Suppose someone fails of certification and then accuses the certifying authority of being opposed to his sort of economics?
>
> [Howard Ellis to Arthur Smithies, 1 Feb. 1954, AEA Papers]

A group of Wisconsin economists considered the issue worth examining, but added:

> Admittedly there are many charlatans and quacks in the field, but we think the setting of rigid standards that would harden lines in the profession to the advantage of present job-holders is a danger that must be avoided.
>
> [P. T. Ellsworth to Calvin B. Hoover, 16 Oct. 1953, AEA Papers]

In 1958 yet another effort by Copeland to activate the issue was defeated in the executive committee 'after considerable debate' (Proceedings 1959, p. 507), and even then the subject was not yet dead. As Secretary Bell reported the following year,

> the recognition of the economist as a professional man [sic] compared with the statistician, accountant, lawyer, doctor, engineer, may be of considerable importance to practitioners . . . especially in anticipation of income tax debates.
>
> [Proceedings 1960, p. 668]

After all, if economists would not look after their own economic interests, who would? Unfortunately for the activists, circumstances in the early postwar decades called for caution, a preference for defence over attack.

The first manifestation of official AEA interest in academic freedom for more than thirty years occurred in 1947, in the form of a reaction to efforts to blacklist certain economics texts expressing supposedly radical (e.g., Keynesian) views of American capitalism and the functioning of the economy. It also marked the beginning of considered and protracted efforts to withstand the growing pressure of extreme anticommunist attacks on the academic community. These attacks gathered force in the so-called McCarthy era, exerting damaging effects on freedom of speech, enquiry, and

451

publication and inhibiting teaching, professional work outside the class-room, and nonprofessional activities.[28]

It is impossible to determine how far the Association's initial decision to take up the textbook issue in 1947 reflected a new climate of opinion on the part of the executive committee or rather the leadership of President Paul Douglas, a man not inexperienced in political combat. In 1941 Secretary Bell had refused an invitation from the AHA to support a textbook resolution due to be published in the *American Historical Review*,[29] but six years later the AEA circulated a statement to 770 colleges and universities, both to department heads and to regents or chairmen of boards of trustees, on behalf of its members, affirming that

> university and college teachers must have the untrammeled right to select for use in their teaching and research such textbooks as they, [and] no others, believe will promote the purposes which their courses are intended by the teachers to serve.
>
> [Proceedings 1948, p. 533; Douglas to Bell,
> 30 Oct. 1947, AEA Papers]

Some universities objected to the phrase 'no others', and President Joseph Schumpeter expressed misgivings when he was asked to sign the resolution, which was circulated during his incumbency. However, he was evidently appeased when Bell explained that in doing so he would be 'merely performing an Association function and not intervening on his own' (Bell to Seymour E. Harris, 12 Apr. 1948, AEA Papers). Bell sympathized with Schumpeter, fearing that the response to the resolution might prove 'embarrassing', and both were anxious lest a 'crusading spirit' should be displayed by the new committee of ex-presidents appointed

> for the purpose of making public the position of the Association concerning academic freedom; to refer appropriate cases to the AAUP; and to give their own judgment on specific grievances referred to the Association.
>
> [Secretary's Report, Proceedings 1948, p. 533; Bell to Schumpeter,
> 20 Feb. 1948, 19 Mar. 1948; Schumpeter to Bell, 22 Mar. 1948: 'God
> grant them the gift of discretion.']

The apparent reversal of the AEA's habitual practice of leaving academic freedom cases to the AAUP had no immediate effect, for the committee decided to confine itself to issues arising from efforts to censor or ban textbooks and related matters (Proceedings 1949, p. 594). However, after the executive committee empowered three professors to draft a resolution in 1950 on the loyalty oath requirement in California, 'expressing the sense of the members present' at the annual meeting (Proceedings 1951, p. 765), the Academic Freedom Committee was strengthened and instructed to consider preparing 'a tentative preliminary statement of general principles, together with an appropriate definition of the proper scope of academic and professional freedom' (Proceedings 1952, p. 718). Other parts of the resolution reveal the continuing uncertainty as to the Association's proper role in these matters, and during the next few years when various 'ad hoc' and 'exploratory' reports were published, the Ad Hoc Committee on Freedom of Teaching, Research, and Publication in Economics acknowledged that the Association had taken a much less 'strong and independent' line than the AHA, APSA, and the American Psychological Association. Nevertheless, after presenting at length the arguments for and against various courses of action, the committee still considered it inadvisable to prepare and publicize an AEA 'declaration of principles of academic freedom for economists' or to 'investigate and report upon specific cases'. Instead, the committee merely proposed to issue an annual report 'on the status of the professor, including information on current attacks on freedom and apparent threats to freedom, on the conditions that promote freedom and those that discourage it' (Proceedings 1954, p. 737), and the executive duly gave its approval.

This modest, if not timid proposal, reflected the belief that the AEA lacked the resources, opportunity, and experience to undertake investigations of reputed violations of academic freedom. To those who deplored the AAUP's ineffectiveness, the response was that it would be wiser to reinvigorate that body than to duplicate and thereby possibly undermine its work, or even possibly to establish 'a joint secretariat' to perform the AAUP's original functions (Proceedings 1954, p. 736). The committee endorsed the limited estimate of the profession's status and potential influence contained in Howard Bowen's AEA report, *Graduate Education in Economics*, which it quoted:

> The economists of the United States are a small heterogeneous group without strong professional consciousness or powerful professional organization. They face public attitudes that are often indifferent and sometimes hostile. Their status as viewed by the public is lower than that of other learned professions.
>
> [Ibid.]

During the later 1950s a somewhat more positive stance was adopted by the newly formed Committee on Academic Freedom and Civil Liberties (note the absence of the word *status*) under the chairmanship of Fritz Machlup, an ardent and effective champion of the AAUP. Its more aggressive, even crusading tone is evident in its 1959 report on the 'disclaimer affidavit',[30] and had Machlup been in a more strategic position at the beginning of the decade the AEA would probably have adopted a more determined and constructive policy in this sphere. This is suggested by the evident relish with which Machlup's committee reported Paul Sweezy's victory in the Supreme Court, after Sweezy had been 'sentenced to jail in New Hampshire for refusing to answer questions, in a state investigation of subversion, regarding a lecture on the subject of socialism which he delivered in a course at the University of New Hampshire'.[31] These quoted words were contained in a note that Sweezy had asked the managing editor of the *AER* to publish, a request that caused the editor some concern. 'Do I take the responsibility,' he wrote,

> for publishing every item of this sort involving an economist, in the form written by the complainant, describing his point of view of threats or actions that have the effect in his judgment of impairing his academic freedom or civil liberties? If so, do I attach to these items as published an editorial note disclaiming all responsibility for their factual accuracy? Do I stand ready to provide space also for replies and comments of others who cite different facts or place a different interpretation upon the facts from that given by the complainant?
>
> [Proceedings 1955, p. 680, n. 3]

In the early 1960s interest in questions of academic freedom declined, and the Academic Freedom and Civil Liberties Committee apparently ceased to function once the executive committee had publicly endorsed the AAUP's statement of principles on academic freedom and tenure – albeit with some reservations on the tenure aspect (Proceedings 1963, p. 690). Nevertheless the subject would not go away. As the result of a strongly worded resolution approved at the 1974 annual meeting, after considerable debate and amendment, a new standing Committee on Political Discrimination was established (Proceedings 1975, pp. 44–6) and in fact still exists. By contrast with previous practice, this body seems to have been inspired by a particular case and, unlike its predecessors, it has conducted investigations of alleged breaches of academic freedom – though naturally with less experience and resources than the AAUP. However, to judge from the Association's records, the results have not generally been satisfactory, although it must be conceded that there is no unambiguous criterion of effectiveness in this difficult field.

IV

As the Association's scale and financial resources have grown,[32] so too have the range and variety of services it has undertaken on its members' behalf. Some of the present activities would obviously astonish the founder members, such as the arrangement of group flights to meetings, while others might shock them, for it is by no means easy to prescribe the limits of propriety for a scholarly organization.[33] The AEA's charter and bylaws have provided some safeguards, as we have seen, but at times the pressure for innovations has been strong enough to oblige the executive committee to consider novel ways and means of meeting the members' wishes, even to the extent of introducing constitutional amendments. Such pressure was especially acute within the AEA, as in other American social science organizations, during the later 1960s and 1970s when there was severe social conflict over such issues as poverty, urban conditions, racial discrimination, women's rights, and the Vietnam war. In this period the Association's traditional nonpartisanship clauses were invariably invoked against those who called for public policy statements, and were usually enough – combined with inertia – to defeat such proposals.

The most acute internal crisis in the AEA's history arose in 1968, a year of serious unrest both on and off campus. After the Chicago police's brutal treatment of demonstrators at the Democratic convention in the summer, which was widely reported on television and in the press, many members demanded that the 1968 annual meeting either be moved away from Chicago or be cancelled, as a gesture of protest. Opinions on the matter were deeply divided, both in the executive committee and in the general membership. After careful and anxious consultations, president Kenneth Boulding decided to go through with the original plan. Boulding, a man of highly developed moral sensibilities, who could not be charged with lack of sympathy for liberal and radical causes, explained his and the executive's motives in a moving letter sent to all members. The protesters organized a breakaway movement in Philadelphia, the first of its kind, at which several hundred supporters enrolled in the newly formed Union for Radical Economics, and attendance at the regular meeting dropped substantially. There was, however, no recurrence of such a division.

On the whole, by comparison with other scholarly associations, especially those in the social sciences, the AEA weathered this stormy period with relatively little damage (Bloland and Bloland 1974). Yet there is substantial justification for the charge that the Association has been 'somnolent', functioning without vitality at the level where 'life is preserved but not pronounced' – though the same critic concedes that the organization's 'moribundity . . . has not harmed, and may possibly have enhanced, the rewards and power of economists' (Orlans 1973, pp. 25–9).

It is certainly true that the tradition of nonpartisanship has frequently served as a device for the avoidance of difficult and controversial issues, and that the effort to maintain this tradition has occasionally produced curious anomalies. For example, the executive committee violated the rule in 1930, when it expressed approval for a Public Documents Bill then passing through the Senate (Proceedings 1931, p. 271), and earlier endorsed a petition for congressional funds to assist scholars travelling abroad, presumably on the grounds that, like pressure for the reduction of postal charges on academic publications and like concerted efforts to improve the Census or the supply of official statistics, these were noncontroversial matters of professional interest to all members. Yet the executive committee refused to give official support to the peace movement after World War I or the proposal in the 1960s to establish a national foundation for the social sciences comparable to the National Science Foundation. Apparently these issues were too partisan. The AEA's unwillingness to take more decisive action on questions of academic freedom or professional ethics presumably stems from the same set of attitudes that has dominated the Association from its early years.

This criticism, if such it is, is not directed merely at the executive committee. In the relatively calm but controversial debate about the desirability or otherwise of holding meetings in states that had failed to ratify the Equal Rights Amendment one dissatisfied member rightly stressed that the executive committee's opposition to change could presumably be overcome by means of a referendum. But as usual there was comparatively little support for such a drastic step. This episode demonstrated the difficulty of avoiding partisanship, for both action and inaction could be interpreted as a commitment to one or other side in the dispute.[34]

It is possible to mention only a few of the Association's numerous activities on its members' behalf, most of which have been uncontroversial, yet deserving of extended consideration. For example, the annual meeting has steadily been transformed from the original, small gathering of colleagues and friends into the present-day vast conglomerate. Expanded well beyond the AEA itself, it incorporates numbers of separate organizations operating under well-established but flexible agreements (since the formation of the Allied Social Science Association in the 1930s as an amorphous, quasi-independent, and self-financing federation), and innumerable specialist subdisciplines, intellectual and research groups. As is well known, much of the most important business and many of the most valuable intellectual exchanges occur outside the formal sessions, much of it related to the formal and informal job (so-called slave) market. But the extent of initial planning and complex administrative management, much of it undertaken by unpaid volunteers, and the occasional difficulties involved in selecting sites and drawing the line between the professionally acceptable organizations or groups and the outsiders, are matters unknown to, and indeed undreamt of by, the majority of AEA members.

Another essential species of activity is publishing which for the AEA, like any other scholarly or scientific body, is part of its *raison d'être*. Here the range, variety, and expense of the Association's activities far exceed the bounds of the founders' imagination, and although part of this large topic has been sketched elsewhere (Coats, 1969), that account focuses only on a few major items. The crucial shift from the original monograph series to the *AER* in 1911 has already been mentioned (*supra*, p. 443). A second major turning point was the launching of the *Journal of Economic Literature*, which rapidly became an indispensable abstracting, reviewing, and bibliographic source, and supplier of invaluable surveys of the state of the art in general economics and in a succession of special fields. Again, even a short list of AEA publications should include the magnificent *Index of Economic Articles* (originally *Journals*) which is also essential to a science that, in Whitehead's memorable phrase, 'hesitates to forget its founders'. (Whether economics is accordingly 'lost', as Whitehead would have inferred, is hardly a matter for examination here.)

Another general category of AEA activities involving publications that can be broadly termed informational has included studies of graduate education and the structure of the profession, research on the nature and functioning of the labour market for academic and nonacademic economists, the publication of job advertisements, and the provision of facilities for contacts between economist job seekers and prospective employers.[35] For several years the AEA drew on the international network of economists in the operation of a screening project for foreign students, in an effort to ensure that they were adequately equipped to benefit from graduate study in the USA; and for more than twenty-five years this function has been performed by the Economics Institute, a quasi-independent organization which has had AEA support and cooperation. Many such ventures would not have been possible without the great increase in financial resources available from the leading foundations and the federal government, and it is important to record, however briefly, that from its early days the AEA has repeatedly provided expert advice and guidance in the design and development of the Census and other categories of governmental statistics.

From its inception the AEA has demonstrated an intermittent interest in the improvement of economics teaching both at the high school and at the college level, and of course some of its publication activities have been designed to raise the level of the general public's knowledge of economic affairs. Yet surprisingly enough, there was no systematic interest in what is now termed economic education until after World War II. It began partly as a direct outgrowth of wartime experience and was considerably expanded after the first Sputnik with the establishment of the National Task Force on Economic Education. This body sponsored a year-long TV course on economics which was shown nationally in 1962–3, and again in 1963–4, and as the Association's co-sponsorship was publicized there were inevitably some who expressed misgivings both about the content of the course and about the general principles involved.[36] In 1965 a fruitful link was established with the Joint Council on Economic Education, which has enabled the Association to exert a considerable influence in the field through its representatives on the council without committing the Association as a body. Indeed, representing the profession in dealings with federal, state, and local government agencies on educational issues soon became such a flourishing activity that the AEA members expressed concern at the volume of work involved. On a different level, there was also an increasing volume of systematic research on the economics curriculum and teaching methods, which led one prominent participant to express surprise that nothing of the kind had ever been undertaken previously (Reynolds 1969, p. 239).

Throughout its history the heterogeneity of the AEA's membership has always made it difficult to cater to all their diverse needs and interests, but the nature of the problem has changed markedly over time. The initial divisive tendencies arising from the size of the country have been overcome partly by improvements in transport and communications, and partly by the emergence of a series of regional associations. After an early set of unsuccessful experiments with branch societies (Coats 1960), the national body has neither sought to control these regional offspring nor has it granted them formal affiliation. The *AER*'s original problems arising from the large number of nonacademic subscribers gradually became of diminishing concern as the *Review* and the Association gained recognition, and as the number of qualified economists outside the higher education system expanded, especially during and after World War I. Although there have been recurrent complaints that the *Review* is too esoteric and academic and the experiment of launching another periodical with a wider appeal is now under way, the hegemony of the academic leadership has never been seriously challenged. A somewhat more serious threat, if such it is, has come from the natural process of the growth, specialization, and compartmentalization of knowledge, which, as early as the 1920s, led some leading economists to wonder whether their subject was disintegrating. That danger was partially offset by the revival of interest in general theory during the 1930s, reinforced by the mathematization of the discipline. The prestige of theory and the growing use of mathematics have been conceptually and technically unifying forces for most of the profession, although there has been a lasting division between the mathematically inclined economists and their more literary and historically minded fellow professionals.

There has, of course, been a rapid proliferation of specialties and subdisciplines, each with its own group of practitioners, some with their own organization and periodical. The 22 category classification used in the *Index of Economic Articles* gives a clear indication of this process of subdivision. But unless the aggregate size of the profession begins to decline – as well it may now that the long postwar academic boom has peaked – these developments need not entail any loss of support for the national parent-body. Awareness of this problem is evident in Bell's comment on a 1955 poll concerning the timing and character of the annual meeting:

> If the AEA is to remain the professional association and learned society serving all economists, we must make its membership so attractive and useful that no formally trained economist can afford not to join and we should make its services so available and so valuable to students and non-professional economists that they, too,

will find membership an asset even though they may belong to other associations as well.

[*AER* 1956, p. 599]

As with every national and scientific organization, the AEA's officers have always been aware of the difficulties of retaining the loyalty and support of their variegated and geographically scattered membership, and of representing their collective and several interests as fairly and comprehensively as possible. Since the end of the predominantly Keynesian era in the 1960s, amid the widely discussed 'crisis' in the discipline, there has been an intensification of doctrinal, methodological, and policy disagreements and a growing interest in the profession's structure, functioning, and public reputation. Charges that the AEA is controlled by a limited 'orthodox' establishment group can be traced back at least to the 1890s (indeed there is evidence at the founding of the desire to limit entry to those who could be expected to work together congenially), and in the post-1945 period these complaints have been supported by statistical analyses of the composition of the executive committee, editorial boards, institutional affiliations, authorship of papers at the annual meetings and in the *AER* and articles in the leading journals.[37]

Whether this is simply an unavoidable – and, as some would aver, a healthy – state of affairs is far too delicate and complex a matter to be examined here. It is surely the case that a scientific and scholarly organization will inevitably be run by those generally recognized as the leaders in the field; and although this is essentially a circular argument, it is equally clear that questions of scientific validity and merit cannot be settled simply by recourse to the ballot box, especially in an organization that has no entry qualifications. The AEA's records repeatedly reveal its officers' and representatives' many efforts to discover and encourage able economists in more remote and less prestigious institutions, and to recognize the existence and rights of heterodox and minority (including specialist) groups within the profession. Perfect justice and wisdom are not to be expected in this world, even among professionals devoted to optimizing or maximizing satisfactions. Nor can one expect perfect consistency in the operations of a society with a constantly changing governing body and only one, or at most two, semipermanent officers with distinctly limited powers. (Unlike many other national associations, the AEA refused to appoint a full-time permanent executive secretary.) Nevertheless, there is evidence of continuing and perhaps increasing dissatisfaction with the ruling body of neoclassical economics, of which the AEA is the largest and most influential organizational embodiment. Whether this is simply a passing phase, a by-product of the growth in the scale and complexity of the profession, and the increasing standardization of graduate training programmes in the post-1945 period, may become clear in the course of the AEA's second century.

During the past two decades three distinct special-interest groups have arisen within the profession and made their presence felt – radicals, blacks (or minority group economists), and women – but their relationships with the AEA, and its responses, have differed significantly in each case. The radical economists emerged as a vociferous minority in the late 1960s demanding improved professional opportunities with respect to scholarships, training programmes, the curriculum, career prospects, representation at the national meetings, and of course the abandonment of the AEA's traditional nonpartisan policy. But although a splinter group within the movement caused serious disruption at the 1969 annual meeting (Proceedings 1970, pp. 487–9), most of the radicals have apparently wished to have no truck with the national organization because they viewed it as too orthodox and procapitalist. Consequently they never sought its support or a share of its resources. In this sense they have not been treated any differently from other doctrinal subgroups such as the institutionalists, libertarians, and post-Keynesians, which have their own periodicals and organization.

However, the same cannot be said of the minority group economists. Curiously enough, the initial 'Statement of Concern' published by the Black Caucus (Proceedings 1970, pp. 527–9) reflected the mood of the times and was indistinguishable from contemporary radical economists' pronouncements. It focused attention on three 'central issues' requiring corrective action: Social and Racial Bias, Professional Bias, and Lack of Social Responsibility; and it concluded with a challenge to the AEA 'to correct its errors of omission and commission' (ibid., p. 529). Nevertheless, before long the group settled down to the more modest constructive task of improving the educational and training opportunities and facilities for its constituents through the summer programme organized by the Committee on the Status of Minorities in the Economics Profession, with the aid of financial support from the Association and outside agencies. No doubt its leaders felt that the basic situation was so unfavourable to minority groups that their position could be ameliorated only by working gradually from the ground up, through the existing system rather than against it.

Different again has been the approach adopted by CSWEP, the Committee on the Status of Women in the Economics Profession, a body inaugurated at the 1971 annual meeting. A natural by-product of contemporary social concern and increased interest in the structure and functioning of the profession, CSWEP has taken up an unabashedly propagandist and advocatorial stance, and has been unambiguously critical of the prevailing status quo. Yet it has consistently operated under the AEA's auspices, and with the organization's direct and indirect support; and it has consistently adopted a scholarly and scientific approach to its task.[38] CSWEP's annual reports to the Association contain an impressive volume of revealing new data and analysis of the functioning of the profession, and the position of women therein, and the group has worked effectively in increasing women's visibility, improving information flows and communications among its constituents, and shedding new light on the workings of the labour market both within academe and beyond. It may, indeed, serve as a model of what a responsible activist group can achieve within the AEA. Yet CSWEP's political commitments must also be recognized as potentially embarrassing to the Association, given its open links with the National Women's Political Caucus, and its participation in the agitation over the ERA, mentioned earlier.

V

The foregoing account, though far from complete, is designed to convey a broad impression of the AEA's contributions to the economics profession, and to raise some questions about its proper role as a scholarly and scientific organization. For example, to cite the Statement of Purpose now printed annually in the Proceedings, is it enough for the Association to assume 'no responsibility for the opinions of those who participate in its annual meetings'? Surely its members and the general public are entitled to an assurance that the meetings will maintain an acceptably high (or at least a minimum) standard of scholarly and scientific quality and professional integrity? The 'encouragement of perfect freedom of discussion' surely does not imply a complete absence of constraints, whereby in principle every crank or advocate of a popular nostrum is entitled to a hearing? Some misguided outsiders have indeed interpreted the AEA's statement of purpose in this way. But of course the procedures for organizing the programme and the Proceedings provide safeguards of professional quality.

An equally sensitive problem arises with the claim that 'the Association *as such* takes no partisan attitude, nor does it commit its members to any position on practical economic issues' (emphasis supplied). Undoubtedly this convention has often protected the AEA and its officers from embarrassment and from involvement in potentially divisive controversies over issues and policies on which there are deep disagreements among its members. Nevertheless, nonpartisanship is a policy: like other policies it has practical consequences, and the AEA's insistence on preserving its neutrality has frequently precluded it from taking action that could have benefited its members and the profession at large. As Graham's wartime proposals on the focusing of informed opinion implied:

> Professions *profess*. They profess to know better than others the nature of certain matters, and to know better than their clients what ails them and their affairs. This is the essence of the professional claim. . . .
> The client is not the true judge of the value of the services he receives,

461

furthermore the problem and affairs of men are such that the best of professional advice and action will not always solve them.[39]

The executive committee and its officers would not deny their responsibility to ensure that their nominees, and the members of their selected subcommittees, which report on a variety of subjects of considerable professional and public significance, are both professionally qualified and likely to perform in a manner compatible with scholarly and scientific standards. As in other intellectual disciplines, such standards are neither fixed nor perfectly explicit and unambiguous; yet is it sufficient for the AEA to pretend that it has no collective responsibility for the specification of professional standards and monitoring of professional behaviour? The heterogeneity of its membership undeniably complicates the situation, especially now that so many qualified economists are employed in nonacademic positions. Yet this also reinforces the case for a more positive policy, one that need not involve any violation of the Association's traditional nonpartisanship with respect to policy issues. If the AEA cannot or will not represent and protect the profession's collective interest, who will? Several of the other leading social science societies have taken a more open and active positive stand on these issues of professional concern.[40]

This is certainly not the place to initiate yet another discussion of the relationship between positive and normative elements in economics, or the links between theory and policy. Nor is it implied that in scholarly and scientific affairs majority rule should decide, even if voting is restricted to what has been called 'the community of the competent' (Haskell 1977). Nevertheless there is a practical issue that should not be evaded, given the repeated efforts to persuade the AEA's executive committee to adopt more positive policies with respect to public policy. As Secretary Bell, a cautious man (like most of the secretaries), conceded in 1947:

> The Association cannot keep aloof from public issues. We are gradually working our way into a pattern of keeping the Association's skirts clean while enabling its members to be more active in matters of public policy.
>
> [Bell to Douglas, 22 Feb. 1947]

As the executive committee reported in 1961, the dilemma has been that the Association has not been organized to undertake 'professional jobs', although in many respects it is the most appropriate body to do so (Proceedings 1961, p. 597), and the pressure to expand its activities has increased recently. Only two years ago the executive committee proposed that some of the prospective financial surplus should be utilized for 'a portfolio of projects essentially dealing with the American economics profession as it relates to the rest of the world' (Proceedings 1984, p. 431), a form of words that few could regard as unduly restrictive. In the event, although various proposals were advanced, none met with 'general approbation' in that body. This is hardly surprising, given the committee's constantly changing membership, which reduces the incentive for decision making and long-range policy planning.

What, it may be asked, should the AEA do for the economics profession that it is not already doing? It is surely not the historian's duty to answer this question, but it is appropriate to recall some of the suggestions referred to in the preceding pages, such as: the certification of economists; the accreditation of economics courses; improvement of the preparation of economists for the public service; the defence of members suffering from infringements of academic freedom or discrimination of any kind; the publication of consensus statements or expert reports on current policy issues; additional informational activities and improvement of employment facilities, hiring practices, etc. These are perennial questions, raised again and again. They deserve deliberate and systematic review by the Association, together with a public restatement of its position. A less controversial activity in conformity with the AEA's original statement of principles, one not mentioned previously here but repeatedly raised by groups of members, is the sponsoring of research projects, including efforts to coordinate existing research activities and to raise funds for substantive projects currently being neglected.[41] The reluctance to move the Association's offices to Washington, DC, or to establish an outpost there, has undoubtedly limited the AEA's collective capacity to make an impact on public thinking and action; nevertheless, the possibility of influencing public thinking and action is still alive. Indeed one of the most novel developments in recent years has been the AEA's participation in the Consortium of Social Science Associations (COSSA) formed in 1982, in order to lobby against prospective cuts in the federal social science research budget. Such action might well have been deemed inappropriate or unconstitutional fifty years ago.

CODA

Like the disciplinary profession it represents, the AEA is constantly evolving in response to a changing environment, and the past affords no secure guide to the future. The Association may not have been active enough to suit some tastes, but the volume and variety of activities have expanded remarkably, especially since World War II. If more needs to be done, the remedy lies in the members' hands. The beginning of a new century is surely a good time to re-examine the Association's strategy.

As Ely recalled in his understandably complacent and characteristically egocentric address at the fiftieth anniversary celebration (Ely 1936), fewer than fifty people attended the inaugural meeting; he began with a single office, 12 by 20 feet, which served as the locus of the secretarial, editorial, and publishing functions; he enjoyed no remuneration or personal assistance; and he was advised that economics constituted no foundation for a career! Few would choose to return to that shoestring era. Moreover, there is something heartwarming about Ely's continuing exuberance. At the semicentennial celebration, despite his 81 years, he had two children under five by his second marriage. Geriatric philoprogenitiveness is not, of course, an index of scientific fecundity; if inspiration for the collective purpose is needed, we must, above all, look to the Association's future rather than to its past. The beginning of a new century is surely a good time to consider the prospect before us.

NOTES

* This essay is part of a general unofficial history of the Association. The views expressed are the author's.

I wish to record my appreciation of the financial support received from the executive committee and the invaluable cooperation and advice provided by several present and past officers and editors.

1 There is a vast and ever-increasing literature on the definition, functions, and growth of professions in modern society which can only be hinted at here. For the present purpose it is sufficient to follow the current convention and treat the AEA as a professional organization without trying to place it exactly on the learned society–fully professional continuum. As will become clear, the AEA's founder-members were certainly aspiring professionals, whereas their post-1945 successors have obviously been reluctant to pursue professional goals to the fullest extent possible. Few present-day nonacademic economists are strictly independent professionals; many economists are employees in bureaucratic organizations, including educational institutions; and the precise status of non-unionized academics vis-à-vis university and college administrators, presidents, and boards of trustees has long been the subject of controversy and conflict. No reference will be made here to the professionalization of academic economists in business schools, who are presumably more vocationally oriented than those in liberal arts divisions of universities, although the subject might repay investigation. For useful introductions to the literature on professions, in addition to the sources cited below, see Parsons 1968; Millerson 1964; Vollmer and Mills 1966; and Goode 1957.

2 Johnson (1972, p. 15). According to Magali Larson (1978, p. xvii), professionalization involves 'an attempt to translate one order of scarce resources – specialized knowledge and skills – into another – social and economic rewards. To maintain scarcity implies a tendency to monopoly; monopoly of expertise in the market, monopoly of status in the system of stratification.' As will appear later, economists have become increasingly aware of these considerations during the past half century or so.

3 For pertinent reservations about the application of the term *professional* to late-nineteenth-century American academics, see Veysey, 1979.

4 (Brubacher and Rudy 1976; Veysey 1965; Metzger 1985.) According to the official US Historical Statistics, the number of institutions of higher education grew from 563 in 1870, to 977 in 1900, and 1,041 in 1920. Concurrently the number of faculty expanded from 5,553 to 23,868 and 48,615, respectively, while the number of Ph.D. degrees granted increased from 1, to 382, and 615.

5 The German universities' preeminence in scholarly and scientific research was

widely recognized in the later nineteenth century. Between 1865 and 1900 thousands of young Americans went to Germany for advanced study, and many qualified for a German Ph.D. degree. Yet despite the powerful German intellectual impact on American academic life (Herbst 1965; Dorfman 1955), and the influence of German models on Johns Hopkins, MIT (via the *Technische Hochschule*), and the early business schools, no general effort was made to replicate the German university structure and curriculum, its relationship to the state, or its élitism.

6 Notable examples among the AEA's early officers were Franklin Giddings (a vice-president) and Edward A. Ross (secretary), who became leading sociologists, and Charles H. Hull (treasurer) who was primarily a historian.

7 Higham 1965, p. 20. There is a somewhat different account of this period in Link, 1985.

8 Curiously enough, 1895 was also an anxious time for the AEA's leaders, owing to a threatened regional split of membership largely, but not wholly, for geographical reasons (Coats 1960).

9 A proposal to elect a businessman as president was seriously considered in 1899, but not implemented. Some nonacademic members made significant contributions in the early years, giving papers at annual meetings or serving as council members or vice-presidents, and one, Frederick B. Hawley, a New York merchant and cotton broker, was treasurer from 1891 to 1895. But the academic constituency remained firmly in control and there was never a hint of a takeover by the nonacademics. By 1909, when the two Associations met jointly to celebrate their quarter century, the AHA's membership was about 2,500, almost twice as large as the AEA's.

10 A scheme to locate the AEA's operations at the Brookings Institution was carefully explored, but the fact that Brookings was a policy-oriented organization was an obvious deterrent. The proposal to establish a consolidated editorial and administrative headquarters either in Washington (but not at Brookings) or elsewhere was approved in principle and was actively explored throughout the 1930s, though nothing eventually came of it. As noted later, the *American Economic Review* was edited from Washington during World War II, but this was strictly a temporary arrangement.

11 By the end of the 1890s the economics profession was 'national, hierarchically organized, and dominated by senior, mostly eastern economists in major universities. Standardized professionalization procedures gave the leading professors a large measure of control over the mobility and advancement of junior scholars. A maturing network of communications through organizations and journals that were accepted both within the profession and outside it as authentic forums for professional economists gave even more authority to the top academics in important schools who selected editors and officers' (Furner 1975, p. 258).

12 Coats 1960; Ely 1887, 1936, 1938. An earlier, more detailed draft prospectus for a Society for the Study of National Economy had already been circulated in 1885 by Edmund J. James and Simon N. Patten of the University of Pennsylvania, under the influence of James' mentor, Johannes Conrad, a founder of the *Verein für Sozialpolitik*. However, this prospectus was far too Germanic and interventionist to gain sufficiently widespread support. Its sponsors accordingly backed Ely's scheme (Fox 1967; Dorfman 1949; Furner 1975).

13 Ely's management of the AEA's affairs was highly personal. As Ely advised his young successor, Edward A. Ross, in 1892: 'You will find that you never make any headway if you submit minor matters . . . to the Executive committee. You must go ahead and do a great many things on your own responsibility, this is

465

what I did, and what I think everyone does who is successful in such positions' (Rader 1966, p. 39). Ely proselytized both for the Association and for various reform causes, earning high praise from social gospel clergy, severe criticism from conservative commentators, and embarrassing his academic peers. For example, he identified socialism with Christianity and informed the working class that 'Christ and all Christly people are with you'; and his mild criticisms of organized labour were overshadowed by his exaggerated commendation of the Knights of Labor published in the year of the Haymarket bomb incident (ibid., ch. 3).

14 President of MIT, formerly a Civil War general, head of the Federal Bureau of Statistics, superintendent of the Census, and professor of political economy at the Sheffield Scientific School affiliated with Yale University, Walker was the perfect choice as titular head of the AEA for its first seven years. In addition to his established international standing as an economist he linked the 'old' and 'new' generations. Moreover he was very critical of the established laissez-faire orthodoxy, and he strongly welcomed 'such moral support from fellow workers in political economy as might come from formal association and concerted action'. Francis A. Walker to Ely, 30 Apr. 1884, in AEA archives (Coats 1960, p. 558; Newton 1968).

15 Adams, Andrews (president of Brown at the time), Bemis, Commons, and E. A. Ross (whose case is referred to later) were either dismissed or obliged to leave. Ely survived a public investigation of his conduct and views. The best introductions to the voluminous literature on these cases are Furner 1975; Hofstadter and Metzger 1955.

16 In many ways the Ross case was a freak. An able, highly regarded, and well-connected scholar, Ross's flamboyant style, refusal to heed warnings from friends and colleagues, and wilful flaunting of the university authority's ban on political activities made him an obvious target for Mrs Stanford, the university's most influential trustee and virtual proprietor. Yet in speaking out for free silver and against coolie immigration, and in forecasting public ownership of the railroads, Ross was dealing with topics within the range of his professional competence. Both his determination to publicize the reasons for his dismissal and his ambivalent relationship with President Jordan were further unusual features of the affair (Hofstadter and Metzger 1955; Furner 1975; Ross 1936).

The American interpretation of academic freedom differed significantly from the German conception, from which it was derived. It focused on freedom of teaching rather than research, emphasized the professor's expertise, and stressed freedom for extramural utterances as an aspect of civil liberty rather than merely a professional prerogative (Hofstadter and Metzger 1955). Unlike several other national social science associations, the AEA, as an organization, has never made formal statements on these matters on behalf of its members.

17 The letters and resolution to appoint a committee are in the *American Economic Review*, Mar. 1913, *3*(2), pp. 255–8; Mar. 1914, *4*(2), pp. 197, 199; Dec. 1914, *4*(4), p. 534. For the context see Metzger 1973, pp. 146–8.

18 The first report to the AAUP by the Committee on Academic Freedom and Academic Tenure was printed in the *American Economic Review*, Mar. 1916, *6*(2), pp. 230–6.

19 Coats 1969. During this period the diversity of beliefs and interests among the AEA's members and their wide geographical dispersion led to persistent disagreements about the choice of location for the annual meeting, which reflected dissatisfaction with the disproportionate influence of the leading eastern academic institutions. In 1895 there was even the threat of a regional split in

the Association (Coats 1960). The decision to launch the *Review* rather than to convert one of the existing journals into an Association publication was generally seen as an assertion of national as against local and sectional interests.

However, Edwin R. A. Seligman, a balanced man and a strong supporter of the Association, feared that the establishment of an AEA periodical would be divisive, and 'entirely at variance with the scientific spirit which has animated us all in giving editorial duty to the Association' (Seligman to Henry W. Farnam, 30 Nov. 1902, AEA Papers). He may have been influenced by the fact that his own university, Columbia, published the *Political Science Quarterly* which frequently included articles on economics.

20 Dewey aimed to publish articles on 'subjects of immediate and widespread interest . . . treated by seasoned minds in a scholarly way' rather than theory, which was the province of the *Quarterly Journal of Economics*. His belief that 'we have been living too much on theoretical hypotheses in the past, and there is a vast amount of testing to be done before we are going to make substantial progress in understanding the economic structure' has a distinctly modern sound (quotations from editorial correspondence in Coats 1969, pp. 59–60).

21 For instance, the proposals to classify civil service personnel between economists of various grades and noneconomists, or to distinguish between professional and nonacademic economists.

22 The practice of electing the president, vice-presidents, executive committee, and representatives on the Social Science Council and the American Council of Learned Societies by mail ballot from a list of nominees submitted to members by the nominating committee was introduced in 1933, in response to a petition initiated by Morris Copeland with 127 signatures presented at the annual meeting the previous year. This was evidently a delayed response to accumulated dissatisfaction with the existing procedure whereby the committee, selected by the president, had presented a list of candidates to the annual meeting, one for each vacancy. Although members could make suggestions to the nominating committee, whose names were published in the June *AER*, complainants argued that there should be a choice of candidates and an opportunity for members to express their preferences, whether or not they attended the meeting. In 1923 Paul Douglas's proposal that Veblen should be elected president had led the executive committee to appoint a special subcommittee to consider alternative electoral procedures, but they proposed no change. In 1925 a petition with 220 signatures, many of them of leading AEA members, proposed Veblen's election, even though he was not an Association member and was regarded by some as a philosopher or sociologist rather than an economist. However, Veblen declined the offer, and efforts to create the position of honorary president for him or to organize an AEA-sponsored festschrift came to naught (Proceedings 1924, p. 154; 1925, p. 126; 1926, p. 329; 1934, pp. 186–8, 192; Dorfman 1934, 1973).

One concern with the new system was that good candidates, if defeated once, would not be willing to run again for office. This appears to have happened in some cases. The records suggest that there had been only one actively contested election for the presidency under the old regime.

23 On the basis of the evidence in the Association's records – which though full, may be incomplete – there is no reason to doubt either that the committee performed its work thoroughly and conscientiously, or that it reached a just verdict. One complication was that the principal charges did not refer to the Association's own publications, and as ex-Secretary Frederick S. Deibler wrote to President Arthur F. Burns, 8 May 1959: 'The implication that the officers of

the Association are in some way guardians of the unpublished ideas of its members is beyond me' (AEA Papers).

Nevertheless, it seems clear that the Association adopted a half-hearted policy, neither rejecting the case on the grounds that such an investigation would exceed its proper functions, as in an earlier instance, nor, once it decided on action, undertaking a full-scale judicial type of inquiry. The proceedings dragged on into 1963, and although justice was probably done, it could hardly be seen to be done (Proceedings 1960, p. 622; 1963, p. 690).

24 Members of both groups began to appear on the list of presidents from the early 1960s.

25 King's proposal met with a decidedly mixed reception from members of the editorial board; consequently Dewey decided against publication. Homan wrote: 'King's procedure is absurd, and the fact that a certain number of persons have assented to a few elementary propositions has no signficance whatever. . . . The report seems to me to have no scientific value and to represent a corruption of the quantitative method.' Albert B. Wolfe, subsequently president of the AEA, agreed that the sample of opinion was unrepresentative, adding, 'When King submitted the first questionnaire to me I sized the whole thing up as being cooked up by the bunch of busy bodies in the New York University and that is still the way I regard it' (Homan to Dewey, July n.d., and 31 Aug. 1934; Wolfe to Dewey, 1 Aug. 1934, both in AEA Papers). It was reported that King eventually published a booklet entitled *A Handbook of Accepted Economics*, but it was not reviewed in the *AER*.

26 There is no systematic study of the role of economists in the federal government during or since the New Deal. One curious incident worth noting was the inclusion in a deficiency appropriations act of Congress for the Office of Price Administration of a clause stating that an executive officer formulating policies must have business experience. For a sample of economists' reactions to this anti-academic move see Nussbaum and Schweitzer 1943, pp. 906–7; Lonigan 1944, pp. 356–8.

27 The study of graduate education was published by Howard Bowen in the *AER*, Sept. 1953.

28 Lazarsfeld and Thielens 1958; McIver 1955; Stewart 1950. For an account of the difficulties faced by one future AEA president and Nobel prizewinner, see Brazer 1982. I wish to thank Mark Perlman for bringing this story to my attention.

29 Merle Curti to Bell, 15 May 1941; Bell to Curti, 20 May 1941, in AEA papers. In 1946 Bell had rejected a plea for intervention when Major Glenn McConagha of the US Air Force pointed out that the *Chicago Tribune* and certain other newspapers had published so-called 'perversive' passages from the text he was using. Bell turned to President Joseph S. Davis for advice, saying that even if the Association chose to act as a body it could not do so quickly enough; but he suggested that some of the past presidents might be consulted (McConagha to Bell, 26 Sept. 1946; Bell to McConagha, 3 Oct. 1946; Bell to Davis, 3 Oct. 1946, AEA Papers). It appears that no action was taken.

30 'It is distressing that so many politicians, administrators of colleges and universities, and even some academic scholars lack the perception and the historical knowledge to understand why oath requirements, and non-disloyalty oaths in particular, are offensive to supporters of academic freedom. . . . They do not understand that it is demoralizing for a student to derive pecuniary advantages from affirming that he does not hold subversive beliefs; that it is inconsistent with the impartial search for truth to be by oath "committed" in favor of or in

opposition to particular positions; that an institution of higher learning ought to refuse the admission of students who have "forsworn" any beliefs or attitudes, even if the teachers themselves have come to reject these beliefs or attitudes; that an oath should never be taken lightly and that the requirement to sign a series of affidavits over the years cannot but help reducing the respect for affirmations under oath; that loyalty to the principles of American government can never be shown by taking a loyalty oath, or a non-disloyalty oath, but only by rejecting the imposition of belief oaths' (Proceedings 1960, p. 114).

31 Sweezy, longtime editor of the *Monthly Review*, and widely respected in the academic profession, was one of the two most distinguished American Marxist economists at the time.

32 The membership rose from 2,301 in 1920 to 4,145 in 1945 and reached a peak of over 26,000 (including subscribers) in 1983. In that year the Association's operations revenue exceeded $1.7 million and its total securities and cash stood at $3,225,960. The AEA's investments had risen from $4,000 (at cost) to $103,000 (market value) by 1945 and passed the half million mark by 1967.

33 For example, one member of the executive committee wondered whether in securing car rental discounts for its members the Association was demonstrating a 'trend towards commercialism' (Proceedings 1981, p. 436). Earlier there were those who thought that the introduction of group insurance for members was inconsistent with the purposes of a professional association (Proceedings 1967, p. 681).

34 As in the Ross case, a semiofficial meeting was organized to enable the members, including the then current president, to express their feelings without, it was hoped, compromising the Association. But of course here, as elsewhere, this practice eliminated the possibility of bringing the Association's weight and authority, as a body, to bear on either side of the issue (Proceedings 1979, pp. 337-8, 380-1; 1980, pp. 429-30).

35 One would have thought the provision of facilities for contacts between economist job seekers and employers an uncontroversial activity, but at one time several members protested at the decision to use state rather than private employment agencies.

36 In a characteristically witty and penetrating dissection of the TV programme citing numerous passages likely to be objectionable to many economists, George J. Stigler lamented the AEA's sponsorship. Curiously enough, more than twenty years earlier he had acknowledged that one of the aims of teaching was to engage in 'discreet propaganda for "good" economics'. Evidently here, as elsewhere, the quest for consensus had not yet reached its goal (Proceedings 1963, p. 653; 1940, p. 419).

37 The following examples, from a large and stimulating recent literature, must suffice for the present purpose: Barbash 1982; Canterbery and Burkhardt 1983; Eagly 1974; Leijonhufvud 1973; Ward 1972. Charges of this kind have been staple features of institutionalist and Marxist writings. Nowadays they have more substantial documentary backing.

38 Would it be sexist to note the occasional emotive references to the 'bleak', 'distressing', and 'disheartening' conditions the committee encountered, and its supporters' 'warm' and 'wonderful' responses? Alongside this must be set the research organized by the committee and the volume of new publications it has produced or encouraged. In a year when the AEA has its first woman president-elect it is interesting to note that women figured much more prominently in the American economics profession up to the early 1920s than during the interwar years (Libby 1981, 1984).

Like the women, the blacks have provided, through the National Economic Association, valuable data on the supply of economists from their own group (Simms and Swinton 1981).

39 Hughes 1965. This citation seems especially apt given Ely's view at the inaugural meeting, that 'it is difficult to win support for an organization that professes nothing'. The principles of nonpartisanship and avoidance of policy statements have, some would argue, precluded the association from 'professions' of scientific principle and practice to which its members are entitled.

40 Orlans 1973, ch. 3. For recent reviews of the situation with respect to professional ethics see Winkler 1985; also more generally, Abbott 1983. The contention that economists are 'a bunch of kept cats' (to cite a session title from a regional economic association some years ago) is obviously debatable. It is effectively argued in Herman 1982, who claims that the demand for economic expertise has recently become increasingly 'conclusion- or ideology-specific' (p. 284). Similar complaints have also been made of the natural sciences. Relevant here is the AEA's reluctance to confront this issue openly and systematically, despite repeated proposals that it should do so.

41 The sponsoring of research projects was seriously considered in the late 1920s and early 1930s, and again, in a somewhat different form, during the past decade.

REFERENCES

Abbott, A. 'Professional Ethics', *Amer. J. Soc.*, 1983, *88*(5), pp. 855–85.

American Economic Association, Papers, Northwestern U.

Barbash, J. 'The Guilds of Academe', *Challenge*, Mar./Apr. 1982, *25*(1), pp. 50–4.

Bernard, L. L. and Bernard, J. *Origins of American Sociology: The Social Science Movement in the United States*. NY: Thomas Crowell, 1943.

Bloland, H. G. and Bloland, S. M. *American Learned Societies in Transition. The Impact of Dissent and Recession*. A report prepared for the Carnegie Commission on Higher Education. NY: McGraw-Hill, 1974.

Bowen, H. 'Graduate Education and Economics', *Am. Econ. Rev.*, Sept. 1953, *43*(4), pp. 1–223.

Brazer, M. C. 'The Economics Department of the University of Michigan: A Centennial Retrospective', in *Economics and the World Around it*. Ed.: S. H. Hymans. Ann Arbor: U. of Mich. Press, 1982, pp. 133–279.

Brubacher, J. S. and Rudy, W. *Higher Education in Transition. A History of American Colleges and Universities 1636–1976*. NY: Harper & Row, 1976.

Canterbery, E. R. and Burkhardt, R. 'What Do We Mean by Asking Whether Economics Is a Science?' in *Why Economics Is Not Yet a Science*. Ed.: A. S. Eichner. NY: M. E. Sharpe, 1983.

Church, R. L. 'Economists as Experts: The Rise of an Academic Profession in the United States, 1870–1920', in *The University in Society*. Vol. II. *Europe, Scotland and the United States from the Sixteenth to the Twentieth Century*. Ed.: L. Stone. Princeton, NJ: Princeton U. Press, 1974.

Coats, A. W. 'The First Two Decades of the American Economic Association', *Amer. Econ. Rev.*, Sept. 1960, *50*(4), pp. 555–74. Reprinted in this volume, pp. 205–24.

——— .'The Political Economy Club: A Neglected Episode in American Economic Thought', *Amer. Econ. Rev.*, Sept. 1961, *51*(4), pp. 624–37. Reprinted in this volume, pp. 225–38.

——— . 'The American Economic Association, 1904–29', *Amer. Econ. Rev.*, June 1964, *54*(4), pp. 261–85. Reprinted in this volume, pp. 239–63.

——— . 'Henry Carter Adams: A Case Study in the Emergence of the Social Sciences in the United States, 1850–1900', *J. Amer. Stud.*, 1968, *2*, pp. 177–97. Reprinted in vol. I in this series.

——— . 'The American Economic Association's Publications: An Historical Perspective', *J. Econ. Lit.*, Mar. 1969, *7*(1), pp. 57–68. Reprinted in this volume, pp. 264–79.

Dorfman, J. *Thorstein Veblen and His America*. NY: Viking Press, 1934.

——— . *The Economic Mind in American Civilization*. Vols III–V. NY: Viking Press, 1949, 1959.

——— . 'The Role of the German Historical School in American Economic Thought', *Amer. Econ. Rev.*, May 1955, *45*(2), pp. 17–28.

——— . *Thorstein Veblen: Essays, Reviews, Reports. Previously Uncollected Writings*. Clifton, NJ: Augustus Kelley, 1973.

Eagly, R. V. 'Contemporary Profile of Conventional Economists', *Hist. Polit. Econ.*, 1974, *6*(1), pp. 76–91.

Ely, R. T. 'Report of the Organization of the American Economic Association', *Publications Amer. Econ. Assn.*, First Ser., Mar. 1887, *1*, pp. 5–46.

——— . 'The Founding and Early History of the American Economic Association', *Amer. Econ. Rev.*, Mar. 1936, *26*(1), pp. 141–50.

——— . *Ground under Our Feet*. NY: Macmillan, 1938.

Everett, J. R. *Religion in Economics, A Study of John Bates Clark, Richard T. Ely and Simon Nelson Patten*. NY: King's Crown Press, 1946.

Fetter, F. A. 'Economists and the Public', *Amer. Econ. Rev.*, Mar. 1925, *15*(1), pp. 13–26.

Fine, S. *Laissez-Faire and the General Welfare State. A Study of Conflict in American Thought, 1865–1901*. Ann Arbor: U. of Mich. Press, 1964.

Fox, D. M. *The Discovery of Abundance – Simon N. Patten and the Transformation of Social Theory*. Ithaca, NY: Cornell U. Press, 1967.

Furner, M. O. *Advocacy and Objectivity: A Crisis in the Professionalization of American Social Science, 1865–1905*. Lexington: U. of Kentucky Press, 1975.

Goode, W. J. 'Community within a Community: The Professions', *Amer. Soc. Rev.*, Apr. 1956, *22*(2), pp. 194–200.

——— . 'Encroachment, Charlatanism and the Emerging Professions: Psychology, Sociology, Medicine', *Amer. Soc. Rev.*, Dec. 1960, *25*(6), pp. 902–14.

Haskell, T. L. *The Emergence of Professional Social Science. The American Social Science Association and the Nineteenth Century Crisis of Authority*. Urbana, IL: U. of Illinois Press, 1977.

Hawkins, H. *Pioneer: A History of the Johns Hopkins University, 1874–1899*. Ithaca, NY: Cornell U. Press, 1960.

Herbst, J. *The German Historical School in American Scholarship. A Study in the Transfer of Culture*. Ithaca, NY: Cornell U. Press, 1965.

Herman, E. S. 'The Institutionalization of Bias in Economics', *Media, Culture and Society*, July 1982, *4*, pp. 275–91.

Higham, J. *History. Professional Scholarship in America*. NY: Harper Torchbooks, 1965.

——— . 'The Matrix of Specialization', in *The Organization of Knowledge in America 1860–1920*. Eds: A. Oleson and J. Voss. Baltimore: Johns Hopkins U. Press, 1979, pp. 3–18.

Hofstadter, R. *Social Darwinism in American Thought*. Rev. ed. Boston: Beacon Press, 1955.

——— . *Anti-Intellectualism in American Life*. NY: Knopf, 1969.

——— and Metzger, W. P. *The Development of Academic Freedom in the United States*. NY: Columbia U. Press, 1955.

Homan, P. 'Economics in the War Period', *Amer. Econ. Rev.*, Dec. 1946, *36*(2), pp. 855–71.

Hughes, E. C. 'Professions', in *The Professions in America*. Ed.: K. Lynn. Boston: Houghton Mifflin, 1965.

Johnson, T. J. *Professions and Power*. London: Macmillan, 1972.

Kiger, J. C. *American Learned Societies*. Washington, DC: Public Affairs Press, 1963.

Larson, M. S. *The Rise of Professionalism: A Sociological Analysis*. Berkeley: University of California Press, 1978.

Lazarsfeld, P. F. and Thielens, W. Jr. *The Academic Mind. Social Scientists in a Time of Crisis*. Glencoe, IL: The Free Press, 1958.

Leijonhufvud, A. 'Life among the Econ', *Western Econ. J.*, Sept. 1973, *11*(3), pp. 327–37.

Libby, B. S. 'American Women Economists before 1925'. Unpublished paper presented at the History of Economics Society meeting, 1981.

——— . 'Women in Economics before 1940', in *Essays Econ. Bus. Hist.*, Vol. III. Ed.: J. Soltow. 1984.

Link, A. S. 'The American Historical Association, 1884–1984: Retrospect and Prospect', *Amer. Hist. Rev.*, Feb. 1985, *90*(1), pp. 1–17.

Lonigan, E. 'The Professors *versus* the People: Comment', *Amer. Econ. Rev.*, June 1944, *34*(2), pp. 356–8.

McIver, R. *Academic Freedom in Our Time*. NY: Columbia U. Press, 1955.

Metzger, W. P. 'Academic Tenure in America: An Historical Essay', in *Faculty Tenure*. A Report and Recommendations by the Commission on Academic Tenure in Higher Education. W. R. Keast, Chairman. San Francisco: Jossey Bass, 1973.

——— . 'The Academic Profession in the United States', in *The Academic Profession*. National Disciplinary and Institutional Settings. Ed.: B. R. Clark. Berkeley: University of California Press, 1987, pp. 123–208.

America'. Unpub. ms.

Millerson, G. *The Qualifying Associations*. London: Routledge & Kegan Paul, 1964.

Newton, B. *The Economics of Frances Amasa Walker: American Economics in Transition*. NY: A. M. Kelley, 1968.

Nussbaum, F. L. and Schweitzer, A. 'The Professors *versus* the People', *Amer. Econ. Rev.*, Dec. 1943, *33*(4), pp. 906–7.

O'Connor, M. J. L. *Origins of Academic Economics in the United States*. NY: Columbia U. Press, 1953.

Oleson, A. and Voss, J. *The Organization of Knowledge in America 1860–1920*. Baltimore: Johns Hopkins U. Press, 1979.

Orlans, H. *Contracting for Knowledge*. San Francisco: Jossey Bass, 1973.

Parrish, J. B. 'Rise of Economics as an Academic Discipline: The Formative Years to 1900', *Southern Econ. J.*, July 1967, *34*(1), pp. 1–16.

Parsons, T. 'Professions', in *International Encyclopedia of the Social Sciences*. NY: Macmillan, 1968. Vol. 12, pp. 536–47.

Proceedings and Papers, *American Economic Review*.

Rader, B. J. *The Academic Mind and Reform: The Influence of Richard T. Ely in American Life*. Lexington, KY: U. of Kentucky Press, 1966.

Reynolds, L. 'The Efficiency of Education in Economics: Discussion', *Amer. Econ. Rev.*, May 1969, *59*(2), pp. 239–40.

Ross, D. 'Socialism and American Liberalism: Academic Social Thought in the 1880s', in *Perspectives in American History*, vol. XI, 1977–8, pp. 7–79.

——— . 'The Development of the Social Sciences', in *The Organization of Knowledge in America 1860–1920*. Eds: A. Oleson and J. Voss. Baltimore: Johns Hopkins U. Press, 1979, pp. 107–38.

Ross, E. A. *Seventy Years of It: An Autobiography*. NY: Appleton Century, 1936.

Sims, M. C. and Swinton, D. H. 'A Report on the Supply of Black Economists', *Rev. Black Polit. Econ.*, Winter 1981, *11*(2), pp. 181–202.

Stewart, G. R. *The Year of the Oath*. Garden City: Doubleday, 1950.

Stigler, G. J. 'Round Table on Problems in the Teaching of Economics', *Amer. Econ. Rev.*, Feb. 1941, *30*(5), pp. 416–21.

——— . 'Elementary Economic Education', *Amer. Econ. Rev.*, May 1963, *53*(2), pp. 653–9.

Veblen, T. *The Higher Learning in America. A Memorandum on the Conduct of Universities by Businessmen*. NY: B. W. Huebsch, 1918.

Veysey, L. R. *The Emergence of the American University*. Chicago: U. of Chicago Press, 1965.

——— . 'The Plural Organized Worlds of the Humanities', in *The Organization of Knowledge in America 1860–1920*. Eds: A. Oleson and J. Voss. Baltimore: Johns Hopkins U. Press, 1979, pp. 51–106.

Vollmer, H. M. and Mills, D. L. eds. *Professionalization*. Englewood Cliffs, NJ: Prentice Hall, 1966.

Ward, B. *What's Wrong with Economics?* NY: Basic Books, 1972.

Winkler, K. J. 'Brouhaha over Historians' Use of Sources Renews Scholars' Interest in Ethics Codes', *Chronicle of Higher Education*, Feb. 1985, *29*(21), pp. 9–10.

24

THE MARKET FOR
ECONOMISTS IN BRITAIN,
1945–75

A preliminary survey*

> If the proper study of mankind is man, then the proper study of
> market economists is surely the market for economists. In decrying
> the imperfections of other product and labor markets, we would be
> delinquent without an occasional look at our own.
>
> (Somers, 1962, p. 509)

By contrast with their American counterparts, British economists have
displayed remarkably little systematic interest in the market for their
services. It is tempting to attribute this to complacency, for there has been
a sustained high demand for professional economists from universities,
government and business throughout most of the post-war period; however,
the same is broadly true of the USA and many other countries. In part,
the Anglo-American difference reflects the backward state of manpower
and planning studies in Britain, where the first official *Survey of Qualified
Manpower* (1971) must be set against the US National Register of Scientific
and Technical Personnel, which has provided comprehensive data on compensation since 1964, and the National Professional Register, containing
information on ages, employment and salaries of professional economists.
The antecedents of these sources can be traced back at least to the early
1940s. Beyond this, however, there is a sociological explanation (Williams,
Blackstone and Metcalf, 1974, p. 13), for American scientists and scholars
generally have been better organized and more self-conscious professionally
than their transatlantic peers. In the case of economics this is evident from
a comparison of the founding and early history of the American Economic
Association and the Royal Economic Society (Coats, 1960, 1964, 1968);
while more recently and specifically, the American profession's market
orientation has been apparent ever since the first Round Table Conference
on the subject at the 1958 AEA meeting.[1]

British economists may, perhaps, have been deterred by the difficulties
of defining an 'economist' or an 'economics profession', whereas the AEA
undertook this task, albeit somewhat reluctantly, in response to the Federal

Government's wartime decision to establish a Roster for Scientific Personnel. Indeed, a major recent study of American economists' salaries provided a systematic analysis of seven different definitions of an economist based on coded data derived from National Register questionnaires (Tolles and Molichar, 1968).[2]

The absence of accepted definitions and adequate data on the British situation creates obvious difficulties. For the present purpose the principal requirements for inclusion in the economics profession are an academic qualification in the subject (as a minimum entry condition) and a job title which acknowledges the specialism. Both criteria present problems, but no more sophisticated definition can be realistically applied to the patchy and inconclusive information available. Job descriptions or labels are dependent on personnel practices, which may be unsatisfactory for scholarly purposes, while intractable difficulties arise from the need to prescribe occupational and disciplinary boundaries, e.g. between economics and statistics. The mathematization of economics and the growth of econometrics have increased the substitutability of economists and statisticians for some purposes; yet it is advisable not to blur the distinction, because the history of the two professions has differed markedly and the inclusion of statisticians within economics would simply raise further borderline problems, e.g. affecting mathematicians, operations researchers, accountants, etc. Consequently statisticians have been excluded, apart from economist/statistician private sector posts in the section on salaries.

I THE SUPPLY OF ECONOMISTS

The first task is to examine the available data on degrees in economics or related subjects, as a basis for estimating the potential supply of recruits for 'professional' employment.

Table 1 shows the output of university degrees in economics and related subjects for the academic years 1949/50 to 1974/5. Unfortunately there is no consistent post-war series and there are serious difficulties in interpreting the data. Some universities (notably Oxford) offer no single honours economics degree, and the 'economics' content of single honours degrees, not to mention joint honours, has differed markedly from time to time and place to place. Thus the early post-war London University B.Sc. (Econ.), which was awarded externally by several provincial University Colleges, was an umbrella social science course with variable doses of economics. The apparent decline in the number of economics degrees between 1950/1 and 1953/4 may reflect the replacement of London degrees by specialist provincial degrees in specific social science disciplines. More recently, the growth of economics has been accompanied by a proliferation of courses in 'applied' fields, which no longer come under the general 'economics'

Table 1 First degrees in economics and related subjects awarded by universities in the academic years 1949/50 to 1974/5

Academic year	Single Honours degrees in economics in year		Joint Honours degrees containing economics awarded in year	Degrees in PPE awarded during academic year	First degree economics students attending institutions of further education
	(1)	(2)	(3)	(4)	(5)
1949/50	427	–	102	–	–
1950/1	325	–	117	–	–
1951/2	331	–	60	–	–
1952/3	307	–	43	–	–
1953/4	275	–	54	151	–
1954/5	290	–	72	178	–
1955/6	549	–	67	165	–
1956/7	298	–	109	156	–
1957/8	600	–	112	195	–
1958/9	656	–	140	206	–
1959/60	638	–	170	191	–
1960/1	625	–	166	201	–
1961/2	687	–	175	302	–
1962/3	724	620	186	235	–
1963/4	812	753	234	245	–
1964/5	963	807	148	219	–
1965/6	–	1111	–	–	1578
1966/7	–	1385	–	–	1802
1967/8	–	1411	–	–	2065
1968/9	–	1313	–	–	2068
1969/70	–	1420	–	–	2080
1970/1	–	1895	–	–	2562
1971/2	–	2131	–	–	2673
1972/3	–	2102	–	–	2470
1973/4	–	1968	–	–	2172
1974/5	–	1859	–	–	1794

Sources: Cols 1, 3, 4: *Returns from Universities and Colleges in receipt of a Treasury Grant* (annual). Col. 2: *First Employment of University Graduates* (annual). Col. 5: *Statistics of Education*, vol. 3 (annual).

Note: Totals relate to the number of students pursuing degree courses mainly at polytechnics during the year, *not* to degrees awarded. CNAA degrees are included.

rubric. The task of disentangling the total number of 'economists' from PPE or joint honours degrees is insurmountable; and even if the various series were precise and consistent, they would not necessarily represent an actual index of recruits to the profession since many students studied the subject without reference to prospective career choices. The UGC publication, *First Employment of University Graduates* gives some impression of the percentage of single honours graduates entering the labour market[3] (cf. Table 3), and the final column, based on somewhat crude and arbitrary assumptions, suggests that less than one third of 'straight' economics graduates became professional economists (i.e. civil service, further and higher education, sections of industry and commerce). No comparable data are available for the 1950s, when the market for economists and the occupational choices facing joint honours graduates were quite different. As their training was generally wider than that of single honours graduates they probably tended to enter teaching, social work or non-professional posts,[4] either from choice or from inability to find suitable professional employment.

Table 2 Indices of post-graduate study, 1949/50 to 1974/5

Year	Full-time students of economics and applied economics engaged in work for a higher degree during the year (1)	Full-time students of PPE engaged in work for a higher degree during the year (2)	Higher degrees awarded in economics during the year (3)
1949/50	200	–	–
1950/1	182	–	–
1951/2	189	–	–
1952/3	193	–	–
1953/4	218	106	–
1954/5	229	110	–
1955/6	224	114	–
1956/7	225	143	–
1957/8	269	199	–
1958/9	262	224	–
1959/60	272	150	–
1960/1	291	180	–
1961/2	338	174	–
1962/3	335	166	93
1963/4	431	200	139
1964/5	469	219	151
1965/6	–	–	189
1966/7	–	–	281
1967/8	–	–	375
1968/9	–	–	375
1969/70	–	–	426
1970/1	–	–	395
1971/2	–	–	480
1972/3	–	–	459
1973/4	–	–	579
1974/5	–	–	606

Source: See Table 1, col. 5

Notes: Cols 1 and 2 refer to numbers of students engaged in higher study during year. Col. 3 refers to higher degrees awarded during year. In respect of part-time students it has been impossible to extract any coherent series. In the early period, we have figures only of the number of students engaged in part-time study of economics and 'near economics' in any year. It would be foolhardy to attempt to convert this into a 'full-time equivalent' series. From the mid-sixties we have data relating to the number of degrees awarded, without distinguishing the type of programme followed.

The statistics clearly demonstrate the increasing importance of a higher degree. Both the number of students engaged in further study and the number of post-graduates expanded remarkably, especially from the later 1960s, a trend noted with approval by the Civil Service Department.[5] There was a significant peak of economics post-graduates in the mid-1960s when, as shown later, the demand for professional economists was growing most rapidly (Westoby, Webster and Williams, 1976, ch. 1, also Table 2).

Making due allowance for the limitations of the data, including the changing status and number of degree-granting institutions, there was no marked upward trend of graduates in economics and 'near economics' until the mid-1950s.[6] There was, however, a considerable expansion through the sixties – a trend possibly understated, given the growth of 'applied' subjects and courses in non-university institutions – which reached a peak in 1971/2 (see Table 1). This expansion was accompanied, in the later stages, by an increasing proclivity to post-graduate study and research (cf. Table 2).

In addition to new graduates, a profession can enhance its numbers by recruiting more senior persons, a practice likely to occur in periods of sustained high demand. Such related numerate professions as accounting and banking may have provided experienced recruits, possibly with some re-training (as in the case of the Civil Service), and it is worth noting that the *Survey of Qualified Manpower* assessed the total stock of economists in 1966 at 14,000+. The basis of this estimate is unknown, though of course it would include a proportion of pre-war graduates. However, in the absence of more detailed information any such estimate must be largely guesswork.

II DEMAND

(a) From the universities

Broadly speaking, the economics profession has three main branches: academic, governmental and business.[7] While the numbers in the first two can be measured approximately, this is hardly possible for the private sector.

The data on academic economists derived from the annual *Commonwealth Universities Yearbooks* must be treated with caution (cf. Table 4). A broad definition has been adopted, including a number of subjects and descriptions which might be termed 'near economics'.[8] Only full-time university teachers of economics are included (e.g. those designated as such in Oxford and Cambridge), and double counting has been avoided where an individual is known to hold two or more posts.

Table 4 reveals a rapid expansion in the late 1940s and early 1950s, as the universities readjusted to peace time, a slower expansion to 1956, and an acceleration thereafter. There has also been a marked change in the content of economics teaching and an especially rapid growth in the number

Table 3 Distribution between further education, training and employment of students who qualified with first degrees in economics in the period 1962/3 to 1974/5

Year	Total graduating (1)	Undertaking further research or training (2)	%	Overseas students returning home (3)	%	Available for employment (4)	%	Gained home employment (5) %	Gained home employment (5)	Non-professional categories[a] (6)	Potentially in professional employment (7)	Col. 7 as a percentage of col. 1
1962/3	620	76	12	57	9	411	66	55	344	149	195	31
1963/4	753	198	26	55	7	483	64	52	390	160	230	31
1964/5	807	181	22	55	7	539	67	55	441	161	280	35
1965/6	1111	275	25	69	6	705	63	48	536	199	337	30
1966/7	1385	370	27	83	6	875	63	45	627	221	406	29
1967/8	1411	354	25	89	6	916	65	45	631	245	386	27
1968/9	1313	289	22	42	3	916	70	49	638	225	413	31
1969/70	1420	324	23	41	3	991	70	45	643	262	381	27
1970/1	1895	444	23	58	3	1283	68	38	719	391	328	17
1971/2	2131	526	25	30	1	1441	68	42 / 4	890P[b] / 83T	477	413	19
1972/3	2102	502	24	34	2	1376	66	42 / 5	874P / 101T	454	420	20
1973/4	1968	405	21	74	4	1367	70	44 / 6	859P / 110T	484	375	19
1974/5	1859	405	22	94	5	1256	68	40 / 6	836P / 106T	450	386	21

Source: University Grants Committee, First Employment of University Graduates.

Notes:

a. 'Non-professional' refers to categories of employment other than professional economists.

b. P = permanent, T = temporary.

of appointments in applied fields, a trend that would certainly appear more dramatic if colleges of technology and polytechnic posts were included.

Table 4 The number of university teaching posts in economics, 1947–74

1947	166	1961	414
1948	215	1962	429
1949	215	1963	471
1950	n.a.	1964	501
1951	254	1965	537
1952	266	1966	619
1953	286	1967	691
1954	307	1968	801
1955	320	1969	814
1956	319	1970	853
1957	323	1971	874
1958	351	1972	902
1959	367	1973	984
1960	367	1974	1031

Source: Commonwealth Universities Yearbooks.

(b) From the government

The main problem here is how to distinguish between those specifically employed as professional economists (e.g. Economic Assistants, Economic Advisers and Senior Economic Advisers) and the many civil servants with degrees in economics employed within the Administrative, Executive or Research Officer classes. During the 1960s efforts were made to concentrate the latter in such 'relevant' departments as the Treasury, Trade and Industry, Transport, Overseas Development.[9] The growth of social science university graduates has necessarily increased the proportion of these economically trained non-specialists.[10]

The Statistician Class also contains many individuals with economics qualifications, for until the comparatively recent growth of academic courses in statistics most of its recruits had studied statistics either within a mathematics or an economics programme, or by post-graduate degree or diploma.[11] The recent expansion of model building and other quantitative projects has brought civil service economists and statisticians closer together, and their contributions are sometimes virtually indistinguishable. However, official grading procedures make it possible to identify civil service professional economists *per se* fairly accurately. Table 5 reveals that the complement was fairly stable between 1945 and 1964, whereas the second half of the 1960s witnessed a dramatic expansion as the government made more intensive and extensive use of economic expertise. Prior to 1964, civil service economists tended to be fairly high level generalists based in the Economic Section of the Cabinet Office until 1953, when the Section was transferred to the Treasury. A few economists were 'bedded out' as high level general advisers in specific departments or international agencies.[12] However, under the new Labour government, from October 1964 there was a determined effort both to increase the numbers employed and to widen the range of available skills. New divisions or units were formed, and the new Departments of Economic Affairs and Overseas Development rapidly acquired substantial professional contingents. With the creation of the Government Economic Service, in January 1965, the Director of the Economic Section became responsible for all the economic specialists in government, and this represented a significant advance in the professionalization process. Towards the end of the 1960s, and more especially with the decline in the numbers and attractiveness of non-governmental employment opportunities, there was a growth of civil service career orientation and a decline in the proportion of temporary or short service staff – a proportion which had been exceptionally high in the earlier post-war decades. During the expansion phase many relatively senior and experienced economists had joined the government from universities and business, arousing expressions of discontent from some existing staff.[13] The fact that some of the newcomers had marked political sympathies with the Labour administration aroused suspicion of these 'irregulars' and fears of the politicization of professional economics in government.[14] In due course these anxieties waned; nevertheless the situation had been transformed as the Civil Service became a major consumer of economic expertise. The number of professional economists in government increased fifteenfold from 1964 to 1975, a process that has been sarcastically called Britain's 'Economics Miracle'.[15] During the same period the number of government statisticians grew more than threefold.

Table 5 also gives an indication of the numbers of agricultural economists. The figures are shown separately, in brackets, as these specialists have had a distinctive history. They were graded separately and excluded from the Government Economic Service until September 1975.[16]

(c) From business

The business community is so large and heterogeneous that there is little hope of obtaining precise data on the numbers of economists. Hence this section must necessarily be brief and sketchy. The first survey of the field,

Table 5 Economists in government, 1949–75

	Professional economists (1)		Administrators with economics degrees (2)
1945	10		–
1946	12		–
1947	14	(19)	–
1948	15		–
1949	17		–
1950	17		11
1951	19		26
1952	16	(20)	35
1953	18		42
1954	20		48
1955	18		51
1956	16		58
1957	14	(19)	66
1958	14		71
1959	12		76
1960	14		90
1961	15		} 114
1962	16		
1963	19	(25)	125
1964	21.5		142
1965	42		157
1966	76.5		–
1967	109.5		–
1968	138.5		–
1969	170.5	(34)	–
1970	236		–
1971	251		–
1972	268		–
1973	282		–
1974	n.a.		–
1975	352	(42)	–

Sources: Col. 1: Treasury, Civil Service Department, and Agricultural Departments' records. Col. 2: Treasury papers.

Notes:

Col. 1. The numbers represent individuals in post, not complements. The method of calculation was changed between 31 December 1973 and 1 January 1975. The figures in parentheses represent agricultural economists, who were separately graded up to 1 September 1975.

Col. 2. Includes only direct entrants 1950–65 and class-to-class transfers 1956–65. No allowance for retirements, deaths and resignations, or for administrators with economic degrees who entered before 1950.

by the Business Economists Group (Alexander, Kemp and Rybczynski, (1967)), drew attention to the tendency for economists to be promoted into 'general management posts', thereby exacerbating the difficulties of defining a 'business economist'. Other difficulties are the variety of functions the economist is required to fulful, and problems of career structure which impair the prospects for the emergence of a distinct profession of business economist (see pp. 53–4, 11–18 and 57).

Like the universities and government, business has absorbed increasing numbers of professional economists.[17] There was a sharp increase in demand in the immediate post-war years; a period of relative stability into the mid-1950s; and thereafter a steady expansion, which accelerated sharply towards the mid-1960s. This period also witnessed a rapid expansion in overseas demand and in the domestic demand for econometricians and statisticians.

III ECONOMISTS' SALARIES

While there are some data on economists' salaries which give an indication of general movements in demand and supply, they are insufficient to provide precise indications of relative shifts in the demand and supply of the three main categories: university, government and business.

Movements of the minimum point of the beginners' scale for university staff (Assistant Lecturer to 1969, Lecturer thereafter) are shown in Table 6, column 1. This is not, however, an accurate index of starting salaries since new appointees are paid according to age, qualifications and experience, hence the series merely reveals the trend of minimum salaries. There is, moreover, some evidence suggesting that the average level of qualifications has changed during the period, and above-minimum salaries are offered to desirable recruits in periods of scarcity.[18]

Similar problems arise in the case of government economists. Table 6, column 2 shows the minimum point on the Economic Assistant scale. The data are most reliable for the 1966–75 period, when the Civil Service first became a large scale consumer of newly graduated economists. Before that time the majority of government economists were academics employed on short-contract appointments, often with individually negotiated contracts – often including a 'disturbance allowance' in recognition of removal and other special expenses – at the Economic Adviser level. Hence Table 6 does not give a reliable indication of market conditions.

Table 6 Starting salaries for economists (£ per annum)

Year	Academic (1)	Civil servant (2)	Business (3)
1947	300	360	
1948	–	360	
1949	400	400	
1950	–	400	610
1951	–	400	
1952	–	400	
1953	–	400	
1954	–	400	
1955	550	470	615
1956	–	580	
1957	700	605	
1958	800	635	
1959	–	655	
1960	900	675	790
1961	–	750	
1962	1000	788	
1963	–	818	
1964	1050	841	
1965	1105	885	1245
1966	–	965	
1967	1240	996	
1968	–	1051	
1969	1350	1145	
1970	1491	1196	1570
1971	1641	1435	
1972	1764	1530	
1973	1929	1928	
1974	2118 }+ threshold	2229	
1975	3174 } payments	2860	3200

Notes:

Col. 1. Minimum of range for Assistant Lecturer 1947–66 and Lecturer 1966–75. *University Development, 1952–7* (Cmnd 534, 1958), *University Development, 1957–62* (Cmnd 2267, 1963), *University Development, 1962–7* (Cmnd 3820, 1969), *University Development, 1967–72* (Cmnd 5728, 1973), (1 January of year), 1973–5 from *Statistics of Education*, vol. 6.

Col. 2. Minimum of range for Economic Assistant including London weighting, from *Imperial Calendar*. (In some instances, the figures given may be out of date as a result of delays in publication.) 1971–5 figures from Civil Service Department.

Col. 3. Advertisements in *The Economist* (see text).

Even less is known about the salaries of business economists, although two indexes are provided in Tables 6 and 7 based, respectively, on a sample of job advertisements in *The Economist* and on figures provided by the Department of Employment. The *Economist* data refer to posts advertised for graduates up to 25, with no previous experience, who can be regarded as roughly equivalent to Assistant Lecturers or Economic Assistants.[19] The figures represent averages of the minimum points in the advertised salary

Table 7 Percentage change in median earnings of business economists compared with figures for all non-manual employees and for all workers

Period	Age of respondents							Approximate changes in average salaries non-manual employees (a)	Observations exceeding (a)	All worker index (b)	Observations exceeding (b)
	25 or under	26–30	31–35	36–40	41–45	46–50	50+				
1964-8	45.0	58.1	34.9	22.4	57.1	21.3	–	26.1	4/6	27.7	4/6
1968-9	24.1	10.2	15.5	8.5	5.7	13.5	–	7.9	5/6	8.3	5/6
1973-4	33.2	26.5	16.1	25.0	12.0	36.5	-2.3	11.6	6/7	13.1	5/7
1974-5	7.1	7.2	9.7	12.5	6.7	-13.8	20.0	25.6	0/7	29.2	0/7

Source: Department of Employment – based on unpublished material.

ranges and obviously cannot be regarded as constituting a representative sample – if only because many of the earlier advertisements mentioned no salary. The data in Table 7, based on Business Economist Group surveys, are derived from small and probably unrepresentative samples, and some of the respondents may have already moved from strictly 'professional' posts into general management.

Some additional insight can be derived from data on the grade structure (i.e. the proportion in each grade) of university economists, as compared with that of the whole university teaching staff.[20] The most striking feature is the relative stability of the two populations, despite the rapid increase in their size during the period, and important changes in the number and character of universities. This stability is doubtless the result of policy decisions on the part of university authorities. However two specific divergences require comment. First, there was a significant reduction in the percentage of Assistant Lecturers in Economics between 1953/4 and 1961/2, whereas no comparable trend is evident in the aggregate figures. The rate of recruitment of economists dropped perceptibly during that period, especially in 1954–7, when the number of university economists increased by only 16 (see Table 4). Two explanatory hypotheses can be suggested: (a) owing to excess demand, university economists were promoted more rapidly, possibly because the salary scales compared unfavourably with those of business economists; (b) in the aftermath of the post-war restocking boom fewer Assistant Lecturers were needed as the 'post-war bulge' worked its way up the hierarchy. In this connection the rising proportion of Senior Lecturers/Readers after 1958/9 and the relatively high proportion of Professors are noteworthy (see Table 8). Incidentally, Table 1 shows that the number of students was stagnating during this period.

The second general divergence is the sustained relatively high proportion of economist professors, possibly because they were in greater demand, both inside and outside the groves of academe, than most of their peers.

As with university staff, government economists' salaries were fixed broadly, if not exactly, in conformity with those of administrators.[21] However the numbers were so small up to the later 1960s, and the proportion of short-contract staff was so high, that a detailed comparison between economists' and administrators' salary and career structures would be pointless. The salaries of individual civil servants were published only in the early post-war years, and above minimum salaries often had to be paid to recruit staff of sufficient quality.[22] Structural comparisons can be misleading in this case because the rapid rate of growth of numbers means that in later years there was a disproportionate percentage in the junior grades. However, Tables 9 and 10 provide some basis for such a comparison.

Table 8 The career structures of university teaching staff in (a) economics and
(b) all subjects, 1953/4 to 1974/5

| | | | | | | | Assistant | |
| Year | Professor | | Senior lecturer/Reader | | Lecturer | | lecturer | |
	(a)	(b)	(a)	(b)	(a)	(b)	(a)	(b)
1953/4	16	14	14	17	51	56	19	13
1954/5	14	14	13	17	58	56	15	13
1955/6	14	14	13	17	60	56	13	12
1956/7	14	14	13	18	61	56	11	12
1957/8	15	14	15	18	62	56	8	12
1958/9	15	14	15	18	62	57	9	11
1959/60	15	13	17	19	58	56	9	12
1960/1	16	13	17	19	58	56	9	12
1961/2	15	13	21	20	53	55	12	12
1962/3	14	13	21	21	51	56	14	10
1963/4	15	13	20	21	49	55	17	11
1964/5	16	13	18	21	48	54	19	13
1965/6	15	11	20	20	· 48	54	17	15
1966/7	15	12	19	20	52	55	15	13
1967/8	14	12	18	19	50	56	17	13
1968/9	13	12	16	20	53	57	17	11
1969/70	15	12	17	20	69	68	–	–
1970/1	15	12	17	20	68	67	–	–
1971/2	15	12	17	21	68	67	–	–
1972/3	16	11	18	20	67	69	–	–
1973/4	15	11	17	21	68	67	–	–
1974/5	16	12	18	23	66	65	–	–

Source: (a) *Commonwealth Universities Yearbooks* (annual). (b) *Statistics of Education*.

Table 9 A comparison of the career structures of government economists and
government administrators

	Administrators (% in grade) (1)	Economists (% in grade) (2)
Under Secretary and above	15	12
Assistant Secretary or equivalent	32	15
Principal or equivalent	43	34
Assistant Principal or equivalent	10	38

Sources: Col. 1: *The Civil Service*, vol. 4, *Factual, Statistical and Explanatory Papers*, p. 38. (Data refer to 1 April 1967.) Col. 2: Civil Service Department, 'A Statistical Review of the Economist Class and the Employment of Economists in Government Service: pre-1960 to 1969'. (Includes seven responses in 'Not Indicated' category distributed between all groups. Data refer to 1 January 1968.)

Given the absence of institutional rigidities, salary figures for business economists should, in principle, provide a more accurate index of market conditions, and despite their limitations, the *Economist* data (Table 6,

Table 10 A comparison of career structures of government economists and government administrators

	Administrators (% in grade)	Economists (% in grade)
Under Secretary and above+	6	7
Assistant Secretary	19	15
Principal	64	40
Higher Executive Officer (A)	3	22
Administration Trainee	8	16

Source: PRISM (Personnel Record Information System for Management) Civil Service Department, 1 January 1975. These data are not strictly comparable with those listed in Table 9 owing to the post-Fulton introduction of the Open Structure

column 3) support the hypothesis that the demand for economists eased in the 1950s as university recruitment slowed down and the salary differential between business economists and administrators/lecturers narrowed. The high starting salary differential favouring business economists in the late forties also suggests that there was excess demand.

The post-1964 Department of Employment data suggest that the demand for business economists (and, by extension, all other professional economists too) was well maintained during the sixties, with rising earnings in most age groups for all three categories of economists.[23]

The inadequate primary sources can be supplemented by information on the careers of social scientists by *subject of degree* – not, it must be noted, by *occupation* (Westoby *et al.* 1976 *passim*). Responses to sample questionnaires by 1950, 1951, 1961 and 1967 graduates from 13 British universities permit comparisons of annual earnings of men with first degrees in various subject groups from 1960–72 (cf. Table 11). These show that the 1959–61 cohort started the decade of the 1960s well and were still favourably placed in 1972 relative to their contemporaries in other subjects, (Westoby *et al.* 1976 p. 11). Moreover, professional economists did usually well, even though the differential advantages had declined by comparison with the early fifties. Generally, over the post-war period economists have lost much of their salaries leadership, and in recent years market conditions have favoured their employers (with some exceptions, e.g. experienced civil service economists during the late 1960s). Table 12 reveals the occupational spread of economics graduates in the early 1970s, by which time the initial salary differential had narrowed considerably. Table 6 suggests that in the early 1950s, a time of slow university expansion, business economists' starting salaries were, perhaps, roughly 50 per cent above those in academic or government employment. Like the Civil Service, business may have preferred to recruit relatively high level generalist economists in the early post-war period, but as the relevance of economic expertise became more widely appreciated more hierarchically structured business units were established. The 1966 Business Economists Survey reveals that 62 per cent

Table 11 Relative salaries of male social science graduates by cohorts and subject, 1960-72

Year of salary	Cohort	Business studies	Economics	Geography	Politics	Psychology	Sociology
1960	1950-1	117	142	100	103	150	112
1964	1950-1	110	153	100	109	128	118
	1961	89	110	100	106	111	110
1968	1950-1	114	138	100	99	159	122
	1961	109	121	100	101	108	117
	1967	111	110	100	143	107	94
1972	1950-1	120	144	100	81	109	124
	1961	128	127	100	111	131	122
	1967	143	115	100	115	104	93

Source: Westoby *et al.* (1976), p. 12.
Note: In each year the earnings of geographers in the relevant cohorts equals 100.

Table 12 Percentage of social science graduates in various occupational categories by subject, 1972

Subject	Industry, commerce and administration	Independent and profesional	Teaching in higher education	School teaching	Other and unknown	Sample no. (= 100%)
Business studies and commerce	75.7	6.8	10.5	4.2	2.8	204
Economics	47.6	19.6	17.2	6.9	8.8	336
Geography	20.2	17.6	13.1	37.8	11.3	455
Politics	37.4	9.9	26.7	15.1	10.9	78
Psychology	22.5	42.1	21.9	7.2	6.3	105
Sociology	53.7	5.7	18.8	16.6	5.5	155

Source: Westoby *et al.* (1976), p. 16.

of all respondents were in the 20-35 age group, (Alexander *et al.* 1967, p. 4).

As lifetime earnings are at least as important as starting salaries in revealing market conditions, the trend of earnings at given stages in an economist's career shown in Table 11 represents a valuable addition to our knowledge. But, unfortunately, as Tables 11 and 12 refer to *subjects*, not to *occupations*, they do not enable us to distinguish earnings from employment as a professional economist *per se*, rather than from other numerate professions, such as accountancy or computing. Moreover it seems that business economists tended to look to high level careers in general management rather than in their professional specialism, as a means of maintaining their career momentum, (Alexander *et al.* 1967, p. 84).

IV CONCLUSIONS

What conclusions emerge from this survey, apart from the obvious limitations of our knowledge and the need for more detailed research? The evidence suggests that after a considerable early post-war excess demand for business economists (Table 6), graduates in economics gained higher salaries than other social scientists (Table 11). A period of limited recruitment in the mid-1950s was followed by a sustained expansion in job opportunities up to the early 1970s, a movement fuelled by the growing output of economics graduates. While differentials in starting salaries had narrowed considerably by the late 1960s, there is considerable evidence that the government found it difficult to recruit experienced economists during both the early and the late 1960s.[24]

The market for economists in Britain has clearly changed very markedly during the 25-year period. University-trained economists enjoyed favourable career promotion prospects not only in academic life, but also in business and, eventually, in government. Numbers grew so rapidly and the proliferation of sub-disciplines and related subjects was so great that the profession was losing its pre-war 'collegial' character and becoming multi-centred and more hierarchical. While enjoying favourable employment prospects and a considerable measure of public esteem, some of the attractions and excitement of earlier, more turbulent days may have been lost.

This review has, of necessity, been retrospective; but some thought must be given to the present and the future. Now that the Department of Employment is taking a genuine interest in manpower planning, and the status and value of universities is the subject of public controversy, the economics profession has an obligation, as well as a vested interest, to provide the basis for informed discussion of its past record and prospective contributions. The Royal Economic Society, Association of University Teachers of Economics, the Society of Business Economists, and any other professional bodies should take a much more active role in market research and forecasting, for it seems clear that the limited traditional functions of sponsoring journals and holding conferences are no longer sufficient to meet members' needs (for background data see Coats and Coats, 1973). By taking a more active interest in the market for economists they would both be enhancing their own relevance and fulfilling their professional responsibilities.

APPENDIX

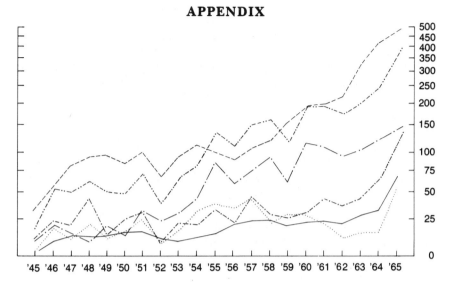

Source: Alexander et al. (1967), p. 58.

Fig. 1 Demand for economists 1945–65

Notes: advertisement columns of *The Economist*. – – – – , total academic posts; ∙∙—∙∙ , total business economists, ∙–∙–∙– , government and public bodies; ∙—∙ , extractive, manufacturing industry and distribution; ∙∙∙∙∙∙ , qualification in statistics/econometrics; ——— , total business economists' posts abroad.

NOTES

* Co-written with A. E. Booth. This exercise is a by-product of research on the changing role of economists, statisticians and agricultural economists in British government since 1945 directed by Professor Coats and financed by the Social Science Research Council. We greatly appreciate the co-operation of many past and current civil servants and also, with respect to this paper, the comments of three experts on educational and manpower questions: Professors Mark Blaug and Gareth Williams, and Mr E. G. Whybrew of the Unit for Manpower Studies, Department of Employment.

1 *American Economic Review Papers and Proceedings*, May 1959. In 1970 the Association organized another Round Table Session on the Academic Labour Market. Cf. *American Economic Review Papers and Proceedings*, vol. 61 (May 1971), pp. 305–33.

2 See Study IV, 'Who are the Economists?', pp. 123–53. Tolles argues that 'No modern profession is in greater need of precise definition than the economics profession. While an economist clearly has something to do with economising the means of satisfying wants, popular usage has extended the field of "economics" from its original sphere of providing financial advice to a sovereign downward to the conduct of any private business operation, outward to the analysis of consumer, welfare, labour, and population problems and inward to any of the logical or statistical techniques used in analysing public or private

491

operations which involve material welfare' (op. cit. p. 123). The AEA's recommended definition of an economics profession appears in the 1948 handbook, published in the *American Economic Review*, vol. 30, no. 1 (January 1949), pp. 341–3. See also the 1955 Handbook and supplementary note on 'The Profession of Economist: Educational Requirements and Career Opportunities', *American Economic Review*, vol. 67, no. 4 (July 1957), pp. 307–9; Williamson (1971), chap. III; Stigler (1965), pp. 32–3; and Coats (1975).

British academic interest in the operation of the labour market for highly qualified manpower has recently awakened. For example, Halsey and Trow (1971); Williams, Blackstone and Metcalf (1974); Greenaway and Williams (1973); Kelsall, Polle and Kulm (1970). See also the considerable literature on general university development and student unrest.

3 Professor Gareth Williams has indicated the limitations of this source. There is no account of graduates from the non-university sector; the figures present only a 'snapshot', taken a few months after graduation, and offer no information about lifetime careers; when graduates delay initial entry into the labour market to search for the right job, they are recorded as not having gained employment; and the UGC returns yield no information on salaries. 'Graduates and the Labour Market', *The Three Banks Review* (September 1973), pp. 10–12. Also relevant to this study is the failure to present joint honours degree data in more detail.

4 In 1965/6, for example, 17.1 per cent of joint honours graduates went on to train to be teachers, and 2.3 per cent to train for social work. For economics graduates the figures were 5.6 per cent and 0.5 per cent respectively.

5 The Select Committee on Expenditure (Education and Arts Sub-Committee) was told: 'Increasingly in the economics profession – and here the United Kingdom is following the lead of the United States – a first degree is insufficient because the advance of the subject continues to be so rapid. More and more young economists are recognising this and are coming to the Civil Service after taking a higher degree: the Government Economic Service welcomes this.' *Investigation into Postgraduate Education*, Minutes of Evidence, House of Commons Papers, 1973.

6 The 1955/6 figure in Table 1 is exceptional and may be erroneous.

7 There is, of course, as much debate (and as little agreement) on the term 'economics profession' as 'economist'. See note 2 above.

8 Polytechnic and college posts have been omitted but demand from the non-university sector was at fairly low levels until the middle and late sixties. As far as university staff is concerned, we have included all those whose title included the word 'Economics', except in the cases of 'agricultural economics' and 'economic history' (in order to try to preserve some consistency with the market for government and business economists). Thus, staff in 'Social Studies' departments, for example at East Anglia, City and Bradford, are not included.

9 Cairncross (1968), p. 7. At one stage in the early 1960s there was a discussion of the possibility of offering differential grants in favour of economics graduates in order to expand the number of potential professionals. However, this proposal was turned down on the grounds that it would be regarded as an unwarrantable interference with university affairs.

10 *The Fulton Report on the Civil Service* (Cmnd. 3638, 1968), p. 28 came out strongly in favour of the recruitment of social scientists for administrative work (which was to be divided into two broad groups – economic/financial; and social), and recommended that, 'the relevance to their future work of the subject matter of

their university or other pre-service studies should be an important qualification for appointment'. However, the government rejected this suggestion.

11 It is worth noting, however, that a significant proportion of the present Statistician Class has been promoted from the executive ranks and has had no academic statistical training. Moser (1973), p. 83.

12 Agricultural economists and economists recruited to the Research Officer Class were, however, always an exception to this generalization. They tended to be employed on specific projects (such as the Annual Agricultural Price Review) and were directly involved in the collection, analysis and application of data.

13 The Association of First Division Civil Servants *Monthly Notes* throughout 1965 expressed concern about the career prospects of economists in the Civil Service before the influx of outsiders became very substantial.

14 The major rebellion came, however, with the appointment of Professor (now Sir Claus) Moser to succeed Sir Harry Campion as Head of the Central Statistical Office. The First Division Association published its correspondence with Sir Lawrence Helsby and letters of complaint, in *Monthly Notes* (February–May 1967).

15 Hutchison (1977), p. 66. See also the interesting figures quoted on pp. 162–3.

16 For background information see Coats (1976).

17 The authors drew their data from job advertisements in *The Economist*, and paid due regard to its impressionistic character. We reproduce their graph here in the Appendix.

18 Williams, Blackstone and Metcalf note a fall in the proportion of lecturers in *social science as a whole* with 'firsts', but a rise in the proportion with a Ph.D. between 1961/2 and 1969/70 (1974, p. 96). With regard to starting salaries, the polytechnics have recently taken to advertising posts on the Lecturer II rather than the Lecturer I scale (though this has little to do with scarcity of potential recruits as compared with university/polytechnic relativities).

19 The limitations of this series are obvious. They are taken from advertisers in only one journal, not from the whole population of business economists, and many of these advertisements were of no use because they failed to supply the relevant age and salary information. Since a distribution curve of the minima of salary scales tends to have at least two peaks, it is probable that the sample includes both new recruits to the profession and those who are on the market for the second time with a minimum of experience (or who had completed a further degree).

20 The figures for economists are taken from the annual *Commonwealth Universities Yearbooks*, but the data are unreliable, especially at the Lecturer/Assistant Lecturer level. Most universities gave full names of staff in all grades; a number named only Lecturers and above, merely supplying numbers of Assistant Lecturers; others listed no Assistant Lecturers for long periods (for example, Birmingham 1954–62). It is possible, therefore, in some cases that either both grades were included in a single category or Assistants were omitted completely. Data on university staff as a whole are taken from *Educational Statistics for the United Kingdom* (annual from 1970 – relating to 1967 – but with statistics dating from the early 1950s in the first edition).

21 Grade equivalents were, for most of the period: Economic Assistant = Assistant Principal; Economic Adviser = Principal; Senior Economic Adviser = Assistant Secretary.

22 The supply of professional economists of sufficient standing to fulfil the requirements of the Administrative Class was, and is, limited. We have mentioned the 'disturbance allowances' paid to entice university economists to taste the forbid-

den fruits of government (above p. 483), and this, typically, would include elements for removals, a 'London weighting', and compensation for delayed promotion prospects. The government wanted academics of about thirty years of age, nearing Senior Lecturer/Reader status. Such individuals were obviously afraid of being 'out of sight, out of mind' of the universities, which remained their main points of career reference. Their publication prospects would, of course, have been much less in government than in the universities.

23 The demand from the government may have been the crucial factor in maintaining relative salary levels into the seventies, since salaries of other professional groups began their downturn much earlier. See Table 7 for data on economists.

24 Note especially that median earnings amongst Business Economists grew most rapidly in the 26–30 and 41–45 age groups between 1964 and 1968. It may well be that government recruitment of Economic Advisers and of Directing Grades resulted in tightness in this section of the market. (See Table 7.)

REFERENCES

Alexander, K.W.J., Kemp, A.G. and Rybczynski, T.M. (1967). *The Economist in Business*. Oxford: Basil Blackwell.

Cairncross, A. (1968). 'The Work of an Economic Adviser'. *Public Administration*, vol. 46, p. 7.

Coats, A.W. (1960). 'The First Two Decades of the American Economic Association'. *American Economic Review*, vol. 50 (September), pp. 555–74. Reprinted in this volume, pp. 205–24.

—— (1964). 'The American Economic Association, 1904–29'. *American Economic Review*, vol. 54 (June), pp. 261–85. Reprinted in this volume, pp. 239–63.

—— (1968). 'The Origins and Early Development of the Royal Economic Society'. *Economic Journal*, vol. 78, pp. 349–71. Reprinted in this volume, pp. 313–37.

—— (1975). 'The Development of the Economics Profession in England: A Preliminary Review'. In *International Congress of Economic History and History of Economic Theories* (ed. L. Houmandis). Piraeus: Piraeus Graduate School of Industrial Studies.

—— (1976). 'The Development of the Agricultural Economics Profession in England'. *Journal of Agricultural Economics*, vol. 27, no. 3, pp. 381–92. Reprinted in this volume, pp. 419–32.

—— and Coats, S.E. (1973). 'The Changing Social Composition of the Royal Economic Society 1890–1960 and the Professionalization of British Economics'. *British Journal of Sociology*, vol. 24, no. 2 (June), pp. 165–87. Reprinted in this volume, pp. 338–60.

Greenaway, H. and Williams, G. (eds) (1973). 'Graduates and the Labour Market'. *The Three Banks Review* (September).

Halsey, A.H. and Trow, M. (1971). *The British Academics*. London: Faber.

Hutchison, T.W. (1977). *Knowledge and Ignorance in Economics*. Oxford: Blackwell.

Kelsall, R.K., Polle, A. and Kulm, A. (1970). *Six Years and After*. Sheffield: Higher Education Research Unit, Sheffield University.

Moser, C.A. (1973). 'Staffing the Government Statistical Service'. *Journal of the Royal Statistical Society*, series A, vol. 136.

Somers, G.S. (1962). 'The Functioning of the Market for Economists'. *American Economic Review, Papers and Proceedings* (May), p. 509.

Stigler, G.J. (1965). *Essays on the History of Economics*. Chicago: University of Chicago Press.

Tolles, N.A. and Molichar, E. (1968). 'Studies of the Structure of Economists' Salaries and Income'. *American Economic Review Supplement*, part 2, pp. 123–53.

Westoby, A., Webster, D. and Williams, G. (1976). *Social Scientists at Work*. Guildford: Society for Research into Higher Education, University of Surrey.

Williams, G., Blackstone, T. and Metcalf, D. (1974). *The Academic Labour Market, Economic and Social Aspects of a Profession*. Amsterdam: Elsevier.

Williamson, H.F. (1971). *Opportunities in Economics Careers*. New York: Educational and Books Division of Universal Publishing and Distributing Corporation.

25

INTRODUCTION TO
ECONOMISTS IN GOVERNMENT:
AN INTERNATIONAL
COMPARATIVE STUDY

I

The essays collected here represent a preliminary effort to open up a new field of comparative social science research – the systematic study of the activities and influence of professional economists in modern government. This introduction is designed to provide a general background to the individual country studies that follow, and to highlight some of the themes and problems which recur in the subsequent chapters.[1]

It is important at the outset to stress the exploratory character of these studies which, in a number of countries, have involved opening up hitherto uncharted territory that cuts across several distinct academic disciplines. The unevenness of the essays, of which the authors are only too well aware, is largely attributable to the impossibility of adequately covering so extensive and multifaceted a subject within a limited space. In several cases the inaccessibility or absence of relevant evidence (e.g. government documents bearing directly on economic policy decisions) and the unwillingness of officials and policymakers to discuss their experiences, have precluded the investigation of certain topics, while in other cases the contributors have deliberately examined in detail certain aspects that were of special relevance in their chosen country. Greater comprehensiveness and uniformity of treatment, with some concomitant risk of forcing the material into a preconceived mould, could undoubtedly have been achieved by means of a more elaborate and lengthy research undertaking. On the other hand, there is much to be said in favour of presenting preliminary findings as early as possible in a field which holds out so much promise for future researchers. Admittedly the studies published here go only part of the way towards filling the vast gaps in our knowledge of the context in which and the methods by which the government economist applies his expertise. Nevertheless we are confident that the results will not only be of interest to students of recent economic history and policy, public administration, and the sociology of the professions and bureaucracy, but will also provide important new insights into recent developments in economics of value to those responsible for the training of economists and their recruitment and deployment in the public service.

Needless to say, the selection of countries included here is by no means representative. As is not unusual in collaborative research exercises, the final choice is attributable partly to design, partly to chance. Nevertheless the range and variety of case studies will suffice to provide a basis for provisional generalizations and an inducement to others to explore the rich potentialities for future research both in the countries represented here and elsewhere.

II HISTORICAL BACKGROUND

Although 'economists' of one sort or another have tendered advice to governments from time immemorial, the practice of employing any significant number of professional economists in government did not become widespread until World War II. This was a watershed in many countries, both in official economic and social policy, and in the development of economics as an academic discipline and as a policy science. The subsequent expanding demand for government economists is but one manifestation of an increasingly complex social division of labour which characterizes modern industrial society,[2] and it has been directly encouraged by the adoption of more interventionist economic and social programmes by a wide spectrum of political regimes, all of which require skilled officials to undertake the increased functions and responsibilities involved.[3]

These trends are apparent in all the countries examined here, though the timing and pace of change have not been uniform. Thus in Italy, Japan, Norway and, for different reasons, Israel, war or the transition to peacetime conditions brought a sharp break with the past. In Hungary the economists' position was directly affected by events of the mid-1950s, while in Brazil the turning point was delayed for roughly another decade. Even where there was no radical change in the political and economic system, as in Australia, Britain, and the USA, or where the bureaucracy remained essentially intact, as in India, the role of economists expanded markedly under the influence of Keynesian ideas, with or without a mild dose of socialist planning. There was a widespread belief in the possibility of achieving a much higher and more sustained level of activity than in the 1930s, and it seemed probable that economists could contribute to the fulfilment of this objective.

III THE SUPPLY OF 'ECONOMISTS'

(a) Definitions, numbers, and academic qualifications

The definition of 'economist', and the calculation of the numbers of persons to be included under this heading, constitute the most fundamental and intractable problems encountered in this research. There is no generally accepted definition and no internationally recognized set of standards by which to measure unambiguously the number of qualified professional economists. The relevant conditions vary from country to country, and during the postwar period there have been considerable, sometimes rapid changes in the content and quality of economics teaching and research. Variations in undergraduate requirements are especially significant in those countries where there are few graduate economists available for government employment. At the level of graduate training, especially with respect to 'core' courses, there has been a measure of standardization, and local cultural traditions are at least partly offset by the desire to emulate the international standards set by American or western European institutions – though these obviously do not apply with equal force in Communist countries.

After considerable discussion among the contributors it became clear that there was no simple satisfactory solution to this problem. Consequently each participant in the project has made an independent judgement of the appropriate definition of 'economist' and the minimum entry qualifications for the profession on the basis of his personal knowledge and experience. In certain countries where the educational conditions are likely to be less familiar to most readers (e.g. Brazil, Hungary, Italy) somewhat more information on student numbers and academic courses is provided. However, it should be noted that course titles which appear similar on paper may in fact be quite dissimilar in practice, as is apparent from a recent comparative study of economics curricula in European countries.[4] In the case of Japan and Italy the specific content of university training is irrelevant, since it plays no part in the placing of new entrants into the civil service.

When all the appropriate qualifications have been made, certain general features of the educational background are apparent. In the early postwar years some countries' educational institutions were much better equipped than others to provide a supply of qualified economists for the public service, and there has been a fairly general long-run rise in the levels of analytical rigour and technical skill involved in their training, albeit with some concomitant losses resulting from excessive specialization. Once a significant growth of demand occurred, the supply usually responded fairly rapidly, especially where substantial public funds were available. Brazil and Hungary provide especially striking examples of this process, which has also occurred in some less developed countries (e.g. India), where the role of foreign-born and foreign-trained native-born economists has been particularly significant. There has, however, been no precise correlation between the quality and extent of educational provision, the reputation of the economics profession, and the growth in the numbers and importance of a country's economists in postwar government. (The UK affords a noteworthy illustration of the divergencies between these variables.)

Here, as elsewhere in economics, mere numbers are deceptive. A tiny handful of strategically placed individuals with direct access to powerful decisionmakers may, of course, be far more influential than a mighty host of trained economists located in the middle and lower bureaucratic ranks. Nevertheless, in the following chapters considerable attention has been paid to these modest toilers in the vineyards, for they have been unduly neglected in the published literature, much of which emanates from senior ex-government economists who have concentrated on the higher-level advisory functions. There is, moreover, a general tendency among academic economists to underestimate the extent to which the formulation as well as the implementation of policy is undertaken in the middle levels of the government machine. A study of the tasks performed at these levels, where most of the employment opportunities for economists occur, provides a more representative impression of the economists' contributions to the expanding economic and social functions of government.

(b) Functions

All governments perform economic 'functions'. But they do not all recognize 'economists' as a distinct category of personnel, nor do they all designate certain positions as economist 'posts', to be occupied only by those with recognized academic qualifications. Moreover, while the categories of personnel, functions, and posts may be conceptually distinct, they are not necessarily so in practice. Qualified 'economists' may be appointed or promoted into general administrative or executive posts which call for little or no economic expertise. Furthermore, it is virtually impossible to define economic 'functions' precisely: at the margin they shade imperceptibly into other types of work (general administration, routine collection of economic intelligence and statistics, etc.); and an individual economist's activities may change over time according to his experience, the development of his knowledge and skills, and the demands imposed on him.

Economics may be termed a vocationally non-specific subject; its relations with other disciplinary professions and the division of labour between them are not static. They will depend, among other things, on the structure and style of the bureaucracy, on the objectives and methods of government policies, and – a point unduly neglected – on the prevailing perceptions of the professional economist's potential contributions on the part of political leaders and those responsible for civil service personnel management.

Needless to say, while all these aspects are touched on in the following country studies, they have not all been examined in detail. It will be obvious to readers that certain tasks reserved for economists in some bureaucracies are performed in others by personnel with few or no formal qualifications, and one of the most basic questions motivating this enquiry is this: Why do governments employ any professional economists? What are their special skills, knowledge, and claims to expertise – if any? Well before the end of the volume it will become clear that the answers to these questions are by no means as clear as some economics textbook writers suggest. Economics is not so esoteric a subject as to be wholly inaccessible and incomprehensible to the layman. Many intelligent civil servants without formal training in the subject have proved themselves capable of 'learning by doing' ('sitting by Nellie' is the appropriate British civil service colloquialism), and it is a well-known cliché that most government economic work requires no more than sophomore (i.e. second-year American undergraduate) economics – with the added proviso that the individual may require several additional years' study and practice before he has fully assimilated this intermediate-level analysis.[5] Many economic problems call for general intellectual qualities, judgement, and experience, rather than advanced technical or professional knowledge. Hence economic specialists have no claim to monopoly privileges, particularly in the field of decision-making or policy advice, one of the central issues in several of the following studies.

(c) The market for economists

In the market for the professional economist's services the central government is seldom, if ever, a monopsonist. At least until the early 1970s, and in some cases beyond that period, there has been a high and sustained postwar demand for economists on the part of academic institutions, business, and non-governmental public agencies at home and abroad. More recently, when certain segments of the market have been less buoyant, the demand from provincial and municipal governments has been expanding in some countries. Hence in considering the availability of economists for central government employment or other official posts some attention must be paid to their alternative employment opportunities.

Unfortunately there is a serious dearth of reliable data on relevant market conditions, especially in the business sector, and bewildering complexities arise in any attempt to make intergovernmental comparisons, partly because of marked differences in official personnel practices. In some countries bureaucratic standards and procedures are lax, appointments are politicized, and competitive bidding occurs. In other instances established personnel policies are carefully managed by officials and monitored by civil service trade unions with the aim of preventing inequities between different individuals or categories of staff. These obstacles can often be overcome or circumvented by strong ministers, especially in emergency conditions; and even in normal times it is usually possible, without corrupt practices, to create occasional or short-term posts for consultants or 'special advisers' attached to a minister, committee, or commission of enquiry – although such appointments usually constitute a very small proportion of the total.

Given the severe limitations of the available evidence, the variety and changeability of market conditions, and the lack of uniformity of bureaucratic procedures, the contributors to these studies have usually been forced to rely on impressionistic judgements based on their personal experience or, in some cases, on interviews with civil servants and past or present government economists. Nevertheless one or two preliminary general observations may be helpful at this stage.

In the British and American cases there have been substantial numbers of short-term government economists, primarily at the upper levels in the USA, but also at the middle levels in Whitehall, whereas in most of the other countries the great majority of such personnel have been permanent officials. The relative attractiveness of government and non-government (primarily academic) employment for economists has varied over time and is determined by a subtle combination of pecuniary and non-pecuniary considerations – including the opportunities for promotion, personal and intellectual independence, freedom to publish and mix with other professionals, and the prospect of exerting an influence on public policy. Over the long run the gap between government and academic economists has narrowed, owing to a combination of developments within the discipline, changes in the nature and scope of government responsibilities in the economic and social spheres, and the increasing feedback effects of government work, and ex-government economists, on the academic community's and general public's conception of the civil service. References to all these matters will be found in the following studies.

(d) General social and cultural attitudes towards intellectuals, professionals, and experts

In any international comparative study of this kind some attention must be paid to national social and cultural attitudes towards economists and other experts, specialists, or disciplinary professionals. In some countries economists and other social scientists are regarded as a strange new breed, to be considered alongside natural scientists and technologists. In traditional humanistic cultures the educational system may be ill-equipped to provide the necessary resources and training facilities for social scientists, and those who obtain the requisite qualifications may find that their rewards, roles, and status are inferior to those of personnel trained in more traditional subjects.[6] In such situations the influence of economists trained in Europe or the USA has often been crucial prior to the development of an indigenous economics profession.

In the British civil service, which left a strong imprint on the Indian bureaucracy, the traditional preference for the 'all rounder' over the specialist inevitably restricted the latter's career opportunities and may have discouraged some men of exceptional ability, ambition, or energy from seeking a civil service career, thereby confirming the generalists' preconceptions that most specialists were of an inferior intellectual calibre. In Australia, by contrast, a deep-rooted anti-élitist attitude imposed barriers to the recruitment of graduates into the civil service during the interwar period, but did not discourage specialization within the organization. Indeed, those with specialist post-entry academic qualifications often rose more rapidly through the ranks. Generally speaking, in northern and western Europe and the USA, unlike Britain, expertise was fully recognized, and special qualifications were an asset in securing senior posts; while in Brazil, the relative position of economists and technocrats in the public service, as in society at large, improved rapidly as a result of powerful support from an authoritarian government, a situation not uncommon under such regimes.[7]

Bureaucratic procedures and styles usually reflect the national culture, as do higher educational institutions, for it can be said of them, as of governments, that the nation gets the universities it deserves. However, as subsequent chapters reveal, an inhospitable cultural climate can be overcome, given sufficient determination and resources.

IV PROFESSIONALISM AND BUREAUCRACY

(a) General issues

Economists in government are necessarily members of a large organization and must accordingly to some extent work in cooperation with, though not invariably in close proximity to, other public servants (some of whom may be professionals) and politicians. They may, of course, be employed in specialist research units where they are comparatively uninhibited by the customary constraints of organizational life, but in such cases they will usually be away from the centres of power and unlikely to be able to exert much influence on the organization's policies or its day-to-day activities. By contrast, the higher the professional rises in the bureaucratic hierarchy the more likely he is to be drawn into its operations and to be working in direct contact with senior bureaucrats and/or politicians. In such circumstances conflicts of loyalty and interest are more likely to arise.

Whereas a professional in a bureaucracy has a dual loyalty, to his profession and to his employer, the bureaucrat has no such problem. In the interests of his career, if for no more laudable motive, he will naturally tend to identify himself with the organization's goals, accept its conventions, and acquire a mastery of its procedures.[8] To the professional, however, adaptation or socialization into the bureaucracy poses certain dangers, including the loss of professional independence and initiative, intellectual obsolescence resulting from total immersion in day-to-day routines, with the consequent inability to keep in touch with new developments in his specialist field, and possibly even the corrupting influence of bribery, power seeking, and politicization.

In this section some indication of the relevance of these issues to the following case studies will be provided, though once again it is necessary to forewarn the reader that it has proved neither possible to achieve nor desirable to aim at complete uniformity of content and structure.

(b) Economics as a profession

Economics is one among a number of modern professions which, unlike their traditional predecessors – law, medicine, and the church – do not have strict controls on entry, formal codes of ethics, or effective methods for disciplining their members. Nevertheless they possess the essential internal and external requirements[9] – namely, that their members are subjectively aware of themselves as professionals and are recognized as such by those who use their services and by the public at large. As in other cases, this recognition is based on the possession of degrees and other qualifications which are not readily accessible to laymen; and it takes the form of specialized appointments, high remuneration, delegation of responsibility or authority, and a measure of social esteem.

The professionalization of economics has not hitherto been subjected to detailed comparative study,[10] but it would be generally agreed that a recognizable corps of professional economists emerged within the academic community in Britain and the USA around the turn of the century, but somewhat later in many other countries.[11] The usual indications are the appearance of specialist learned societies, scholarly periodicals, and academic degrees. Government employment, with its hierarchical gradations of title, status, responsibility, and emoluments, has markedly accelerated the process and has also helped to arouse a sense of professional self-consciousness and *esprit de corps* among economists, both in the public service and in the academic world, where the postwar expansion has led to increasing specialization and division of labour within the discipline.

While professional economists may be said to share a common culture which is circumscribed by certain accepted conventions, ideas, and methodological rules, they do not constitute a tightly organized or homogeneous community. On the whole, academic training in economics has not been so rigorous, at least until recently, nor the socialization process so effective, as to engender a sharp differentiation between economists and other social scientists, statisticians, operations researchers, mathematicians, etc. Nor are they immune from lay judgement on technical matters on the grounds that the laity is presumed incompetent to comprehend their arcane knowledge or evaluate their performance, although some more technical branches of the discipline (e.g. mathematical and econometric model building) possess this character.

In fact the professional economists' relations with the public – including non-economist bureaucrats and politicians – have often been uneasy, for many laymen have firm preconceived ideas about economic affairs and unwarranted confidence in their own ability to prescribe solutions to current economic problems. Some of those most outspokenly hostile or sceptical towards economists' expertise have also been inclined to exaggerate their influence on public policy. When economic affairs have been proceeding smoothly and prosperously, economists have generally been in popular favour, and they have usually been willing to take at least some of the credit for the situation. By contrast, when economic conditions have deteriorated, they have correspondingly received undeserved blame.

Several of the studies in this volume (e.g. those of the USA, Australia, Brazil, and Israel) provide clear indications of the postwar rise and subsequent deflation – whether mild or serious – of the professional economists' public reputation. In some instances the initial upswing was directly associated with the prestige or influence of a particular individual or 'school' of economics (e.g. J. M. Keynes in Britain, Australia, India, the USA, and also Canada; Don Patinkin in Israel; Jan Tinbergen in the Netherlands; and Ragnar Frisch in Norway, where the Oslo School's reputation has remained remarkably high throughout the postwar era). In the case of Brazil (as to a lesser extent with Greece under the so-called Colonels' Regime) the economists' rise to power and influence occurred under a military government determined to use its powers to improve the country's economic performance. Similar experiences can be recorded in other South American countries (e.g. Mexico), where authoritarian regimes have been favourably disposed to economists and other technocrats.[12] But here, as in more democratic societies, exaggerated expectations which carry the economics profession on the crest of a wave of public enthusiasm (as in the USA and, to a lesser extent, in Britain during the 1960s) are all too often followed by a reaction when the high hopes are dashed – with obvious consequences for those involved. This, indeed, is one of the reasons for the much discussed 'crisis' in economics in the late 1960s and early 1970s,[13] a state of affairs that has not yet been fully resolved.

504

(c) Some relevant features of modern bureaucracy

According to Max Weber's classic analysis, bureaucratic organizations involve specialized and differentiated administrative roles; recruitment, transfer, and promotion by universalistic criteria of achievement, rather than by ascription; reliance on full-time salaried officials; and administrative decisionmaking within a context of hierarchy, responsibility, and discipline.[14] Needless to say, practice often diverges substantially from this 'ideal type', for example in the extent to which the organization functions smoothly and efficiently, and is free from political interference, corruption, nepotism, etc. One of the principal aims of this series of studies is, while acknowledging the differences between Weber's model and the complex realities of twentieth-century government, to examine how and with what effects economists function within modern bureaucracies.

As might be expected, the studies included here reveal a wide variety of experiences. In Britain, India, and to a lesser extent Australia, the advent of professional economists into government encountered some resistance from a stable, politically neutral, and well-entrenched traditional body of 'intelligent laymen' generalist administrators; and strong exogenous forces (e.g. depression, war, or the pressure of a determinedly innovative government) were sometimes required before any significant number of economists rose to positions of influence within the bureaucratic hierarchy. In Norway, where the traditional nineteenth-century European 'juristenmonopol' prevailed until World War II,[15] the subsequent rise of professional economists was so remarkably frictionless that a 'harmony model' has been found applicable. Numbers are important here, for while one or two influential advisers (e.g. in a European-style ministerial 'cabinet') may be added to an existing organization without much affecting its main operations or internal structure, more significant changes may be required when, as in the USA and Britain, considerable numbers of short-service or temporary specialist professionals are added. In the British case the reliance on short-term economists was due both to shortages of suitably qualified personnel and to the politicians' and established bureaucrats' unwillingness to create sufficient attractive niches for the professionals. It was not until the numbers reached a critical minimum size that it became necessary to provide formal procedures for the recruitment, deployment, and promotion of economists, a development that was accompanied by an increased measure of professional autonomy and self-control. In the USA, where, by long-established convention, a sizeable number of senior posts have been reserved for political appointees, most of whom come and go with changes in the political leadership, it was easy to find suitable slots for professional economists right up to and including cabinet rank.[16] These outsiders were, of course, obliged to collaborate with the corps of lower-level permanent officials, some of whom were certainly qualified to be regarded as professional economists;[17] but this does not seem to have generated much friction. Some of the effects of these short-term arrangements on the relationships between academic and government economists will be noted later in this introduction.

At this point it is appropriate to refer to the situation in those countries where the bureaucracy makes no provision whatever for specialist posts for professional economists. In Japan this deficiency is offset by a regular system of in-service training and secondment for selected officials, whereas in Italy the problem is handled on an *ad hoc* basis by calling upon outside advisers, usually university professors, and utilizing the resources of specialist research institutes and agencies. Whether these arrangements are sufficient to meet the need for economic expertise is a matter for conjecture. It would, indeed, be ironic if the research embodied in these studies were to suggest that the vastly increased employment of economists in postwar governments was in fact an unnecessary luxury. The performance of the Japanese economy may be cited by some, superficially, as supporting evidence; but few observers are likely to argue that the same applies to Italy. There is, in fact, no necessary or observed correlation between the number of professional economists in a government and that country's growth rate, notwithstanding some cynics' contention that the relationship is an inverse one!

In-service training both for professionals and for generalist administrators has become increasingly fashionable in recent years. The elaborate preparation provided for senior French civil servants at the Ecole Nationale d'Administration has been much admired in Europe and elsewhere. In Britain determined efforts were made in the 1960s, especially in connection with the work of the Fulton Committee, to modernize the public bureaucracy, with somewhat mixed success;[18] and in the USA there have been many experiments with graduate instruction in public administration and, more recently, policy analysis and other supposedly relevant disciplines. With respect to economics, the value of in-service training for generalist administrators dealing with economic and social problems and needing to communicate with social scientists has been widely recognized; and the mounting volume of statistical information and analysis has put an increasing premium on numeracy as well as the traditional verbal and literary skills. In all these respects economists have proved themselves valuable both as 'new generalists' and as specialists; and in many governments (as illustrated in the cases of Norway and Hungary in these studies) they have been supplementing and even competing for positions with traditional jurists, who for so long enjoyed a monopoly of the highest positions in European bureaucracies.

As the role of professionals and experts increases in modern government, economists, like other categories of staff, find themselves dealing and occasionally competing with other professionals, often in so-called 'mixed divisions'. In the more technical activities, such as model building or investment appraisal, they often work alongside statisticians, mathematicians, operations researchers, accountants, or engineers. Chance, convention, and the influence of personalities necessarily affect the type of working relationship, but when economists move in significant numbers into a field hitherto regarded as the prerogative of a particular category of staff, friction is likely, especially when the newcomers question the effectiveness of existing procedures or resource allocations in such a way as to imply that the incumbents had not really thought seriously about their activities. Hostile reactions are almost inevitable when the application of cost-benefit analysis, planned programme budgeting, or policy analysis and review threatens well-established official procedures, hierarchical responsibilities, and career prospects. In a number of countries the rise of the economists has caused serious resentment, partly because of their combination of expertise and adaptability. But it is the belief that they have occasionally arrogantly exceeded the limits of their competence that has led one critic to coin the term 'econocrats'.[19]

(d) Professional ethics and standards

One valuable social and intellectual by-product of the large-scale employment of economists in government has been the heightened sensitivity to problems of professional ethics and standards, issues which in earlier periods were considered, if at all, only indirectly in the course of methodological debates about the nature and scope of economic science or the relationship between the 'art' and the 'science' of political economy (latterly explained in terms of 'positive' and 'normative' economics).[20] Government service has not merely stimulated a collective self-consciousness, it has also provoked constructive discussion of the profession's social responsibilities, especially in the policymaking process.

Broadly speaking, during the 1950s and 1960s there was a marked surge of professional self-confidence among economists, especially in Western countries, but also more generally, where the successful avoidance of a postwar slump and large-scale unemployment was widely attributed, rightly or wrongly, to the effective application of Keynesian doctrines in the public policy arena. More recently much of that optimism has been dissipated with the reemergence of significant unemployment combined with slower economic growth and serious inflation, and there has consequently been a good deal of heart searching about the nature and limitations of the economist's knowledge and its applicability to practical problems.[21] Experience of government employment has led many economists to adopt a healthy scepticism about earlier simplistic textbook descriptions of economics as a 'positive' science, and the familiar dichotomy between 'ends' and 'means' now appears much less clear-cut than was once the case.

Given the generally accepted interpretation of the nature and objectives of science it might seem that all the professional economist need do in dealing with policy issues is to abide by the 'rules of the game'[22] – that is, to be honest about the limitations of his knowledge; to refrain from presenting his personal judgements or predilections as though they were scientific truths; and to recognize the dangers of subjectivity, even in empirical matters. But such worthy counsels may not be capable of implementation in practice if only because the economist is a human being, with imperfect knowledge, and insufficiently aware of his personal and professional prejudices, or at least incapable of deciding how far to discount them in making policy recommendations. Contrary to earlier teachings, more often than not policy objectives are controversial, conflicting or incompatible, or obscure, sometimes as a result of deliberate concealment by policymakers. Moreover, they invariably transcend the boundaries of economics, as traditionally defined. Economic theory is abstract, limited in scope, and capable of a remarkable variety of extensions, adaptations, and interpretations which constitute a source both of strength and of weakness in policy debates. Beyond this, the available data on relevant past and current conditions are usually incomplete and unreliable; the future is uncertain; forecasting methods are far from satisfactory; and it is usually difficult to know how far ahead to trace the implications of any policy proposal. In short, the list of difficulties is formidable.

In seeking a code of professional conduct for government economists it is helpful to distinguish between internal and external dimensions.[23] With respect to the former, the economist wastes his time if he proposes policies which cannot conceivably be adopted; but within the constraints of his job he must set out the various policy options fully and honestly and present his recommendations. If his advice is rejected, he should accept defeat, lick his wounds, and live to fight another day. But if he repeatedly accepts defeat passively, in the hope of future victories, he will run the risk of reducing his effectiveness to the point where he becomes not merely neutral, but neuter. On the other hand, if he fights too fiercely, he will quickly become *persona non grata* and be either by-passed or dismissed.

Considered from an external standpoint, an adviser also has responsibilities to the public, by explaining the government's philosophy and policy objectives, but in so doing it is obviously difficult to draw the line between partisan advocacy and merely instructing or informing the public and his fellow professionals.[24] At times the economist can preserve his integrity only by remaining silent when faced with official policies of which he strongly disapproves, and if his silence proves embarrassing or unacceptable to his employers, he should resign. Whether, and if so when, to resign, and whether to resign silently or loudly in a blaze of publicity, are matters to be left to his professional conscience. But resignation, however conducted, is a once-for-all decision, a confession of failure, and a gesture unlikely to

508

have any effect on policy. Some cynics maintain that government employees are merely or mainly involved in rationalizing policies that make little or no economic sense, but which have been adopted solely for reasons of political expediency. This suspicion is reinforced by the contention that there is a self-selection process whereby radical, eccentric, or highly original individuals are discouraged from entering or, if they enter, from staying in government employment. Government employees serve the ruling sociopolitical establishment and doubtless reflect the views of the dominant professional group in the discipline. However, if there are regular changes of government regime, changes of economic advisers may merely suggest that each administration is getting the advice it wants, rather than detached or independent professional opinion. And the wider and more contentious the divisions within a disciplinary profession, the more plausible this suggestion appears.

The preceding paragraphs of course apply with special force to the most senior economic advisers, those who are closest to the centres of power and political decision, and the issues involved have been richly demonstrated in a series of publications by former members of the President's Council of Economic Advisers in the USA, a body which has displayed a unique combination of professional and political participation in economic policy-making. Economists serving in the middle and lower ranks of the hierarchy seldom face such acute problems of professional integrity; but they, too, can become frustrated and embittered if their contributions are repeatedly ignored or misused and their recommendations rejected. If they remain in public service indefinitely under such circumstances their sense of professional commitment will be impaired and they will become indifferent, lacking in drive and imagination. The higher civil servant economist may experience similar reactions, especially if he knows that his political master regards him as incompetent or his proposals as objectionable. He may for a time console himself with the thought that politicians come and go, and there is consequently a temptation to hold on for a while in the hope that matters will improve. Alternatively he may seek a transfer to another department, overseas mission, or international agency. But such an escape is simply cowardly in a situation where the minister wilfully and repeatedly ignores the evidence of forecasts, and deliberately deceives or withholds information from the public. In some governments secrecy is effectively maintained (though officials may be serving ministers who deliberately 'leak' information when it suits their purpose); and eventually, in extreme cases, the economist may have no option but to violate the official secrecy regulations if he deems it his duty to expose a dishonest or incompetent politician or senior official.

By comparison with non-economist bureaucrats the government economist may be subject to special temptations because he has access to confidential data (e.g. which may affect the course of share prices), and he may be more aware of the costs of bad policies. Moreover, he is often directly in the firing line because the economic policies are controversial and dependent on predictions known to be subject to significant but indeterminate margins of error. Given his dual loyalty to his employer and to the values and standards of his profession, the tension between them may at times become unbearable. In such circumstances his links with academic economists may be not only a source of comfort but also an ever-open escape route – especially in those cases noted earlier where exchanges between universities and government are frequent and well established.

With respect to standards of professional performance it is clear that academic criteria are not necessarily relevant to public-service employment, where the emphasis is on 'useful' knowledge, in some sense of that vague expression. Nevertheless, in recent years it seems clear that the gap between academic and government economics has been narrowing significantly in many countries, and the proportion of genuine intellectual innovations originating within government agencies has been growing markedly – though of course it is difficult to confirm this impressionistic judgement. This is especially likely where an idea or technique is directly dependent on the author's knowledge of the practical functioning of the economic system and its institutions. Government experience, it is said, has greatly stimulated the translation of economic analysis and research into operating rules for public policy, and into quantifiable concepts. And if government employment has served to narrow the long-standing gap between theoretical and applied economics, this is a contribution of no small importance.

Government economists tend to believe, with some justification, that their contributions are undervalued by the economics profession, as contrasted with brilliant new theories or technical achievements which have little or no conceivable practical application.[25] Most of the profession's accolades go to academic members, partly because government economists' work cannot be readily evaluated, since so little of it is published or even completed in publishable form, owing to the pressure of work. And in rare cases where a government economist becomes known to the public he may be found guilty by association with policies determined by others against which he has offered unsuccessful resistance. Strictly speaking, the work of academic economists and the work of government economists are not merely different, but incommensurable, and it may be proper to speak not of one profession but two – with business economics as a possible third category.

V THE POLITY

(a) The political system

In considering the political context within which the government economist performs his duties the relevant considerations include such elements as the degree of stability, adaptability, and conflict or consensus; the stage of economic development; and the position on the spectrum of control extending from democracy to authoritarianism.[26] As noted earlier, in the brief historical period covered in these studies, new states emerged in India and Israel, while Italy, Japan, and Norway underwent significant transitional changes during or after World War II, and Hungary and Brazil somewhat later. Moreover, in almost all the cases considered here the political system has been at times under such pressure for economic and social change – usually as the result of a combination of overeager political leadership and rising public expectations – as to warrant serious consideration of the dangers of political overload. And the economists, as a professional group, have usually been directly involved in efforts to reconcile and achieve a complex interrelated set of economic and social objectives.

Professional economists constitute a subgroup within the political culture – whether as political leaders, members of legislatures, government employees (our primary concern in these essays), journalists, or scholars – and like other subgroups they have their own attitudes and conventions, which both reflect and react on the wider community. Where political socialization is advanced there are unlikely to be marked disparities between the economists' norms and values and those of the political leadership and bureaucracy, although there may be transitory periods of discord when circumstances are changing rapidly – when, indeed, the economists may be either leading innovators or resistant to developments which they regard as disruptive to previously established economic and social goals. They are, on the whole, more likely to be in harmony with the polity where secularization is well advanced – that is, where rationality, analysis, and empirical relevance are evident in political action. (These conditions were lacking in Hungary during the early postwar years, in Brazil prior to the mid-1960s, and in Italy throughout most of the post-1945 period.) Where traditional orientations and attitudes have been displaced by more dynamic decision-making processes (for example in less developed countries undergoing rapid modernization), the economist is likely to be able to make significant contributions to the gathering and evaluation of information, the setting out of alternative courses of action, the selection of one or more of the most feasible options, and the effort to assess the outcomes.[27] In such situations, however, the economic adviser is liable to work under severe constraints owing to the mismatch between political objectives, administrative conditions, and available resources.

(b) The structure of government

The government economists' functions and effectiveness obviously depend directly on the positions they occupy in the official structure. The number of conceivable variants is so great that the studies presented here have concentrated on the principal economic policymaking units or agencies – e.g. key departments such as the Treasury, and the Ministry of Finance and/or Economic Affairs; the planning bureau (if there is one); the central bank; specialist economic advisory agencies; or such 'para-statal' bodies as play an important role in economic decisions. Even this brief list suggests the impossibility of dealing in detail with more than a few major components of the machinery of government, and the scope for more extensive studies is obvious. Of particular interest is the comparatively recent utilization of economists in 'social' departments (e.g. education, health, and social security), not to mention much more obviously economic ministries as defence, transportation, agriculture, labour, and overseas trade. Beyond this, in recent years there has been a substantial growth of employment opportunities for economists and other professionals in state, provincial, and municipal governments. Hence it is hardly necessary to emphasize that we are only beginning to scratch the surface.

Among the organizational factors affecting the economist's work are these:

a. his level in the system – technical tasks usually being performed in the lower and middle reaches, whereas at the 'top of the office' functions and responsibilities more closely resemble those of generalist administrators, and even of political appointees;
b. whether he is an isolated adviser or specialist, a member of a team, or merely one of many suppliers of economic expertise from within or outside the organization;
c. the size and influence of the department or agency employing him; of course similar specialist functions occur in several different branches of government and nominal similarities may conceal practical differences – e.g. owing to variations in departmental policies;
d. the degree of politicization of the bureaucracy and the economic service;
e. the extent of the government's interventionist policies – e.g. whether primarily macroeconomic or microeconomic.

Economic forecasting may serve as an example of the range of possibilities, for this may or may not be centralized and will have varying relationships with the central statistical service and the key policymaking committees or councils. The nature and extent of contact between forecasting and model-building units and other parts of the bureaucracy which supplies them with data is another variable; so is the extent to which forecasts are published – a matter which directly affects the relationships between forecasters, politicians, and the public.[28]

Enough has been said to reveal that the economist's activities and influence are necessarily determined to a large extent by the context in which he works, and there is no ideal organizational structure that will maximize his effectiveness. Most government economists prefer to occupy a position in or close to the centre of decisionmaking, but an effective contribution is dependent on an appropriate relationship between the level of activity, the flow of information, and the area of responsibility.

VI CONCLUSION: THE ROLE OF ECONOMISTS IN POLICYMAKING

For many readers the main interest in this collection will be the assessments in the following studies of the nature and effectiveness of the professional economists' contributions to policymaking. Such an interest is understandable enough, given the importance of the economic problems governments have encountered during the period in which significant numbers of professional economists have been employed as civil servants and policy advisers.

Without seeking to anticipate the conclusions to be drawn at the end of the collection it is appropriate at this stage to discount exaggerated expectations by noting some of the serious difficulties facing those seeking to assess the 'influence' of professional economists in government.

The main point, perhaps, is to emphasize that in a strict sense there is no such thing as 'economic policy', for policy is always affected in some degree by non-economic as well as economic factors, and it always has implications and effects which transcend the narrow and somewhat artificial boundaries of the economist's field. Why, then, should we expect to get precise answers to questions about the influence of economists on policy?

Effective policymaking involves at least three distinct phases: a correct diagnosis of the problem, which depends on accurate information and comprehension of the economic processes at work; the formulation of appropriate and feasible policy recommendations; successful implementation of those recommendations. Needless to say, the process may break down in any one or all of these phases, owing to lack of information, imperfect knowledge of economic processes, inability to predict the future, adoption of 'wrong' policy recommendations (which, for various reasons, may be second or third best from the economist's standpoint), time lags, and inefficiency in implementation – which may be thwarted or distorted by any one or a combination of political, administrative, or legal obstacles.

On the other hand, successful policy (however defined) may be due to a favourable conjuncture of economic, political, bureaucratic, and professional elements – including no small measure of good luck, especially with respect to timing.[29]

Broadly speaking, given the political setting and the bureaucratic system, the effectiveness of any group of professionals involved in the policy process depends on a number of readily specifiable conditions,[30] including:

a. the nature of their expertise;

b. the extent to which their expertise is recognized (i.e. the 'authority of knowledge' accorded to them);

c. their access to centres of power and information (especially that which they exclusively control or generate);

d. their skill in communicating with their clients, and in coalition forming;

e. the degree to which their recommendations accord with the prevailing political and bureaucratic climate of opinion;

f. their effectiveness in 'working the machine', i.e. comprehending and manipulating the norms, procedures, constraints, and culture of the administration;

g. the extent of their ability to avoid involvement in areas where they cannot help, or where no clear solutions are available.

The case studies that follow cannot, of course, be expected to cover all these aspects systematically. The nature of the problem is indicated by the lighthearted proposal by one penetrating observer of the Whitehall scene who suggested that the Royal Economic Society should compile a record of official lifetime averages by which to gauge individual economists' success in making predictions. He concluded, after a thorough survey of the record, that the average performance is roughly correlated: negatively with ideological dogmatism, party-political fervour, and subservience to fashion; neither clearly positively or negatively with mathematical and geometrical facility; and positively with institutional experience and with knowledge of historical cases and institutional, administrative, and political processes.[31]

These remarks, it should be noted, were based on the published record of economists many of whom had, admittedly, spent periods in government employment. How much more difficult it would be to compile a score sheet for those involved within the bureaucracy whose performance is not or cannot be recorded![32] How can one assess the impact of an economic adviser whose recommendations are fed into and become lost in the policy-making process? Is he to be held responsible for sound policies badly executed, or recommendations overruled, reversed, or ignored by politicians more concerned with catching votes than promoting economic welfare? Over what time span should the effects of his recommendations be considered if they are detectable, and how far can he legitimately be blamed for failures due to unforeseeable developments beyond his control?

Needless to say, not all these questions will be answered, or indeed even asked, in the essays presented here. But they will help to suggest why the study of economists in government is both fascinating and important.

NOTES

1 Several readers of earlier versions of this introduction, whose constructive comments and criticisms are hereby acknowledged, have remarked that the underlying preconceptions are Western (i.e. Anglo-American). This bias is admitted,

and remains, despite efforts to compensate for it. It is to be hoped that others can be persuaded to present an alternative perspective on the subject.

2 As William Goode has observed, 'an industrializing society is a professionalizing society'. Cf. 'Encroachment, Charlatanism, and the Emerging Professions: Psychology, Sociology, Medicine', *American Sociological Review* 25 (1960): 902.

3 For a broad multi-country survey of these developments see, for example, Andrew Shonfield, *Modern Capitalism* (London, 1965).

4 J. F. H. Roper, *The Teaching of Economics at University Level* (London, 1970).

5 Cf. the widely quoted remarks by Alain Enthoven reproduced in William R. Allen, 'Economics, Economists, and Economic Policy: Modern American Experiences', *History of Political Economy* 9 (1977): 73. There are, of course, some exceptions to this general dictum, but Allen's article provides a highly stimulating compendium of views on the matter.

6 There are stimulating reflections on the influence of cultural factors on the organization of top-level economic advisory functions in Henry C. Wallich, 'The American Council of Economic Advisers and the German Sachsverstaendigenrat: A Study in the Economics of Advice', *Quarterly Journal of Economics* 82 (Aug. 1968): 349–79.

7 Unfortunately the studies that follow do not include a genuinely underdeveloped country. For a relevant, and exceptional, study of this type see B. D. Giles. 'Economists in Government: The Case of Malawi', *Journal of Developmental Studies* 15 (Jan. 1979): 216–22.

8 Of course, bureaucrats are heterogeneous. See, for example, Robert Putnam's useful distinction between the 'classical' and the 'political' types and comments on the decline of the former in Germany, Sweden (also Norway), and Italy in the postwar period. Cf. his essay in Mattei Dogan, ed., *The Mandarins of Western Europe: The Political Role of Top Civil Servants* (New York, 1975), pp. 87–126. As Reinhart Bendix has noted, the element of 'trust' involved in professional judgements is, at least in principle, at odds with the requirement of 'accountability' in administrative actions, which implies distrust. A modern government relies on both professional and administrative skills, 'but to be responsible it must necessarily check on the discretionary judgements that are indispensable for both professional work and good government'. Cf. 'Bureaucracy', *International Encyclopedia of the Social Sciences*, 2 (New York, 1968): 214.

9 On professions and professionalization see, for example, Talcott Parsons, 'Professions', *International Encyclopedia of the Social Sciences* (New York, 1968), 12: 536–46; H. M. Vollmer and Donald L. Mills, *Professionalization* (New Jersey, 1966); and Phillip Elliott, *Sociology of the Professions* (London, 1972).

10 See, however, my 'The Development of the Economics Profession: A Preliminary Review', in L. Houmanidis, ed., *International Congress of Economic History and History of Economic Theories* (Piraeus: The Piraeus Graduate School of Industrial Studies, 1975), pp. 277–90; 'The Development of the Agricultural Economics Profession in England', *Journal of Agricultural Economics* 27 (Sept. 1976): 381–92 (reprinted in this volume, pp. 419–32); and 'Reflections on the Professionalization of Economics' (Newcastle University, New South Wales, 1980).

11 This is not the place to discuss whether economists of earlier periods, such as the exponents of *Kameralwissenschaft*, should be regarded as professionals. It is, however, appropriate to note the parallels between contemporary government economists and the 'consultant administrators of the mercantilist era'. Cf. Joseph A. Schumpeter, *History of Economic Analysis* (New York, 1954), part II, ch. 3.

12 There is a suggestive analysis of the differences in economists' roles between an authoritarian and a democratic regime in Roderic Ai Camp, *The Role of Economists*

in Policy-Making: A Comparative Case Study of Mexico and the United States (Tucson, Ariz., 1977).

13 For general reviews of this episode see, for example, Walter W. Heller, 'What's Right with Economics?' *American Economic Review* 65 (March 1965): 1–26; and A. W. Coats, 'The Current "Crisis" in Economics in Historical Perspective', *Nebraska Journal of Economics and Business* 16 (Summer 1977): 3–16 (reprinted in vol. I in this series). For evidence that the discussion is not yet closed see the special issue of *The Public Interest* (1980) in which a dozen authors, including several leading economists, examine 'The Crisis in Economic Theory' (also available in book form in Daniel Bell and Irving Kristol, eds, *The Crisis in Economic Theory* (New York: Basic Books, 1981)).

14 See Weber's classic essay on 'Bureaucracy' in H. H. Gerth and C. Wright Mills, *From Max Weber, Essays in Sociology* (New York, 1946), pp. 196–244.

15 For general background see John A. Armstrong, *The European Administrative Elite* (Princeton, 1973).

16 More extensive research would, of course, reveal many examples of political influences on the appointment of economists and other civil servants. For a fascinating example, not included among the studies in this volume, see Georges Stienlet, *Economists and the Civil Service System: The Belgian Case* (Centrum voor Economischen Studien, Katolieke Universiteit te Leuven, 1978).

17 In recent years the growing demand for technical and professional expertise has led to some changes in the boundaries between political and established posts in Washington. Cf. Hugh Heclo, *A Government of Strangers* (Brookings Institution, Washington, D.C., 1977).

18 The critics' major contention was that Britain's senior civil servants were inadequately equipped 'to tackle the political, scientific, social, economic and technical problems of our time', *The Civil Service: Report of the Committee, 1966–68*: *Chariman, Lord Fulton*, Cmnd 3638 (London: HMSO, 1968), vol. 1, paras. 31–2. As the Head of the Civil Service conceded in 1970, since the war it was 'not so much that generalism has been found inadequate, as that the particular skills covered by that description have either been overtaken by events or seem to require a great deal more formal training as well as experience, and to be supplemented by the skills and experience of people formally dubbed "specialists" '. William (Lord) Armstrong, *Personnel Management in the Civil Service* (London: HMSO, 1971), p. 2.; also his *Professionals and Professionalism in the Civil Service* (Welwyn Garden City, 1970), pp. 5–19.

19 Peter Self, *The Econocrats and the Policy Process: The Politics and Philosophy of Cost-Benefit Analysis* (London, 1975). The author is especially concerned with the misuse of cost-benefit analysis.

20 The best general account of these issues is to be found in T. W. Hutchison, *Positive Economics and Policy Objectives* (London, 1964). See also his *Economists and Economic Policy in Britain 1946–1966* (London, 1968); and my two essays: 'Value Judgements in Economics', *Yorkshire Bulletin of Economic and Social Research* 16 (Nov. 1964): 53–67 (reprinted in vol. III in this series); and 'Methodology and Professionalism in Economics: A Subordinate Theme in Machlup's Writings', in Jacob S. Dreyer, ed., *Breadth and Depth in Economics: Fritz Machlup – The Man and His Ideas* (Lexington, Mass., 1978), pp. 23–35.

21 Cf. the sources referred to in note 13, *supra*. Also T. W. Hutchison, *Knowledge and Ignorance in Economics* (London, 1977), pp. 1–8.

22 However, as Michael Polanyi has wisely observed, 'all formal rules of scientific procedure must prove ambiguous, for they will be interpreted quite differently

according to the particular conceptions about the nature of things by which the scientist is guided'. *Personal Knowledge* (Chicago, 1958), p. 167.

23 In the discussion of these matters I have drawn freely on Walter W. Heller, *New Dimensions of Political Economy* (Cambridge, Mass., 1966), ch. 1, and my unpublished 'Report of Discussions' at the Royaumont Conference on the Role of the Economist in Government, April 1974, sponsored by the Ford Foundation.

24 The most valuable brief account, focusing on political as well as more narrowly ethical issues, is the American Economic Association symposium published in *Challenge*, March/April 1974, pp. 28–42, entitled 'How Political Must the Council of Economic Advisers Be?' The participants included Herbert Stein, James Tobin, Henry Wallich, Arthur Okun, Eileen Shanahan (chairman), *et al.*

25 There are, of course, exceptions to this generalization. Moreover, the situation depicted in the text may be changing. In Britain for example, a number of current and ex-government economists have been awarded life peerages, knighthoods, and other honours during the past two decades and have been honoured by their professorial colleagues. In India it is now customary to elect a government economist as President of the Indian Economic Association in alternate years. More generally, it is obvious that the prestige of the academic profession varies considerably from time to time, place to place, and discipline to discipline.

26 This and the next paragraph are based on Gabriel A. Almond and G. Bingham Powell, Jr, *Comparative Politics: A Development Approach* (Boston, 1966), esp. chs. 1, 2, 11; and the essays in Joseph La Palombara, ed., *Bureaucracy and Political Development* (Princeton, 1963; 1967).

27 Cf. the article by Giles, cited note 7 *supra*, which contains references to Zambia, Lesotho, and Swaziland, as well as Malawi.

28 For example in Sweden there is virtually complete publicity of forecasts by the governmental, but independent, Swedish Business Cycles Institute. Its forecasts are based on the assumption that government policy will remain unchanged, and they appear together with the Finance Bill published by the Ministry of Finance, in which the Minister gives his opinion of prospective developments. In Britain the long-standing refusal to publish official forecasts has recently been abandoned, and outside users now have access to the official Treasury model.

29 As Walter Heller conceded, in recounting the story of a famous American policy decision, 'it was the Council's good luck . . . to have the 1964 tax cut come when the economy was still moving forward'. Had it occurred as an offset to an incipient downturn 'we would have lost the force of the *post hoc ergo propter hoc* reasoning that has undoubtedly been gaining popular acceptance for positive fiscal policy'. Cf. his essay 'Economic Policy Advisers', in Thomas E. Cronin and Sanford D. Greenberg, eds, *The Presidential Advisory System* (New York, 1969), p. 36. The complexities of the American political and legislative system had in fact significantly delayed the implementation of the tax cut. For a somewhat less sanguine interpretation of the episode see Harry G. Johnson, 'The Keynesian Revolution and the Monetarist Counter-Revolution', in Elizabeth S. Johnson and Harry G. Johnson, *The Shadow of Keynes: Understanding Keynes, Cambridge and Keynesian Economics* (Chicago, 1978), p. 193.

30 This approach will doubtless strike some readers as excessively taxonomic. For a recent attempt to introduce a more theoretical approach see Alan Peacock, *The Economic Analysis of Government and Related Themes* (Oxford, 1979), esp. pp. 213–42.

31 Hutchison, *Economists and Economic Policy*, p. 262.

32 This is especially true of those contributions which entail the prevention or modification of foolish or harmful actions, a process which Alan Peacock has

expressively termed 'damage minimization'. As William R. Allen has stated, American economists in government have reported that 'incredibly important decisions were being made with incredibly insufficient information by incredibly unanalytical people'. In such situations the economist's function is to 'keep them from doing something dumb, just completely dumb'. Op. cit., pp. 79–81. This recalls the impressions of British economists in the generalist environment of Whitehall in the early postwar years.

26

BRITAIN

The rise of the specialists

I INTRODUCTION AND HISTORICAL BACKGROUND

One of the most striking features of Britain's history has been the continuity of her ideas and institutions. Political, economic, and social change has usually been slow and gradual, and even world wars seem more often to have accelerated existing trends than to have brought about fundamental changes of mood or direction. This makes it peculiarly difficult to decide where to begin an account of the post-1945 expansion of the role of the economist in government. One obvious starting point is the publication of J. M. (later Lord) Keynes' *General Theory of Employment, Interest and Money* (1936), which is generally acknowledged to be the most important book written by an economist in this century. But there is an obvious danger of exaggerating the influence of any single individual thinker on the subsequent course of events, more especially as there is still vigorous and seemingly endless controversy about the precise antecedents, character, and significance of the *General Theory*, the relationships between Keynes' own ideas and those of his disciples the Keynesians, and the validity and influence of Keynesian economics.[1]

Fortunately, the details of this controversy need not concern us here. Even his most ardent critics acknowledge that Keynes' ideas exerted a powerful and direct impact on both the scientific community and the prevailing conception of the ends and means of economic and social policy. Moreover, as Keynes himself was continuously engaged throughout the 1930s in public debates about current economic and social problems and in government advisory work, some account of the context and nature of his influence on prewar, wartime, and immediate postwar affairs up to his untimely death in 1946 is unavoidable.

From the present standpoint the most relevant phase of Keynes' prewar career was his work through the Economic Advisory Council established by the second Labour government in January 1930, as part of the official machinery for handling the acute unemployment problem.[2] The council itself did not survive the 1931 crisis, for it uneasily combined a 'representative' group of businessmen and trade unionists with a 'technocratic' group of experts who, as Winston Churchill observed in 1930, could examine complex matters 'requiring high, cold, technical, and dispassionate or disinterested decision'.[3] However, that same year the Prime Minister, Ramsay MacDonald, accepted Keynes' proposal to create a Committee of Economists to diagnose current problems and propose possible remedies.[4] Other committees followed, especially the Committee on Economic Information which functioned from 1932 to 1939, and together they constituted the major channels through which economic expertise reached high Treasury officials, some of whom eventually proved responsive.[5] The results were by no means dramatic or immediate in policy terms. The process was one of permeation rather than conversion, and it was somewhat impaired by disagreements among the experts.[6] Nevertheless, it was through these committees that academic economists, especially Keynes himself, effectively undermined the notorious 'Treasury view' well before the *General Theory* had made its full impact.[7] It was a valuable learning experience for both sides, one that paid rich dividends in wartime, for example, in accelerating the acceptance of Keynes' policy proposals.

In organizational terms the council and the committees were precursors of such wartime organs as Stamp's Survey of War Plans, the Central Economic Information Service, and, far more important, its two offspring: the Economic Section of the War Cabinet Offices and the Central Statistical Office, both of which will be more fully considered below. The beginnings were necessarily modest, for there is clear evidence of powerful civil service opposition during the 1930s to any proposals to expand the technocratic element significantly or to create any substantial number of specialist posts for economists. The economist members of the Council were, of course, part-time advisers or consultants who retained their academic posts; and their full-time economist staff was confined to one senior member, H. D. (later Sir Hubert) Henderson, plus two juniors on the payroll and a third unpaid assistant.[8] Outside this tiny band there were also a small number of other civil servants who could legitimately be regarded as competent economists, most notably R. G. (later Sir Ralph) Hawtrey, whose official title was Director of Financial Plans, at the Treasury, from 1919. Also, following a short-lived post-1918 experiment with a General Economic Department at the Board of Trade, the post of Chief Economic Adviser to the Government was created;[9] but as it transpired, this official played little if any part in domestic economic policy for most of the period, being primarily occupied with quasi-diplomatic functions associated with imperial and international economic relations.

Before turning to the war and postwar periods one further notable prewar development must be recorded, namely, the creation of a professional economist unit in the Ministry of Agriculture, in 1934, and in the Department of Agriculture for Scotland.[10] This innovation was completely ignored in the recent scholarly study of the Economic Advisory Council, an ommission reflecting the authors' acceptance of the conventional preoccupation with high-level Keynesian macroeconomic policymaking. There are, of course, other important functions for economists in government, and the Ministry of Agriculture experiment constitutes further evidence that professionals were beginning to gain a foothold in official circles. In organizational terms, the agricultural economists were the first group of recognized economists employed within a government department, as contrasted with Henderson's unit in the Cabinet Office, which was designed to service a group of advisory bodies composed of outsiders. The location of the experiment in agriculture is also historically significant, for during the interwar years the government developed a more actively interventionist policy for agriculture than for any other sector of the economy, and this formed the basis of an expanded wartime and postwar agricultural policy which generated an unbroken tradition of agricultural economics and statistics up to the present. The personnel employed in the prewar period were engaged on modest, indeed sometimes literally down-to-earth, tasks which have typically been ignored or looked down on by other economists. Yet it was in the Ministry of Agriculture, rather than in the Cabinet Office, that the predecessors of today's vastly expanded army of departmentally based government economists are to be found.

In World War II, as in 1914–18, the exigencies of the situation generated an urgent demand for relevant economic ideas, techniques, and data, and this time the economics profession was much better equipped to make a constructive contribution. The broad intellectual foundations of macroeconomic policy had been laid and with respect to economic expertise there was direct continuity of personnel and approach in the transition from peace to wartime. The initial buildup of the administrative apparatus was slow and hesitant, even for a time after Churchill succeeded Neville Chamberlain in May 1940, but there gradually evolved an expanding and flexible organization for coordinating production, allocating scarce labour, materials, and shipping space, and controlling prices and production. However, even at the peak of the process the machinery of government fell some way short of full-scale centralized economic planning.[11]

Between 1939 and 1945 qualified economists and statisticians enjoyed unprecedented opportunities for government employment.[12] Oddly enough, although Keynes was drafted into the Treasury as an economic adviser early in the war, he never became a salaried civil servant. Yet from his informal position he came to exert a major impact on official thinking and on the aims and direction of policy until his death. His collection of articles *How to Pay for the War* (1940), which incorporated such seminal concepts as 'the inflationary gap' and 'output potential', constituted the intellectual basis of Kingsley Wood's innovative Budget of 1941. An associated development from the same general source was the first official wartime effort to construct estimates of national income and expenditure by Richard Stone and James Meade, also in 1941.[13] From that time onwards the expanded conception of the role of the budget as a central tool of economic policy and the data provided in the national accounts became integral components of wartime and postwar economic management. The relegation of monetary policy to a subordinate role was also largely due to Keynes, who argued persistently and effectively in favour of so-called cheap money.

The explicit wartime commitment to Keynesian peacetime goals was made in the path-breaking 1944 White Paper on *Employment Policy*, which announced the government's acceptance 'as one of their primary aims and responsibilities the maintenance of a high and stable level of employment after the war'. While conceding that in proposing this extension of state control over the volume of employment the government was 'entering a field where theory can be applied to practical issues with confidence and certainty only as experience accumulates and experiment extends over untried ground', the document went on to disclose the intention to 'establish on a permanent basis a small central staff qualified to measure and analyse economic trends and to submit appreciations of them to Ministers'.[14]

In the present context this declaration is of symbolic as well as practical significance, since it both acknowledged the success of the technocratic component in wartime economic policymaking and also guaranteed its survival into the postwar era. The general character of the economists' wartime contribution can be described briefly, since it can be explored in the available secondary sources.[15] Shortly before the outbreak of hostilities three members of the aforementioned Committee on Economic Information were brought together to form the so-called Stamp Survey of Financial and Economic Plans, which helped to provide some guidance in the initial transition from peace to war.[16] Several months later the Survey was expanded, by the inclusion of additional economists and statisticians, to form the Central Economic Information Service, which was located in the Cabinet Offices rather than the Treasury because of the broad range of its responsibilities. This body in turn was divided early in 1941, on Churchill's orders,[17] to form the Economic Section, which continued in existence (after its transfer to the Treasury in 1953) until 1969, and the Central Statistical Office, which still survives in a greatly expanded form. The immediate motive for the division was Churchill's determination to establish a single authoritative supply of statistics, for he had been exasperated by the provision of conflicting departmental estimates. But the organizational details are less important than the fact that once the Economic Section came directly under the aegis of Sir John Anderson, as Lord President of the Council, its prestige, effectiveness, and influence soared. Anderson was not merely a great administrator; he also commanded Churchill's confidence, and under his leadership the Lord President's Committee became, in Churchill's words, 'a parallel cabinet concerned with Home Affairs'.[18] Anderson took his economic experts seriously, although he did not, of course, always follow their advice; and as the members of the Economic Section and the Central Statistical Office were increasingly enlisted to provide expert advice on a wide variety of departmental and other committees, their influence spread. As Lionel (later Lord) Robbins, the Director of the Economic Section for most of the war period, has revealed in his autobiography,[19] the dons rapidly gained practical experience, working alongside other temporary and permanent officials. Instead of intermittent contributions in the form of briefs and reports which might be ignored or dismissed by ministers and senior officials, they became active participants in the discussion and formulation of policy. In the special circumstances of the wartime emergency, and with the additional weight provided by their association with Anderson, they played a far greater role than they could have done in more leisurely peacetime conditions, when the goals of policy are less simple and direct. Nevertheless, the wartime practice set a precedent which decisively affected postwar developments.

One of the most unexpected features of the British case is the fact that the economists' acknowledged success in wartime and the conscious adoption of full employment as a major postwar policy objective did not automatically generate a substantial demand for professional economists in the peacetime civil service. During the first two postwar decades macroeconomic management was undertaken with the aid of only a handful (i.e. less than 20) professional economists. Perhaps even more surprising, however, was the dramatic transformation of that situation after the Labour government's election in October 1964, during which time the number of professional economist posts in Whitehall grew approximately twentyfold to a peak of 390 in 1979 (cf. Table 1).[20]

Table 1 Economists and statisticians in the British Civil Service

Year	Economists[a]		% change since 1950	Statisticians[b] No.	% change since 1950
	No.				
1950	17	(37)		104	
1964	21.5	(46.5)	26 (26)	128	23
1970	208.5	(242.5)	1226 (661)	266	293
1975	365		2150	477	459
1980	379		2229	538[c]	517

Notes:

a. Compiled from information supplied by the Treasury and the Ministry of Agriculture and Fisheries. The figures in brackets include agricultural economists who were not part of the Government Economic Service until 1974. The basis of calculation differs from that in Table 2, below.

b. Compiled from information supplied by the Central Statistical Office.

c. 1979 figure.

This transformation cannot be explained simply in political terms, even though the change of administration was followed by a major effort to redirect economic and social policy and a determination to 'reform' the civil service, a long-cherished objective of the British left. It is, of course, broadly true that the Labour Party has been more favourably disposed towards economic planning and technocratic interventionism in economic and social affairs than the Conservatives; but if politics had been the sole determinant, there should have been a substantial number of economists employed under the postwar Labour regime, from 1945 to 1951, and a diminution rather than a continuing upward trend during the Conservative government of 1970–4.

Politics aside, there are various other reasons for the peculiarities of the British postwar experience to be considered in the following paragraphs. Briefly, they include: overconfidence in the efficacy of high-level peacetime macroeconomic management, stemming largely, no doubt, from the acknowledged success of the wartime Economic Section and the almost unquestioned dominance of Keynesian views of economic policymaking up to the 1970s; the absence of any clear conception of peacetime economic planning on the part of the postwar Labour government;[21] rapidly waning official, public, and even socialist enthusiasm for direct economic controls; the long period of Conservative rule from 1951 to 1964, and especially the 1950s, when conscious efforts were made to reduce the extent of government intervention and the size of the civil service;[22] difficulties on the supply side, owing to the reluctance of many of the temporary wartime civil servants to remain in government employment after the end of hostilities; a continuing shortage of trained economists in the 1950s and early 1960s relative to the rising demand in the universities and in business;[23] the unfavourable public image of the civil service, compounded by official reluctance to offer specialists preferential pay and conditions; the heavy reliance on temporary or short-service professional economists, which tended, at least for a time, to obscure the long-term problems on the supply side; and the prevailing generalist, so-called 'intelligent layman' or amateur tradition in government employment, which restricted the opportunities for specialists to rise through the hierarchy and participate in top-level decisionmaking.

This is a formidable catalogue; not all of the items it contains can be fully considered here. The post-1964 transformation reveals that at least some of the earlier obstacles could have been overcome, given sufficient determination and foresight on the part of ministers and senior civil servants. But to leave the explanation at that point would be to overlook the fact that already from the early 1960s there had been perceptible changes both in the government's view of economic planning and in the official attitude towards the employment of specialists, especially economists, within the government. On a political level, the manifest failure of the economy to grow at a satisfactory rate led to a shift from the loosely managed 'welfare capitalism' of the 1950s to a revival of interest in economic planning, largely modelled on French experience. This change, described by a perceptive French observer as 'the conversion of the conservatives',[24] led to the establishment of the National Economic Development Council, with consequences for the economics profession which will be considered later. Almost simultaneously, within the Civil Service, there was a conscious drive for improved efficiency in management under the direct influence of the Plowden Committee on the Control of Public Expenditure, which reported in 1961, but also, more fundamentally, as a by-product of widespread dissatisfaction in Parliament and in Whitehall with the existing administrative organization and utilization of resources. While the immediate effects on the government economists' position were limited, even after the reorganization of the Treasury in 1961–2, the longer-run implications were much more significant. However, instead of pursuing such matters now, thereby extending this chronological introduction, it is appropriate to consider these items later under topical subheadings.

II THE SUPPLY OF ECONOMISTS: DEFINITION; QUALIFICATIONS; NUMBERS; MARKET CONDITIONS

In the absence of a generally accepted definition, the term 'economist' is used here to describe a person with a recognized academic qualification in the subject and a job title which acknowledges the specialization. This is the most appropriate criterion from the standpoint of professionalization, since the assignment of a suitable designation is *ipso facto* recognition of the need for trained expertise in the performance of the functions involved. However, as applied in British central government the term may be considered unduly restrictive, since for most of the postwar period the bulk of official economic work, from low-level routine functions to high-level economic decisionmaking, has been undertaken by non-economists. It is true, of course, that some members of the élite generalist Administrative Class had taken undergraduate courses or even degrees in economics, but in many cases they soon lost touch with their academic background while occupying a sequence of administrative posts. Promotion within the hierarchy was determined more by on-the-job performance than by educational qualifications. Given the anti-specialist ethos of the central bureaucracy, which reflected traditional educational prejudices, it is clear that the majority of key decisionmakers in postwar Britain, including ministers, Governors of the Bank of England, and heads of the nationalized industries, have had no formal training in economics. It should, however, be conceded that there is no conclusive evidence that trained economists necessarily make the best economic decisionmakers!

Unlike the situation on the European continent, there has been no direct link between the training of economists and lawyers in Britain. But given the comparatively low cultural status generally accorded to technical and scientific education both in the academic world and in the civil service, it is easy to understand why the number of government economists and statisticians was so low at the end of the war and grew so slowly during the first two postwar decades.[25] Although some British universities have awarded specialist degrees in economics since the early years of this century, the practice is not yet universal. Indeed Oxford, one of the most prestigious institutions with a strong tradition of supplying graduates for the public service, has no 'single honours' degree in economics, the Modern Greats (or PPE) course comprising a variable mixture of studies in Philosophy, Politics, and Economics. While this may well be an admirable preparation for entrants into the generalist Administrative Class, it is by no means adequate as a training for economic specialists. Moreover, it is impossible to determine, without specific information, how much economics training any given Oxford PPE graduate has received; and the same is broadly true of the holders of early postwar London University B.Sc. (Econ.) degrees and the innumerable 'joint' degrees still awarded by many universities. For civil service recruits in the first two postwar decades the quality of the degree (and, some would add, the institution by which it was awarded) was usually far more important than its subject matter. This was not true of statisticians or agricultural economists; but the majority of early postwar recruits to the Economic Section were employed as high-level economic administrators and advisers, rather than technicians. By today's standards many were deficient in mathematical and quantitative techniques, and it was not until the mid-1960s that any significant number of civil servants had obtained the master's or doctor's degree in economics – a by-product of the slow development of postgraduate research and instruction in Britain.

However, in this as in other respects conditions were changing rapidly during the 1960s. Early in that decade there was a growing demand for experienced academic economists in their thirties or older who could occupy middle-rank posts and command the respect and attention of senior officials. Unfortunately, such individuals were not only few in number but also, in some cases, reluctant to enter the public service at a time when the universities, the main focus of their career aspirations, were entering a rapid expansionist phase. By going to Whitehall they would not only be out of sight, out of mind, but their publication opportunities would be restricted and, consequently, also their academic promotion prospects. Younger economists were, admittedly, somewhat less scarce. But there were few opportunities for apprentices in the only specialist unit, the Economic Section, which was deliberately kept small, whereas if they entered a large government department they could hardly expect to make a significant impact at a junior level, especially as they were liable to become immersed in routine administrative duties.

Several ways of relieving the shortage were considered as part of the growing effort to improve the quality and efficiency of management. One novel suggestion was the provision of preferential postgraduate awards for economics graduates, the argument being that this was the stage at which professional career decisions were made. However, this scheme was rejected both as a potential interference with university autonomy and as an invitation to other specialist groups to claim comparable treatment. For young entrants with few or no qualifications in economics or statistics, a small number of cadetships or bursaries were provided, and attempts were made to place Executive and Research Officers with economics training in appropriate posts. Most significant, however, was the establishment of the Centre for Administrative Studies in 1963, designed to provide short courses in economics for generalists to enable them to perform economic functions more effectively and to enhance their ability to communicate with the few recognized government economists. In addition, refresher courses were provided for administrators who had previously studied economics.[26]

These developments constitute significant evidence of a growing awareness of the need for more specialists, not merely economists, in the public service, a change of outlook which was followed by a variety of efforts to improve the in-service training facilities for civil servants. Hence, when the reforming zeal of the new Labour administration was added late in 1964, it gave a strong impulse to a movement which was already under way. Several years earlier the Conservatives' 'conversion' to economic planning had given birth to the National Economic Development Council, a public agency outside the main departmental structure, but drawing in part on data and expertise supplied by the regular civil servants. The Council's office, Nedo (or Neddy) as it soon became known, quickly built up an economic staff almost as large as that in the Treasury, and when the Department of Economic Affairs was created in 1964, after the change of government, most of the Nedo economists moved into the new ministry. There was also a rapid buildup of economists in the newly established Ministry for Overseas Development, and an even more dramatic development was the appointment of three prominent academic economists, Thomas (later Lord) Balogh, Robert Neild, and Nicholas (later Lord) Kaldor, as special advisers to the Prime Minister, Chancellor of the Exchequer, and Inland Revenue Department, respectively. This innovation caused a mild sensation at the time, and its implications for the professionalization of government economics will be considered below. At this stage, however, its significance for the supply of economists must be emphasized, for it revealed the government's determination to give them a more prominent and influential role in the formulation and implementation of policy. Some of those who had hitherto dismissed the civil service as an unsuitable arena for the exercise of their talents responded readily to the determined efforts now being made to seduce them from their ivory towers. Most of the new recruits were temporary, which was already the established practice for members of the Economic Section; but because many were not enlisted through the normal recruitment procedures, they soon became known as 'irregulars'.[27] One important lesson was that if the conventional personnel practices could be overcome, stretched, or circumvented and if the prospect of government employment could be made to appear stimulating enough,[28] then obstacles to growth in the supply of economists which had hitherto been deemed insurmountable could in fact be overcome.

Although the invasion of the irregulars was essentially a short-term response to an immediate demand, it proved to be the onset of a remarkably rapid and sustained upsurge in the number of economists in Whitehall.[29] Those officials responsible for personnel matters were, it is true, anticipating a long-run increase in the numbers of economists and statisticians; but no one seems to have foreseen how fast or how far it would go – partly, no doubt, because the new government's political position was decidedly shaky at first, and it was thought that if the Conservatives were returned, the process might be halted or reversed. With the benefit of hindsight, however, it is clear that the process was affected not only by changes in political attitudes and the official view of the role of specialists in government but also by more general trends in the market for economists.

To sum up a complex story the full details of which are still unclear,[30] it appears that a marked expansion in the output of economics graduates from the early 1960s through to the early 1970s was accompanied by a sustained growth of their job opportunities, whereas more recently the slackening of demand both from business and from the universities, coupled with increases in civil service salaries and favourable pension provisions, has greatly enhanced the relative attractiveness of government employment. As will be indicated later below, there has been a growth of career-mindedness on the part of Whitehall economists during the present decade, whereas up to the early 1960s the professionals in the Economic Section had usually regarded their government experience as a temporary intermission in a permanent academic career. In this respect, as in others to be noted below, the differences between British government economists and statisticians have narrowed, for the latter have almost invariably regarded the civil service as a lifetime career.

III GENERAL SOCIAL AND CULTURAL ATTITUDES TOWARDS INTELLECTUALS, PROFESSIONALS, AND EXPERTS

The dramatic increase in the numbers of civil service economists, statisticians, and other professionals during the past decade or so may suggest that there has been an underlying transformation in traditional anti-special-ist social and cultural attitudes. However, it is far from easy to assess the precise extent and significance of this movement, especially as the civil service is one of the more entrenched and prestigious of British institutions, and its reform has been a hotly debated matter, especially since the early 1960s.

No doubt the roots of recent changes in social and cultural attitudes must be sought in the wartime emergency when the general desire for postwar reforms which would ensure that wartime sacrifices were not in vain contributed to a markedly leftward shift in public opinion.[31] The enthusiastic reception of Sir William (later Lord) Beveridge's welfare state proposals, and the general acceptance of full employment as a major policy objective, entailed a commitment to more active interventionist policies for the sake of greater economic and social equality, as well as prosperity. In the educational field the postwar expansion and democratization of the universities, and the shift towards the social and natural sciences and technology, constituted manifestations of a modernization process which might have been more rapid but for the slow rate of economic growth (by European standards), for this severely limited the resources available for educational experiments. And in these circumstances the delayed impact of modernization on the civil service itself seems somewhat less surprising.

From the standpoint of civil service reform, by far the most important single postwar landmark is the Fulton Committee's report of 1968, although enough has already been said to indicate that significant internal develop-ments were already under way some years before that date. Unfortunately the question of the extent to which pre- and post-Fulton changes have effectively modernized and professionalized the civil service, which was one of the Committee's principal avowed aims, is still highly contentious; so too is the related question of the extent to which the highest ranks of the service have been opened to able candidates from broader social back-grounds. A massive recent House of Commons review of the post-Fulton decade concluded that the pace and extent of change had been disappoint-ingly slow, and even some of the senior officials who gave evidence expressed regret and even bewilderment at the apparent failure of their efforts to correct the heavy statistical bias among new entrants in favour of independent (i.e. fee-paying) schools, Oxford and Cambridge universit-ies, and arts graduates, as contrasted with social and natural sciences graduates.[32]

Various explanations of this state of affairs have, of course, been offered. Civil servants, on the defensive, have naturally stressed the difficulties of transforming a vast bureaucratic organization within a short period, whereas overeager reformers have blamed bureaucratic inertia or deliberate resistance to change. Some of those specialists whose salaries, conditions of service, and promotion opportunities have, at least until very recently, improved out of all recognition, have been inclined to express dissatisfaction because their gains have fallen short of their rising expectations. Casual empiricism suggests that while conditions are now in many respects (and especially for specialists) remarkably different from those obtaining in the 1950s, Britain still lags well behind the USA and most northern and western European countries in respect of the role accorded to professional economists in government. It seems that the persistence of traditional cultural and social attitudes, as reflected in bureaucratic styles and procedures, has significantly delayed the impact of modernization, even though there has lately been a rapid closing of the gap.

IV PROFESSIONALIZATION

(a) Economists, statisticians, and agricultural economists

Operational definitions of professionalization are difficult to formulate and apply, but there seems little reason to doubt that the Keynesian revolution and the subsequent wartime and postwar activities of economists in government have done more than anything else to enhance the public reputation and influence of the economics profession in Britain. Although there is evidence that professional self-consciousness was growing among the economists around the turn of the century, their principal organization, the Royal Economic Society (RES) adopted a distinctly limited and cautious policy until the later 1960s.[33] This is true whether it is compared with the American Economic Association or its closest British counterparts, the Royal Statistical Society (RSS) and the Agricultural Economics Society (AES). The statisticians' organization is stronger and more venerable and has been more active, for example, in petitioning the government on behalf of its members, usually with the object of obtaining additional resources for the improvement of official statistics; and shortly after the war the RSS shocked a number of leading economists, who were members of both organizations, by proposing to establish qualifying examinations for statisticians.[34] A comparable proposal for economists would probably have been unthinkable, and in the event the economists succeeded in thwarting the scheme. The agricultural economists, despite their limited numbers and lower prestige, also developed a more active organization in the 1930s then the RES, largely owing to their collective association with and dependence on the Ministry of Agriculture, a link which stimulated their sense of professional solidarity and *esprit de corps*.[35] At least as far as the pre-1965 period is concerned, a broad comparison of the three groups reveals that in each case the degree of professional coherence, organization, and self-consciousness within the civil service has roughly paralleled the situation outside.

There are obvious reasons why British government statisticians were organized and professionalized in advance of the economists. Their numbers were greater; they had a recognizable shared technical expertise; and they were, as a group, more civil service career oriented than the economists, most of whom were, until very recently, on temporary or short-service appointments. A coordinated and systematized body of official statistics is obviously indispensable, and since World War II the evolution of centralized Keynesian-type national income accounting has reinforced the need for a unified statistical apparatus and centralized management of statistical staff throughout the public service. The Central Statistical Office was the natural focus for coordination and management, but owing to the established tradition of departmental autonomy in staffing matters, those organizational functions were necessarily performed by persuasion and convention rather than by formal authority. From the later 1960s, however, the effective influence of the CSO increased through the Head of the newly formed Government Statistical Service.

The need for formal organization of agricultural economists was much less pressing than for statisticians because their numbers were smaller and they were mainly concentrated in two departments.[36] As long as the economists were, to all intents and purposes, confined to the Economic Section and severely limited in numbers, informal management was sufficient. It is true that after the Treasury reorganization of 1962 they were increasingly 'bedded out' within Treasury divisions and were working alongside non-specialist administrators. Management panels for economists and statisticians were in fact established before the hectic influx of irregulars in the early months of the new Labour government, but that development made it necessary to provide a more effective administration of the expanding but still scarce supply of economic expertise. In an effort to introduce a measure of order and system A. K. (later Sir Alec) Cairncross, the Director of the Economic Section and Economic Adviser to HM Government, was made Head of the newly formed Government Economic Service early in 1965, in addition to his economic advisory duties. But although the Treasury ultimately controlled the funds available for staff appointments, in practice Cairncross possessed limited powers to control or direct the new wave of temporary officials, though he endeavoured to check the proliferation of specialist economist units, which were rapidly becoming fashionable. More important than the details of these developments is the fact that the new arrangements, though initially designed to meet immediate needs, accelerated the progress of professional autonomy and self-control within the government machine. The need for specialized knowledge in managing the appointment, placement, and promotion of specialist personnel was reinforced by a trend away from the macroeconomic generalists who had predominated in the Economic Section towards microeconomists, a movement encouraged by the increasing attention already being paid to economic planning and regional development from the early 1960s. Cairncross found it virtually impossible to act as central recruiting agent and manager of a proliferating corps of specialists in economic forecasting, transport, industrial, and development economics while simultaneously performing his duties as Economic Adviser to the government. The employment of professional economists spread from the Treasury through the obvious economic departments to education, health and social security, foreign affairs, and defence – branches of government which hitherto had employed no professional economists whatsoever. The creation of the Civil Service Department (CSD) in 1968 to take charge of establishment (i.e. personnel) matters formerly undertaken by the Treasury, also contributed to the extension of professional autonomy. The economists and statisticians came to be regarded as 'well-managed classes' who did not require detailed supervision or control at a time when CSD officials were preoccupied with other more pressing matters.

Oddly enough, when the Government Economic Service was established, the agricultural economists were excluded, initially on the grounds that they were a specialist cadre who could not, like other economists and general administrators, move from one department to another if required to do so. This was an increasingly unrealistic contention at a time when, as already noted, the development of specialization among other government economists was proceeding apace.

(b) Professional self-consciousness, organization, ethics, neutrality

It is difficult to generalize about the effects of these processes on the development of the economists' professional self-consciousness. Despite the limited numbers employed in the Economic Section up to the mid-1960s, it would be erroneous to suggest that they were not professionally self-aware, even though most of them regarded the academic rather than the civil service community as their sociological reference group. They fully appreciated that they occupied a privileged position close to the centre of the policymaking process, and probably also realized that they were regarded by some officials, including statisticians and agricultural economists, as semi-academic theorists or backroom boys rather than operational civil servants.

With the growth of scale there inevitably developed a measure of specialization, division of labour, and hierarchy which had been largely absent in the Economic Section. From the later 1960s the Economist members of the First Division Association of civil servants became more concerned about such matters as pay, career management, and promotion, and in recent years the practice of annual semi-formal negotiations with the Head of the Government Economic Service has become customary.

Prior to the mid-1960s the professional economists in Whitehall were too few to exert any effective group pressure, had they sought to do so. In fact, they seem to have had a modest conception of their individual and collective role. In his *Autobiography* Robbins recalled that the Economic Section's wartime success had been due in considerable measure to its members' willingness to make themselves useful to ministers and senior officials, and to their acceptance of established civil service values and traditions.[37] Had they differentiated themselves too sharply from their non-economist colleagues, claiming special attention or consideration because of their knowledge or insight, they would presumably have encountered greater resistance and correspondingly diminished their impact. Robbins' successors, James Meade and Robert Hall (later Lord Roberthall), seem to have adopted the same general approach, and the latter seems even to have gone out of his way to minimize the need for any substantial number of professional economists in government.[38]

In retrospect, while this professional modesty may have enhanced the economists' initial acceptance and ensured them a place near the heart of the economic policymaking process, it may have inhibited the long-run perception of the need for their services within departments. Their general situation certainly changed little during the 1950s, but after that time a more favourable climate prevailed both within and outside the main departmental structure. In this respect a notable development was the appointment of an experienced economist, Sir Robert Shone, as the first Director-General of the National Economic Development Office. Through his Economic Director, Sir Donald MacDougall, who was already well-known as an academic and ex-government economist, a substantial staff of general and industrial economists was assembled with unprecedented speed, and although the organization was outside the established departments, it was close enough to exert a significant indirect demand for economists in Whitehall itself. There was both cooperation and some rivalry with existing departments, which were put under added pressure to adopt a more thorough and professional approach to the preparation and presentation of economic policy proposals. Nedo was prominent in the campaign for increased economic growth during the years 1962–4, and on Labour's accession to power in October 1964, MacDougall moved to the Department of Economic Affairs to take charge of economic planning and public affairs under a new Permanent Secretary, Sir Eric (now Lord) Roll, another internationally known economist with both academic and governmental experience. MacDougall took with him most of his Nedo economists, and both in the DEA, and from 1969 as Head of the Government Service, his economic staff expanded rapidly. Unlike Cairncross, his immediate predecessor in the Treasury, MacDougall had no misgivings about working in charge of a large body of professionals.[39]

While the DEA was designed as a major economic department to challenge the Treasury's supremacy, other substantial groups of professional economists were assembled, most notably in the Ministry of Overseas

Development, from 1964, and at the Ministry of Transport, from 1966. In both instances an enthusiastic minister, Barbara Castle, provided the initial stimulus; but in both cases the process became cumulative, largely because of the professionals' desire to work with their own kind. These examples were subsequently followed in other departments, though in a less spectacular manner.

By comparison with their American peers British economists have expressed remarkably little concern about questions of professional ethics or integrity arising from government employment. Doubtless the well-established respect for civil service neutrality has shielded them from most of the dangers that are only too familiar to their counterparts in some other countries; and some weight must be accorded to the practice of 'inning' and 'outing' which enhanced the short-service academic economists' feelings of independence and reduced the risks of professional obsolescence to which the permanent civil service economist is subject. There was, however, one period when the threat of political interference loomed large in Whitehall, namely when Balogh, Neild, and Kaldor were appointed to top-level advisory posts and were followed by an influx of irregulars, many of whom also appeared sympathetic to the new Labour government. For a time Cairncross's position as the chief government economist seemed to be undermined, if not actually jeopardized, while those of his colleagues who did not fear the taint of politicization nevertheless resented the intrusion of inexperienced newcomers, however academically distinguished, who were appointed above their heads. In practice, however, the initial over-anxiety soon died away. Almost all the government economists benefited in some degree from the boom in the demand for their services, and it was not always possible to distinguish politically motivated irregulars from economits who could have (or indeed had) been appointed to the pre-1964 Economic Section. After a phase of uneasiness and dislocation, compounded by the hectic pace at which the new administration set about its ambitious programme, conditions soon settled down with regulars and irregulars working smoothly alongside each other. Professional solidarity and *esprit de corps* may have prevailed over short-term disturbances. Within two or three years many of the more prominent 'political' economists (as they were known in official circles) left the civil service, often somewhat disillusioned by their failure to transform Whitehall as completely as they had overoptimistically expected,[40] while others, who acquired a taste for government work and became fully assimilated into the Whitehall community, stayed on and became permanent civil servants.

Apart from the increase of scale, one other permanent legacy remains from this period – the practice of appointing Special Advisers to ministers whose function is to provide technical as well as political advice, somewhat on the lines of continental ministerial 'cabinets'. Their numbers have been small, and they have usually been selected by and attached to specific ministers on a temporary basis, but their influence may well have been considerable, for they can interpret official recommendations and, when disagreements arise, take a much stronger line than regular civil servants if they choose to do so. By no means all the Special Advisers have been economists. But it was probably the economists who led the way, and it is noteworthy that despite severe Conservative criticism of Labour's irregulars, the practice of appointing Special Advisers was continued after the Conservatives regained office in 1970.[41]

(c) Relations with other professionals

The rapid expansion of the professional economist cadre in Whitehall was accompanied by broadly similar trends among other professional groups, but as yet there is little detailed comparative analysis or commentary on the process. Given the growth of professional autonomy and self-control it would be surprising if tension and friction had been entirely absent. For example, during the Fulton Committee's investigation a merger of the economist and statistician classes was seriously contemplated but was eventually abandoned, largely because the statisticians feared it would work to their detriment.[42] In other instances the introduction of economists into departments aroused opposition or misgivings among entrenched professional groups such as the road engineers in Transport, where the process was sudden and dramatic in the later 1960s, tax inspectors in Inland Revenue, or prison officers in the Home Office. In some respects the response was not essentially different from that of generalist administrators, who, it has been said, 'have tended to resist any development of specialization, save in limited and pragmatic ways which can be combined with the maintenance of their generalized career opportunities'.[43] Additional problems may arise when the newcomer claims or is supposed to possess superior powers of formal analysis, since his advent implies that the incumbents 'have been sitting around for years mindlessly carrying on their activities without ever asking whether what they were doing was worthwhile or whether there might not be better ways to do the same thing'.[44]

During the past decade and a half there have been two parallel, and at first sight contradictory, trends in Whitehall professionalization. As noted earlier, the extent of professional recognition, autonomy, and self-control has grown substantially, but at the same time there has also been an increasing number of 'mixed divisions' in which a variety of professionals work side by side either under a professional head or under a generalist administrator. Such a development is doubtless inevitable, given the increasing complexity of modern society and governmental processes. Yet this intermingling and collaboration has not been accompanied by a blurring or obliteration of professional distinctions. In other words, with varying degrees of success methods have been devised to reconcile organizational

535

flexibility and efficiency with the needs and interests of the participating professional groups.

V THE LOCATION, FUNCTIONS, AND SPREAD OF GOVERNMENT ECONOMISTS

As so few professional economists were employed in Whitehall during the first two postwar decades, it is hardly surprising to find that apart from occasional outside consultants, the nationalized industries, local government, and even the Bank of England were virtually without economists at the time. There were, admittedly, one or two exceptions to this generalization which can be ignored for the present purpose;[45] and it is worth noting in passing that local government employment in Britain, unlike central government, has not been dominated by the amateur or 'intelligent layman' tradition. Engineers and lawyers have often held key positions in county and municipal bureaucracies.

Something must, however, be said of the Bank of England both because of its potentially strategic importance and because in some respects it epitomizes the British situation. As is well known, the Bank has had a long and proud history, and even after its nationalization in 1946 it retained for a time much of its former independence. During the war period, when concern with materials and manpower shortages took precedence over purely financial considerations, the Bank was responsible for exchange controls and the sterling area, and its officials played a significant role in the vital discussions of postwar international trade and payments proposals. Their misgivings about the outcome appeared to be confirmed by the 1947 convertibility crisis, and thereafter the Bank acquired a virtually autonomous position on certain policy matters. For much of the early postwar period it remained almost aloof from Whitehall. Despite the secrecy surrounding its activities, it is known that the Governor occasionally gave advice (e.g. on Bank rate changes after the initial 'cheap money' period) directly to the Chancellor of the Exchequer without the intermediation, sometimes even without the knowledge, of the Economic Adviser to the Government.[46] During the 1950s there seems to have been a kind of tacit division of labour between the Economic Section and the Bank – partly, no doubt, because of Keynesian ideas, which were interpreted as assigning monetary policy a role subordinate to fiscal policy in the economic management process, but also because the Section's primary functions and reputation had evolved in wartime, when monetary and financial matters had been relegated to a secondary place. Yet another reason is the fact that up to 1960 the Bank seems to have been 'positively averse to economics'.[47] Although in 1933 it had appointed an Economic Adviser (Professor Sir Henry Clay, who retained that office until 1944) and one other economist, it actually reduced its economic and statistical staff in wartime and was devoting fewer staff resources to domestic matters in the 1950s than in the 1930s. Its personnel were often recruited from the City of London or directly from independent schools rather than the universities, and though many probably took elementary economics as part of the Institute of Bankers' qualifications, the level of their formal knowledge was usually distinctly limited.

The publication of the Redcliffe Committee's Report on the Working of the Monetary System in 1950 'marked the beginning of a change, which gathered momentum in the succeeding years'.[48] There was a virtually complete rethinking of the Bank's role. The provision of monetary and financial statistics was transformed; the Bank began to employ economists and other specialists in its general office and to publish data and commentaries on economic affairs. In the past two decades cooperation with the Treasury has greatly improved, especially since the Bank recruited a number of distinguished economists into its higher policymaking positions, some of them former members of the Economic Section.[49] Here too the professionals' encroachment on the intelligent laymen's domain has been inexorable, if inordinately belated. And in the process the Bank has lost some of its traditional independence.

One of the by-products of this history is that even during the 1960s and to a somewhat lesser extent in the 1970s, the Treasury was seriously undersupplied with monetary expertise, a state of affairs doubtless reflecting both the customary division of labour with the Bank and the persistence of the Keynesian focus on fiscal rather than monetary matters. Until quite recently the Treasury's econometric forecasting models apparently contained no monetary equations whatever. Thus there has been no parallel between Britain and those countries where the central bank has been both an integral component in the policymaking process and a major supplier of economic expertise to the government.[50]

As already indicated, prior to the mid-1960s British government economists were concentrated mainly in the Economic Section and actively engaged in the policymaking process at a variety of levels. Unfortunately, owing to the restrictions imposed by the Official Secrets Act, it is impossible to provide a detailed description and evaluation of their roles and influence. Nevertheless, a reliable general impression can be derived by extrapolating from accounts of the wartime experience, by piecing together published reports, and by interviews.

The Economic Section's postwar position was determined largely by wartime precedents and by decisions taken before the end of hostilities. Before agreeing to succeed Robbins as Director, Meade obtained an assurance that the Treasury's wartime economic advisers – Keynes, Lord Catto, D. H. (later Sir Dennis) Robertson, and Henderson – would not remain indefinitely, and that he would, ex officio, have a place on the crucial Budget Committee. This was probably the Section's most important single means to exert an influence on policy throughout the 1950s. While the Section was still in the Cabinet Office Meade was invited by the Chancellor, Hugh Dalton, to approach him directly whenever he wished; and Hall retained that right after the Section moved into the Treasury in 1953. Yet neither seems to have availed himself of this privileged access in practice, believing that it would be more likely to arouse official suspicion and hostility than if he worked in the customary way through the senior Treasury staff, who were in almost daily contact with the Chancellor.

Other members of the Section also worked mainly by assimilating themselves into the established administrative processes rather than by direct assertion or by seeking special facilities. They played a major role in the preparation and production of the postwar Economic Surveys and became deeply involved (together with some of the CSO statisticians) in the slowly developing economic forecasting machinery. In addition they attended a variety of official policy committees and their subordinate, usually interdepartmental, working parties; wrote briefs and memoranda on current issues, sometimes directly for ministers; made independent studies of topical and prospective problems; prepared materials for ministerial speeches and replies to parliamentary questions; and made themselves generally useful to administrators. Theirs was a very flexible organization – a kind of high-level fire brigade, ready to be deployed against almost any economic emergency, equipped with little or no supporting technical or clerical staff, but able to draw on a kind of accumulated goodwill and cooperation from a variety of government departments and agencies. In the early postwar period when the Section's future was still in doubt, they were, in a sense, on trial. While often seeming academic in tone and inclination, they knew that their effectiveness and impact depended on their ability to be relevant and constructive – for example, by becoming involved in issues at an early stage, before official attitudes had hardened. Their success, which seems to have been considerable, probably depended less on their specialized academic knowledge and professional skills than on their individual qualities and abilities – e.g. tact; patience; adaptability; the capacity to work quickly under pressure; the ability to communicate with non-specialists; skill in the arts of persuasion; a sense of timing; grasp of bureaucratic procedures and conventions, or more colloquially, the capacity to 'play the machine'; appreciation of the problems of administrative feasibility and political practicality; recognition of the limits of one's professional expertise; and sheer stamina. In general, the Section's members seem not only to have avoided arousing the traditionalists' hostility; they also won the confidence, respect, and occasionally even the admiration of their official colleagues, some of whom have paid generous tribute to the lessons they learned from collaborating with economists. This undoubtedly helps to explain part of the rising demand for economists (and to a lesser extent, statisticians) in

538

the 1960s as their supporters moved up the civil service hierarchy and used their influence to create new technical or economic advisory posts.

By present-day standards most of the economists employed in Whitehall in the first two postwar decades were, by virtue of their academic training and mental outlook, closer to the generalist than the specialist end of the spectrum. Unlike the agricultural economists and statisticians, they were generally regarded as economic administrators rather than mere technicians. In some degree this reflects the fact that economics is a more value-oriented subject, more sensitive to political considerations than more narrowly technical disciplines; and as is well known, at the higher official levels administrative appraisal contains a relatively large economic component and a smaller technical component, whereas the nature of technical appraisal varies less with changes of administrative level. As Hall remarked, reflecting on the predominantly macro preoccupations of the 1950s, 'the special province of the economist is the economic system as a whole, and the relations between the workings of its different parts'.[51] In a similar vein one of the most outstanding early postwar generalists, Lord Bridges, acknowledged the economist's potential contribution to the coordination of policy by remarking that 'it is economic factors more than anything else which have compelled departments to work together'.[52]

At present there is insufficient evidence on which to base a judgement of the economists' effectiveness. But in the early postwar years it seems clear that one of their most important functions was 'damage minimization', as one leading economist recently put it, by correcting the fallacious economic reasoning employed by non-economist officials.[53] An indication of the need for economic education in the Treasury at that time is provided by the official who subsequently admitted:

> I was flung in at the deep end. I learnt about exchange rates through the process of reading briefs on devaluation. I learnt about budgets by making and preparing one as Secretary to the Chancellor. I did it knowing I had not the faintest idea of the basis on which the Budget was put together. I did not even know what a deficit was. It came as a great flash of light when someone told me that what you did when you had a deficit was borrow.[54]

That confession may not reveal a typical situation. But there are certainly retired Permanent Secretaries of economic departments who generously acknowledge how much they learnt 'sitting by Nellie', i.e. alongside articulate trained economists. And the changing climate of opinion in the Treasury over the whole period is suggested by a leading government economist, who remarked in the mid-1970s:

> Nowadays economic language is talked throughout the Treasury. And instead of the economists feeling strange, it is the administrators, who

do not know any economics, who feel embarrassed. . . . And the fact that the top people are economically trained means that you have to put up a decent economic argument . . . and this is the way it should be.[55]

The spread of economic literacy has certainly gone much further in the Treasury than in most departments, but there were evidently still some embarrassed administrators recently even in that enlightened citadel. As with the growth of numeracy and familiarity with the handling and interpretation of statistics, there has been a veritable revolution in Whitehall during the postwar period, and its effects will continue to be felt long after the mere expansion of numbers has ceased.[56]

The progress of economic literacy and numeracy has undoubtedly been very uneven, and dependent on a chance combination of personalities and circumstances. At times, as with the creation of new departments like the DEA or the Ministry of Overseas Development or divisions within established departments such as the Ministry of Transport or the Board of Trade, the dissemination of economic ideas and data has increased suddenly. In other cases, however, a lone economist has been imported into a department because a minister or senior official had the vague notion that it might be helpful 'to have a tame pundit around the place'.[57] Such an individual has had to find his own way around, learn the ropes, and spend considerable time explaining in elementary terms the kind of analysis and advice he can provide. Needless to say, the results have often been meagre, especially until the newcomer has won the confidence of significant colleagues and discovered how to keep his ear close to the ground without losing his dignity. Sometimes the initiative for such an appointment comes from outside the department, e.g. from the need to deal with an international agency, or closer to home, from the need to defend expenditure proposals under Treasury fire. Indeed, it is not unlikely that in some instances the initiative has come from the Treasury itself in the form of a gentle hint that unless the department's expenditure proposals are more skilfully presented and more cogently argued in future they are unlikely to be approved.[58] There have even been unfortunate instances when the new appointee has come directly from the Treasury, arousing suspicions that he has been planted as a spy.

During the past decade or so the economists' functions in Whitehall have changed markedly for a variety of reasons: the increase of specialization, division of labour, and other organizational developments consequent upon the growth of numbers; the introduction of new and more complex techniques – most notably in the vastly expanded forecasting process, but also in the widespread use of such tools and approaches as cost-benefit analysis, output (or planned programme) budgeting, investment appraisal, and econometric model building; the growth of specialist operational and research units in the larger departments; and the increasing range, variety, and detail of government's intervention in economic and social affairs. Of course there are still economic administrative tasks of the kind undertaken in the heroic days of the Economic Section, especially by the increasing number of economists in senior posts where the distinction between purely economic functions, administration, and policymaking becomes unavoidably blurred.[59] But given the scale and complexity of the current bureaucracy, such economic administrators nowadays often have substantial managerial as well as advisory responsibilities. In this respect the functions of senior economists are becoming more like those of senior statisticians, many of whom have normally had charge of considerable numbers of subordinate technical and supporting staffs. By contrast, the Economic Section's personnel often worked in isolation or in pairs.

The development of more interventionist policies, especially since the revival of enthusiasm for economic planning in the early 1960s, has contributed to a major shift of emphasis in the utilization of professional economists from broad macroeconomic management towards more specific and detailed microeconomic work. Admittedly the distinction between macro- and microeconomic issues is difficult to sustain in practice; the two are in many cases interdependent, and there has been no simple abandonment of the earlier type of Keynesian macroeconomics despite mounting reservations about its theoretical foundations and practical effectiveness. But in recent years the main growth in demand for economists, both as technicians and as economic administrators, has been in the formulation, implementation, and evaluation of specific policies focused on some one aspect or segment of the economy. A case in point is the development of regional policy, where the success of any given measures will depend crucially upon their applicability to the special conditions and problems of the area concerned, as well as their general analytical soundness and compatibility with other current policies.[60] Hence in many macroeconomic policy issues there is a need for detailed factual knowledge of the subject matter, whether it be an area, an industry, a mode of transport, or an aspect of economic and social life such as housing, education, or health. To say that most departmental economists are engaged on micro- rather than macroeconomic activities may be an oversimplification, especially as some are technicians whose contributions consist of the application of their specific skills to any of a wide variety of problems. Nevertheless it is clear that the changing character of government economic work, as well as the growth of numbers, specialization, division of labour, and professionalization, have combined to reduce the gap which at one time differentiated the general economists (or economic administrators) from the departmentalized specialists in agricultural economics. And indeed, curiously enough, it is arguable that since the initial British approach to the EEC, a major new departure in economic and political affairs with especially important implications for the agricultural sector, the trend in agricultural economics has been in the opposite direction to the trend in government economics generally – namely, away from their established preoccupation with the microeconomic details of domestic agricultural production and pricing towards a broader concern with the role of agriculture in the national and international setting. Here too there has been a shift of emphasis rather than a sharp break with the past. But as in other branches of government economic work, it has been accompanied by considerable advances in analytical sophistication and technical complexity.

In addition to changes in their functions, there has been a remarkable 'spread' of economists beyond the Treasury, in which they were for so long concentrated. The extent of this movement is indicated in Table 2, which lists the main concentrations[61] of economists and statisticians in the mid-1970s. Some of the implications of this movement for the economist's working conditions (e.g. whether he is a loner or a member of a substantial unit or team) have already been mentioned.

VI THE NATURE OF THE POLITICAL SYSTEM AND BUREAUCRACY; THE ROLE OF ECONOMISTS IN POLICYMAKING

At the beginning of this study the continuity of British history was stressed, and this theme is also relevant when considering the general characteristics of the political and bureaucratic environment in which the professionaliz-ation of government economics has evolved during the past four decades. Throughout that period the political system has been democratic (doubtless somewhat less so in wartime and in the immediate postwar transition); government has been dominated in succession by two major parties which, for all their superficial differences and mutual antagonisms, differ much less in their practice than in their ideology or rhetoric; the balance of political support has shifted remarkably little, with the consequence that Parliamentary majorities have at times, at least until the present (1980) government, been disturbingly small and uncertain, and it is not too much to say that there has been a fundamental consensus – admittedly with some significant changes of emphasis and differences in detail – on the basic objectives of economic and social policy. Indeed, for these and related reasons, many observers maintain that the continuity – in other words, the inability to shake off the shackles of the past – has been the major reason for Britain's inability to escape from her depressingly persistent economic problems, such as a slow rate of economic growth; a low level of manufac-turing productivity; inadequate investment and technological innovation; outdated managerial and labour attitudes and practices; balance of pay-ments weakness; excessive overseas financial and political commitments (until recently); and a general lack of economic and social capacity to adapt to the demands of twentieth-century modernization.[62]

This is obviously not the place to embark on a general survey of postwar British economic and social history, especially one coloured unduly by the justifiable disappointments of the past decade or so. From the standpoint of the 1930s there have been substantial achievements, notably a steadily rising standard of living, and the avoidance of serious depressions and

Table 2 Major concentrations of economists and statisticians in the British Civil Service, 1974 and 1980

Government Economic Service			Government Statistical Service[d]		
	1974[a]	1980[b]		1974	1980[e]
Department of the			Department of the		
Environment	73	(60)	Environment	45	68
Department of Trade			Department of Trade		
and Industry	43	(44½)	and Industry	78	57
Treasury	58	(65½)	Treasury	7	12
Ministry of Overseas			Ministry of Overseas		
Development	29	38	Development	14	15
Department of			Department of		
Employment	20	21	Employment	20	42
Department of Health			Department of Health		
and Social Security	14	20	and Social Security	30	42
Department of Energy	10	20	Ministry of Agriculture,		
			Fisheries and Food	12	18
Foreign and			Ministry of Defence	37	32
Commonwealth Office	10	9			
Scottish Office	9	24[c]	Central Statistical		
			Office	56	55
Education	7	7	Office of Population		
			Censuses	32	29
			Civil Service		
			Department		
			Home Office	17	25
			Inland Revenue	14	21
Others	17	81	Others	52	96
TOTAL	290		TOTAL	442	520

Notes:

a. Compiled from Government Economic Service Directory, 1974. There were also 23 economists in the Ministry of Agriculture, Fisheries and Food, and 11 in the Department of Agriculture and Fisheries, Scotland, who were then excluded from the GES.

b. Data applying to 1 October 1980, supplied by Government Economic Service. These figures do not include economists on loan outside the GES; on study leave; in Nedo or Administrative posts; and those recruited by the Price Commission and other non-departmental bodies.

c. The Scottish Office figure includes agricultural economists in the Department of Agriculture and Fisheries, Scotland. The agricultural economists in the Ministry of Agriculture, Fisheries and Food are included in the table among 'other' economists.

d. Compiled from Government Statistical Service Directory. It should be noted that the Statistician Class in the British Civil Service is broadly parallel in salary and status to the Economist and Administrative Classes.

e. Data supplied by the Central Statistical Office.

widespread unemployment. With respect to the present subject, changes in the size, composition, and structure of the civil service and the educational system have been significant, even though too slow and gradual in the early postwar decades. Within the government machine there has been a significant breakdown of anti-specialist prejudices and a corresponding readiness, on the part of senior civil servants and ministers of both parties, to place more reliance on qualified social scientists, technologists, and other experts in making policy decisions.

The temptation to draw significant parallels between the rapid expansion of the Government Economic Service in the past decade or so and the concurrent rise in the trends of inflation and unemployment has, of course, proved irresistible to some commentators. On occasions it has provided harmless amusement in the form of references to the 'plague of economists' in Whitehall[63] which unduly flatter the economics profession by exaggerating its influence (much as socialist and sentimentalist historians overstated the pernicious influence of the classical economists in the early nineteenth century). From another standpoint, however, the matter cannot be dismissed so lightly, for serious scholars have attributed at least part of Britain's ills to the failures of Keynesian economics and the bad advice given by government economists, and even to a species of *trahison des clercs* on the part of the professional establishment, especially Cambridge and Oxford members.[64]

Needless to say, these important but highly controversial contentions cannot be adequately explored here. Despite a veritable flood of analysis, interpretations, reminiscences, journalistic disclosures, and scholarly studies of Britain's postwar economic ideas and policies, we still lack detailed knowledge of when, how, and to whom economic advice was offered, and precisely how far, if at all, it entered into the decisions actually taken.[65] The combination of an (at least partially) effective Official Secrets Act, a strong and sustained tradition of civil service anonymity, and a predominantly consensual style of administration[66] constitutes a significant obstacle to scholarship. In some instances – such as the economists' unsuccessful efforts to persuade the Wilson government to devalue the pound between 1964 and 1967 – the general content and thrust of economic advice and its reception are well known. But this was an unusual episode and on the whole – for example, by comparison with the USA[67] – British students of economic thought and policy labour under serious handicaps.

However, despite these difficulties, some broad concluding observations can be made about the changing postwar role of British government economists. As professionals, they now play an enormously increased role in policymaking in the broadest sense of the term – which includes the choice of policy objectives and assignment of weights to them; the selection of means to attain those ends; and the implementation and adaptation of existing policies in response to changing circumstances. Underlying the decisions there is now infinitely more relevant economic and statistical data, which are nowadays prepared and presented in a much more sophisticated form and analysed in more subtle and varied ways. Doubtless not all of this represents a net gain, for the proliferation of analyses and data may generate confusion and indecisiveness on the part of policymakers, especially when there is a babel of conflicting voices. Indeed, it is appropriate at this point to note the tendency, especially among scholars, to exaggerate the deliberateness and rationality of the policymaking process, which can be countered by reference to Cairncross's timely warning that 'The atmosphere of a large government department is frequently almost indistinguishable from that of the loony bin. I use the term in no pejorative sense; it is simply one of the facts of official life.'[68]

On the same occasion Cairncross referred to the temptation to exaggerate the influence of policy and the danger of neglecting the non-economic factors involved, considerations that have been especially important in recent British history. The predominantly 'consensual' relations between British ministers and top-level civil servants encourage 'mutual political protection', a practice based squarely on the traditions of collective ministerial responsibility and bureaucratic anonymity. Changes of government, however sudden or unexpected, have only temporarily affected this state of affairs,[69] even in the most dramatic postwar instances when the Labour Party came to power in 1945, and again in October 1964, supposedly with deep-rooted suspicions of the bureaucratic machine and a fierce determination to change the course of postwar history. In the latter episode, as always, the civil servants prepared themselves for the new regime by studying the campaign programmes and endeavouring to predict and clear the ground for new policies, some of which were discussed in private with leading members of the opposition before the election. As with so many potential British revolutions, the accompanying efforts to politicize the government economic service and reform the bureaucracy proved to be disappointing to their most ardent proponents.

The manifest failure of Labour's attempt to shift the balance of power within the bureaucracy by creating the DEA as a counterweight and policy-making rival to the Treasury is yet another example of the underlying continuity of the British system of government.[70] Curiously enough, some of those who are most critical of civil service traditionalism and most anxious to accelerate its reform also recognize that 'The greater the professionalism and expertise of our bureaucracy the greater its power. So we need to match any increase in civil service professionalism by at least a corresponding increase in the capacity of our Ministers and Parliament to control our bureaucratic machine.'[71] Yet while there has been a widespread tendency to overrate the importance of bureaucrats and experts – a view that the economists themselves have too seldom discouraged[72] – there is no doubt that in a democracy the ultimate responsibility must be with their masters, the politicians, and through them the electorate. In the British case it appears that in addition to the inertia of the past we have suffered unduly in recent years from short-term administrative and political disruptions consequent upon changes of government. As Michael Stewart has noted in a cogent analysis of the structural, technical, management, and political influences on the course of events,

> Incoming government have spent their first year or two abolishing or drastically modifying the measures – often quite sensible – of their predecessors, and pressing ahead with the measures – often unrealistic or irrelevant – which they have formulated in opposition. After a year or two they have come to closer terms with reality, and changed course, but by that time much harm has been done, and the benefits that would have accrued from continuing the policies they inherited have been lost.[73]

To the extent that this diagnosis is correct the remedy lies not in the sphere of economics, but in the need for more responsible opposition and the development of a degree of bipartisanship with respect to the primary ends and means of economic policy. British postwar experience suggests that this desirable objective is unlikely to be attained either easily or rapidly. While economists have undoubtedly learned much in that time about the complexities of policymaking processes and the intractability of economic and social problems, in dealing with such matters they necessarily tend 'to direct their attention to facets that can be illuminated by the methods of inquiry they find congenial. Their instruments are efficient within a range; but they often choose to ignore what lies outside it. . . . So it happens that, on occasions, their inquiries do not penetrate beyond the periphery of fundamental problems.'[74] Nevertheless, despite the undeniable limitations of economics as science – limitations that become the more obvious as economists participate more actively and continuously in government – it is clear that they can make a constructive, if usually modest, contribution to public affairs.

VII CONCLUDING REFLECTIONS

This study began by emphasizing the continuity of British ideas and institutions. In the light of events since the general election in May 1979 it may be appropriate to conclude by asking whether this generalization still holds good, for there have recently been significant, even seemingly dramatic, changes in government attitudes and practices. The first government in our history to be led by a woman Prime Minister has so far displayed an unusual determination to reverse the decline of the British economy (in itself no novel objective) by adopting strong policies that represent a conscious and deliberate break with the past. The fact that these policies are widely believed to be wholly or largely inspired by an economist – an American, Professor Milton Friedman – is of added interest from the standpoint of these studies. And as Mrs Thatcher's administration has the largest Parliamentary majority for some years, and therefore (at least on paper) the political means to implement her party's campaign promises, the current experiment is likely to be of great interest to future students of economic thought and policy.

It is, of course, much too early to judge how far this apparent discontinuity is either real or lasting. The current severe economic recession, though obviously not confined to Britain, has been accompanied here by unprecedentedly high interest rates, a sharp increase in the value of sterling, a high level of bankruptcies, and the worst unemployment since the early 1930s. How far the government is directly responsible for these conditions – some of which are novel, while others simply represent an accentuation of existing trends – is a matter of intense controversy. But whatever the verdict, the shift towards monetarism, loosely defined, raises important theoretical and practical questions about the government's ability to measure and control key monetary variables. Moreover, it entails a significant change from the earlier approach, according to which monetary factors were not ignored but were regarded as 'peripheral to the forecast mainly because examination of past relationships suggested that their influence was not strong'.[75]

Post-mortems on this period may eventually shed new light on the role of economists in British government, but these investigations, like the present study, will doubtless continue to be severely inhibited by the Official Secrets Act.[76]

There have, however, been several recent developments relevant to our subject which are worth noting by way of conclusion. Firstly, it is clear that the peak in the numbers of professional economists and statisticians in Whitehall has been passed, partly as a result of the government's determination to reduce public expenditure and the size of the civil service. Secondly, unlike the first two postwar decades, the days of 'inning and outing' are virtually over: almost the entire corps of professional economists in Whitehall now consists of career civil servants. Thirdly, while the present government has continued the practice of appointing special advisers – not all of whom, of course, are economists[77] – the latest appointee as Head of the Government Economic Service, Professor Terry Burns (formerly of the London Business School) has had no previous experience of working in the civil service. Unlike his predecessors, most of whom had earned reputations both as academics and as experienced economist-administrators, Burns is a leading econometrician and forecaster. As an isolated case, his appointment can hardly be regarded as a portent of politicization, even though many of the career professionals would probably have preferred to see the promotion of an insider. But whatever his impact on policy may be, Burns' arrival in Whitehall is further evidence that highly technical economic expertise is now securely placed at the top of the generalist bureaucracy.

NOTES

1 For example, the essays in Don Patinkin and J. Clark Leith, eds., *Keynes, Cambridge and the General Theory: The Process of Criticism and Discussion Connected with the Development of the General Theory* (Toronto, 1978); also T. W. Hutchison, *Keynes Versus the 'Keynesians'?* (London, 1977); and Elizabeth and Harry G. Johnson, *The Shadow of Keynes* (Oxford, 1979).

2 Howson and Winch, *The Economic Advisory Council 1930–1939.* I have drawn heavily on this source in this and the following paragraph.

3 In his Romanes Lecture, *Parliamentary Government and the Economic Problem*, quoted by Howson and Winch, p. 155.

4 Howson and Winch remark that 'this must have been the first occasion that an official body consisting entirely of economists was entrusted with such a far ranging brief' (op. cit., p. 47). It should be noted that the work involved investigatory as well as merely advisory functions.

5 This was especially true of Sir Richard Hopkins and Sir Frederick Phillips. Hopkins, who became Permanent Secretary of the Treasury from 1942 to 1945, was a defender of the 'Treasury view' in 1930, but became a wholehearted supporter of Keynes from the autumn of 1940. Ibid., pp. 151–2.

6 The economists who served on one or another of the committees included A. L. Bowley, G. D. H. Cole, H. Dalton, D. H. MacGregor, A. C. Pigou, L. Robbins, D. H. Robertson, J. Stamp.

7 The 'Treasury view' was an expression coined by Keynes to describe the official opposition to expansionist anti-depression measures. Cf. Howson and Winch, pp. 18, 27.

8 The three junior members were H. V. Hodson, Colin Clark, and Piers Debenham. For a short time R. F. (later Lord) Kahn was Assistant Secretary to the Committee of Economists.

9 Between 1919 and 1946 this post was held, successively, by Sir Hubert Llewellyn Smith, Sir Sydney Chapman (sometime Professor of Political Economy at Manchester), and Sir Frederick Leith-Ross.

10 See Coats, 'The Development of the Agricultural Economics Profession in England', esp. pp. 382–5 (reprinted in this volume, pp. 419–32). The first 'economic student and investigator' post was created in 1924, and three qualified assistants were appointed in 1934.

11 Cf. Hancock and Gowing, *British War Economy, History of the Second World War.* This is, of course, but one of a series of official histories of wartime economic and social affairs.

12 For a useful general account of this period see Winch, *Economics and Policy*, ch. 12, 'Keynesian War Economics and Post-War Plans'. Also the general survey by Leruez, *Economic Planning and Politics in Britain*, chs. 1 and 2; and the essays by wartime government economists in Chester, *Lessons of the War Economy.*

13 At that time an earlier pioneering effort was unknown. Cf. *Inland Revenue Report on National Income; with an Introduction by Richard Stone* (Cambridge, 1977). See also Stone's essay, 'The Use and Development of National Income and Expenditure Estimates', pp. 83–101.

14 Cmd 6527, London, HMSO (1944), p. 26. In fact the permanence of the central staff, in the Economic Section, was not assured until the early 1950s.

15 In addition to the works by Winch, Leruez, and Chester, already referred to, the account in Lord Robbins, *Autobiography*, ch. 8, is especially valuable. Research into this period is already well under way. Important new material has recently become available in Donald Moggridge, ed., *The Collected Writings of John Maynard Keynes*, vols. 22–4 (London 1978, 1979).

16 The members were Lord Stamp, H. D. (later Sir Hubert) Henderson, and H. (later Sir Henry) Clay.

17 The instruction is reprinted in Winston Churchill, *The Second World War* (London, 1949), vol. 2, app. A, p. 608. Robbins gives a vivid impression of the economists' dissatisfaction with the situation before they came under Anderson's wing. The personnel had been largely recruited by A. F. Hemming, who had been on the secretarial staff of the prewar Economic Advisory Council committees.

18 Cf. his statement in the House of Commons, 24 Feb. 1942, quoted by Chester, p. 9. For comments on Anderson's role and influence see, also, Robbins, p. 175, and the biography by Sir John Wheeler-Bennett, *John Anderson, Viscount Waverley* (London, 1962).

19 Robbins, *loc cit.*

20 The reasons for this remarkable expansion are considered briefly below. For relevant background material see Booth and Coats, 'The Market for Economists in Britain, 1945–75: A Preliminary Survey', pp. 436–54 (reprinted in this volume, pp. 474–95).

21 For a useful review of the literature on this subject see Leruez, ch. 2; also, for valuable details on the immediate postwar situation, Bernard Donoughue and G. W. Jones, *Herbert Morrison: Portrait of a Politician* (London, 1973).

22 The numbers in the Administrative Class, which included the highest-level officials as well as economists and statisticians, fell from 4,600 in 1950 to 3,400 in 1964, and rose again to 4,000 by 1970. *Annual Abstract of Statistics*.

23 Cf. Booth and Coats, 'The Market for Economists in Britain, 1945–75' *op. cit.*

24 Leruez, ch. 3. The subsequent developments are well treated in chs. 4 and 5. See also the valuable recent study by P. Meadows, 'Planning', in F. T. Blackby, pp. 402–17. This volume is the work of a team of economists under the auspices of the National Institute of Economic and Social Research.

25 For a more detailed account of the matters discussed in this and the next paragraphs, see Booth and Coats, 'The Market for Economists in Britain, 1945–75'; *op. cit.*

26 Cf. Desmond Keeling, 'The development of Central Training in the Civil Service 1963–70', *Public Administration* 49 (Spring 1971): 51–71.

27 Brittan, 'The Irregulars', pp. 329–39. See also Shanks, 'The Irregular in White-hall', in Streeten, pp. 244–62.

28 It is worth noting that a substantial group of economists was easily recruited for Nedo at a time when government departments were finding it very difficult to recruit economists. When the Department of Economic Affairs was established, late in 1964, the Nedo economists were transferred to it virtually en bloc, as mentioned above.

29 Cf. Table 1.

30 Cf. Booth and Coats, 'The Market for Economists in Britain, 1945–75', *op. cit.*

31 For an excellent general account of the process, see Addison, *The Road to 1945*.

32 *House of Commons, Expenditure Committee, Eleventh Report, 1976–77, Civil Service* (London, HMSO).

33 Cf. A. W. Coats, 'The Origins and Early Development of the Royal Economic Society', *Economic Journal* 78 (June 1968): 349–71; A. W. Coats and S. E. Coats, 'The Changing Social Composition of the Royal Economic Society 1890–1960

and the Professionalization of British Economics', *British Journal of Sociology* 24 (June 1973): 165–87. Both reprinted in this volume, pp. 313–37 and 338–60, respectively.

34 The evidence was published in *Journal of the Royal Statistical Society* 109A (1946), esp. pp. 490–502. The growth of the Statistician Class is discussed in Sir Roy Allen, 'On Official Statistics and Statisticians', pp. 509–26.

35 Coats, 'The Development of the Agricultural Economics Profession in England' this volume 419–32.

36 That is, the Ministry of Agriculture and Fisheries and the Department of Agriculture for Scotland.

37 Robbins, *Autobiography*, p. 184, where he stressed the need 'to become part of the machine and accept its logic rather than pretend to some special status. . . . If we had not been prepared to conform to the normal rules and normal routine, or if those who ran the machine had been hostile, the experiment would have failed.'

38 Cf. Sir Robert Hall, 'The Place of the Economist in Government', p. 122, where he remarked that 'there is no obvious reason why most of those who are engaged in activities within the province of the economist should themselves be professional economists'. For a valuable insight into Hall's position within the government machine, see the article by one of his junior colleagues, Robin Marris, 'The Position of Economics and Economists in the Government Machine', pp. 759–83.

39 For Cairncross's views on this point, see his 'On Being an Economic Adviser', p. 290. In fairness to MacDougall's predecessors it should be noted that whereas recruitment was a *sine qua non* of success with new ventures such as Nedo or DEA, it was always subordinate to the main economic advisory responsibilities of the Director of the Economic Section. It was not until 1969 that any formal provision was made for the recruitment and personnel management functions of the GES.

40 This overoptimism was not merely a manifestation of political bias or reforming zeal; it also reflected the contemporary wave of enthusiasm for new models, concepts, and techniques in economics in the heyday of what is usually termed 'positive' economics. This tide of professional self-confidence receded rapidly in the early 1970s.

41 For instructive insights into the role of Special Advisers, see Mitchell, 'Special Advisers', pp. 87–98.

42 Other reasons included the recognition that the respective functions and spheres of the two groups were distinct, even though on some matters they worked closely together. The economists were by no means unanimously in favour of a merger. From the standpoint of professionalization the issue is of interest, since the two groups resisted the bureaucratic urge for order and administrative simplicity for the sake of preserving their respective professional interest and identities.

43 Self, *Administrative Theories and Politics*, p. 182.

44 Heclo and Wildavsky, *The Private Government of Public Money*, p. 283.

45 For example, Sir Ronald Edwards, formerly a Professor of Industrial Economics at the London School of Economics, was head of the Central Electricity Board. Another LSE economist and former Economic Section member, Ralph Turvey, served as a consultant and economist in the same organization. The National Coal Board has also occasionally had an economist on its staff.

46 There was a famous, though still officially secret, conflict between the Bank and the Treasury economists in the mid-1950s over the proposal to introduce

convertibility of sterling. The Bank was eventually defeated after a protracted struggle.

47 'The Work of the Economic Intelligence Department', *Bank of England Quarterly* (Dec. 1976), p. 436. This is by far the best published account of the Bank's economic and statistical work. It gives vivid hints of the interwar resistance to infection 'with the ideas or the language of an economist'. A 1925 memorandum proposing the appointment of an economist stated: 'He should be fully qualified, as far as degrees etc., indicate; must not be a crank, and must have the gift of applying economics to practical affairs. A man chosen from the Cambridge School, if under the influence of Mr. Keynes, might perhaps have acquired this desirable aptitude; but if he had also followed this Economist in his progressive decline and fall, dating from the "Tract on Monetary Reform", he would be worse than useless' (ibid.). On the matters in this and the next paragraph I am indebted to Professors Leslie Pressnell and Richard Sayers.

48 Ibid., pp. 436, 440–6.

49 They included C. MacMahon and J. C. R. Dow, both of whom had served in the Economic Section. Dow is now a Director. It should be noted that the comments in the text refer to top-level policymaking staff. According to figures published in *The Economist*, 15 June 1974, the Bank's staff of economists had grown from 12 to 45 in the preceding dozen years. However, the precise status and functions of this staff are not known to this writer.

50 As, for example, in Mexico. See Roger Ai Camp, *The Role of Economists in Policy-Making: A Comparative Case Study of Mexico and the United States* (Tucson, Ariz., 1977), esp. p. 55.

51 Hall, 'The Place of the Economist in Government', p. 125.

52 Sir Edward (later Lord) Bridges, *Portrait of a Profession* (Cambridge, 1950), p. 23. As Martin Albrow has remarked, 'It is only a slight exaggeration to argue that a professional will come closer to the centres of power and influence the more he relinquishes his specific professional function . . . such a process is built into the professional career as the professional role widens to include administrative and other duties . . . professionalism may enhance the listening ability of the official, but it increases his distance from the noise' (*Bureaucracy*, London, 1970, pp. 149, 177). In this sense the early postwar economists were probably less 'professional' than their more technically sophisticated successors of the 1970s. But economics has at least, until recently, usually been a vocationally non-specific discipline; hence its suitability as a component in the administrative decisionmaking process.

53 See, for example, I. M. D. Little, 'The Economist in Whitehall', esp. pp. 35–6. This seems to have been a common experience at that time.

54 Anon., quoted in Heclo and Wildavsky, p. 41.

55 The author of this remark wishes to remain anonymous.

56 As noted by Lord Armstrong, who has since retired as Head of the Civil Service, 'over the time that I have been in the Civil Service, I have seen a really quite remarkable revolution in the attitude of the decision-takers to the kind of information they require, and this has been followed by a very large increase in the number of statisticians in the Government service' ('Management Training', p. 96).

57 This is an actual quotation from an interview.

58 There is a penetrating discussion of this and related matters in Heclo and Wildavsky, *passim*.

59 As Sir Alec Cairncross has noted, any economist who believes that he and his professional peers can successfully take over the management of economic policy,

'has never been present at the kind of discussion between economists, administrators, and ministers, at which it is by no means uncommon for the economist to talk politics, the administrators to talk economics, and the ministers to discuss administrative problems'. See his 'Economists in Government', p. 203. In 1969 there was only one economist post at Under Secretary level and above, apart from the Head of the Government Economic Service. By 1977 there were four such posts in the Treasury alone, and fifteen throughout the civil service.

60 For an account of the employment of economists in one major region, see Coats, 'The Changing Role of Economists in Scottish Government', pp. 399–424 (reprinted in this volume, pp. 580–605).

61 Government Economic Service staff were also employed at that time in the Cabinet Office (Central Policy Review Staff), Civil Service Department, Customs and Excise, Ministry of Defence, Office of Fair Trading, Home Office, Board of Inland Revenue, Royal Commission on the Distribution of Income and Wealth, Welsh Office, Civil Aviation Authority, Commission for Industrial Relations, Office of Manpower Economics, Monopolies Commission, National Economic Development Office, Post Office, and Price Commission.

62 It should perhaps be added, given the experience of the later 1970s, that some other leading countries appear to be encountering somewhat similar problems, albeit in a less acute form.

63 Cf. M. M. Postan's well-known article of that title originally published in *Encounter*, 1968, and reprinted in his *Fact and Relevance: Essays on Historical Method* (Cambridge, 1971). An amusing editorial in the *Guardian* (25 July 1974) discussed the correlation between the number of economists in government and the growth of such undesirable phenomena as inflation, airline hijackings, and terrorist outrages, suggesting that 'if it can be shown that the value of money varies inversely in proportion to the quantity of advice received, an important watershed in the field of economic theory will have been passed'.

64 See, for example, Harry G. Johnson, 'Keynes and British Economics', in Milo Keynes, ed., *Essays on John Maynard Keynes* (Cambridge, 1975), pp. 108–22; T. W. Hutchison, *'Positive' Economics and Policy Objectives* (London, 1964), esp. the concluding chapter; also his *Economics and Economic Policy in Britain, 1946–1966*.

65 Of course in many cases it is impossible to know exactly what occurred and why. As Cairncross has remarked, 'it is often very hard even for those at close quarters with policy-making to know what does in the end shape the decisions that ministers take – or, still more, do not take. . . . Where the issue is in dispute, who except the minister (or even including the minister) knows what clinched the matter? It is very rarely that one can say with confidence that the decision would have been different if *x* had not been there. The people who think they know and say so may, in fact, be ill-qualified to judge.' *Essays on Economic Management*, p. 210.

66 For a good recent example from a large literature see Christoph, 'Higher Civil Servants', in Dogan, ed., pp. 25–6. There is an excellent account of the upper-level civil service working atmosphere and relationships in Hecio and Wildavsky, *passim*.

67 See, for example, the very detailed documentation used by the contributors to Craufurd D. Goodwin, ed., *Exhortation and Controls: The Search for a Wage-Price Policy, 1945–1971* (Washington, 1975).

68 From an unpublished paper, 'Writing the History of Economic Policy' (1970), quoted by permission. For a useful discussion of the role of rationality (which economists tend to overrate) and other elements in policymaking processes see

Geoffrey Hawker, R. F. I. Smith, and Patrick Weller, *Politics and Policy in Australia* (University of Queensland Press, 1979), ch. 1, and sources cited therein.

69 This is in marked contrast to the situation in Belgium. Cf. Drs G. Stienlet, *Economists and the Civil Service System: The Belgium Case* (Centrum voor Economische Studien, Katolieke Universteit te Leuven, 1978).

70 Some of the postwar structural changes in Whitehall have been changes of nomenclature and form rather than substance, and it is noteworthy that the post-Fulton removal of establishments (i.e. staffing) matters from the Treasury to the CSD has not been an unqualified success. A return to the status quo ante-1968 is by no means unlikely.

71 Lord Crowther Hunt, Evidence to the *House of Commons Expenditure Committee*, op. cit. n. 32 *supra*, 3:1108.

72 During the 1960s some economists encouraged false public expectations by exaggerating their ability to influence the course of policy. A few years later when the now familiar combination of inflation and unemployment became obvious, they were given a disproportionate share of the blame for policy failures.

73 Michael Stewart, *The Jekyll and Hyde Years: Politics and Economics Since 1964* (London, 1977), p. 241. There is support for this emphasis on the disturbing effects of repeated policy changes in the editor's concluding 'General Appraisal' in Blackaby, esp. pp. 652–3.

74 G. C. Allen, *The British Disease* (London, 1976), p. 19.

75 Blackaby, p. 628.

76 Despite considerable public pressure during the past decade or so this measure remains virtually intact. With respect to the machinery of government there are other significant signs of continuity. As in the mid-1960s the opposition, through the Fabian Society, is once again examining proposals for the reform of the civil service, including suggestions concerning the role of special advisers and the powers of the Prime Minister. At the same time the government is reported to be reviewing the Fulton Committee's reforms with a view to abolishing, or reducing the role of, the Civil Service Department, by restoring to the Treasury control over personnel management. *Plus ça change, plus c'est la même chose.*

77 The latest (i.e. November 1980) appointment of an economist Special Adviser, in this case to the Prime Minister, is Professor Alan A. Walters of the Johns Hopkins University (formerly of the LSE).

BIBLIOGRAPHY

Addison, Paul, *The Road to 1945*. London, 1975.

Allen, C. G. 'Advice from Economists – Forty-Five Years Ago'. *Three Banks Review* (June 1975). Reprinted in his *British Industry and Economic Policy* (London, 1979).

Allen, Sir R. 'On Official Statistics and Statisticians'. *Journal of the Royal Statistical Society* 133A (part 4, 1970): 509–26.

Allen, W. R. 'Economics, Economists, and Economic Policy: Modern American Experiences'. *History of Political Economy* 9 (1977): 48–88.

Anderson, Sir J. *The Organization of Economic Studies in Relation to the Problems of Government*, Stamp Memorial Lecture. London, 1947.

Armstrong, Sir W. (later Lord). *Professionals and Professionalism in the Civil Service*. Welwyn Garden City, 1970.

——. *Personnel Management in the Civil Service*. London: HMSO, 1971.

——. 'Management Training for Statisticians and Opportunities to Enter Top Management'. *Journal of the Royal Statistical Society* 136 (part 1, 1973): 95–9.

Blackaby, F. T., ed. *British Economic Policy 1960–74*. Cambridge, 1978.

Booth, A. E., and A. W. Coats. 'The Market for Economists in Britain, 1945–75: A Preliminary Survey'. *Economic Journal* 88 (1978): 436–54. Reprinted in this volume, pp. 474–95.

——. 'Some Wartime Observations on the Role of the Economist in Government'. *Oxford Economic Papers* 32 (July 1980): 177–99. Reprinted in this volume, pp. 556–79.

Brittan, S. 'The Irregulars'. In R. Rose, ed., *Policy-Making in Britain: A Reader in Government* (New York, 1969), pp. 329–99.

——. *Steering the Economy: The Role of the Treasury*. London, 1971.

Brown, R. G. S. *The Administrative Process in Britain*. London, 1970.

Cairncross, Sir A. 'On Being an Economic Adviser'. Reprinted in *Factors in Economic Development* (London, 1962), pp. 272–91.

——. 'The Work of an Economic Adviser' (1967) and 'Economists in Government' (1970). Reprinted in *Essays in Economic Management* (London, 1971), pp. 184–96, 197–216.

Chester, D. N., ed. *Lessons of the War Economy*. Cambridge, 1951.

—— and F. M. G. Willson, *The Organisation of British Central Government 1914–1956*. London, 1957.

Christoph, J. P. 'Higher Civil Servants and the Politics of Consensualism in Great Britain'. In M. Dogan, *The Mandarins of Western Europe: The Political Role of Top Civil Servants* (New York, 1975), pp. 25–62.

Coats, A. W. 'The Development of the Economics Profession in England: A Preliminary Review'. In L. Houmanidis, ed., *International Congress of Economic History and History of Economic Theories* (Piraeus: Piraeus Graduate School of Industrial Studies, 1975), pp. 277–90.

——. 'The Development of the Agricultural Economics Profession in England'. *Journal of Agricultural Economics* 27 (Sept. 1976): 381–92. Reprinted in this volume, pp. 419–32.

——. 'The Changing Role of Economists in Scottish Government Since 1960'. *Public Administration* 57 (Spring 1979): 399–424. Reprinted in this volume, pp. 580–605.

Coddington, A. 'Economists and Policy'. *National Westminster Bank Quarterly Review*, Feb. 1973, pp. 171–88.

Devons, E. *Papers on Planning and Economic Management*. Edited by Sir A. Cairncross. Manchester, 1970.

Dow, J. C. R. *The Management of the British Economy 1945–60*. Cambridge, 1964.

Hall, Sir R. 'The Place of the Economist in Government'. *Oxford Economic Papers*, n.s. 7 (June 1955): 119–35.

Hall, R. L . 'Reflections on the Practical Application of Economics'. *Economic Journal* 69 (Dec. 1959).

Hallett, G. 'The Role of Economists as Government Advisers'. *Westminster Bank Review*, May 1967, pp. 2–20.

Hancock, W. K., and M. M. Gowing. *British War Economy, History of the Second World War*, United Kingdom Civil Series. HMSO, 1949.

Hargrove, E. C. *Professional Roles in Society and Government: The English Case*. Beverly Hills, 1972.

Heclo, H. and A. Wildavsky. *The Private Government of Public Money*. London, 1974.

Henderson, P. D. 'The Use of Economists in British Administration'. *Oxford Economic Papers*, n.s. 13 (Feb. 1961): 5–26.

Howson, S. and D. Winch. *The Economic Advisory Council 1930–1939: A Study in Economic Advice During Depression and Recovery*. Cambridge, 1977.

Hutchison, T. W. *Economics and Economic Policy in Britain, 1946–1966*. London, 1968.

Jewkes, J. 'Second Thoughts on the British White Paper on Employment Policy'.

In *Economic Research and the Development of Science and Public Policy* (New York, 1946).

Keeling, C. D. *Management in Government*. London, 1972.

Leith-Ross, Sir F. W. *Money Talks: Fifty Years of International Finance*. London, 1968.

Leruez, J. *Economic Planning and Politics in Britain*. London, 1975.

Little, I. M. D. 'The Economist in Whitehall'. *Lloyds Bank Review* 44 (April 1957): 29–40.

Marris, R. 'The Position of Economics and Economists in the Government Machine: A Comparative Critique of the United Kingdom and the Netherlands'. *Economic Journal* 64 (Dec. 1954): 759–83.

Mitchell, J. 'Special Advisers: A Personal View'. *Public Administration* 56 (Spring 1978): 87–98.

Moser, C. A. (Sir Cl.). 'The Statistician in Government: A Challenge for the 1970's'. *Transactions of the Manchester Statistical Society*, Session 1970–1, pp. 1–39.

—— 'Staffing in the Government Statistical Services'. *Journal of the Royal Statistical Society* 136A (part 1, 1973): 75–88.

Peacock, A. *The Economic Analysis of Government, and Related Themes*. Oxford, 1979.

Postan, M. M. 'A Plague of Economists'. Reprinted in *Fact and Relevance: Essays on Historical Method* (Cambridge, 1971).

Robbins, Lord. *The Autobiography of an Economist*. London 1971.

Roll, E. 'The Uses and Abuses of Economics'. *Oxford Economic Papers*, n.s. 20 (Nov. 1968): 295–300. Reprinted in his *The Uses and Abuses of Economics, and Other Essays* (London, 1978).

Salter, Sir A. J. *Slave of the Lamp: A Public Servant's Notebook*. London, 1967.

Seers, D. 'Why Visiting Economists Fail'. *Journal of Political Economy* 70 (Aug. 1962): 325–8.

Self, P. *Administrative Theories and Politics*. Toronto, 1972.

——. *Econocrats and the Policy Process: The Politics and Philosophy of Cost-Benefit Analysis*. London, 1975.

Shanks, M. 'The Irregular in Whitehall'. In P. Streeten, ed., *Unfashionable Economics: Essays in Honour of Lord Balogh* (London, 1970), pp. 244–62.

Stone, R. 'The Use and Development of National Income and Expenditure Estimates'. In D. N. Chester, ed., *Lessons of the War Economy* (Cambridge, 1951), pp. 83–101.

Thomas, H., ed. *Crisis in the Civil Service*. London, 1968. Essays by R. Opie. 'The Making of Economic Policy', pp. 53–82; and D. Seers, 'The Structure of Power', pp. 83–109.

Williams, A. *Output Budgeting and the Contributions of Micro Economics to Efficiency in Government*, CAS Occasional Paper No. 4. London, 1967.

Wilson, H. 'Statistics and Decision-Making in Government: Bradshaw Revisited'. *Journal of the Royal Statistical Society* 136 (part 1, 1973): 1–16.

Winch, D. *Economics and Policy: A Historical Study*. London, 1969.

27

SOME WARTIME OBSERVATIONS ON THE ROLE OF THE ECONOMIST IN GOVERNMENT[1]

I

The employment of professional economists in government is now an accepted, if occasionally controversial, fact of twentieth-century life, and since the 1930s their numbers have grown apace both in advanced countries and, more recently, in many underdeveloped countries, too.[2] In the British case two periods stand out as turning points – World War II and the mid-1960s. During the intervening years, however, the number of civil service posts for professional economists remained virtually constant despite the fact that the value and significance of their contributions to the war effort had been generally acknowledged.[3]

Various reasons for this hiatus can be offered, such as: the overall shortage of qualified personnel, in relation to the expanding demand from universities and business;[4] conditions within the bureaucracy, including traditional resistance to the use of specialists, unattractive career opportunities for economists, and efforts to reduce the number of public servants; and changes in the aims and methods of economic policy, of which the waning enthusiasm for economic planning in the 1950s is a relevant instance.[5] In addition, some weight must be assigned to a factor which has hitherto been generally overlooked, namely, the economists' own conceptions of their prospective role in the peacetime machinery of government.

The discussion of this matter came to a head during a more general examination of the organization and functions of government, especially those administrative divisions and departments which had been created in response to wartime exigencies. During World War I a similar administrative explosion had occurred and its implications had been reviewed towards the close of hostilities by the famous Haldane Committee on the Machinery of Government. Following this precedent, the 1942 War Cabinet resolved that a ministerial committee consisting of Sir John Anderson, Sir Stafford Cripps, Sir Kingsley Wood, Viscount Samuel and Herbert Morrison be established 'to enquire into the responsibilities of the various Departments

556

of the central executive Government, and to advise in what manner the exercise and distribution of its functions should be improved'.[6] The investigative work was undertaken by a committee which considered the economists' prospective peacetime position and functions in the light of the wartime experience. The economists themselves contributed directly to these deliberations and their views consequently provide valuable insights into their individual and collective professional self-images.

Prior to the outbreak of hostilities very few professional economists had been involved in British government. The only departments to employ groups of professional economists were the Ministry of Agriculture and Fisheries and the Department of Agriculture for Scotland,[7] but throughout the 1930s high ranking Treasury officials had been privy to the discussions of the Economic Advisory Council and several of its offspring, most notably the Committee on Economic Information, which had a tiny staff of professionals in the Cabinet Office.[8] Under these arrangements leading economists such as H. D. Henderson, J. M. Keynes, W. Layton, D. H. Robertson, L. Robbins, J. Stamp and others had been able to provide first hand evidence of the value of economic advice. With the outbreak of war the machinery for professional economic advice was formalized. The Committee on Economic Information begat the so-called Stamp Survey of Financial and War Plans, which in turn gave way to the Central Economic Information Service (CEIS). Towards the end of 1940, it was decided to split the CEIS into two parts – the Central Statistical Office (CSO) and the Economic Section (ES) – and after a spell of frustration and apparent irrelevance the latter body, under the direction of John Jewkes and subsequently Lionel Robbins, acquired a central role servicing the Lord President's Committee chaired by Sir John Anderson, which became the supreme body coordinating the home front and general economic policy.[9] In addition the Prime Minister's Statistical Section, under Professor Lindeman, operated alongside (and sometimes across) the ES and CSO in the Cabinet Offices, while groups of professional economists and statisticians were recruited into various departments – most notably Henderson, Keynes, Robertson and Lord Catto in the Treasury.[10] Clearly some of these developments were temporary, and would disappear at the end of hostilities, possibly without trace, as had been the case with most of their 1914–18 predecessors. But there was a widespread determination to avoid as far as possible the mistakes of the post World War I experience, and it was against this background that the future role of the economists was considered.

II

The Ministerial Committee on the Machinery of Government held its first meeting on 12 November 1942, at a time when economic and social policy, particularly the methods and organization required to achieve postwar full employment, was already the subject of active debate.[11] On 1 December, Sir William Beveridge's Report on *Social Insurance and Allied Services* appeared, and was followed by an extraordinary outburst of popular enthusiasm which annoyed and embarrassed those Ministers and civil servants who were anxious to avoid premature commitments to grandiose peacetime policies.[12] The level of public and official interest in economic and social questions remained high throughout the next two years, during which time the path-breaking *Employment Policy* White Paper was issued in June 1944, and Beveridge's own, far more explicit and ambitious, *Full Employment in a Free Society* was published in November of that year.[13] Under these circumstances the question of the economists' contribution to peacetime government obviously could not be viewed simply as a technical matter; it was inextricably bound up with much wider issues arising from the discussion of postwar economic and social policies and the organizational provisions required to implement them.

During the 1930s the persistence of mass unemployment was generally recognized as the most pressing economic problem, and numerous solutions were proposed, ranging across the politico-economic spectrum from the orthodox liberal-market approach to various forms of socialist economic planning.[14] Towards the end of the decade a broad but vague consensus in favour of more active state intervention was emerging, and this trend was substantially reinforced during the early war years by a markedly leftward shift in public opinion.[15] The details of this movement cannot be considered here, although in retrospect special interest attaches to the evolution of the Keynesian approach to macroeconomic management, which came to dominate postwar economic thinking and official practice.[16] But it is important to note that this outcome and its implications were by no means clearly discernible to those involved in the Machinery of Government Committee's proceedings.

As a by-product of the wider debate about the role of the state in economic and social affairs, proposals designed to enhance the economists' contribution to policy-making were repeatedly aired during the interwar years. Most of the leading economists who participated in government activities had only limited faith in the wisdom and competence of the politicians and civil servants responsible for economic policy. Undoubtedly some of the proposals designed to bring economic expertise to bear on the policy-making process were vague and ill-adapted to the administrative and organizational realities of official life. But from the early 1920s the need for an Economic General Staff (EGS) was repeatedly argued, often by analogy with the Committee of Imperial Defence.[17] Beveridge was the most persistent advocate of this scheme up to the mid-1940s, having initially advanced it in 1923 in the *Nation and Athenaeum*, a liberal journal edited by Henderson under the control of a company chaired by Keynes. Beveridge himself had no direct hand in the vigorous propagation of the idea in the so-called Liberal 'Yellow Book' of 1929, entitled *Britain's Industrial Future*, or in the detailed proposals to the Prime Minister, Ramsay MacDonald, later that year by Henry Clay, Keynes, G. H. D. Cole, Stamp, J. A. Hobson, Layton and others, in the course of the discussions leading to the establishment of the Economic Advisory Council. But after the Council's early demise, partly because it embodied an uneasy compromise between 'representative' and 'technocratic' elements, all that remained was the series of occasional advisory committees which had only an insignificant input of expertise from established civil servants trained in economics. This state of affairs was undoubtedly acceptable to many senior civil servants, who tended to oppose novel organizational arrangements and were suspicious of economists, believing (like many of their post-1945 successors) that they should be 'kept on tap, but not on top'. But during the later 1930s there was mounting criticism from observers like Beveridge and Cole, whose dissatisfaction with traditional civil servants was reinforced by their faith in social scientific expertise and desire for more active interventionist policies.[18]

Without overrating Beveridge's importance or influence, it is worth reviewing his ideas briefly not only because his shifts of opinion are revealing but also because his views were familiar to Ministers and civil servants, some of whom were anxious to exclude him from the high government offices which he so eagerly sought. As José Harris has shown in her excellent biography, during the 1920s Beveridge became 'markedly less "bureaucratic" and more "technocratic" in his approach to public policy', as he abandoned his earlier belief in a 'benevolent administrative state', and 'turned more and more to social science – and particularly to economics – as the tool that would solve the problems of society'.[19] His initial EGS proposal envisaged a body of professional economists headed by 'a person of high authority in the science' to review and coordinate the various departmental programmes and to advise the government on such matters as unemployment, tariffs and trade.[20] From the official standpoint, of course, advice is one thing, coordination quite another, especially if it involves powers to implement the recommendations emanating from the coordinating agency. In his original conception advice seems to have figured more prominently in Beveridge's mind than coordinating powers; but as the slump of 1929–32 undermined his confidence in market processes, he began to revert to more interventionist policies, partly under the influence of the Webbs' enthusiasm for Soviet economic planning.[21] Beveridge himself did not, of course, swallow the Webbs' ideas initially, but he became increasingly aware of the problems involved in preserving political democracy while pursuing *dirigiste* economic policies. In a broadcast in May 1935 he reiterated his belief in the need for an EGS to coordinate economic policy and advise a small group of Ministers who should, if possible, be freed from departmental responsibilities,[22] and during the next few years he gradually came to favour a more active planning role for economists within an interventionist framework. In 1938 he conceived the EGS as

> a group of civil servants ... with nothing whatever to do except to think about the future and plan the future; with no daily function at all ... not allowed to do anything but think; with adequate resources for thinking, that is to say, with enough money to be able not only to employ their own staff on making investigations, but to induce economists in the universities and elsewhere to divert their minds from other-world problems to problems of the present world; with access to all the information and resources of Government departments, and, finally, with authority to influence the Government, while leaving the final decision to the Government.[23]

Precisely how this 'think tank' was to avoid being ignored as a species of research body concerned with long-run issues that would inevitably be given lower priority than the pressing issues of the day – according to the well-known principle of government economics, that 'the important must always give way before the urgent' – was not made clear. Beveridge recognized that the Economic Advisory Council's members had been too preoccupied with other tasks, and that the various departmental intelligence and research divisions had failed to take a coordinated, aggregative view of the kind that could only be formulated at the centre of the government machine.[24] But at this stage Beveridge had no conception of Keynesian economic management – which he did not in fact embrace until 1943–4. Hence it took the early period of the war with its dramatic expansion of government activity, the influx of academic economists into Whitehall, and the disappearance of the mass unemployment which had hitherto occupied so much of Beveridge's intellectual energies – to push him a stage further towards the socialist type of economic planning favoured by Cole and the Webbs. As he told the Engineering Industries Association in July 1942,

> On the face of it, the experience of 1920–1939 suggests that the former methods of peace are unlikely to accomplish [the maintenance of full employment] with even tolerable success, and that there are probably two unavoidable conditions for the maintenance of productive employment after the present war, namely (a) continuous fluidity of labour and resources, and (b) continuance of national planning.[25]

The implications of this form of economic organization for the EGS are clear from Beveridge's talks on his insurance scheme. In December 1942, he declared

> If, for instance, we want to maintain employment in this country, one thing we have to do is make a design of how all the productive resources of a country ... can be used after the war in meeting needs

which we know will exist. That is what is called national planning. . . .
The body I look to to make such a design is what I call an Economic
General Staff, somebody to plan our economic life . . . just as a military staff plans a campaign.[26]

Even at this late stage he did not specify the size, composition, precise powers and functions of an EGS, but he did refer to deficiencies of contemporary civil servants and the need for a new type of administrative organization, 'different types of people and different types of training'.[27]

When he eventually appeared before the Machinery of Government Committee in October 1943 (significantly, eleven months after their deliberations had begun),[28] Beveridge discussed the possibilities of expanding the role of economists in government in terms of two alternative hypotheses. On the first assumption, that the prewar economic system underwent no fundamental modification, he reiterated his early ideas for a small, centrally placed, coordinating body with an advisory function. His second hypothesis, however, presupposed that the economic system be state-controlled to maintain full employment, and consequently entailed a radical reconsideration of existing administrative arrangements. Much would follow from the need for a single minister responsible for economic policy.

His functions would include those at present discharged by the Treasury but he would be concerned not merely with the national budget, but with the national income as a whole and his annual budget statements would be of a very different character. . . . In a Treasury with extended responsibilities of this kind the Minister would clearly need to include among his advisers a large planning and intelligence staff of expert economists.[29]

At this point Beveridge may not yet have been persuaded by the Keynesian revolution, to which he was converted by the young Keynesians then engaged on his full employment study.[30] Hence he was probably still committed to the centralized supply-side planning of the war economy, although he may have envisaged that the large planning staff he proposed would be involved in detailed macroeconomic analysis and forecasting work of the type which the Treasury has fully embraced in the past decade or so.[31]

While Beveridge appears as the single most persistent advocate of the need for economic expertise in government, he undoubtedly weakened his case by the uncertainties and shifts in his social policy views. More seriously still, the impact of his arguments was diminished by the official reactions against his aggressive personality and his reputation for publicity-seeking in disseminating the results of his social services report. Given the official resistance to radical conceptions of postwar government[32] Beveridge's later, more ambitious, ideas were bound to be watered down in practice.

III

The Machinery of Government Committee provided the economic liberals (i.e., those opposed to a major expansion of state intervention in the peacetime economy) with ample opportunity to propose alternative visions of postwar economic policy and the economist's position therein. In January 1943 Robbins prepared a lengthy memorandum 'Notes on the Role of the Economist in the Future Machinery of Government' which reflected his experience as Director of the ES during the preceding year.[33]

Robbins began significantly by dissociating himself from those who, like Beveridge (to whom he did not directly refer) advocated a more ambitious *dirigiste* conception of the organization of central government economic policy-making. Denying that there had been a 'radical revolution' in the state's economic functions in wartime he rejected proposals to create

> outside of the departments, a gigantic economic general staff consisting of professional economists and statisticians who should draw up plans and then, presumably with some authorization from the Cabinet, proceed to issue orders to the various departments, as the Supreme Command is said to issue orders to the various armies under its direction.

Such projects he added, though 'flattering to my profession', were neither acceptable in practice nor desirable in principle. And doubtless the loaded word 'gigantic' combined with the concept of a central group of experts 'issuing orders' to departments, albeit with a rubber-stamped authorization from a Cabinet which did not really grasp the issues as stake, was well calculated to evoke a hostile response from most defenders of democratic and civil service traditions.

After reviewing the historical background and present position of the ES, Robbins turned his attention to the future, a future in which, he observed, he would play no part in policy-making as he intended to return to academic life. For those who remained, he warned that 'the economic problems of war are child's play compared with the problems which will emerge as soon as the single object of war disappears'.[34] Whatever might be said on the issue of 'totalitarian' economic planning, even the most liberal society would need more coordination of economic policy measures than in the interwar period. In this of course, Robbins was in substantial agreement with Beveridge and most of his fellow economists. In Robbins' scheme, however, responsibility for economic policy would rest unequivocally with the Cabinet; but some preparatory sifting of the issues on an official level was also required. It was, he continued, an inescapable fact that

> dispersed initiative at the departmental level does not necessarily lead to coherence and consistency in policy as a whole. . . . The economic problem is essentially a single problem although it has many facets.

For, in the last analysis, the economic problem is the rational (i.e., consistent) disposition of resources; there can be no pluralistic action here. And if, as is often the case, there is conflict between the objectives of different departments, then unless there is, somewhere some organ for analysing matters from a wider point of view, the material on which Ministers may be called upon to take decisions will be incomplete.

Hence some kind of machinery was required, such as an official body staffed by civil servants, some of whom would have had a full training in economics. Robbins came to this conclusion with some diffidence, though with great firmness because, he said, although economics was an essentially simple subject, 'without systematic training in the application of such platitudes, the most acute minds are liable to go astray'. The members of this official body should be free from daily departmental concerns and be attached to a Minister or group of Ministers directly responsible for economic policy. He clearly favoured retaining a position at the centre of the administrative machine; but, failing that, the Section's responsibilities should perhaps be assigned to the Treasury, where it would have behind it

> the driving power of a department of State already accustomed to organize a coordinating function in a very important sphere. It would command the services of men who . . . are already trained to adopt an approach of some generality to the problem of economic policy. And it would mean that, through the position of the Chancellor of the Exchequer in the Cabinet itself, there would be automatic and continuous representation of the coordinating point of view.

However, although this argument would be strengthened by the reassertion in peacetime of the importance of the money measure, coordination

> would need to be applied in a more comprehensive sense than in the old context of Treasury control. Not the effect of particular measures on the national *budget* but rather the effect on the national income would be the ultimate focus of concern in the system I am suggesting. Such a development, however, sometimes seems to be already on the way. Already in the development of the wartime economy, Treasury policy has come to be framed more and more against a background of computation of national income and expenditure. We should only need to travel a little further along this road before the transformation of the nature of policy becomes fully manifest, and the Treasury would emerge, not as a Ministry for government bookkeeping in the narrow sense, but rather as a Ministry of general economic policy. . . . In such a Ministry the present functions of the Economic Section

(and others to which we do not aspire), would be, presumably, performed by the general department.

The head of the peacetime ES, Robbins added, should be qualified to direct the more academic side of the research, so as to get the best out of the academic members of his staff; but should preferably be recruited by promotion from inside, since an outsider would not know the ropes, and might have the 'somewhat inflexible habits of a man with settled status'.

Robbins' memorandum has been quoted at length because it was an authoritative and influential statement of issues of fundamental importance to the role of the economist in government, and because it provided an accurate forecast of the postwar solution adopted in practice. His modest evaluation of the economist's current and potential contribution to governmental processes was calculated to appeal to his audience of senior officials and Ministers, and was entirely compatible with the prevailing generalist ethos in Whitehall. Moreover, it conveys an accurate impression of the outlook of a generation of professional economists who were, by present-day standards, few in number, poorly organized, lacking in collective self-consciousness, and disinclined to emphasize their technical skills.[35] Robbins' scheme differed from Beveridge's both in its underlying social philosophy and because, unlike Beveridge, he had by this time adopted a broadly Keynesian conception of economic management. Robbins' solution went well beyond Beveridge's earlier ill-defined ideas of the role of an EGS in a largely non-interventionist state; yet it did not arouse the fears and suspicions evoked by Beveridge's later planning proposals. Robbins' wartime experience enabled him to be much more specific in discussing the economists' position and functions in the governmental apparatus. His proposals incorporated the expanded wartime view of the nature and significance of the budget, which gave economists much greater potential influence at the centre of government without, however, exaggerating their role in the decision-making process. It was a singularly effective document which received the wholehearted support of such key officials as Norman Brook and Edward Bridges.[36]

IV

Robbins was not, however, without his critics, most notably Sir Hubert Henderson, whose official experience extended back to World War I and included periods of service with the EAC, the CEI, the Stamp Survey and the wartime Treasury. On his appointment to the EAC he had been described as 'a good critical mind, but deeply political and not very constructive',[37] and in the next few years he became increasingly disenchanted with economic theory, while his 'pessimism concerning the efficacy of certain types of government economic policy was increasingly at odds with the Treasury's growing awareness of the need for macroeconomic management'.[38] His response to Robbins' memorandum directly reflected his personality and outlook, for while he conceded that a small corps of professional economists might play a useful role in peacetime economic policy-making he was apprehensive at the prospect of disagreements among them, stemming mainly from political rather than strictly professional differences. His conception of the kind of advice sought by Ministers may be viewed as cynical, or perhaps merely realistic and percipient, since it foreshadowed the post-1966 introduction of 'irregulars' and 'Special Advisers' into Whitehall.[39]

> Under ordinary peace conditions the issues on which economists differ may be leading issues of party controversy; so that the Ministers to be advised are in effect committed on the one side or the other by virtue of their political position. Under such conditions, the last thing Ministers want is ostensibly expert advice, the broad effect of which is that they are in the wrong and their political opponents are right. What they want are (1) arguments on their side of the case which may be useful as munitions in debate, and (2) advice as to what is the best course to pursue in a detailed application of a pre-determined line of policy. For both these functions, economists doubtless have their uses, though neither represents very satisfactory or happy scope for exercise of their higher faculties.

Henderson suggested, by implication, that a *cabinet* of politically oriented central economic advisers might be acceptable in peacetime; yet he also considered that within government departments economists could function as impartial civil servants. However,

> the general run of economists are not very well endowed with the marvellous chameleon-like adaptability of the capable civil servant; so that if and when our affairs are again conducted on the basis of a party dog-fight, the condition indicated could probably only be attained by changing the *personnel* of the Central Economic Section *en bloc* with each change of Ministry. . . . This difficulty does not apply in serious degree to the employment of economists in particular departments; and I entirely agree that there should be more of them than formerly.

His conclusion was cautious rather than adverse. Like Sir Frederick Leith-Ross, the Chief Economic Adviser to the Government, Henderson believed there was a case for retaining the ES in its present form after the war on an experimental basis, but that 'it would be a mistake to try to give it an established place in our machinery of government until we have had a few years of post-war experience'.[40]

Henderson's reservations about the role of economists in a central coordi-

565

nating body were reinforced from a different standpoint by Sir Donald Fergusson, Permanent Secretary to the Ministry of Agriculture and Fisheries. He, too, favoured the employment of professional economists within departments, presumably on the basis of his experience with the agricultural economists in his own Ministry.[41] But as official head of the department which had been conducting a vigorous campaign against the wartime ES,[42] Fergusson consistently argued throughout the Machinery of Government enquiry that central coordination should be exercised only by Ministers, whose task would be facilitated by relieving the departments of those executive responsibilities which could be undertaken more effectively by boards, committees or commissions. Like Henderson he distinguished between the political and the technocratic dimensions of the problem, maintaining that the new tasks of long-term planning should as far as possible be removed from the highly politically-charged atmosphere of central government and assigned to technical experts with time to devote to such matters. In the present instance he suggested that:

> The creation of a section of personal or specialist advisers who have no responsibility for the carrying out of Departmental policies and who are in a position decisively to influence the views of prominent and powerful Cabinet Ministers is bound to cause difficulties and such difficulties arise with special force when the Minister concerned has no Department and therefore no Departmental advisers.

Unlike Henderson, Fergusson was less concerned about the economists' political biases than the fact that they functioned as irresponsible experts influencing (and possibly blinding) policy-makers with their 'academic discussions'.[43] The fact that any economists tended to belong to particular schools of thought did not matter provided that they had

> full opportunity to give free expression to their views on economic matters whether those views appear to support or conflict with Departmental policy and at the same time are themselves intellectually honest and level headed and recognize that there are other considerations besides economic ones which have to be taken into account.

He shared the conventional civil service prejudices against advisory and coordinating agencies dissociated from departmental responsibilities and especially objected to a situation where economic advisers had more direct access to a member of the War Cabinet than 'the responsible Civil Servants in the Departments concerned'. Yet others have recognized that the ES's wartime achievements were largely attributable to the fact that its members and their chief – the Lord President of the Council – were freed from departmental responsibilities, and could therefore take a broader view of economic affairs.[44]

V

In the event Henderson's and Fergusson's views did not go unchallenged. An administrator, Sir George Gater of the Colonial Office, responded that Henderson exaggerated

> the extent to which Civil Servants do violence to their consciences in advocating policies which commend themselves to their political masters of the moment.... I think Sir Hubert confuses the willingness of the Civil Servant to carry out loyally instructions with which he does not agree, with a willingness to submit evidence which he thinks would be acceptable.

He also made the perceptive point that if party differences were to become so deep that 'conscientious economists who have served one Government found it impossible to serve the other, it seems quite certain that there can be no economic planning in this country'.[45] This observation discloses the difficulty in wartime of envisaging how far planning policies would be the subject of political conflict after the armistice, and the uncertainties attaching to the meaning and scope of the concept of 'planning'.

Keynes, too, commented at length on Robbins' memorandum,[46] providing a corrective to the misgivings expressed by his critics. Like others, Keynes believed that more economists should be located within departments; but he also stressed the need for a more senior and weighty central contingent for individual departments necessarily saw only part of the general situation. A central group should provide: (1) advice to the economic coordinating Minister or Committee independent of that offered by departments (a situation Fergusson was especially anxious to avoid), and (2) comprehensive advice on such macroeconomic matters as the level of income, employment and investment which 'cannot very conveniently be studied within the walls of Departments which are in a position to see only a part of the picture'.[47] Keynes laid special emphasis on this latter function, believing it had been unduly neglected by others supplying evidence to the Machinery of Government Committee. He then turned to the 'vitally important' question whether the economists advising on (2) should be attached to the Treasury or the Cabinet Office, a matter which Robbins had considered with great care and concern. Having been employed in the Treasury, Keynes recognized its need for advice on microeconomic issues, and therefore concluded that it would require a distinct, but smaller group of its own working in close cooperation with the Cabinet Office economists. Such was, in effect, the wartime organization, and Keynes explicitly noted that the Cabinet Office economists would have to consider a wider range of issues than their Treasury counterparts.

With respect to staffing and recruitment, Keynes favoured the appointment of 'inners-and-outers' on secondment from universities for periods of three to five years – which in fact became the prevailing postwar practice up to the later 1960s. He implied that there should be no such distinct species as the 'government economist', but did not specify whether this rule should also apply to the chief economic adviser.

> It will not be possible to attract or keep the best men unless they are allowed to retain some measure of academic freedom even during their sojourn in Whitehall, subject to their reporting confidences and information obtained in the course of their official work, and to the general use of discretion and not unnecessarily expressing opinions outside on matters which they are simultaneously advising inside. . . . It will be important not to make service in Whitehall too much like a visit to the tomb. . . . Civil servants will have to appreciate that they are dealing with people who have not been broken in when young and who will, indeed, only be useful if they have in fact developed dangerous powers of self-expression.

Keynes doubtless appreciated that permanent civil servants were subjected to the pressures of day-to-day work to the point where their vision and imagination became constricted, and he relished the freedom he derived from his own freelance position. By contrast, Robbins took a more favourable view of the generalist administrator and saw certain advantages in a mixture of permanent and temporary personnel.

> [I]n years to come there is likely to be an increasing proportion of younger civil servants who have degrees in the Social Sciences; and although there is much to be said for the view that fairly frequent recruitment from outside would be particularly appropriate in such a body, there is also much to be said for having a stiffening of young permanent civil servants with the requisite training in economics. They will be better acquainted with the snares and pitfalls of official life, and their knowledge of the peculiar administrative problems of the different departments would be at once useful to the Section as a whole, and educative to their more academic colleagues.

Keynes' commitment to the idea of a central ES composed mainly or entirely of university economists on secondment reveals that he was little concerned about either the divisions of opinion among economists or the outsiders' difficulties in learning how to 'work the machine' – problems that have been more serious in the past few years than Keynes foresaw. In characteristically optimistic fashion he lightly dismissed Henderson's apprehensions about the political divisions among the professional economists, noting that in so far as their appointments were short-term 'no doubt governments will be given the opportunity of changing the complexion of their economic advice fairly rapidly if they wish to do so'. Yet if seriously meant, this remark overlooks a number of awkward problems. For example, would the chief economic adviser and his entire team be viewed as replaceable, in the manner of a European Minister's *Cabinet* or US President's Council of Economic Advisers? Or, if some were to be retained, in the interests of continuity, who would decide who should stay or go? Would such a system imply the emergence of a sharp differentiation between departmental economists employed on technical, politically neutral topics, who would presumably have established civil service status, and the central 'political' team who would presumably be 'purged' from time to time?[48] Would the political economists at the centre be able to work harmoniously with the conventional non-political senior administrators in the Treasury and other departments (especially if, as Henderson pointed out, there were periodic changes of personnel and political coloration); and would the politicization of the central economic service represent the beginning of a gradual erosion of other areas of traditional civil service neutrality, a tendency liable to encounter determined resistance both inside and beyond Whitehall?

But while Keynes, under the pressure of other more urgent affairs, may not have fully considered the implications of his remarks, the significance of his support for Robbins' essentially liberal views should not be underestimated. The *dirigiste* conception of the EGS had been decisively defeated, and two of the leading wartime economists had supplied detailed, coherent suggestions for the maintenance of a small, specialist central group of professionals to coordinate departmental policies and take a more active innovative role in demand management.

VI

In their report to Ministers,[49] the Official Committee of the Machinery of Government Committee declared themselves generally in favour of Robbins' proposals for a flexible method of collecting data and coordinating economic advice which did not, as he had put it, 'provide for an economic planning dictatorship'. The report depicted the EGS proposal in exaggerated terms as a body 'presided over by an economist who would be endowed with immense power to dictate policy'. Such a body would be not merely 'impracticable' but also 'alien to any form of Parliamentary Government'. This interpretation was, of course, unfair to Beveridge who did not, in fact, appear before the Committee until October (after its report was drafted but before the final version was submitted to Ministers). His views apparently had no effect on the Committee's conclusions.

A curious feature of the document, explained by the fact of a concurrent enquiry into the role of scientists in government, was the Committee's approving reference to a letter in *The Times* of 19 June 1943 from a group of scientists who had declared that 'No social problem can be solved solely by the methods of science. A scientific and soulless technocracy would be the worst form of despotism.' These considerations were said to apply 'with even greater force to the economist' not, as might be supposed, because his discipline was more technocratic, but because it was less so. The economist's 'claim to specific authority is less clear than that of the scientist', the report contained. The subject lacked 'exactitude'; it was more concerned with 'scientific theory than with facts ascertained by scientific method'; its practitioners belonged to divergent 'schools of thought'; and it was

> so close to politics that there is a temptation for the economist to identify himself with a partisan point of view, which fits ill with the traditional impartiality of those who are called upon to advise Ministers of a Government constituted on party lines.

However, this indictment was not a preamble to a general warning against the employment of economists; merely a reminder that they should 'not have the final say in policy making'. The report acknowledged that economists had 'made important contributions within Departments' and recommended that in peacetime departmental economists should be accorded 'sufficient status' to ensure that their advice would be taken into consideration.

On the crucial question of the nature and extent of the economists' coordinating role, the Committee was sufficiently conscious of the risks of professional and political disagreements to argue that the future arrangements should be dependent on 'the progress made towards uniform opinion and the ability of economic advisers to appreciate the political background at the high level at which they work'. The possibility that uniformity of opinion might reflect doctrinal dogmatism rather than scientific consensus seems not to have occurred to the Committee,[50] whose report revealed little grasp of the more quantitative and technical background to Keynesian macroeconomic management. However, in effect they conferred their blessing on the *status quo*, suggesting cautiously that

> The functions of the Central Economic Section should be limited to those which it performs at present, namely investigations into spheres which are not covered exclusively by one Department such as manpower, national income and expenditure, employment. It should act as a liaison body between the economic advisers of the different Departments.

Whether this 'investigative' activity would include advice on demand management was not specified. No new functions were proposed for the ES, nor significant increases in staff or changes of titles.

Here, as elsewhere, the Machinery of Government Committee displayed a remarkable belief in the continuity of wartime administrative arrangements. On Keynes' 'vitally important' question of the location of the ES

570

they again favoured the *status quo* for the time being, dismissing the possibility of placing it in the Treasury or Board of Trade on the grounds that the ES should

> work to a Ministerial Committee responsible for co-ordination rather than to a single Minister, however closely his departmental duties may be connected with economic problems.

In so saying they dismissed the possibility of converting the Treasury into a more comprehensive coordinating Ministry of Economic Affairs, on the lines suggested by the Keynesian conception of the expanded role of the budget in economic management. Such a proposal would presumably have aroused too much opposition from other departments, and at this time the Treasury had not yet recovered from the wartime decline in its importance in the overall structure of government. The point is however noteworthy, given that the ES was moved into the Treasury in 1953, a change that meant less in practice than in principle.[51]

With respect to staffing, the Committee put its faith mainly in economics-trained permanent officials. As Keynes and others had suggested, academic recruits were to be welcomed on a temporary (e.g., two- to five-year) basis and salaries would have to be comparable to those for higher academic posts with additional compensation for deprivation of non-pecuniary university attractions. Further inducements would include opportunities to publish, within the limits of the Official Secrets Act, and retention of university superannuation provisions during government service. It was hoped that middle-rank academics could be found to work as economic advisers within departments, while the top ES posts were filled either by promotion from within, as Robbins had suggested, or occasionally by outsiders. Hence Robbins' notion of an ES staffed by 'conformists' working within departments was preferred to the more aggressive, confrontational model which Keynes seemed to have in mind. In general the report tended to underplay the economists' technical contributions while looking more to the quasi-administrative type akin to the traditional civil service generalist – which helps to explain the concern about the overlap between economics and politics.

VII

While the Committee's Report presumably settled the main issues, at least for the time being, some were reopened shortly after when the adoption of the *Employment Policy* White Paper in 1944 gave the economists a fresh opportunity to sell themselves as specialists providing essential technical expertise. The discussion is worth considering both as another stage in the pre-history of postwar economic management and as a further source of insight into the economists' wartime conception of their prospective contributions to government.

John Jewkes, who had directed the ES before he moved on to the Ministry of Reconstruction, produced a paper entitled 'Next Steps for Carrying into Effect the Government's Long Period Policy for Maintaining Employment'.[52] Confessing that he 'came somewhat timidly to the ideas of the White Paper' – an admission of interest considering his vitriolic postwar attacks on economic planning[53] – Jewkes emphasized the ES's need for staff who could communicate effectively and act responsibly when faced with the difficult choices involved in advising Ministers. The Section's head should have direct access, for there should be as few intermediaries as possible in matters where vested interests inevitably arose. Moreover he must have high status:

> At least equivalent to that of the Chiefs of Staff in wartime. No War Cabinet could make a major decision of strategy without closest consultation with its Chiefs of Staff. The danger is that peacetime Cabinets will feel competent to embark on economic strategy without any more assistance from their economic experts than a few papers which, if they are short enough to be read, will certainly be too short to be informative.

The inescapable conclusion was that the unit should be in the Treasury.

> Effective powers to coordinate within Whitehall are not a matter of granting formal responsibility for that purpose; they are much more a matter of prestige and status built up over a long period by the calibre of officials, access to information and the ultimate control exercised through finance. If the new organization were set up outside the Treasury then the two parts of a common policy [employment policy and fundamental budgetary provision] would be torn apart by administrative arrangements.

Jewkes therefore argued for a new Treasury division headed by a man of affairs with practical experience of business and finance, a working grasp of economics and statistics, and a high degree of administrative capacity. The technical staff would consist of specialist economists and statisticians who would operate primarily in the realm of ideas, which did not fit into any conventionally disciplined or hierarchical organization. Jewkes considered it essential to attract and retain competent specialists within the machinery of government to help prevent mass unemployment. Consequently, somewhat like Keynes, he advocated special privileges for such a staff, including greater freedom of expression, more leisure time, and facilities for free discussion with university staff. How far these specialists would be able to exercise their 'higher faculties' (to cite Henderson's term) is a matter for conjecture, since Jewkes did not explain, though it was con-

sidered in James Meade's memorandum referred to below.[54] Moreover
Jewkes did not even refer to the coordinating function which figured so
prominently in the Machinery of Government Committee's proceedings.
Essentially Jewkes was anxious to provide the Treasury with its own departmental economists, thereby detracting significantly from the ES role in the
macroeconomic policy-making process.

These administrative responsibilities were seized on by James Meade in
his reply to Jewkes. Having devoted so much time to the 1944 *White Paper*
Meade endeavoured to place Jewkes' suggestions within the wider context.

> If the group of economists was to be in the Treasury, should they be
> solely concerned with employment policy? If not, there would be no
> room for an Economic Section outside the Treasury. If so, there would
> be no group to give advice on other important issues, or a separate
> group giving advice on problems other than employment policy.

Meade conceded that he did not know the solution to this problem which,
in effect, raised the question whether employment policy and economic
coordination were coextensive or even identical. The matter was not, however, as simple as Jewkes had maintained. For example,

> Your draft does not bring out the fact that in addition to the 'brains
> trust' functions of a group of economists and statisticians, there is a
> most important central administrative function. Who is to be respons-
> ible for seeing that departments have a good armoury of imaginative
> schemes for public investment, ready planned to a point at which
> they could be quickly put into effect?

Meade was, of course, trying to illustrate the variety of contributions a
peacetime ES could make beyond the provision of advice in the general
sense of that term. To a present-day reader his example was perhaps
unfortunate since it recalled the wider type of public works discussion of
the interwar and pre-1914 years, rather than a single component in a
Keynesian type policy framework. A contemporary economist would be
more likely to illustrate the need for coordination by referring, for example,
to the task of reconciling departmental expenditure proposals with forecasts
of such major aggregates as inflation or the value of sterling, or alternatively
the task of reconciling monetary, fiscal and balance of payments policies.
In 1943 there was evidently some doubt whether the economists were to
be used to coordinate the movement of the economy (in the sense of
studying the interrelationships between the numerous variables involved)
or coordinate the work of different government departments (which, if
it was to be at all effective, would necessarily impinge upon traditional
departmental autonomy). There was a strong Whitehall tradition against
centralized direction.

VIII

What emerges from the foregoing? Most conspicuous in terms of economists in government *per se* is the general consensus in favour of employing economists in departments. Why was this not accomplished? Several explanations suggest themselves. There were obvious difficulties on the supply side, but supply is merely a function of price. The Treasury was unwilling to give highly favourable salaries and conditions of employment to attract specialists at a time when university restocking and recruitment by industry and the numerate professions made academic and business employment attractive to economists in both the short and the longer terms.[55] But there was undoubtedly also an absolute shortage of *suitable* economists (that is, combining requisite competence, personal and non-professional qualities and willingness to conform to civil service styles and procedures) with interests in economic policy, especially outside the field of macroeconomic management. Many economists were genuinely relieved to be away from Whitehall in the comparative peace of the university environment. A civil service career was not an especially attractive prospect to the professional social scientist at a time when promotion and career prospects appeared much better in the administrative grades.

There were also demand side problems. Lee admirably documents the strong urge for continuity in civil service machinery at the end of the war.[56] It was thus unfortunate that many of the larger groups of economists in Whitehall were in war- or reconstruction-related activities, which were rapidly wound up after 1945.[57] To have employed economists in departments in peacetime would have required both a spirit of innovation and considerable effort and flexibility from establishment officers in the recruitment of specialists. In the event, neither existed. Senior officials disliked novelties and were anxious to preserve departmental organization and autonomy.

Perhaps the economists themselves ought to have tried harder to create a bigger place for their specialist skills in government; in 1943 they certainly spoke modestly of their contributions to policy-making and failed to emphasize their technical expertise. But at this early stage the implications of Keynesian macroeconomic management – that is, the practice – had not yet been fully grasped by officials and probably not by the economists themselves. Much of the blame must be placed with the administrative overreaction to the ideas put forward by Beveridge. Most of the contributors to the Machinery of Government exercise went to a great length to undermine Beveridge's position. There was definite, even wilful, confusion between 'coordination' and 'direction' and a severe misrepresentation of Beveridge's views. With the benefit of hindsight much of the discussion in 1943 seems woolly and ill-considered.

But by the time of the *Employment Policy* White Paper, economists had much more self-confidence and a belief in the usefulness of their *technical* expertise in government. A number, of course, were the bright young men who had worked with Keynes during the thirties. It must have been tempting for them to believe that the commitment to full employment and the place for high-level specialist economic advice marked the achievement after a decade of pressure of all the goals which the Keynesians had set themselves. Having achieved one major breakthrough, it is perhaps unreasonable to have expected government economists to take one more step and exert pressure to see that the departments had adequate provision of economic advice. The high work load on the ES and the frenetic atmosphere in Whitehall towards the end of the war made it impossible to devote much time to this sort of activity. Moreover, there runs through Keynes' writings an élitist outlook which assumes that almost all economic problems can be effectively remedied by a small, centrally placed group of academically excellent advisers.[58] For a variety of reasons economists in government decided to settle for what was offered. They had already begun to close ranks and submerge professional and political disagreements as a means of strengthening the reputation of the discipline in upper civil service circles.[59]

Thus, economists seemed content to consolidate their position in government. The gains made during wartime were not to be lost, but nor were significant advances to be sought.

NOTES

1 Co-written with A. E. Booth. This paper is a by-product of research financed by the SSRC under the direction of Professor A. W. Coats on the role of the economist in British government 1940–70. We are indebted to Mr J. M. Lee of Birkbeck College, London for allowing us to see his monograph, *Reviewing the Machinery of Government 1942–52: An Essay on the Anderson Committee and its Successors* (1977). Copies are available from him.

2 See, for example, T. W. Hutchison, *Economists and Economic Policy in Britain 1946–1966: Some Aspects of their Interrelations* (1968) and A. W. Coats, Economists in Government, A Research Field for the Historian of Economics, *History of Political Economy*, vol. 10 (1978).

3 However, informal advice from economics-trained administrators did increase. See A. E. Booth and A. W. Coats, The Market for Economists in Britain, 1945–75: A Preliminary Survey, *Economic Journal*, 86 (1978), 444 (reprinted in this volume, pp. 474–95). On the significance of the war effort, see W. K. Hancock and M. M. Gowing, *British War Economy* (1949), pp. 220–3.

4 Booth and Coats, op. cit.

5 The term 'planning' is, of course, ambiguous. A good discussion of the various nuances in relation to British experience in the twentieth century can be found in Jacques Leruez, *Economic Planning and Politics in Britain* (translated by Martin Harrison) (1975).

6 PRO CAB 87/73, Ministerial Committee on the Machinery of Government, First Meeting, 12 Nov. 1942.

7 A. W. Coats, The Development of the Agricultural Economics Profession in England, *Journal of Agricultural Economics* 27 (1976) (reprinted in this volume, pp. 419–32).

8 Susan Howson and Donald Winch, *The Economic Advisory Council 1930–1939* (Cambridge 1977).

9 Lionel Robbins, *Autobiography of an Economist* (1971), ch. 8.

10 On the PMSS, see G. D. A. MacDougall, The Prime Minister's Statistical Section, in D. N. Chester (ed), *Lessons of the British War Economy* (1951). On Keynes and co. in the Treasury, see R. S. Sayers, *Financial Policy* (1956), especially chapters 2 and 3.

11 José Harris, Social Planning in Wartime, in Jay Winter (ed), *War and Economic Development: Essays in Memory of David Joslin* (1975), pp. 244–5 and 251–2. (Hereafter, *Social Planning*.)

12 Paul Addison, *The Road to 1945* (1975), ch. 5.

13 José Harris, *William Beveridge: A Biography* (Oxford, 1978), p. 438 (Hereafter *Biography*); Addison, op. cit., ch. 5; W. H. Beveridge, *Power and Influence* (1953), p. 331.

14 See Leruez, op. cit., ch. 1.

15 Addison, op. cit., *passim*.

16 The prewar background to Keynesianism can be found in Howson and Winch, op. cit.

17 This paragraph attempts to summarize some of the arguments of Howson and Winch, op. cit., pp. 9ff.

18 See, for example *Biography, passim*, G. D. H. Cole, *The Machinery of Socialist Planning* (1938), and the subsequent references to Beveridge in this paper.

19 *Biography*, pp. 311, 314.

20 W. H. Beveridge, An Economic General Staff, *The Nation and Atheneum*, 29 Dec. 1923 and 5 Jan. 1924. The proposal to establish a body whose function was confined to 'thinking' is curious from someone with Beveridge's background and practical experience. Apart from its sheer novelty, such a body was bound to be ignored, or not taken seriously by Whitehall officials.

21 *Biography*, p. 325.

22 Reprinted as ch. 7 of *Planning Under Democracy* (1936).

23 In Sir Ernest Simon (ed), *Constructive Democracy* (1938), pp. 141–2.

24 Beveridge rejected as 'inadequate' the Economic Advisory Council because its members were too busy with other tasks; the various departmental research and intelligence divisions because of their failure to take a coordinated aggregative view; and the Industrial and Economic Advisers already in post because of their failure to accomplish the necessary tasks. Ibid, p. 141.

25 Reprinted as chapter 5 of *The Pillars of Security and other Wartime Essays and Addresses* (1943). This extract can be found at p. 45. As José Harris notes, Beveridge bombarded government departments with 'offers of assistance' early in the war, and wrote to Attlee, Bevin and Morrison after Churchill assumed power in May 1940 'once again offering his services and spelling out the need for an Economic General Staff', *Biography*, pp. 317–18.

26 *The Pillars of Security*, op. cit., p. 92. The broadcast formed chapter 7 of *The Pillars of Security*.

27 Ibid, p. 93.

28 Beveridge noted in his autobiography that he was 'boycotted' by Ministers and civil servants soon after the publication of his Report see *Power and Influence*, op. cit., pp. 323–4.

29 PRO CAB 87/71 meeting held 12 Oct. 1943.

30 *Biography*, p. 435.

31 Note that Beveridge welcomed the recommendation in the *Employment Policy* White Paper to keep the Economic Section as the acceptance of a place for an EGS. See *Full Employment in a Free Society: A Report by William H. Beveridge* (1944), pp. 258–9.

32 We owe this point to Mr J. M. Lee, op. cit., *passim*.

33 PRO CAB 87/72. Memorandum dated 25 Jan. 1943. There are several drafts of this document, some of which contain revisions in response to comments and suggestions from Robbins' civil service colleagues, both established and temporary.

34 Robbins subsequently elaborated this argument in the *Economic Problem in Peace and War* (1947).

35 For the views of Pigou and Keynes on economics and policy see Howson and Winch, op. cit., pp. 161–3. For Henderson's views see pp. 564–7.

36 Bridges, at this time Secretary to the Cabinet, and Brook his deputy, were obviously powerful men at the top of the civil service hierarchy and their support was very important, if not crucial, in the decision to retain the ES. However, Robbins' memo must have lacked some clarity for Sir Horace Wilson, Permanent Secretary to the Treasury, believed that Robbins 'really has in mind an EGS' (PRO CAB 87/72 Memorandum of 2 Feb. 1943). But Wilson was by this time very much persona non grata with Churchill who could not abide him. His views were accordingly less important.

37 Howson and Winch, op. cit., p. 25 (quoting the ILP weekly *New Leader*, 14 Jan. 1930); Henderson had been Joint Secretary of the EAC from 1930 to 1934; a member of the CIE 1931–9 and the Stamp Survey 1939–40; and a Treasury economist since 1939.

38 Howson and Winch, op. cit., p. 164.

39 See, for example, Sam Brittan, The Irregulars, in Richard Rose (ed), *Policy Making in Britain: A Reader in Government* (New York 1969), and Michael Shanks, The Irregulars in Paul Streeten (ed), *Unfashionable Economics: Essays in Honour of Lord Balogh* (1972), 244–62; Joan Mitchell, Special Advisers: A Personal View, *Public Administration*, vol. 56 (1978).

40 This is a paraphrase of Leith-Ross' views from the Draft Report of the Official Committee, para. 11. He believed that there was a real danger of conflict between a Central ES and heads of departments. Curiously enough, Professor H. J. Laski, who might have been expected to adopt a more radical position, shared Fergusson's practical and constitutional objections to an EGS which 'would usurp the position of Ministers by presenting them with cut and dried policy'. Also from the Draft Report of the Committee.

41 As the agricultural economists constituted the pioneers among departmental economists it is worth citing Fergusson's conception of their duties. 'To prepare *objective* studies' of the relevant economic problems as a basis for departmental policy 'and to give objective and unbiased economic advice to the Permanent Secretary and Minister on these problems'. To explain to them the meaning and significance of 'papers on economic subjects originating outside the Department'. To provide Ministerial and Departmental briefs 'in the form either of economic criticisms of proposals made in Parliament or by other Departments or of such economic arguments as can be adduced in support of the Department's own policies or activities'.

42 Fergusson had strongly objected to the ES support for the Ministry of Food in its efforts to keep down the cost of living when the Ministry of Agriculture was trying to maintain or increase prices and farm profits in an effort to maximize

food production. One economist in Food jokingly recalled that the battle with the Ministry of Agriculture occupied far more of their energy than that with the Germans!

43 During anxious consideration of the tariff question in 1931–2, when Fergusson was Private Secretary to the Chancellor of the Exchequer, Neville Chamberlain, he had warned that 'once economists are let loose on a topic of this kind, they are sure to disagree and your committee will be side-tracked into academic discussions'. Howson and Winch, op. cit., p. 98.

44 See, for example, the discussions of the ES activities in Hancock and Gowing, *loc. cit.*, and Robbins, *Autobiography of an Economist*, ch. 8.

45 Memorandum dated 12 March 1943. Gater emphasized the need for trained economists in the Colonial Office and 'much regretted that the various attempts which have been made to add to our staff persons with an adequate economic training have hitherto failed'. This remark is of interest because the Colonial Office was one of the few postwar departments to employ economists, albeit in small numbers and at a fairly low level, before the 1960s. Gater added that 'any economic organization inside the Colonial Office itself would stand in very much the same relationship to the rest of the office as the Economic Secretariat planned by Professor Robbins would stand in relation to the general adminis- tration of the country'. This statement suggests that such an organization would occupy a higher position than the Economic Intelligence unit in the postwar Colonial Office.

46 Memorandum dated 9 April 1943.

47 Keynes does not really spell out what he meant by 'advice' at this level; there is obviously a requirement to estimate the relevant magnitudes statistically, and, secondly, to assess trends and forecast future movements. In these stages statisticians were vital but Keynes did not attempt to comment on the division of responsibilities between the ES and the CSO.

48 This problem has occurred over the political complexion of the US Council of Economic Advisers. The literature is voluminous, but for a stimulating review of the issues, see the discussion, How Political Must the Council of Economic Advisers Be? in *Challenge*, March–April 1974. For a comment from a British standpoint, see Sir Alec Cairncross, *Essays in Economic Management* (1971), pp. 206–8.

49 Draft Report of the Official Committee.

50 Some of the most severe recent critics of postwar British economics have seized upon the predominance of Keynesian ideas and policies as a major source of weakness. For example, Harry Johnson, Keynes and British Economics, in Elizabeth S. Johnson and Harry G. Johnson, *The Shadow of Keynes: Understanding Keynes, Cambridge and Keynesian Economics* (Oxford 1978), pp. 203–20.

51 The matter was discussed on several occasions before the final decision was made partly because the postwar relations between the ES and the Treasury seemed to be working smoothly, despite the shift of power back to the Treasury, and because senior officials wished to ascertain whether this would continue to be so under a Conservative government. Nevertheless, when the transfer occurred it was discussed at length by the economists, in correspondence between Sir Robert Hall, then Director of the ES, and his predecessors Robbins and Meade, who gave it their blessing.

52 A copy of this correspondence survives in PRO T230/70.

53 *Ordeal by Planning* (1948) and *New Ordeal by Planning* (2nd edition 1968).

54 PRO T230/69, Meade to Jewkes 29 July 1944.

55 Those economists who entered business and professional employment in the

early postwar years enjoyed a definite salary advantage over other social scientist contemporaries, and over subsequent entrants into professional economist employment. See Booth and Coats, op. cit., 445–52. Reprinted in this volume pp. 445–89.

56 Op. cit., *passim*, but especially his concluding remarks at pp. 144–5.

57 For example, the Ministers of Aircraft Planning and Economic Warfare employed economists on war-related activities. Economists in the Board of Trade's Industries and Manufactures Division I were involved in large part in drafting the outlines of the Board's reconstruction policies and consequently also had a limited immediate usefulness to government. Another large group was found in the Ministry of Food, but they had experienced some difficulty in integrating themselves into the work of the department. Thus, only the Ministry of Agriculture and the ES remained as major employers of government economists.

58 In the Machinery of Government exercise, for example, Keynes suggested that the Treasury could make do with no more than two economists. At a more general level, see Elizabeth Johnson's essay in *The Shadow of Keynes*, pp. 1–16.

59 Note, for example, the reconciliation between Robertson and Keynes, Robbins and Keynes, and the broad similarity of the proposals on employment policy formulated by the Keynesians who were helping Beveridge and the Keynesians who were advising the government. Harry Johnson has suggested that this closing of ranks led to far too much unanimity and mutual protection and has been to the great detriment of British economics. *The Shadow of Keynes*, pp. 203–20.

28

THE CHANGING ROLE OF ECONOMISTS IN SCOTTISH GOVERNMENT SINCE 1960[1]

INTRODUCTION AND BACKGROUND

In any general survey of postwar developments in the employment of professional economists in British government, the advent of the Labour administration, in October 1964, is the most obvious watershed. Several of the incoming ministers immediately created special high-level economic advisory posts, and within the next few months there was a dramatic increase in the number of economist appointments at a variety of levels in a number of different departments – especially in the new Department of Economic Affairs and the Ministry of Overseas Development. This proved to be the beginning of a spectacular expansionary trend which continued after 1970 under the Conservative government, and it would be unwise to underestimate the novelty and importance – at least for the economics profession – of this movement. Nevertheless, closer inspection of the pre-1964 Whitehall situation reveals that the demand for economic and statistical expertise was already growing perceptibly from the beginning of the decade, partly under the influence of the marked revival of interest in economic planning and regional economic development. This entailed changes in both the nature and the scale of the demand for economists, and foreshadowed major new developments in both the utilization and the management of specialist categories of civil service personnel.

A study of the Scottish dimension of this process is especially appropriate, for a number of reasons. As is widely recognized, the Scottish Office has played a pioneering role in the evolution of regional economic development policies and economic planning programmes, especially since the early 1960s, and therefore provides special insights into one major aspect of the growing demand for government economists and statisticians. In addition, although the Scottish situation possesses certain characteristics which differentiate it from Westminster and Whitehall, it can in some respects be regarded as a microcosm of the larger British political and bureaucratic system. And, given its limited scale and partial isolation, it presents a manageable field for investigation.

In this paper attention is focused on the principal reasons why and the processes whereby the number and functions of professional economists – both civil servants and outsiders – expanded so substantially in Scotland during the period under review. Some reference will also be made to the effects of these developments on the demand for statistical information and expertise. But before plunging into the details of the story, it is necessary to provide a brief introduction to the Scottish 'political system'.[2]

This wider context is an integral part of the story, since political considerations exerted a powerful and direct influence on the formulation and evolution of policies designed to correct the backwardness of the Scottish economy. Postwar action in this field has involved Whitehall departments, the Scottish Office, Scottish pressure groups, local authorities, industry, banks and financial institutions. There is a distinctively Scottish decision-making process stemming from the special relationship between the Secretary of State for Scotland – whose responsibilities are so wide that he has been referred to as Scotland's 'Prime Minister' – and other Cabinet members. The structure of government in Scotland results from an uneasy and ever-shifting compromise between a purely London-based and an Edinburgh-based system, and the expansion of the British government's responsibilities for economic and social affairs in the postwar decades has produced a persistent tendency, compounded of political pressures and administrative expediency, to transfer functions and responsibilities from Whitehall to the Scottish Office. In practice the process of change has been fairly gradual, so that its long-term implications tended to be overlooked until the growth of Scottish nationalism and the prospects of devolution drew attention to it. As Kellas noted, owing to the combination of strong nationalist vested interests and the flexibility of the powers over organizational matters accorded to the Scottish Secretary of State, this steady accretion of functions and responsibilities has taken place without the frequent and disruptive bureaucratic reorganizations which were taking place in Whitehall.

By comparison with the much vaster, more complex, and highly departmentalized Whitehall machine, the Scottish civil service is relatively compact, self-contained, and modest in scale, despite the recent expansion. It is therefore easy for the senior officials to develop a sense of coherence and unity of purpose which is of considerable value in any efforts to develop coordinated policies for the Scottish region. At all levels the majority of staff are Scots who display a natural and proper preoccupation with Scottish interests and affairs as a whole, often extending well beyond the duties and responsibilities of their respective ministries. According to a well-informed academic commentator the personnel of St Andrews House, the locus of the Scottish Office:

are much more accessible to the general public than those in Whitehall, and that their work is carried out before a critical audience in Scotland, in a way in which the work of Whitehall civil servants is not. . . . The officials in St Andrews House therefore work in a world of divided loyalties. Unlike their counterparts in Northern Ireland, they do not belong to a distinctive administration with its own Parliamentary and popular base. They are recruited and promoted on the same basis as officials in Whitehall. Yet they think of their careers almost entirely in Scottish terms.[3]

As Kellas remarked, the limited scale of the Scottish Office produces both strengths and weaknesses:

It provides for Scotland, a bureaucracy derived from, and knowledgeable of, its people and their special needs. For the men who staff it, it gives some technical problems not present in Whitehall relating to Parliamentary business and liaison with other departments. The type of work which they do makes them generalists rather than specialists, although they remain within the same department to a much greater extent than do civil servants in Whitehall. This has given the Scottish Office in recent years an overall sense of direction lacking in much of Whitehall, and certainly in any region in England.[4]

In the evolution of regional policy during the past two decades it seems clear that the peculiar strengths of the Scottish political system have outweighed the disadvantages. As Mr A. B. Hume, Secretary of the Scottish Development Department, remarked to the members of the Commission on the Constitution, in 1969:

The fact that we are a nation and concerned with our welfare, and have organs of the press and so on to express this led to more thinking in academic circles as well as in government and in other fora about our needs. . . . Certainly we in St Andrews House constituted one focus of forward thinking, and I cannot think of an appropriate Ministry in Whitehall at that time which could have had the responsibility either for doing that [i.e. regional planning] or for promoting that in an English region.[5]

Given the breadth of the Secretary of State's responsibilities it was possible:

to put plans together over a whole field so that they coalesce and can then be followed out one by one so that they complement each other. This has been done in at least two White Papers, one on central Scotland and a later one on Scotland as a whole. That is a general advantage . . .[6]

According to an earlier witness, J. H. McGuinness, the dynamic Assistant

Under-Secretary of State responsible for regional development, all the assessments for those White Papers:

> and the resultant decisions reflected the Scottish Office's assessment of the importance of public investment, particularly of highway investment and housing in support of economic growth, involving large expenditures of money. All these were incorporated as deliberate instruments of policy, and although these were collective decisions of Government, the preliminary work was done by the [Scottish Economic] Planning Board and the Departments participated in it. This represented a definite new move forward to take account of Scotland's special economic conditions.[7]

THE TOOTHILL REPORT AND THE DEVELOPMENT OF SCOTTISH REGIONAL POLICY

The distinctive characteristics of the Scottish system of government sketched in the preceding paragraphs help to explain why the professionalization of economics in the Scottish bureaucracy has been so closely associated with the development of regional policy and economic planning. The most obvious turning-point in the story is the publication of the Toothill Report – by a committee of the Scottish Council (Development and Industry) in November 1961.[8] This document was a direct response to the widespread concern at the economic difficulties of the Scottish economy during the late 1950s, and it was but one of a long series of attempts to enlist government support for new methods of relieving persistent unemployment, modernizing an outmoded industrial structure, and fostering economic growth. As far back as the 1930s Scots had actively supported government-sponsored industrial estates, a scheme which became an integral feature of the early development area legislation, while the so-called Cairncross report of 1952, issued by a committee of the Scottish Council,[9] had emphasized the inadequacy of policies designed merely to relieve unemployment. In advocating more positive measures this document introduced the concept of growth areas (or poles) which became a key element in official policy during the 1960s. The Toothill Report proved to be even more timely, since its publication coincided with a sudden burst of British enthusiasm for planning for economic growth, and in harmony with contemporary thinking it specifically emphasized the economic, as opposed to the social aspects of regional development.[10] Although the Scottish Council is a private body, composed of representatives of employers, trade unions, local authority associations, and individuals, it was in close touch with official thinking, especially through its civil service 'assessors'. Scottish Office officials contributed directly to the writing of the Toothill Report, and although they lacked the power to implement its proposals without Whitehall's sanction, the combined pressure of internal and external Scottish forces obviously facilitated its ready acceptance as the basis of subsequent policy.

In the present context, special interest attaches to chapter 22 of the Report, which recommended the effective transfer of additional economic and industrial responsibilities from Whitehall to the Scottish ministers, on the grounds that the existing organization of duties under the Secretary of State was not 'well calculated to promote the coordination of activities related to economic development'. A new department, headed by a Scottish Minister for Economic Affairs, was needed to carry out, among other duties, 'the Secretary of State's non-statutory responsibilities for the general oversight of the Scottish economy and his statutory functions relative to town and country planning, roads, electricity and water'. The current situation, whereby the Secretary of State was dependent on the supply of statistics from the Board of Trade, Ministry of Labour, and other Whitehall departments, was clearly inadequate. He needed 'an economic information and research unit within his own departments to study and advise on economic and industrial matters generally'. Its duties should include the following:

> Continuing analysis of the economy and of the general measures required to ensure its health and growth;
> Advice on the coordination of economic and industrial policy in Scotland;
> Advice on the broad lines of investment policy in Scotland and on the economic implications of the programme of public investments;
> Advice on the wider economic implications of major questions before departments;
> Advice on the implications of national economic policy for Scotland and, where necessary, on the desirability of modifying its application in Scotland.

The new unit should work closely with appropriate sections of the Treasury in London and with the research departments of other ministries, and its first task should be to review the progress of Scottish statistics and to consider what improvements were required.

These recommendations virtually constituted a blueprint for subsequent developments in the Scottish administration. Admittedly it was almost a decade before a full-scale economics and statistics unit was created, and the review of Scottish statistics to which the Toothill Committee attached so high a priority proved to be, at least in the short run, a non-event.[11] Nevertheless it is to Toothill – and, no doubt, to the influential voice of its Vice-Chairman, Thomas Wilson, Professor of Political Economy at the University of Glasgow – that we must look for the antecedents of the Scottish Economic Planning Department, which was established in 1973.

From an organizational standpoint the first major post-Toothill development was the formation of a new Scottish Development Department (SDD) in 1962.[12] This new body absorbed certain functions hitherto performed by the Scottish Home Department and the Department of Health for Scotland, and it included a division responsible for General Economic Development, Town and Country Planning under the direction of J. H. McGuinness, as Under-Secretary, and also, for a time, the Scottish Statistical Office. The Secretary of the New SDD, Douglas Haddow, became a key figure in the subsequent evolution of economic policy making, and his elevation to the post of Permanent Under-Secretary of State for the Scottish Office, as a whole in 1964 – a position he held until his retirement in 1973 – symbolized the central importance attached to regional development policy. Within the SDD a Scottish Development Group was created as an inter-departmental forum to provide a coordinated approach to economic development problems, and in late 1963 it produced the *White Paper on Central Scotland* (Cmnd 2188), its first major planning exercise. By 1964 the expansion of economic functions and responsibilities led to the creation of a Regional Development Division (RDD) outside the four main Scottish Departments but directly under Haddow. This Division was not a conventional executive department, but rather 'a staff group which keeps its eye on all sorts of things',[13] and its head, McGuinness, was in a position to concentrate on economic matters as responsibility for physical planning remained within the SDD. When Sir Douglas Haddow became Permanent Under-Secretary of State McGuinness succeeded him as Chairman of the Scottish Economic Planning Board, a coordinating body comprising senior officials in Scotland concerned with economic affairs plus senior officials of the Whitehall Departments concerned with Scottish economic and physical development,[14] such as the Departments of Industry, Employment and Energy (to use their present titles). The new board played a leading part in the preparation and drafting of the *White Paper on the Scottish Economy 1965–70* (Cmnd 2864). The senior Scottish Office officials who were members of the Board also drew upon the external advice provided by the specially appointed Scottish Economic Planning Council[15] and attended meetings with the panel of economic consultants.

Thus by the mid-1960s the basic machinery of Scottish economic policy making had been established, and its subsequent expansion[16] provided the context within which the growing demand for professional economists and statisticians was expressed. It is now time to consider the impact of these demands on the civil service organization and personnel.

Immediately following the publication of the Toothill Report there were detailed official discussions of the best method of implementing the proposals contained in chapter 22. A suggestion that the new unit's primary functions should be statistical rather than economic was rejected, for it was felt that priority must be given to the provision of expert economic advice if the Secretary of State's staff was to exercise the necessary persuasion with other departments having professional economic support, a contention suggesting that professional economists were already presumed to have some weight in Whitehall deliberations. There were complaints that undue emphasis had been placed on employment-creation as a means of assisting the Scottish economy, irrespective of whether there was economic justification for the additional jobs; and the underlying reasoning had been sloppy. There was no shortage of tasks for the new unit. It would have a coordinating function similar to that performed in Whitehall by the Economic Section of the Treasury, and would supply technical expertise parallel to that provided by physical planners and the specialist staffs in other Scottish departments, such as agriculture and health. It would be desirable to establish links with Treasury economists 'not least in order to avoid the danger of ministers receiving conflicting professional economic advice'. However, there would be no point in setting up a backroom unit divorced from the application of theoretical principles. Economics should be regarded not as a 'hierophantic mystery', but as a technique of fact-finding and appraisal which would be of direct value to an administrative manager. Some administrators felt that the Economic Section's contributions often suffered from an ivory tower angle of vision. Moreover, much of its work had been too general to be applicable to Scotland, and it had not, in any case, been brilliantly productive.

Nevertheless, despite these misgivings an approach was made to the Treasury Economic Section, in which it was noted that as far back as 1946 the Lord President of the Council (Herbert, later Lord Morrison) had suggested that the Scottish Office needed a qualified economist and supporting staff to present the economic aspects of Scotland's problems to the government in a proper form. The suggestion had been welcomed in Edinburgh, but it had proved impossible either to second a member of the Economic Section or to recruit an academic economist for work on Scottish economic problems. Instead, a Scottish administrative civil servant with qualifications in economics had been appointed, but this experiment was abandoned in the early 1950s.

As it transpired the recruitment problem was no easier a decade later. Discussions were held with the recently installed economic adviser to HM Government, A. K. (later Sir Alec) Cairncross, who was very familiar with the Scottish situation, having just completed a decade as Professor of Economics at the University of Glasgow. However, it is worth noting his revealing comment that throughout that period his department had not received a single request for advice from any of the Scottish government departments. This had surprised him, for he had rather expected to be under considerable pressure to provide research and advisory staff for government work, and on taking up his chair in 1951 he had actually promised the Vice-Chancellor not to become too much involved in carrying out research for the Edinburgh departments! This lack of contact between the university and the government broadly reflects the situation throughout Britain in the 1950s, when interest in economic planning was at a low ebb.

Early in 1962, when the Permanent Under-Secretary of State in the Scottish Office, Sir William Murrie, sought his assistance, Cairncross was already experiencing serious difficulties in obtaining professional economists of the right calibre for his own Economic Section. The demand for the Section's services was growing apace and he was being encouraged to expand his staff so that some professional economists could be seconded to other parts of the government on special assignments. Thus the appeal for help from the Scottish Office was but one of several, not all of which could be met simultaneously; and it did not have the highest priority. Cairncross therefore proposed that the Scottish Office should seek assistance from the Scottish universities, either by employing academic economists on a part-time basis, or by commissioning specific research projects. There were precedents for these practices in Whitehall, especially the former. However the Scottish Office officials were anxious to have a full-time professional economist as well as a reinforcement of their statistical staff. But given the acute shortage of qualified economists willing to enter the civil service at a time when the demand for their services was growing perceptibly in Whitehall, it proved impossible to find a recruit of the requisite maturity and experience. The Scottish officials were unwilling to appoint a young up-and-coming economist with little or no experience of government; they were seeking a person of established reputation, whose advice would carry weight in Whitehall departments. They therefore considered whether it would be appropriate to appoint a good administrator with an economics background and much experience of economic policy matters. However, Cairncross considered that for a post of the kind proposed a practising professional economist should be appointed, and in this he was no doubt concerned to maintain the professional standing of the Treasury Economic Section. He may also have been aware of the earlier abortive experiment with a non-economist administrator.

Cairncross's argument that the work required could only be undertaken by professional economists won the day, and the Scottish officials therefore decided to build up the staff of economists and statisticians in the Scottish Statistical Office – though in fact it was some years before this aim was achieved. They hoped to avoid the risks involved in appointing some high-powered person who, while he was finding his way about the official machine, might have thought that he had not enough to do, and might otherwise have felt frustrated. In addition, in support of the permanent staff, they decided to enlist the heads of departments in the Scottish universities to form a panel of consultant advisers to the Secretary of State on matters affecting the Scottish economy, an arrangement which would facilitate subcontracting of research work to the university departments involved.

THE ECONOMIC CONSULTANTS

This is the background to the establishment of the Scottish Advisory Panel of Economic Consultants, a body which has no postwar counterpart elsewhere in British government, although it bears some resemblance to the Economic Advisory Council of the 1930s[17] and to several of the numerous bodies of experts established in other countries during this century. It is, of course, impossible to assess the consultants' influence on decision making, given the lack of access to policy documents of the last thirty years. Nevertheless, the creation and functioning of this body is of interest as an administrative device designed to offset the severe shortage of professional expertise within the permanent ranks of civil servants, and it still exists – albeit in a somewhat modified form – despite the recent expansion of the number of professional economists and statisticians in the Scottish Office.

The initial press announcement sketched the background of Scottish economic problems requiring expert attention, and stated that the consultants' advice would be sought under one or other of the following three heads:

a. *Scottish Office Responsibilities*: advice on matters, particularly programmes of investment, handled by one of the Scottish Departments, e.g. the economic implications of particular programmes of road development, new towns, or major housing projects, etc.
b. *UK Department Responsibilities*: advice on the impact in Scotland of particular policies or proposals, e.g. port developments, specific major industrial proposals, railway developments, etc.
c. *General Economic Policy*: advice on the impact on Scotland of alternative general economic policies such as fiscal policies, commercial treaties, and the Common Market.

It was also assumed that the consultants might wish, either individually or collectively, to initiate advice on current matters, and that the liaison arrangements would enable a degree of interchange between the universities' research work and the department's studies to be undertaken as the basis of government policy and executive action. Official cooperation would be provided in the form of appropriate factual and other material and advice with any current university research, so as to produce the most immediate practical results.

Like any new departure, the introduction of consultants posed certain problems which, it was feared, might prove to be a source of embarrassment. The new body might, for example, be regarded as an encroachment on the universities' independence or an attempt to teach them their business, and there was uncertainty whether the consultants would be regarded as policy makers, and consequently subjected to embarrassing newspaper questions and comments. Subsequent experience reveals that these initial fears were unwarranted, and there was evidently general satisfaction with the arrangement. At first there were only three consultants – Professors Thomas Wilson and Donald J. Robertson of the University of Glasgow and Professor Archie Duncan Campbell of Dundee University – possibly because it was felt that a larger gathering would be subject to diminishing returns. In 1965 Treasury permission was sought to increase the number to five, partly in the interests of geographical balance, by adding Professor J. N. Wolfe of the University of Edinburgh and Professor Max Gaskin of Aberdeen to the original trio. About that time Professor Wilson retired, partly because of his concurrent commitments as economic consultant to the Northern Ireland government, and later Professor K. W. Alexander of Strathclyde University joined the team.

During the next few years the composition of the Panel remained constant, until 1971, apart from the addition of an industrialist, Mr Desmond Misselbrook, by which time the corps of professional economists and statisticians in the Scottish civil service had increased substantially. So, too, had the number of Scottish universities and their economist staff. It was felt that a return to the original, more informal consultative arrangements was desirable and a two-tier system was introduced, comprising a nuclear group of three consultants – Professors Alexander, Campbell, and Wilson (who was again available) – who would meet the ǀPermanent Under-Secretary of State every two months immediately prior to each meeting of the Scottish Economic Council, and a larger panel of about twelve members, from which individuals could be invited on an *ad hoc* basis according to their specialist expertise and the particular issues on which advice was to be sought. These gatherings were to be held less frequently than meetings of the nuclear group, according to the flow of papers coming forward, and the attendance of civil servants was to be restricted to those directly concerned with the day's agenda. With the core trio it became the practice to have wide-ranging discussions of the current situation, government policy measures, and their likely effects on Scotland, while day-to-day business was handled by the permanent staff.

These new arrangements reflected the changes which had taken place since the early 1960s, both within and outside the government sector. As the number of Scottish academic and civil service economists had increased considerably, the need for generalized economic wisdom of the kind provided by the original three consultants had diminished. The number of specialized studies and policy activities had grown remarkably, and various links had been established between the Scottish Office staff and university and other research bodies. Nevertheless, as the range and variety of the government's economic and social activities was still expanding, the consultants continued to be regarded as a useful supplement to the expertise of the growing corps of professionally qualified officials.

The original panel of consultants had met monthly, eleven times a year, and had considered a remarkably large and varied collection of subjects. Most of the papers and reports presented to them reflected current official matters either within one or other of the Scottish or Whitehall government departments, or from one of the many other official bodies concerned with Scottish affairs. The Scottish Economic Planning Board and the Scottish Economic Planning Council were regular suppliers of business, and the topics ranged from broad issues of economic development to detailed schemes involving particular districts, towns, industries, or social projects. The consultants also provided valuable advice on the background preparations to the 1963 and 1965 White Papers.

In practice they took a less active and initiatory role than had originally been expected, for the original trio were extremely busy men already occupied as chairmen of or advisers to various official bodies, while also performing their regular university duties. In the early years their work was serviced by a junior official (with the rank of economic adviser) who was entitled economic liaison officer, a man who already had academic qualifications in economics and planning and experience of government work. He performed a variety of duties arising from his position as a channel of communication of economic and statistical advice both within the civil service network and between government officials and the many public and semi-public bodies and private individuals concerned with economic and social affairs. He was required to establish and maintain close contact with the Scottish Statistical Office statistician; to liaise with the Treasury Economic Section, supply them with notes on the Scottish aspects of any general economic questions; to give advice to the SDD on the Scottish implications of British economic policy; and to serve as a link between the academic consultants and the civil service. The range of his activities expanded inexorably during the 1960s with the growth of the Scottish Office's economic and social functions, and his post constituted the seed from which we can trace the subsequent development of professional economic work in the Scottish civil service. By 1964, when the RDD was established, it was felt that the time had come to form a properly equipped economic and statistical unit. However before discussing the nature and significance of this organizational innovation[18] it is appropriate to consider the work of the economic consultants, whose activities the economic liaison officer was initially appointed to serve.

The consultants' contribution to the policy-making process was, in the nature of the case, limited, and as the volume of official economic and statistical work expanded these limitations became increasingly apparent. Apart from the sheer bulk of paper to be considered at their monthly meetings there was a problem of timing, since some documents concerned matters already decided or not yet ready for decision. Experience elsewhere has shown that if economic advice is not forthcoming at an early stage, before official attitudes have hardened, it is likely to be ineffective, for it is difficult to halt or reverse the bureaucratic machine once the wheels are turning. The basic problem was to get as far as possible away from 'cauld kale' and as close as possible to 'stop press'. The full-time officials had insufficient time to prepare papers specifically designed for the consultants' meetings, and they were consequently forced to rely on those arising from a variety of civil service sources which did not necessarily fit into the consultants' schedule. One possible solution was to have irregular meetings timed so as to maximize their effectiveness, but this proved impossible to arrange; yet although individual consultants were approached directly from time to time on matters falling within their specialist fields, these contacts were not regarded as sufficient to justify the abandonment of the established schedule.

On the whole the consultants' meetings were regarded as a useful forum for discussion, rather than an integral and indispensable component of the decision-making process. They were, in several senses of the term, an educational experience for the officials involved, who benefited from the opportunity to receive critical analysis of a kind not always to be found in the conformist atmosphere of a civil service department. In cases where a department's views were undecided, or where there were disagreements between departments or officials, the consultants' views could be decisive, while on matters where the department wished to confirm the wisdom of a preconceived position the consultants' 'imprimatur' was welcomed. More generally, it is easy to underestimate the value of detached expertise. Civil servants are often expected to produce simple answers to questions from ministers or from the general public, and they wished to ensure that no such answers were available before committing themselves. Discussions with the consultants were frequently helpful in this respect, for example by pointing out that the controversial issue of labour migration to and from Scotland was compounded of the mixture of motives of innumerable individuals who made up the gross stream in both directions.

On the other hand, some officials found the consultants' contributions too academic or too generalized. Without criticizing them individually or questioning their expertise, they doubted the value of a general airing of issues on which specific and clear-cut advice was needed. Much of the material presented to the consultants did not lend itself to point-by-point examination and comment. Moreover, some of the officials who regarded the consultants as a superfluous cog-wheel in the machinery of discussion would have resented any effort to give them a more detailed and decisive role in the decision-making process.

There are, of course, many reasons why disagreements and misunderstandings can arise between civil servants and professors, and occasional consultants, whether from universities or elsewhere, necessarily have their limitations. Nevertheless, the sheer longevity of the Scottish Advisory Panel of Economic Consultants provides some evidence of its perceived value to officials. Suspicion of ivory tower academics may not have been far below the surface, as for example when Sir Douglas Haddow assured a parliamentary committee that:

> We have . . . contacts with economic consultants, with professors in Scottish universities, and so on, some of them with very considerable industrial as well as economic experience; *they are not academic economists by any means.*[19]

Yet the officials were certainly not merely seeking compliant 'yes' men. They genuinely welcomed discussion, even on those occasions where the academic approach introduced less immediately relevant considerations, for it was difficult to institutionalize the role of the *agent provocateur* in an official bureaucracy.

Scottish officials wished to get a representative cross-section of academic advice, but there was only a limited number of professors with specialist knowledge of the Scottish economy or with the requisite experience or professional interest in the application of economics to government problems, especially in the early 1960s. Some of the potential consultants were unwilling to become directly involved in government policy issues, for fear of compromising their academic independence. And although they were given only limited access to restricted documents, the consultants had to sign the Official Secrets Act, and their status as economic advisers, even if only part-time and occasional, may have been somewhat inhibiting to them. As the universities expanded it was suggested that the number of consultants might be increased, and that attendance might be staggered, or alternates appointed; but, as noted earlier, officials preferred to retain the existing arrangements until 1971. In this case at least there is no evidence for the cynical belief that some ministers deliberately surround themselves with a considerable number of economic advisers in the confident expectation that they will cancel each other out, or provide a rationalization for any conceivable policy recommendation. Yet there is some evidence that Scottish officials had, at least initially, shared the widely held view that any group of economists could be expected to disagree among themselves, and they had been agreeably surprised by the degree of consensus which they had encountered in practice.[20]

For most of the period the consultants' meetings have been chaired by the Permanent Under-Secretary and the attendance has included the Chairman of the Scottish Economic Planning Board, other Scottish Office officials, and the Scottish Regional Controllers of the Ministry of Labour and the Board of Trade. Since the modification of the system in 1970–1 the number attending has been reduced substantially. Distinguished academic or civil service economists other than the consultants have appeared very occasionally, and in very recent years the Secretary of State for Scotland, or the Minister of State, had presided – an experience which, it is thought, has been of considerable value to them.

THE GROWTH OF PROFESSIONAL STAFF AND THE ROLE OF STATISTICS

Although a considerable proportion of this paper has been devoted to the consultants, the main professional contributions to Scottish government economic and statistical work necessarily came from regular civil servants. About 18 months after the appointment of the economic liaison officer it was clear that an increase of professional economic staff was required to deal with the explosion of interest in economic planning, both within and outside the government machine. Regional development policy had become more fashionable not only in Edinburgh, but also in Whitehall, especially as a by-product of the work of the National Economic Development Council and its professional staff, who had been busily initiating studies and conducting enquiries which necessarily increased the permanent civil servants' workload.[21] Moreover, after the advent of the Labour government, in October 1964, the process received an added boost with the creation of the Department of Economic Affairs, whose substantial and energetic staff of professional economists soon gave considerable impetus to regional planning throughout Britain. In Edinburgh, the economic consultants' work had demonstrated the need for more background material for assessments of the economic implications of various aspects of government policy and it was felt that the Scottish Office should play a more positive role in a period 'bubbling with research and activity'. Within the civil service, economic expertise was called for in the analysis of studies undertaken by the development group, to provide periodic reviews of economic progress in Central Scotland and advice on specific matters of government policy affecting Scotland. The economic liaison officer was grossly overloaded and it was felt that the expansion of his work had paved the way for the establishment of a more substantial corps of economic advisory and research staff.

However it was no easy task to fulfil this intention. The Treasury was cautious, as ever, for there had already been a considerable investment of resources in Scottish economic affairs, when account was taken of staff working on these problems in the Ministry of Labour, Board of Trade, and the Department of Agriculture for Scotland. Moreover, Treasury establishments officers were not sure that professional economists were needed, rather than administrators, agricultural economists, or research officers. The Scottish request for additional staff came at a time of rapidly expanding demand for expertise of all types and Cairncross, as Head of the Government Economic Service (GES), which was created early in 1965, had to take account of the needs of many other departments and fields of research.

About that time in Whitehall it was not too difficult to find good young economic assistants; but there was a 'most appalling shortage higher up', and the only feasible solution was to recruit able young economists and train them within the civil service. It was felt that if too many established university economists moved into government service there might be short-run benefits, but these would have to be weighed against the reduction of academic teaching and research, and it seemed that especially in a burgeoning field like regional economic development this might prove harmful in the long run.

Against this background it is hardly surprising that the Scottish staffing problem was not easily resolved, even though the RDD was created in 1964 and its staff was transferred from the SDD to the Scottish Office, where it came directly under the new Permanent Under-Secretary, Sir Douglas Haddow. Despite the determination to 'go all out' to get a university economist on a five-year contract there were no immediate changes in the complement of professional economists and statisticians. Part of the delay was due to a protracted administrative debate about the relationships between economists and research officers resulting from the creation of the GES, for economic assistants and assistant research officers had been working together both in Scotland and in the DEA. The parallel problem of the respective roles and status of agricultural economists, which was the subject of some friction in Whitehall,[22] created no difficulties in Scotland, for the new economic liaison officer, G. F. Hendry, a former principal agricultural economist, was transferred to the GES on taking up his new post. There may, however, have been some difficulty in obtaining Treasury permission to establish a new economic unit in Edinburgh under a senior economic adviser, partly because it was feared that other regions would demand parallel units. It was suggested that the staff should include a statistician as well as economic assistants, a practice that was then unusual outside the agricultural departments, and Cairncross saw no objection to this arrangement. Indeed, at that time in Whitehall there was active discussion of a proposal to merge the economist and statistician classes,[23] and although this was not implemented there has subsequently been a growth in the number of mixed divisions combining several categories of professional staff headed by a professional or an administrator, whichever seemed most appropriate given the personnel available.

Staffing problems of this kind are neither dramatic nor exciting, and they consequently tend to be neglected in discussions of economic policy. Yet in any bureaucracy matters of rank and status have operational significance, and the issue in this case was not merely that of the weight to be attached to the new unit, but also the difficulty of recruitment in Scotland owing to the geographical distance from the main sources of supply. As it transpired, this difficulty was circumvented. The economic liaison officer, G. F. Hendry, became assistant secretary responsible for Transport questions and general economic advice in the Regional Development Division, and his successor as economic liaison officer, P. M. Scola, who had also previously been employed as a principal agricultural economist, was transferred from the Department of Agriculture for Scotland and re-graded as an economic adviser, despite his nominal ineligibility for the GES.

The next significant organizational change in the Scottish Office was the creation of the Economics and Statistics Unit within the RDD, in 1970.[24] But before considering this development it is advisable to review the reasons for the slow growth of Scottish statistics in the post-Toothill era.

The need for improvements in the range and quality of Scottish official statistics had been widely recognized long before the Toothill Report by academics, civil servants, and even, on one occasion, by a Scottish minister. As early as 1949 the Secretary of State for Scotland had invited the Director of the Central Statistical Office to investigate the situation. In his report, Harry Campion emphasized the need to provide a more centralized control of Scottish official statistics and to appoint a professional statistician to give expert advice to all the departments concerned. However two years passed before a statistician Mr J. Grant was appointed to take charge of the Scottish Statistical Office (SSO), and the proposal to appoint an assistant statistician was repeatedly turned down prior to 1960.

Unlike some government departments the Scottish Office did not normally collect a large volume of data from primary sources, and it therefore had no need for a large executive and clerical staff to process the data. But considerable analysis and interpretation was required before the statistics acquired from secondary sources could be used for official purposes, and professionally trained personnel were needed for this purpose. As in other Scottish departments it was necessary to cover a very wide range of subject matter, and in dealing with Whitehall departments a person of sufficient rank was required to deal with London-based officials who were reluctant to undertake the requisite time-consuming collection and extraction of date. Moreover there had been strong resistance to any proposals to collect Scottish statistics independently.

Nevertheless, despite these obvious difficulties there was no expansion in the Scottish Statistical Office's professional staff throughout the 1950s and 1960s. This was partly due to the acute shortage of statisticians, which manifested itself much earlier than the shortage of trained economists referred to earlier.[25] Another reason was that from 1946, when the statistician class was established with entry conditions and pay scales equivalent to those of the administrative class, Campion's determination to maintain high entry qualifications inevitably had the effect of restricting the supply of suitable candidates. In the Scottish Office the attempt to recruit an additional statistician was abandoned as hopeless in 1963, and instead efforts were made to secure the appointment of an Assistant Research Officer with statistical qualifications.

As noted above,[26] after the RDD was placed directly under the Permanent Under-Secretary in 1964 Cairncross was prepared to support the appointment of a statistician within an economics and statistics unit. It was acknowledged that the statistical work had grown beyond the capacity of the lone statistician in the SSO, and that departments other than SDD were developing their own independent statistical units. It was suggested that a new unit should be formed within the Scottish Office consisting of two sections, one concerned with economic assessment, the other with the provision and interpretation of the requisite statistical material. It should be headed by a senior economic adviser (SEA), supported by two main grade professionals and an infrastructure which would enable the SEA to participate more fully, and with the appropriate status, in all major national policy issues bearing on regional development and discussed at that level in such Whitehall departments as the DEA and the Treasury. By that time, of course, the number of professional economists in Whitehall was expanding very rapidly and the Scottish civil servants were anxious not to be 'upstaged' by their Whitehall counterparts.

During the next two years there was a steady but unspectacular growth of the professional economic staff by means of internal promotion and transfer, and by the appointment of the first economic assistant to enter the Scottish civil service via the GES recruitment mechanism.[27] However the proposal to establish an economics and statistics unit seems to have remained dormant until late 1969, partly owing to organizational difficulties.

In March of that year, by which time the economic unit comprised an economic adviser and two assistants, its work was described as:

> imparting economic advice on a wide range of subjects including unemployment, Industrial Development Certificates, EEC matters, SET and the effects of major fiscal and economic measures, the provision of secretariat functions for the Secretary of State's Economic Consultants; liaison with the UK planning machinery; and the study of the economic implications of regional studies in Scotland and elsewhere.

By December the proposal to combine the economics branch with the statistical resources of the SSO into a single economics unit in the charge of an SEA was revived, and was put into effect early in 1970 with the appointment of Dr R. G. L. McCrone, initially on a two-year secondment from Oxford. This organizational change was obviously influenced by McCrone's availability; and as it transpired, his arrival represented a turning point in the professionalization of economics in the Scottish civil service. McCrone had been an outspoken advocate of the need to improve Scottish statistical data. Towards the end of his *Regional Policy in Britain* (1969) he concluded that:

Everything comes back to the shortage of data on the case for regional policy. . . . In part the shape of policy is determined by the strength of the social and political pressures to which the regional problem gives rise; but the economic analysis on which it might be based is often too weak to exert much influence over it. In particular, this is due to the comparative neglect of this subject in economic theory and to the gross inadequacy of the statistical data which is necessary not only for an analysis of regional economic conditions but to provide a basis for choosing between different policy alternatives and to assess the effects of policy on growth, income levels, and the economic structure of regions.[28]

This passage embodies the economist's claim for a central place in the policy-making process, and in appointing McCrone the Scottish Office officials presumably realized the kind of professional they were getting. The demand for an improvement in Scottish statistics was not new; many earlier examples can be quoted from the literature and from public statements; but the record shows that there was evidently a reluctance to will the necessary resources, doubtless because the administrators' conception of the need fell far short of the economists' view. In this context it is pertinent to compare McCrone's views with the evidence given by Haddow and McGuinness to the two major official inquiries into Scottish affairs which were held in the same year as his book was published. When invited to comment on the urgent need for improved Scottish statistics Haddow replied:

I have the misfortune to have been a mathematician and I have a grave suspicion of many statistics. If a national plan for Scotland were drawn up with the full statistical apparatus that was available to those who drew up the National Plan for Great Britain in 1965, I would only hope that the fate of the plan would not be similar. I have not personally – I do not know whether Mr. McGuinness may have more refined feelings – found myself frustrated in any significant extent by the absence of statistics except occasionally when it comes to answering certain questions by Members of Parliament.[29]

In answer to a later question he pinpointed the difference between the administrator's judgement and that of the specialist:

Of course any statistician and in my experience any economist would say 'it would be nice to know . . .' and then reel off a lot of statistics that were not on the table that afternoon. There are of course difficulties. The figures of actual employment are not as up-to-date as we would like. The categories are not as up-to-date as we would like. These are not problems of Scotland versus England; these are problems involved in the mechanism for collecting statistics of this kind at all. We are very conscious and are reminded very often of the load that is put on firms by the great variety of demands for statistics and information that reach them from government departments.[30]

Needless to say, McGuinness agreed. Not, he asserted, just out of loyalty to his superior, but because:

the facts are that no part of the British Isles in my experience has a bigger statistical coverage than we have in the Digest (of Scottish Statistics). . . . I can say quite honestly that we have never been hampered by lack of statistics.[31]

Nevertheless, it seems undeniable that the provision of qualified statistical staff had fallen far behind the needs of the Scottish situation. By the early 1970s regional policy had developed well beyond the growth areas stage when decisions had been based, in McCrone's words, on 'the demands of political expediency tempered by little more than hunch as far as the economic criteria were concerned'.[32] The deficiencies of data were such that it was often impossible to establish the actual situation within a given region, let alone devise appropriate specific policies and assess their effects after a suitable time lag. Officials were unable to meet the ever-growing demands of politicians and the public for information and new policies, and the problem was exacerbated by the fact that many forms of government intervention entailed specific discriminatory advantages or disadvantages, and were consequently highly controversial. The lack of reliable data inevitably meant that public discussion was often confused and inconclusive. Economists in the Scottish civil service were unable to develop adequate economic forecasts or to employ such relevant techniques as cost-benefit analysis, largely because they were unable to construct the requisite technical relationships.

When these matters were considered by the *Commission on the Constitution* they inevitably became associated with questions of devolution and the possibility of Scottish independence. But it is worth stressing that the demand for Scottish data did not necessarily involve these wider issues. In response to questioning based on his book *Scotland's Future – the Economics of Nationalism*, McCrone denied that it was practicable to separate the two economies. Moreover, he considered that:

It is a fact of life that England is the major trading partner [and] the general outline of regional policy and development must be determined centrally. There would be room for some control of public expenditure at regional level, but the pattern of incentives and the scheduling of areas as problem areas etc., must be done centrally. Otherwise areas would compete with each other.[33]

ORGANIZATIONAL CHANGES

The establishment of an economics and statistics unit within the Regional Development Division of the Scottish Office in 1970 was, as we have seen, the result of a long-term expansion of the government's economic and social activities within the region. It was headed by McCrone, as senior economic adviser, supported by two permanent economic advisers, one of whom, P. M. Scola, was the former economic liaison officer, and one statistician, A. M. Burnside. There was also a third economic adviser post, on a two-year basis, for the economic work on the West Central Scotland Plan, which was then just starting under the direction of a steering committee comprising both central and local government nominees. By November 1971 the staff also included three senior economic assistants, three economic assistants, and a separate branch responsible for Scottish economic statistics, comprising a statistician (Burnside, who was in effect the successor to J. Grant) and an assistant statistician. Some of the staff on the West Central Scotland study team acquired permanent status in the Scottish Office on the completion of the Plan, since new posts were required for the increasing volume of work. In 1970 the Scottish Statistical Office had disappeared from the imperial calendar, being replaced by a separate Statistical Services Division within the Scottish Office, under a chief statistician, W. J. Fearnley. Fearnley was given overall responsibility for the coordination of statistics throughout the Scottish government departments, and became 'professionally responsible' for the statistical staff under McCrone. This latter arrangement has become increasingly common in the civil service in recent years, and is a significant minor indication of official acknowledgement of the degree of professionalization in the government service.

At the outset the Economics and Statistics Unit's three other branches were responsible for:

a. General economic questions affecting Scotland;
b. Fiscal and monetary policy, employment, transport, steel and other nationalized industries; and
c. Economic aspects of the West Central Scotland Study.

The wide range of issues covered by the first two of these branches helps to explain why Scottish government economists have tended to regard themselves as generalists rather than specialists, and why they have complained about the lack of time for research or studies in depth. In this respect their position was comparable to that of staff in the Economic Section of the Treasury, at least until the early 1960s.

The creation of the Scottish Economic Planning Department (SEPD) in June 1973 was a major new development, albeit a logical one given the organizational expansion of the preceding decade. The Prime Minister (Mr Heath) assigned special responsibility for North Sea oil matters in Scotland to the Minister of State in the Scottish Office (Lord Polwarth), and in support of this Haddow's successor as Permanent Under-Secretary of State, Sir Nicholas Morrison, decided to establish a fifth Scottish department in view of the steadily increasing role which Scottish ministers were playing in economic affairs. This process, especially as a result of North Sea oil, required the support of more than a single under-secretary division in RDD. Hence the SEPD was created, under Mr T. R. H. Godden as Secretary (with deputy secretary rank), an administrator with considerable direct experience in economic affairs. McCrone's division was brought into the SEPD and a second under-secretary division was created to bring together various other economic functions previously undertaken in SDD, including responsibility for the Highlands and Islands Development Board, the new towns, the Tourist Board, the two electricity boards, and transport.

Needless to say, these changes meant an enhancement of the status and importance of the Scottish Office's economic and statistical staff. When McCrone succeeded McGuinness as head of RDD in the autumn of 1972, with the post of under-secretary and chief economic adviser, another ex-academic economist, Graham Reid, succeeded him as senior economic adviser. McCrone's dual title reveals his explicit combination of administrative and professional responsibilities, which was still comparatively unusual in British government. Haddow had obviously favoured this change, which doubtless reflected both his respect for McCrone and his recognition of the professional economists' contribution to Scottish affairs. With the creation of the SEPD the following summer McCrone's group of divisions formed the nucleus of the new department and the economics and statistics unit worked to Godden, rather than being a free-standing unit directly under the Permanent Under-Secretary of State. Nevertheless, the new arrangement provided every assurance that professional economic advice would be taken fully into account in the policy-making process.[34] Of course, in these matters the role of personalities is usually quite as important, if not more so, than formal organizational structure and functioning.

The expansion of the economics and statistics unit's duties within the SEPD is indicated by the following range of activities, at the end of 1975:

Branch 1: Regional policy; EEC matters; Scottish Development Agency.

Branch 2: Employment; economic situation; industry; tourism; rural development; construction industry.

Branch 3: Regional reports and other planning matters; local impact of North Sea oil; new towns; ship building; housing policy; urban regeneration.

Branch 4: Scottish economic statistics; index of industrial production.

Branch 5: Local transport planning; air services and airports; Scottish transport group; ports; railways; roads.

Branch 6: Energy policy, including North Sea oil.

With the transfer of the Department of Industry Office for Scotland, based in Glasgow, to the SEPD the Industrial Development Division was created, becoming the third under-secretary division. This Division took over the responsibility for financial assistance to industry in Scotland under section 7 of the Industry Act, and there was a much greater ministerial involvement in industrial policy issues generally. Its economic staff included two senior research officers – who have subsequently been replaced by an economic adviser and a statistician – under a senior principal, and their work was akin to that undertaken in the economics and statistics unit. In mid-1975 the statisticians in Branch 4 were considered to be grossly overloaded since any aspect of economic statistics affecting Scotland could fall within the Branch's remit, and there was a great deal of committee work in Whitehall representing the Scottish Office interest in particular statistical proposals. There were also a number of major topics on which considerable additional work was required, such as the analysis of the effects of public expenditure and the explanation of the relationships between broad Scottish macro-economic aggregates.[35]

Unlike the situation in Whitehall, where the economists were mainly preoccupied with macro-economic management up to the early 1960s, and subsequently became increasingly involved in micro-economic affairs, developments in Scotland since the Toothill Report have largely proceeded in the opposite direction. This was of course partly due to the absence of separate macro-economic data on the Scottish economy, but also more particularly to the fact that the political and administrative division of labour between Whitehall and Edinburgh inevitably meant that the responsibility for macro-economic management lay in London.

Despite its growth, until quite recently the economics and statistics unit continued to bear traces of its origins as a small unit looking to Whitehall, rather than a fully independent Scottish entity. This was due less to mere size than to the fact that much of its work consisted of comment on and reactions to work initiated by Whitehall departments relevant to the Scottish situation. Given the range of issues, much very general comment is provided on a large number of specific problems. The opportunities for research are still very restricted,[36] owing to the limitations of staff; but the scope of Scottish Office responsibilities means that the variety of topics on which economic advice is sought is wider than in many Whitehall departments. The tradition of close cooperation with the Scottish universities and non-governmental research organizations, has done something to offset the pressure of the unit's operational responsibilities. There is still comparatively little contact with the Scottish agricultural economists, whose work is relatively self-contained, but the collaboration is likely to increase in the future, as well as the contributions of economists to hitherto neglected areas, such as health and education. In the long run there is a possibility that economists may be bedded out in various Scottish departments of state, and links with professionals in planning and transport and with administrators in finance are likely to develop further. But the shorter-run horizon is dominated by the implications of Scottish devolution, or the creation of a Scottish Assembly, even separatism, which has already expanded the range of issues under consideration by Scottish civil servants. A great deal of preparatory economic work has already been undertaken and the demand for economic statistics has grown significantly. Thus the situation is still fluid, and a further increase in the employment of professional economists and statisticians may take place, notwithstanding the currently stringent constraints on the expansion of the bureaucracy.[37]

Scottish Office economists and statisticians are still an outlying part of the Whitehall machine, and senior officials necessarily spend much of their time commuting between London and Edinburgh. Yet the growth in the organization of the GES and Government Statistical Service and the development of central management of recruitment and career planning have by no means overcome the sense of isolation felt by some Scottish professionals. They feel with some justification that the Whitehall machinery is insensitive to their special needs and interests. Geographical separation means that their career and promotion prospects are somewhat circumscribed, even perhaps for those willing to transport their home and family to the deep South. However, professional conditions and prospects have greatly improved during the 1970s, and with the development of central interviewing and promotion procedures in the Whitehall-based GES Scottish staff have been included within the established network of staffing services. And whatever may be the outcome of current political manoeuvres, the demand for economic and statistical expertise will undoubtedly be sustained.

CONCLUSIONS

This paper began with some reflections on the distinctive characteristics of Scottish government. It is fitting to conclude by noting that the recent growth in economic and statistical expertise in Scottish government represents part of a wider movement affecting public bureaucracies not merely in Britain but throughout the world. In the past decade or so there has been widespread discussion of Britain's lag behind other advanced industrial countries in this aspect of the modernization process, a lag often explained in terms of our anti-specialist cultural tradition. There had, however, been a remarkable dearth of detailed studies of the professionalization of this vital field of government activity.

As indicated earlier, once the demand for a more interventionist planning policy gathered momentum it encountered not only conventional organizational inertia but also a serious shortage of qualified personnel. Yet in many respects the Scottish civil service proved responsive to the changing exigencies of the situation, albeit after some delay, and provided a lead which was followed elsewhere in Britain. The post-1961 period saw the evolution of an effective organization which helped to lay the foundations of a worthwhile economic plan, as the Toothill Committee had recommended. It was not simply a technical unit to play about with unemployment statistics and the index of industrial production. Although the initial expedient, the panel of economic consultants, was innovative and constructive, it inevitably proved to be inadequate. Regional policy is ill-defined and almost indefinitely extensible in scope, and the growing pressure to expand the government's economic and social functions and responsibilities has necessitated a consequential increase in the provision of expert advice, analysis, data collection, and interpretation.

Unfortunately, owing to the restrictions imposed by the Official Secrets Act, it is impossible to gauge how effectively the growing corps of professional economists and statisticians has been utilized. Moreover, even if all the files were open to scrutiny it would still be difficult to assess their impact on policy without numerous interviews with the relevant surviving *dramatis personae*. Economic advice and statistical data are but two of several inputs into the policy-making process; and the acceptability of advice often depends almost as much on the supplier's personal characteristics as on his professional ability. Even when such advice is not ignored or brushed aside for political reasons it may be rejected on administrative grounds, or because its implementation would be too slow to meet the needs of the situation, or because the ultimate decision maker lacks courage or imagination. Nevertheless, during the postwar period there has been a remarkable growth in the demand for the technical analysis and statistical data without which policy making is merely a matter of guesswork, and there is substantial indirect evidence that the contributions of professional economists and statisticians in the Scottish Office have been welcomed and valued both by ministers and by senior administrators.

NOTES

1 This paper is a by-product of a larger study of the changing role of economists, statisticians, and agricultural economists in British government since 1945, undertaken with the aid of a grant from the SSRC. It is based largely on official documents, interviews, and correspondence which cannot be quoted directly owing to the Official Secrets Act. My former research assistant, Dr Alan Booth, now of the University of Sheffield, provided some of the documentation, and I am also indebted to a number of civil servants for their valuable advice and assistance. Dr R. G. L. McCrone, of the Scottish Economic Planning Department, provided innumerable constructive comments and rigorous criticisms of earlier drafts. Needless to say, mine is the sole responsibility for the final version.

2 Cf. James G. Kellas, *The Scottish Political System* (Cambridge University Press, 1973). Kellas uses the term 'political' to describe the distinctive set of Scottish institutions within the British political and administrative structure which respond to the region's interests, prepare and execute government decisions, and adjudicate disputes.

3 H. J. Hanham, 'The Development of the Scottish Office' in J. N. Wolfe (ed.) *Government and Nationalism in Scotland*, Edinburgh UP, 1969, p. 69.

4 Kellas, op. cit., p. 83.

5 *Commission on the Constitution*, 1969–72, 30 Sept. 69, p. 37.

6 Ibid., p. 38. The documents referred to are the *Central Scotland Plan 1963* (Cmnd 2188) and the White Paper on the *Scottish Economy 1965–1970* (Cmnd 2864, 1966).

7 Ibid., 29 Sept. 69, pp. 26–7.

8 *Inquiry into the Scottish Economy 1960–61*, Edinburgh, 1961.

9 *Report of the Committee on Local Development in Scotland*, Edinburgh, 1952.

10 For background material cf. Jacques Leruez, *Economic Planning and Politics in Britain*, London, 1975, part 3; and Gavin McCrone, *Regional Policy in Britain*, London, 1969. Also Kellas, op. cit., p. 171.

11 Cf infra, pp. 593ff. for an account of Scottish developments in statistics.

12 A clear and concise account of the evolution of 'The Machinery of Economic Planning in Scotland' up to 1969 is contained in the Memorandum submitted by the Regional Development Division to the House of Commons *Select Committee on Scottish Affairs* (1968–71), 23 Apr. 69, pp. 1–9.

13 *Select Committee on Scottish Affairs*, op. cit., 28 Apr. 69, Qu. 117.

14 Before becoming under-secretary in charge of the division of General Economic Development, Town and Country Planning, in the Scottish Development Department, McGuinness had been under-secretary in charge of Town and Country Planning in the Department of Health for Scotland, of which T. D. Haddow had been the Secretary.

15 The Council was set up in March 1965. It consisted of 23 members and a Vice-Chairman appointed by the Secretary of State, sitting under the Secretary of State as Chairman. The terms of reference and 1969 membership are set out in the Memorandum cited above in note 12.

16 *Supra*, pp. 599ff.

17 Susan Howson and Donald Winch, *The Economic Advisory Council 1930–39*, CUP 1976.

18 *Supra*, pp. 599ff..

19 In answer to a question put by the *Select Committee on Scottish Affairs* Session 1968–9, Minutes of Evidence, 22 Apr. 69. Qu. 169. In a private letter Sir Douglas has confirmed that in the early years the consultants' opinions and advice were valued highly by senior officials, and played a formative role in policy making, a view endorsed by Professor Thomas Wilson. More recently, however, the consultants have undoubtedly played a more limited role.

20 Cf. Haddow's replies to questions from the Select Committee, op. cit., 23 Apr. 1969, Qu. 222.

21 For an account of the creation and activities of the National Economic Development Council see Leruez, op. cit., chapters 4, 7, 8.

22 Agricultural economists have had a distinctive history in government service, and on the formation of the Government Economic Service they were excluded. For a general account see my article, 'The Development of the Agricultural Economics Profession in England', *Journal of Agricultural Economics* vol. XXVII 1976, pp. 381–92 (reprinted in this volume, pp. 419–32).

23 House of Commons, Session 1966–7, Estimates Committee 4th Report, Government Statistical Services, HC 246.

24 *Supra*, p. 599.

25 Cf. *supra*, p. 593. In Scotland, as in Whitehall, there was a desire for staff qualified in economics with statistics, rather than statistics *per se*, but suitable recruits were lacking. Like the economists, the statisticians had rank and pay scales formally equivalent to that of the administrative class, although there were very few posts at the upper levels of the hierarchy. Both professional groups were determined to resist dilution of their ranks, for example by recognizing the equivalence of economic assistants and research officers (many of whom had degrees in economics) or by the promotion of executive officers experienced in statistical work into the statistician class. Whether justified or not, these restrictive attitudes necessarily restrained the growth of civil service professional posts in economics and statistics.

26 *Supra*, p. 594.

27 Prior to this time all the Scottish civil service economists had been recruited in Scotland.

28 McCrone, op. cit., pp. 219, 273.

29 *Select Committee on Scottish Affairs*, 23 Apr. 1969, Qu. 54.

30 Ibid., 28 Apr. 69, Qu. 164.

31 Ibid., 28 Apr. 69, Qu. 165. The views of Haddow and McGuinness were subsequently echoed by a senior Treasury administrator, Vinter. However a Senior DEA economist, H. Cole, while recognizing the shortage of professional staff and conceding that economists could not have all the information they wanted, referred to the 'severe problem in relation to the whole of regional economics and of Scottish economics' resulting from data deficiencies. Ibid., vol. 22, Qu. 280 and 788.

In evidence to the *Commission on the Constitution* Dr W. S. Robertson, for the Scottish Council (Development and Industry), stated that the RDD had a sufficient range of 'specific executive professional knowledge', but that a quantitative increase of staff was necessary. Op. cit., *Minutes of Evidence*, IV, 5 May 1970, p. 93.

32 McCrone, op. cit., p. 211. See also pp. 240, 246.

33 *Commission on the Constitution*, 5 May 1970, Qu. 490, 500. Some members of the Commission thought that Scotland should have a separate budget and its own balance of payments accounts. McCrone considered that the Scottish budget of 1969 had been produced 'largely in response to the political situation, rather than in response to the demands of economists'. It was 'a useful document, and I would like to see an estimate of this kind prepared from time to time so that one had a check on the flows of Government expenditure'. Ibid., Qu. 484, 486.

34 McCrone's position as Chairman of the Economic Planning Board reinforces the point.

35 One topical and rapidly growing area is North Sea oil, on which the new Branch 6 works closely with the Department of Energy in Whitehall.

36 It was felt that subjects had to be picked up and put down with great frequency. Consequently it was difficult to build up a substantial body of expertise on many particular subjects, and virtually impossible to have a true research function as distinct from a day-to-day advisory role.

37 Kellas, op. cit., p. 204. See also p. 194.

29

ECONOMISTS IN
GOVERNMENT

An historical and comparative perspective*

Despite the vigorous revival of research in the history of economics during the past two decades, most present-day professional economists are woefully ignorant of the development of their discipline, and the long tradition of economists' involvement with government. Consequently it may come as a surprise to learn that Adam Smith, who is so often misleadingly depicted as the originator of *laissez faire*, described political economy as 'a branch of the science of a statesman or legislator'.[1] Nor was this just another aberration on the part of a great thinker unencumbered by the consistency said to be the hobgoblin of little minds. On the contrary, since the bicentennial of *The Wealth of Nations* scholars have reemphasized that Smith's definition of political economy was fully compatible with his intellectual vision and intentions.[2] In this respect he was in accord with his contemporary, Sir James Steuart, who is often portrayed as the last of the British mercantilists; and like Smith's predecessors, most continental European economic writers of the time adopted a broadly similar view. The beginnings of formal economic instruction in that region occurred largely under the rubric of Staatswissenschaften – the sciences of the state.

As is well known, the subsequent progress of modern scientific economics was closely intertwined with the rise of economic liberalism. Yet even in the heyday of British classical economics, with its predominant bias against state intervention, most of its leading exponents were involved in affairs of state either directly – by occupying government positions for a time, or occasionally serving as official or unofficial economic advisers, or indirectly – through active and often influential participation in policy debates, by no means invariably on the *laissez faire* side. Here, too, as in so much else, Smith served as a model. Despite his powerful advocacy of 'the obvious and simple system of natural liberty' and severe criticism of 'that insidious and crafty animal', the politician, he not only provided economic advice but also served for twelve years as Commissioner of the Customs in Scotland. Despite his belief in free trade Smith was not a mole but an active collaborator – 'a competent and dedicated practitioner of mercantilism', according to the most recent students of this episode.[3] Behind Smith stood a long list of predecessors involved in government at least as far back as Sir Thomas Gresham in the Elizabethan era, and including such important seventeenth-century economic writers as Malynes, Misselden, Mun, Downing, Child, and Locke. After Smith the distinguished roster includes McCulloch, Senior, James and John Stuart Mill, Marshall, Foxwell, Ashley, and Hewins. Henry Fawcett is exceptional. Having occupied the chair of Political Economy at Cambridge he served as an MP and Postmaster General in one of Gladstone's administrations, while Leonard Courtney, briefly Professor of Political Economy at University College, London, later became a cabinet member. That Jevons, too, briefly acted as an unofficial economic adviser has only recently been appreciated.[4]

To extend this list into the twentieth century would prolong it intolerably, and include Keynes, whose multifarious government activities suffice to fill an entire lecture series. Enough has been said to establish the initial historical point: that British economists have long been involved with government despite a determined effort, since the later nineteenth century, to portray economics as an autonomous, positive a-political discipline. And of course much the same applies to their counterparts in most other countries. On the European continent it was by no means unusual for leading economists to become ministers or directors of the state Statistical Bureau. In Austria, for example, there was a saying that first-rate economists become professors in Vienna, whereas second-rate ones become Ministers of Finance!

With the enormous expansion of the economics profession's interest and participation in government activities all over the world, the orthodox a-political conception of economics has come under increasing attack, and not only from Marxists, Radicals, and Institutionalists. The term political economy has come back into vogue. There is now a growing body of systematic theoretical and empirical research on the interrelations between economics and politics, for example on the political business cycle.[5] And it is no coincidence that the most recent award of the Nobel Prize has gone to James M. Buchanan for his contributions to this work.

In this lecture I am chiefly concerned with the implications, for the economics profession, of the vastly enlarged role played by economists in many governments since the Great Depression of the 1930s and, more especially, during and since World War II, although I can deal with only some aspects of this large subject. I believe this concern would have been shared by the distinguished man whose name is commemorated in this lecture series. Richard Charles Mills was one of a small pioneering group of economists in and out of government in Australia during that period, who laid the foundations for subsequent expansion. The strength of those foundations is clear from Dr Petridis's valuable Australian contribution to a ten-country comparative study of economists in government which I edited some years ago,[6] from which it appears that economists have exercised a significantly greater influence on Australian government than have their peers in many other lands.

Considering the historical record, some cynics in the audience may wonder whether this should be a source of pride. But, let me warn you against an oversimplified, mechanistic, or technocratic view, to which some professional economists subscribe, that there is a one-to-one correlation or a causal connection between the number of economists in a country's government and the level of its economic performance. Sometimes, in fact, it is suggested that the correlation is inverse; but this too flatters the profession.

According to a current economist joke, one of many, a foreign observer is watching the annual May Day parade in Moscow, and after the troops, tanks, and missiles have passed by he sees serried ranks of men in grey suits. 'Who are they?' he asks his host. 'Ah: they are the economists. It's amazing how much damage they can do!' As with all such stories there is a grain of truth here. Bad advice based on erroneous theory, inaccurate data, unreliable forecasts, failure to appreciate the time lags involved in modifying accepted ways of thinking and acting, insensitivity to considerations of political and administrative feasibility – all these may lead to the adoption or attempted implementation of unconstructive or positively harmful policies. However, there is also another side to the account, for which Alan Peacock has coined the expression: 'damage minimization'. Unfortunately for the historical record, and the economists' collective reputation, this contribution – which I believe is highly significant – rarely leaves clear traces in the official documents. As anyone who has enjoyed the brilliant BBC series *Yes Minister* will attest, senior bureaucrats, including economic advisers, can often discourage, and sometimes even prevent ministers from making fools of themselves.[7] As one British interwar Permanent Secretary of the Treasury is said to have remarked, after losing a long argument with his master: 'Well, Minister, if you must do such a silly thing, must you do it in such a silly way?' No doubt the story has grown in the telling; but it has the solid ring of truth.

Needless to say one must beware of stereotyping, according to which bureaucrats are always on the side of inertia, determined to preserve the status quo, and eager to maximize their 'on the job leisure' – another Peacock coinage.[8] By contrast, politicians are always in a hurry, eager to make a dramatic impact on their department, their cabinet colleagues (especially the Prime Minister), Parliament, the party, the press, and even the country at large. Advocacy of slow, cautious, unspectacular piecemeal change has only a limited political payoff.

However, in practice the interactions among the participants in the policy process are usually more subtle and complex than either the stereotypes or *Yes Minister* suggest. This can be illustrated by two telling quotations from Sir Alec Cairncross, one of Britain's most experienced ex-government economists. Any economist who believes that he and his professional peers could successfully take over the management of economic policy, Cairncross observes,

> has never been present at the kind of discussion between economists, administrators, and ministers, at which it is by no means uncommon for the economists to talk politics, the administrators to talk economics, and the ministers to discuss administrative problems.[9]

And for those who seek to gauge the impact of economists, or indeed any individual or group, Cairncross elsewhere remarks that

> it is often very hard even for those at close quarters with policy-making to know what does in the end shape the decisions that ministers take – or, still more, do not take. . . . Where the issue is in dispute, who except the minister (or even including the minister) knows what clinched the matter? It is very rarely that one can say with confidence that the decision would have been different if x had not been there. The people who think they know and say so may, in fact, be ill qualified to judge.[10]

To some members of the audience, especially academic economists lacking government experience, Cairncross may seem guilty of wilfully blurring the roles and relationships between politicians, administrators, and economists; yet consideration of policy-making processes from the 'inside' completely exonerates him. Contrary to the economistic view presented in innumerable texts on the theory of economic policy – especially those suggesting the main task is to ensure equivalence between the numbers of policy 'instruments' and policy 'targets'[11] – life in government service seldom, if ever, conforms to Max Weber's classic 'ideal type' analysis of bureaucracy. In practice, policy-making processes are rarely rational; they are dominated by complexity, contingency, uncertainty, and muddle. While the individual participants may be rational according to their own lights, the multiplicity and variety of lights may be as confusing as those at a disco. The policy process has been aptly described as,

> a multi-person drama going on in several arenas, some of them likely to be complex large-scale organizational situations. Decisions are the outcome of the drama, not a voluntary, willed, individual instial action. 'Drama is continuous. Decisions are convenient labels given *post hoc* to the mythical precedents of the apparent outcomes of uncertain conflicts.'[12]

Rational policy may be especially difficult to achieve in the field of macro-economic management,

> in which there is no simple or permanent solution and where the

definition of what has to be solved will determine the range of possible answers. . . . The economy needs constant adjustment, although it is always affected by forces not wholly subject to the control of a single government. As one economic problem is temporarily alleviated another emerges. One year's solution may create the next year's problem. Further, there is seldom unanimity about the choice of the best policy: different actors may have perspectives that are so diverse that a variety of proposals can be presented, each of which can be legitimately defended, with reconciliation between them almost impossible.[13]

No wonder economic policy problems have been termed 'wicked'.

Turning to the context in which economic policy is considered (decided would perhaps be too explicit a term), let me again cite Cairncross, who has warned that

The atmosphere of a large government department is frequently almost indistinguishable from that of the loony bin. I use this term in no pejorative sense; it is simply one of the facts of official life.[14]

In crisis situations 'the important must always give way to the urgent'; and in some sectors of government the crisis atmosphere is endemic. American economists have vividly described this problem in William Allen's brilliant article on 'Some American Experiences'. The sheer lack of time to think, to undertake a sober and deliberate assessment of the issues and policy options, inspires such terms as, 'quick draw specialists', 'shooting from the hip', or 'putting out fires'. He cites a staff economist on the Council of Economic Advisers who was instructed at 11 am to prepare an analysis of 'the economic payoff from the Peace Corps' by 4 pm; and another who wryly commented that: 'In the academic world, you think now and decide never; and in the government it's just exactly the other way round.'[15]

From the abundant literature recording the irrational elements in high-level policy making I recommend the voluminous published diaries of two British cabinet members, Richard Crossman and Barbara Castle; and for horror stories David Stockman's recent revelations of the Reagan administration are surely unsurpassed.[16] Even after discounting heavily for sensationalism designed to maximize sales, it is an extraordinary tale of confusion, contradiction, dishonesty, deception and self-deception, incompetence, and incomprehension leading to unprecedentedly irresponsible fiscal indiscipline. In this case the economists are walk-on characters rather than leading players, but a crucial role is occupied by a budgetary forecast – directly dependent on economic assessments – which is so wild that it became known as Rosy Scenario. Once settled, and later only slightly revised, it formed the basis of later negotiations over proposed budget cuts, most of which proved to be abortive. Indeed, what Stockman calls a 'magic asterisk' was put against items, included as expenditure cuts, which were to be decided in the future. And if Stockman's mode of presentation makes the story seem too fantastic let me cite an entirely different, though in one respect parallel example from an unimpeachable source, Charles Kindleberger, one of the most recent Presidents of the American Economic Association. In arranging the Marshall Plan, he recalls:

> once we got to a 5.2 billion figure for the first year, I defended it to the death. And any time I had to make a change in anything, I changed something else to keep it, simply because if we changed that number every day, we'd know that the whole thing would come unstuck. Somebody made up a joke that those computers . . . produced 5.2 billion on every problem for a long time after . . . it was the only number they could come up with. I'm ashamed of that.[17]

It was essential to preserve the figure intact, otherwise the Plan's political opponents would have had a field day.

Before considering the range of economists' functions in government, the variety of contexts in which they work, and some of the attributes they require if they are to be effective, let me first say a little more about the political context and relationships with clients, many of whom are non-economists.

One of the many disturbing features of Stockman's account is the insights it provides into the relationship between the economic adviser and the clients, another matter in which the idealized concept of neutral, objective, scientific analysis and data presentation is wholly unrealistic. By comparison with the performance of other postwar Presidents, as revealed in interviews with former Chairmen of the Council of Economic Advisers (CEA),[18] President Reagan's responses were often lamentable. Apart from lapses of memory, which have become only too familiar in recent months, he demonstrated an exceptional inability to grasp issues or appreciate arguments, often drawing a conclusion opposite to that intended by the persuader. Objectional words like 'Medicare' triggered off rambling monologues; he responded to anecdotes rather than concepts, so that the most effective medium of communication was via 'folksy *Reader's Digest* stories'; and on one memorable occasion a major argument favouring defence expenditures was clinched by the production of large-scale cartoons![19]

Lest all this should seem a figment of Stockman's fevered and frustrated imagination let me quote a passage attributed to an earlier President, Warren Harding, who, after listening to his advisers arguing over a tax issue protested:

> I can't make a damn thing out of this tax problem. I listen to one side and they seem right, and then – God! – I talk to the other side and they seem just as right, and here I am where I started. I know

611

somewhere there is a book that will give me the truth, but, hell, I couldn't read the book. I know somewhere there is an economist who knows the truth, but I don't know where to find him and haven't the sense to know him and trust him when I find him. God! What a job![20]

As Gardner Ackley, a former CEA Chairman, has observed: 'the effective transmission of economic understanding depends not only on the attributes of the transmitter but also on the intellect and desire to learn of the intended recipient.' Unfortunately 'public officials are mostly just our students grown older; many of them still can't or won't learn'.[21]

The importance of the President's views and capacity in this sphere has been stressed by Herbert Stein, Chairman of the CEA under President Nixon. The President, he says, should be seen as

the dominant decision maker in economic policy, as the judge of economics and economists, and as the major figure attempting to set the psychological tone of the economy. In those senses he is the nation's chief economist.[22]

By comparison with other post-World War II Presidents, whose relationships with professional economists have been the subject of fascinating and revealing studies, Reagan has adopted very strong positions. Again quoting Stein, by no means a 'liberal' in American economic terms, Reagan

has chosen a rather eccentric school of economics and economists. . . . In relations with the Congress he has been unusually insistent that only the precise program he has proposed will solve the nation's problems. He has been unusually explicit in public advice and direction to the Federal Reserve. And he has vigorously played the role of public spokesman and salesman for the economic program.[23]

Like Roosevelt before them, no post-1945 President could afford to be indifferent to economic affairs; but the degree of interest and enthusiasm displayed has varied considerably.[24] Kennedy and Ford seem to have been the most willing consumers of economic analysis and expertise, whereas Johnson responded positively only when clear political issues were at stake, while Nixon, who certainly had the requisite intellectual capacity, was bored by economic discussion. Thus it may not be entirely coincidental that two of the worst examples of policies undertaken against the weight of economic advice – Johnson's refusal to recommend higher taxes to pay for the Vietnam War, and Nixon's insistence on imposing the first ever peacetime wage and price controls – occurred in those administrations. Reagan's lack of concern about the enormous deficit, and his wilful refusal to support a tax increase, led to the most serious deterioration in the relations between a President and a CEA Chairman (Martin Feldstein) in the Council's history, raising the question whether that body would survive.[25]

The character and structure of the governmental system largely determines how far and through which channels professional advice can be brought to bear on economic policy.[26] Relevant features of the political context include: the degree of stability, adaptability, and conflict or consensus; the stage of economic development; and the position on the spectrum of control extending from democracy to authoritarianism. Where there are strong opportunities or pressures for political, economic, and social change – for example, when new states are formed, or after a major war (especially in the case of occupied or defeated countries), or where a strong, perhaps military, regime has taken over after a political revolution, runaway inflation, or other extremely disruptive experience – then the scope for economists to perform as technocrats may be unusually great. Unfortunately, as Richard Mallon has noted in his revealing study of Argentina,

> those who are most adroit at seizing power are seldom as adept at managing an economy. . . . Furthermore, the use of force instead of compromise to impose policies is almost bound to polarize sectoral clashes and the struggle over income shares into extremist political ideologies. This outcome can only be avoided by broadening effective political and economic participation which, even if carried out by a benign one-party or military dictatorship, requires the strengthening of mediative institutions capable of resolving interest group conflicts. . . . [However] it is easier to advocate a role for nonnormative economic policymaking than it is to provide a cogent explanation of how to put it into practice.[27]

Similar conclusions emerge from Alejandro Foxley's analysis of *Latin American Experiments in Neoconservative Economics*. He shows that although, in principle, structural–institutional changes and macro-economic adjustment policies 'can be handled if the authoritarian regime is able to suppress political opposition and discontent', the achievements of such regimes have fallen far short of expectations, both in political and in economic terms.[28]

Some of the early pioneers of econometrics, notably the Norwegian Nobel Laureate, Ragnar Frish, believed that the development of more scientific, quantitative methods would so enhance our knowledge of the economy that much of the confusion and wasted energy generated in political debate could eventually be eliminated. Once the operations of the economic machine were fully understood politicians would be able to concentrate on ends, leaving means to the technicians. This is a seductive argument. Even Keynes, who warned that

> the pseudo-analogy with physics leads directly counter to the habit of mind which is most important for an economist to acquire[29]

613

claimed, in 1932, that

> For the next twenty five years, in my belief, economists, at present the most incompetent, will nevertheless be the most important group of scientists in the world. And it is to be hoped – if they are successful – that after that they will never be important again.[30]

Fortunately for the profession, this kind of success seems no nearer than it did half a century ago; possibly owing to their sustained incompetence.[31]

A brief reference to the structural differences between Britain, Australia, and the USA may serve to illustrate some possibilities. In the first two, the presence of cabinet members in parliament, and the hierarchical relationships among the departments of state, mean that in principle effective control over economic affairs rests with the Prime Minister and the Treasury. That department, in both countries, has evolved since the inter-war years from an agency primarily concerned with traditional budgetary accounting into the central locus of economic management, acquiring major responsibilities consequent upon the vastly enlarged scope of government in economic and social affairs. In both cases since World War II the 'Treasury Line', to cite Greg Whitwell's term, has been both very influential and at times intensely controversial, as the doctrinal emphasis has shifted from an initially strong Keynesian approach to a less interventionist, somewhat monetarist viewpoint.[32] Despite complaints of official secrecy in both countries the discussion of these matters, both within government and outside, has been more open in Australia than in Britain, although it is not clear whether this reflects differences in bureaucratic cultures rather than the influence of professional economists. In Britain fears that the introduction of high-level political/economic advisers into the Wilson government, in October 1964, would entail the politicization of the government economic service proved to be exaggerated;[33] but similar fears have been expressed during the Thatcher regime.

In the USA, the situation is far more complex. The federal government is vast and balkanized, and the component parts are intensively competitive.[34] Although the Secretary of the Treasury is the administration's chief spokesman on economic affairs, the separation of powers between the executive and Congress, and the separation of responsibilities for fiscal and monetary policy between the Treasury and the Federal Reserve Board respectively, enhances the likelihood of tension, if not conflict over economic policies, virtually guaranteeing periodic major policy inconsistencies. In this context the CEA, as a device for institutionalizing the provision of economic expertise, is unique. It places professional economists at the political centre of a global power, threatening their scientific neutrality and straining their professional integrity. The question: 'How political should the Council of Economic Advisers be?' inevitably arises.

This issue was aired by a panel of ex-Council members at the 1973

American Economic Association meetings, but it has been a matter of intermittent concern ever since the Council's inception in 1946.[35] The first Chairman, Edwin Nourse, had tried, with only limited success, to serve the President while preserving his scientific neutrality and impartiality. He is said to be the original subject of Harry Truman's plea for 'a one-armed economist'. Nourse's deputy, Leon Keyserling, later his successor, had no such inhibitions; he was an enthusiastic propagandist, and his behaviour was so unpopular in some quarters that the Council's future was in serious jeopardy at the outset of the Eisenhower administration. Among later Chairmen Walter Heller and Herbert Stein were especially active in educating the public in favour of official policies, and the misgivings about the Stein–Nixon relationship probably inspired the AEA discussion mentioned earlier. Could the Council members, especially the Chairman, be the President's men (or women) without being 'a bunch of kept cats'? Various behavioural percepts or guidelines have been suggested, which usually distinguish between 'internal' and external conduct.[36] A key issue is whether – and if so when and how – a council member should publicly defend an official economic policy or action that he or she had opposed vigorously in private. To remain silent is another option, but at times the silence may seem deafening. To accept defeat, on the principle of you win some, lose some, is one option; but as Cairncross once observed, if one is too often neutral one eventually becomes neuter. *In extremis* there is always resignation; but this is an admission of defeat, possibly creating an opening for a genuine 'kept cat', or leaving economic policy to amateurs, with damaging consequences for the Council and the profession. And even here there is the question whether to quit quietly or loudly.

The dangers of such situations for the economics profession need no emphasis. Beyond harmless jokes about the dearth of good Republican economists – some of them emanating from Republicans[37] – there has been a growing politicization of the Federal Reserve System's economists, although monetary policy is supposed to be independent of Executive and Congressional politics – itself a debatable issue. When it was thought that a number of so-called new Keynesian economists were dominating the Fed's Open Market Committee, a rival group of monetarists established their own Shadow Open Market Committee and published a number of effective technical and political critiques of the Fed's forecasts, its economic staff, and its decision-making processes and their outcomes.[38] Underlying these disagreements were conflicting ideological and professional conceptions of the stability of the economy – the Keynesians and other interventionists believing that macro-economic management was essential to preserve stability whereas their critics argued that discretionary policies were not merely ineffective, but positively destabilizing. With such disputes, no wonder there has been a loss of public confidence in the economics profession, and also a loss of self-esteem among many of its practitioners.

So far I have concentrated mainly on the top-level economic advisers. Below them, however, within the bureaucracy, are innumerable lesser professional economists performing a bewildering variety of tasks, by no means all of a strictly 'professional' character. The scale and timing of the growth of these personnel has been very uneven.[39] In the Netherlands, Norway, and Australia, as in the USA, economists seem to have been readily accepted as part of the machinery of government ever since the depression of the 1930s. In much of Europe, including France, the Mediterranean- and German-speaking countries, jurists were the predominant category of bureaucrats during the nineteenth century, and in many lands they maintained their hegemony until well after 1945. However, Britain, which did not have law school training as the main source of supply of civil servants, provides the classic case of an advanced industrial country whose public service put up an effective resistance to the rise of specialists. The entrenched cadre consisted almost exclusively of élitist, anti-technocratic so-called intelligent laymen. Despite the general acknowledgement that trained economists had made a major contribution to the war effort, especially through the small Economic Section of the War Cabinet Offices under the direction of Lionel Robbins, but also in many other parts of Whitehall, there was no disposition to enlarge their role after 1945, and some hesitancy about preserving the Section intact.

In this situation, as Robbins recorded in his *Autobiography of an Economist*, the economists' success was largely due to their willingness to make themselves useful to ministers and senior officials, and to their acceptance of established civil service values and traditions. Robbins stressed the need

> to become part of the machine and accept its logic rather than pretend to some special status. . . . If we had not been prepared to conform to the normal routine, or if those who ran the machine had been hostile, the experiment would have failed.[40]

This exposes one aspect of the classic problem of specialists in the bureaucracy. If they differentiate themselves too sharply from their generalist colleagues, or from other professionals in the bureaucracy, claiming special attention or consideration because of their knowledge or insight, they are liable to encounter resistance, and a correspondingly reduced impact. However, if they become too completely socialized, they lose the qualities and abilities that come from a distinctive background, species of knowledge, and set of skills.

The fact that the Economic Section remained small, and the number of designated economist posts in the whole British Civil Service did not rise above 20 for nearly two decades after World War II, suggests either that the wartime economists had not made a sufficiently strong case for the expansion of their role, or that the existing generalist cadre was remarkably effective in resisting encroachments on its territory. There was, in fact, a

616

steady, unspectacular growth in the number of generalists with some economics training. But for most of the period the general atmosphere remained uncongenial to specialists, and the recognized economic administrators (as Cairncross has called them) had to exercise their talent for damage minimization by countering, and where possible correcting the fallacious reasoning of the economic illiterates, many of whom were blissfully aware of the limitations of their own 'do-it-yourself' (DIY) economics, as it has recently been termed.[41]

A telling example of the need for economic expertise in the Treasury is the official, later to become Head of the Civil Service, who subsequently admitted:

> I was flung in at the deep end. I learnt about exchange rates through the process of reading briefs on devaluation. I learnt about budgets by making and preparing one as Secretary to the Chancellor. I did it knowing I had not the faintest idea of the basis on which the Budget was put together. I did not even know what a deficit was. It came as a great flash of light when someone told me that what you did when you had a deficit was borrow.[42]

Some twenty years later, in the mid-1970s, after the great influx of professional economists following Harold Wilson's election in October 1964, matters were very different. As a leading government economist remarked,

> Nowadays economic language is talked throughout the Treasury. And instead of the economists feeling strange, it is the administrators who do not know any economics, who feel embarrassed. . . . And the fact that the top people are economically trained means that you have to put up a decent economic argument . . . and this is the way it should be.[43]

In considering the demand for and supply of economists in government attention must be paid to national social and cultural attitudes towards economists and other experts, specialists, or disciplinary professionals. These attitudes may, of course, change over time, as illustrated by the gradual acceptance of economists in Whitehall during the post-1945 period and, some would argue, the increasing suspicion of economic experts in the USA since the turn of the century.[44] Where the indigenous educational system fails to generate the necessary supply of trained personnel the influence of foreign advisers and training institutes, and opportunities for postgraduate education in the USA or Europe may largely fill the gap until the local supply situation improves.[45] In Australia, for example, an anti-élitist attitude imposed barriers to the recruitment of graduates into the public service during the interwar years, but did not discourage specialization within the organization, whereas in India the British civil service tradition and the cult of the 'all rounder' were dominant.[46] Where oppor-

617

tunities for specialization in government economics have been restricted, persons of unusual ability, ambition, and energy may have been discouraged from seeking an official career, thereby confirming the generalists' belief that specialists are of an inferior intellectual calibre. In authoritarian regimes, as for example in Latin America, the demand for technocrats may at least temporarily raise their status and career opportunities by comparison with more traditional bureaucrats.[47]

Much has been written about the nature of economics as an intellectual or scientific discipline, but there has been comparatively little systematic study of what economists in non-academic employment actually do, and – what is more pertinent – what they can do better than non-economists. Economics is a vocationally non-specific subject. It is difficult to identify tasks that economists are uniquely equipped to perform, and this has both advantages and disadvantages, for they can be employed either as specialists – for example, in an econometric forecasting or research unit – or as generalists, where their distinctive knowledge, skills, and aptitudes enable them to collaborate with and/or substitute for administrators. As specialists they are necessarily in competition with other specialists, for example, statisticians, operations researchers, mathematicians, etc., and the increased emphasis on mathematics and quantification has reduced the distinction between the more technocratic type of economist and these other specialists in numeracy. The economists' relationships with administrators have usually become closer as they are assimilated into the bureaucracy, as indicated earlier.[48] In this process their combination of verbal and numerate skills is crucial; so is their capacity to think broadly in terms of the allocation of resources, foregone alternatives, costs and benefits (both in narrow pecuniary terms and more generally in terms of societal implications).[49] It is a commonplace of the literature on economic policy making that the majority of economists in government rarely utilize the more sophisticated and esoteric ideas and techniques which they have been required to master during their apprenticeship, and it is useful to distinguish between at least three overlapping categories of economists' tasks:

(i) low level routine or clerical work, including data compilation;
(ii) strictly professional work – for example, forecasting, economic analysis, policy formulation and implementation;
(iii) higher level administrative, managerial, or decision-making functions.

Any such classification is necessarily rough and ready, but although various efforts have been made to apply supply and demand analysis to the economists' inputs and outputs in government, they have not been conspicuously more successful.[50] Moreover, the widespread blurring of the distinction between professional and non-professional activities makes it virtually impossible to provide accurate comparative statistics on the number of economists employed in different national (or for that matter, state and local) governments.

The organizational factors affecting the economist's work can be categorized in various ways.[51] A simplified classification would include:

(a) his or her level in the system – more technical tasks usually being performed in the lower and middle reaches, whereas at the 'top of the office' functions and responsibilities more closely resemble those of generalist administrators and political appointees;

(b) whether he/she is an isolated adviser or specialist, a member of a team, or merely one of many suppliers of economic expertise from within or outside the organization;

(c) the size and influence of the department or agency employing him/her; of course similar specialist functions occur in several different branches of government, and nominal similarities (for example, job descriptions) may conceal significant practical differences owing to variations in departmental staffing procedures;

(d) the degree of politicization of the bureaucracy and the economic service;

(e) the extent of the government's interventionist policies, for example, whether primarily micro- or macro-economic.

As is well known, there was a great increase in the number of economists in government during and after World War II, in the so-called Keynesian era, when macro-economic issues were the main focus of attention, and more recently these issues have been the centre of intense professional controversy. The economists' manifest inability to offer workable solutions to the problems of domestic inflation, unemployment, and slower productivity growth during the 1970s and 1980s largely explains both the loss of faith in economic management, especially 'fine tuning', and the widespread sense of professional crisis. International economic conditions have also presented an additional range of intractable problems. However, as economic interventionism increased a growing proportion of government economists became involved in micro-economic affairs (admittedly the distinction between macro and micro issues is not always clear in practice), and recent survey research has revealed a significantly greater degree of professional consensus on micro- than on macro-economic issues.[52] Curiously enough, the recent ideological shift away from interventionism towards more market-oriented policies has not – at least as yet – led to any significant decline of government interest in micro-economic affairs, or in the demand for economists to deal with them. On the contrary, in the sphere of de-regulation, for example, economists have played an important role in devising, promoting, and implementing policy. They are, after all, by professional training and bias disposed to advocate increased efficiency and reliance on market forces.[53] Thus the ideological shift of emphasis away from macro- to micro-economic issues has enabled the economists to demonstrate their usefulness once again, and it may conceivably do something to brighten up the profession's somewhat tarnished image. Broadly speaking, given the political setting and the bureaucratic system, the effectiveness of any group of professionals involved in the policy process will depend on a number of readily specifiable conditions, including:

(a) the nature and range of their expertise;
(b) the extent to which their expertise is acknowledged – that is, the 'authority of knowledge' accorded to them;
(c) their access to centres of power and information – especially that information which they generate or exclusively control;
(d) their skill in communicating with their clients, and in coalition forming;
(e) the degree to which their recommendations are compatible with the prevailing political and bureaucratic climate of opinion;
(f) their skill in 'working the machine', that is, comprehending and manipulating the norms, procedures, constraints, and culture of the bureaucratic (that is, administrative) system;
(g) their skill in avoiding involvement in matters where they cannot help, or where no clear solutions are available.

What qualities are required for success as a government economist, beyond technical competence? No brief list will suffice, given the wide variety of economic, political, and bureaucratic conditions and the range of tasks the economist may be called upon to perform. From the extensive literature on the subject it is clear that among the valuable qualities are:

> tact; patience; adaptability; the capacity to work quickly under pressure; the ability to communicate with non-specialists in a variety of circumstances and at differing levels of audience comprehension; skill in the arts of persuasion; a sense of timing; grasp of bureaucratic procedures and conventions – that is, the capacity to 'play the machine'; appreciation of the problems of administrative feasibility and political practicality; recognition of the limitations of one's professional expertise; and sheer stamina.

Needless to say, this combination of virtues is seldom to be found in any one person, which explains why exceptional capacity in this difficult work is so rare. Nevertheless it is appropriate to ask how far the typical professional economist's training prepares him or her for employment, whether temporary or permanent, in the public service.

This is a highly pertinent question at the present time, given the chorus of complaints about graduate education in economics, both from within and from outside academia, and the possibility that the training of professional economists has since become the subject of systematic investigation in the USA. Of course American conditions and practices are not typical; but they are influential, hence the results of a recent (as yet unpublished) survey of graduate students in leading American university economics departments are of considerable interest. When asked: what qualities make for success in the graduate programme? the most striking responses were those revealing the low importance attached to such matters as (in descending order): interest in and ability at empirical research; a broad knowledge of economic literature; and – lowest of all – 'a thorough knowledge of the contemporary economy'.[54] These responses confirm the worst misgivings of those experienced former government economists who believe that contemporary professional training in the discipline is too heavily biased towards highly abstract theory and sophisticated quantitative techniques. An overdeveloped confidence in the persuasive value of logical analysis, especially if it is combined with technical arrogance, can be a serious obstacle to effectiveness in a bureaucratic context where ability to work in a team and knowledge of institutional procedures, processes, and constraints are vital. Much of the literature on economists in government, especially that dealing with the role of the economic adviser, argues that it involves more art than science, and judgement in such matters as 'a feel for the real world', a knowledge of what governments can or cannot do, sensitivity to the problems of drafting and administering legislation, and

> judgment on how close to get to the political process, on when political costs outweigh economic ones, and on when the battle is lost so that one should keep quiet even if one believes one knows better than the politicians what can be done to achieve objectives.[55]

Whether, and if so how far, prospective recruits for government economic work should be instructed in these matters, and how far the existing patterns of graduate education in economics should be modified to take account of them, are questions that cannot be considered adequately here. Probably some desirable qualities like 'judgement' can only be acquired, if at all, by experience on the job, while some of the requisite skills of the practitioner are highly personal. Nevertheless it is difficult to believe that the potential feedback effects of government work on academic education in economics should be ignored. The rich available literature on which this paper has drawn provides many valuable insights into a lengthy and complex process of collective professional learning-by-doing, the results of which, at least in recent years, have been chastening.

It is difficult to believe that only two decades ago even so hard-headed an observer as George J. Stigler could claim that

> economics is finally at the threshold of its Golden Age – nay, we already have one foot in the door. . . . Our expanding theoretical and empirical studies will inevitably and irresistibly enter into the subject of public policy, and we shall develop a body of knowledge essential to intelligent policy formation. And then, quite frankly, I hope that

621

we become the ornaments of democratic society whose opinions on economic policy shall prevail.[56]

Unfortunately the present mood is much less heady, not only because the discipline's limitations are nowadays much more generally recognized, but also because it is acknowledged that policy-making processes are far more complex than previously supposed, that the number of participating organizations has increased alarmingly, and that the economist's world has in many ways become much more difficult to understand, let alone manage.[57] There is still no reason to doubt that economists have much to contribute to public enlightenment, to government and business policy, and even to the maintenance of stability and growth in the international economy. But that contribution now appears to be a good deal more modest than it seemed twenty years ago.[58]

According to Walter Heller, an outstanding practitioner of economics in government, government experience has greatly stimulated the translation of economic research into operating rules for public policy, and into quantifiable concepts.[59] A great deal of constructive economic research is now undertaken in government departments and agencies, and if it has served to narrow the long-standing gap between theoretical and applied economics that is a contribution of no small importance. Government economists tend to believe, with some justification, that their contributions are undervalued by the profession, as contrasted with brilliant new theories or technical achievements which have little or no conceivable practical application. Most of the profession's accolades do indeed go to academic members, partly because government economic work cannot be readily evaluated, since much of it is not published nor even completed in publishable form owing to the pressure of work or official restrictions. Hence government economists cannot usually acquire a just status in the profession's 'reputational system'. When such an economist becomes well known to the general public it may be for some conspicuously unsuccessful or unpopular policy – guilt by association even with a policy which he may have unsuccessfully resisted! Damage minimization is not invariably a complete success.

Nevertheless, the volume of literature and the number of prestigious lectures and addresses by prominent current and former members of the government economic establishment,[60] suggests that the professional status and role of economics and economists in government may be growing, even while a more cautious assessment of their value prevails.

At the beginning of this lecture I linked political economy with Staatswissenschaft – the science of the state. It is therefore appropriate to conclude with a quotation from an Australian practitioner of this science (or art?) of more than a century ago:

Our lawyers must study law, our doctors must study medicine and surgery, our clergy must study theology and bibliology, and give proof of competent knowledge of these subjects before they are allowed to enter their several professions, in order that the interests of the public may be protected against the wild work of ignorance. Why then should state-craft be the only profession in which no special preparation – no study of its principles – is demanded?[61]

Whether this applies to late-twentieth-century economics in government I leave you to judge.

NOTES

* Text of the 15th R. C. Mills Memorial Lecture delivered at the University of Sydney on 10 June 1987. This lecture has also been published in part in *Economic Papers*, and is republished here by kind permission of Professor Coats, Professor Peter Groenewegen of the Faculty of Economics, The University of Sydney, and Professor David Collins, Editor of *Economic Papers*.
1 Smith (1776, 1976) Introduction to book IV.
2 Winch (1983) (1978), Haakonssen (1981).
3 Anderson, Shughart, Tollison (1985); Tollison (1985) p. 920.
4 White (n.d.).
5 For example Frey (1978) (1983), Tufte (1978). As Herbert Stein has remarked: 'the Employment Act of 1946 may or may not have succeeded in its goal of introducing economics into politics, but it certainly succeeded in introducing politics into economics'. (1986) p. 7. The same applies to the British and Australian White Papers of 1944 and 1945.
6 Petridis (1981) in Coats (1981).
7 For the text see Jay and Lynn (1984).
8 Peacock (1979) p. 241.
9 Cairncross (1971) p. 203; cf. Schultze (1982) p. 65.
10 Cairncross (1971) p. 210.
11 See Tinbergen (1956) and Theil (1968) and the critical comments on this 'technocratic-elitist' approach in Frey (1983) chapter 11.
12 Hawker, Smith, Weller (1979) p. 21, quoting Schaffer (1977) p. 148.
13 Ibid. pp. 151–2.
14 Cairncross (1970). An Australian economist has compared the economic adviser's role to that of a veterinarian charged with the task of mating elephants. 'First, everything is done at a great height; secondly, a whole lot of roaring and screaming goes on; and third, you have to wait at least two years to see any results.' (Hewson, 1981, p. 46).
15 Allen (1977) pp. 50, 51. Nor is this experience confined to the USA. The Australian economist quoted earlier recalls having been instructed 'to develop a detailed case for devaluation' in about half an hour. Fortunately he had already drafted a paper on the topic for another purpose; but the example illustrates the need to be as prepared as possible for any likely eventuality, and some unlikely ones too. (Hewson, 1981, p. 57).
16 Crossman (1975–7); Castle (1980–1); Stockman (1987).
17 Allen, op. cit., p. 67. For a somewhat similar story in the Heller regime see Hargrove and Morley (1984) p. 211.
18 Hargrove and Morley (1984) *passim*.
19 Stockman (1987) pp. 50, 54, 99, 310, 315, 373.

20 Orlans (1982) p. 5.
21 Ackley (1982) p. 208. For a valuable general treatment of the problems of dealing with ministers see, for example, Weller and Grattan (1981) *passim*.
22 Stein (1981) p. 57. For a more extended treatment see Stein (1984).
23 Stein (1981) p. 57.
24 The following comments are based on Hargrove and Morley (1984).
25 For an earlier phase of uncertainty about the Council's future see Hargrove and Morley (1984) p. 95ff.; also Flash (1965).
26 It is not uncommon for ministers, some of whom have been professional economists, to have professional economists as official and unofficial personal advisers. There is a valuable comparative analysis of this species in Walter (1986). See also Mitchell (1978) for one economist's personal experience.
27 Mallon (1975) p. 163.
28 Foxley (1983) p. 186. See also Camp (1977).
29 Quoted by Whitwell (1986) p. 173.
30 Keynes (1982) p. 37.
31 For example Stein has noted that 'the number of economists in Washington increased by 60% from 1980 to 1983, adding: "I wonder whether President Reagan knows that." ' (1986) p. 6. He estimates that the size of the 'economics industry' is about the same as that of the motion picture industry, which is, like economics, involved in producing a combination of information and entertainment. (p. 1).
32 Whitwell (1986); Hughes (1980). It has recently been suggested that the Australian Treasury is now encountering more competition in respect of economic advice than hitherto. (Shann, 1986). On the British situation see Coats (1981) p. 26ff.; Brittan (1971); Heclo and Wildavsky (1974).
33 Cf. Coats (1981); Brittan (1969).
34 And reportedly becoming more so. For example, Rivlin (1987); Stein (1986); Bosworth (1980). For a general survey see Barber (1981).
35 Shanahan *et al.* (1974) pp. 28–42. For background see Flash (1965); Hargrove and Morley (1984).
36 For example, Heller (1966) chapter 1; Leman and Nelson (1981–2) pp. 97–117; Verdier (1984) pp. 421–38; Wallich (1982); and the numerous references in Nelson (1987). The general relationship between economics and policy analysis is relevant.
37 Hargrove and Morley (1984) pp. 319, 416. When the Republicans introduced price controls in 1971, appointing their own economists to implement them, J. K. Galbraith likened it to appointing the Vatican to run a birth control programme. Fels (1986) p. 11.
38 For example, Lombra and Moran (1980).
39 This and the next two paragraphs are based on Coats (1981).
40 Robbins (1971) p. 184.
41 Henderson (1986).
42 Coats (1981) p. 52.
43 Ibid. p. 53.
44 Nelson (1987) p. 52ff.
45 For examples of the problems encountered see Rosen (1985); Jones (1986); Abbott (1976).
46 Coats (1981) chapters 3 (Petridis), 4 (Ambirajan).
47 See Coats (1981) chapter 11 (Haddad).
48 *Supra* pp. 616.
49 The economist's habit of thinking in terms of interdependencies and the system-

wide effects of specific policy measures is often cited as a major asset. For example, Henderson (1986) p. 107. There is some concern that an overemphasis on technique in professional training 'may work to the detriment of the more historical and philosophical elements in an understanding of the economy'. Cairncross (1981) p. 13. See also Peter Self's attack on the misuse of cost-benefit analysis (1975). On the question of training see below pp. 620–1.

50 Cf. Coats (1978) p. 312; Peacock (1979) part IV; Cairncross (1981) chapter 1. This matter is discussed in several other works cited in the references, for example, Ackley, Cairncross (1971), Carney, Fels, Fisher, Hewson, Hargrove and Morley, Nelson, Stein (1986), Wallich, Walsh.

51 For example, Ackley has referred to six basic and six subordinate organizational variables. (1982) pp. 212–16.

52 For example, Brittan (1973); Samuels (1980); Frey *et al.* (1984).

53 Nelson (1987). In policy making there is often a conflict between considerations of efficiency, argued by economists, and considerations of equity, to which politicians are sensitive. This is the so-called 'big trade-off'. Cf. Okun (1975).

54 Colander and Klamer (1987); Klamer and Colander (1989). The qualities deemed most important were: ability at problem solving (a somewhat ambiguous category), and (slightly lower) excellence in mathematics. Much lower valued were knowledge of a particular field, and ability to make connections with prominent professors!

There is a marked contrast between the demands on the graduate students surveyed and the qualities desired by Australian public service employers of economists, as revealed in Abelson and Valentine (1985).

55 Neville (1981) p. 9; also pp. 1–2. Many other similar citations could be provided.

56 Stigler (1966) p. 17.

57 Bosworth (1980); Rivlin (1987) makes various proposals designed to simplify the Washington policy process, which has been termed 'hydra-headed'.

58 By 1976 George Stigler had modified his views dramatically, arguing that 'economists exercise a minor and scarcely detectable influence on the societies in which they live'. (1982) p. 57. Quoted by Fels (1986) p. 1.

59 Heller (1966) p. 60.

60 It is of interest that Alice Rivlin, President of the American Economic Association in 1986, the first woman to hold that office, has had a distinguished career in the public service.

61 E. C. Nowell (1872), quoted in Goodwin (1966) p. 586.

REFERENCES

Abbott, G. C., 'Why Visiting Economists Fail: An Alternative Interpretation', *Public Administration, 54* (Spring, 1976) pp. 31–43.

Abelson, P. W. and Valentine, T. J., 'The Market for Economists in Australia', *Economic Papers*, The Economic Society of Australia, 4 (December, 1985) pp. 1–16.

Ackley, G., 'Providing Economic Advice to Government', in J. A. Pechman and N. J. Simler, *Economics in the Public Service. Papers in Honor of Walter W. Heller* (New York: Norton, 1982) pp. 200–34.

Allen, W. R., 'Economics, Economists, and Economic Policy: Modern American Experiences', *History of Political Economy, 9* (Spring, 1977) pp. 48–88.

Ambirajan, S. 'India: The Aftermath of Empire', in Coats (1981) *infra* pp. 98–132.

Anderson, G. M., Shughart II, W. F., and Tollison, R. D., 'Adam Smith in the Customhouse', *Journal of Political Economy, 93* (August, 1985) pp. 740–59.

Barber, W. J., 'The United States: Economists in a Pluralistic Policy', in Coats (1981) *infra* pp. 175–209.

Bosworth, B., 'Re-establishing an Economic Consensus: An Impossible Agenda?', *Daedalus, 109* (Summer, 1980) pp. 59–70.

Brittan, S., 'The Irregulars', in R. Rose (ed), *Policy-making in Britain: A Reader in Government* (New York: Macmillan, 1969) pp. 329–99.

——, *Steering the Economy: The Role of the Treasury* (London: Penguin, 1971).

——, *Is There an Economic Consensus? An Attitude Survey* (London: Macmillan, 1973).

Cairncross, Sir A., 'Writing the History of Economic Policy', unpublished paper, 1970.

——, *Essays in Economic Management* (London: 1971).

——, 'Introduction', and 'Academics and Policy Makers', in F. Cairncross (ed), *Changing Perceptions of Economic Policy. Essays in Honour of the Seventieth Birthday of Sir Alec Cairncross* (London: Methuen, 1981).

——, 'Economics in Theory and Practice', *American Economic Review Papers and Proceedings, 75* (May, 1985), pp. 1–14.

Camp, R. A., *The Role of Economists in Policy Making: A Comparative Case Study of Mexico and the United States* (Tucson, Ariz.: University of Arizona, 1977).

Carney, T., 'The Social Scientist as Policy-Maker: Reflections on Australian Experiences', Academy of the Social Sciences Symposium, 1986. (Unpublished)

Castle, B., *The Castle Diaries* 2 vols (London: Weidenfeld and Nicolson, 1980–1).

Coats, A. W., 'Economists in Government: A Research Field for the Historian of Economics', *History of Political Economy, 10* (Summer, 1978) pp. 298–314.

—— (ed), *Economists in Government. An International Comparative Study* (Durham, N.C.: Duke University Press, 1981). The Introduction from this work is reprinted in this volume, pp. 496–518.

—— (ed), *Economists in International Agencies. An Exploratory Study* (New York: Praeger, 1986).

Colander, D. C. and Klamer, A., 'The Making of an Economist', *Journal of Economic Perspectives, 1* (Fall, 1987), pp. 95–111.

Crossman, R., *The Diaries of a Cabinet Minister* vols I–III (London: H. Hamilton, 1975–7).

Fels, A., 'The Social Scientist as a Member of Statutory Bodies', Academy of the Social Sciences Symposium, 1986. (Unpublished)

Fisher, N. W. F. 'Social Scientists as Policy Advisers: A Consumer Assessment', Academy of the Social Sciences Symposium, 1986. (Unpublished)

Flash, E. S., *Economic Advice and Presidential Leadership* (New York: Columbia University Press, 1965).

Foxley, A., *Latin American Experiments in Neoconservative Economics* (Berkeley: University of California Press, 1983).

Frey, B. S., *Modern Political Economy* (Oxford: Martin Robertson, 1978).

——, *Democratic Economic Policy. A Theoretical Introduction* (Oxford: Martin Robertson, 1983).

——*et al.*, 'Consensus and Dissensus among Economists: An Empirical Inquiry', *American Economic Review, 74* (December, 1984) pp. 986–94.

Goodwin, C. D., *Exhortation and Controls: The Search for Wage-Price Policy, 1945–71* (Washington, D.C.: The Brookings Institution, 1975).

——, *Energy Policy in Perspective: Today's Problems, Yesterday's Solutions* (Washington, D.C.: The Brookings Institution, 1981).

Haakonssen, K., *The Science of the Legislator. The Natural Jurisprudence of David Hume and Adam Smith* (Cambridge: Cambridge University Press, 1981).

Haddad, P. R., 'Brazil: Economists in a Bureaucratic–Authoritarian System', in Coats (1981) *supra* pp. 318–42.

Hargrove, E. C. and Morley, S. A., *The President and the Council of Economic Advisers* (London: Westview Press, 1984).

Harris, S., 'The Role of Microeconomic Theory in Policy Formulation', in Harris and Maynard (eds), *infra* pp. 27–59.

—— and Maynard, G. (eds), *Economic Theory and Public Policy*, Centre for Applied Economic Research, CAER paper no. 12 (August 1981).

Hawker, G., Smith, R. F. I., and Weller, P., *Politics and Policy in Australia* (St Lucia: Queensland University Press, 1979).

Hawkins, R. G. and Fitzgerald, V. W., 'The Potential Contribution of Econometric Modelling', in Neville (ed), *infra* pp. 11–33.

Heclo, H., 'OMB and the Presidency – The Problem of "Neutral Competence" ', *The Public Interest, 38* (Winter, 1975) pp. 80–98.

—— and Wildavsky, A., *The Private Government of Public Money* (London: Macmillan, 1974).

Heller, W. W., 'What's Right with Economics?' *American Economic Review, 65* (March, 1965) pp. 1–26.

——, *New Dimensions in Political Economy* (Cambridge, Mass.: Harvard University Press, 1966).

Henderson, D., *The 1985 BBC Reith Lectures: Innocence and Design: The Influence of Economic Ideas on Policy* (Oxford: Blackwell, 1986).

Hewson, J. 'The Role of the Advisor', in Neville (ed), *infra* pp. 46–67.

Holmes, A. S., 'Macro, Micro and Modelling – What Else?', in Neville (ed), *infra* pp. 34–45.

Hughes, B., *Exit Full Employment: Economic Policy in the Stone Age* (London: Angus & Robertson, 1980).

Jay, A. and Lynn, J., *Yes Minister* (New York: Parkwest Publications, 1984).

Jones, G. W., 'The Role of the Western Social Scientist as Policy Adviser or Consultant in Asia', Academy of the Social Sciences Symposium, 1986. (Unpublished)

Kearl, J. R. *et al.*, 'A Confusion of Economists?' *American Economic Review, Papers and Proceedings, 69* (May, 1979) pp. 28–37.

Keynes, J. M., 'The Dilemma of Modern Socialism', *Political Quarterly* (1932) reprinted *The Collected Writings of John Maynard Keynes, 21; Activities 1931–39*, D. Moggridge ed (London: Macmillan, 1982) pp. 33–8.

Klamer, A. and Colander, D. C., *The Making of an Economist* (Boulder, Colo.: Westview Press, 1989).

Leman, C. K. and Nelson, R. H., 'Ten Commandments for Policy Economists', *Journal of Policy Analysis and Management, 1.* (1981–2) pp. 97–117.

Lombra, R. and Moran, M., 'Policy Advice and Policy Making at the Federal Reserve', in K. Brunner and A. H. Meltzer (eds), *Monetary Institutions and the Policy Process, 13*, Carnegie–Rochester Conference Studies on Public Policy (Amsterdam: North Holland, 1980) pp. 69–91.

Mallon, R. D., *Economic Policymaking in a Conflict Society. The Argentine Case* (Cambridge, Mass.: Harvard University Press, 1975).

Mitchell, J., 'Special Advisers: A Personal View', *Public Administration, 56* (Spring, 1978) pp. 87–98.

Nelson, R. H., 'The Economics Profession and the Making of Public Policy', *Journal of Economic Literature, 25* (March, 1987) pp. 49–91.

Neville, J. W. (ed), *Economics, Economists and Policy Formulation*, Centre for Applied Economic Research, CAER paper no. 13 (September, 1981) pp. 1–11.

Nowell, E. C., 'Political Economy', *Monthly Notices of Papers and Proceedings of the Royal Society of Tasmania*, in C. D. Goodwin, *Economic Inquiry in Australia* (Durham, N.C.: Duke University Press, 1966).

Okun, A., *Equality and Efficiency. The Big Trade Off* (Washington, D.C.: Brookings Institution, 1975).

Orlans, H., 'Academic Social Scientists and the Presidency: From Wilson to Nixon', *Minerva* 24 (1986) pp. 172–204.

Peacock, A., 'The Oil Crisis and the Professional Economist', *Sir Ellis Hunter Memorial Lectures* (York: University of York, 1970).

——, *The Economic Analysis of Government and Related Themes* (Oxford: Martin Robertson, 1979).

Petridis, A., 'Australia: Economists in a Federal System', in Coats (1981) *supra* pp. 69–97.

Rivlin, A., 'Economics and the Policy Process', *American Economic Review, 77* (March, 1987) pp. 1–10.

Robbins, L., *The Autobiography of an Economist* (London: Macmillan, 1971).

Rosen, G., *Western Economists and Eastern Societies. Agents of Change in South Asia, 1950–1970* (Baltimore: Johns Hopkins Press, 1985).

Samuels, W., 'Economics as a Science and its Relation to Policy: The Example of Free Trade', *Journal of Economic Issues, 14* (March, 1980) pp. 163–85.

Schaffer, 'On the Politics of Policy', *Australian Journal of Politics and History, 23* (1977) pp. 146–55.

Schultze, C. L., 'The Role and Responsibilities of the Economist in Government', *American Economic Review, 72* (May, 1982) pp. 62–6.

Self, P., *Econocrats and the Policy Process: The Politics and Philosophy of Cost-Benefit Analysis* (London: Macmillan, 1975).

Shanahan, E. *et al.*, 'How Political Must the Council of Economic Advisers Be?' *Challenge*, March/April, 1974, pp. 28–42.

Shann, E. W., 'Economic Policy Formation: Policies and Institutions', unpublished paper, 15th Conference of Economists, Monash University, 25 August, 1986. Revised version published in *Canberra Bulletin of Public Administration, 53* (December, 1987).

Smith, A., *An Inquiry into the Nature and Causes of the Wealth of Nations*, R. H. Campbell and A. S. Skinner (eds) (Oxford: Clarendon Press, 1976).

Stein, H., 'The Chief Executive as Chief Economist', in W. Fellner (ed) *Essays in Contemporary Economic Problems. Demand, Productivity and Population* (Washington, D.C.: American Enterprise Institute, 1981) pp. 53–78.

——, *Presidential Economics. The Making of Economic Policy From Roosevelt to Reagan and Beyond* (New York: Simon & Schuster, 1984).

——, 'The Washington Economics Industry', *American Economic Review. Papers and Proceedings, 76* (May, 1986) pp. 1–9.

Stigler, G. J., 'The Economist and the State', *American Economic Review, 55* (March, 1965) pp. 1–18.

——, 'Do Economists Matter?' in his *The Economist as Preacher* (Oxford: Basil Blackwell, 1982).

Stockman, D. A., *The Triumph of Politics. The Inside Story of the Reagan Revolution* (New York: Avon, 1987).

Theil, H., *Optimal Decision Rules of Government and Industry* (Amsterdam: North Holland, 1968).

Tinbergen, J., *Economic Policy: Principles and Design* (Amsterdam: North Holland, 1956).

Tollison, R. T., 'Economists as the Subject of Economic Inquiry', *Southern Economic Journal,* 52 (April, 1986) pp. 909–22.

Tufte, E. R., *Political Control of the Economy* (Princeton: Princeton University Press, 1978).

Verdier, J. M., 'Advising Congressional Decision-Makers: Guidelines for Economists', *Journal of Policy Analysis and Management, 3* (Spring, 1984) pp. 431–8.

Wallich, H. C., 'Policy Research, Policy Advice, and Policy Making', in R. E. Lombra and W. E. Witte (eds), *Political Economy of International and Domestic Monetary Relations* (Ames: Iowa State University Press, 1982) pp. 237–53.

Walsh, C., 'The Role of the Social Scientist as Policy Adviser to Public Servants and Politicians', Academy of the Social Sciences Symposium, 1986. (Unpublished)

Walter, J., *The Minister's Minders. Personal Advisers in National Governments* (Melbourne: Oxford University Press, 1986).

Weller, P. and Grattan, M., *Can Ministers Cope? Australian Federal Ministers at Work* (Richmond, Victoria: Hutchison, 1981).

White, M., 'Some Issues in Taxation and Coinage: W. S. Jevons as Government Adviser 1869–71', unpublished mss.

Whitwell, G., *The Treasury Line* (Sydney: Allen & Unwin, 1986).

Winch, D., *Adam Smith's Politics. An Essay in Historiographical Revision* (Cambridge: Cambridge University Press, 1978).

——, 'Science and the Legislator: Adam Smith and After', *Economic Journal, 93* (September, 1983) pp. 501–20.

Woolley, J. T., *Monetary Policy. The Federal Reserve and the Politics of Monetary Policy* (Cambridge: Cambridge University Press, 1984).

INDEX

630

Harrod, Roy F. 107, 119, 162, 184, 185, 188, 385
Harvery, William 'Coin' 282
Haskell, Thomas L, 145, 434, 437, 462
Hawkins, H. 436
Hawley, E.W. 182
Hawley, Frederick B. 465n
Hawtrey, Sir Ralph G. 123, 520
Hayek, Friedrich A. 116, 184, 376, 377, 381–6
Headlam, Stewart 297, 299, 300
Heath, Edward 599
Heller, Walter W. 395, 407, 517n, 615, 622
Hemming, A.F. 549n
Hempel, C.G. 76n
Henderson, Sir Hubert D. 520, 521, 537, 557, 558, 564–5
Hendry, G.F. 594
Herman, E.S. 399, 470n
Hewins, W.A.S. 93, 103n, 110, 114, 116–17, 119, 128n, 361–9, 370nn
Hewson, J. 623n
Hexter, J.H. 376
Hicks, John R. 194–5, 381, 385, 388n
Hicks, Ursula 183
Hicks-Beach, Sir Michael 126
hierarchy in economics 45
Higgs, Henry 125, 323, 325, 326, 332n, 335n, 336nn
Higham, John 145, 437
Hobson, J.A. 114, 121, 127n, 129n, 181, 361, 559
Hofstadter, Richard 120, 144, 439, 440
Hogben, Lancelot 377
Hollander, Jacob 265
Holst, H.E. von 214
Homan, Paul 159, 166, 171n, 269–73, 277nn, 278n, 447, 448, 468n
Hoover, Calvin B. 451
Hopkins, Sir Richard 548n
Howey, Richard S. 79n
Howson, Susan 548n
Hoxie, Robert 231, 284
Hubbard, J.D. 262
Hull, Charles H. 442, 465n
Hume, A.B. 582
Hutchison, Terence W. 106, 108–9, 113, 126n, 141, 146, 398, 410
Hutt, W.H. 62n, 82, 96–8, 104nn, 386, 390n
Hutton, Graham 374

Hyndman, Henry M. 298

idealism 114
ideology 17, 396–8
imperial preference 93
implicit theorizing 110
Index of Economic Journals 155–68, 195–6, 457, 458
Indian Economic Journal 163
individualism 24, 73
innovation (discovery), intellectual 20, 39; in maginal revolution 66–71
Institute for Economics Research (Brookings) 40, 254–5, 270, 449
Institute for Research in Land Economics and Public Utilities 243, 446
Institute of Statistics (Oxford) Bulletin 183
institutional economics 118, 396
instrumentalism 17
intellectual authority, role in development of British economics of 82–98, 108–9; 115, 121, 138–42
internationalization of economics 135, 146–7, 406

Jaffé, William 70, 146
James, Edmund Janes 206, 217nn, 231, 232, 438, 465n
Jameson, J. Franklin 288n
Jenkins, Hester 344, 347
Jenks, Jeremiah W. 214, 251
Jevons, William Stanley 119, 146, 316, 607; on influence of authority 90, 94, 101n, 121, 140; and marginal revolution 63, 66, 69, 70, 71, 73, 80n
Jewkes, John 557, 572–3
Johnson, Elizabeth S. 52n
Johnson, Harry G. 25, 27, 28, 32n, 42–4, 52nn, 139, 141, 149n, 150n, 187–8, 372, 401, 406, 579n
Johnson, Lyndon B. 612
Johnson, T.J. 399, 420
Jones, A. 422
Jones, D. Caradog 344, 347
Jorgenson, E.O. 258
Journal of Agricultural Economics 182
Journal of Economic Abstracts 264, 274
Journal of Economic Literature 191, 264, 274, 456–7
Journal of Political Economy (JPE) 156–67 *passim*, 264, 268, 269, 282